The Report

of the

Commission of Inquiry

Concerning Certain Matters

Associated with

The Westbank Indian Band

John E. Hall, Q.C.
Commissioner

Maureen E. Cowin
Executive Secretary

John F. Rowan, Q.C.
Counsel

1988

Commission of Inquiry
Concerning Certain Matters
Associated with
the Westbank Indian Band

CANADA

Commission d'enquête
concernant certaines
questions liées à la
bande indienne de Westbank

Commissioner
John E. Hall, Q.C.

Commissaire
John E. Hall, c.r.

TO HER EXCELLENCY
The GOVERNOR GENERAL IN COUNCIL

MAY IT PLEASE YOUR EXCELLENCY

By Order-in-Council PC-1986-1816 dated August 12, 1986, I was appointed to inquire into certain matters associated with the Westbank Indian Band and certain matters relating to the Department of Indian Affairs and Northern Development. I now beg to submit the attached Report.

Respectfully submitted.

Commissioner

April 1988

C.P./P.O. Box 48766, Succursale Bentall Station
Vancouver, Canada V7X 1A6

Table of Contents

Westbank Reserve 10 looking north along Okanagan Lake. The floating bridge to Kelowna, B.C. is at the right.

Reserve 10 looking southwest. Highway 97 traverses the Reserve at left centre, passing the new Band office in the middle of the photograph.

Mobile home park development on Westbank Reserve 9. McDougall Creek Estates (Toussowasket) is at centre right and Westview Village (formerly operated by Park Mobile Home Sales Ltd.) is to the left.

Several mobile home park developments on the shores of Okanagan Lake, Reserve 9.

Shelter Bay Marina on Reserve 10 near the Kelowna bridge. Above is the Lakeridge Subdivision developed by the Westbank Band.

Tourist facilities, including Wild'N'Wet Waterslide at centre left, on Reserve 9. The reconstructed Highway 97 is in the foreground.

SUMMARY

This Commission of Inquiry was assigned two particular tasks. Its first task was to investigate certain matters of controversy surrounding the management of the Westbank Indian Band and the relationship of the Department of Indian Affairs and Northern Development to the Band between the years 1975 and 1986. Additionally, under this heading, the Commission was requested to look into the activities of lessees and residents of the reserve lands of the Westbank Indian Band during the same period.

The second task assigned to the Commission was to consider the Indian Act, R.S., c.I-6, the existing primary legislation governing Indian Affairs, and to recommend any changes to that Act, to the management of Indian lands and monies, or to policies and procedures of the Department of Indian Affairs and Northern Development that were deemed to be appropriate. I was also asked to consider and recommend remedies for any specific problems that might be disclosed during the course of the Inquiry, having regard to the government's policy of supporting and strengthening Indian self-government on Indian lands.

The Order-in-Council establishing this Commission of Inquiry is included in Appendix E of the Report. Therein the terms of reference are fully set out.

The Westbank Indian Band is located just outside of Kelowna, British Columbia. The Department of Indian Affairs and Northern Development (hereinafter referred to as "the Department") is a federal department under the direction of the Minister of Indian Affairs and Northern Development. The Headquarters of this Department is located in Ottawa/Hull and the regional office is located in Vancouver, British Columbia. The district office of the Department which deals with the Westbank Indian Band is located in Vancouver as well.

At the outset of the Inquiry, I decided that it would be desirable to hold hearings in the Westbank area to give those interested the best opportunity to be heard. In addition, I held some hearings in Vancouver. All persons who sought standing before the Inquiry were granted standing, and funding was made available to allow for the legal representation of former executives of the Westbank Indian Band as well as the current executive and members of the Band. The Department of Indian Affairs and Northern Development was represented by counsel throughout the course of the Inquiry. Mr. Fred J. Walchli, formerly the Departmental Regional Director General in British Columbia, was also represented by counsel. The Westbank Indian Band

and its development company had considerable dealings with the failed Northland Bank; accordingly, the liquidator for the Bank sought and was granted standing at the Inquiry.

This Inquiry was not an examination of one specific event, but rather concerned several issues that occurred over a lengthy period. It considered some 11 years in the history of the Westbank Indian Band and the Department of Indian Affairs and Northern Development. Over this 11-year period, the Westbank Indian Band made substantial economic progress. Because of their location, the Reserves of the Westbank Indian Band were well situated for residential development. Between 1975 and 1986, there was a very substantial growth in the number of mobile home parks located in the Okanagan Valley (particularly in the Kelowna area), due to its generally pleasant climate and its location halfway between Vancouver and Calgary. The Westbank Band shared in this growth, with population increases in both B.C. and Alberta and transportation improvements greatly enhancing the value of the Band's lands in recent years. The pictures at the beginning of this Report give an overview of the geography of the inhabited Reserves of the Westbank Band.

The Band's economic progress was aided in 1983 when it received several million dollars from a reserve lands cut-off claim. In the period 1982 to 1984, large sums of money accrued to the Band and more particularly to some Band members, as a result of a project to upgrade the provincial highway which traverses Reserves 9 and 10. Because of the Band's improved economic situation, it was able to be more aggressive in obtaining better banking treatment. It is not always easy for Indian bands or individuals to obtain good financial services. In late 1982, the Band took a substantial share position in the Northland Bank, and began to become an increasingly large depositor. At the same time, the Band and its development company were granted substantial lines of credit and began entering into sizeable loans. Chief Ronald Derrickson was also dealing with the Bank in his personal capacity and became a substantial borrower. In the spring of 1984, Chief Derrickson became a director of the Bank, resigning in August 1985, just prior to the demise of the Bank. The failure of the Bank resulted in the deposits in the Bank (standing to the credit of the Band or the Band company) being put in jeopardy. The Bank ceased paying interest on deposits. The Band thereafter refused to pay interest on loans owed to the Bank. As it turned out, the amount of money on deposit was not vastly different from the amount owing in loans, and that matter is apparently being worked through at the present time, although at the conclusion of the evidence in the Inquiry it had not yet been finally resolved.

The Chief of the Westbank Indian Band between 1976 and 1986 was Ronald M. Derrickson. By accident or design, Mr. Derrickson had become something of a "media figure" over the years. He was viewed by some as a capable administrator and skilled businessman. Others, both within and outside of the Band, viewed him as a petty tyrant who could bend the Department to his will to the advantage of himself and his family.

When Chief Derrickson came to power in the summer of 1976, he discovered a number of problems. A major development initiative, Lakeridge Park, located on Reserve 10 near Okanagan Lake, was in serious financial trouble. This ambitious residential subdivision had been commenced under the administration of his brother, former Chief Noll Derriksan. It had not progressed nearly as well as had been hoped. When Ronald Derrickson became Chief, the project was heavily in debt and sales of lots were weak. At the same time, his brother Noll's mobile home park (Toussowasket) had just been completed and was having serious financial woes. Built with the assistance of government funds, it was overloaded with debt and had a high vacancy rate. Various other mobile home parks were being operated or contemplated by non-Band members. Some were not well managed and many were returning what seemed to Chief Derrickson to be grossly inadequate rents.

One feature of Indian land that made it desirable to developers was that there was relatively little by-law regulation of the land. Chief Derrickson felt that this was an area that needed study and possible improvement. He believed regulation could generate income and ensure better quality developments. Chief Derrickson was not a man to hide his light under a bushel. He had been relatively aggressive in acquiring land for his own use and he was determined to pursue an aggressive policy in getting a better return on Reserve lands from the lessees operating mobile home parks. Unbeknownst to these lessees, a very new broom indeed had arrived.

As it happened, Mr. Derrickson became Chief at a time when a different system of Departmental administration came into effect. This change was necessitated by the closure of district offices of the Department of Indian Affairs. This was also the time when Mr. Fred J. Walchli took over as Regional Director General in B.C. Mr. Walchli had a background in land management and was keenly interested in improving the economic return on Indian lands.

Chief Derrickson was not viewed with universal acclaim in his own house (the Band). Some members of the Band considered him to be power-hungry and intent on the too rapid development of Band lands. Undoubtedly there was an element of jealousy present for he has been financially successful in the conduct of his own business affairs, but there also appears to have been a feeling of unease by some Band members that the Band was being hurried forward at an unreasonable pace. Some saw opportunity, others foresaw a looming train wreck.

Geographically, Indian reserves are islands that are located in provincial seas. Some provincial laws of general application may apply, but many do not. Under the Canadian constitution, the federal government has responsibility for Indians and Indian lands. The tenure of Indian land is different from that of non-Indian land. Essentially, Indian land may not be sold by individuals but can only be leased. This can make it desirable for lower cost developments (a developer is not forced to lay out a large sum of purchase money), but it also ensures a continuing relationship of lessor and lessee that can and did lead to friction between Indian locatees and mobile home park operators at Westbank.

One subject that troubled the Westbank Band was the asserted jurisdiction of the B.C. Rentalsman, a functionary who had authority to control rents for residential tenancies in British Columbia in the late 1970's and early 1980's. Chief Derrickson wanted the Rentalsman and all his works banished from the Reserves without delay. Only then, in his view, could Reserve lands return a proper economic rent. Tenants at the mobile home parks fiercely resisted this. A comprehensive rentalsman by-law under which the Band could appoint its own rentalsman was purportedly enacted, but was apparently disallowed by the Department. The jurisdiction of the B.C. Rentalsman was sustained by the courts. This Rentalsman controversy played a large role in the Toussowasket mobile home park story told in Chapter 2 of this Report.

By-laws were enacted to raise revenue and to better control development on the Westbank Reserves. These by-laws predictably brought howls of outrage from some mobile home park operators. Chief Derrickson became the lead negotiator for rents on the Reserve and in many cases also had a personal interest in the land involved. He undertook to raise rents significantly. This too provoked complaints from several lessees. Allegations were made that the Chief wished to bankrupt the park operators so that he could have the improvements in place accrue to himself or the other parties for whom he was negotiating.

A mobile home park owners' association was formed in 1982 in response to a number of initiatives taken by the Chief in 1981. Acrimonious relations existed between the Band executive and a number of park operators. Some park operators questioned the ethics of the Band executive, and in particular, Chief Derrickson. Complaints were conveyed to Members of Parliament and the media carried stories about conflict at Westbank.

In the summer of 1982, an individual assaulted Chief Derrickson at his home in Westbank. The individual was arrested and later sentenced to a substantial term of imprisonment. Shortly after his arrest, the police established that he had acted on the instructions of some third party or parties. Chief Derrickson was certain in his own mind that this "hit-man" had been directed by certain of the mobile home park operators. This incident and the resultant charges created an outburst of media attention in British Columbia and nationally. Attitudes hardened. Chief Derrickson viewed himself as surrounded by a host of enemies. Mobile home park operators who had entered into agreements with the federal government to lease Indian land viewed transfers of authority over such leases to the Band executive as a failure to live up to the terms of the agreements. There were suspicions that the Department of Indian Affairs was corrupt or negligent. Many park operators came to feel that the Chief was power-hungry and determined to oust them from the Reserve lands and reap the benefits of their improvements.

At the same time that the mobile home park controversies were outstanding, the failure of the Northland Bank in September 1985 occasioned acute anxiety to many Band members who had never really understood or been kept properly apprised of financial transactions. They feared financial ruin from the machinations of the Chief. Many of these machinations existed largely in the minds of certain Band members, but because information on financial matters had been jealously hoarded, a considerable amount of misinformation and rumour was circulating.

In 1986, dissident elements within the Band, spurred into action in part by a non-Indian "consultant", vented their frustrations in some strongly worded petitions to the Minister, suggesting grave improprieties on the part of the Chief and Band administration. It was alleged that the local Department of Indian Affairs was either supine or corrupt and could not be trusted to give an accurate version of affairs at Westbank.

The Department was beset by growing demands from various Indian groups throughout Canada. It was operating under an Indian Act that had not been substantially updated since it was enacted in 1951. This governing statute does not reflect the major changes in Indian society in the past 35 years. The Department was going through a difficult transition period of devolution of power to Indian governments.

During the first 70 years of the twentieth century, Indian issues tended not to be a high profile area, but Indian people became much more vocal and politically active in the 1970's. This was particularly true in British Columbia where there were various controversies and internal quarrels between different groups and factions. The Department came to be viewed by many Indians as a dismal relic of the nineteenth century standing in the way of progress. In 1975, a number of district offices throughout British Columbia were occupied by Indians dissatisfied with the present state of affairs. The Department acted on their demands to close some district offices. Thereafter, matters of local administration were increasingly managed from Vancouver. Modern transportation and communication facilitated this process of more central administration, but clearly some local "on the ground" awareness of conditions at individual reserves would be lost.

On balance, these changes were positive, but at times the Department tended to lose touch with local concerns.

With regard to the Westbank situation, the Department felt it was being pilloried unfairly. It wished to have the air cleared and to have some consideration of new directions in policy, as well as possible statutory change. It had gone through a period of quite dramatic policy change with very little statutory alteration. I comment further on these matters in Section II of this Report.

Previous studies and reports had been commissioned concerning affairs at Westbank, but it was felt that previous investigations had lacked sufficient powers of compelling document discovery and testimony to achieve the best results. It was felt that a full inquiry was needed to resolve the issues at Westbank, as well as to examine certain broader issues of Departmental policy and possible statutory change. This Inquiry was constituted in August 1986 to consider Westbank specifically and the Departmental concerns generally.

I found at Westbank an exemplification of much that causes tension between Indian and non-Indian people in Canada. Indian people were more or less invisible in Canada for much of the twentieth century. Living on reserves, they were a people set apart and were often treated as second class citizens. Given the economics of earlier times, their lands usually were not economically desirable. By and large, they were not a factor in the economic life of Canada.

After World War II, Canadian society underwent a number of changes. Affluence increased, as did social consciousness. Indian lands became more valuable, sometimes as a result of underlying oil or gas deposits, but more usually because of proximity to expanding urban areas. Westbank was in the latter category. Land that had marginal utility became and is becoming more capable of enhanced utilization. There is a progression of leasing from agricultural uses and sign leases, through mobile home parks and recreational uses, to full scale residential and industrial uses.

The process of growth and change is one that always generates a certain amount of controversy and tension. At Westbank, there has been economic tension between Indian lessors and non-Indian lessees. There were jealousies and controversies between different factions in the Band. The Department was in a state of transition from the older "Indian agent" style of management to a new approach of granting greater autonomy to local Indian governments. Westbank had the fortune or misfortune to be rapidly escalating its economic activity at a time when the Department was moving away from active involvement in the management of individual bands. With regard to leases and leasing activity at Westbank, there was a very real vacuum of authority. One witness said Westbank was on the "cutting edge of change". At times, largely because of the personalities involved, it resembled a battle zone.

I heard from most of the Westbank mobile home park operators. Some could get along with Chief Derrickson, some could not. Getting along with the Chief involved what appeared to some to be capitulation. The Department was placed in a difficult position, but by failing to grapple more decisively with troublesome issues, it allowed the situation at Westbank to become increasingly explosive. The increasing wealth and political power of certain members of the Derrickson family caused resentment among some Band members. The Band administration elected to become involved in a major way with the Northland Bank. The collapse of that bank was a catalyst that caused a great amount of controversy to erupt at Westbank. There had been the earlier violent assault on Chief Derrickson that received wide publicity. There were increased calls for an inquiry to discover the real facts at Westbank concerning lessee issues and financial matters of concern to the Band and Band companies.

I found that the mobile home park operators did have some legitimate complaints. The Department was not always adhering to the terms of their leases in the setting of rents. The Band introduced a by-law regime in a chaotic fashion and there appeared to have been an absolute failure by the Band to undertake prior consultation with those affected. The Department failed to make clear to either the park operators or the Band executive what were the spheres of authority of the Department and the Band — confusion persisted and controversy grew.

While Mr. Leonard Crosby, the head of the Mobile Home Park Owners' Association, was far too extravagant in his attribution of evil deeds and motives to Chief Derrickson, there was a core of fact to his allegation of failure by the Band administration and the Department to adhere to lease terms concerning rent revision and to his allegation that the Band rentalsman by-law was misrepresented as being in force when it was not. Unfortunately, some of the highly charged allegations emanating from Mr. Crosby and those members of the Band who comprised an "Action Committee" were viewed too credulously by certain parliamentarians. These individuals, believing their constituents, took an alarmist view of events at Westbank. There were problems at Westbank and in the Department of Indian Affairs, but not of a serious criminal nature.

The most pervasive problem I found was that of conflict of interest. It seemed to be a concept virtually unknown (or wholly ignored) at Westbank. The Department, while professing to have standards in this area, could on occasion demonstrate remarkable lapses in enforcing these standards in the field. The problem is and always will be a source of continuing difficulty in human affairs. It will come to the fore in developing economic societies. The familial nature of many Indian bands makes the conflict situation even more delicate and difficult in Indian government. The problem will be increasingly seen in bands as they become more active economically. I think the recommendations I make to address this problem in Section II of the Report can contain the problem. The publicity of this Report concerning the obvious lapses at Westbank can also be a powerful force for the application of correctives at the Department and band levels throughout Canada. As I note elsewhere in my Report, Ronald Derrickson failed during his tenure as Chief to be sensitive to conflict of interest issues.

Indian band government must be run in an orderly and businesslike fashion. That is what self-government demands. This will create a climate of confidence among band members and it will ensure better relations between the band and outsiders dealing with the band. Open government which is free from conflict of interest concerns is the ideal to be sought. At Westbank, there was a strong and wilful Chief who failed to act always in a procedurally correct manner. It was the old problem of a government of men and not a government of laws.

I found no corruption in the Department of Indian Affairs, but I did find failures to come to grips with problems and bureaucratic fumblings. The Department was not vigilant in seeing that conflicts of interest were avoided. It failed to answer the concerns of lessees about rent setting difficulties. It should always be remembered that the dramatic changes in Indian Affairs in the period 1975–85 made it an intensely difficult period for Department personnel. I heard faint suggestions from some quarters that the lives of Indians would be improved only if the Department were abolished.

It is quite unrealistic to demand that the Department be abolished. It performs and will continue to perform very valuable functions. Bands that have the ability should be encouraged to accept the fullest measure feasible of self-government, but many bands are going to continue to need wide ranging support from the Department. The key factor to keep in mind is that various groups in Indian society are at very different stages of progress due to accidents of geography and history. Different regions have different needs, and I have made recommendations for some statutory and policy changes to accommodate the differing needs and aspirations of the various groups served by the Department.

There will be inevitable tensions between Indian and non-Indian groups. In practical terms, this means conflict between Indians and governments. Some issues will be susceptible of a political solution, others may become the subject of litigation in the courts. These tensions are and will continue to be painful to all concerned, but they are doubtless a necessary concomitant to the passage of Indian people from a lesser to a greater status in Canadian society. In the second section of my Report, I have made specific recommendations for statutory and policy changes that seem to me appropriate at this time.

A Commission of Inquiry has many functions. I think that most of the participants in this Inquiry have now a greater knowledge of themselves and of the relevant facts. That knowledge will be invaluable to them in their future conduct so that certain errors and excesses of the past may be avoided. Persons in political life will be more conscious of the fact that caution and circumspection are called for when allegations of wrongdoing are made to them. The Department of Indian Affairs is subject to many diverse pressures. Sometimes the noise level exceeds the substance level. I have made suggestions for dispute resolution methods that can hopefully winnow out matters of controversy that should not become high profile political issues.

Indian affairs in Canada were long neglected. In more recent times, they have received a great deal of attention, perhaps in some areas a surfeit of attention. Issues such as self-government cannot be worked through too hastily. There is a necessary process of searching for solutions. This Inquiry, coupled with the current reviews under the aegis of the Office of the Comptroller General, can provide insights and highlight needed changes. The legislative base is rudimentary and not entirely suited to the more complex modern conditions we live in; changes would be very helpful in some areas. Hopefully, the Inquiry has cleared the air at Westbank and can, by its recommendations, indicate some changes and initiatives that will allow better administration in the future.

SECTION I

The Westbank Indian Band

Chapter 1

Introduction

This Commission of Inquiry was appointed by Order-in-Council dated August 12, 1986. The Inquiry was asked to investigate certain matters of public controversy concerning the Westbank Indian Band between 1975 and 1986. It was also asked to consider possible changes to the Indian Act and Department of Indian Affairs and Northern Development policy, and to comment on any specific problem areas disclosed during the course of the Inquiry. I held hearings at Westbank, B.C. and at Vancouver, B.C. commencing in late 1986 and continuing through to the summer of 1987. The preamble of the Order-in-Council is as follows:

> WHEREAS certain matters associated with the Westbank Indian Band of Kelowna, British Columbia have been the subject of public controversy;
> WHEREAS there have been allegations of impropriety on the part of officials of the Department of Indian Affairs and Northern Development (DIAND) and of Councillors of the Westbank Indian Band (Band) in connection with the affairs of the Band;
> AND WHEREAS three reviews of these matters have been conducted and the resulting reports have been submitted to Ministers of Indian Affairs and Northern Development without resolving the concerns relating to these matters;
> THEREFORE, the Committee of the Privy Council . . . advise that a Commission do issue under Part I of the Inquiries Act . . . appointing Mr. John E. Hall of Vancouver, British Columbia to be Commissioner to inquire into and report on the circumstances of, and factors contributing to, the above-mentioned controversy, allegations and concerns. . . .

The major areas of interest to the Commission included transactions relative to lands at Tsinstikeptum Reserves 9 and 10 of the Westbank Indian Band, Band finances, the structure and exercise of Band government, and the enterprises and activities of commercial lessees of the Reserve lands.

The Westbank Indian Band has been, in British Columbia, one of that group of bands on the "cutting edge" of the changes that are occurring and will continue to occur in matters concerning Native people in Canada. At the same time, it would be no overstatement to say that in the past twenty years there has been a revolution in the thinking of the Department of Indian Affairs and generally, in matters pertaining to Indians. As with all revolutionary change, or indeed any substantial change, tensions and controversies are created as the old order gives way to the new.

Mr. Cecil Branson, Q.C., counsel for Mr. Fred Walchli, former Regional Director General of the Department of Indian Affairs and Northern Development, put this in vivid terms in his closing submission to me. He said:

> When you have devolution or self-government and turn over power to someone else who it is thought ought to have that power, there are bound to be problems in transition — the breakup of the British Empire proved this.

As noted in the Order-in-Council, there have been previous examinations of certain matters concerning the Westbank Indian Band. Reports of these examinations have been submitted to previous Ministers of the Department of Indian Affairs and Northern Development. These reports were available to myself and to counsel.

I read over these reports to generally familiarize myself with the background at Westbank. However, it was the view of the Commission Counsel, Mr. John Rowan, and myself, that the fairest method of dealing with our task was to avoid hearsay and to rely upon direct testimony. This was the basic course we followed. Of course, there were many documents filed from lawyers, departmental officials, and others to furnish a narrative of what was happening in specific areas over the years. If we had insisted on calling a witness to comment on each of those documents, this Inquiry would have extended into the next decade.

We were able, I think, to adhere to the practice of largely avoiding hearsay evidence. That is, we were able to hear and see the witnesses. Cross-examination rights were fully afforded. People were given an opportunity to speak to issues that concerned them. We could have heard more and we could have heard less. Here, as in all matters of human affairs, we had to exercise some judgement as to what was material or useful and what was not. Matters that initially appeared in one guise often appeared very different in light of later and fuller evidence. We endeavoured to make the Inquiry a searching one without prying unduly into the private affairs of individuals. I did not intend to and indeed I could not go into detail on all areas covered. I have selected those I believe material for inclusion in my Report. Here, too, there must be a pruning process or the resultant report would extend to the same length as the evidence.

The findings and recommendations concerning the first phase of the Inquiry on the subject of the Westbank situation are based on the evidence seen and heard during that phase of the Inquiry. The comments and recommendations under the second phase of the Inquiry, sometimes called Part IV and pertaining to possible changes to the Indian Act and in Department of Indian Affairs and Northern Development policy or procedures, are based on a consideration of written and oral material made available to myself and Commission staff. Certain matters touched on in the first phase obviously provided background information for the second phase.

History of the Westbank Indian Band

In order to appreciate the setting in which relevant events occurred, it is desirable that I set out a brief history of the Westbank Indian Band.

The Westbank Indian Band is one whose reserves, Tsinstikeptum 9 and 10, are situated on lands located opposite the City of Kelowna on the west shore of Okanagan Lake. The Kelowna area was settled by non-Indians about 120 years ago and the initial economic focus revolved around agricultural pursuits. At the present time, the area continues to exhibit considerable agricultural activity, with fruit farming being perhaps the largest sector. But today both Kelowna and the surrounding area are much more than just a farming region, given the very attractive physical environment. The Okanagan Valley has attracted, and will doubtless continue to attract, a growing population. Many people find it to be a good place for retirement living. It is a place with considerable development potential that has grown steadily in the past twenty years.

This growth trend has had obvious implications for the Okanagan Valley generally, and in particular has had a dramatic impact on the use of lands of the Westbank Indian Band and its members. The lands reserved for the Westbank Indian Band, being Tsinstikeptum 9 and 10, were not, until the relatively recent past, particularly desirable tracts of land. These two reserves, comprising about 2400 acres, are located on bench lands above the shore of Okanagan Lake. (A third, distant reserve, Mission Creek Reserve 8, consists of only five acres and is uninhabited.) The land is arid unless irrigated, and while it is possible to grow crops on it, the value of the land has in the past two decades become greatly enhanced by its possibilities of development for housing and business enterprises.

This is a not uncommon pattern in the history of Indian reserves in British Columbia. In many cases lands reserved for Indian bands were perhaps those of less value for agriculture. They may also have been less easily accessible, being on the distant side of a lake or river that had attracted some settlement. However, with the passage of time and the growth of population in the province, many of these lands have become, because of their location near growing urban areas, highly desirable lands and greatly enhanced in value. These situations occur most frequently in the central interior, the Lower Mainland area, and Vancouver Island. Together with the growth of a sense of political purpose in Indian people, these historic factors have combined to make some quite dramatic alterations in matters relating to Indian bands and Indian lands.

The Westbank Indian Band as a separate entity came into being relatively recently. That may be a factor, albeit a minor one, in certain controversies I examined.

The Westbank Band currently numbers approximately 250 members. It is historically and culturally part of the larger linguistic group of Okanagan Indians. The Okanagans traditionally inhabited an area stretching roughly from the head of Okanagan Lake in British Columbia to Spokane, Washington. In Canada, the Okanagans comprised a number of bands, including the Okanagan Band, the Penticton Band, the Westbank Band, the Osoyoos Band, and the Upper and Lower Similkameen Bands. There are also bands of Okanagan Indians south of the border in Washington State. In 1846, an international boundary divided the Okanagan nation, or people, at the forty-ninth parallel. However, there was a certain amount of intermingling which continued after the boundary was drawn, and cultural and familial ties continue today between the Okanagan people of British Columbia and those in Washington State.

The Westbank Band recently has been recognized as a distinct band under the Indian Act. Prior to 1963, the Westbank group was part of the larger Okanagan Band. In 1963, members of the Okanagan Band living on the reserves near Westbank requested that they be constituted a separate band. On October 18, 1963, pursuant to the provisions of Section 17 of the Indian Act, the federal government provided for separation of the Westbank Band from the Okanagan Band. At the time of that division, the population of the Westbank members approximated 165. That was about 20 percent of the then total Okanagan Band membership (765). Existing reserve lands were divided between the two bands as follows:

Okanagan Band:

Okanagan I.R. 1	25,284.43 ac
Otter Lake I.R. 2	62.00 ac
Harris I.R. 3	148.29 ac
Priests Valley I.R. 6	83.00 ac
Duck Lake I.R. 7	429.15 ac
	26,006.87 ac

Westbank Band:

Mission Creek I.R. 8	5.00 ac
Tsinstikeptum I.R. 9	1,544.59 ac
Tsinstikeptum I.R. 10	768.34 ac
	2,317.93 ac

The reserves allocated to the new Westbank Band comprised a logical geographical grouping. Reserves 9 and 10 are situated on the west side of Okanagan Lake between Kelowna and Westbank. Mission Creek Reserve 8 is a small uninhabited reserve on the east side of the lake adjacent to Kelowna. Historically, Tsinstikeptum Reserves 9 and 10 were the home of the Indians now known as the Westbank Band. The reserves were established in 1888 by Peter O'Reilly, an appointed Indian Reserve Commissioner for British Columbia. Originally these lands were part of ten reserves established for the Okanagan Band. The main reserve, Okanagan 1, is located at the head of Okanagan Lake.

Reserve 9 originally had been surveyed to include approximately 2400 acres. Mission Creek Reserve (8) was originally 55 acres. In 1913, a Royal Commission on Indian Affairs for the Province of British Columbia held hearings concerning reserves in the Okanagan area. The Commission had been appointed pursuant to a federal-provincial agreement signed in 1912, known as the "McKenna-McBride Agreement". The Commissioners were empowered to make recommendations on reserve size and location in order finally to resolve all outstanding issues in that regard between the Province of British Columbia and the Government of Canada. The Commissioners recommended that Reserves 8 and 9 be reduced. Following this recommendation, approximately 820 acres were "cut-off" from Reserve 9 and 50 acres were "cut-off" from Reserve 8. The cut-off lands later became the subject of litigation between the Westbank Indian Band and the federal and provincial governments. A settlement was achieved in 1983, resulting in certain lands and funds passing to the Band.

There were a number of reasons for separation of the Westbank group from the Okanagan Band. When the Department of Indian Affairs grouped the Indians living at Westbank together with those living at the head of the lake, it did so perhaps more because of administrative convenience than because of historical links. Although the two groups shared a common language and heritage, the distance between them was a natural division in earlier times. Historically, Indians residing near Westbank had had their own Chief or sub-Chief. Clearly, geographical isolation from the main population would be a major factor in the impetus to separate the Westbank Band from the larger group.

In 1957, residents on Reserves 9 and 10 petitioned the Indian Agent at Vernon for separate status. They noted that since they were approximately 50 miles from Reserve 1, where the Band Council convened, they had difficulty in having due regard paid to local concerns by Council. The councillors, who were all residents of the Reserve at the head of the lake, were said to be not sufficiently interested in the affairs of the people residing at Westbank. The Indian Agent, Mr. David Hett, forwarded the request together with his recommendation in favour of separation to the Indian Commissioner for

British Columbia. Mr. Hett confirmed that the Indians at Westbank were not adequately represented on the Okanagan Band Council (there were then no councillors from Reserves 9 or 10). He felt that the group at Westbank was capable of governing their own affairs and that the grant of separate status would enhance the welfare of the residents of Reserves 9 and 10. The Department did not take any concluded action on the request at that time. The status quo remained until 1962–63, at which time separate status was conferred on the Westbank group.

In addition to problems caused by geography, there were apparent philosophical differences between the Okanagan Band Council and the band members at Westbank. Some members residing on Reserves 9 and 10 were anxious to take greater economic advantage of their proximity to Kelowna. They wanted to lease their lands for commercial purposes. The Okanagan Council was generally opposed to the long-term leasing of their reserve lands. The residents of Reserve 1 were generally engaged in farming and their lands were well-suited for that purpose. Although not all the members resident on the Westbank reserves wanted commercial development, there was virtual unanimity on the issue of separation. The Westbank people generally felt that their concerns were given a low priority by the Okanagan Band Council. There was a feeling that they were not receiving their fair share of funds provided by the Department of Indian Affairs. That feeling is not unknown beyond the boundaries of Westbank. It has sometimes been noted by premiers of this province that they feel the central government is not sufficiently attentive to local issues.

In 1963, the issue of separation had come to the forefront. A special committee was organized from among the members resident on the Westbank reserves, in order to further promote the request for separation. Band members active on the committee included Ted and Margaret Derrickson, J. Norman Lindley, Alex and Mary Eli, Henry and Millie Jack, and Francis Swite. Another petition was sent to the Department of Indian Affairs asking for the division of the Okanagan Band by the creation of a new Westbank Band.

The sentiment of people at Westbank in favour of separation remained. Lack of adequate representation on the Okanagan Band Council, coupled with the difficulty of attending Council meetings due to the distance between the two communities, persisted as major grievances of the Westbank group.

In addition to continuing concerns over lack of adequate representation, an economic issue arose that sharply divided the Okanagan Band. A new floating bridge had recently been constructed, providing a direct link between Reserve 10 and Kelowna. The City of Kelowna expressed an interest in expanding the municipal boundaries to include Reserve 10. There was also a proposal to lease a substantial amount of land on that reserve for a college site. Many residents at Westbank wanted to take advantage of the commercial development potential of their reserve lands. The Chief and Council of the Okanagan Band continued to be hesitant to commit themselves to long-term leasing. They were unenthusiastic about the proposed college site lease. The District and Regional Offices of the Department of Indian Affairs were mindful of the sentiments of the Westbank group. Meetings were organized in order to persuade the Okanagan Band Council to move on the development proposals. The Westbank group also sought more representation on Council. It was suggested that one or two councillors be elected from Westbank. The Okanagan Band Council declined to accommodate these Westbank requests for representation. They continued to oppose the possible college development lease.

A vote was conducted on the question of the Westbank group separating from the Okanagans. Voters at the head of Okanagan Lake outnumbered those at Westbank by approximately four to one. The results of the vote were close — 49 percent in favour to 51 percent opposed. Ninety percent of the eligible voters at Westbank had cast ballots, virtually all in favour of separation. Only about one-third of the eligible voters on the other Okanagan reserves had cast ballots. There were just enough opposed to defeat the proposition. The federal government eventually exercised a discretion in favour of a division, probably because of the very strong sentiment at Westbank. Additionally, Westbank was becoming very much an economic area of its own.

Details of the division of land and money assets were largely completed by 1964. That year, the first Westbank Band Council was elected. It was composed of J. Norman Lindley as Chief and Harry Derrickson and Margaret Derrickson as councillors. Mr. Lindley served as Chief until 1968, when Noll C. Derriksan was elected to that office. The new Band office building on Reserve 10 is named in honour of former Chief Lindley. Noll Derriksan served as Chief from 1968 until 1974, when Mr. Lindley again took over. He was succeeded in 1976 by Ronald M. Derrickson. Although they spell their names differently, it should be noted that Noll C. Derriksan is the elder brother of Ronald M. Derrickson. Their parents are Ted and Margaret Derrickson.

The first ten years after separation were very much growing and learning years. Band members Mrs. Mary Eli and Mrs. Millie Jack gave evidence before the Commission, both having served on Council during the years following division. Mrs. Jack noted that much time was devoted to establishing an administration that could manage programs such as social assistance, education, and housing. These programs were even then beginning to be transferred from the exclusive jurisdiction of the Department to local Band administration. The pace of development on the Reserves had not been as great as may have been anticipated at the time of separation. But the Band was now a separate entity and had achieved a greater measure of control over its future course. It was located in a favourable position compared to many bands in that its lands were more likely to attract the attention of developers because of proximity to Kelowna.

The Importance of Land

The importance of land to the Native Indian people cannot be overstated. Besides its spiritual or emotional significance to them, it is truly the very cornerstone of their economic well-being. Section 2(1) of the Indian Act defines "reserve" as follows:

> . . . a tract of land, the legal title to which is vested in Her Majesty, that has been set apart by Her Majesty for the use and benefit of a band;

The concept, broadly speaking, is of a parcel of territory set aside for the communal benefit of a group of people comprising an Indian band. The concept of reserve land is that it be essentially inalienable, and that it be kept in perpetuity for the benefit of that band which has the use of the reserve. Although the concept of an absolute or fee simple interest in land is not spelled out in the Indian Act, there is provision in it for an individual band member to obtain what is called a Certificate of Possession. Section 20(2) of the Act reads as follows:

> The Minister may issue to an Indian who is lawfully in possession of land in a reserve a certificate, to be called a Certificate of Possession, as evidence of his right to possession of the land described therein.

While that interest is not, as noted, a fee simple interest, it has in practical terms much similarity to such an interest in land. A person holding a Certificate of Possession is usually referred to as a "locatee". Section 58(3) of the Indian Act reads as follows:

> The Minister may lease for the benefit of any Indian upon his application for that purpose, the land of which he is lawfully in possession without the land being surrendered.

The process of surrender, of which more later, is a method whereby an Indian band may authorize officials of the Department of Indian Affairs and Northern Development (hereinafter often referred to as "the Department") to lease Indian lands in a reserve upon such terms and conditions as may be approved by the band. It should be noted that where a proposal is made to lease band land, the consent of the electors of the band is required to the necessary surrender. That is not the case, of course, where what is being considered is a lease of a locatee's land.

There was a time when absolute surrenders were made. Those days are long past and, as a matter of practice, conditional surrenders are now normally used to effect leases of some definite duration.

Where a member of an Indian band is lawfully in possession of a tract of land located on a reserve, he or she is entitled to request the Minister to grant a lease of that land to a third party under the provisions of Section 58(3) of the Act. Again, as a matter of practice, the Department is currently reluctant to consent to leases in excess of 21 years under the provisions of this section. That policy is criticized by some Indian people.

As noted above, Indian land generally cannot be sold to outsiders, but it may be leased for a stipulated term to a third party who is not a band member. It is thus not possible for an outside party to buy a piece of land on an Indian reserve and put a development on it. Land can only be leased. The freedom to deal with a lease can in practice be much less extensive than is the case with owned land. In a certain sense, a developer can feel pressured because of this form of tenure. If the lease is lost, the improvements may pass from his possession to that of the locatee. It would be idle to pretend that these tenure issues did not contribute to some of the tensions that arose at Westbank. While development on leased land has attractive features to some developers, it also has hazards. Those hazards are not always apparent at the outset of a project.

A form of development that has become quite popular on Indian lands in areas adjacent to urban settlements in British Columbia is that of mobile home parks. This type of development on Indian land has certain advantages from the developer's point of view. The developer is not obliged to purchase a parcel of land. Instead, a developer is able to lease, for a fixed term, Indian lands located on a reserve. On those lands a development can be constructed, at less initial capital cost than would have been the case had he or she been obliged to purchase a freehold interest in land for such a facility. This is so because hitherto it usually has been cheaper to lease Indian land than to purchase (or lease) non-Indian lands. That state of affairs may by now be a thing of the past. To the extent that this means Indian people are getting a fairer return on their land, this is a good thing.

Leasing Indian land has other implications. Indian land is subject to some disadvantages from a developer's point of view. Thus, it may not be the case that absolute parity of rentals compared to non-Indian lands is justified. Appraisal of the value of Indian lands appears to me to be a more difficult task than the appraisal of non-Indian land. Non-alienability and absence of taxation are but two features that cause there to be some significant differences between the two types of real estate. I will comment later on certain issues relating to development, taxation, and related matters concerning Indian lands.

From the point of view of an Indian person in possession of a tract of land on a reserve under a certificate of possession, the desirability of entering into a lease with a developer is that a cash return is therefore generated from that tract of land. Additionally, long-term improvements may be made. The surrounding area may be enhanced by proper development. However, according to Section 28(1) of the Indian Act, an individual Indian band member may not directly lease his or her land to a third party non-Indian. Section 28(1) reads:

> Subject to sub-section (2), a deed, lease, contract instrument document or agreement of any kind whether written or oral, by which a band or a member of a band purports to permit a person other than a member of that band to occupy or use a reserve or to reside or otherwise exercise any rights on a reserve is void.

Undoubtedly a significant policy concern underlying the Indian Act and its predecessors was that Indian persons were not to be imposed upon or cheated by non-Indians. Given that general concern, it was made mandatory for any transactions relating to the disposition of Indian lands to require the involvement of the agency responsible at the material time for the administration of Indian affairs. That legal requirement is still in effect. However, in practice, there has been considerable alteration in the sense that Indian persons and bands now have a much more active role to play in the governance and disposition of their lands. The Act provides that leases of Indian land should be executed by an official acting on behalf of Her Majesty the Queen in right of Canada. In practice, that official is a member of the Department of Indian Affairs. Where bands have been granted more ample authority over land matters pursuant to Sections 53 or 60 of the Indian Act or by special statute, the practice may be somewhat altered.

Nevertheless, the basic concept is that the federal government holds Indian land in a fiduciary capacity for individuals or a band and is, in law, the party lessor. But whatever the legalities are, the commercial world follows its own course and, in fact, leases of Indian lands are similar to leases of non-Indian lands. A developer will approach a band or a band member to ascertain if a contractual arrangement can be entered into for leasing a parcel of land. If an agreement can be reached, documentation is prepared and a lease is duly entered into. But the lease, as executed, is not between AB, an Indian band member, and XY, a non-Indian, but rather between Her Majesty the Queen as lessor and XY as lessee.

Although, in fact, AB has leased the land to XY, in point of law, the direct legal relationship is between the federal government and the lessee. In such a situation, there is obviously some divergence between the situation in fact and the position reflected in the legal documentation.

There is thus a certain artificiality to the transaction in the sense that the basic business arrangement is between AB, the Indian entitled to possession of the tract of land, and XY the lessee, but this is not reflected in the documentation where Her Majesty and not AB is the lessor. It is, of course, not unknown in the non-Indian world for agents or nominees to be involved in commercial leases. Such a situation would arise where, for instance, the trustee of a minor beneficiary entered into such an arrangement with a lessee. In the latter case, however, there would often be no direct dealing between the beneficiary and the lessee, whereas in a situation involving a member of an Indian band, the reality is usually otherwise. There, the band or band member has many of the attributes of ownership but is not generally able to directly lease Indian reserve land.

The interposition of the Department of Indian Affairs and Northern Development between the band member and the third party lessee has considerable historic underpinning and justification, but I think that it does from time to time cause certain tensions and difficulties. There has always existed a very real possibility of confusion as to just who has particular responsibility or authority relative to the various issues that may arise under a lease of Indian land. There was a time when Indian people had very little control over such matters in practice. But over the past twenty years that situation has changed quite dramatically in British Columbia.

It would be to ignore reality to fail to note that practices regarding leases of Indian lands in the 1950's and 1960's differed from those in the 1970's and 1980's. This was particularly true of desirable lands near urban centres, such as the reserves of the Westbank Indian Band. There was certainly a suggestion in the evidence I heard from a number of sources that the posture of the Department as landlord in earlier times was less vigilant than in the recent past. The Department, as a landlord, was undoubtedly viewed as a much more "easy" landlord than would be the case in more recent years. Yet, to be fair to all parties, these were early days in the economic development of reserves in British Columbia and the perception of matters economic in Indian affairs then was dramatically different in a great many ways from what it is today.

As noted, Indian lands have certain desirable features from a developer's point of view. The capital cost requirements can be lighter. There may be less regulation, and that also appeals to developers. Land values on the Westbank Reserves 9 and 10 were considerably lower in the 1950's and 1960's than was the case in the late 1970's and into the 1980's. There was no particular planning regime in the 1960's. By-laws were unthought of. It was an uncomplicated era in some senses, but later, out of events that originated in that uncomplicated era, rather serious complications were to arise.

Early Development on the Westbank Reserves

Prior to 1970, there was relatively little development on either Westbank Reserve 9 or 10. The earliest registered leases, from the

1930's through to the 1950's, were virtually all short-term agricultural leases. Many Band members gained their livelihood working in the fruit and vegetable industry. Certain Band members engaged in small farming operations during this time. Indeed, agriculture still contributes to the economy of the Westbank Band. For example, Mr. Ted Derrickson on Reserve 9 and the Swite family on Reserve 10 are actively involved in farming. However, by the 1960's some members of the Westbank Band were beginning to seek out commercial and residential development as a more substantial source of income.

The new floating bridge that spanned Lake Okanagan linking Reserve 10 directly to Kelowna greatly increased the development potential of both Reserves. The City of Kelowna was viewing Reserve 10 as a possible suburb within its expanding municipal boundaries. These events and concepts were evolving about the time that the Westbank group separated from the Okanagan Band. Certain of these factors may have acted as a catalyst in the decision to form a separate Westbank Indian Band.

On February 17, 1965, about one year after separation from the Okanagan Band, Westbank Band members voted to surrender Reserve 10 for leasing purposes. This was done to accommodate a plan referred to as the "Grosvenor Laing Development", an ambitious proposal for developing the entire Reserve. However, as the details of the development were more closely scrutinized by Department officials, it was decided that the return to the Band members would be insufficient. Mr. Fred J. Walchli testified that his first assignment (as a Land Use Officer with the Department) was to review the Grosvenor Laing proposal. He recommended against the plan because he felt there was too much uncertainty as to whether the Band would get a fair return on their land. An overview of the proposal was that development costs would be the first charge against any return, thereafter management fees were to be paid to Grosvenor Laing, and any resulting profit would be split 50/50 between the developer and the Band.

After the concept of the Grosvenor Laing development had been abandoned, another group of developers came forward with a similar proposal. According to Mr. Walchli, this new proposal on behalf of Catamount Developments suffered from many of the same defects as the Grosvenor Laing plan. Although it was an improvement over its predecessor in that it allowed for Indian involvement on the board of directors and more attractive revenue-sharing, it was still viewed as creating too great a risk to the Band's valuable land holdings. Consequently, it was not allowed to proceed.

Only minor development occurred on Reserve 10 during the surrender period. A portion of waterfront had been leased for a marina development, and another small parcel adjacent to the bridge had been leased for a retail enterprise. Okanagan Regional College Council had leased a substantial lot for a college site in 1965, but relinquished it in 1973.

Reserve 9 had been surrendered for leasing in 1967 under similar conditions to those governing Reserve 10. There was not a great deal of leasing activity on Reserve 9 during the surrender period. A portion of Reserve 9 which fronts on Okanagan Lake had been the subject of some tent and trailer park development. Mr. Leonard Crosby had commenced constructing a development. Mr. Noll Derriksan attempted to develop certain of his locatee lands through a corporate vehicle, West-Kel Holdings Ltd. West-Kel held the head lease on lands which were later sub-leased to the developers of a proposed mobile home park often described as Westview Village or Park Mobile Homes. This was adjacent to the area of Mr. Derriksan's own Mt. Boucherie Mobile Home Park. In addition to such commercial leasing, there were some shorter-term agricultural leases, and there was consideration given to developing a speedway racetrack on Reserve 9.

Virtually none of the lands which had been leased during the surrender period on Reserves 9 or 10 were Band lands. Consequently, virtually no funds accrued to Band revenue as a result of the surrender exercise. The surrender could be viewed as a tentative step in the direction of Reserve development. Ultimately, it was fortunate that the proposed development on Reserve 10 did not proceed, as I believe the Band members are better off today with the great increase in land values that has occurred over the past 15 years. In December 1972, both Reserves 9 and 10 were returned to reserve status.

Under the terms of surrender of both reserves, revenues generated from leased parcels were to accrue to the locatees who had held the lands prior to the surrender, or to the Band as a whole in the cases where unallotted lands were leased. Although a surrender of reserve lands normally has the effect of removing all individual locatee interests, under the terms of the Westbank surrenders, former locatees retained a beneficial interest in their lands. Individuals continued to buy and sell these interests during the surrender period. However, no new allotments were possible. At the time the lands were returned to reserve status in 1972, the Band Council reallotted lands to individuals based on the historic beneficial interests. Lands that had been leased during the surrender maintained the status of surrendered lands until those leases expired or were cancelled. This later had some significance relative to the possible application of Band by-laws to such land — questions arose as to whether surrendered land was in the category of reserve land under the Indian Act.

Although the strategy of surrendering the entire Reserves for development was abandoned, the push for development was very much alive in the early 1970's. The federal government had undertaken programs in the late 1960's to improve the social and economic status of

Native persons. An Economic Development Program was launched at that time, the object being to encourage Indian entrepreneurship and the efficient development of reserve lands. The Westbank Band was still of a mind to see Reserve 10 developed in a comprehensive way under a community plan. A study, known as the "Interform Plan", was undertaken in 1973 to determine the optimum future development for both Reserves. The plan recommended that Reserve 10 be fully developed as a planned community, and that Reserve 9 should be used for Band housing as well as for agricultural, recreational, and commercial purposes.

The Community Plan for Reserve 10 was in structure and concept similar to the earlier plans noted above. However, it was now to be undertaken in stages by a development company to be formed by the Band. It envisaged primarily residential uses of varying densities together with a supporting town centre, a golf course, and associated recreational facilities. Some commercial uses, including an existing marina and store, were to be permitted under certain controls. It was recommended that locatees on Reserve 10 sell their lands to the development company and receive in return shares in the development. Both Band and locatee lands were to be included in the project. The concept of the plan apparently had a reasonable measure of support from the locatees of Reserve 10, although a number of locatees had substantial concerns about specific aspects of the plan. The land pooling concept was never achieved, but the Band did begin to formulate future development on both Reserves that was generally in accord with the Interform concept.

By 1973, the Westbank Indian Band Development Company had been formed to begin developing the land resources of the Band. Noll Derriksan, Chief of the Band in this period, began planning for the first residential subdivision on Reserve 10, the Sookinchute, or Lakeridge Park, development. To that end, a large block of Band lands above Lake Okanagan was surrendered. A long-term head lease was entered into with the Westbank Indian Band Development Company. This company undertook to develop the subdivision and to make lease payments to the Band. It would obtain its revenue from long-term sub-leases of individual lots. The Company's Board of Directors was comprised of appointed Band members. The project was to be financed by way of conventional financing, including long-term residential mortgages. It was conceived as a high quality residential development, a concept that has been fulfilled.

The subdivision ran into difficulties at the outset such as cost overruns and financing uncertainties. There also appeared to be a general resistance in the housing market to long-term leaseholds on Band land. By the time Ronald M. Derrickson became Chief in October 1976, the project was in some disarray. By virtue of financial assistance from the Department, coupled with an aggressive marketing strategy (and perhaps assisted by a general upswing in the local economy), the company began to overcome these early problems. Although it is difficult to be precise as to how much money this project generated as ultimate profit to the Band, it has been generally viewed as an economic development success story by both the Band and the Department of Indian Affairs and Northern Development.

While the Band, through its company, was thus developing Reserve 10, development of mobile home parks became more active in the Okanagan Valley generally and in the Kelowna area in particular. This activity was occurring particularly on Reserve 9. The parks that had been established in the late 1960's and early 1970's were expanding and others were being started. As early as 1974, Noll Derriksan, through his company Toussowasket Enterprises Ltd., had, with the assistance of the Department, undertaken plans for development on his locatee land of a mobile home park that he intended to operate. This park, later known as Mount Boucherie Mobile Home Park, was to be a high quality park. Actual construction of the park began in 1976. The project was subject to financial problems from an early date, details of which are provided in Chapter 2 of this Report.

At the time that Ronald M. Derrickson was first elected as Chief in 1976, the Westbank Indian Band and certain of its members had begun projects to develop reserve lands. However, two of the major Indian-owned initiatives, Lakeridge Park and Toussowasket Enterprises, were in rather dreary economic condition at this time. Mr. Derrickson said about Lakeridge in his evidence: "we came to the . . . conclusion that the company was bankrupt and it was unsalvageable". He was persuaded by Mr. Walchli to try to salvage it and in fact it was salvaged and became a good development. The development of this residential subdivision continues at present.

Significant Persons

In the period 1975–86, three people stand out as major figures in the history of events at Westbank. Those people are Mr. Leonard R. Crosby, a lessee of lands on Reserve 9, Mr. Ronald M. Derrickson, Chief of the Westbank Indian Band from 1976 through 1986, and Mr. Fred J. Walchli, Regional Director General in B.C. of the Department of Indian Affairs for the period 1976 through 1983. Various storms (or perhaps at times just thunderclouds) rumbled about Westbank. The three above-noted noted men were centrally involved in the various controversies that emanated from Westbank.

Mr. Crosby had become interested in developing a retirement complex on lands held by Mr. Derrickson. This was in about 1969 when he was still a member of the R.C.M.P. Later, the project changed to a mobile home park. Mr. Crosby appears to be a competent operator. Although he and Mr. Derrickson have, to put it mildly, had their differences, the latter acknowledged that Mr. Crosby's operation has been well-run and a credit to the Reserve. He was somewhat less commendatory of some other operations.

Mr. Derrickson grew up on Reserve 9. His parents, people of some stature in the community, farmed and still farm on the Reserve. Mr. Derrickson has lived through an era of dramatic change in Indian affairs. It would be fair to say that he is not wholly typical of Indian society. He has been actively involved in economic and political activities. He became interested in acquiring land on Reserves 9 and 10. He sought political office. In 1976 he was elected Chief. He possesses drive. He is not long on humility. His style can be highly confrontational. He has not had an easy life because he straddles two worlds. He gets things done but diplomacy is not his forte.

Mr. Walchli was born in Prince George and took his schooling there and at UBC. He has training in land economics and management. He worked in industry and for municipal authorities prior to joining the Department of Indian Affairs and Northern Development in 1966. Immediately prior to joining the Department, he worked for two years as a land inspector in Prince George with the provincial Department of Lands and Forests. His initial job with the Department of Indian Affairs and Northern Development was as a land use officer. When he took over as Regional Director in B.C. in 1976, there was considerable upheaval in Indian affairs in B.C. These were not easy times in which to preside. Mr. Walchli is currently a senior federal negotiator for land claims.

It is desirable to let these three parties speak for themselves to some extent. I set out hereafter excerpts of their evidence. Because these people are central to any meaningful narrative of events at Westbank, it is necessary to understand who they are and what they perceived themselves to be doing. By allowing them to use their own phraseology, one can get a sense of the individuals and their backgrounds.

How Mr. Crosby came to be a lessee on lands at Westbank Reserve 9 is set out in the following excerpt of his evidence:

> Q Mr. Crosby, I'd like a little biographical detail about you at first. You were formerly a sergeant in the Royal Canadian Mounted Police, were you not?
> A Yes.
> Q And you were stationed in Kelowna in about the years 1967 and '68?
> A Yes, I was.
> Q And about that time you became interested in acquiring some land on the Indian Reserve No. 9?

A Yes.

Q And you made application for some land?

A Yes, I did.

Q Can you tell us about the land you applied for at that time, where it was situated and what it was?

A It's on the southeast corner of No. 9 Reserve. It borders on to Boucherie Road, and that is on the north side of Boucherie Road, and it consisted of approximately three and a half acres.

Q And that's at the west end of the Indian Reserve No. 9, is it not?

A Yes.

Q And in relation to the lake, the lake is, in fact, south of your property?

A Yes.

Q You made application then in or about the year 1968 for three and a half acres of land?

A Yes, that's right.

Q And who were you dealing with at that time, to acquire that land?

A I had been talking to Ron Derrickson.

Q And was he, to your knowledge, the locatee of the three and a half acres at that time?

A I believe so.

Q And you made application then by this letter, No. 1 in this group of documents, and a lease was executed and delivered to you in the year 1969?

A That's right.

Q And I refer you now to document No. 2 in the group of documents.

A Yes, document No. 2 is a copy of a telex that I received from the administrator of land in Ottawa, and it bears the date 11th of December 1969.

Q And in that document, or No. 2, you were advised that a lease had been executed and would be forwarded to you through the Kootenay Okanagan Indian Agency.

A Yes. . . .

Q What were the significant terms of the lease that you entered into in 1969?

A It was a fifty-year lease. The rent for the first five-year period was $800 a year, I believe.

Q And when it came to revisions of the rental what did the lease provide for?

A It provided for arbitration.

Q All right. And I refer you now to document No. 3(a) and No. 3 in the volume of documents. No. 3(a) appears to be a document dated the 25th of August 1969. Included in it and on the signature page, it would be about the sixth page, it appears to have been executed by yourself, by Ronald Derrickson, by Herbert Taylor Vergette on behalf of the Department, or the Minister, or the Crown. It appears to be signed by the Chief and Councillors of that time. Do you have that before you?

A Yes, I do.

Q Is that the lease that you executed for your original three and a half acres?

A Yes.

Q All right, just going through the significant terms: There's $800 as a rental. There is a sketch showing a 3.75 acre parcel. Do you have that?

A Yes.

Q And Boucherie Road is to the south of your parcel, I take it?

A That's correct.

Q And at the top of the page, that's the western boundary of the parcel?

A Yes it is.

Q Now, who drew this lease or do you know?

A I don't know for sure.

Q All right. It was not drawn by your lawyer?

A No.

Q I refer you to page 2. There is, in the first full paragraph, after the word "provided" there are mechanics that are incorporated into the lease for rent revision. Do you see that?

A Yes.

Q All right. Would you explain to the Commission what your understanding of that clause was and what your input was into the drawing of that clause?. . .

A The main part of that matter was that in any future — or the determination of rent for any future five-year period, that is after the first five-year period, the annual payment is reflecting the increase, if any, in the market value of the unimproved land to be paid by the lessee to the lessor. Such amounts shall be agreed upon by the locatee and the lessee and in the event no agreement should be reached by arbitration with the locatee and the lessee, each selecting one arbitrator, and the two arbitrators so selected choosing a third and the decision of the majority of the three arbitrators shall be final.

Q Now that provision was agreed upon by you, by the locatee and by the Crown or the Department of Indian Affairs, is that correct?

A Yes.

Q And the idea behind that clause was the concept that you would not pay any increased rental based on any improvements that you placed upon the land?

A That's my understanding, yes.

(Transcripts: Volume I, pp. 5–10)

Thus it was that Mr. Ronald M. Derrickson and Mr. Leonard R. Crosby became known to each other and entered into legal relations, one with the other. Or perhaps more accurately, one might say that they were prevented from entering into direct legal relationship, one with the other, by the provisions of the Indian Act, and that that may in turn have led to many of the problems that later surfaced between them. Interposed between the two was the Department of Indian Affairs and Northern Development. Later on, following his retirement from the police force in 1971, Mr. Crosby arranged to lease additional land from the father of Ronald Derrickson, Ted Derrickson. Mr. Crosby told me of the improvements he began on the land.

Q What type of financing did you arrange for the development of this property?

A I used my own funds initially, but all of those weren't immediately available when I first commenced and I had some financing from the Kelowna and District Credit Union.

Q Did you grant a mortgage over the property at that time?

A No, I think my first financing was by way of personal guarantee. There wasn't a mortgage registered against it.

Q What buildings did you put on the property?

A The first building we constructed was a duplex building, approximately 1600 square feet, one bedroom on each side, with a carport and a small sundeck.

Q Did you do any levelling of this land?

A Yes, we did some, before building the duplex, but not the whole acreage initially.

Q When was the duplex completed?

A To my recollection my brother was the first occupant of one half of it and I think that was approximately Christmas, 1971.

Q What else did you do to develop that property?

A Well, we had to get power onto the property and put in water lines. We roughed in a gravel road initially.

Q And the source of your water was not the lake, but the well you had dug?

A Yes. . . .

Q Now, you continued to develop that property of three and a half acres. You put in a duplex. Did you put in other buildings?

A Not in '71, but I recall we did put in the basement for the second duplex, that is all the cement work. I think that was in 1972.

Q Was there any further development done in that period of time?

A No. We were working at it all the time, mostly my father-in-law and I. There was a — we also built my brother's house or started to build it. I think that was in the period of '72 to '73.

Q And in the first five-year period of that lease, how much building did you do on the property?

A That's between '69 and —

Q Say '74.

A — '74. I believe we largely completed my brother's house, and the first duplex would be finished and the second duplex commenced. And we've done a lot more site work. There was an awful lot of earth to move to fill the ravines.

(Transcripts: Volume I, pp. 12–14)

By the mid-1970's the direction of the enterprise had shifted. Mr. Crosby now wished to develop a mobile home park. He said some problems arose relative to the lease and that he was not well treated by the Department of Indian Affairs over an arbitration clause:

Q All right. Now, did you have many discussions, and I'm now talking about the years 1974 and '75, with the locatee of the land, Ron Derrickson?

A On one or two occasions, but not protracted discussions.

Q All right. Now, I'd like to ask you about something else in this letter. Do you recall there was an arbitration clause in the lease that you signed?

A Yes.

Q Now in the first paragraph of this letter it refers to an inability to arbitrate and also the Department's acceptance of a contractual arrangement that cannot be honoured. Do you see that?

A Yes.

Q I direct your attention also on the second page of the letter to the clause that says:

"Arbitration as outlined in the lease is inoperative."

A That's right.

Q All right. Would you tell us about what discussions you had with respect to the arbitration of the revised rent or a new rent?

A Well, it's just as the letter states, the Department representative adopted the view that the arbitration — the reference to arbitration in the lease was inoperative. They couldn't or wouldn't use it.

(Transcripts: Volume I, pp. 20–21)

Mr. Crosby came to believe the Department was not living up to the terms of the lease. He felt the Department should go to arbitration on the rent, but the Department thought otherwise. The arbitration clause was poorly drawn and there was some basis for the Department saying that it was "inoperative" — perhaps "inadequate" would have been a better term. It was clearly difficult to implement.

Q And it appears that the Department fixed a rent at $2100 per year in the letter, and then it's stroked out, and $2675 is written in in September 6, 1974.

A That's correct. And in their letter on the 9th, that's 10E, dated the 9th of September 1974, there's a P.S. at the bottom,

"In our letter to you dated September 6, 1974 in connection with lease 69–2249 the new rental is shown as $2100. This should read $2675."

Q Can you elaborate on that for us, please, or can you tell us anything more about it?

A I took it that he was drawing to my attention that there'd been a typographical error.

Q In any event, that lease — those letters were not acted on, were they? A new arrangement or a new deal was made.

A Yes.

Q Would you tell us about that, please?

A Well, I think we'll come to those letters in a moment, but we didn't seem to be getting — be able to resolve the difference of opinion as to what the rent should be, so I needed an arbitrator and I wanted the Department to see that the rest of the lease was lived up to.

Q Did the Department name an arbitrator?

A No.

Q And there was no arbitration?

A No, there was not.

Q However, you later, in that year or the year following, entered into further negotiations for a lease, did you not?

A Yes, at that time, since we couldn't seem to agree or get the arbitration matter in progress, I offered to sell them my leasehold interest and leave the property, but this never came about nor did I receive an offer of any sort in reference to his offer to sell to them. . . .

Q In any event, up until the period of 1975 or 1976 you had not started to develop any form of mobile home park?

A No.

Q I refer you to letter No. 13, a letter to Ronald Derrickson, the 5th of July 1975, which reads as follows:

"After our last conversation I contacted Mr. Hulley at the Vernon office and he offered to see you within a few days and was to contact me. However, I believe he no longer acts in his former capacity.

I believe we are close to being able to settle our mutual differences, however, we appear to have a communications problem and to assist in that regard may I suggest that you ask your brother Noel or your father if he would mind contacting me for a short meeting in order that I can convey my current thoughts on the matter of rent to you through a third party who I believe has the confidence and esteem of both of us."

Now, what was happening at or about that time?

A We still hadn't resolved the rent issue and we had been discussing the enlargement of the area I leased from about three and half to approximately seven and a half acres.

We were close to an agreement on what rent would be suitable to him for the seven and a half acres, but it's my recollection that Ron was not the locatee of that land at that time. I believe that the land belonged to his father or was under the locatee or certificate of possession of his father.

Q You were thinking at that time of leasing an additional parcel of three and half or four acres?

A That's right.

Q You were thinking at that time, then of creating a mobile home park?

A Yes.

Q And to your knowledge or belief at that time Ron Derrickson was not the locatee of the property adjacent to you, but his father, Ted Derrickson, was the locatee, do I have that right?

A That was my understanding, yes. I eventually did lease this additional four-acre piece of land. When the locatee status changed I don't know.

(Transcripts: Volume I, pp. 21–26)

Around 1975 momentous changes were occurring in Indian affairs in B.C. There was a considerable degree of unrest, and relations between the Department and bands were becoming more tenuous — some district offices were closing. Mr. Crosby testified about this as follows:

Q Now, the next letter in this bundle of correspondence is from the Department. It's number 14. It's dated July 16, 1975 and it directs

you to make payments under your lease not to the Kootenay
Okanagan District Office but to a Vancouver office of the
Department of Indian Affairs.

A That's correct.

Q Can you tell us what has happening at or about that time?

A The district office, as this letter says, is closed. That is, the office
in Vernon closed at that time.

Q Okay, and that office closed at that time and has never reopened?

A No.

(Transcripts: Volume I, p. 27)

Ultimately, Mr. Crosby, through his company Golden Acres Ltd.,
acquired a lease of about 7.5 acres in 1976. He testified about the terms
of the lease:

Q Now, let's just deal with the significant parts of this lease, No. 23.
It was a lease for forty-five years?

A Forty-five years, seven months. Yes.

Q And there's payment of rent of $1400, and then the rent for the
first five-year term, I take it looking at page three, was an annual
rent of $3500?

A That's correct.

Q And then you had in there on page three a formula for establishing renewal rents for revised rents for the future.

A Yes.

Q All right. Did you have any input into the drawing of that
formula?

A Yes. When we had agreed as to the new area and the new rent,
then I was in Vancouver and I don't know for certain who it was
that I was speaking to, but it was in relation to the preparation of
the lease and I was insisting that the lease contain words which
would acknowledge the development, or the authorization of the
development had already been done; also that it was to be a land-
only lease.

Any future renewal of rent in any future five-year period would
be in respect to land only and they were to ignore any improvements that I'd made on the property. Also there was a discussion
and I was saying in effect that I wanted some assurance that any
future land rent would not be so excessive that it would be
impossible for me to carry on with the lease.

Those generally were the things that I was asking or insisting
that should be included in the new lease.

(Transcripts: Volume I, pp. 37–38)

During 1974–76, there were discussions back and forth between Mr.
Crosby, Mr. Derrickson, and officials of the Department as to whether
Mr. Crosby would go forward with his development plans or whether
Mr. Derrickson would buy Mr. Crosby's completed developments.
Ultimately Mr. Crosby entered into a new lease in 1976. The lease was
different from leases current today. It provided for setting lease rates
based on applying bank prime rates to appraised land value. It also
provided that "the level of income being generated by the tenant from

its use of the land will be taken into account". As well, the lessee consented to observe by-laws, regulations, etc. of "every federal authority or agency applicable to the land and improvements".

These clauses loomed large in later controversies between Mr. Crosby and Mr. Derrickson. The concept of a percentage rent surfaced in a letter from Mr. Crosby to Mr. Kerr of the Department dated April 19, 1975. A dispute over this later led to a rupture of relations between Mr. Crosby and Mr. Derrickson — this breakdown had the unfortunate result that dialogue ceased and acrimony increased. However, strains in the relations between the two men could be perceived as early as July 1975 when Mr. Crosby wrote to Mr. Derrickson seeking to involve a third party and suggesting "your brother Noel [Noll] or your father" as a mediator of sorts. This is a theme we shall see again in the form of Mr. Crosby seeking to deal not with Mr. Derrickson but with officials of the Department.

During a period of dramatic and intense change, 1974 through 1976, came the advent of Mr. Ronald Derrickson as Chief of the Westbank Indian Band. He gave evidence before the Commission commencing on June 5, 1987. He described his early life, how be became interested in Band affairs, and what he aspired to do for his Band and Native people in general:

Q Mr. Derrickson, what is your present age?
A I am 45.
Q And what is your present occupation?
A I am a businessman.
Q Where were you born and raised?
A I was born in the Kelowna General Hospital, and I was raised on the Westbank Indian Reserve.
Q Mr. Derrickson, could you tell us where your parents were raised?
A My father was born in Winfield and was raised in Westbank, as far as I know. My mother, I think, was born in Ashcroft and was raised at St. Mary's Mission in Omak, Washington, and I guess, her remainder of life, she looked after me.
Q Mr. Derrickson, what are your earliest recollections of life on the Reserve in Westbank?
A Well, I guess my earliest recollections are somewhere in the late 1940's, and I think life on our Reserve then would be consistent with a non-serviced, rural — very rural area — Indian Reserve. It was generally, the most of homes, I guess at that time, none of the homes had running water, none of the homes had bathrooms, some of them never had homes.
   You know, our people were nomadic, they followed work. I myself, we worked for the Chinamen in the vegetable gardens. We worked thinning and worked in apple orchards, anywhere we could make a buck to eat.
Q Could you tell us a little bit about what your recollections are in reference to employment on the Reserve in those early days?
A Well, there is basically two to three types of employment offer to a Native Indian in those days; that was working in the vegetable and

fruit industry in this valley with large canning facilities. We never got the privilege of working in the canning facilities, we worked out on the farms in the sun. They worked, like I say, the vegetable gardens, the orchards; some of the Indians went to work in a logging camp. That wasn't very much in the early days.

We were generally nomadic in nature. We had to move around the area where the jobs were and small farmers.

Q Mr. Derrickson, what is your earliest recollection of where you lived, or the house that you lived in upon the Reserve?

A Well, the first one I remember was a one-room shack, somewhere just off of Boucherie, I would say, north of Boucherie Road, where the Boucherie Pub is right now, and my dad's vineyard is — the one-room shack that had no running water and no bathrooms in it.

Q Did you live in that particular area for most of your younger life?

A I lived down in that area all my life.

Q Mr. Derrickson, do you have any recollection in the early days on the Reserve, as to what the policing was like on the Reserve?

A Well, the original police used to be the Provincial Police. As far as Indian is concerned, I guess it's like most government bodies, they are the enemy, because, you know, the Indian, in my mind, and as I grew up, seems to always get the short end of the stick when they were involved. I'll give you an example.

When the police used to come for sport on Saturday nights and they used to come to the Reserve and kick in a few doors on the Reserve to find out if there was any Indians drinking, because in them days, the Indians weren't allowed to have liquor.

Q What is your early recollection in reference to your schooling?

A My brother, Noll and I, were one of the first Indians ever allowed to go to a public school in Westbank, and it was tough.

Q How long did you go to that particular school, Mr. Derrickson?

A We went there the first grade one of our schooling, and then it was so rough on us that our folks pulled us out and sent us to St. Mary's Mission in Omak.

Q Now, your brother Noll, is older than you are?

A Yes.

Q But you both started school at the same time?

A That's right.

Q And you both started school in Westbank?

A Yes.

Q Tell us about the type of difficulties that you had in that first year of schooling.

A Well, all Indians were made to sit at the back of the class. You know, for example, when the teacher would ask the question of the student, and if an Indian put his hand up you know, he'd just look like a dope sitting there with his hand up, because nobody would ask him a question. It got better as years went by, but not much better during my time I was in school.

Q Now, a decision was made by your parents to remove from that school after the first year?

A That's right.

Q And where did you go then?

A St. Mary's Mission.

Q Where's that?

A Omak, Washington. It was, I guess, I don't know what the term for that school would be, an Indian residential Catholic school, with all the Catholic dogma and trimmings, I suppose.

Q And how long did you remain at that school?

A A year.

Q And then what happened?

A Well, it was worse than the public school, so we came back to the public school.

Q How long did you remain in the public school?

A I left public school in the middle of grade nine.

Q What gave rise to you leaving school at that time?

A I was entered in the University — in those days they had a University program — I don't know if it's the same, it's been so many years since I've seen the inside of a school. The principal removed me from the University program, so I thought there wasn't much point; I wasn't getting along very well with him anyways, so I just left.

Q Was there a particular incident that gave rise to you leaving in reference to that particular program that you were involved in?

A Yes. There was a violent incident that made me suddenly decided I had better make an exit.

Q Did you ever return to school after that?

A No. Yeah, I went during the early '50's, or the mid-'50's, there was a national report, and I can't remember who it was done by, but basically the report said that the education and the housing situation with Indian people was deplorable, and there was a great surge of conscience and the non-Indian sympathy for the Indian people had grown at such a rate, they decided to give a bunch of Indian kids a chance to learn something.

So, I was chosen as one of the children — or young teenagers — to go to the University of British Columbia, to attend a six-month extension course in agriculture, so they figured they'd get us back into the fields somehow.

Q And did you attend that course?

A I did.

Q Is there anything that particularly sticks in your memory that happened during the course of that time at UBC, that you can recollect today?

A Well, that was the first time I ever met Senator Len Marchand. He heard I was in the school; he heard there was an Okanagan Indian down there, and he came to see if I had, you know, enough pairs of socks and two pairs of pants for a change. He was going through the University on an Agriculture course then.

Q And that was the first time you were involved with Senator Marchand, is it?

A That's the first time in my recollection that I remember Senator Marchand. Of course, he wasn't a Senator then.

Q Mr. Derrickson, when did you first start working?

A As soon as I could, I guess, get my butt between two rows of onions, you know.

Q How old would you have been then?

A Five or six.

Q After you finished school, what did you do?

A I went to work in logging camps and orchards, whatever, ranches, you name it, wherever there was a job and where they would hire me, I would work.

Q How long were you involved in the logging business?

A Off and on, four or five years.

Q What did you do next as far as employment was concerned?

A It's so long ago, it's hard to remember, but I started welding in Vancouver for Wagstaff Hoists, and then I got into a Union by getting into the shop. Then as a union member, I travelled all over Canada, and the northern west half of the United States, doing service work for Wagstaff Hoists.

Q Did you take an apprentice program in welding?

A That's right.

Q And you completed that course?

A Yes.

Q And that was your employment for a number of years, was it?

A That was — well, that's the only profession I ever gained.

Q What type of days and hours did you work in reference to that particular business?

A Well, you know, in the boom days of '60's, when they were building oil pipelines and pulp mills all over the country, I worked eight hours on and eight hours off, almost seven days a week for six months. I worked when they build the Northwood Pulp Mill in Prince George, I worked from the time it opened until the time that W.A.C. Bennett cut off the overtime, then there was no use working there, you know, it was a hard place to — Prince George wasn't my favourite place for a Native son to be.

Q Mr. Derrickson, was it during that period of time that you started to garner somewhat of a capital base?

A I saved as much money as I could get my hands on. What I saved, I bought land with.

Q Did you have a plan at that time, in reference to what you were going to use that capital for?

A Well, I don't know at that age, if I was bright enough to have a plan, but, you know, I intended to — I was experiencing — trying to experience business, so I was looking at anything that I could make a fast buck at. The only thing that had been drummed into my head from the time I was born was my dad said that the land doesn't go away. If you buy it, it will be there tomorrow. So, you know, that was, basically, the first thing that I started to look at.

Q At that period of time when you were away working, was your father involved in the management of looking after a series of land parcels on the Westbank Indian Band Reserve?

A Yes. My father was always very ambitious in regard to having a large land base, and he has a large land base together. In fact, I can remember the Indians used to call him the "Commissioner" and the "Baron", you know, jokingly, because he had all this useless land. Like, some of it is still useless today. But, I can tell you, none of us are going to give up any.

Q Did you start acquiring or buying land during this period of time?

A Yes.

Q And you bought land at that time, mainly on the Westbank Indian Band Reserve, is that correct?

A Mainly, except for one other parcel I got involved in with a group of Kelowna businessmen, and they gave me my first lesson in knowing what the hell you're doing before you get in it, because they skinned me for everything I had.

Q Mr. Derrickson, during the 1950's, could you tell me what your recollection is of how the administrative part of the Westbank — what is now the Westbank Indian Band operated? I realize it was the Okanagan Band at that time, but could you tell me how the administration of the Band operated?

A Well, I wasn't very much interested in them days. I was more interested in getting enough money for lunch, but, you know, my recollection that my parents were very involved, and that they had tried, unsuccessfully, for some years with the Okanagan Indian Band to get some kind of representation — even a Councillor — elected to represent the interests of the Westbank Indian Reserve.

It was a joke. They laughed. I mean, there was no way we were going to get representation for anything, period, up there. So, as I remember, the initial committee was Francis White and my dad, and Mary Eli and Millie Jack, and Bert Wilson, who started lobbying. I think in them days, and I can't remember offhand, the big guy in Indian Affairs was called the "Commissioner", and I think, eventually after a lot of lobbying and votes of both Bands, it was agreed that we could leave the Okanagan Reserve, and we formed our own Reserve.

Q Did you have any experience in dealing with the Indian agency in Vernon, during the period of time it existed?

A No. I was like any other Indian. I pretty well went along with what they told us to do, and pretty well respected what they told us to do in those days.

Q Mr. Derrickson, was there much in the way of communication between the Natives that were in the Westbank Indian Band area and the Okanagan Band, or the agency office in Vernon, during that period of time?

A Well, I don't know. If you had an agriculture lease or something, you went up there and, other than that, I don't really know. I know that you couldn't do much; you couldn't fence; you couldn't put up wire. I know that a truck would come along every couple of years with the deck of the truck full of paint, and it was all the odd colours that no other — I guess all the paint companies wanted to get rid of and give the Indians the orange and purple, and green, bright green paints.

So, I guess that's become part of our heritage, having bright houses. . . .

Q Mr. Derrickson, what are your first recollections of your dealing with the Department of Indian Affairs, and who were you dealing with?

A Well, in respect to, I guess the very first dealings with the Okanagan Indian agency and the first guy, I remember, was Dave Hett. I can remember trying to get some barb wire from him for my dad's house, and he wouldn't give me any and it made me so upset he wouldn't give me any barbed wire, but the guy had just taken 40 rolls out of there before me and I only wanted 6 rolls. I think that was the first interaction I ever had with the Department of Indian Affairs and I lost, so I never did get my wire.

Q Were you dealing, at that stage, with an Indian Agent in Vernon in the early years?

A Yes.

Q How would you characterize the attitude and the response of the Indian Agent, in reference to Native people, at that point in time?

A Well, some of them were very good. Dave Hett, you know, he was from the old school. I think he might have had a bit of a military background because it was traditional that those people in the military would, when they retired from the military, they would come and they would work for Indian Affairs, and you could see that. You know, they were very disciplined in their manner and their ways, and very short, you know. We were expected to, you know, really were expected — the same thing is expected today, only they do it a little more eloquently.

Q They set rules and you followed them?

A Pretty well, pretty well. The Indians are — they are an enterprising race. They learned how to sneak around them and do things without them. I learned just as well as the rest of them, you know. In the old days, you couldn't even sell any of your produce or your cattle without their permission. But hell, we didn't pay no attention to them, we'd sneak off and do it without them. And we still don't pay much attention to them.

Q Except for when you go on fishing trips down to the Regional office?

A Well, I mean, you have a responsibility if you are a Chief or a Councillor of a Band, to try and better your people and to look after your various programs. Any time, in the early years, there was really not much going on around here, I mean, you could all meet at the local restaurant or something and talk about what could happen, but eventually we got to a point where we went down to see what could happen, you know. And we'd go down on our little fishing trips to Indian Affairs in Vancouver, this was after the District office was closed, just to see what was available. I mean, it was a learning experience. We'd try to get on a first-name basis with everybody.

Generally, most of the technical bureaucrats were very helpful to the Indian people and would really try. I would say, probably, nine out of ten officials in the Indian Affairs were very good and very helpful, but it was very frustrating to deal with them and they were generally frustrated, because of the policies and the rules and the laws, and it's always been my complaint that the Indians are guided by 5 percent law and 95 percent policy. . . .

Q Mr. Derrickson, what is your recollection as to when the Band split, with the Okanagan Band, as to what transpired then, as far as the Westbank Indian Band was concerned?

A Well, even though there was divisions in our Reserves back then, our people knew well and good that in order to get away from, I mean, I guess to make a long story short — we hated each other less than we hated them up there. So, we had to kind of come together to get away from them up there, and we did — or they did, you know, I was just a kid.

Once we got divided from them, we elected the new Chief and Council. I think our first Chief and Council was elected by acclamation, but I can't remember.

Q Now, once that Band was separated and formed here, did you, when you were in Westbank, or at home, or at your property, did you take part in Band meetings and Band activities?

A Yes. I very, very ever seldom ever missed a meeting, the Band meetings of this Band, since I can remember. Not especially because I wanted, because our parents made us go, you know, we didn't have much choice in the matter. It was like going to church when we were younger. . . .

Q . . .Your first venture into Band government was in 1976, is that correct?

A That's right.

Q You ran against Norman Lindley?

A That's right.

Q And you were elected Chief?

A That's right.

Q Now, I would like you to tell us as to what your involvement was or what your focus of interest was in the first few months after you became Chief.

A Well, basically to find out where the Band was, to review the records and with particular emphasis on the Band's development company, the Westbank Indian Band Development Company.

(Transcripts: Volume LXV, pp. 9625–9695)

As noted above, the 1970's were times of very significant changes for Indian people both in British Columbia and in Canada generally. Mr. Fred J. Walchli gave evidence before the Commission in March 1987. He said he joined the Department of Indian Affairs and Northern Development in 1966 as a land use officer. He said that, prior to 1966, he had worked as a land inspector for the Department of Lands and Forests in Prince George. He was approached by Arthur Laing, a federal Cabinet minister responsible for Indian Affairs. Mr. Laing had expressed concerns about the way Indian lands were being managed and encouraged Mr. Walchli to join the Department of Indian Affairs and Northern Development. He described the situation when he arrived as follows:

Q Would you describe briefly the state of the Department at that time?

A My role at that time was primarily in dealing with land problems, and I suppose the first thing that struck me when I joined the Department was the general attitude toward the management of Indian lands. The feeling seemed to be that Indian lands had very little value, that if they did have any value, then we should take whatever proposal came along and try and lease it out.

There was no thought given to standards of development, arriving at proper rent rates, and no such thing as rental reviews, except on reviews that were no longer acceptable, like ten- and twenty-year periods. In any event, the approach seemed to be to accommodate the lessee, not the Indian.

The Indian people were starting to object to this in a big way. They were starting to enter into their own agreements which were what we called buckshee leases. The Okanagan was particularly bad for that, but all throughout British Columbia and indeed Canada there were a number of bands who had virtually taken over leasing out their own lands. They entered their own agreements, collected their own rentals.

They had no written agreements; certainly they weren't registered by the Department, and part of my role was to try and regularize a lot of those agreements.

Q That is what you called "buckshee agreements"?

A That's correct.

(Transcripts: Volume XXXI, pp. 4233–4234)

In 1969, Mr. Walchli was appointed the Regional Superintendent of Economic Development. He said about the land holdings situation generally in the Okanagan:

Q Could you give a brief overview of your work involving the Okanagan District, in particular with regard to land use during the period from '66 to '69?

A Well, this was one of the areas that we had most trouble with in British Columbia. The amount of land held by Indians is around 830,000 acres, of which 200,000 is in the Okanagan/Kootenay area, and another 200,000 in the Kamloops area. So half the land is in the southern part there, and in the Okanagan we had very bad situations.

On the Okanagan Reserve out of Vernon the whole lakeshore had been leased out in terms of buckshee leases, and of course the health authorities were pressuring us to develop some standards and get control of the situation. In Westbank we had one or two of the lessees, particularly on the Tomat properties, and Leo Matte, there was Shady Camp was the other one, I think — we were trying to undo deals that the Indians had already entered into, because we couldn't accept them because the standards weren't right, the lease fees weren't right, and Arthur Laing at the time was signing every lease, and he just wouldn't accept them until he was sure there was a proper development plan that went with it.

Then in terms of going through to Penticton we had a case where the airport had been taken during the war, had never been compensated — the Indians had never been compensated. We had a lot of problems trying to regularize that situation.

There were a number of leases on Skaha Lake which were regarded as unacceptable. We had a problem with the railroad through Penticton. Then, of course, we had Osoyoos. The bands there were trying to go ahead with a similar development to Grosvenor-Laing. They had another group of people in there, and we ended up rejecting that proposal because it didn't meet the type of standards we insisted upon.

There were highway right-of-way problems where the province had taken land without ever compensating the Indians, no agreements in place. It was a bad scene. I spent the first three years most of the time going through the Okanagan trying to correct a lot of these problems.

(Transcripts: Volume XXXI, pp. 4239–4240)

Mr. Walchli left British Columbia and was in Alberta from 1974 to 1976. He returned to British Columbia in mid-1976. This was after the closure of the Vernon office. He outlined the situation when he arrived.

Q So, Mr. Walchli, you took up your position as Regional Director General July 2, 1976. How many reserves, and what was the structure of the government of the Indian peoples at that time?

A Well, there were 1621 reserves. If you refer to the map here, and it's not very good —

Q You have a map above you, yes?

A All these little dots represent reserves. There's 194 bands in British Columbia. There were 192 at the time, but later on two of them subdivided. I know one of them subdivided, and two more.

Anyway, we ended up with 194 bands. Now, when I took over in British Columbia I took over after the long hot summer of '75.

Q We'll go into that later.

A But what I found in British Columbia was a situation where the relationship of the Indians was extremely bad. The Department, because of what happened in 1975, had in fact become almost non-functional to the extent where the contact between the Indians and the Department was on an occasional basis.

Our staff would go out to the reserves if they were requested to, but otherwise they preferred not to. Indian people generally had given up on the Department at that point. In fact, they wanted the Department completely removed from their life.

(Transcripts: Volume XXXI, pp. 4247–4248)

Mr. Walchli went on to note that this was a time of considerable change in the dynamics of the Indian bands and the Department. He said that Indian people were seeking to take on more administration of programs.

A As we introduced programs, the bands began to take advantage of them. Throughout the British Columbia region we started introducing welfare programs and housing and so on, and they became very interested in development, all facets of development, social and economic.

But as they became more schooled in understanding the dynamics of development, they began to want to take over from us. Now, the band councils at that time had very little authority. The Department of Indian Affairs virtually did all the programming, or developed all the programs on the Reserves.

We administered the welfare; we administered the education; we provided the bus services; we built the houses and so on. The Indian band council was nothing more than a group of people who would advise the Department on where development was to go, and approve certain Band Council Resolutions relating mostly to land and the trust functions, but also approving certain programs.

(Transcripts: Volume XXXI, pp. 4251–4252)

He described what lead to what he described as the "uprising in '75". As noted earlier, the period 1974–75 was one of stormy relations between Indian people and the Department in B.C.

> A So you had a situation by 1974 which basically had seen Indian Affairs move forward with the transfer of programs — or not transfer of programs — rather the implementation of programs virtually under Indian Affairs' control.
>
> We had band councils who began to realize that development was the way to go, but they wanted to control the development. They wanted to manage it. We had a provincial organization, an Indian organization, which had become divorced from their members and were pursuing initiatives which the membership did not support.
>
> But because the money was going to the provincial organization and because the bands didn't have any control over it, they began to have quite a problem of — a problem arose between the two which actually became quite acrimonious. In fact, it led to the uprising in '75.
>
> THE COMMISSIONER: Who were the combatants in that particular contest?
>
> THE WITNESS: In '74?
>
> THE COMMISSIONER: Yes. You said there was some sort of controversy or dispute. Who were at each other's —
>
> THE WITNESS: Well, you had two sets of things happening. The bands were down on the Department because we would not turn control over to them fast enough, and you had the bands starting to turn on the Union of Indian Chiefs because they were not able to control that organization, and they felt that organization was not providing the kind of services that they were designed to do, and they objected very strongly to the idea that the federal government would provide up to $2 million a year to a provincial organization in which the membership had no control of.
>
> (Transcripts: Volume XXXI, pp. 4256–4258)

Mr. Walchli said that when he arrived back in British Columbia as Regional Director General there was considerable disaffection and confusion in the Indian community. Many people in that community were advocating complete divorce from the Department.

> A ...The result of all this was a total collapse in British Columbia of the Indian organizations; the Union of B.C. Indian Chiefs collapsed. The district councils were removed. What was left were the Indian bands with virtually no control over the Department of Indian Affairs at that point, and almost seemingly taking the point of view that from here on in, if they could not get it legally, they were simply going to assume control of their lives.
>
> Now, they were going to make the point with the Department and with their own membership that they were no longer going to rely on the Department of Indian Affairs, and as part of the national period of discontent, as the caravan was marching on

Ottawa, each region was confronted by Indians who occupied offices or led confrontations of one kind or another.

In British Columbia, the summer of '75, seven of our district offices were occupied. The regional office was occupied, three of the district offices were closed for good, and the Indians rejected government funding.

So from the summer of '75 until the summer of '76 when I arrived here the Department and the Indian people had all but broken off relationships, and there was very little development going on on reserves. As well, the Indians had decided to demonstrate to the Department they could go it alone without government funding.

That was the situation I found in 1976 when I got here.

(Transcripts: Volume XXXI, pp. 4263–4264)

Mr. Walchli noted that a significant shift in policy was undertaken by the Cabinet and the Department of Indian Affairs and Northern Development in 1976. By 1976, cooler heads were prevailing and it was evident that the Department and Indian people could not carry on satisfactorily under the old regime but neither were Native people in a position to entirely dispense with Departmental assistance. Mr. Walchli spoke of the changes around that time.

A ...Perhaps the most significant event that took place that year was when the Cabinet approved the Indian Government Relationships Paper...

Q That, in your view, was a significant watershed in the relationships?

A Very much so, because it did a number of things. First of all, the 1969 White Paper had proposed a new direction which had virtually seen the federal government removed from having any trust responsibility, and had turned over the responsibilities either to the province or to the Indian people themselves.

The Indian people had accused the government of following integrationist and assimilation policies, which they found not acceptable. This paper then was designed to answer a lot of concerns that the Indian people had, as well as to set a new direction and a different way of dealing with the Indian people.

You'll note the first — or one of the major statements in the policy talks about the new concept being "one of Indian identity within Canadian society rather than a separation from Canada society or assimilation into it."

This was the government response to the White Paper. They now formally recognized that the Indians had a place in the sun, and that the intent was to develop a new relationship based on transferring to Indian people the control of programs and the management of programs.

Now, the document did a number of things. First of all, I want to point out this was approved by the Cabinet, not just by the Department, and it was issued under the instructions of Judd Buchanan; and all regions were commanded to take into account the new directions in the way they organized and delivered programs.

It was to be sort of the underlying philosophy for the development of policies, as well as to the delivery of programs. Now, there's a few important things in it. Basically from here on in there was to be mechanisms set up across the country at the band, provincial and national levels where Indian people would be consulted and have an involvement in the policy-making and in the program development, and also have a lot of say in how programs were delivered to the reserves.

The paper is broken into two areas which really deals with the policy, and then the question of program development and delivery.

(Transcripts: Volume XXXI, pp. 4265–4267)

Mr. Walchli said that the thrust of the policy of the Department at the time was to transfer programs as quickly as possible.

What was happening in British Columbia, as described by Mr. Walchli (and it was not confined to British Columbia alone, of course) was a very profound change in the relationship between the federal government and Indian people. That profound change spilled over into relationships between third parties such as lessees of reserve lands and Indian people. If it had been true that the Department was a somewhat somnolent landlord, that assumption could no longer be made. The old verities, good or bad (and the goodness or badness probably depended on the perspective from which one viewed these matters) were being swept away, and a new era was being born.

The years 1975–86 were years of progress but they were also years of increasing acrimony. The winds of change were sweeping through Westbank — not surprisingly there was conflict and controversy. Rapid change often causes discomfort. Additionally, periods of rapid change put stresses on people and systems that may cause both to malfunction at times.

Many of the problems arose from personal conflicts of individuals on and about the Reserves. Mr. Ronald Derrickson was often at the centre of controversy. He wore many hats — Chief, locatee, negotiator, land manager, etc. He was a man for all seasons but, like many men of action, he caused in some others quite strong reactions. Relations between him and certain mobile home park lessees became increasingly acrimonious — Mr. Crosby complained to Departmental officials and politicians about what he perceived as problems relative to lessees and Band and Departmental administration. Mr. Walchli was the Chief Executive Officer in B.C. for the Department during a period of change and controversy.

The 1980's were turbulent times at Westbank. In 1984, Mr. Derrickson became a director of the ill-fated Northland Bank. A number of mobile home park lessees were embroiled in controversies over leases. Highway 97 was being widened and considerable sums of compensation accrued to Band members for lands taken. A significant settlement regarding cut-off land was achieved and a large block of land at Gallagher's Canyon was purchased by the Band. Reserve water supplies (and proper fire protection) were becoming of increasing concern. A spacious new office building, partly for Band offices and partly for business rentals, was erected on Reserve 10.

During the years 1975–86, much correspondence was directed to various Ministers of the day. Press reports were made of controversies involving the Reserves. Statements were made in Parliament. Certain members of the Band formed an "Action Committee" to have the Chief removed. A violent physical attack was made on Chief Derrickson in the spring of 1982 and widely publicized court proceedings followed.

Certain problems at Westbank may be common to all bands undergoing rapid change — to that extent, the events there can hold valuable lessons for other bands and the Department. However, a great many of the matters I looked at at Westbank seemed to arise out of the local situation.

Chapter 2

Toussowasket (Mt. Boucherie Park) and Related Matters

Toussowasket Enterprises Ltd., sometimes also known as Mt. Boucherie Mobile Home Park or McDougall Creek Estates, has generated considerable controversy over the years at Westbank. Between 1975 and 1982, a substantial mobile home park was built on lands held by Mr. Noll C. Derriksan, a former Chief of the Westbank Indian Band and the brother of Mr. Ronald M. Derrickson (who was Chief from 1976 to 1986). During those years a considerable amount of federal money was allotted to this project, and it was suggested in some quarters that Noll Derriksan had received unjustifiably favoured treatment from the Department of Indian Affairs, thereby greatly enhancing his capital and income position.

Toussowasket Enterprises Ltd. (hereinafter called "Toussowasket") had been incorporated in 1971 by Noll Derriksan. He and his mother, Margaret Derrickson, were shareholders. For my purposes, the narrative commences in 1974. Noll Derriksan was the locatee of real property on Reserve 9, where he proposed to develop a mobile home park. Heritage Realty Projects Ltd. of Vernon was engaged to be the general adviser and overseer of the project. Toussowasket obtained a lease from Her Majesty the Queen of a portion of the lands held by Mr. Derriksan as locatee. These lands are located at the edge of Reserve 9 near Mt. Boucherie, within easy reach of Kelowna. The lands are adjacent to Highway 97 and are immediately next to Westview Village Mobile Home Park, an operation owned and operated for several years by members of the York family. Relations between Mr. Derriksan (also locatee of the Westview lands) and the Yorks were strained at times.

The term of the Toussowasket lease was for thirty years from November 1, 1974. Heritage Realty Projects Ltd., project overseer (hereinafter called "Heritage"), proposed that financing be provided by means of an Indian Economic Development Fund (IEDF) loan as well as a loan from the Federal Business Development Bank (FBDB). Heritage was under the direction of a Mr. Weir, formerly of the Department. He had been the Land Use Officer at the Vernon District Office who dealt, inter alia, with the initial Crosby lease.

It was felt, in 1974 and 1975, that the area of Kelowna was not sufficiently serviced by mobile home parks and that the venture proposed by Mr. Derriksan could be a profitable one. Loan financing was in fact obtained through the Indian Economic Development Fund and the Federal Business Development Bank. FBDB was in the first security position and IEDF was the second-place secured lender. Correspondence indicates that, when construction was occurring in 1976, the projected construction costs proved to be too optimistic — the costs of the project began to spiral. By late summer 1976, the first phase of the mobile home park had been completed, albeit with cost overruns, and the park began operations.

By that time, there seemed to be a decline in the demand for mobile home park accommodation in the Okanagan, which meant it was very difficult to operate the park with any degree of profitability. The debt obligations of Toussowasket at that time were substantial. There was approximately $195,000 owed to the IEDF and approximately $170,000 owed to the FBDB. Mr. Derriksan had guaranteed payment of all of the former and a part of the latter. As well, the park had to pay an annual rental to the locatee and there were outstanding sums still owed to parties who had helped build the project. These included Donaldson Engineering Limited ("Donaldson" — head contractor) and Underwood & McLellan (engineers). It appeared that the amount of more than $50,000 owing to Donaldson was for extra costs not originally provided for in the contract.

The amount of money contributed to this project by way of equity injection was said to have been $40,000 from Noll Derriksan (letter of Weir to McGillivary). Some of this was apparently bank borrowings. Mr. Derriksan also provided the land for the project. That is a notional contribution in the sense that he did not then put out cash for the purchase of the land but furnished land to the project on a rental basis. This land had been purchased for a few thousand dollars in about 1969. From any point of view, the project was thinly financed and top-heavy with debt. This debt load caused continuing difficulty after 1976.

The original concept had been that Toussowasket would operate the Mt. Boucherie Mobile Home Park and in turn would pay an annual rental to the federal Crown which would pay the rental money to the Indian locatee, Noll Derriksan. Whether or not any funds would flow to Mr. Derriksan by way of rent would, of course, be directly dependent upon the success or lack of success of the mobile home park. In May 1976, Noll Derriksan had agreed with the Department that he would not take any rent until Toussowasket was in a position to pay it without impairing the viability of the project. In December 1976, Messrs. Peter Clark and Fred Walchli (of the Department) determined that they could not recommend an additional loan of $50,000 for the project as had been requested by Mr. Derriksan. A memorandum covering the subject said:

> After an extensive study of the project, it was determined that the average cost per pad is excessively high; that the total of the present financing exceeds the projected ability of the project to pay both principal and interest; and the additional loan requested would not be

sufficient to cover outstanding invoices due and loan interest due. The request is therefore declined. (My underlining)

(Exhibit 114, Document 64)

Mr. Leonard Crosby, President of the Mobile Home Park Owners Association, suggested that one reason the Mt. Boucherie Mobile Home Park got into trouble was because the park was built to a higher standard than was economical when it was built. In other words, it may have been a park that was designed to be too high-priced for the market it was to service. It was a difficult position for the locatee and the Department. The project needed more money, but unfortunately the existing debt load was so high that it was already impossible to service the debt. More debt would simply have driven the project deeper into financial woe. To put it colloquially, "a fine mess".

This situation, of course, raises the problem of developments on Indian reserve land and assistance by governmental agencies to such developments. On the one hand, it is highly desirable that Indian entrepreneurship be encouraged and assisted; on the other hand, it should be done so that market economies are observed to a reasonable extent. Also, it can be fundamentally unfair if one enterprise is given a large amount of government funding and another nearby private enterprise is forced to exist entirely on private sector financing. This sort of problem is, I am sure, not confined to Westbank. The problems that occurred in connection with this venture provide material for useful study in this whole area of what government can or should do in this sector of Indian enterprise. Toussowasket was a fledgeling chick of economic enterprise on the Westbank Reserve — some might have been inclined at times after 1976 to call it an albatross around the neck of the Department.

It must always be remembered, however, that banks have not been historically favourable to lending on Indian projects and therefore a certain amount of government backing is often needed to generate economic activity on reserves. To the extent possible, it is probably desirable for government to be more often a guarantor than a direct lender — that helps to ensure some realistic analysis of the economics of the venture in the early stages.

There were serious and continuing problems with regard to the economic viability of the project from the very beginning of operations. Mr. Ronald M. Derrickson, in his evidence, was inclined to be critical of Heritage, the managers of the project. Management of the park seemed to be a continuing problem — Mr. Walchli said in his evidence, "For whatever reason, the management of the court was not up to what was required from '76 on 'til about '81". The facts would seem to support his comment.

Mr. Noll Derriksan did not testify and give us the benefit of what was in his mind for the project, but undoubtedly the project offered substantial benefits to him with no great outlay of capital and with substantial assistance from government financing. In addition to the stated contribution of $40,000 in cash to the project, I have noted that he had provided a contribution by way of land valued at $95,000. This was land whereon he was the locatee. The debt to equity ratio was always high and it was to become higher.

To add to the miseries of the project, a corporation that had entered into an agreement relative to leasing mobile home pads from Toussowasket, Homco Industries Ltd., ran into economic difficulties and was not able to carry on as initially envisaged. A report on the park project, done apparently in the first half of 1977 by Stewart C. Wong for the Department, indicates continuing problems with the park and little likelihood of economic viability in the foreseeable future.

6. UNDERLINE{EXPECTATIONS FOR 1977}
   Unless the owners are able to find private capital to pay outstanding construction invoices or make alternative arrangements with their debtors; and unless the remaining lots are rented early in 1977, the owners will become substantially in default of their loan repayments.
   Thirty lots have been leased to Homco which company has been having financial difficulties. However, they were recently granted an extension by their creditors for a five year period.
   In considering requirements for 1977 the company obviously requires additional assistance to the extent of $75,000, but the affairs of the company are such that it cannot carry any more debt.
   As a result, no additional financing can be considered, so far as the company is concerned. (My underlining)
                                        (Exhibit 116, Document 78)

The underlined comment above succinctly states the essential dilemma of the enterprise. The outstanding invoices relative to the building of the park were not satisfied and in early 1978, Donaldson Engineering Limited commenced suit against Toussowasket. Donaldson eventually recovered judgement in April 1979 for approximately $55,000 for services rendered as main contractor on the project. The judgement was ultimately obtained by default and although there were faint suggestions in the evidence that Donaldson had not done a good job, I was satisfied that it had performed its tasks in a competent manner.

From the point of view of all concerned, including the locatee and majority shareholder of Toussowasket, Noll Derriksan, the golden dreams of Toussowasket had very much turned to dross. Neither the IEDF nor the FBDB had any likely prospect of being repaid the monies that they had advanced, the land was not producing any rental return to the locatee, and the locatee remained liable on his personal guarantee, although the collectability of that guarantee was very much in doubt. On June 8, 1978, then Chief Ronald M. Derrickson (brother of Noll Derriksan), sent the following telegram to Fred Walchli:

> This is to advise you that we have met this day with the solicitor for Noll C. Derriksan and the solicitor for the Westbank Indian Band. In his general opinion, the company Toussowasket Enterprises Ltd. is insolvent and does not have the ability to make any payments at all. Tax Department is taking action to recover four years taxes never paid. In order to protect the personal financial position of the locatee we request that you telex our office back this day with immediate cancellation of the lease.

On June 16, 1978, Noll Derriksan, on behalf of Toussowasket, requested the Department to forgive the IEDF loan "in an attempt to keep the company operating and to meet all accounts as they come due". The Department was not prepared to agree to this course of action.

On June 20, 1978, the sum of $17,000 was advanced by way of a grant from the Department to defray legal costs and engineering analysis costs connected with the defence of the outstanding claims of Underwood & McLellan, the project engineers, and Donaldson Engineering. Concurrently with these developments, a proposal was being considered to extend the term of the original lease from 30 years to 65 years in order to enhance the use of the land for purposes other than mobile homes and to enable better financing to be obtained by conventional means. Everyone was casting about for some solution to this continuing problem.

A perceived difficulty in changing the use of these approximately 27 acres of which Mr. Derriksan was the locatee is indicated in a letter from Mr. Poupore, Director of the Lands Branch in Ottawa, to Mr. Peter Clark, of the B.C. Region, on November 30, 1978. Mr. Poupore says:

> We have doubts about the proposed change of the use clause in this lease. Non-Indians living in a mobile home park should have very little long range or permanent impact on the lifestyle of the Indian community. However, if this use is expanded to include permanent residences, an influx of non-Indians occupying such permanent residences will undoubtedly affect the reserve as a whole. Any development plans which will affect the lifestyle of the Indians, for whom the reserve was set apart, must be presented to all members of the Band so that they may decide whether they wish their reserve to be used for such a purpose. As you know, we have received advice from our legal advisers in the past in which they have pointed out the pitfalls of long term major developments on locatee land, without the approval of all the members of the Band.

While we are sympathetic with the Regional Office's desire to safeguard the monies loaned by the Federal Government on this project, we wonder whether this is sufficient reason to even consider this new scheme. It is our view that we have a responsibility to the Indian people as a whole and that this obligation must be given precedence over our efforts on behalf of individual band members. At the same time we must ensure that protection of the Indian band's interest in its lands is seen as paramount to the recovery or protection of loan funds.

(Exhibit 116, Document 113)

Mr. Poupore's letter does highlight one problem that development raises for reserves. If the greater part of the reserve is developed, then its essential character may change. This is no different from changes facing any community but it does illustrate that the length of leases is a very relevant concern for all members of an Indian band in that the duration and conditions of leases can very much alter the local environment. Mr. Poupore also notes in his letter the dilemma facing the Department's regional office in choosing whether to go deeper into the project or to abandon it.

By February 1979, the FBDB was calling Noll Derriksan on his guarantee and was also demanding payment from Toussowasket of the $190,000 then outstanding on their loan. Prospects for reduction of the liabilities were dim. What had started out as an attempt to launch a viable business was proving to be a financial headache for all concerned.

The increasingly unhappy situation is outlined in a letter of February 23, 1979 from Mr. Armitage of the Department of Indian Affairs to the Department of Justice.

Potential loss and the reputed poor attitude of Mr. N. Derriksan have caused some harm to the Indian cause so far as the Federal Business Bank in Kelowna is concerned and possibly the regional office in Vancouver. In an attempt to retain some good will, we may be willing to split the net rental between the bank and ourselves.

The mobile home park has a considerable number of vacancies at present; 26 rented, 33 vacant. The park, if it could be sold, would be at a distressed price, probably not even sufficient to pay the FBDB loan. Present indications are that the demand for spaces will improve after another two/three years time. Then the receiver/manager may well sell the park with a very low vacancy rate maximizing the price to be obtained. Even so, it is questionable whether the proceeds would repay both loans totalling approximately $400,000.

(Exhibit 116, Document 116)

In March 1979, the FBDB appointed as receiver Mr. A.D. Stewart, C.A., of Kelowna. As reflected in an interim accounting by Mr. Stewart for the period from March to August 1979, the enterprise continued to be of marginal economic viability and was certainly not generating enough revenue to properly service the debts or to return any funds to the locatee by way of rent.

An unaudited schedule of development costs dated April 30, 1980, which was done by Lett, Trickey and Co., Chartered Accountants, indicated that the development costs of the project then aggregated over $500,000. However, in November 1979, Mr. Marsh, of the Department of Justice, had advised Mr. Van Iterson of the B.C. Region of the Department of Indian Affairs in Vancouver that "while the matter is complicated, we have come to the conclusion that much of the Crown's security and that of FBDB is, from a practical point of view, worthless." This was, of course, very gloomy news to the secured lenders.

By March 1980, the relationship between FBDB and the Department of Indian Affairs was being strained by the insistence by the Bank that the Department take action to ensure that the bank debt was repaid. The Bank let it be known to the Department that if the situation was not resolved, they would look very unfavourably in the future on loans to Indian bands or to Indian individuals in British Columbia.

Ronald M. Derrickson testified that he was very unhappy with the way in which the receiver appointed by FBDB had been conducting the business of Mt. Boucherie Park. By Band Council Resolution dated July 14, 1980, the Band Council requested that the lease dated November 1, 1974 in the name of Toussowasket Enterprises Ltd. be cancelled. For obvious reasons, the Department of Indian Affairs was most unwilling to effect cancellation of the lease. Cancellation would mean destruction of the underlying security for the IEDF and the FBDB loans.

The situation at that time reflects the sort of conflict of interest position in which the Department can find itself. On the one hand, by reason of its perceived obligations to the Band member, Noll Derriksan, and in its capacity as landlord under the lease, its position would tend to favour termination of the lease. But if it took this course of action, the outstanding secured loans (over $200,000 directly owed to the Crown under the IEDF loan and $225,000 indirectly owed to the Crown through FBDB) could be rendered uncollectable. Additionally, of course, the fact of the lease being cancelled and the likely destruction of any security for the FBDB loan would undoubtedly have a negative impact on the possibility of future financing by FBDB for Indian enterprises.

Although Noll Derriksan does not appear to have taken any major public role in events, his brother, the then Chief, Ronald Derrickson, was actively involved in the matter and was obviously at odds with the receiver/manager, Mr. Stewart. On October 6, 1980, then Chief Derrickson notified the receiver that the rent due the locatee was being increased retroactive to November 1, 1979 and was being set at $44,500 per annum. He also reminded the receiver that rental payments had not been received for the years 1977 and 1978 and demanded prompt payment with interest. On October 14, 1980, the receiver/manager, Mr.

Stewart, responded to the Chief advising him that Toussowasket had an assignment of rentals from Mr. Derriksan and that sums owing on account of rent were to be satisfied by crediting the appropriate amounts to a shareholder's loan of Mr. Derriksan. The receiver took the position that all rents were therefore current. The original rental assignment apparently had been made to assist in obtaining funding from IEDF.

By the fall of 1980, the situation was showing some improvement. The park was generating enough revenue to repay part of the principal on the FBDB loan but not enough to properly service and retire all outstanding debts and to return the required sum due as rental to the locatee, Noll Derriksan.

Former Chief Derrickson testified concerning this matter before the Commission as follows:

A ....Homco's other companies in Ontario and Saskatchewan got into financial difficulty, even though this plant here was doing well financially. Homco went into bankruptcy and he had an agreement that they would pay him $1,500 for every lot he produced.

Well, number one, he got the bottom of the spiral. He had to build it to standards higher than anyone else on the reserve, and the fact that he had consultants who left a lot to be desired, and some of the construction and engineering work left a lot to be desired.

I mean, it was a hopeless situation from the start. My first impression of that park was it should go into bankruptcy, even more so than Lakeridge Park. I always maintained that belief it should be let go into bankruptcy.

Q Now, what steps did you take to try and resolve that particular problem as far as Toussowasket was concerned?

A Well, I tried to force it into bankruptcy, but I wasn't getting much cooperation, simply because the Department didn't want to see bankruptcy occur on something that they felt could be viable.

Some of the technicians at Indian Affairs put together a package where Noll would, based on the figures from the receiver — and I'd looked at the figures the receiver had produced and it showed that the park was getting deeper into debt every year. They tried to convince me that maybe over 13 years Noll, if he gave up the the park completely, if they kept it in receivership for 13 years that it would eventually come to a place where it would start paying off.

I said that was a ridiculous situation.

Q Now, did you ask the Department to do a detailed review of that particular project?

A I think I asked the Department to do a — at our initial meeting with Fred Walchli I think we asked them to do a detailed review on Lakeridge Park, which was called the Sookinchute Development.

That he agreed, and he agreed to support us. He agreed to support us financially so that we could get the — I think there was current outstanding bills at that time, over and above the loans, but there was bills that were 90 days in arrears or longer of $185,000, and I'm just saying this from memory.

Q Did Noll Derriksan, prior to you becoming involved in this particular problem, did Noll make a number of proposals to your knowledge to the Department to try and resolve this particular financial problem?

A Yes.

Q Now, eventually a proposal came forward after a number of discussions back and forth between Noll and the Department; eventually a proposal arose that the Band became involved in.

A Now, we're talking about the trailer park or Lakeridge Park?

Q No, the trailer park, Toussowasket.

A Okay.

Q Now, first of all, can you tell us how that particular proposal arose, how it came about?

A Well, again, I don't have the use of the files, so I have to go from memory. I hope you appreciate that. I don't have the benefit of files.

It's my understanding, from my memory, we got to a point where we were going to take a very, very strong position in regard to that park. It was not going to be in receivership for 13 years. The Locatee was receiving no rent, had never received any rent to my knowledge, and every proposal he put forth had been denied.

I don't know the reasons. I guess there was some politics on it. I think one of the facts was that Noll had had a write-up in some magazine that professed him to be a millionaire, when indeed he had no cash.

So, we wanted to put it into bankruptcy and we were making waves with the Department. We told them that we were going to make application to the courts and force it into bankruptcy regardless of what they thought or said.

Q Now, had you followed that route, Mr. Derrickson, based on your understanding of the way that might have worked, what would have been the end result had you been successful in putting it into bankruptcy?

A The end result would have been that, number one, Noll would have got his park free and clear of all debt. I don't think politically, it's never happened before, the Department could have stood the criticism of a trailer park like that going bankrupt and then giving it to somebody else.

Even if they did, if they took the most drastic action, at least he would have been entitled to his rent, which was better than what he was getting. I always figure if you see a situation in business and if you see you can get the advantage, and you see more eggs in your basket in a negotiation you take full advantage.

I felt that the bankruptcy was the best route to go; that there was more benefits for the locatee through bankruptcy than a reorganization.

(Transcripts: Volume LXV, pp. 9709–9712)

Such a course of action (bankruptcy) would have had certain obvious benefits for the locatee, but from the point of view of the Department and the FBDB, the results would have been very unfavourable. The FBDB had suggested that the Department sort out the loan problem or face very substantial restriction of FBDB lending to Indian persons in B.C. While Mr. Walchli was quick to point out to FBDB that such a policy might be hard for a body such as FBDB to adhere to, he was nonetheless keenly aware that the bankruptcy of Toussowasket could have a very chilling effect on bank lending practices to Indian individuals and bands in British Columbia (and doubtless elsewhere in Canada).

While it might be said that the Chief and Council at Westbank were holding a gun to the head of the Department, it could also be said that the gun was partly primed and loaded by the Department itself when it entered into the venture in the mid-1970s. One should not, however, be overly critical of the Department, for one of its mandates is to encourage more economic enterprise on behalf of Indian people. It apparently was the case that the advisers to the locatee believed that this would be a viable project. Looked at in retrospect, the project may well not have been subjected to a sufficiently rigorous economic analysis at the outset and, as we have seen, the project continued to suffer from management and financial deficiencies until 1980.

In the summer of 1980, the Toussowasket situation was in a most unsatisfactory state. The Department was casting about for some method to resolve a matter which had generated a great deal of ill will on all sides. Regardless of the errors of the past, the then existing situation required that some solution be imposed to avoid further deterioration.

Mr. Walchli testified that he felt that it would be a good thing to have the Band take over the operation of the park. He attempted to persuade then Chief Derrickson to interest the Development Company in taking on the project.

> Q Now, those matters about which you just gave evidence on the questioning of the Commissioner, Mr. Walchli? Just to continue from what you said, they arose out of the beginning note, the telex of June 8, 1978, document 100, and then you also spoke of document 131, the April 18, 1980 letter of yourself, and followed, I think, by personal discussions that you had with Mr. Derrickson, Chief Derrickson, late '80 and January '81?
>
> A That's correct, yes.
>
> Q Is there anything to elaborate on that, what the nature of those discussions were, or were they just as you described them to the Commissioner a moment ago?
>
> A Well, the discussions between myself and the Chief began to take on a serious approach to this in 1980, in the latter part of 1980.

He really was pushing the idea that we should simply let the thing go into bankruptcy and that once the bankruptcy was cleared away, then Noll Derriksan would in fact be able to take back the court and set up under a different arrangement, a different company and a different lease and continue to operate it.

I rejected that. I told him that that would be a last resort; we should first try and explore the idea of the Band acquiring an interest, and he was agreeable to that.

Q Okay. Carrying on then with document 145. That is a memo of March 11, 1981. I understand that to be a summary of a proposal?

A That's correct. Jack Rennie had been assigned at this point to start working with the Band, and this was the type of proposal that he'd worked up.

Q There is some figuring on the bottom in hand. Do you see that, Mr. Walchli?

A Yes, that's correct. That's really the amount of money that is owing on Toussowasket at that point in time. You'll note that there's a principal of $197,350.00, and interest which was accrued to March 31st, '81 as being $100,543.07, for a total of $297,893.00

There's a further figure which says how much interest it's costing per day. It's $56.77. . . .

Q There's another document following that which appears to be part of that. It's a contribution arrangement.

A Yes, that's correct.

Q That is something that is prepared preliminary to the contribution agreement going into force, in effect, I take it, is it?

A Yeah, we always do what we call an analysis of the proposal, in the jargon of the Department a "work-up sheet", and this really was designed to do that, to lay out the proposal and to indicate the conditions which would apply for the contribution agreement, and also to stipulate or state the reasons for the transaction, which is on the following page.

Q Okay. Then we have at 146 an interim accounting from the receiver for period March 20, 1979 to March 31, 1981. I note the Federal Business Development Bank were paid $50,000. IEDF doesn't appear on that.

A That's correct. What they were doing at that point in time was merely operating the park, and any of the proceeds or the profits were going to paying off their loan. IEDF did not receive any consideration from Mr. Stewart.

The other thing I think is important is it shows that even during that period of time, which was two years, from March 20, 1979 to March 31, 1981, the park really was not — or was just barely generating enough revenue to cover the Federal Development Business loan, and there were no funds left over to retire any portion of the IEDF loan. . . .

Q And then 147, a letter to Chief Derrickson from the FBDB just indicating, I guess, the amount outstanding and the amount in arrears at that time?

A That's correct.

Q And they need a certain amount, $49,226.90 to bring this account to a current position. Was that done?

A Not at that point, no. Oh, sorry, just shortly after it was. This was the letter that the bank sent to the Band, and I think four or five days later the Band actually brought the account into good standing. . . .

Q Then we've set out the final account of the receiver, document 149.

A Right.

Q Now, why is he doing that at that time?

A Well, the agreement that the Band had struck with FBDB was that once the Federal Development Bank loan was brought into good standing, then the receiver's term of duty was completed. He's simply advising us that his duties are over as of May 19th, 1981.

Q Okay. Then document 150 is an agreement between Toussowasket, WIBDC, Noll Derriksan and the Band?

A That's correct.

Q Can you summarize that for the Commission?

A Well, this agreement really was designed to enable the Band to acquire the 50 per cent interest in Toussowasket. Now, this included not only the parcel of land which the trailer park was on, which was Lot 32–2, but it also included the part that was not developed, 32-2-1, and an option to acquire Lot 33–1.

Now, what this does is simply — it's an agreement in which the vendor, Toussowasket, agrees to sell a 50 per cent interest in and to the lease, and the purchaser wished to purchase this interest.

So the approach that the Band were following was that they were going to acquire their interest by obtaining a 50 per cent interest in the leasehold of Toussowasket.

Q They were not going to acquire any interest in the company?

A No, not as such.

Q All right, okay. And the consideration: "The Band agreed to assume responsibility. . ." — under "C" there — ". . .on behalf of the vendor for the payment of all monies due and owing under the second mortgage". That's the IEDF loan?

A Right, and they also agreed to bring the Federal Business Development loan into good standing, and they took over 50 per cent of Noll's personal guarantee.

THE COMMISSIONER: The guarantee with regard to the FBDB?

THE WITNESS: That's correct, yes. At that point it was a $50,000 guarantee. They took over repayment of FBDB's loan, 50 per cent of that. They took over 50 per cent of the personal guarantee, and they agreed to pay off the total IEDF loan. Then, of course, it sets out the responsibility for completing the court and managing it.

THE COMMISSIONER: What was the state of the park at that time, Mr. Walchli? Obviously they'd had financial difficulty in the sense it wasn't generating really enough cash flow to even service its debts. The receiver, Stewart, was managing it. Was there a — I don't suppose they were building anything at that stage, were they?

THE WITNESS: No, there was no construction taking place. There was just a certain amount of maintenance being done, and that's all. The court itself at that point in time owed IEDF around $300,000. It owed FBDB $216,000; over $500,000 worth of debt.

THE COMMISSIONER: It just hadn't panned out as originally envisaged by the first plans that had been put forward, because as I understood it, from what Mr. Branson led by way of evidence I think two weeks ago, when it was envisaged it was going to be a self-supporting operation, it would pay its debts, and it would reach a certain size. Obviously it hadn't come anywhere near that by '81, had it?

THE WITNESS: No. What had happened is that there were a number of problems right from the outset with the court. The initial feasibility study done by Heritage Realty had underestimated the cost of development. . . . (My underlining)

(Transcripts: Volume XXXV, pp. 4726–4732)

In a memorandum on the subject of Toussowasket, in early 1981, to Mr. J. W. Evans, Director of Economic Development, Mr. Walchli gave instructions as follows:

The Westbank Band Council have decided to take over the Toussowasket Park. They're requesting that assistance be given from the Department in putting forward such a proposal. They have specifically asked for Jack Rennie to help them. Would you please assign Mr. Rennie to this project.

In the spring of 1981, a contribution agreement was entered into between the Department and the Westbank Indian Band whereby the Department agreed to contribute to the Band up to $300,000 over a period of years. The Band agreed to undertake liability for 100% of the IEDF loan and to undertake liability for 50% of the FBDB loan and 50% of the guarantee of Noll Derriksan. The Band or Band Company was to obtain a 50% interest in the venture, and also undertook to construct an additional phase or phases of the park to bring it to "completion". An agreement was entered into at about the same time between Toussowasket, Westbank Indian Band Development Co. Ltd., Noll Derriksan and Westbank Indian Band whereby the Development Company would be the actual purchaser of the half interest in the lease.

The entry of the Band and its development company into the picture heralded better days for Toussowasket. It emerged from a slough of financial despond to become a more successful operation. The park was expanded. But Band involvement had required the promise of additional federal funds of $300,000 — by now the amount of federal funds committed and to be committed was in the range of $750,000. Mr. Walchli, then Regional Director General in B.C., felt that on balance, no other course of action was preferable.

The matter of Toussowasket appears to have been a subject of considerable discussion before the Standing Committee on Indian

Affairs and Northern Development in 1982. The following exchange occurred between members of the Committee and Mr. Walchli at a meeting of May 26, 1982. Mr. Walchli had been called back from holiday to meet with the Committee and was probably not fully prepared to deal with the matter. For instance, he told the Committee that the $300,000 of the contribution agreement was used to satisfy all creditors, but in fact the unsecured creditors were not paid. The tone of the meeting was at times quite critical of Mr. Walchli and his relationship to Chief Ronald Derrickson and Noll Derriksan.

Mr. Oberle: Thank you. Mr. Chairman. Let me first express our appreciation for Mr. Walchli's efforts in coming here. I know that you have probably interrupted a personal holiday, and we certainly appreciate your co-operation. I would like to begin by asking Mr. Walchli some questions and perhaps make a little bit of an opening statement. Mr. Walchli, when we were meeting in Vancouver, and prior to that, in meetings here which led to the decision of the committee to travel to Vancouver to examine the situation that many of us felt was peculiar to that part of the world, myself and my colleagues began to harbour the impression that there was something wrong with the administration of the department's affairs in British Columbia. It is not that everything is rosy in the rest of the country, but there were some very peculiar problems in British Columbia. Unfortunately, the testimony we received in Vancouver did not allay, at least in my mind, my conviction that there are some peculiar problems, or some problems that are peculiar to British Columbia.

Generally, I have the impression that you have sort of your own system; it is a paternalistic system, but that is the nature of the act under which you operate. But when I looked at the objectives that are stated in the department's estimates, you are achieving some of these objectives but you are achieving them for a select few Indian people. There is a disproportionate number of Indian people and tribal councils and band councils in British Columbia that have achieved quite a degree of self-sufficiency and self-administration, but there are others as well who need a lot of help. I get the impression, from testimony we have received and documents we get from time to time from a variety of sources, that you are all too ready to help those who do not need your help any longer. They told us: Look, we already have engineers, and this and that, working for us in the district councils and we do not see any evidence that the bureaucracy in Vancouver are getting rid of their responsibility or reducing their staff that we have hired ourselves. So the people who get all the help from you do not need it any more. They are telling us, get Walchli off our back, and the people who need your help are not getting it.

Rather than going through a tedious process to show you, in the testimony, how we arrived, or how I arrived, at this assessment of your role in Vancouver, I would like to show you an example and maybe we could ask you to explain to us a particular case. In doing that, I would like you to cast your mind to the so-called, as we call it, "Westbank Caper". Westbank is a reserve near Kelowna where a brother of a chief by the name of Derriksan received some economic help from your department back in 1976. You became involved shortly after you arrived on the scene in Vancouver. I think close to $300,000 was involved. The idea was to lease a parcel of land from the reserve and convert it to a trailer court. A fellow by the name of Noll Derriksan became the president of the operation. His mother, Margaret Derriksan, held one share and was the secretary of the company.

Things did not go very well right from the beginning, but to make a long story short, because I would like you to elaborate and fill in the gaps, the department was not very successful in getting any repayment of this.

Before I go further, I should tell you that I compare this particular situation with a situation in Fort Ware, for instance, where I travel and I see old people freezing to death or cold because they do not have any firewood or the generator has broken down and there is no electricity. Another old family is sitting on the floor of a shack, 40 below outside, eating porcupine legs, because they no longer have any food left. That is what I am comparing the situation with.

So here is an old Derriksan, obviously one of the favourite sons of paternalists in Vancouver. He is having a lot of trouble repaying his loan. In fact, he has not made a payment on it, either in principal or in interest. So the situation gets rather difficult and dicey. Then you get a lawyer who suggests — as Derriksan is not only unable to repay your loan, but is also having trouble satisfying his other creditors — that you make another loan, this time to the Indian Band. Incidentally, the chief of the band at that point is the brother to Noll, Ron Derrickson, whom I see has received money from time to time — at least in one instance — to travel with you to Ottawa. I see an expenditure of $4,000 travel expenses to that particular person. I would like to see the chief in Fort Ware travel someplace and tell his story. It would shock a lot of people.

The notion was kicked around, that the department should make another loan, this time to Ron Derrickson, on behalf of the band. This is the story I got, so you might be able to fill me in. The idea was to buy 50 per cent of the shares of the brother's company. The brother's company would become a shell, and it would hold all the liabilities, but the assets would be transferred to a new company. Indeed, I see in a document here, in a print-out, that $100,000 has been allocated to that particular band. As I understood it, the payment was to be made over three years at $100,000 a year. The band would now be a 50 per cent shareholder in the scheme, and the money that is being paid to allow the band to buy in to this incredibly lucrative enterprise would, of course, be used to retire the department's obligation in the first place.

If that is true and that coincides with facts — or if it is even close — you know, of course, that this is highly irregular — if not illegal in terms of the constraints of the Financial Administration Act. You can see, with that background, why we are increasingly nervous sitting here putting our stamp of approval on the departmental estimates on Monday, when these kinds of things are going on.

You have, no doubt, a bunch of favoured sons out there, who have helped you out of all kinds of political problems by collaborating with you in starting this regional forum, by going into a deal which would be known as an Indian Economic Development thing which as far-reaching Utopian consequences including that of self-government. All of this, if nothing else, is terribly premature, because according to my information, it is not until later on this year that the government intends to table some guidelines with respect to the development of an Indian government.

I am glad that Mr. Savill is here, because he understands and knows the problems which I see daily, or everytime I go home. He knows the situation at Lower Post, Ingenika, Fort Ware, Blueberry, and at Doig River. Here I am begging on my knees to find $250,000 to assist in the rural electrification program that would bring electricity — one of the most basic elements — into the Doig River Reserve. When I see this kind of squandering of public money, sir, I am less than amused. I would like you to make some comments. If my information is wrong, I will just be too pleased and excited to be corrected.

Mr. Walchli: First of all, Mr. Oberle, I would like to respond to the allegation that we are discriminating against certain bands and favouring others. That is just not the case.

If you take a look at the per capita breakdown of all the departmental funds going into B.C., you will note that most of the bands are getting their fair share of those dollars.

Now, we did a breakout here a year ago which looked at the equalization of those payments and, to quote there on what you are talking about, the central area has 15 per cent of the population and are getting 15.1 per cent of the funds. You will find that every district is fairly close to a fair share in their funds. The one exception is the coastal district in Prince Rupert. It is not getting its fair share of the funds at this point, and there are good explanations for it. But the point I make is that we have attempted, and have done so over the last five years, to distribute those funds equally across the region. I have figures to support that.

Second, in terms of actual help from the department, we have transferred to tribal councils a lot of the responsibility for providing their own advisory services. Along with that has gone $6 million. So I think it is not fair to suggest that we have given certain tribal councils money and others we have not. Each tribal council has had a fair share of that budget.

In terms of our own support services, they are available to bands upon request. Some bands are very good at coming to us and asking for help. Others are not. We do not foist ourselves upon any band, if they do not want us. So I think it is a totally unfair allegation that, in some way, we have favorite sons to whom we attempt to provide more funds than to others.

Let us go to Westbank, because that seems to be an issue here. Let us talk about it. I am going to put the whole story on the table. First of all, on the development proposal. This trailer court we refer to was developed and funded at a time when I was not in the British Columbia region. It was a new venture by an Indian band at that time, particularly Noll Derriksan, to go into the trailer court business. There were some costly mistakes made in terms of the cost of engineering. Also, it came on stream at a time when the economic development situation was such that they could not market those trailer lots. The result was that the company ended up in a deficit position at the very outset. It should have been the subject of a stabilization grant in the way other bands were stabilized in British Columbia. It was not.

Mr. Oberle: Excuse me. Are you telling me now the loan was made to the band or to the individual?

Mr. Walchli: To the individual.

Mr. Oberle: You said the word "band".

Mr. Walchli: I am sorry. I meant to say the individual. At that time, there were a lot of economic development projects in trouble across Canada. The department introduced a stabilization program to stabilize those projects worth saving. We did not do that for this particular project. The assessment at the time was that it could stand on its own feet. That proved not to be the case. It went into receivership by FDB and, for two years or a little longer, they administered that trailer court. The one thing they did not do in those two years was to raise the rents the way other rents were going up around the country. So the result was that, even if the company could have made money, it was not allowed to do so. It continued to lose money.

There were a number of other problems with it. First of all, it was a lease issued over a locatee land — land which should have been surrendered and was not for reasons I do not understand. The problem then was that in order to foreclose on that development, we would have been into quite a legal problem. So that was one reason we had to look at how to solve it without going through the courts.

Mr. Oberle: But you said it had already been foreclosed by the bank.

Mr. Walchli: No. It had gone into receivership. It had not been liquidated. So that was one problem. The other one was the FDB had not raised the rents; therefore, it could not sustain the debt load it was carrying.

The third problem was that the band itself was proposing new sets of guidelines in terms of quality of development, and were insisting that the rents on that whole reserve be brought up to a market rent. But this was not possible under the arrangement.

We did an assessment of that project and came to the conclusion that the project was a good one.

It was a well-constructed trailer court and it had the potential to provide revenue to the owners. But we could not find it in our guidelines or within our policy to contribute a further $300,000 to Noll Derriksan per se. What we decided to do then was to tell Derriksan that he would have to be prepared to give up half interest in that trailer court and that the band would in turn acquire 50 per cent ownership. As a result, the money, 50 per cent of the revenue, would go into the band coffers for use by band members to pay for their own services.

We agreed to provide $300,000. The Band Development Company put up another $450,000, which was their own money, and between the two we were able to liquidate all the debts on that trailer court operation and put it into a viable position. Derriksan himself has lost

50 per cent ownership in that company and 50 per cent of his land holdings on which the trailer court is set. So he did not get a single nickel from us. Ron Derrickson did not get a single nickel from us, the Westbank Band did.

Mr. Oberle: What you are just telling me is precisely what I told you happened, except that you are making the story worse. You are now saying that you gave the band another $300,000 —

Mr. Walchli: That is right.

Mr. Oberle: — with which they acquired 50 per cent of the trailer court. Did any of the $300,000 get back to you in terms of interest and principal on the first loan?

Mr. Walchli: There is a debt load on that and I do not have the exact figures. But there was a debt load to the FDB. There was a debt load to private creditors and there was a debt load to Indian Affairs. We agreed to put up $300,000, the band agreed to put up $450,000, or thereabouts, and out of that they retired the total debt. Our money was used to pay the FDB and the private creditors.

Mr. Oberle: So you have not got any of your initial money back.

Mr. Walchli: It was one pot of money, Mr. Oberle. It was to retire the total debt of that trailer court.

Mr. Oberle: So you now have $600,000 in that venture and poor Noll Derriksan, even though he lost 50 per cent of it, no longer has any debts. You paid them off for him.

Mr. Walchli: No, the point I am making is that it was the band company. Not the Westbank Band Council but the band company that bought a 50 per cent interest in that trailer court. Now the revenue from that, instead of going to Noll Derriksan, goes into the band.

Mr. Oberle: Who is the president of the Band company?

Mr. Walchli: At the moment they have a board of directors, Noll Derriksan and the other band councillors on that band council, but —

Mr. Oberle: I see. So he is sure he is his own director.

Mr. Walchli: — the shares are held by the Westbank Band.

Mr. Oberle: Well, that just simply makes the problem that much worse.

Could I ask you to comment on a letter — I am sure you have a copy of it — which was written by. . .?

Mr. Walchli: Mr. Oberle, if I may point out, if that had gone into bankruptcy, then the money owing the department, the department would have had to pay it anyway.

Mr. Oberle: That does not provide me with any source of comfort. Nor does the fact that a lot of other projects were in trouble throughout the country. That is no excuse.

Mr. Walchli: It may not be an excuse but it is a fact of life.

Mr. Oberle: Well it certainly is not.

I have a letter here which was written by a consultant, I think it is a departmental consultant. I will just read one paragraph of it to you. I know you are not a stranger to it:

This project was developed primarily as a retirement fund for the locatee Noll D. Derriksan. The proposal was to create a development consistent with the master plan of the reserve which after payment of loans would create a good source of annual income as a form of a retirement plan.

I have financial statements of this Noll Derriksan here. He is shown to have an income of $44,890 from land holdings, and from the sale of paintings. Although I am told he is not really an artist, he is a manager of a section, of the B.C. Arts and Crafts Centre.

So he has an income from there. He is obviously one of those people who would fit into that category of the favourite son, of which I spoke earlier. The accountant says that if Derriksan were to have to pay income tax like any other person in Canada does who is not an Indian earning his money on reserve, his annual income would be in the neighbourhood of about $150,000. In fact, his life-style would bear that out.

(Minutes of the Standing Committee on Indian Affairs and Northern Development, May 26, 1982, pp. 55:5 to 55:10)

Mr. Walchli said he "was going to put the whole story on the table". He did not. By the time he spoke to the Committee in late May 1982, a proposal had been made and accepted to have the Band Company trade the half interest in the mobile home park for land of Noll Derriksan located on Reserve 10.

It appears from the dialogue between members of the Committee and Mr. Walchli that there was some misapprehension on the part of some members as to the magnitude of the problems confronting Mr. Walchli in 1979–80 on this project. Significant government funds had been allocated to the project and the partly completed project was in receivership and was generating barely enough revenue to pay operating expenses. Chief Derrickson, to assist his brother, Noll Derriksan, the locatee, was proposing to put the enterprise into bankruptcy and was urging that the Department cancel the lease. Mr. Walchli, with considerable justification, viewed these eventualities as little short of disastrous. He said in his evidence before the Commission that if the park were put into bankruptcy "it was very doubtful, in fact, whether there'd be any assets that were available to us after a bankruptcy".

As I noted earlier, the Department was in a most unhappy position. If they allowed the operation to go under or if they terminated the lease, at least three undesirable events would ensue. The IEDF loan likely would be lost. The FBDB loan would almost certainly not be repaid and this could have negative repercussions for other Indian projects. A locatee would inherit the improvements and be put in a position to thumb his nose at creditors. As a result, the Department could well face criticism for showing gross favouritism to one band member of one Indian band to the prejudice of other bands and members. Indeed, that is precisely what was put by Mr. Oberle to Mr. Walchli at one point during the Committee meeting of May 26, 1982:

So here is an old Derriksan, obviously one of the favourite sons of paternalists in Vancouver. He is having a lot of trouble repaying his loan. In fact, he has not made a payment on it, either in principal or in interest. So the situation gets rather difficult and dicey. Then you get a lawyer who suggests — as Derriksan is not only unable to repay your loan, but is also having trouble satisfying his other creditors — that you make another loan, this time to the Indian Band. Incidentally, the chief of the band at that point is the brother to Noll, Ron Derrickson, whom I see has received money from time to time — at least in one instance — to travel with you to Ottawa. I see an expenditure of $4,000 travel expenses to that particular person. I would like to see the chief in Fort Ware travel someplace and tell his story. It would shock a lot of people.

(Minutes of the Standing Committee on Indian Affairs and Northern Development, May 26, 1982, pp. 55:6)

Obviously members of the Standing Committee were concerned, and rightly so, with the spectacle of one member of one band apparently getting so much when so many individuals and bands in Canada were in very poor shape economically. It appears that some members of the Committee felt a degree of outrage at the situation at Mt. Boucherie Mobile Home Park. But as I have said, Mr. Walchli was facing a troublesome problem at Westbank — he was in a difficult position in 1980 and 1981 with regard to this failing mobile home park and it is difficult to see what more satisfactory solution he could have devised than to get the Band or its company to take over the park in an effort to complete it and resurrect its fortunes. If the Band could be induced to take over the project, improve it, and ultimately salvage it, then a host of unpleasant events could be avoided. Mr. Walchli had been engaged in 1980–81 in efforts to induce the Band to undertake reponsibility for the project. He felt the Band had demonstrated capability because of the turnaround it had achieved on the Lakeridge Subdivision between 1978 and 1980. This was the high-quality subdivision located on Reserve 10 above Okanagan Lake.

The Band was not willing to take over the project unless a substantial financial contribution was provided by the Department. Mr. Walchli signed a Contribution Agreement wherein the Department agreed to provide such assistance up to a maximum amount of $300,000. Although it was submitted by counsel for the Department that there was a requirement in that Agreement to complete development at the mobile home park within 18 months, I was not able to find any clear provision in either the Contribution Agreement (May 5, 1981) or the four-party Agreement (May 20, 1981) where this requirement was spelled out. There seems to have been a general understanding that the Band company would further develop the park but the obligation to do so seems only to be spelled out in a later agreement of April 23, 1982. For ease of reference, I set out hereafter a copy of the May 5, 1981 Contribution Agreement. It was later amended.

CONTRIBUTION AGREEMENT

BETWEEN:

HER MAJESTY THE QUEEN IN RIGHT OF CANADA AS REPRESENTED BY THE MINISTER OF INDIAN AFFAIRS AND NORTHERN DEVELOPMENT

(Hereinafter referred to as the "Minister")

AND:

THE WESTBANK INDIAN BAND,

(Hereinafter referred to as the "Recipient")

MAILING
ADDRESS: P.O. Box 850, Westbank, B.C. V0H 2A0

CONTRIBUTION
AMOUNT: $ 300,000.00

PURPOSE:

To purchase a 50% interest in the leasehold interest held by Toussowasket Enterprises Ltd. and a first refusal to a leasehold interest in an additional 15 acres adjoining the property.

FINANCING:

"Application of Funds"	"Source of Funds"
Purchase of leasehold interest $300,000	Department of Indian Affairs $300,000

TERMINATION: This Arrangement shall terminate on the 30th day of June, 1984, subject to any other provisions of this Arrangement.

DISBURSEMENT:

1. On the Recipient's acceptance of this Arrangement and the completion of all legal documentation, a disbursement of $100,000 will be made.

2. The Recipient shall provide a statement of expenditures with full disclosure of all disbursements during the period, plus a revised expenditure plan before any subsequent payments can be released.

3. The Recipient agrees to refund to the Department all funds not expended or committed for the purpose by cheque payable to the Receiver General for Canada.

EXPENDITURE
PLAN:

Prior to March 31, 1982	April 1, 1982 to March 31, 1983	April 1, 1983 to March 31, 1984
$ 100,000	$ 100,000	$ 100,000

Funds will not be disbursed in any fiscal year until the Band's Financial Audit has been received and approved by the Department.

OTHER:

1. The Recipients shall provide accrued interests towards financing the Purpose, as follows:

   Accrued Interest on the outstanding balance of the debt owed by Toussowasket Enterprises Ltd. to the Indian Business Loan Fund on an annual basis commencing March 31, 1982.

2. The Recipient shall observe the following additional conditions under which the Contribution is made:

   The Westbank Indian Band shall enter into an agreement with Toussowasket Enterprises Ltd. that all payments made to Toussowasket Enterprises Ltd. from funds paid under this Arrangement shall be used to reduce the debt owed by Toussowasket Enterprises Ltd. to the Indian Business Loan Fund including principal and accrued interest.

GENERAL
CONDITIONS:

1. All funds contributed in this Arrangement will be subject to an annual financial audit to the Minister's satisfaction to be provided by June 30th for each year ended March 31st.

2. The Minister reserves the right to cancel or suspend any disbursement relative to this Contribution at any time should circumstances warrant such action.

3. All schedules required pursuant to this Arrangement, and attached hereto, form an integral part of the Arrangement.

4. The approval of the funds, which are the object of this Arrangement, are subject to appropriations being approved by Parliament during each fiscal year of the Arrangement.

5. Any funds not disbursed by March 31st of each fiscal year must be returned to the Receiver General for Canada.

6. This offer is open for the acceptance of the Recipient until June 30, 1981, after which it shall become null and void.

7. The Recipient shall keep and maintain accounting records during the life of this Arrangement in a form satisfactory to the Director General and permit or arrange for the Director General, or any person authorized by him, to examine those books and records at any time.

8. This Arrangement shall not be assigned.

9. Disbursements made by the Recipient, pursuant to the Arrangement for honoraria, professional and administrative services and all other expenses, must be supported by invoices itemizing time and charges.

10. The Recipient agrees to provide a summary report of activities undertaken during each quarter of the period covered by this Arrangement. The report should address the degree of attainment of the objectives of the program.

11. No member of the House of Commons may be admitted to any share of this Contribution or to any benefit to arise therefrom.

There was later to be considerable debate over the question of whether this contribution agreement was for the purpose of the Band buying an interest in the mobile home park enterprise or for the purpose of paying down the debt owing, inter alia, to IEDF. It could be plausibly argued that it was a bit of both. The debate or argument that waxed over this issue is reminiscent of the vexed questions of causality in the law of torts wherein learned lawyers debate the niceties of ultimate and proximate causes.

Plainly, a major object of the contribution agreement was to ensure repayment of the IEDF loan. But it was also a practical way of getting the Band to take on the project and, hopefully, to make it work. Mr. Ernest E. Hobbs, former Director of Economic Development in Ottawa for the Department, was eminently correct in his assessment that the contribution agreement was being inappropriately used to pay back the IEDF loan, but he of course was looking at the matter only through the lens of economic development policy. Mr. Walchli was faced with a multifaceted problem. He felt able to fit the contribution agreement into a permissible category of aid to the Band to acquire a 50% interest in the economic enterprise of the mobile home park. Or perhaps I should say, the highly uneconomic enterprise prior to 1981!

Although the disagreement between Messrs. Hobbs and Walchli generated a fair amount of sound (and perhaps fury), the course pursued by Mr. Walchli offered a way out of the morass the Department found itself in. He may have worked around the rules somewhat but he was faced with a most unhappy situation and acted in an endeavour to solve the troublesome Toussowasket problem.

After the advent of Band Company direction of the enterprise, matters progressed far better at the mobile home park. In part, this was fortuitous. The years 1980–82 were a time of rapid increase in land values and an acceleration of economic activity generally in B.C. In retrospect, the period had certain aspects of economic mania, the fallout from which is often economic hangover (B.C. has not proved an exception to the usual pattern). All concerned with Toussowasket were fortunate that the demand for accommodation increased just as the new park expansion got under way. Perhaps the more dynamic direction of then Chief Derrickson also played a role in the reversal of fortunes. From being in a very bad state financially, it could be said that by 1982–83 Toussowasket was becoming a healthy enterprise. The course taken by Mr. Walchli resulted in the economic resuscitation of the floundering enterprise and satisfaction of the debts owed to secured creditors. Unsecured creditors were not so fortunate, but it seems most unlikely, as submitted by counsel for the former Band executive, that they would have been paid if bankruptcy had ensued. Of course, the surrender of the lease in April 1982 made the case of the unsecured creditors utterly hopeless.

The Toussowasket matter in its many facets and long duration had an influence, not always for the good, on what happened at Westbank in the late 1970's and early 1980's. It will be remembered that the origin of the Mt. Boucherie Park was a joint initiative of the former Departmental official, Mr. Weir, and the former Chief of the Westbank Indian Band, Noll Derriksan. By 1980, the federal government or its agencies had outstanding debt on the project of something in the order of $500,000. There were unpaid development bills outstanding on the park, which was only partly completed. Rancorous relations existed between the FBDB and the Department because of the sad experience relative to this park. That ill feeling threatened to spill over to the economic disadvantage of bands throughout the province and indeed even throughout Canada. What was to be done? In effect, the Department was trapped in a situation where it desperately needed a path out of the morass of debt and discord that surrounded Toussowasket.

As I noted earlier, Mr. Walchli had discussions in late 1980 wherein he urged then Chief Derrickson to become involved with the Park. The Chief demanded a substantial financial contribution if the Band or the Band company were to become involved. A contribution agreement (set out above) was eventually signed in May 1981. Undoubtedly, participation by the Band in the enterprise and the subsequent escalation in the fortunes of the project — the Band and Band company took the matter through to substantial completion — relieved Mr. Walchli of a host of difficult problems surrounding this matter. The success of the project no doubt also enhanced Chief Derrickson's own view of his business abilities — he told me that he had been able to work out a very favourable arrangement with a Kelowna mobile home vendor to pay a considerable sum of money as reservation fees for mobile home pads on the newly developed area at Mount Boucherie Park. These fees are sometimes colloquially called "patch fees". They were apparently a considerable source of income to park owners in the buoyant times of 1980–81. With the injection of these sums and the additional $100,000 immediately contributed by the Department under the contribution agreement of May 1981, the fortunes of Mt. Boucherie Mobile Home Park improved dramatically. The longer-term picture improved too because of an upsurge in demand for mobile home park accommodation in the Kelowna area. Mr. Walchli was undoubtedly pleased that Band involvement in both the Lakeridge subdivision and the Toussowasket park had been fruitful. The latter especially had been a source of concern to the Department for several years. But as the evidence developed, it appeared to me that matters surrounding Toussowasket had a fallout effect that influenced other events which in turn caused further controversy at Westbank.

The Toussowasket matter had, in my view, a relationship to what I shall call the York-Derrickson controversy. It should be noted that Mt. Boucherie Mobile Home Park is directly adjacent to and contiguous with the Westview Village Mobile Home Park, sometimes also known as Park Mobile Homes Ltd., an enterprise run, as previously mentioned, by members of the York family. The individuals managing the park from 1978 to 1982 were Mr. Bruce York and his wife, Henriette York. Henriette York gave evidence before the Commission but Mr. York was not available due to illness. Mrs. York was an articulate witness and was able, with the aid of numerous documents, to outline a general history of the mobile home park from its inception in the early 1970's.

One Larry York had been involved in the area from the early 1970's. He had been developing a mobile home park and had been engaged in the sale of mobile homes at the location leased from West-Kel Holdings on Westbank Reserve 9. There also was a sales outlet in or near Kelowna for a period of time. The mobile home park and sales office were located adjacent to Highway 97 on land held by Noll Derriksan as locatee. It was my impression that Mr. Derriksan was one of the most active members of the Westbank Band in seeking leasing and business opportunities in the early 1970's. The park was generally referred to by witnesses as either Park Mobile Homes or Westview Village. Mr. Derriksan was, of course, also the locatee at Mt. Boucherie Park, the history of which is set forth above.

Those individuals actually running the park prior to 1977 had not been particularly desirable operators, according to Mr. Ronald Derrickson. He said that the park had not been built to a high standard and was not well maintained. Additionally, the existing sub-lease between the York company (Park Mobile) and Mr. Noll Derriksan's company (West-Kel) was not a particularly favourable one and became less favourable as time passed. The Westview Village (York) Park was a direct competitor of the (Derriksan) Mt. Boucherie Park, and, it appeared, a rather low-cost competitor. It will be remembered that the Mt. Boucherie Park was said to have been built to a quite high standard at considerable cost. Mr. Walchli had noted to the Standing Committee that, in his view, the Mt. Boucherie Park was a well-built court. One had here the inherent tensions of a relatively low-cost operator next to a relatively high-cost operator. The Park Mobile enterprise appeared more successful than the Mt. Boucherie enterprise. It must have been somewhat galling to both Noll Derriksan and then Chief Ronald Derrickson to see the York operation proceeding in reasonably good economic fashion while Mt. Boucherie (Toussowasket) languished in economic distress. To put it in colloquial terms, there was no love lost between the Yorks and Chief Derrickson or his brother, Noll Derriksan.

As outlined in the evidence of a sometime co-venturer of the Yorks, Mr. Nick Dachyshyn, the Yorks were obligated to have the mobile home park completed to a certain degree by a specified date in 1981 or face possible forfeiture of the sub-lease. Mr. Dachyshyn, however, grew so frustrated with the endless delays and impediments he encountered in 1980–81 that he eventually gave up and left the Kelowna area. A picture emerges of certain of the Yorks being less than ideal lessees, but a picture also emerges of the then Chief and Council behaving towards their proposed development plans in a fashion that was frustrating to the developer. In some ways, the problems and controversy flowing from the Park Mobile development are illustrative of how problems can arise on leased Indian reserve land. It is a case that can usefully be studied by Departmental officials and bands to avoid future troubles on developing reserves.

I heard about the rather curious incident of the allotment of an old unused Band roadway to Messrs. Noll Derriksan and Harold Derickson. Mr. Ronald Derrickson, Chief at that time, professed that he was concerned about maintenance of and snow clearing from the road and that because of this continuing burden on the Band, the road was allotted to the two adjoining locatees. He noted that there was a payment made to the Band of $1,400 arising from the road allotment. The road issue was made more contentious by a perhaps less than perfect provision in the original lease to preserve access to all parts of the Westview property through and over this roadway bisecting the property. The Band allotted part of the road to Noll Derriksan, one effect of which was to give Noll Derriksan a legal position that could enhance his bargaining position vis-à-vis the Yorks. It was my view that he would be glad to improve his position because of the fact that the sub-lease was becoming less desirable as time passed after 1976 through to 1982.

It was not long after the time of this allotment that relations between the Yorks and Ronald Derrickson and Noll Derriksan appear to have become more strained. There were plausible reasons for the allotments of the roadway to the adjoining locatees, but I saw no compelling reasons. I think the allotment did more harm than good because it could be construed by the lessee as a lack of evenhanded action by Council — why, for instance, as a sensible precaution, was not the lessee asked if it had any comments on the matter prior to this allotment?

As I noted earlier, the Park Mobile operation was located on Reserve 9 adjoining Highway 97 and contiguous to Mt. Boucherie Park. At the time of the original leasing of the land in 1971, the leased area had been "surrendered" land. The surrender question was later to have repercussions on the question of the applicability of Westbank Band by-laws to the Park Mobile operation. There has long existed doubt about the application of by-laws to surrendered land, according to Mr. David Sparks, a Departmental official with expertise in this area. As noted in the Introduction, there was a period in the late 1960's and early 1970's when Reserves 9 and 10 had been surrendered in the hope that major leasing arrangements could be concluded. These hopes were not realized. However, any leases entered into in that period were arguably different from normal locatee leases of reserve land because the terms of the Indian Act leave room for doubt as to whether "surrendered" land is "reserve" land within the meaning of the Act. Hopefully, this uncertainty will be resolved by certain proposed amendments to the Act that are currently in the parliamentary process.

The 1971 lease had some rather special rental provisions in that up to 1976, the rent was to be higher than after 1976. The rent was fixed in the lease for the first ten years from 1971 to 1981. The rental in the first three years was to be $15,000 a year. Rent for the next year was to be $19,000 a year and in 1975–76 was to be $23,000. Then for five years from July 1976 until June 1981, it was to be $12,000 a year. The lease provided that the rent for the eight succeeding five-year periods after 1981 would be set at a fair market rent to be negotiated immediately before the commencement of each five-year period. In the event that an agreement could not be reached, the matter would be referred to the Federal Court. In 1977, just when Noll Derriksan's woes at Mt. Boucherie were commencing, his lease income from Park Mobile was about to take a substantial dive downward.

The lease also contained the following term, which became of considerable significance later on:

> the lessee agrees that it will have, by the end of the tenth year of the term hereof, completed a minimum of 260 mobile home pads or sites and have expended a total of not less than $450,000 on its development on the said premises failing which the lessor shall have the right to cancel the present lease on thirty days notice without further recourse by the lessee.

It was also contemplated in the lease that a concurrent sub-lease would be granted to Trojan Developments Ltd. In 1971–72, Trojan Development ran into financial problems and had to abandon the sub-lease. This operation had been under the direction of a Mr. Young. Henriette York said only a few mobile home pads had been completed in that early period.

Mr. Larry York of Park Mobile Home Sales Ltd. (hereinafter sometimes called "Park Mobile") had apparently some existing financial relationship to Trojan Developments and in October 1972, another sub-lease was entered into between West-Kel (Derriksan) and Park Mobile (York). This sub-lease was for a period of forty-eight years and eight months. The payment terms paralleled those in the head lease, which had a fifty-year term. There was a difference in duration in that the first rental period (fixed) of the sub-lease extended until October 1982, since the first year of the ten-year term under the York sub-lease had commenced in October 1972. This sixteen-month difference in duration between head lease and sub-lease later caused much controversy when there arose a debate over just when a new rent was to be fixed for the succeeding five-year period. This controversy generated quite a blizzard of correspondence between the solicitors involved for the respective parties.

The new sub-lease also contained this clause:

> Notwithstanding anything herein contained, except for the approvals required in paragraph 8 herein, it is agreed that the grantee shall have the sole and exclusive power and authority on behalf of the grantor to deal directly with the lessor under the lease relative to any matter arising under the lease or with respect to development on the land and the grantor shall not undertake any negotiations or communications with the lessor unless specifically requested to do so by the grantee.

It appears that this provision contemplated that Park Mobile would be dealing directly with the Department of Indian Affairs relative to certain matters arising under the lease. Mr. Larry York signed the lease on behalf of Park Mobile. From 1973 through 1976, Park Mobile went on with development on the land leased from West-Kel and also carried on a mobile home sales operation at Kelowna. For a time, a Mr. Charles Satiacum was involved with the operation. Henriette York said that Mr. Larry York and Mr. Charles Satiacum did extensive development to the park in the mid-1970's. Bruce and Henriette York came on the scene as park operators in 1977; almost from the outset, there were difficulties.

In April 1977, Mr. Satiacum ceased to be involved in the Park Mobile business and the shareholders of the enterprise then became Messrs. Bruce York, Glen York, and Stanley Lawrence York. From financial statements of Park Mobile at that date, it appears that the amount of money required to be spent under the head lease in development of the park had been expended, but the requisite number of pads had not yet been installed. The stipulated number had to be in place by the summer of 1981 in order to preserve the lease (and sub-lease) in good standing. The sub-lessee, Park Mobile, had undertaken in its sub-lease to complete the necessary construction and to expend the necessary monies stipulated in the head lease. This requirement lay at the heart of later problems. The urgent need of Park Mobile to complete the development and the apparent reluctance of the Band executive (particularly on the part of the Chief) to expedite matters relative thereto contributed to continuing ill feeling on the part of the sharehold-ers of the lessee company.

Around the time of Mr. Satiacum's retirement and the takeover of the park by the Yorks in 1977, relations between the parties seemed to become increasingly acrimonious. In April 1977, correspondence was exchanged between the solicitors, Larson and Co., on behalf of the Yorks and Mr. Warren, solicitor to West-Kel, relative to alleged breaches of the lease. In May 1977, Noll Derriksan, president of West-Kel Holdings Ltd., wrote directly to Mr. Fred Walchli, the Regional Director General, concerning this lease. It seemed to me somewhat unusual that a locatee would think it appropriate to write directly to the head of the B.C. Region in connection with his problems over a lease. Generally speaking, I doubt that such would occur. I realize that it is desirable that chief executives not be isolated from the activities of their department, but orderly business would be impeded if this practice became the order of the day. But it must be remembered that Tous-sowasket (and to some extent Lakeridge) had involved Mr. Walchli in getting to know Noll Derriksan and Ronald Derrickson. He came to know them and he was favourably impressed certainly by Ronald Derrickson. It may have been perceived that he was treating them as court favourites. There was, to put it in mild terms, considerable intensity in Indian politics in B.C. in the 1970's. Perhaps unconsciously, Mr. Walchli allowed himself to become identified as a Departmental official who was quite close to Ronald Derrickson and his brother. It is always a difficult and delicate task for a chief executive who must to some degree be accessible to all, and yet not perceived as too accessible to some. I think this was a particularly difficult task in B.C. in the late 1970's, when there was a very fluid situation in Indian politics in B.C. Some of the perceptions of wrongdoing that emerged from the Toussowasket affair could be said to be flawed, but there was some foundation for suspicion in the sense that Mr. Walchli did have a considerable measure of contact with Ronald Derrickson and Noll Derriksan. Some felt he was too solicitous of their welfare.

In June 1977, Mr. Warren sent to Park Mobile through their solicitors a notice to quit and a demand for possession. This was but an early salvo, albeit a fairly heavy one, in what would continue as a state of more or less constant confrontation for several years. Around this time, a Department study was commissioned on behalf of Noll

Derriksan — the engineers were instructed not to communicate with the Yorks. There seemed to be growing mutual mistrust. The Department was becoming more involved in the vortex of ill feelings that was growing out of the Park Mobile situation.

In May 1977, Mr. Warren sent to Mr. Larson a letter pointing out that a former Band roadway through the park was now owned by the locatee of the leased land, Noll Derriksan. This road had on it, according to the evidence, encroachments which had been constructed by Park Mobile or by their tenants or predecessor in title, Trojan. As noted above, it was said that there had been problems with maintenance of the road as well as complaints from Band members about motorcycles and skidoos on the road. Ronald Derrickson said in his evidence that allotment of the road had realized $1,400 for Band coffers. The allotment was completed in May 1977, just prior to the arrival in the Department of Mr. Peter Clark. The allottees were the adjoining locatees, Harold Derickson and Noll Derriksan. The timing of the allotment was unfortunate in that it coincided with a hardening of relations between Noll Derriksan and the Yorks.

Mr. Clark said in his evidence that this road was no longer needed for access and was therefore allotted to the adjacent landowners, Noll Derriksan and Harold Derickson. However, Mr. Walchli, in his evidence before the Commission, said that this later became one of the considerations in the mind of the Department regarding problems with the FBDB security on Mt. Boucherie. He said:

> You will recall when we looked at the plans that Sandy McDougall put on the board the road access was actually transferred to Noll Derriksan some time earlier, but it was not part of the lease agreement. So without that access the trailer park was land locked. (The reference is to Mt. Boucherie.) (My underlining)
>   (Transcripts: Volume XXXV, p. 4828)

It appears from a letter of January 27, 1977 from Chief Derrickson, that access to Highway 97 from that road had been cancelled by the Department of Highways, but at least in the mind of Mr. Walchli, Noll Derriksan's ownership of the roadway created some question as to the viability of the Mt. Boucherie lease and hence proper enforcement of FBDB security. This matter, of course, came to a head later when debate arose between the Department of Indian Affairs and FBDB as to what was going to be done with regard to the defaulted loan on Mt. Boucherie Park. The fear of the Department was that the locatee and the Band could frustrate any effective dealing with the lease which was the basic security for the loans against the Park. The roadway was one factor. Another was the problem of getting Band consent to assignment of the lease.

The Department had been required to give its consent to the allotment of this roadway to the adjoining landowners to make an allotment effective. Given the later acrimony between the locatee, Noll Derriksan, his brother, then Chief Ronald Derrickson, and the Yorks, the timing of this transfer of the roadway was a matter that Commission Counsel submitted should be looked at very critically. Should the Department have given its consent to this allotment? Counsel submitted that it was unwise of the Department to give its consent.

Mr. Clark said it was a routine request. He saw nothing out of the ordinary in it. As the matter was presented to the Department, there appeared to be valid reasons for a transfer of the roadway to the adjoining locatees. Ronald Derrickson said that it would relieve the Band of its maintenance or snow removal obligations, although one wonders just what degree of responsibility would be placed on the Band by keeping this as a roadway. It did not appear that it was being maintained by the Band as a road in any event. From the state of encroachments on the roadway, it appeared not to be able to be utilized as a road. The Okanagan is not noted as a severe snowbelt, so snow clearing responsibilities could not be viewed as a matter of substance.

The objection to allotting this roadway was that it changed the character of the particular land from road designation to a state of ownership by the respective locatees. Since the road bisected a portion of Park Mobile Home's leased land, it gave to the locatee, if so inclined, a more absolute form of dominion over the land. For instance, the locatee could erect a fence, plant crops, put up a row of trees, and the like. It could result in an enhancement of the legal ability of the locatee to make life difficult for the surrounding lease holder. For instance, in a letter that Mr. Clark wrote to Mr. Noll Derriksan in November 1978 he said:

> I'm advised that in the absence of a mutual agreement that steps to prevent Park Mobile Home Sales Ltd. from using land in which they have no interest, such as a fence, should be taken. (My underlining)

Mr. Clark said, when asked about that letter,

> ...It was one of the ways, I think, in the negotiation that there were areas there which I think were causing some concerns which could have been fenced off without causing any major problems. I understood that was feasible to do although apparently it wasn't economic.
> Q And of course the erection of a full fence would have prevented the people that were landlocked from getting anywhere.
> A Right.
> Q Were you prepared to go that far yourself, or was that just a negotiating tool?
> A No. I think there were one or two roads across that piece of property that — it wasn't as if the road was being used in a lineal part at all, but there were one or two accesses that were across the road, which as I understood, was still being used and there was no

great problems with, on the north/south I imagine, rather than the east/west.

Q Were you proposing here that — were you considering at that time that those accesses be fenced?

A No.

(Transcripts: Volume L, pp. 7172–7173)

This evidence of Mr. Clark I find difficult to comprehend — I believe Mr. Clark was here suggesting that a fence be put up to put pressure on the park operator — Mr. Derriksan had been complaining to Mr. Walchli about this problem and Mr. Clark, his subordinate, was casting about for ways to solve the simmering controversy. The Department also bore some responsibility for the problem since it had unwisely consented to this allotment in 1977.

Unfortunately, we were not able to hear from Mr. Sheldon McCullough, the official of the Department who approved of the allotment, because of his health problems. It appears that he was oblivious to the potential problem when he recommended Departmental consent to the allotment. Mr. Clark could not give details of the Department's thinking since he did not arrive until shortly after allotment of the roadway. Mrs. York said, when asked about the roadway:

Q When did you find out and when did you first obtain the knowledge that Noll Derriksan asserted title to this roadway? Was it only after you became a shareholder in the —

A Oh yes, it was in that one letter, but even at that point I myself didn't think that a band member became owner of a road, the Band road. I just — that was my own way of thinking. I didn't think that band roads became private property of band members. Obviously I was wrong.

(Transcripts: Volume XIV, pp. 1970)

There is nothing to criticize in a band allotting band roads to whomever it chooses, but it should be done in such a way that the status quo ante is not altered. That principle was wholly ignored in this case by both the Band Council and the Department. Mrs. York was unpleasantly surprised to find that the ownership of the roadway was now in Noll Derriksan, the locatee. Nevertheless, it was quite improper for Park Mobile or park tenants to be placing encroachments on a roadway which was not part of the leased land. The Band was the authority orginally in control of the road and as a matter of law, they or the Department would have had the right at any time to demand that these encroachments be removed. By May 1977, it was in the control of Noll Derriksan as locatee. By this time he was interested in seeing if his lease position could be improved. The Yorks would not be enthusiastic about making any alteration to the lease arrangements that would be less favourable to themselves.

Clearly, the transfer of the Band road to Noll Derriksan would be a circumstance that could lead the Park Mobile proprietors to believe that they were not playing "on a level field". Therefore it was unfortunate that the Department consented to this allotment. Mr. McCullough may not have been as fully informed as he ought to have been by the Band as to who had lease holdings in the area, but I think where roadways are concerned, that there are usually potential issues of access, and prudent practice would be to ascertain there are no interests overlooked. As noted, the Band always would have had the right to deal with any encroachments on the road. This allotment to Mr. Noll Derriksan could be interpreted by the lessees as providing an unfair advantage to the locatee. Where an existing lease is in place, the Department must be scrupulously careful not to disturb the balance of the status quo between the lessor and the lessee. Here that status was disturbed and became another issue of contention between people who already had many issues arising between them. Its natural tendency was to cause the Park Mobile owners to question the bona fides of the Band executive and the Department. That is the one thing that governments cannot afford — those subject to governmental action may disagree with a particular governmental action but it is a problem of an entirely different order when parties question the integrity or motives of government. This roadway issue had the tendency to cause the Yorks to harbour suspicions that they were subject to capricious action by the Band.

As I noted above, there was an interplay between Toussowasket and the Park Mobile situation, which situation later became full of acrimony. It will be recalled that by 1977 the fortunes of Noll Derriksan's park, Mt. Boucherie, were in a state of serious disarray. Directly beside this park was the Park Mobile operation. It was just at that time that the rent on Westview Park (Park Mobile) was reduced for the next five years. The rental scheme for the first ten years, (1971–81), appears to have been designed to encourage full development of the site. By 1977, the rental arrangement was becoming less favourable to the locatee in the sense that his cash return was being diminished and would be diminished for several years.

Noll Derriksan was in possession of a failing park (Mt. Boucherie), while the Yorks were running a park that was generating a reasonable income from mobile home sales as well as from pad rentals. But the York operation was, as of 1977, returning to Noll Derriksan a decreased rental and was going to do so for the next several years. It is clear to me that, commencing in or about 1977, Noll Derriksan, abetted by his brother, Ronald Derrickson, was intent on getting a new and better lease arrangement in regard to the Park Mobile leased land. Two letters that I set out hereafter as an addendum to this chapter give the flavour of the controversy that was going on in the spring of 1977. (Documents 27 and 30 from Exhibit 51)

Significantly, on May 2, 1977, a letter was sent from Warren and Company on behalf of West-Kel (Derriksan) to the solicitors for Park Mobile (York) containing the following proposal:

> In an effort not to jeopardize your client's investment, West-Kel Holdings Ltd. is prepared to implement the following: 1) the property shall be appraised by two appraisers, one selected by your client and one selected by our client; 2) the average of the appraisals shall be taken and against such average there shall be applied an annual rental of 9.5%. The new lease agreement shall be entered into for the benefit of your client and our client, the details of which shall be subject to the aforementioned meeting. (My underlining)

On May 11, 1977, Mr. Warren again wrote to Mr. Larson making a proposal that Lot 31, adjoining Mt. Boucherie Mobile Home Park, be deleted from the existing sub-lease and that a new appraisal be done and a new rent fixed for Lot 32. In October 1977, Mr. Derriksan wrote to Mr. Walchli demanding that the Department have encroachments on the aforementioned roadway removed. On November 8, 1977, Mr. Clark wrote to Park Mobile in care of their solicitors, requesting immediate action to remove enroachments from the land comprising the old roadway. He said in his letter, inter alia,

> alternatively, you may arrange to meet with the locatee landowner, Mr. N. Derriksan and Band Council to retain use of these lands on terms and conditions to be established in conjunction with this Department. (My underlining)

I would infer, as did counsel to the Department, that the underlined portion is a reference to the Minister's ultimate jurisdiction over lease arrangements.

As early as November 1977, action was being taken by West-Kel in the courts to attempt to cancel the sub-lease. These efforts were unsuccessful. A court doubtless would be reluctant to order forfeiture of the sub-lease of such a substantial operation as Westview Village Mobile Home Park for the sole reason of some encroachments on the former Band roadway. Bruce and Henriette York must have been greatly concerned to find themselves facing cancellation of the sub-lease almost immediately after their arrival at Westbank. Noll Derriksan was apparently becoming frustrated by the unsatisfactory state of matters at Mt. Boucherie. Both parties got off on the wrong foot and never did seem to be able to establish good relations thereafter.

The parties were apparently close to settling their dispute in the summer of 1978 when agreement was reached for an increase in rent from $1,000 a month to $1,500 a month. But the settlement negotiations appeared to founder over the issue of whether or not the roadway was to be included in the proposed settlement. Mr. Warren said in a letter of July 31, 1978 he sent to the solicitor for Park Mobile,

> We reject your suggestion that there was ever any intention of including within the terms of the settlement agreement, a settlement of the trespass and encroachment on Tsinstikeptum Reserve #9 by Park Mobile Homes Sales Ltd. Indeed, I remind you that the author specifically informed you during our settlement negotiations that the firm of Warren, Ladner was not authorized or instructed to deal in any way with the problems related to the 66-foot roadway. The undersigned made specific reference to this matter in order that your office and your client could determine whether it desired to negotiate separately on the two disputes.

Mr. Clark of the Department had given his approval to a form of settlement and apparently was of the view that all matters between the parties were settled. In the event, no settlement was concluded and the dispute continued. There were quite a number of solicitors successively involved for both parties and matters were not ultimately resolved until 1984. The resolution, in effect, was a divorce — the Yorks sold the park to a new owner, Mr. John Ross. My impression from considering all of the correspondence, court proceedings, and testimony concerning this long-running matter was that there was a considerable reservoir of ill feeling on both sides. Such things, I suppose, are inevitable in human affairs, but it is still disappointing to see so much unedifying acrimony.

In the summer of 1982 occurred a truly shocking incident. Ronald M. Derrickson was set upon in his home at Westbank by an assailant and was severely injured. This matter and its resultant charges has already been dealt with by the Criminal Courts and I do not wish to trench on conclusions reached in earlier proceedings where evidence was led and conclusions were arrived at based on evidence heard by other tribunals. However, it is abundantly clear that the assailant of Chief Derrickson did not drop from the sky by chance. The individual who was found to have actually committed this brutal assault was a person known to relatives or associates of relatives of Mr. Bruce York. The assailant came from Edmonton and relatives of Bruce York were located in that city. A Mr. Tsu of Kelowna pleaded guilty to a charge in connection with the attack, but Bruce York and his relatives were acquitted of conspiracy charges laid arising out of the assault. I heard evidence from a Ms. W. that after the assault (and after conspiracy charges had been laid) Bruce York was heard to offer compensation to someone if they would agree to plead guilty to the crime. This conversation occurred in Edmonton, she said, at the residence of relatives of Bruce York. That, in and of itself, obviously proves nothing against Bruce York. Such evidence could be admissible at law to support an inference that a person possessed a guilty mind concerning the crime, but it could be equally consistent with a legitimate wish to avoid any entanglement in criminal charges. Ms. W. said in her evidence before the Commission in answer to questions from counsel for the former Band executive:

> Q What did they indicate had gone wrong in reference to this hit?

A Well, at first they didn't know, they just announced that something had gone wrong and somebody had gotten shot.

Q Were there any discussions at that initial meeting, if I could just take you back for a moment, in reference to the nature of the business transaction, or what type of relationship they were involved in with Mr. Derrickson?

A Yes. There was some reference made to a lease on a trailer home, and that Ron had reneged on the lease and that they were out to get him, or something along those lines. It's been a long time ago.

Q What do you recall the next incident involving this matter as being, after that?

A When the charges were laid.

Q All right. Can you tell me what happened then?

A Yes. They were sitting in the basement, discussing that —

Q Now, if I could just stop you there, when you say "sitting in the basement", was this, again, at Larry York Senior's residence?

A Yes.

Q In the City of Edmonton?

A Yes.

Q All right.

A St. Albert, actually.

Q St. Albert?

A Mm-hmm.

Q And you were present?

A Yes, I was.

Q And who else was present at that particular discussion?

A Bruce York, he came in from Kelowna; flew in from Kelowna. There was also Larry York Junior; Larry York Senior; Murray; myself, and Olga Petrov, which is Larry York Junior's girlfriend at that time, it's now his wife.

Q And all these people were present at this conversation that took place?

A Yes.

Q All right. Would you tell me what was discussed then?

A What was discussed was that Larry York Junior should take the —

THE COMMISSIONER: When you speak of charges, Miss W., as I understand matters, there was a chap called Cooper, who had been arrested shortly after this incident in Kelowna. I think he was charged with attempted homicide; is that the charges you are talking about, or are you talking about charges that were laid against Mr. Bruce York, and I think maybe Larry York, and others?

THE WITNESS: No. There was charges apparently laid against Cooper, fairly subsequent, like, almost right away after the incident happened. But, it was some time before, if I remember correctly, it was sometime before charges were laid against Larry York Junior, Larry York Senior, and Bruce York.

THE COMMISSIONER: Fine. Now, when you speak of "charges" that you were present at a conversation, is that the second series of charges you are talking about?

THE WITNESS: That's the ones against the York family, yes.

THE COMMISSIONER: Okay. Yes, all right. All right, now I understand. Yes, carry on.

Q And there were discussions about those particular charges?

A Yes, there were.

Q And you were present?

A Yes, I was.

Q Could you tell me what was discussed?

A What was discussed was Bruce York offered Larry York Junior an amount of money, I can't quite remember whether it was $30,000 or $50,000, but it was a large sum of money for him pleading guilty to the charge, and letting the other two go.

Q Was Larry York Junior prepared to accept this money and plead guilty?

A No, he wasn't. He said that he would do that if there was a larger amount of money. I remember distinctly that he said that he was looking at perhaps three to five years, and for him to take a charge like that, he'd have to get paid more than that.

Q And was that the first time that you had met Bruce York?

A Yes.

(Transcripts: Volume LXIX, pp. 10331–10335)

This assault incident and subsequent court proceedings related to it cast a somewhat lurid glow over events at Westbank. It must always be an object of regret when parties seek to take the law into their own hands. That incident was obviously evidence of aberrant thinking. But because of the tremendous publicity such a matter inevitably attracts, this appears to me to have been a large factor in giving undue prominence to various disputes and controversies at Westbank. It raised to a remarkable degree the profile of Ronald Derrickson and the Westbank Indian Band. From that day forward, the Chief and Band had great "news value". This is not always a desirable state of affairs. Sensational publicity can have quite unforeseen consequences.

This whole incident and its fallout would obviously have been a further factor to exacerbate the already difficult relations existing between the Band executive and the operators of Park Mobile. There was no suggestion that Henriette York had anything to do with this whole disgraceful incident — indeed, I had the impression from her evidence that she could never understand just what led the various parties to manifest such animosity to each other. She appeared to be a woman of good sense and good will.

On another front, in September 1978, the Westbank Indian Band had sought approval under Section 53 and Section 60 of the Indian Act to manage their surrendered and reserve lands respectively. Mr. Clark wrote on this subject to Mr. Joe Leask, another member of the Department, on November 6, 1979. He said, inter alia:

since the issuance and approval of this Band Council Resolution by the Westbank Band Council we have continued discussions related to the advisability and necessary procedures to affect such control and management as the record shows there's been a history of difficulties related to the disposition and development of lands held by members of the Westbank Band.

The experience gained by the Band through their Band Development Company and the Lakeridge Park subdivision which is on surrendered land, is evidence that there is a competence to effectively manage these lands. I therefore recommend that the request to the Westbank Band Council for the Minister to appoint the Band Council to manage, sell, lease or otherwise dispose of surrendered lands under Section 53(1) of the Indian Act be approved. — Such authority should be limited to the surrendered lands on Tsinstikeptum Reserve #10. (My underlining)

The surrendered lands on Reserve 10 chiefly comprised the Lakeridge Park subdivision located above Okanagan Lake. This is a housing, as opposed to a mobile home park, development. It is a high-class residential subdivision that is a credit to the Band.

The Department, ignoring Mr. Clark's above advice, on October 6, 1980 appointed the Westbank Indian Band to exercise Section 53 authority over all surrendered lands on its reserves at Westbank. The effect was to give to the Westbank Indian Band authority over the management and administration of the leased land whereon Park Mobile was situate. On October 15, 1980, Mr. Walchli wrote to Park Mobile advising them that he had been informed that they were commencing development improvements in breach of Westbank Indian By-law 1979–15, relating to development, and that since no proper plan was approved they were to cease and desist from construction. Since the Band had been given authority over surrendered lands, there seems no apparent reason for Mr. Walchli to write on the subject — it may be, however, that it was simply a case of overlap. I again found it somewhat surprising that Mr. Walchli would involve himself in this matter even if the Department had responsibility for dealing with the land — I would have expected it to fall more suitably within the purview of a less senior member of the Department. Having someone in the position of Mr. Walchli dealing with this relatively minor issue could lead the lessees to suspect the worst.

For the Department to grant authority over all surrendered lands, including as it did the Park Mobile lands, in the circumstances existing in 1980, was probably not the prudent course to adopt. There was, as noted by Mr. Clark, some history of prior trouble, and given the controversy existing between the Yorks, the locatee Noll Derriksan, and his brother, the then Chief, this was once again a situation where the status quo was being changed in a way that could give lessees an impression of a failure by the Department to have due regard to existing lease arrangements. The blanket grant of authority was indeed not considered desirable by the regional official, Mr. Clark. Perhaps the proverbial distance between Ottawa and B.C. contributed to this lapse.

I have earlier noted the evidence of Mr. Dachyshyn about the problems he encountered in 1980 and 1981 with regard to obtaining approvals for expansion of the Westview Village Mobile Home Park. This expansion was, as we have seen, necessary in order that the lessee meet certain construction requirements imposed under the head lease of 1971. Failure to complete by the deadline could imperil the continuance of the sub-lease covering the park.

In September 1980, apparently in a state of near desperation about the lack of progress on the park expansion, Mr. Dachyshyn and Mr. Bruce York sought to enlist the aid of a Mr. John Steward. Apparently Mr. Steward had promised to engage a law firm to sort out the development and by-law problems that the Park Mobile people were encountering with the Westbank Indian Band Council. On October 9, 1980, Chief Derrickson wrote to Park Mobile saying:

> We have on file a letter signed by yourself and Nick Dachyshyn appointing Mr. Grant Maddock of Okanagan Planning and Engineering Ltd. to be your sole agent to finalize all approvals in regard to your extension. Mr. Maddock set up a special meeting with the Westbank Indian Band Council where all plans would be reviewed. There were several preliminary meetings with the Westbank Indian Council and Mr. Maddock, the final meeting was with the intention of trying to finalize or clearly define those areas needing to be fulfilled for final approval. <u>Before this meeting took place we were informed by Mr. Walchli that a Mr. J. Steward had been appointed as your sole agent to deal directly with the Department in regard to obtaining these approvals.</u>
>
> We have therefore had several meetings and telephone conversations with the Department of Indian Affairs, and we have established that the complete files on Park Mobile Home Sales including all problems will be subject to complete review in regard to the present facility and approvals, any encroachments or complaints by West-Kel and/or the locatee as well as several complaints made to this office by residents of your park. (My underlining)

On September 26, 1980, Chief Derrickson sent to Park Mobile a letter in the following terms:

> Enclosed please find copy of a news clipping which will be of interest to you. We also advise that all lands on Indian Reserve #9 are unsurrendered.

Attached to the letter was a newspaper article with the heading "B.C. Rentalsman Scalped by Indian Act". The article dealt with the proposition that the Provincial Rentalsman had no jurisdiction over Indian lands. The sending of the letter could be construed as a not very subtle statement by Mr. Derrickson that he intended to take a more aggressive stance with lessees and tenants of mobile home parks.

One can see from these letters the possibility of further suspicion. The Park Mobile operators could get the impression that the head of the Department in B.C., Mr. Walchli, was passing on everything to the Chief. This is an example of the undesirability of the Department head involving himself in matters at this level. A suspicious person might well say — "what on earth is the head of the entire B.C. Region doing involving himself in this lease problem — the Chief or his brother must have a tremendous amount of influence with him". Additionally, the letter enclosing the clipping seemed to indicate that the Chief meant to be more, not less, assertive. If the lessees came to feel that Mr. Walchli was too compliant where the Chief was concerned, their apprehensions would have been much increased.

On October 27, 1980, Mr. Walchli again wrote to Park Mobile in strong terms telling them to remove their encroachments on the former roadway. This, of course, was when Mr. Walchli was urging the Chief and Council to step in and assist with the Mt. Boucherie Park problem which was worrisome to the Department and which threatened to permanently impair relations between FBDB and the Department (and Indian entrepreneurs). I can appreciate that Mr. Walchli would want to maintain good relations with Ronald Derrickson, but for him to involve himself personally in this lease dispute was to court the possibility of giving a very unfortunate impression that he was allowing himself to become unduly partial.

There was a meeting held in early November 1980 at the Westbank Band office. According to Mr. Dachyshyn, there was a bit of a scene between the Chief and a fire marshall. The Chief demanded that the person in question leave the meeting. Apparently one of the issues to be discussed at the meeting was the vexed question of fire protection — this was a legitimate concern of the Chief, but the matter would hardly be advanced by diatribe as opposed to rational discussion.

Q What happened at that meeting?
A Well, we started to discuss the plan, and tried to get to the problem of why he rejected the water system, and he stated his case, and then the Assistant Dominion Fire Marshall, he didn't get up, but he got into a discussion where, according to all codes, requirements, water reserve, the gallons-per-minute that the pump pumped, and that the system as far as his regulations were, was sufficient.
Q What was the response of any of the parties there to that statement?
A Well, it took about two or three — maybe five or ten seconds — Chief Ron asked him who he was, what he was doing there, and he could just pick up his bag and he gave him two minutes to get out of there, or he would call somebody and have him removed.
Q What happened then?
A The gentleman left.
Q Did the meeting continue?

A Yes.

(Transcripts: Volume LXVIII, p. 10202)

This sort of behaviour by the chief executive officer of the Band, aside from being petulant, was scarcely of the sort to dispel the already deep suspicions that the Park Mobile people harboured about the Band administration. It also highlights just how undesirable it was for the Chief to involve himself so directly in a matter where his brother was the next-door competitor of (and actively engaged in litigation with) Park Mobile. Here was a clear example of a conflict of interest but everyone, including Departmental people, seems to have been oblivious to it. Mr. Grant Maddock of OPEC Engineering, in answer to questions from counsel for the former Band executive, said this about relations between the parties as he, an outsider, saw them around this time:

A Well, there was a couple of things that were causing difficulties. One was the right-of-way, and I know that was a sore point. It looked like it was going to go to court over it, and also the new standards.

  I know that Larry York was very discontent with the Band and Council at that time because of the new by-laws that were being brought in.

Q Mr. Maddock, were you involved in those actual discussions and negotiations that were ongoing at that time?

A No, I was only a third party to what was being said and the discontent that was going on.

Q Did you have an discussions with Mr. Larry York in reference to his reaction to the Band over these by-laws?

A Yes, I did.

Q How would you assess that particular reaction?

A He was very upset. There were many words that were said that were I would say derogatory about the Chief, specifically about the Chief at that time.

Q And that was Ron Derrickson?

A Yes.

Q Did it become an extremely difficult and tense situation as a result of that to deal with this problem?

A I would say it was getting to be that way, yes. It was to the point that there were court actions being contemplated from both sides.

(Transcripts: Volume LXI, pp. 8805–8806)

Eventually Mr. Maddock grew tired of the wrangling and refused to carry on. I can appreciate his sense of frustration with all parties who seemed more intent on scoring points than solving the outstanding issues.

In December 1980, the Park Mobile owners engaged a Mr. Falkenberg to be their consultant to attempt to get the planning completed so that they could adhere to the terms of the original lease, which terms required them to have a specified number of pads in place by the summer of 1981. It appears that his efforts were successful for the requisite number of pads seem to have been completed at Westview sometime in the summer of 1981.

Throughout that year the various lawsuits were continuing. On July 3, 1981 Mr. Warren wrote to Park Mobile advising that they were in default under their lease because they had not constructed the minimum of 260 mobile home pads on the demised premises by June 30, 1981. He said:

> You should be aware that the failure to construct the minimum number of pads by the aforementioned date will be reflected in the rent renewal in the event you are still the tenant on the property.

The fear of the Park Mobile operators that they would be held strictly to the terms of the lease appeared to be materializing. Although it appeared that the Yorks had succeeded in getting the required pads completed (more or less on time) to avoid lease forfeiture, they could not be sure that this was the case if Mr. Warren should receive instructions to litigate this issue. This was just one more element of uncertainty they faced.

In the fall of 1981, there was a general meeting held by the Band executive with mobile home park lessees relating to the question of by-laws. The lessees were informed of a new by-law regime that was to be put in place. It was quite a comprehensive plan. Mr. David Sparks of the Department had assisted the Band in drafting appropriate by-laws to address what was perceived as a regulatory vacuum on the Reserves. I deal with some questions relating to by-laws elsewhere in this Report. This meeting had good and bad elements. It was proper for the Chief to notify lessees of the new regime, but it might have been better to have greater and earlier consultation with those affected so that people felt they were part of the process. To the greatest extent possible, it would be desirable if bands could be sensitive to the concerns of lessees on reserves. If a new by-law regime is to be brought in, it seems to me that it would be desirable to have discussions with lessees about the parameters of regulation. Lessees may not always be happy with by-laws (in fact they often will be unhappy) but if they are consulted, I think that friction can be lessened. I have observed elsewhere that Mr. Derrickson was a man of action. This is a desirable quality in a leader in that it ensures that things get done, but in this instance, Mr. Derrickson might have been wiser to do some preparatory consultation before presenting the lessees with a fait accompli. I must observe, however, that the mobile home park association at Westbank seemed at times to seek to undermine the Chief by complaining to third parties. Local disagreements should generally be settled at the local level and it was unfortunate that a litany of complaints to third parties occurred as opposed to direct dialogue between Band executive and lessees.

In September 1981, the Westbank Indian Band sent a bill to Park Mobile for $14,500 for development fees charged pursuant to the new Band development by-law. Park Mobile refused to pay these fees and has continued to refuse to pay them to the present day. One of the live issues between the parties was the question of whether by-laws could apply to "surrendered" land. There also appeared to be some question as to the applicability of this by-law to the works in question. I hope recommendations made in Section II of my Report can quiet that sort of issue relative to surrendered lands in future.

In the early part of 1982, there was correspondence between solicitors for the Band and solicitors for Park Mobile concerning the payment or non-payment of various fees. In March 1982, Mr. Flanagan of the Warren, Ladner firm wrote to Mr. MacDonald, the then solicitor for Park Mobile, indicating that, because of various alleged breaches by Park Mobile, there would be no business licence issued to them, and accordingly they could be subjected to penalties. Throughout that spring and summer, there was an ongoing controversy between the Band, B.C. Telephone, B.C. Hydro, and Park Mobile over whether or not services could or should be installed at any park extensions. Chief Derrickson purported to forbid access to Reserve 9 for installation of services at the new Park Mobile development. He said that he did this to have the Yorks comply with Band by-laws and press them to pay development and other fees. The Yorks objected to the imposts. One unfortunate by-product of this contest was inconvenience and worry occasioned to tenants of the mobile home park. There seemed to be some confusion over the status of the land on Reserve 9 because on May 19, 1982, Chief Derrickson wrote to B.C. Hydro advising:

> This is to advise that the property concerned is presently leased to West-Kel Holdings Ltd. and sub-leased to Park Mobile Home Sales Ltd. and is not surrendered. (My underlining)

On June 3, 1982, Mr. Munro, then Minister of the Department, wrote to Mr. Fred King, M.P.:

> A couple of the mobile home parks on the reserve are lands surrendered for lease. The portions not under this provision are returned to reserve status leaving leased areas surrendered lands. In October, 1980, under Section 53 of the Indian Act I appointed the Westbank Band Council to manage the surrendered lease lands as my agent. I understand that the Westview Village Mobile Home Park is surrendered lease land and I assume that the Band Council is exercising its authority to manage this leasehold under the 1980 delegation of authority. The Westview Village Mobile Home Park is operated by Park Mobile Home Sales Ltd. under lease from West-Kel Holdings Ltd. which in turn leases the lands from the Crown. (My underlining)

It does not appear that the assertions in the two letters about the status of the lands can be reconciled to stand together. Once again, such patent inconsistency could excite suspicions.

On June 5, 1982, Henriette York wrote to the Minister, the Honourable John Munro, apparently as a result of a letter earlier sent from the Minister's office to a tenant of Westview Park who had written to the Minister complaining about his inability to get telephone service. Mrs. York said in her letter:

> The band has used every conceivable means in attempting to cause us to be in violation of our lease, and to prevent us from conducting our normal business. One of the means used is to allege that we have not paid the fees necessary under their By-law #1979–15. This allegation did not arise until October 1981, some months after the original permits were obtained. In October 1981 we received a letter from the Band demanding $14,500 in additional permit fees. The Band also caused a copy of a Band Resolution to be sent to B.C. Hydro and B.C. Telephone forbidding them from entering Band Reserve land leased to Park Mobile Homes to install any Hydro meters or telephone service.
>
> We called the Westbank Indian Band Council to set up a meeting with Chief Ronald M. Derrickson, and had the meeting set for 1:00 p.m. on April 3, 1981. Upon arriving we were told the Chief could not meet with us, but Brian Eli, a council member, and Harold Derickson, license inspector, would meet with us. They offered to reduce their fees to $50 for each lot, as a processing fee. There were 88 lots, so that is $4,400, and they would forgo the additional $10,000 "Inspection Fees". We asked that if we accepted that offer would this be all that was demanded, and would it result in Hydro service. We were assured that it would. Mr. Minister, there is no mistake in relating this conversation as we have a verbatim transcript of it. Within an hour after returning to our office, Harold Derickson phoned me to state that the Chief had over-ruled, and the full amount had to be paid. In October, after the Band Council Resolution was sent to Hydro and B.C. Telephones, the Band requested information on the cost of the expanded park. This was supplied. Thereafter, they raised the amount required to $23,432.51.
>
> We feel there is no legal basis for such demands, and we are prepared to contest the matter. By-law #1979–15 has according to the information from your department, never been approved by yourself. They choose rather to try and force payment by preventing public utilities from servicing us. To date, Mr. Minister, you have, possibly without realizing it, assisted the Band in doing that.
>
> Mr. Minister, other Mobile Parks were expanded immediately prior to our expansion and also immediately afterwards, and no such exorbitant fees have been asked of them. There were no changes in the By-laws during that period. All we are seeking is equal treatment. Mr. Minister, are you seriously suggesting that we are at fault, as indicated in your Bianchini letter, for not yielding to what in my opinion is attempted extortion.

> What we did do in an attempt to reduce or eliminate the civil damages being done is to offer to put the disputed fees in trust awaiting a ruling on the matter. Please note a copy of our solicitor's letter to the Band's solicitor, dated Feb. 12, 1982, which is attached. Also attached is a copy of a Band letter dated May 7, 1982, containing their latest demand for full fees of $31,494.09.

The tone of the letter discloses that the people actually running the park, Bruce and Henriette York, felt that they were getting unfair treatment from Band officials. The controversy involving Park Mobile was a continuing and bitter one. It had spread to involve the Minister in Ottawa and public utilities in British Columbia.

The spring of 1982 was also the time when there arose a serious question of finance concerning Mt. Boucherie Park. In May 1981, an agreement had been signed by the Department for contribution to a maximum amount of $300,000 to be payable over three years. That was part of the arrangement arising from discussions held between Mr. Walchli and Chief Derrickson in 1980 and 1981, as a result of which the Band development company took an interest in the Mt. Boucherie Park with a view to further developing the park.

This contribution agreement had been brought to the attention of Mr. Ernest Hobbs, Director of Economic Development for the Department, in the fall of 1981. This matter, like several I encountered at Westbank, seemed to have a political component in that the source of the complaint to Mr. Hobbs was apparently an Indian leader who was not then sympathetic to either Chief Derrickson or the B.C. Region of the Department. Mr. Hobbs began inquiries as to the legality and propriety of this contribution agreement in view of the fact that it could be an infringement of the policy of not permitting Indian Economic Development Fund loans to be repaid from other Economic Development Funds. I gathered this was a policy founded on comments of the Auditor General of Canada. Mr. Hobbs outlined his position questioning the propriety of the contribution agreement under cross-examination by counsel for the Department. His evidence is as follows:

> Q All right. Well, isn't it necessary, Mr. Hobbs, to look beyond the dry words of the purpose, to purchase a 50 per cent interest, to find out the reason for that purpose in order to understand what's going on?
> A Well, I believe it is. I believe one needs to look at the entire contribution arrangement to understand what's going on.
> Q And isn't it necessary to find out whether there is indeed an economic enterprise on the Reserve lands, to find out whether the reason for the purchase is to save that economic enterprise?
> A Well, that's certainly one of the considerations, yes.
> Q And do you still take the position, that if that's the dominant underlying reason for the purchase which is spelled out in this contribution agreement, do you still take the position that if one of

the effects of that is to pay off the IEDF loan that there isn't authority to enter into that?

A I take the position that it is impermissible to have a contribution agreement, using government monies, a condition of which is to ensure that an IEDF loan is repaid, because there is no authority to use Economic Development contribution monies, or in fact any other contribution monies of the Department in order to meet that condition.

Q But there is authority to use contribution monies to save an economic enterprise on Reserve lands?

A There certainly is that.

Q All right. If one of the things that needs to be done in an orderly business sense, and that is to take care of the secured debt, do you take the position that, because one of those secured debts is an IEDF loan, that the contribution arrangement must be halted, cannot go ahead? Do you go that far?

A Well, I think in fact if you look at my memorandum of March the 30th, 1981, you will see — or 1982, I suppose it is — you will see that I didn't in fact take that position. What I took was a position that I required all of the documentation in order to be able to understand the full nature and purpose of this arrangement.

As far as the other aspect of do I take the position that it is not possible to use the contribution funds for the purpose of repaying an IEDF loan, yes, I take that position. As I said earlier, it is not myself that wrote these regulations. It's regulations of the Government of Canada, to the extent that those regulations are written in such a way as to preclude something happening, notwithstanding its apparent desirability.

My understanding is that the only way that one is in a position to do this is to use the authorities which have been put in place, presumably with due consideration by people who had the authority to put them into place, to accomplish the desirable ends.

There is a way in which that can be done in terms of forgiving or deleting or reducing loans which are due to the Crown. That was a way which was available to be accomplished here.

In fact, in this particular case it had been considered earlier, prior to my arrival in the Department, and had been turned down as going through that process, as the result of the fact that it was not considered to be a loan which should be forgiven or reduced by the Crown as a result of the type of security which the Crown held on it.

(Transcripts: Volume LXIV, pp. 9457–9459)

On March 30, 1982, Mr. Hobbs sent a telex to Mr. Walchli in Vancouver advising him not to disburse the remaining funds under that agreement until the matter had been fully reviewed. Mr. Hobbs was not the direct superior of Mr. Walchli in a line sense, but he was a senior official with authority in the Economic Development area. Persons who could give a direct order to Mr. Walchli forbidding him to expend those funds included Mr. Donald Goodwin, Assistant Deputy Minister of the Department. This directive of Mr. Hobbs caused a considerable flurry of excitement. Ronald Derrickson sought immediate support from other

Indian leaders, including Senator Marchand and Messrs. Antoine and Moses. He and the others attended at Mr. Walchli's Vancouver office where there was a conversation by speaker phone with Mr. Hobbs. The result of this conversation was that it was agreed that Mr. Walchli could proceed if he could obtain Mr. Goodwin's approval. Mr. Walchli said that he in fact did receive such authorization and accordingly he proceeded to accelerate disbursement of the remaining $200,000. He viewed this as a matter of some urgency at the time because the monies had to be taken from Department funds that were on hand at the end of March 1982. The government fiscal year ends on March 31. There was no assurance that these funds would be available in the following fiscal year.

April 1982 was a period of considerable activity on many fronts in regard to matters involving Toussowasket (Mt. Boucherie Mobile Home Park). Ultimately, some of the haste generated confusion and suspicions. Mr. Walchli was under considerable pressure from Chief Derrickson to pay over the $200,000, but questions were being raised by Mr. Hobbs. At the end of April 1982, the Toussowasket lease was cancelled. This cancellation was registered May 3, 1982. In March 1982, Mr. Justice Locke (then of the B.C. Supreme Court) had delivered Reasons for Judgement in the case of Toussowasket Enterprises Ltd. v. Effie Mathews et al. This action had been taken by a tenant at Mt. Boucherie Park who was opposed to a rent increase and the B.C. Rentalsman was also involved as a party intervening in the case. The park proprietors sought to increase rents to make the park more economic. Although the judgement deals with a number of issues, one aspect of it sustained the jurisdiction of the Provincial Rentalsman over the tenancies at Mt. Boucherie Park, among other grounds, on the basis that the corporation, Toussowasket, had a separate legal existence and was not to be treated as identical to an Indian person. The learned Justice quoted from an Alberta case which contained the following passage:

> The status of a corporation as a legal entity which exists independently of the character or status of its shareholders is recognized in law.

As a result of this judgement, it was felt that one way to perhaps abate the jurisdiction of the Rentalsman would be to have the corporation cease to be the leaseholder, and to have a direct lease from the Crown for the benefit of the locatee — this, it was believed, would oust the jurisdiction of the B.C. Rentalsman. As I understand it, the Rentalsman later held that this alteration did not deprive him of his jurisdiction but at the time the park proprietors and the Department desired not to be subject to his office in order that more economic rents could be put into effect at Mt. Boucherie. Mr. Walchli spoke of this before the Standing Committee and Ronald Derrickson also noted this problem in his evidence before the Commission. He said that the

Receiver had failed to raise rents during his tenure and that, as a result, the existing rental rates were out of step with comparable parks in the Westbank area.

In the spring of 1982, Mr. Ted Ross of Donaldson Engineering had been endeavouring to have his long-standing judgement against Toussowasket registered in the Indian Land Registry in Ottawa. He had no success. He had, as he said in his evidence, by that time elected to "go the political route", and was in contact with his M.P., Mr. Ron Huntington. Mr. Huntington was a Conservative and the government of the day was Liberal.

Mr. Huntington was apparently questioning Mr. Munro on what was happening with regard to the $300,000 contribution agreement. A letter went from Mr. Leask from the Department in Ottawa to Mr. Clark in Vancouver. It contained the following:

> The question raised by Mr. Huntington on March 24, (1982) concerning the $300,000 contribution agreement to the Band with respect to Toussowasket Enterprises, Mt. Boucherie Mobile Home Estates, is under review. We have asked for background information from our Economic Development Branch in our Regional Office. We expect to have this information within the next few days.

Mr. Hobbs had told Mr. Walchli to hold back payment at the end of March 1982. On April 1, 1982, Chief Derrickson wrote to the Department protesting against any cutback in this funding. In the original contribution agreement, a stated purpose of the contribution agreement was the "purchase of 50% interest in the leasehold interest held by Toussowasket Enterprises Ltd". This was, of course, the lease on the mobile home park.

There was apparently some sentiment within the Band Council at this stage (March and April 1982) to have the Band get out of the mobile home park business entirely. It was felt that it might be wiser to concentrate instead on the development of real estate in the Lakeridge Park area. Ronald Derrickson dealt with this in his evidence:

> A ...In around that time the trailer park owners and some of the trailer park residents were becoming very restless and becoming very active and very vocal. We were starting to get somewhat gun-shy about — I think the question was asked by Brian or Harold or whoever it was there at one of the Council's meetings that what the hell are we doing in the trailer park business; we're supposed to be operating the administration of the Band and we should get the hell out of it.
> So there wasn't much stomach at that time, the fight with the Rentalsman and so forth and all the negative press we had been getting. There wasn't much stomach by the Council and from me for that matter, either, in regard to proceeding with trying to acquire all the trailer parks.

And the other thing; that finances — you know, it was going to stretch the Band to go in and rebuild this Paradise Trailer Park.

So, we had an offer with subjects on it and we let the offer collapse, and then decided that we've had the most success and we can see the better future in Lakeridge Park, that area on number 10. It was decided by the Council what we wanted to do — what we wanted to do, what we'd like to see done was to acquire as much of that area, in fact all of that area surrounding Lakeridge Park on the other side of the highway.

Q I.R. 10?

A This was the area. This was the entire area that we felt we wanted to get in under our control. That's Campbell Road — and all of this, and we acquired basically all of it, eventually.

Q Now, these discussions at the Band Council level arose after you'd made the initial agreement to get involved in the Toussowasket Park, and after you'd made the initial agreement with Noll Derriksan?

A Yes.

Q Now, how did these discussions, first of all, arise with Noll Derriksan in reference to this land swap?

A Well, when the first brilliant idea was thought up, Harold and I went over to Noll's house, and needless to say he threw us out. We had one hell of a big argument and he threw us out.

So, we came back and thought well that one's dead. So, Noll is a different sort in that he'll get mad and be negative at first and then after you give him a while to think about it he will contact you.

So, he contacted Brian and told Brian he wanted to see him and discuss it. Brian came to me and I said well by all means, I'm not going back over there.

So, the deal started there, and Brian would go and negotiate with him and come back to me. The first agreement that Brian negotiated I wouldn't agree to. He kept running back and forth until we had something hammered out.

Q During the period of time that the Band was involved in the operation of this particular park, who managed the funds?

A We at all times managed all the funds 100 per cent. At no time did Noll have anything to do with it, and that was stipulated by me. We had Band monies involved in that park and we couldn't take a chance that anybody else could jeopardize our position by handling those monies.

Q Now, there was a problem that arose over this land swap, and we referred to a number of letters or correspondence previously in this Inquiry in reference to an appraisal that was completed on the property that's known as Lot T, that was Noll's prior to the exchange.

There was a problem that arose from this particular appraisal. Could you tell us what your memory is of that particular concern?

A Well, it was Fred Walchli was the problem, you know. He wouldn't let us make the trade. In fact he went and put caveats on the title. I was furious about it. In fact, I threatened to bring the whole goddamn thing down on his head — excuse my language, the whole thing down on his head when I found those caveats were placed on the title.

But he said it goes both ways. If it's not valuable enough you're not going to trade, and if it's too valuable I've got to let him know. I said if I tell him what it's worth he won't trade. So, you know, I was caught in my mind between the Indian Affairs system.

Anyway, before I would actually agree or before I actually went and told Noll what the value was, I went over and asked him if he would sign a letter, and that letter is somewhere in the files, that he understands that the lot — Parcel T — I don't know what they call it now.

Q Parcel T.

A Yes, this Parcel T was more valuable in the trade. He signed the letter, so then I had no problem with Fred showing him the appraisal after that, because I thought I'd jump one step ahead of him.

Q Did that cause a few problems as far as Noll was concerned?

A No, because he'd signed the letter. He's a big boy. I told him what the value was. I said look the value is higher than what the trade is. He knew enough. He wasn't stupid. He knew that the Band had very little money in this project and that we were getting a bonanza. Why would we do the deal otherwise? I mean, it was a lot of heartache, this whole trailer park situation. . . .

Q Now, this particular trade — I'm not sure whether you were present or not when Councillor Eli gave evidence, but were you involved in the details in reference to the exchange of properties in reference to this trade for the 50 per cent interest in Toussowasket?

A Yes, I was involved. Brian reported to me what they were discussing.

Q Were you aware of the fact that during this negotiation that Noll had an interest in two acres or approximately two acres in Parcel T and wanted to keep part of that parcel?

A Had an interest in it?

Q He wanted to keep an interest in part of Parcel T?

A Oh, sure. Yes.

Q Were you aware of why he wanted to do that?

A He wanted to build an art gallery and some sort of small commercial building to house all his various little businesses that he was doing or contemplating.

I have to be honest, I didn't want him there. I didn't want to be involved with him in that business, simply because it was a cause of blisters that occur between us from time to time, and I wanted it a little more clean and neat.

Q Now, were you also involved at that point in time in reference to discussions with Lucy Swite in reference to the exchange of certain properties with her?

A Mostly — not with Lucy so much. I think I talked to her a few times, but basically with Bob Young, who was her lawyer, and I think on occasion her sister and her brother.

Q Now, without referring to the actual documents in exhibit, but they are, as you know, in as an exhibit in this particular Inquiry —

A Yes.

Q — eventually a deal was made between Noll and the Band in reference to an exchange of parcel T for the 50 per cent interest in the Toussowasket Trailer Park. Is that correct?

A That's correct.

Q It involved a series of exchange of properties whereby Noll ended up with a parcel down on the land and Lucy Swite ended up with a parcel on the lake, and the Band ended up with Parcel T, which is the Band office site?

A Yes.

Q There were certain exchanges of monies and lots involved in that particular transaction as well?

A That's right.

Q It took a period of time before that transaction was eventually concluded after it was initially discussed?

A Well, as usual, with anything we do something seems to happen to always complicate it and make it, I don't know, difficult to understand.

   Lucy had bought this trailer already and I got a phone call from the mobile home lot that she wanted to move it. We hadn't come to an agreement. In fact, at that point in time, I thought there was no deal with Lucy.

   Then her lawyer and her brother phoned me and Brian came in hollering at me about, you know, we've got to do something; they want the trailer out of the lot. So, we were looking for a site for her and she wanted more in exchange of the lot from the Band than we were willing to give.

   I think it was finally resolved between her lawyer and I and then she moved in and took kind of the pressure off there, and that's where it ended up.

(Transcripts: Volume LXV, pp. 9718–9726)

It is not easy to reconcile the documentary evidence concerning certain of these matters with the testimony given. Mr. Walchli said, when questioned by his counsel, "Well at that time we had — towards the third week in April, particularly after we'd received the decision that there would be no financial support from...[the Department to appeal]...the Locke decision, the Band at that point, began to explore with Noll Derriksan the idea of exchanging property".

On April 23, 1982, the Band and Noll Derriksan signed an agreement. This agreement provided that, when full development had taken place at Mt. Boucherie, the Band would trade its interest in the mobile home park for Lot 180 on Reserve 10. This lot was then held by Noll Derriksan as locatee. It was generally adjacent to Lakeridge Park subdivision and was thought to be a likely site for future long-term lease development.

As noted above, the original agreement had been that the Band or its company would purchase a half interest in the lease at Mt. Boucherie Park. Mr. Walchli said that the development of the mobile home park ultimately went faster than was contemplated. He said: "originally we had planned it to take over three years to complete, but the Band through Chief Derrickson actually accelerated the process and it moved much faster that we'd originally thought would be the case". It was proposed, in April 1982, that the lease be cancelled and that the payment be accelerated, and this was in fact done. However, it was done so quickly that the Department itself could not keep abreast of the actual events at Westbank.

On April 29, 1982, Mr. Munro, the Minister, wrote to Mr. Huntington, M.P. Mr. Munro's letter contained the following paragraph concerning the Donaldson judgement and Toussowasket Enterprises:

> You may wish to inform Mr. Ted Ross, the President of Donaldson Engineering and Construction Ltd., that Toussowasket Enterprises Ltd. has been taken out of receivership. The loan with the Federal Business Development Bank has been renegotiated and the one from the Indian Business Loan Fund has been partially paid. Toussowasket Enterprises Ltd. is again an operating company and Mr. Ross is free to pursue his claim against it through the normal legal channels. I trust you will find this useful.

When one compares that to the narrative of events given by Mr. Walchli, it is clear that Mr. Munro was not up-to-date on actual events at Westbank. Obviously, his own staff had not been able to keep him abreast of the rapid developments in the Toussowasket situation. In fact, the Toussowasket lease was terminated by the date of the Munro letter — thus there was nothing for any creditor to seek to realize upon. Because of the dismal financial condition of Toussowasket, it appeared to me doubtful in the extreme that Donaldson would have in any event realized any funds under its judgement. However, by the end of April, not only had the somewhat moribund horse bolted from the stable — the stable itself had collapsed by virtue of the lease cancellation. Mr. Munro was giving an answer to Mr. Huntington based on a state of affairs that had ceased to exist. It was a case of the right hand not knowing what the left was doing. This is, of course, not unknown in government or private enterprise, but such patently incorrect information being furnished to Mr. Huntington could lead people to believe they were not getting the real story.

Mr. Walchli told the Commission that he had not been particularly expansive in dealing with the Parliamentary Committee because he was not certain that the arrangement for the trade of the interest in the park for land between the Band and Mr. Noll Derriksan would go forward. But if that were so, why then would the Department agree to cancel the lease at that date? If in fact the deal did not go forward and the status quo had to be restored, there would have been no existing lease in place to protect the funds that the Band or its company had already expended. Mr. Walchli may have recognized this himself when he had a caveat placed on the lot in question. There was ultimately a period of several months before the exchange was completed and in the interim matters stood in a somewhat uncertain state.

The evidence of Brian Eli, a councillor of the Westbank Indian Band, in this matter is instructive. He said in answer to questions from counsel for the former Band executive:

Q Now, I'd like you to tell us about that particular transaction; in other words, the negotiation that gave rise to the Band acquiring the site which is referred to as the Band office site, and giving up its 50 per cent interest in the trailer park to Noll.

A Well, initially that we became 50 per cent ownership to that lease we got on the trailer park, during that time there was some controversy about the Band's involvement and a lot of bad publicity was out there into the general public.

It was decided that we should try to get out of this business because of all the things that were happening. The Chief and Council were getting blamed for starting all this, instigating this stuff.

Then, at that time, I think we were looking for — we were involved in buying additional land for the Band, and I'd done some research and found out Noll would possibly be interested in trading some land to remove us out of there. Between himself and me we went down and looked at parcel T and —

Q If I could just stop you there. Parcel T is the parcel that the Band office is now located on?

A Yes.

Q How large is that parcel approximately?

A I believe it's around 40 acres. I might be wrong.

Q Carry on.

A Once we viewed that parcel the discussion between me and him was that he'd be willing to trade our share in exchange for the land down there. One of the conditions was that he wanted a two-acre site there for his own business.

He had businesses in Kelowna at the time and he was trying to move them — trying to establish them on reserve where he could be exempted as a Band member having business on reserve, some of the income tax benefits.

From there I went back to the Chief and Council and talked to them and identified the type of discussions I had with Noll. Harold and Ron were there. It was pointed out to me by the Chief and Council, Harold and Ron, that I had to go back and try to get Noll to disagree with the two acres.

Q If you could stop there for a moment. To disagree with the two acres; to withdraw his position in reference to the two acres or to give up the two acres?

A To give up the two acres totally, and if he wanted to start up any businesses that since we were anticipating building this would be an ideal site for it, on number 10, that he could come in with us and we'd rent — we'd put up the building and he could start his own business within our building, such as an art gallery and whatever else he had going.

And he wanted his own personal office there.

Q Now, was that acceptable to Noll?

A Yes.

Q Now, did he want any other consideration in reference to this particular transaction?

A Well, there was — initially it was agreed upon us, between me and him, that our 50 per cent would be given up for Lot T excluding two acres.

I took that back to the Council and said well I've made a deal with him and now what and they instructed me that I'd have to look for — try to go back to him and renegotiate with him to try to find an alternative route to remove those two acres from him.

I then was talking to — I went back and talked to Noll and said that we had a piece of property on number 10 that is — I forget what the exact acreage is, but I think it's about two acres or so — maybe less than two acres.

It's adjacent to the lake. It's parcel FF, 2-B or something like that or 1-B.

Q Could you point out that particular parcel on the map behind you please? That's in the far corner of I.R. 10 next to the lake?

A Yes.

Q All right. Carry on then.

A I took that proposal back to him and he agreed to that, to exclude himself from the two acres from parcel T and accept this property in exchange for the two acres.

I then went back to the Council and they agreed to it and I was finalizing that deal. Other things were happening, too, that happened later. I don't know if you want to get into it.

Q Yes, carry on. What happened then? Did you ever finalize that deal with Noll?

A Yes, it was finalized there.

Q But, did you finalize the deal in reference to the parcel on the lake with Noll?

A Parcel F was actually transferred to him, and during that there was other things happening at the time. An estate on number 10 was being settled at that time and one of the Band members, a lady elder of Number 10 residence, was on an estate which her husband felt he had a right to or he was hoping to receive some land back, because he was the last surviving brother of the individual.

The Department of Indian Affairs settled in the estate on that and it was proved that other Band members had rights to that property and that she no longer had the right to reside there.

Q Mr. Eli, if I could just stop you there for a moment. I hesitate to get into names, but as you're aware this individual has given evidence previously. That was the property that Lucy Swite was seeking an entitlement to. Is that correct?

A Yes. I didn't know if I should say.

Q All right. She has given evidence previously in reference to that matter. Just carry on from there then, please.

Q Okay. I then talked to Lucy. I went down there and had a number of discussions with her, because she was becoming very concerned.

Another Band member was talking to her about the possibility of the new people that were going to receive land, that they were going to chase her off immediately.

I went down to her and assured her that we'd assist her in trying to relocate. I initially offered her a lot in number 9 reserve. I brought her up and showed her one house and she said it was too far and she liked the lake and it wasn't her type of unit she wanted.

So, again I went back and showed her some other land that the Band had bought for a Band subdivision on I.R. 10. Again she said she didn't like that property. It was too far from the lake and that there was nobody around, it's too isolated.

Our final discussion was that she didn't want to build on her own property because of water, sewage and trespassers by the general public.

Q If I could just stop you there for a moment. That parcel of property was the property that was down immediately adjoining the bridge — is that correct — on I.R. #10?

A Yes, parcel Q I think it is.

Q Could you just point that out, please?

A Parcel O.

Q That was the parcel that is immediately adjoining 97 and the bridge?

A Yes.

Q Now, all right. Carry on from there.

A After we talked about the servicing the roads and the housing and the problem of trespassing she didn't want to live down there. After more discussion I pointed out what about parcel FF-1, I believe it was, the parcel that I negotiated with Noll Derriksan — negotiated with him on the other deal — that possibly the Band could give that property and allow her to build on that, make her a deal on that one.

There was discussion about possibly changing titles from one property to another. At that time we indicated that parcel O would be an ideal for — you know, if she wanted to transfer that to the Band we in turn would transfer this one over.

There was other conditions on there. I believe there was setting up the trailer, doing the yard work and doing the moving for her, and a porch and other considerations that we had to give her.

Q Did you eventually arrange that particular trade on that parcel?

A Yes. Eventually it turned out that Lucy Swite, through Ron Derrickson and Lucy Swite's lawyer in Calgary, that they did strike a deal on the transfer of one property to another with considerations for helping set up the trailer, doing the yard, clearing the property and a porch and a few other things that we did for her during the transition period.

We ended up with parcel O. After we did agree to that I went back immediately to Noll and said that I have another deal which I had to work on rush on, and explained it to him, and that this parcel O was what I wanted him to trade us back, give back to the Band, as we will get the title for parcel O for him.

In the meantime Lucy Swite would get parcel FF, and he agreed to that.

Q That was how Noll Derriksan ended up with the parcel of property down next to the bridge, which was unserviced?

A Yes.

Q And is unserviced to this date?

A Yes.

Q Now, did you consider that particular transaction to be part and parcel of the agreement in reference to the exchange of Lot T and 50 per cent interest in the trailer park?

A Yes, because they were happening fairly close to the same time and I was discussing one or another. There was a number of things that were happening at the same time.

Q Was that particular agreement that you negotiated with Noll Derriksan as to the two acre part of Lot T, was that part of the agreement ever documented?

A The two acres that he wanted excluded?

Q Yes.

A No, because I was discussing with him — we had agreed before the documentation was completed that, I believe, that he would not take property within T.

Q Now, all these negotiations throughout you were primarily involved with?

A Yes.

Q Was Ron Derrickson ever involved directly in the negotiations with Noll Derriksan?

A No.

(Transcripts: Volume LVII, pp. 9078–9086)

Mr. Eli, in his evidence, refers to a question concerning a two-acre parcel to be reserved from the large lot held by Noll Derriksan on Reserve 10. There is, however, curiously no reference to this in the agreement of April 23, 1982. Despite Mr. Eli's evidence that agreement with regard to the two acres was reached "before the documentation was completed", I got the impression that it was sometime after April 23, 1982 that an agreement was made whereby Noll Derriksan was given other land instead of the two acres. This exchange transaction had elements of confusion, but on any view of matters, it appears that Noll Derriksan realized significant additional consideration in the ultimate agreement.

It was not until quite late in the evidence before the Inquiry that a later written agreement surfaced, namely an agreement dated October 13, 1982 between the Westbank Indian Band and Noll Derriksan. This agreement provided additional consideration to Noll Derriksan, including a parcel of waterfront land located near the Okanagan Lake bridge at Highway 97, a lot in the Lakeridge Park subdivision, and a cash payment of $15,000. Mr. Eli in his evidence describes the process of moving from the April agreement to the October agreement as one that apparently took much time and negotiation. It remains puzzling to me that there is no reference to any reservation of a two-acre parcel in the original April 23 agreement. Puzzling too is the fact that in a letter of November 18, 1982 from Mr. Walchli to Ronald Derrickson amending the contribution agreement, there is no mention of the October 13, 1982 agreement. This appears to be a deliberate cover-up by the Department of the full extent of the consideration Noll Derriksan received in the exchange transaction. Counsel for the Department described this as an "anomaly". The November 18 letter, coupled with Mr. Walchli's failure to give a full explanation to the Standing Committee in May 1982, could give the unfortunate impression that something wrongful was occurring. It would appear the Department had knowledge of certain of the extra considerations, namely the allotment of Lot F-1 on Reserve 10 because, as disclosed in Exhibit 150, an application to register that allotment went to the Regional Office on November 2, 1982. The absence of Mr. McCullough makes it difficult to assess the precise state of knowledge of the Department at the relevant time. Was the Band Council being less than frank with the Department? Chief Ron Derrickson earlier had neglected to tell the Department about the receipt of patch fees at Mt. Boucherie. I am of the view that the Band Government was not keeping the Department fully advised of the details of the exchange transaction; such failures to keep the Department in the picture had the capacity to embarrass Mr. Walchli and the Department. It was but another example of the problems that seemed fated to occur in the Toussowasket enterprise.

It appeared to me that things moved too rapidly for people to keep abreast of events in the month of April 1982. Aside from the propriety of disbursing the $200,000 when the matter was not fully resolved, it seems to me that it was of doubtful wisdom to agree to cancel the lease so precipitously. For instance, if the arrangement of April 23, 1982 had to be annulled (Mr. Walchli said that he was not sure that he would permit it to go forward), it seems to me that it would not have been possible to return the parties to their original status because the lease had been terminated. As well, the Minister was obviously not being kept informed, and it is unfortunate that his letter to Mr. Huntington contained erroneous information. It was another element that could lead people such as Mr. Ross of Donaldson Engineering to think that there was something improper occurring at Westbank.

It was also undesirable, from the point of view of the Band, to have the lease cancelled, and thus have no security for the funds that they had already advanced in connection with the mobile home park. It was clearly a benefit, of course, to Noll Derrickson to have the lease cancelled and to have the rentals increased on that park. There was here an element of conflict of interest in having Chief Derrickson of the Band dealing with this matter, which so intimately involved his brother Noll Derriksan. Although Mr. Eli seems to have been the main negotiator, Chief Derrickson was clearly involved in the decision-making process relating to the exchange transaction.

It is not wholly clear to me why further consideration was provided to Noll Derriksan by the agreement of October 13, 1982. It is difficult, as

I said, to synchronize the testimony of Mr. Eli and Mr. Derrickson with the written documents of April 23, 1982 and October 13, 1982. I reflected on whether or not Noll Derriksan was giving some consideration to the Band by releasing them from certain obligations to complete works at the park, but I gathered from Mr. Walchli that the new park works were largely completed by the fall of 1982 because the project had moved quite swiftly. The fact was that the Band found itself in the summer and fall of 1982 in the position of not having the security of a lease and if Noll Derriksan was inclined to seek some further consideration, he would have therefore had an enhanced bargaining position. He did ultimately, as noted above, receive significantly more consideration than a single conveyance of one half of the mobile home park. In general terms, Noll Derriksan was receiving immediate benefits in that he was getting cash, highway monies arising from the large parcel at Reserve 10, and the mobile home park and the income from the park. Additionally, Mr. Derriksan was to receive either Parcel "F" or Parcel "O" on Reserve 10. In fact he received the latter, which was on the waterfront adjacent to Highway 97. The Band was getting a large parcel of land suitable for future development. The Band acquisition in this exchange may have been more suitable for development by an entity as opposed to an individual. The Band had a successful track record on Lakeridge and the future development on the new property seems likely to be quite a major undertaking.

I am of the view that if Mr. Walchli was in doubt as to whether or not the exchange transaction reflected in the agreement of April 23, 1982 was going to be allowed to proceed, then he ought to have insisted that the Toussowasket lease not be cancelled. On the other hand, if he was quite certain that the deal was going to go forward, he should have given a more complete and up-to-date description of the current state of affairs to the Standing Committee when he met with them on May 26. The Committee was left with the impression that the Band or Band company still had an interest in the park when the fact was that they had agreed to the exchange of their interest for land held by Noll Derriksan.

It appeared to me that the haste with which matters moved in April was one of the problems here. It does not seem to me that Mr. Walchli and his officials conducted a careful enough analysis of this matter to avoid later potential problems. I can understand everyone's desire to get out from under the problem of the Rentalsman, but was it wise to cancel that lease so quickly? By so doing, Mr. Walchli was certainly placing the Band and the Department in a position where Noll Derriksan could have a distinct bargaining advantage. There was also a problem in that the rapidity with which matters moved could lend an aura of covert action to the entire transaction. Was Mr. Walchli less forthcoming than he might have been with the Standing Committee because he felt that the Department had allowed itself to be persuaded to move before it was ready in April 1982? In retrospect, it may be that Mr. Walchli realized in May that he had moved with undue haste, and that he was therefore somewhat hesitant to deal with the matter in full detail before the Standing Committee. I think that his failure to do so was unfortunate in that it left the record incomplete and could lead to the impression that there was an effort being made to suppress the true facts.

Certainly it is most undesirable to have the Minister of the Department writing to a colleague setting forth facts that are no longer facts. I do not think that Mr. Munro can be faulted for this, but clearly his Department was not keeping him up-to-date on the matter. I rather think that in this instance, for whatever reason, Mr. Walchli allowed the Department to proceed too quickly and that all the details of the arrangement were not sufficiently settled before the Toussowasket lease was cancelled.

Criticism has been directed at Mr. Walchli for his role in affairs at Westbank. In effect, the criticism was that he was being overly favourable to individuals of the well-off Westbank Band to the detriment of other bands in British Columbia that were in desperate economic straits. Mr. Walchli vigorously denied this before the Standing Committee and said he tried to treat all bands and individuals in a consistent fashion.

On one view of matters, Noll Derriksan has received substantial benefit from the Toussowasket venture, but the train of events that resulted in the benefits was set in motion before Mr. Walchli took over in B.C. In 1981, when the Toussowasket problems were longstanding and serious, Mr. Walchli persuaded the Westbank Indian Band to acquire an interest in the mobile home park. There were considerations in the spring of 1982 that made it desirable for the lease to be cancelled. There were also certain reasons why it made sense for a trade of land to be considered in exchange for the interest in the park. Yet, as I noted, it could appear that Noll Derriksan was receiving far too many benefits in this transaction of Toussowasket.

I think that in the spring of 1982, Mr. Walchli allowed himself to be moved too quickly along the path desired by Ronald Derrickson and Noll Derriksan. This gave the unfortunate impression to outsiders, including Mr. Ross of Donaldson Engineering, that there was something improper being done. I have said that it was unlikely that Donaldson could have realized any funds from Toussowasket because it was an unsecured creditor. However, it clearly would have been better if the lease had remained in place until the company had at least had a chance to pursue the suggestion in Mr. Munro's letter. I am not certain that any effort would have succeeded in view of the professed attitude of the Registry officials that they did not feel that the company could obtain registration of the judgement. That aspect of matters (execution by creditors), dealt with in Section II of this Report, is one of the most perplexing problems of developments on Indian lands.

In retrospect, it is unfortunate that Mr. Walchli was perhaps not more definite in his approach to this matter when he was before members of the Standing Committee on Indian Affairs. By that time he was aware that there was a plan for a land exchange. This represented a benefit to Noll Derriksan, but it also could represent a benefit to the Band because they were getting land that had good potential. I am not prepared to characterize this transaction as being one that was necessarily hurtful to the Band. Mr. Walchli said in his evidence that he was not sure he would approve this deal in any event, hence he did not mention it to the members of the Committee. As well, I must say that some members of the Committee were not particularly restrained at times, either then or on earlier occasions, relative to their characterization of the behaviour of Mr. Walchli. Their desire for evenhanded treatment of all bands is an appropriate one, but the Committee does not appear to have had any real understanding of the very difficult situation that Mr. Walchli had faced relative to Mt. Boucherie Mobile Home Park. Mr. Walchli appeared to be reluctant to give an absolutely full explanation of the whole situation, which reluctance was probably the wrong posture to adopt. If the impression is given that something less than the full facts are being provided, suggestions can be made that there is something to hide.

Perhaps an explanation for his reluctance may lie along these lines. Mr. Walchli knew it could be said that, on the surface view of matters, he had shown a degree of favouritism to Noll Derriksan and then Chief Ronald Derrickson. He had been receptive to assisting Ronald Derrickson to advance the Band. This was not an unnatural reaction because Chief Derrickson had been a forward-looking administrator. He had rendered great assistance to Mr. Walchli in bailing the Department out of the Toussowasket mess and had done a good job at Lakeridge. Mr. Walchli was also aware of the rumbling discontent growing between himself and Mr. Hobbs, and may have felt a bit reluctant to dig too deeply into the whole contribution agreement issue, which had recently been the subject of much debate and discussion within the Department and with Chief Derrickson. Later on, when it was discovered that, in fact, Noll Derriksan had received a transfer of the ownership of the entire park, there might well be further questions raised as to the propriety of the transaction. I think Mr. Walchli did himself a disservice by failing to make clear to the Committee in greater detail the past and existing situation at this troubled mobile home park. I think it would have been preferable to have the full history of the transactions narrated in the spring of 1982 so that no one was in any doubt as to what was going on. Once again, fact would have proved a useful antidote to rumour.

Ultimately, as we have seen, Noll Derriksan received considerable benefit. He obtained some cash and became the sole owner of a valuable mobile home park which gave him an income. The park had received a large contribution of government funding. However, the Westbank Indian Band had also received a benefit by obtaining a block of land on Reserve 10 with development potential. Noll Derriksan got immediate benefits. Only time will tell how good an investment the land on Reserve 10 will prove. I hope it turns out to be a favourable one. Given its proximity to Kelowna, I think it is likely that this will be of benefit to the Band in the long-term.

If there are uncertainties as to the dimensions or nature of a transaction, people can misunderstand and rumour and innuendo can result. It may be that some will be critical concerning the amount of money that has accrued to Noll Derriksan from government coffers. But that result was probably foreordained from the day that Heritage Realty and Mr. Derriksan embarked upon the project in the mid-1970's. Mr. Walchli was faced with a fait accompli when he arrived in 1976 and it fell to him to wrestle with the Toussowasket problems over the succeeding years. The course he adopted was one that he need not to be ashamed of, but if he had been less reticent with the members of the Committee, I think that he would have been following a wiser course.

The Toussowasket situation and related issues, such as Park Mobile, appeared to me to be a major focus of much of the controversy that occurred on the Westbank Indian Reserves. The Council, in particular the Chief, saved the Department from an embarrassing situation by taking over the operation of Mt. Boucherie. At the same time, the Department entered into an agreement with the Band to contribute money to help solve the problems. I think the dealings between Mr. Walchli and Chief Derrickson were to have unfortunate consequences in that Mr. Walchli tended to be too uncritical of the wishes of the Chief and it may have affected, perhaps unconsciously, the ability of Mr. Walchli to look at matters in a sufficiently objective fashion. For instance, the whole of the acrimonious controversy with the Yorks went on with a seeming lack of intervention by the Department in a situation that called for an active role at the executive level of the Department. The Department should not interfere with legitimate band government but when matters reach the state they did at Westview Village, to do nothing is to invite trouble, which trouble in fact arose, albeit in a wholly unexpected and shocking fashion. I have earlier noted the lapse of Departmental management in failing to heed Mr. Clark's advice on limiting the extent of surrendered land over which authority was transferred to the Band government.

The matter of Donaldson Engineering should be considered in this context. Mr. Ross from Donaldson Engineering said that because of his inability to get satisfaction through legal means he "went the political route". I think he was also influenced by the possibility that this route might be cheaper, as suggested by counsel for Mr. Walchli. While I can appreciate the frustration Mr. Ross felt, I believe that it is better to keep such matters out of the political arena because it transforms what should be commercial disputes into political disputes, and that is not an orderly way to resolve them. However, there obviously was something seriously amiss in April 1982, for at the very moment that Mr. Munro, the Minister, was writing to Mr. Huntington saying that Mr. Ross would have to pursue his remedies through the courts, the main lease was being surrendered, which action, of course, rendered the proposed legal proceeding completely nugatory. The stated motive was to solve the Rentalsman problem, but one who did not appreciate why this was being done could consider such action to be evidence of gross collusion between the Department and the Band to prevent any hope of realization by creditors.

It seems clear to me that if the enterprise had been allowed to go into bankruptcy (as had been urged by Ronald Derrickson), Mr. Ross's company would not have recovered any funds because of the very poor financial status of the park and the prior rights of secured creditors. However, the destruction of the underlying head lease had the appearance, on the face of it, of pulling the rug out from under the feet of all creditors, including Donaldson Engineering. It again was something that could be (and was) misconstrued and fastened onto as evidence of sinister activity at Westbank. Had matters proceeded in a less hasty fashion, it would have been clear that there were legitimate reasons for the actions taken and that Mr. Walchli was not acting in a corrupt fashion, but was in fact trying to solve some of the continuing series of problems that centred around the Toussowasket project.

Concerning the performance of Donaldson Engineering, it appears to me that the company did a reasonably competent job of the tasks that it had undertaken at Mt. Boucherie Park. There were cost overruns, but I could not conclude on the evidence before the Inquiry that the company was a poor operator. In the end it was not fully paid. That, of course, happens all too often on construction projects. Difficulties of realizing on debts are often greater on Indian lands because of restrictions on alienation of the lands.

This fact raises another issue that surfaced during this Inquiry. There seemed to be a belief or impression that somehow the Department was going to be a financial guarantor of the Toussowasket enterprise. Contractors may face very real problems when they are working on Indian land because there are limited rights of execution against Indian land. Contractors cannot assume that merely because the Department is advising on a project that it will necessarily guarantee payment. If a contractor wishes to assure itself of payment, then it must enter into the proper guarantee arrangements before projects are undertaken. Hopefully, proper legal advice will alert contractors to difficulties that may be encountered because of the special legal status of Indian land.

A potential source of problems is that because the Department is an arm of the federal government, it will be held to a somewhat higher standard than would be the case in ordinary business. There seemed to be some notion abroad that because an agency of the government was involved, it would see to it that the contractor was paid. That is not the law nor is it likely to be the law, but it did appear that there was the impression that somehow this situation was different. This seems a burden that often hangs round the neck of the Department of Indian Affairs and Northern Development. Similar thinking underlies the complaints of some lessees, who also seemed at times to have the misapprehension that somehow the government was going to look after their lease for them. As counsel for the Department pointed out, this would place the Department in a false position — its concern must be for the Band or locatee. However, it is clear that the Department has to adhere to a standard of conduct that is above reproach and it cannot be seen to be engaged in or abetting any sharp practice. Unfortunately, when a department of government is engaged in a business enterprise, it is sometimes seen as being a guarantor of perfection and, furthermore, it is too often assumed that there is no limit to what it can pay.

This matter illustrates again some of the difficulties of having government operate outside of the purely public sector. In the case of Indian Affairs, it is often very necessary for government to be involved, either as a guarantor or as an initial source of funding and so it becomes involved in the commercial process. This may lead to misunderstandings or dashed hopes and the disappointed parties may seek to find fault residing somewhere else than at their own doorstep.

The problems, for instance, that Donaldson Engineering faced bring into focus some of the difficulties with the registry system in effect on Indian lands, which difficulties I comment on in Section II. To the extent that contractors or third party businessmen find that they cannot deal reliably on Indian lands, the cause of Indian people and bands throughout Canada will be injured. The recommendations that I make elsewhere on the registry system are intended to ameliorate problems seen to exist in this area. It does not seem to me that it lies within the purview of this Commission to order a radical restructuring of Indian landholding, but obviously it is desirable that there be full opportunity for orderly and businesslike dealing between third parties and Indian bands and Indian entrepreneurs to foster the better development of Indian reserves and Indian business ventures. Arbitrary or capricious actions must be avoided, as must all appearance of arbitrariness or capriciousness if Indian business and enterprises are to have the best opportunities for success.

It would have been desirable for Mr. Ross of Donaldson Engineering to have been told earlier the full story of what went on in connection with the Toussowasket matter. I doubt if he ever had a true picture of what happened prior to this Inquiry. When the matter is examined in detail, it should be plain to Mr. Ross that no one in the Department was trying to do him harm. But unless he had the whole picture, there was obviously room for him to believe that there was collusion between the Department and Band Council or Mr. Derriksan to avoid payment of a lawful debt. Unfortunately, the members of the Standing Committee were also not given a full and complete picture and they were left in a state where they could think that there was indeed something rotten at Westbank.

Ultimately, the complete facts did not emerge until this Inquiry was held. Before this Inquiry, there did not exist the necessary machinery to examine the Toussowasket matter in adequate detail. Indeed, it was not until late in the hearings that counsel were able to finally determine just what was the total consideration that passed from the Band to Noll Derriksan for the large parcel of land the Band acquired on Reserve 10. The agreement of October 13, 1982 was news to a lot of people. Because the full story of Toussowasket remained obscure until the present time, confusion and controversy continued.

The Toussowasket venture was in many ways a disaster for the Department. It was an early project and like all learning experiences, it generated pain. In the end, it has proved to be a viable project, but at considerable cost in money, heartache, and bad press. There might have been a great deal less controversy at Westbank without the project and all its ramifications, but once started, it proceeded inexorably on its way and became the focus of a series of controversies and confrontations that had wide repercusssions. It was a central event in the Westbank story. I believe that this Commission has unearthed the full facts and concerned parties can at last know just what occurred. And now they know that they know, which is perhaps most important of all!

It is a tale replete with missteps and misunderstandings, but it also demonstrates that intractable problems may require unconventional solutions. Mr. Walchli took something of a risk in trying to salvage the project. The project was improved and the secured lenders paid. However, one result was that Mr. Walchli came to be perceived in some quarters as unduly partial to Ronald Derrickson and Noll Derriksan. This is a continuing problem in Indian Affairs and I am sure Mr. Walchli has much company in this difficulty. I saw no misconduct, but I did feel that Mr. Walchli did not always exercise effective management in his dealings at Westbank. I trust that he has learned that one must take exceptional care to avoid charges of partisanship in this highly charged political scene. In a tense atmosphere, such as the one in which Indian Affairs has operated over the past decade, a high measure of statesmanship is required on the part of Departmental people. I hope that this Inquiry will be of some assistance in pointing out to parliamentarians that the Department is operating in a difficult era. I would hope that it can be made clear to all concerned that partisan politics are to be avoided if the Department is to function in optimum fashion.

LARSON, SMITH & HENDERSON

Barristers and Solicitors

TELEPHONE 763–0307
STE. 3 — 246 LAWRENCE AVENUE
KELOWNA, B.C. V1Y 6L3
CANADA

C.H. LARSON LL.B.
LON L. SMITH B.A., LL.B.
B.R. HENDERSON B.A., LL.B.

OUR FILE   L 1034

May 12, 1977

Warren, Ladner,
Barristers and Solicitors,
256 Lawrence Avenue,
Kelowna, B.C.

ATTENTION: Darrel Warren, Esq.

Dear Sirs:

Re: West-Kel Holdings Ltd. and Park Mobile Home Sales Ltd.

We acknowledge receipt of two letters from you dated May 11, 1977. As I previously advised you verbally, the new owners of the shares of Park Mobile Home Sales Ltd. have injected substantial amounts of money into that Company to ensure that it can meet its debts as they fall due. There are a number of matters in dispute between the Company and some of its creditors. However, we expect those matters to be resolved in a very short time. According to our information the Company is not insolvent.

The present owners would like very much to reorganize the complete financial structure of the Company to ensure its profitability in the future but of course are reluctant to do so in view of the present circumstances with respect to the lease. It would appear from your letter that your client wishes to delay that reorganization further even though part of the reorganization which we have proposed would not include any increase in the indebtedness of the Company or encumbrance on the present lease. We fail to see how the assignment of the mortgage from the Royal Bank of Canada to the Bank of Nova Scotia can effect your client's position and are at a loss to understand why he has refused his consent.

However, it is our understanding of paragraph 9 of the sub-lease that our client does not require the consent of West-Kel Holdings Ltd. to that assignment. As we read it paragraph 9 only requires Park to obtain the consent of Her Majesty. Under the circumstances, we have requested the consent of Her Majesty Queen Elizabeth II as required by clause 9 and intend to proceed with the assignment if consent is granted.

Larson, Smith & Henderson

Warren, Ladner   Page 2

With respect to the matter of a survey we apologize for the misunderstanding that it was Noll Derickson who ordered the surveyors off the property. In fact it was apparently his brother Ron Derrickson. We don't understand what right he has to order people off property that is leased to another individual such as our client, particularly when the specific lease in question requires the survey to be done. We have also contacted the Department of Indian Affairs in Vancouver and they have advised that they fail to see what right he has to deny Park quiet possession of this property. Because Ron is Noll Derrickson's brother, his actions are very suspicious.

If your client's real interest in sending the notice of deficiencies is to have the deficiences corrected under the lease as soon as possible, we would request that you have him do everything in his power to ensure that the Indian Band does not put road blocks in our way because, as you can well appreciate, his actions have already delayed the matter by a considerable period of time.

It has come to our attention that there is growing concern amongst members of the public and the business community that leases of Indian lands lack security. In fact it is our understanding that there was a sign along Highway 97 South warning members of the public not to deal with the Indians within the last several days. No doubt your client will appreciate that if the concern becomes widespread it will be very difficult to find people prepared to lease Indian lands.

In this particular case the land was leased to our client a number of years ago when its value was substantially less than it is now. It was leased on the basis that our client, the Lessee, would, over a period of ten years, enjoy a moderate rent in return for which it would spend substantial sums of money on development of the lands as a mobile home park. It now appears that your client is attempting to recover the land itself, or a substantially higher rental from it, wihout considering the enhancement of its earning potential by virtue of the money which has been spent on developing it by our client. Quite frankly we view this as short sightedness on his part as we have previously indicated. As you are well aware, we are attempting, with all diligence, to cure any deficiencies which exist under the lease. At the moment we do not believe there are any deficiencies of sufficient seriousness to justify our client making an application for re-entry.

In reviewing your letters and the Notice of April 14, 1977, we note that a number of the allegations of breaches of the Head Lease and the sub-lease are vaguely

/3

LARSON, SMITH & HENDERSON

---

described. There seems to be a distinct lack of specificity to the particulars of the deficiences alleged. In your letter of May 3rd, you have conceded that Park Mobile Home Sales Ltd. has corrected only one item in the list of deficiencies. Unfortunately both the Notice and your letters have failed to spell out specifically what deficiencies you allege are still outstanding under items 2, 3 and 9 listed as breaches of terms under sub-lease number 29252. You have also failed to spell out particulars of the breaches which you allege under items 1, 2, 3 and 4 of the head lease.

For example, you have alleged that the trees have been removed without permission for purposes other than that permitted by the lease document. We have in our correspondence indicated that according to the Engineers who have done the work, no trees have been removed except as necessary for purposes of construction of the mobile home park. If your client has a specific allegation of removal of trees without permission which was done for some purpose other than the construction of the park, we would appreciate being advised of it. However, our client as you can well understand cannot correct a problem which is not particularized to the point that he can identify it.

Furthermore our client requires specific notice of other breaches which you allege are still outstanding such as what rubbish or other matter of offensive nature are deposited on Lot 32; what fences which were on the demised premises have not been looked after and why he alleges that development was not first undertaken on those portions of Lots 31 and 32 outlined in blue on Schedule "B". We further require specifics of what you allege are the deficiencies under paragraphs 2 and 3 under the sub-lease so that we can identify the problems which you wish corrected. We have explained that we are of the opinion that these matters are not deficient. If you disagee, we must have a specific explanation so that we can identify the problems.

With respect to the surveyor, you are well aware that we are attempting to have that done as expeditiously as possible. We should point out however, that in years past Mr. York has approached the Westbank Indian Bank Council and requested instructions to do the survey and was told not to bother because of a previous survey which had been done. Again we would point out that as this specific deficiency, if there is one, has continued since 1972 without your client having brought it to our client's attention, we take the position that your client has waived any breach of that term of the lease.

With respect of paragraph 8(A) of the sub-lease, we take the position that that clause has been waived by your client by acquiescence since the inception of the

LARSON, SMITH & HENDERSON

Warren, Ladner   Page 4

---

sub-lease in 1971. Since that time Mr. Derrickson has been in and out of the park and past the park on many many occasions, has seen the construction and has been aware of the continuing installation of mobile homes in the park. At one point during a strike of electricians, construction on the park was at a standstill. Noll Derrickson and Larry York had a conversation at which time Mr. Derrickson asked Mr. York when Park Mobile Home Sales Ltd. would be getting more trailers set up in the park. Mr. York apparently said something about requiring Mr. Derrickson's permission and Mr. Derrickson indicated that he did not need his permission. . . "just go ahead and fill it up as you have to pay the rent somehow." Under the circumstances we take the view that the deficiency has been waived by your client both verbally and by his acquiescence. Insofar as the future is concerned we are prepared to work out with you an agreement which we would have all future tenants sign before they take space in the park. We would also be prepared to work out some sort of procedure which would permit us to obtain approvals by West-Kel and the Department of Indian Affairs. However it has been our client's experience that when he has required the consent of Mr. Derrickson, it has sometimes been very difficult to obtain it. It seems to us that West-Kel's greatest concern should be that the lease price which is agreed upon is sufficient for the amount of space that is being leased. If that is the case we should be able to work out some kind of agreement which would permit approvals to be granted quickly provided that the lease price agreed upon covered a portion of the property of a specified size. We would welcome your comments with respect to that. In the meantime we are enclosing a form of agreement which we have prepared and which we are presently using in another mobile home park for your perusal. We have supplied a copy to our clients, Park Mobile Home Sales Ltd. and requested their comments. We are also forwarding a copy to the Department of Indian Affairs for their comments. We must naturally ensure that the agreement is acceptable to those people who will be prospective tenants of the park. We also understand that the Provincial Government is threatening to enact new regulations to cover mobile home park tenancies which of course will have to be taken into account in due course.

In one of your letters, you have indicated that Park Mobile Home Sales Ltd. is not to establish a mobile home sales office on the park premises. In our view this is a necessary, related, or ancillary service or facility and therefore comes with the provisions of Clause 5(C). As evidence that this is in fact the case, we would point

LARSON, SMITH & HENDERSON

Warren, Ladner   Page 5

---

to Mr. Noll Derrickson's own property, which we understand is on Lot 33 where he has developed a mobile home park. It is our understanding that in conjunction with that, he has leased a mobile homes sales office to a mobile home sales company as a necessary ancillary service or facility to the park. The two seem to us to go together like hand in glove. In any event there is no mobile home sales facility there at the moment and our client has indicated that they will not set one up until that particular matter has been resolved between us.

With respect to the deficiency numbered 11 under the sub-lease, we have provided you with evidence indicating that inspections have been done by the Health Department. We take the view that the clause is uncertain to the point where it would be almost impossible for any Court to say that there has been a violation of it; however we have requested the Technical Services Branch of the Department of Indian Affairs to inspect the installations as soon as possible in order to attempt to satisfy your client.

Also, once the survey has been completed to the satisfaction of everyone, if there are encroachments on any other properties, those will be corrected forthwith. We are advised by Mr. York that some of the problems were created by a previous lessee by the name of Trojan Developments, prior to the lease between Her Majesty and West-Kel. Those problems with respect to Lot 35 were corrected by Park Mobile Home Sales Ltd. to avoid problems with Mr. Harold Derrickson.

With respect to the letter proposing a compromise by way of a new lease which would delete Lot 31 and increase the rent on Lot 32, our answer must necessarily be no. Approximately $170,000.00 has been spent on the development of Lot 31 and our clients are not prepared to donate that to your client along with an increase of rent to be paid on Lot 32. Also the water system for the entire park is located on Lot 31 as is access and our clients feel very strongly the need to control the access and the water supply. Also our clients do not feel that they should agree to pay any substantial increase in rent over the next four years of the lease as they still have the responsibility to complete the development of a large number of mobile home pads in the park which will require the expenditure of a substantial amount of money. We would again suggest that your client should be patient as he will no doubt receive a substantial increase in rental payments when the rent is renegotiated in four years time.

LARSON, SMITH & HENDERSON

Warren, Ladner   Page 6

In closing, we wish to reiterate that since your client has acquiesced in whatever deficiencies there may be for a considerable period of time we are of the view that a Court would be reluctant to grant him re-entry. He has apparently stood idly by for a number of years while substantial amounts of money have been spent on development of the park. We doubt that a Court would allow him to prejudice our client's position to that extent by his acquiescence and then allow him to take advantage of it after such delays. We will therefore strenuously resist any attempt to obtain re-entry. We would however like to have matters cleared up as soon as possible so that the future relationship between the parties can be reasonably amicable.

Yours very truly,

LARSON, SMITH & HENDERSON

per:

        C.H. Larson

CHL/ss
Encl.

WARREN, LADNER   TELEPHONE (604) 763–5643

BARRISTERS AND SOLICITORS   256 LAWRENCE AVENUE
                                       KELOWNA, B.C. V1Y 6L3
DERRIL T. WARREN
HUGH G. LADNER

May 17, 1977   W I T H O U T
                                           P R E J U D I C E

Messrs. Larson, Smith & Henderson   Your File   # L1034
Barristers and Solicitors
3 — 246 Lawrence Avenue
KELOWNA, B.C., V1Y 6L3   By Hand Delivery

Attention: Mr. C. H. Larson

Dear Sirs:

Re: West-kel Holdings Ltd. and Park Mobile Home Sales Ltd.

We acknowledge receipt of your letter of May 12th 1977.

You have raised a number of points in your letter and we shall endeavour to answer them in the same order as that in which they appear in your letter.

1. You have stated that you fail to see how the assignment of the mortgage from The Royal Bank to the Bank of Nova Scotia can affect our Client's position and you are at a loss to understand why he has refused his consent; the consent form required by the Director of Indian – Eskimo Economic Banch of the Department of Indian Affairs and Northern Development requires a statement that the lease in question is in good standing. To execute a consent form for the Bank of Nova Scotia would not only be misleading but dishonest.

2. We have had an opportunity to talk to Chief Ron Derrickson concerning the allegations contained in your letter and Chief Derrickson is forwarding a letter to us indicating the reasons why it is necessary for the surveyors to obtain the consent of the Indian Band prior to the survey being performed. Briefly, the surveyors will have to treaspass on land owned by other Indians or by the Band and as a result of problems in the past it is in the Band's Resolution that they would advise each land owner of the possible trespass. This step would have the effect of preventing any misunderstandings.

3. You have made a number of general allegations which strike personally at Mr. Noll Derriksan and his brother Ron; by innuendo and direct

.... comment you have ...

comment you have indicated that their conduct is less than meritorious; for these reasons our instructions are to proceed with a Notice to Quit in the event the lease deficiencies are not corrected within the time allowed. We have specifically refrained from making comment on your Client and some of the statements which your Client has rendered but we think that if there is to be fault allocated your Client will carry the heavier burden.

4. Your Client is well aware of the breaches of the lease and the deficiencies are sufficiently specific to allow corrections thereof; for example, your Client removed all of the trees along the buffer zone located adjacent to Highway 97. Your Client then filled in this area with excess fill and now proposes to remove it. Surely you are not suggesting your Client does not know that it has done this. Concerning your other requests on page 3 we do recommend that you visit the mobile home park and it will become obvious to you, as it is to your Client, which deficiencies still exist.

5. We have attempted to determine who from the Westbank Indian Band Council gave instructions to Mr. York not to prepare the survey and there is no evidence whatsoever that any such instruction was given to Mr. York.

6. In passing, our Client has continually requested your Client to meet its obligations under the lease; we have secured some correspondence in the Office of another lawyer and the record is clear that every request advanced by our Client to your Client was simply ignored by your Client.

7. Contrary to your Client's undertaking we noted yesterday that a mobile home sales office is now established on the property, apparently set up over the weekend. This is not untypical of the actions of your Client and we would point out to you that the wording under Mr. Noll Derriksan's lease is significantly different from that under the lease held by your Client.

8. You have indicated that Park Mobile Home Sales Ltd. has settled its problems with Mr. Harold Derickson; enclosed herein you will find a letter from Mr. Derickson commenting on the settlement.

9. Having visited the property we are confident that your Client has not spent anything like $170,000.00 on the development of Lot 31. In addition, our Client would certainly provide the necessary assurances that water and access would remain under your Client's control.

WARREN, LADNER   -:3:-   May 17, 1977

Mr. C. H. Larson   Re: West-kel & Park Mobile   Without Prejudice

Yours very truly
WARREN, LADNER

"Derril T. Warren"

DERRIL T. WARREN

Enclosure

DTW: jp

Chapter 3

Land Allotments

The Indian Act defines "Reserve" as:

> ... a tract of land, the legal title to which is vested in Her Majesty, that has been set apart by Her Majesty for the use and benefit of a band;

The definition of "Band" includes the following:

> ... a body of Indians... for whose use and benefit in common, lands,... have been set apart... (My underlining)

From these definitions it is apparent that reserve lands were originally set apart for the use and benefit of all band members in common. The Act also contains a general prohibition against the sale, lease, or other disposition of reserve lands until those lands have been surrendered to Her Majesty by the band for whose use and benefit the reserve was set apart. The surrender procedures are detailed in the Act and require a band vote to be taken on the issue of surrender. Within the framework of this communal interest in reserve lands, the Act also provides for certain individual interests to be created. Section 20 of the Act sets out how an individual band member may acquire lawful possession of reserve lands:

> 20.(1) No Indian is lawfully in possession of land in a reserve unless, with the approval of the Minister, possession of the land has been allotted to him by the council of the band.
> (2) The Minister may issue to an Indian who is lawfully in possession of land in a reserve a certificate, to be called a Certificate of Possession, as evidence of his right to possession of the land described therein.

Section 24 provides that band members may transfer their possessory rights either to the band or to another band member. Whenever the band council conveys band lands to an individual member, regardless of whether or not any consideration passes, that transaction is termed an "allotment". Allotments may be made in exchange for cash consideration or in exchange for other land. An allotment may be made subject to the performance of certain conditions — for instance, requiring improvements to be made within a specified period.

The Minister (in effect, his delegate in the Department of Indian Affairs) must approve any allotment. Only then is an individual band member recognized as being in "lawful possession" of reserve land. A

"Certificate of Possession" is issued as evidence of the individual's lawful possession. A band member in lawful possession of reserve land is referred to as the "locatee" of that land. The locatee obtains an interest in land that may be transferred by sale, or by will. However, the interest can only be transferred to the band or to another band member. The locatee may use his land as he sees fit, subject to the restrictions contained in the Indian Act, regulations made under the Act, or band by-laws. An Indian who has acquired "lawful possession" pursuant to Section 20 of the Act may request the Minister to lease his lands for his benefit, pursuant to Section 58(3) of the Act (the "locatee lease"). If the land is situated so as to be attractive for commercial or residential purposes, a locatee can gain a substantial income from his land under such a locatee lease. Because of the favourable location of the Westbank Reserves, individual rights of lawful possession are very valuable.

Not all bands in Canada use the allotment provisions of the Indian Act in order to give rights of use and occupation to their members. Many bands rely on more traditional communal systems of land holding. However, the only possession by an individual band member that is recognized as "lawful" under the Act is that conferred by allotment made pursuant to Section 20. If an individual is not in "lawful possession", then he cannot request a lease of his lands pursuant to Section 58(3) of the Act.

The Department of Indian Affairs has recognized that a conflict of interest may well arise in instances where a band council was allotting land to a chief or to a member of band council. Since 1975, the Department has had published guidelines to avoid conflict of interest in these situations. The current policy, in effect since 1979, is set out in Program Circular H-3. It reads as follows:

> Where an allocation is proposed for a sitting member of the Council and/or the Chief, where there may appear to be a conflict of interest, the member to whom the lands are allotted should not be a voting member of the quorum. Normally, an allotment to the Chief or a Council member should be ratified by a majority of the electors of the Band at a Band meeting. A subsequent resolution of allotment provided to conform with the specific provisions of this subsection, i.e., "allotted to him by the council of the Band" would not, if signed by the individual as a quorum member, be a conflict of interest. (My underlining)

During the years that Ron Derrickson was Chief of the Westbank Indian Band, he was allotted parcels of land situate on both Reserves 9 and 10. Some of those lands are quite valuable and it appears that the consideration received by the Band was quite modest. It did not appear that the Band adopted the practice of putting the question of these allotments before a Band meeting. The following are instances where allotments were made to Mr. Derrickson.

Lots AA and BB — Reserve 10

Lots AA and BB, located on Reserve 10, were allotted to Ron Derrickson by Band Council Resolution dated October 22, 1976, some two weeks after he was first elected Chief. The lots are located on Okanagan Lake opposite Kelowna. Each lot is approximately four hundred feet long and one hundred feet deep. Mr. Derrickson had earlier acquired the adjacent upland (Lot 111) in 1969. All three parcels are currently under lease to Gabriel Estates Ltd. That company is said to have plans to construct and operate a resort hotel on the property.

In his evidence before the Commission, Mr. Derrickson explained that the allotment in 1976 only confirmed his pre-existing interest in Lots AA and BB. He said that he had previously purchased one of the lots from his brother Noll Derriksan and the other from Norman Lindley. Normally, when one band member purchases land from another band member, the transaction can be effected by a transfer pursuant to Section 24 of the Indian Act. However, before an individual band member can effect a transfer of his lands, he must first have acquired "lawful possession" of these lands. Indian Land Registry records do not indicate any lawful individual interest in Lots AA and BB prior to the 1976 allotment to Ron Derrickson. When Mr. Derrickson was questioned as to how the vendors had acquired legal interest in the lots, he said that they had historical claims recognized by the Band. Mr. Derrickson said that Norman Lindley had occupied one of the lots. The other lot had been occupied by Ron Derrickson's uncle, David Derrickson Senior. Ron Derrickson testified that his uncle's claim had been purchased by Noll Derriksan and that he had later purchased his brother's interest.

None of these previous claims or purchases are recorded in the Indian Land Registry. Mr. Derrickson suggested in his evidence that records of the previous claimants to the lots had been lost following the closure of the Vernon office of the Department of Indian Affairs in 1975. He said that documents concerning the Westbank Band that had been stored at the Vernon office had been destroyed after the office was closed. "Piles and piles of maps were destroyed at the Vernon garbage dump when that office was closed down". However, the Land Registry is located in Ottawa. Any documents which evidenced interest in land should have been recorded in Ottawa following their processing at the Vernon office. The destruction of documents from the Vernon office should not have affected the Land Registry records in Ottawa.

When Council allotted Lots AA and BB to Chief Ron Derrickson in 1976, he was in a position of conflict of interest. Ron Derrickson claimed to have purchased those lands previous to this allotment from individual Band members even though there are no recorded allotments of the lands prior to 1976. The lands in question are valuable beach lots.

They are rendered even more valuable when joined with the contiguous upland lot which had previously been acquired by Ron Derrickson. It is of interest to note that the acquisition of the upland lot (Lot 111) in 1969 was duly documented and recorded in the Reserve Lands Registry. There is no corresponding record of Ron Derrickson's purchase of Lots AA and BB. He did not say how much money he paid for Lots AA and BB, but it is clear that he paid no compensation to the Band for the allotment. Any compensation was paid to individual Band members who had no recorded interest in the lands.

Lots AA and BB form an integral part of the lands now under lease to Gabriel Estates Ltd. The term of that lease is 98 years commencing February 1, 1985, for a total rent of $2,700,000. Rent is to be paid to the locatee in various instalments with the final instalment due in 1994. The lessee additionally paid a premium of $300,000 to the locatee as an inducement for the locatee to consent to the lease. The sums paid and payable under this lease demonstrate that Lots AA and BB are valuable assets. While the lots may have been of considerably less value in 1976, they were waterfront situate near Kelowna and thus quite desirable.

It is difficult to understand why the Department approved this allotment in the absence of a Band vote. Counsel for the former Band executive argued that this was not a "pure allotment" but was rather a "transfer". Given the nature of the Registry records, it appears to the outside observer that it would fall within the guidelines requiring a Band vote. This is a good example of a situation where timely disclosure of this transaction to other Band members would have been highly desirable. I make some suggestions for improvements in this area of disclosure in Section II of this Report.

Lot 13–6 — Reserve 9

On March 5, 1980, Ron Derrickson was allotted Lot 13–6 on Reserve 9 by Band Council Resolution. Lot 13–6 is a small lot of approximately two acres. This lot has approximately 150 feet fronting on 1st Avenue North, the public road which separates Reserve 9 from the village of Westbank. At the time of this allotment Ron Derrickson was the locatee of lands located on either side of Lot 13–6.

The history of this allotment has been documented to some extent in Band Council minutes as well as in correspondence between the Department and the Westbank Band Council. At a meeting of Council held on December 10, 1979, Ron Derrickson agreed to transfer his interest in a permit for the use of certain waterfront lands on Reserve 10 to the Band in exchange for an allotment to him of Lot 13–6. The transaction is recorded as follows:

Concerning BCR 1979–86, the cancelled agreement on Parcel L, I.R. #10, Ronald Derrickson has agreed to cancel this agreement and allow the Band to take over and receive revenue from same in exchange for title to Lot 13–6. Therefore, it was Moved by Councillor Brian Eli, Seconded by Chief Ronald M. Derrickson and carried unanimously that Lot 13–6 be transferred to Ronald Derrickson in exchange for the cancellation of the agreement on Parcel L, I.R. 10.

Ron Derrickson testified that he had held a five-year permit to certain lands described as Parcel L on Reserve 10. Pursuant to this permit, Mr. Derrickson sublet numerous beach lots for summer camping purposes. He said that the business generated between fifteen and twenty thousand dollars per year. At the time that the exchange was made, there were two camping seasons remaining on a five-year permit. Mr. Derrickson explained that the Band wanted to obtain a source of revenue and consequently this deal was struck to exchange unoccupied land for the waterfront property, which generated revenue.

At the time that the transaction occurred there was a seat vacant on the Westbank Band Council. As a result, the Band Council consisted only of Chief Ronald Derrickson and Councillor Brian Eli. Some months later when the allotment was perfected, a second councillor had been elected. He concurred in the Band Council Resolution. There is no record of any further discussion of the matter beyond that found in the December 1979 Band Council minutes.

At one point in the processing of the allotment, the issue of a possible conflict of interest was brought to the attention of the Band Council. In a letter dated February 8, 1980, an employee of the Department of Indian Affairs' Regional Office advised:

> Please note that when an allocation is proposed to a member of the Council, the member to whom the lands are allotted should not be a voting member of the quorum, in order to avoid the possibiliy of a conflict of interest.

A copy of the conflict of interest guidelines contained in Program Circular H-3 was attached to the letter. That policy provided that a band vote should be conducted when an allotment of this sort occurred. There was a Band meeting held on February 21, 1980, but it does not appear that the allocation of Lot 13–6 was brought before the meeting. The allotment was approved by the Department in March 1980.

According to Mr. Derrickson's evidence, the consideration for Lot 13–6 was his relinquishment of the final two years of his permit over Parcel L. He said that surrendering the permit amounted to a significant detriment to himself in the years remaining on it. The Band traded the land located on Reserve 9 to him in perpetuity. Ron Derrickson was thus involved on both sides of this transaction. As Chief of the Band he took part in the decision that the Band required the revenue from the beach lot permit. Any revenue would not be generated immediately as this transaction was entered into in December. It was a decision of Council (of which he was a sitting member) that the transaction was in the interest of the Band. This situation was very like that of a mayor being involved in a land exchange with his municipal government.

There could be questions raised concerning the benefit to the Band of this transaction. The Band was alienating land in perpetuity and receiving in return benefits under a permit with two years to run. The Band could, for instance, have simply waited for the permit to expire and then taken over operation of the business. From the Band's point of view, one advantage of the use of a permit was that it allowed the Band to collect some revenue (rent paid by the permit holder) from its lands without tying them up for a long period of time. Mr. Derrickson said his mother had operated a similar enterprise under permit for some years before he took it over. It may well be that the Derrickson family was involved in this business enterprise for many years, but that does not convert a five-year permit into a perpetual right or interest in the land. Under the terms of the permit he was to pay an annual rent to the Band of $600. The beach lot rentals were said by Mr. Derrickson to be bringing in $15,000 to $20,000 per season. It would appear that this permit would have accrued to him during his tenure as Chief. There was no evidence of Band approval of this transaction.

Mr. Derrickson said that Lot 13–6 was not particularly valuable land. However, that parcel had special value to him as it was located between two other parcels of land that he already owned. By acquiring Lot 13–6, Mr. Derrickson was able to consolidate this land into one block. Some indication of the land's value may be obtained from the amount of compensation paid for the highway taking. Mr. Derrickson received $27,500 for 0.57 acres taken for highway purposes. This lot is near the village of Westbank and near the main highway. It is clearly less valuable than waterfront. I am not disposed to say that the value of exchange was disproportionate or that Mr. Derrickson was trying to steal a march on anyone, but I believe that Band members should have had a chance to comment on the exchange of the permit rights for the land granted on Reserve 9. Mr. Derrickson should have been especially careful to get Band approval since it was he, the Chief, who was getting the land. Once again, he appears to have been blind to an obvious conflict of interest and failed to take steps to ensure that the matter was handled carefully. Here again, the Department appears not to have ensured that there was proper approval by the Band membership.

Lot Q Remainder — Reserve 10

On August 30, 1985, Ron Derrickson was allotted Lots 188 and 190 on Reserve 10, both of which were formerly known as the Remainder of

Lot Q. The allotment was made by resolution of the Band Council. Chief Derrickson did not sign the allotment instrument. At this time, the Band had been granted authority to control and manage its Reserve lands pursuant to Section 60 of the Indian Act. As a result, the Band Council was responsible for allotting Reserve lands and was also the approving authority acting in place of the Minister. The allotment was signed by Councillors Brian Eli and Harold Derrickson, and was subsequently approved by those two Councillors on October 4, 1985.

Prior to the 1985 allotment, the Remainder of Lot Q had been registered in the Indian Land Registry as Band land. During the Inquiry, Mr. Derrickson said that the official records concerning this lot were in error. He said that he had an historical claim to the area and that this was perfected by the allotment.

The history of Lot Q must be considered. In 1964, Ron Derrickson had been granted a conditional allotment of a 12-acre parcel of land in this area. It does not appear there was a legal survey of the land. The resolution simply described the parcel as a 12-acre portion of the Reserve shown in an attached sketch. The sketch differed from the dimensions of the lot eventually surveyed as Lot Q. The parcel defined as Lot Q in the first official survey of Reserve 10 was a 12-acre parcel located on Okanagan Lake at the southern end of the Reserve. It was roughly triangular in shape, with approximately 1000 feet of waterfront. The original sketch showed a more elongated parcel of land stretching further along the waterfront. The first official survey of this Reserve was published around 1970. Following this publication, a further Band Council Resolution was passed requesting that the boundaries of Lot Q be redrawn in accordance with the sketch that had accompanied the 1964 allotment to Ron Derrickson. In 1971, a resurvey of the area was done. A new lot, described as Lot FF, was created. It more closely resembled the original sketch, which reflected the intended allotment to Ron Derrickson. Lot FF was formed out of a portion of Lot Q and other lots which were registered as Band lands. The boundary of the newly created Lot FF cut Lot Q approximately in half, leaving the waterfront portion included in the new lot FF. The back portion of Lot Q became known as Lot Q Remainder. The new Lot FF comprised approximately 20 acres.

Following the de-surrender of Reserve 10 in December 1972, the Band Council realloted any lands which had formerly been in individual possession. Band members who had retained rights in any Reserve lands during the surrender period were realloted those lands upon de-surrender. Based on his equitable interest, Ron Derrickson was allotted the new Lot FF and recorded as the locatee of Lot FF. The Band was recorded as the owner of the remainder of Lot Q.

At the Inquiry, Ron Derrickson claimed that he should have been allotted both Lot FF and the remainder of Lot Q. He said that the lot known as FF did not accurately show all of his property. He maintained that his property included not only the new Lot FF, but also the portion known as Lot Q Remainder. He explained that he had traditionally claimed the property located in the area extending from the waterfront back to the point where the land starts to rise sharply into a cliff. That physical description would include both Lots FF and Lot Q Remainder. Mr. Derrickson further testified that, following the de-surrender of the Reserve in 1972, a committee of Band members was appointed to settle disputed boundary lines. He said this committee had viewed his property and agreed that he was entitled to the lands from the waterfront to the base of the hill. He was not aware of any written document that reflected this decision.

Indian Land Registry records do not support Mr. Derrickson's historical interest in the remainder of Lot Q. Following the 1972 de-surrender of Reserve 10, there was no further resurvey of this property. When the Council reallotted lands according to equitable entitlement, Ron Derrickson was allotted Lot FF. The remainder of Lot Q was not allotted, but it was recorded officially as Band land. Mr. Derrickson explained that he was not allotted Lot Q Remainder immediately following the de-surrender of most of the Reserve because it had been mistakenly included with lands still surrendered for the development purposes of the Westbank Indian Band Development Company (the Lakeridge Park development). Mr. Derrickson stated that, before he could be allotted that land, there had to be a further de-surrender of Lot Q Remainder. He thought that this may have occurred in 1985. Considering the Land Registry records, Mr. Derrickson's claim is hard to follow.

The question of Mr. Derrickson's entitlement to Lot Q arose as a result of highway construction in the area. In 1982, the Provincial Ministry of Highways negotiated for the purchase of certain rights of way on Reserve 10. Compensation was to be paid to either the locatee in possession of lands affected by the highway, or to the Band when the highway crossed Band lands. Ron Derrickson claimed and was paid compensation for lands taken from the Lot Q Remainder. When officials from the Department of Indian Affairs were reviewing the acreages taken and the compensation paid, there was a question raised respecting Ron Derrickson's entitlement to such compensation. At that time, the Registry records in Ottawa showed Lot Q as unallotted Band land.

This discrepancy was one of several land status issues then delaying the transfer of the highway lands to the Province. This issue was apparently resolved as a result of a meeting held in June 1984, minutes of which were entered as an exhibit in these proceedings. They indicate that the purpose of the meeting was to resolve any land entitlement or status issues that were delaying the issuance of the federal Order-in-Council required to transfer the lands taken for highway purposes to the

Province of British Columbia. The meeting was attended by officials from the Department of Indian Affairs and the Ministry of Highways. The Band was represented by Chief Ron Derrickson. According to the minutes, the status of Lot Q Remainder would be resolved by "the Band" agreeing to "confirm the allotment of the whole area to Ron Derrickson by Band Council Resolution". This was eventually done the following summer with the allotment of Lots 188 and 190.

The minutes of the 1984 meeting reveal a conflict of interest in that Ron Derrickson represented the Band at that meeting and apparently agreed on behalf of the Band to resolve the issue of his entitlement to the remainder of Lot Q by having the Band Council allot that property to him. It is not known why the representatives of the Department of Indian Affairs agreed to that resolution of the issue. There was no ratification of this allotment by Band vote. The resolution was not in keeping with Department policy concerning allotments of land to Council members. It can scarcely have escaped the attention of the Department that this was a clear conflict of interest situation — here the Department showed an alarming lack of vigilance. While the Department perhaps could claim not to have been fully aware of certain other instances noted above, it had a representative present at the meeting where this transaction was approved. Its failure to ensure observation of its own published guidelines is surprising, to say the least!

Departmental Policy Regarding Conflict of Interest

The Department of Indian Affairs had policies in place regarding allotments of land, including a specific directive regarding allotments to sitting council members. That policy, as noted above, called for a band vote or ratification of any allotment to a sitting council member. Mr. Peter Clark, former Director of Lands, Revenues and Trusts for the B.C. Region, said in his evidence before the Inquiry that his land officers adhered to the policy described in the program circulars. Policy can be a malleable thing depending on how it is interpreted and applied. Mr. Clark's evidence regarding the implementation of the conflict of interest guideline set out in Program Circular H-3 is indicative of how policy can be misconstrued. It stated that "normally, an allotment to the Chief or Council member should be ratified by a majority of the electors of the Band at a Band meeting".

Mr. Clark expressed his view that because all Band Council meetings at Westbank were open for interested parties to attend, it was sufficient to deal with the issue at a Band Council meeting rather than at a Band meeting. He said that because the Council meetings at Westbank were open and an agenda posted at the Band Council office well in advance of the weekly meetings, this sufficed. Department policy seems to call clearly for a Band meeting as opposed to a Band Council meeting. I got the impression from Mr. Clark's evidence that he perceived no distinction between the two kinds of meetings for purposes of complying with the conflict of interest policy. But there are obvious and important differences. Band meetings are usually called by way of special notice and are convened at a time that is convenient for the majority of Band members to attend. The Westbank Band Council meetings, on the other hand, were generally convened on weekday mornings. While Band Council meetings may be open for all interested Band members to attend, Band members do not have a vote at Band Council meetings. The stated policy seemed to be that a special Band meeting would be held where as many electors of the Band as attended could express their views and vote on the issue. If the majority of the electors of the Band present at a Band meeting ratify the allotment, then any potential conflict problem seems to me to be solved. If ratification is not forthcoming, then presumably the membership is not prepared to endorse the transaction. But the membership is clearly entitled to know what is happening so that they can vote "aye" or "nay".

Due to the commercial value of lands on the Westbank Reserves, it was, and is, important that allotments to Council members be carefully considered. The Department of Indian Affairs recognized that such allotments involve a potential conflict of interest. Accordingly, they prescribed that those allotments should be subject to the scrutiny of band members and requested a band vote to ratify transactions. This policy appears to have been honoured more in the breach than in the observance at Westbank.

I trust that the Westbank experience will serve as a caution to bands and the Department that scrupulous care should be taken to obviate conflict of interest problems. This is one of the more common problems that can occur in bands because of their size and family structures. It is essential for the political health of the band to avoid controversy and rancour arising from perceived favouritism. The Department guidelines are helpful — I believe that they should be universally observed in order to ensure that conflicts of interest do not occur and are not perceived to occur. This area was one where I found that the Department did not conduct itself with distinction. I am not certain why the failures occurred, and I am not able to say in detail how this area can be better dealt with in future. The issue is clearly important and I commend it for immediate study to the Lands, Revenues and Trusts Directorate. It is of practical economic concern and is the sort of matter that should be carefully overseen to ensure that abuses of office do not occur.

Chapter 4

Northland Bank

One issue that generated considerable controversy and caused much uncertainty in the Westbank Indian Band was the matter of the Northland Bank (hereinafter sometimes called "the Bank"). A detailed description of the circumstances that led to the failure of Northland Bank is contained in the *Report of the Inquiry into the Collapse of the CCB* (Canadian Commercial Bank) *and Northland Bank,* published in the fall of 1986. Northland Bank had become overextended and was placed under curatorship in September 1985. The federal inquiry into its demise and that of the CCB was conducted by Mr. Justice Willard Z. Estey, a judge of the Supreme Court of Canada.

This bank failure caused grave concern among members of the Westbank Indian Band who were aware that then Chief Ronald M. Derrickson had been a Director of the Bank and who were also aware that the Band had an investment in and other financial dealings with it. Indeed, it appeared that the term "misappropriation" found in one or more of the petitions of the Action Committee was a reference to the investment or deposit of monies into the Northland Bank. Given the amount of money that was either invested in Northland Bank shares or deposited in it, it is not difficult to appreciate why Band members would be concerned about the state of affairs that existed in the fall of 1985 and continued through 1986 into 1987.

Substantial progress has been made to effect some resolution of the various cross-claims between the Northland Bank, the Westbank Indian Band, and the Westbank Indian Band Development Company. However, even when submissions were being made to the Inquiry in August and September 1987, it was apparent that total resolution of those issues had not occurred.

Concerned Band members had visions of their patrimony vanishing in the wreckage of the Northland Bank. It appears that the problems anticipated may not be as serious as once thought and it now seems that resolution is possible. But it was and remains a worrisome situation for the Band.

One task that this Commission addressed was to attempt to unravel the story of the dealings between the Northland Bank, on the one hand and, on the other hand, the Westbank Indian Band, the Westbank Indian Band Development Company, and Ronald M. Derrickson. In 1984 and 1985 Mr. Derrickson was a director of the Bank. It proved a bit of a tangled web, and on the face of it certain matters could excite suspicion. These required proper investigation to determine whether or not any wrongful conduct had occurred, and specifically whether there had been abuse of office or conflict of interest on the part of any of the then Band executive members.

In order to appreciate what went on vis-à-vis the Band, its Company, and individuals and the Northland Bank, it was necessary to examine events commencing in 1980–81. A group of investors had conceived the idea of constructing and operating a large amusement park near Calgary called Calaway Park. At the time the project was conceived, it was thought that it could be put into operation for an investment of around $12 million. Chief Ronald M. Derrickson became interested in the project and ultimately was a shareholder in it. Northland Bank was to be the main financing bank for the project, although it proceeded to syndicate part of the loan out to partner banks. This project was a large-scale one involving substantial sums of money.

It did not progress well, perhaps most significantly because of a general, catastrophic downturn in the western economy in general and the Alberta economy in particular in late 1981 and through 1982 and 1983. Indeed, even today, the western economy is not nearly as robust as it was in the late 1970's and 1980. Precipitous declines in the price of oil and real estate have caused severe economic distress in western Canada. Commissioner Estey in his Report has discussed the difficulties occasioned to Northland Bank by these declines.

In addition to these external events, it proved not to be possible to build the park for the amount originally estimated and there were quite substantial cost overruns. Ultimately, the cost of the park worked out to be in excess of $20 million. The problems associated with cost overruns on any project were, of course, magnified by the poorer revenue prospects because of the economic recession.

As a condition of obtaining financing for construction of the park, the various shareholders were required to sign personal guarantees for the bank indebtedness. The signatories included Mr. Ronald M. Derrickson. Bank borrowings initially estimated to be in the $6–9 million range had dramatically escalated by the summer of 1982 when the park was about to open.

Calaway Park had the misfortune of opening just when there was this unexpected downturn in economic activity in Alberta. Attendance figures were nowhere near those projected, and of course, given the greatly increased level of debt, it proved increasingly difficult to successfully service the debt and to pay ongoing expenses. By the fall of 1982, the newly opened project was in serious financial trouble and so was placed into a form of "soft receivership". Northland Bank and syndicate banks hoped that they might be able to work out a solution, but it was apparent by the end of January 1983 that matters were going from bad to worse. Accordingly, in early February 1983, Touche Ross came on the scene as a court-appointed receiver.

As detailed at some length in the Estey Report, Northland Bank was faced with a difficult situation. Here was a large loan that had turned non-performing. That circumstance would adversely affect the perceived financial condition of the Bank. It was therefore desirable that the Bank be enabled to restore the loan to performing status. To this end, it entered into negotiations with the original shareholders of the Calaway Park operation, that is, Mr. Derrickson and his co-venturers. These individuals were also placed into a difficult situation because the Bank had called the loan and had demanded payment pursuant to their guarantees. At that stage those guarantees had a potential liability of over $12 million. Several of the guarantors were in no financial position to pay substantial sums, though certain investors, including Mr. Derrickson, did have quite substantial assets. Mr. Derrickson was therefore obviously one of the persons who would have been a financial target to pursue if Northland Bank had intended to seek recovery under the guarantees.

Obviously, Northland Bank, its loan syndicate partners, and the several investors in the Calaway Park operation had a variety of problems to solve. Ultimately, Northland Bank bought out the other syndicate members at a discount. If it could then work out some solution whereby the original investors would continue to support the park and inject more capital, its financial status would be considerably improved. At the same time, if the investors could receive some relief from the immense guarantees overhanging them, they would obviously benefit financially. And, of course, if the park could be made viable, all would benefit from its success.

To some extent, there was a time limit on negotiations because Northland Bank was anxious to have matters in order for its financial year-end on October 31, 1983. Ultimately an agreement was reached. In general terms it involved writing down the park debt to a more manageable level. The old shareholders from Calaway, through a new company called Calalta Amusements, would continue to carry on the operation of the amusement park. Outstanding guarantees were to be written down from as much as $12 million in potential liability to a maximum of $250,000 per individual or individual company.

Northland Bank also undertook to fund certain investors by loans when they were unable to raise equity funds for the project from their own resources. It was anticipated that, by thus setting the debt load lower, the project could be made viable as an ongoing business. The debt could then be retired in an orderly fashion from operating revenues. It appeared that a forced sale of the park would have resulted in a very large shortfall and a concomitant financial loss to be borne by Northland Bank and the guarantors.

While it could be said that individual investors were receiving enormous benefit from having their guarantee liabilities written down so much, it could also be said that the Bank was benefitting in that the investors were going to put in more funds (though much of the new equity would be furnished to the investors through loans from Northland) and were going to endeavour to keep the park going. It was certainly a permissible inference that Mr. Derrickson and his fellow investors were getting large financial benefits in the sense that an onerous liability was being reduced to very moderate proportions. As noted above, it appeared from the information laid before the Inquiry that Mr. Derrickson was one investor who might well have been a major target of the Bank if it sought recovery under the guarantees.

I will now examine events that occurred at Westbank in order to provide an understanding of that aspect of the problem. In the early 1980's, there were negotiations occurring between the Westbank Indian Band and the federal and provincial levels of government over compensation for what is termed a "cut-off" claim. Briefly described, in the early years of this century, certain governmental actions were taken to "cut-off" lands from existing Indian reserves in British Columbia. In the past several years there have been negotiations between some of the bands affected and the two levels of government to arrive at compensation for these cut-off lands. In the case of Westbank, part of the ultimate settlement was in the form of land transferred back to Band control. In addition, a sum of money was provided as compensation. These monies came from the two levels of government.

Between 1982 and 1984, the Westbank Indian Band received cut-off funds totalling about $4.5 million. In addition, there were highway compensation funds of approximately $3 million received by locatees of Reserve 9.

The mechanism for funding these latter payments was as follows. The cut-off funds were utilized to pay out individual locatees. The Band then became the owner of the lands (see Band Meeting minutes, December 1983). In effect, the Band undertook to clear title and convey the land taken from the Crown Federal to the Crown Provincial for highway use. It was, as Mr. Derrickson and Mr. MacSween (of the Provincial Department of Highways) testified, the Band's responsibility to see that the land was conveyed clear of any claims. I deal with this matter of highway land takings in greater detail in Chapter 9 of this Report. It suffices here merely to outline the general course adopted by the Band and its executive.

As noted above, 1982 and 1983 were increasingly difficult years in western Canada. The economic downturn severely affected the Northland Bank. The Bank had many other loans besides Calaway Park which were not in good standing. By the fall of 1983, the Bank was seeking to enhance its capital base by issuing shares. It was anxious to induce new shareholders to put up capital in order to strengthen its equity position. Bank management deemed this move essential if the Bank was to continue as a viable institution.

Mr. H.G. (Byd) McBain, a former vice-president of the Bank, said when shares were being offered, employees were under some pressure to support them. He said: "We were told that there was an offer. I guess — certainly in my case and I know in many other cases, like you really didn't have a lot of choice as to whether you exercised your employee's rights or not". The Bank sent two of its executives, Mr. Martin Fortier and Mr. McBain, to Westbank. When questioned by Commission Counsel, Mr. McBain made the following comments about the transaction in which the sale of shares to the Westbank Indian Band was concluded:

A   Ron Derrickson was one of the individuals that was contacted and asked if he wanted to subscribe.
Q   Why was he prevailed upon to subscribe to these shares? What was the thinking as far as the bank was concerned?
A   Well, we'd seen his balance sheets, of course, and felt that he could afford it. You know, he had indicated some interest in the bank, getting into native banking.
Q   Yes?
A   Whilst nothing had been done at that time, you know, there had been some discussions.
Q   Now, you were dealing with him on a day to day basis, I presume, in the restructuring of the Calaway Park thing about that time?
A   Yes. Well, not necessarily with Ron on the Calaway. I was dealing with him on his own involvement in it. Generally speaking, he wasn't that involved in the restructuring, although he was in the background, of course.
Q   He was interested?
A   Oh, as one of the shareholders, yes.
Q   Yes. What else was happening with Ron Derrickson then? We're dealing about October/November.
A   Yes. That's about the extent of it; that and the purchase of shares. Now, I don't recall the exact date that we did make a sale of shares to him, but I believe it was around this time.
Q   Who made the approach, do you know?
A   Marty Fortier.
Q   You would have been in communication with Mr. Fortier because of your ongoing relationship with Mr. Derrickson, I presume?
A   That's correct.
Q   Were you present at any meeting with Ronald Derrickson in which the purchase of shares in the bank was discussed?
A   Yes, I was.
Q   When and where did those discussions take place?
A   I believe it was about this time, and they took place at the Chief's office on the Reserve.
Q   In Kelowna or in Westbank?
A   Yes.

Q You were present?

A I was present.

Q Was Marty Fortier present?

A Yes.

Q Would you tell us what you recall was said?

A Well, Marty and Ron, as I recall it, had some discussions and Marty and I flew out together to meet with Ron and the two Councillors. Marty had some figures and a bit of a pro forma, I guess, on what they thought that the bank could do and he went through that with the Chief. It was agreed that some shares would be purchased.

Q What was the nature of the figures in the pro forma?

A It showed a pretty good turnaround in the bank, but I just can't recall. I didn't have one of those packages, and I hadn't been involved in the actual sales of the shares at that point. So I'd be just wild-guessing.

THE COMMISSIONER: You said they were meeting with Chief Derrickson and the Councillors. Do you mean the Councillors of the Westbank Indian Band?

THE WITNESS: Yes, Brian Eli and Harold Derickson.

THE COMMISSIONER: Were you ever introduced to those people?

THE WITNESS: Yes, I know them.

BY MR. ROWAN:

Q And you had known them before this meeting?

A Yes, I believe so.

Q What business relationships or dealings had you had with the Council prior to this meeting at which the shares were discussed?

A I don't know if we'd had any at this point. I don't recall the dates when we were doing business with them on a business basis, but I had been out to see Ron. When we were trying to do the restructuring we came out and looked at some of his assets, and I believe I met one or both of the Councillors at that time.

I made so many trips here during my time with Northland that I forget which —

Q Pardon me?

A I made a number of trips during my time with the Northland to Kelowna to visit with Ron and his Councilmen. I can't recall the first time I met them.

Q Now, was the sale of shares to the Band and to Ron Derrickson discussed at the same meeting?

A I believe it was.

Q And what was the outcome of those meetings? There were a number of shares purchased by the Band and there were a number of shares purchased by Ron Derrickson himself, as I understand it.

A That's correct. The discussions with Ron, of course, were simply with Ron Derrickson. The discussions with the Band included the Councillors. I believe they were both present.

(Transcripts: Volume XXXIX, pp. 5402–5405)

The Band then had an investment in a term deposit of approximately $1 million. This represented funds received from the Province as part of the cut-off settlement. It appears from the evidence that this had the character of what is called "Capital money" in the parlance of the Indian Act. Such funds are subject to certain restrictions; generally, they are to be used to purchase or construct capital assets for the benefit of the Band.

On November 23, 1983, Northland Bank authorized a $1 million loan as bridge financing to enable the Band to buy 240,000 shares of Northland Bank stock. As security, the Bank took back an hypothecation of the $1 million term deposit owned by the Westbank Indian Band. The commitment letter was signed on behalf of the Bank by Mr. McBain; Mr. Ronald M. Derrickson, Mr. Brian Eli, and Mr. Harold J. Derickson signed on behalf of the Westbank Indian Band. It appears that the term deposit at that point was located at the Continental Bank, but that was subsequently moved to the Northland Bank.

A document found in Exhibit 81 sets out the Bank's analysis of what the transaction was and who it was with. These comments are contained in the Bank memo:

> The Westbank Indian Band is a wealthy band of Okanagan Indians residing on a Reserve at Westbank, B.C. Under the capable direction of Chief Ron Derrickson the Band is virtually debt free and has accumulated considerable wealth through real estate development on leased land and sale of properties to federal and provincial governments. A recent cut-off settlement negotiated with the two governments will net the Band in excess of $10 million.
> The Band is constantly undertaking projects for the betterment of its members, as evidenced by the recent completion of an ultra modern extended care facility. A good portion of the funds outlined above go to the individual Band members (or in trust until age 19) and to facilities such as a proposed new hockey rink and the extended care facility.
> A portion of the funds, which are still held on a trust basis for the Band, have been pledged as security for this investment facility to enable the Band to participate in the recent bank stock issue.
> Interest will be at prime until December 2, 1983 at which time the deposit will be moved from the Continental Bank in Kelowna to our Vancouver office. At that time the interest will revert to 10% fixed, for a one year period (to match the rate being paid on the deposit). Interest will accumulate for the one year but will not compound.
> It is important to note that all negotiations in the closing of this transaction took place on the Reserve at Westbank.

At the time that this investment decision was made, the Chief of the Band was Mr. Ronald M. Derrickson. The Band councillors were Mr. Brian Eli and Mr. Harold J. Derickson. As described above, around the time of the investment by the Band in Bank shares, Mr. Ronald M. Derrickson was able to arrive at an agreement with Northland Bank whereby his guarantee was reduced from a potential liability of several millions to $250,000.

The Band undertook to purchase Bank stock valued at about $1 million. This was a quite substantial investment. Obviously this situation called for close scrutiny because of the substantial financial benefit that had accrued to Mr. Derrickson by reason of the guarantee reduction.

Ronald M. Derrickson indicated in his evidence before the Commission that he did not wish to unduly influence the other councillors concerning buying stock in the Bank. He arranged for them to meet alone with the representatives of the Bank, Messrs. McBain and Fortier. This was confirmed by the former Bank officers, who gave evidence before the Inquiry. In questioning by counsel for the former Band executive, Mr. Brian Eli and Mr. Harold Derickson gave evidence concerning their participation in the decision as follows:

Q Now, Mr. Eli, you've been present in the course of this Inquiry and you've heard evidence in reference to the purchase of shares of the Northland Bank?

A Yes.

Q Would you please tell us as to what your recollection is as to when the discussions first arose in reference to the purchase of those shares based on my understanding that they were purchased in late November or December of 1983?

A Ron had indicated to us that he had Byd McBain and Mr. Fortier were in the office to discuss the possibility of buying shares, and that he would like myself, Harold to meet them privately and then meet also, myself and Harold, together with them to discuss the possibility of buying the shares.

I first met with them privately, discussed the possibility of buying shares, the dollar figure that we were buying them at and some of the questions that I asked him — our concern at that time was that Northland Bank was indicating to us in a very strong manner and cooperative manner that they were anticipating to put in an outlet for the Band members and the Band itself for deposits where we would be exempt from taxation on our dollars.

This was very attractive to us at that time. In that light I was looking at the possible buying of shares as a very good investment.

Q Mr. Eli, were there discussions at those meetings or prior to those meeting in reference to the potential or the possibility of enticing a bank — maybe not the Northland Bank, but enticing a bank to locate in the Band office building?

A Yes, a number of years the majority of our Band banking was done with the Royal Bank. We were also approaching them. We felt that we had a good promise or acknowledgement that they were, at that time, in the '78/'79 period, or even before that, that they were willing to come and put up a deposit centre at the Band office or at one of our locations that we were trying to get them at.

We already were anticipating the settlement of the cut-off lands and also possibly the settlement of the highways on 9 and 10, so there would be a fair amount of cash coming to the Band itself and individuals.

Also after that, after the problem with the Royal Bank, that they weren't that interested or not going to follow through with their promise of putting an outlet we then approached Continental Bank, which again, they in turn said that they were willing and seriously looking at putting in an outlet again, within the Westbank Indian Band office, which was on Shannon Lake Road, which never came about.

After that discussion Northland Bank was approached — or Northland Bank approached us and we jumped into Northland Bank because they sounded more sincere than the other banks.

Q Were there discussions with the representative from the Northland Bank in reference to a Native banking program?

A Yes. During the time there was a lot of considerable problems with loans to individuals or bands itself, and Band businesses or Band companies or locatees or Band members.

The Federal Business Development Bank around that time had given a statement that they will no longer finance any type of development on reserve property, whether it was regarding an outside developer or a Band business or individuals.

So, the only resource of loans that we had available were the Department of Indian Affairs loans. With Department loans funds it was the taxed amount of dollars that they had available to us, and to get that it was a long process.

You're looking up to maybe six months to eight months to get that loan approved, and then, you know, it's very cumbersome and at that time things were going too slow for us. We were looking for alternate financing from outside sources, so we were looking at trust companies, anything that we could get into.

Q Now, when these discussions took place, and prior to the shares being purchased, where there discussions with the Northland Band representative in reference to Native banking between yourself and them?

A Yes. They wanted at that time to discuss about setting up a Native loans policy, setting up a whole separate program where it would identify and deal with specifically only loans to Bands or Band members on reserve.

Q Mr. Eli, you have reviewed the minutes of the various Band meetings that have been held prior to November/December of 1983. Is that correct?

A Yes, some of them.

Q Now, in your review of the minutes have you been able to determine whether or not there's any documentation referring to discussions prior to November/December of 1983 in reference to purchase of shares in the Northland Bank?

THE COMMISSIONER: Are you speaking here of Band meetings, Mr. McAfee?

MR. McAFEE: Yes. Band meetings, not Band Council meetings.

A The minutes that I've got, I've obtained those through different sources within our own group and I have yet to see the Band minutes that are held at the Band office, and I haven't — the ones I've got aren't, in my mind, completed. I feel that there's some minutes missing.

The minutes — it does not reflect that there was discussions on the shares purchase, but there is discussions regarding purchase of shares but it doesn't identify the Northland Bank.

Q Now, do you recall from your memory, without being able to refresh it from the minutes, do you recall any discussions prior to late November or December at a Band meeting in reference to the purchase of shares in a bank?

A Yes. During several meetings I remember we were talking about the problem of loans within the Band itself and its businesses and with individuals obtaining loans for development on reserve, and that we felt we should be buying into something to get an Indian Native policy for loans on reserve.

We did discuss us possibly buying shares into a trust company or into a bank, whatever was available to us.

Q I would like to now go to Mr. Derickson, if I might...

... Now, Mr. Derickson, were you present when the discussions took place in reference to the purchase of the Northland Bank shares?

A Yes, I was.

Q Could you tell me what you recollect in reference to the discussions on the purchase of those shares? First of all, do you have any recollection of any discussions taking place at the Band level prior to the decision being made to purchase the shares?

A Yes, it was discussed in general terms in relation to a general Band meeting in relation to that Council was wanting to invest in shares and looking at shares or some type of financial institution that would address some of our immediate concerns, alleviate some of our difficulties in raising capital monies for investments or developments and that type of thing.

Q Now, did you have discussions with representatives to the Northland Bank in reference to, number one, the potential of locating a bank branch in the Band office building?

A Yes.

Q Did you have discussions with officers of the Northland Bank in reference to a training program for Band members in the banking program?

A Yes.

Q Did you have discussions with representatives from the Northland Bank in reference to what they could offer by way of a Native banking program prior to you making the decision as to the acquisition of shares?

A Yes.

Q Now, were these some of the factors that you considered when you made the decision to purchase shares in the Northland Bank?

A That's right. That was some of the major things that I was concerned with; the idea of a financial institution on reserve, the Band having some type of investment in there through a share purchase would give us a foot in the door into a financial institution — the idea of a financial institution on reserve where some of our Band members that had monies they could deposit that would be interest free in relation to their — or I guess it would be income tax free in relation to their deposits on their income. This type of thing really appealed to me, because I was working and always have worked and still am in a lot of the job creation programs for the Band. That's one of my main portfolios.

I questioned them and quizzed them in relation to well what benefit is the Westbank Indian Band going to get out of this financial institution if it does take place that we invest, and so we went through the whole gamut in relation that we could end up with members involved in the financial institution in various capacities.

The direct benefit would be to the Band and the Band members, and that was all part and parcel of the decision to arrive at — to say, yes, we should purchase the shares. It sounded like a good, viable operation.

Q Mr. Derickson, during these discussions that you had with representative of the Northland Bank, did then Chief Ron Derrickson insist that you meet with these individuals and discuss this particular transaction with them privately without anyone else present?

A Yes. I mean they both, Mr. McBain and Mr. Fortier were in my office. We probably spent about two or three hours going over the various ramifications and benefits that could be available to the Band in the event we decided to invest and we had a good, long discussion on it.

Q Mr. Eli, did you meet with the representative from the Northland Bank separate and apart from Harold Derickson and from Ron Derrickson?

MR. ELI:

A Yes, I did.

Q And at the conclusion of these various meetings a decision was made by Council which, I assume, was to invest in the Northland Bank?

A Yes. Prior to making that decision the three of us, I and Harold, met with them again together without Ron Derrickson. After the discussion me and Harold had talked about it. Then we went to the Council meeting.

(Transcripts: Volume LXII, pp. 9035–9048)

Mr. Eli further testified in cross-examination by counsel for the liquidator of the Northland Bank as follows:

Q Mr. Eli, first of all, did you, in your position as a Band Councillor, after discussions with McBain and Fortier, believe that, apart from the benefits the Band might receive in the sense of good bank relationships — and then you get in the bank as a tenant and the other matters you discussed — did you also believe that it was good value to buy these shares in the Northland Bank at the price they were being offered at?

A Yes.

Q All right. Was there discussion about that later with the Band Council, in the Band Council?

A Yes. As I stated earlier, I met them privately myself and I joined Harold Derickson in a discussion with him also. Then we went into a Council meeting and agreed to the purchase.

Q Was it the consensus in the Band Council itself that the shares were good value for the price that was being asked for them per share?

A Yes. Without looking or having the Band Council minutes available to me, I believe there was actually a motion passed. I'm not too sure. If I had those minutes I could show it to you.

Q You have them available, but not here at the present time?

A No, I don't have them. They're presently at the Band office, and I think that they are — at different times in the Inquiry McAfee has asked for them.

Q All right. Now, in your evidence — and I mean — if I didn't hear you correctly I'm sure you'll tell me.

   You said that you recalled discussions in the Band Council about buying shares in trust companies or banks. You described various discussions. Was there specific discussions at the Band Council about buying shares in Northland Bank as opposed to any other bank?

A You're talking about the Band Council or general Band meetings?

Q Yes, I'm talking — I'm talking about Band meetings. I'm sorry, I confused you.

A Not specifically, no.

Q Oh, but there was at the Band Council meetings?

A Yes, at the time of the purchase, I think. We, at that time — after we met with them we held a Council meeting shortly right after the discussions.

Q All right. And you recall whether at a Band Council meeting there was actually a motion made which was passed authorizing the purchase of the million dollars worth of Northland Bank shares?

A I believe so. As I indicated earlier, I don't have those documents in front of me, but if I had them I could possibly go through them and see if there is such a document there. I believe there was.

Q You have those documents available to you?

A I said if I had those documents available to me I could look at them and —

Q I'm sorry, I'm confused. Where are they now?

A I indicated just a couple of minutes ago that they're at the Band office and we haven't been able to obtain them. . . . .

Q . . . .Mr. Eli, you're aware, I presume that the Band paid for the shares by way of obtaining a loan from the Northland Bank. Did you participate in negotiations for that loan?

A The loan with the Northland Bank?

Q Yes.

A I was informed through Ron Derrickson, I believe it is.

Q I see. Were you aware that as security for the loan to buy the shares in the Northland Bank, the Band pledged monies in a term deposit at the Continental Bank, where were Indian monies received from an expropriation. You were aware of that were you?

A Yes.

Q Was it ever discussed at a Band Council meeting that the Band was going to pledge that term deposit as security for the loan?

A At a Council meeting?

Q Yes.

A I'd have to look at the files I guess, the Council Minutes.

Q All right. I'd appreciate it if you'd do that.

A Okay.

Q Was it discussed at the Band Council meeting that the Band would have to put up security of some sort for the loan?

A It was probably covered in the Council minutes if there was.

Q You believe that would be in the minutes?

A Yes, I believe so.

Q All right. You'll examine them with Mr. McAfee, will you?

A Yes.

Q All right. Did you have any involvement in the repayment of the loan for $1 million by the Band to the Northland Bank? Are you aware of the circumstances under which it was repaid?

A To the point where — I believe where Ron Derrickson was dealing with the Northland Bank and dealing on our behalf, he would inform us of a decision, whatever happened with the Northland Bank, and it would be discussed in the Council minutes.

(Transcripts: Volume LXII, pp. 9125–9131)

There are certain curious features to the transaction whereby the large block of shares in the Northland Bank was purchased in the fall of 1983. Counsel were not able to find a Band Council Resolution referring to the matter. Mr. Norman Schwartz, the Band Administrator and chief financial officer, did not seem to be very familiar with the details of the transaction. Given the magnitude of it, this unfamiliarity could lend force to the suggestion that there was a sinister quality to the transaction.

After considering all of the evidence, oral and written, I concluded that neither Chief Ronald M. Derrickson nor Councillors Brian Eli and Harold J. Derickson were guilty of an abuse of office in effecting this particular investment.

The situation vis-à-vis Ronald M. Derrickson and the investment in Northland Bank shares was replete with the potential for allegations of conflict of interest. Was it an example of abuse of office on the part of Ronald M. Derrickson or the councillors? I am more inclined to characterize the hasty and undisclosed proceedings surrounding the investment as a lapse in careful procedure rather than as a true "abuse of office". I believe abuse of office connotes matters such as corrupt practice or breach of trust in the context of an investment decision of this sort. I did not perceive that sort of conduct here.

As to conflict of interest, it probably would have been desirable for Mr. Ronald M. Derrickson to have abstained from voting for or against this investment because of his personal Bank dealings. It therefore could be said that he acted in a situation of conflict of interest. But I did not conclude that he had acted from any wrongful or corrupt motive. I think that his participation, while perhaps unwise and unfortunate, does not deserve censure as a breach of trust of his office. I cannot help observing that much difficulty could easily have been obviated had a more orderly and businesslike course been adopted from the outset.

It appears to me that the situation was poorly handled from the point of view of having Band membership informed as to what was transpiring. Likewise, there was no process undertaken to get informed approval from Band members for this very substantial investment. I remain puzzled by the failure of Chief and Council to properly consult with the membership on this issue. Such failure contributed in large measure to the controversy that erupted after the failure of Northland Bank. It is a classic example of the mischief that can accrue from lack of full disclosure.

A subject that arose from time to time during the course of the Inquiry was the extent to which the Band should be consulted on decisions made or to be made by the executive of the Band. Indeed, it appeared to me that even to the present day, disparate groups in the Band are far from unanimity on the degree of disclosure that ought to occur. As a general proposition, it seemed to me that the "outs" wanted everything to be approved by the Band membership, while the "ins" manifested much less enthusiasm for calling general Band meetings to discuss what course of action should be taken or had been taken. That is a pattern found in political organizations throughout the world, and obviously there must be some accommodation made between efficient and effective Band government and the democratic participatory process. In the natural order of things, the executive of a band, or of any government, is expected to perform governing functions — that is why they were elected in the first place. There is always a tension in any democratic organization to steer some sort of a middle course between a rudderless government by referendum and the declaration such as that of the English statesman, Edmund Burke, to his constituents that he would proceed as he thought fit rather than how they might think fit.

Many governmental decisions have to be dealt with confidentially in order to protect the public interest. Likewise, a band government or any other government has to make decisions about general administration that must and should be made by it and not referred for decision to the general membership. To operate otherwise would mean that the band executive would have no real function and effective governmental action would be at an end. It is also necessary, of course, that some decisions be taken quickly in order to achieve the best results.

One example of a case where confidentiality was important was disclosed during the Inquiry. It seemed to me to be an appropriate exercise of executive decisionmaking by the Chief and Council (without Band participation concerning specific details) to work out the details of the purchase of the property known as "Gallagher's Canyon". The Band had earlier, in a general way, endorsed the concept of purchasing additional land with funds received pursuant to the cut-off negotiations. If a vendor of land became aware of the fact that a band government had passed a resolution approving of or requiring the purchase of his piece of property, this obviously could have a severe impact on the price the vendor was asking. And the impact would not be downward! In order to preserve a proper bargaining position, it seems to me necessary that the executive have a relatively free hand in negotiating a land purchase or sale. It would be harmful to the interests of the Band, from a financial point of view, to have it known to a vendor that the Band was fully committed to purchasing a particular parcel of land. Gallagher's Canyon was a good example of a situation where full prior disclosure of a proposed transaction could have harmed the financial interests of the Band. Its general good dictated that the matter be conducted with a certain degree of reticence. I saw virtually no comparison between that situation and the Northland Bank share purchase arrangement.

This latter transaction was a sale of shares. Obviously the Bank was quite keen to sell shares to prospective purchasers. I certainly did not get the impression from the evidence that the shares were in such short supply that there was urgency for an instant decision. The gist of the testimony of the Bank officers and their actions tended to suggest that they, not the Band, were the supplicants.

I remain mystified as to why there was this curious failure to solicit Band views on the purchase. That failure was compounded by failure to inform the Band membership about what had been undertaken in this regard. Had a more open, consultative process been followed in the case of the purchase of Northland Bank shares, a great deal of controversy and rumour could have been stopped at the outset. Full disclosure was obviously required because of the very substantial dealings ongoing between Mr. Ronald M. Derrickson and the Northland Bank.

If the other members of the executive, Mr. Brian Eli and Mr. Harold J. Derickson, were aware of the full extent of Mr. Derrickson's dealings with the Northland Bank, they should have insisted on a far more rigorous course of disclosure and participation by the Band in this matter. Their knowledge would necessarily, of course, be much less complete than the knowledge of Mr. Derrickson, who would be fully aware of his own dealings.

This was clearly a potential conflict of interest situation and had to be dealt with in a scrupulously correct manner to allay any suggestion of misfeasance. Because the sums of money involved (in both instances) were substantial, the matter had to be handled so that no one could suggest wrongful actions or bad motives. In fact, the way in which it was done was virtually an invitation to misconstruction.

Mr. Ronald M. Derrickson was quite vague when he was asked what discussion was had with the Band concerning purchase of the shares. He was questioned on the matter by counsel for the former Chief and executive:

A I might have mentioned it once or twice, the fact that we could make a quick profit. I don't remember offhand, but I'm sure if they were up at that time it would have been on my mind.

Q Mr. Derrickson, prior to the decision being made to purchase the shares, which I understand was late November or December 1983, do you have any recollection of the subject matter of a share purchase being discussed at a Band meeting?

A I can't point to any recollection. There's days I'm sure that it was discussed and there's days I can't remember. So, I really can't point to — you know, I've talked to some of the Band members and they've told me that they were sure it was discussed there and so forth.

But I can't specifically say on so and so a date these were the words that were said. I talked with several of the Band members, including quite a few of them that are here, that said that we discussed the share purchase with them.

(Transcripts: Volume LXVII, p. 9947)

One is left wondering why there was such reticence to bring this matter before the Band to have the investment ratified. Clearly there were many legitimate reasons why a band might invest money in the Northland Bank. Mr. Eli and Mr. Harold J. Derickson have noted above the reasons that impelled them to favour the investment. Those reasons are sensible and supportable. That being so, I find the failure to have proper consultation or at least post-event disclosure wholly inexplicable.

Mr. Ronald M. Derrickson said this when he was asked about the matter by counsel for the former Chief and executive:

Q Now, Mr. Derrickson, that was one of the considerations you had when you negotiated for the purchase of shares in Northland Bank. Are there others that come back to your memory today in reference to why you had a particular interest in purchasing shares of the Northland Bank?

A Well, at the time, unwisely or not, I figured that we would make — that the shares were down, the market was somewhat in a — you know, that the economy at that time was difficult and the shares were down in price.

I thought that the potential of where they had been before, there was potential for us to double our money at least on the shares. They were paying dividends and we received dividends right up until the curatorship was announced.

But the main consideration of buying the shares was, you know, we certainly didn't buy the shares thinking that we would lose the money. We bought the shares thinking that we would make a profit on them, that they would be a good long term investment, but they would also become security.

Although the Bank Act prevented us from using them as security to Northland Bank, we could certainly use them as security at other banks.

One of the things that Indian Bands generally lack is any form of security.

Q Mr. Derrickson, were there discussions with the Northland Bank people in reference to setting up a branch or setting up a deposit service to make it available to the Westbank Indian Band members?

A Yes, but they took the long route around. They were dubious — a little bit redneck maybe in some of their knowledge of Indian business, and keep in mind at that time that we bought the shares they had a major Indian band as an investor.

I think at that time they owned seven or eight per cent. That was the Erminskin Indian Band. They had an appointment and a director. They appointed, I think, their business managers or their lawyers or their director. He represented their interests there.

So it wasn't all completely new and foreign to us, but I think the major consideration was the fact that we would have access and it would open the doors and we would have an ongoing ability to access funds, especially if they located a bank branch on the reserve.

I think, as one of the other Councillors said — I can't remember who — we had entertained and negotiated with — I think they said two banks, but we negotiated with the Royal Bank to open a deposit centre on the reserve.

We negotiated with the Continental Bank, and I've forgotten the other one.

Q Would it be Royal Trust?

A Possibly, I can't remember.

Q Mr. Derrickson, was there consideration in reference to tax benefits as far as Band members were concerned, if you could locate a bank within your new building?

A Well, the consideration was there. That is not a consideration any more, because money earned on reserve, even if you deposit it in a bank, is not taxable any more. There's some court cases that support that.

But, at that time, interest on deposits was a very key thing in our mind. A lot of our members if they have large term deposits — and I can remember one specifically, I won't use their name, had about $500,000 in a term deposit and was receiving about 4.5 per cent return on it.

What we wanted to do was get our Indians in a situation where they could become well aware of the differences in interest rates and to get them the maximum benefit they could from these rates.

Q Mr. Derrickson, at the times that the shares were purchased by the Westbank Indian Band did you have strong personal feelings in reference to the purchase of those particular shares, and in fact, did you purchase shares yourself?

A Well, I had strong personal feelings to a little over a million dollars of my own money went into the purchase of shares in the bank. (My underlining)

(Transcripts: Volume LXVII, pp. 9943–9946)

In fact, the Band purchased another quarter million dollars worth of shares in the spring of 1984. Funds were borrowed from Northland

Bank to do so. In financial matters, as in other matters, all things are relative, but from any point of view this was a significant investment for the Westbank Indian Band. I think it fell very clearly within that class of matters calling for consideration by the Band as a whole. Furthermore, it was of the utmost importance (because of the Chief's peculiar position in that he had extensive dealings with the Bank and was receiving from one point of view substantial benefit from the Bank at about the same time) that there be true, full, and plain disclosure of the whole transaction in a timely fashion. It did not appear to me that the full story of this transaction was revealed until evidence was developed during the Inquiry. This was rather late for Band members to be finding out the whole story of their investment in Northland Bank.

When the Bank failed in September 1985, there was alarm approaching panic among certain members of the Westbank Indian Band. Mr. Ronald M. Derrickson was critical (and there were grounds for his criticism) of the inflammatory language used by the Action Committee and its agent, Mr. Kayban. However, he to some extent was the author of his own misfortune, in that the inexplicable failure of him and his council to frankly and fully inform the Band in a timely fashion about matters concerning investment in Northland Bank was a large contributing factor to much of the concern and misinformation that appeared to swirl about the reserve. If a matter is left obscure, as this was, wrong inferences can and usually will be drawn. The lack of information on this subject would lead people who were concerned to suspect the worst, and they did. This, I believe, played a large role in creating the hysterical tone of the allegations given currency through Mr. Kayban. The best cure for rumour is usually fact. If Band members had had a true appreciation of the facts in 1985 and 1986, I think a great deal of hyperbole would have been avoided.

Based on my analysis of the evidence and submissions related to the investment in the shares of Northland Bank, I think there were many legitimate reasons why the investment in shares in the Bank could have been advantageous to the Westbank Indian Band.

It is too often true that banks are reluctant to lend funds to Indian people or Indian enterprises. Banks are not necessarily to be criticized for this reluctance because they have had some bad experiences. Banks are not in their conception or in their operation usually viewed by themselves or others as charitable institutions. They exist to provide a profit to their shareholders. There are, as we know, problems with the taking of security on Indian land or on chattels located on Indian land. All these matters affect the issue of whether or not an Indian person or band will have easy access to lending and capital markets, in particular to banking connections. The desire of the Westbank Chief and Council to enhance their relationship with a chartered bank in order to help them fund persons and enterprises was laudable and worthy. Likewise, it was laudable that Chief Derrickson later undertook to be a director of the Bank. We need more Indian leaders, not fewer, doing this sort of thing.

I therefore find it puzzling that he was reluctant to involve the Band in this decision, or to be frank with them as to particulars of the investment. Given that he had extensive dealings with the Bank, if matters were left unexplained or uncertain, many unfavourable inferences could and would be drawn against him by others in the Band who were not in possession of the facts. It is, to put it mildly, unfortunate that the whole story did not come out prior to the Inquiry.

One other matter that calls for comment in connection with the purchase of shares in the Northland Bank is that there appears to have been no financial analysis done on this investment. In the Band by-law establishing the position of Band Administrator, one task given is to act jointly with the Band Treasurer for the purchase and sale of securities by Council, and generally to have control and supervision of all matters respecting Band finances. It was clear from the evidence that Mr. Norman Schwartz, Band Administrator, was not involved in evaluating the investment in the shares.

Mr. Schwartz said when asked by Commission Counsel about the Northland Bank investment:

Q Now, in or about that time, and I'm talking about the end of 1983, the Band invested a substantial amount of money in the Northland Bank. There was about a million dollars borrowed and used for the purchase of shares in the Northland Bank. Do you remember that?

A I remember we have shares in the Northland Bank, yes.

Q Can you tell me how the decision was arrived at to invest the money in the Northland Bank?

A Well, to be honest with you, I was not involved in the decision. The Chief and Councillors made that decision themselves, and I think they were together with a lawyer at the time, and I was not present.

Q Was there any legal advice taken that you know of? Do you know the lawyer that was involved at all?

A Graham Allen, I believe, was the legal adviser at that time.

Q Did you ever meet a Mr. Byd McBain?

A I have met Byd McBain once, but I don't know him on a personal basis.

Q Did you meet him about the time that the shares were bought in the Northland Bank?

A I couldn't say that for sure.

Q Did you discuss the purchase of shares in the Northland Bank with Chief Derrickson?

A I think that it was reported to me, yes, that we had shares in the bank.

Q A million dollars worth?

A I think it was a fraction over a million, or in that area. That was the value. I don't think they paid that much for the shares.

Q Did you discuss with the Chief or any of the members of the Council about any advantages or disadvantages of buying shares in the Northland Bank?

A No, I did not because, you know, when you get into the politics of the Band you're — I'm not involved. I think that that was a political sense.

Q Do you consider that was a political decision or just a plain investment decision?

A Well, it was an investment, and it was the Band's money. I don't think that the administrator should be involved in that particular area.

Q Well, other than I see you're charged with some duty with regard to the purchase of securities.

A Oh, yes. Well, I am, sure. I have many charges with the — right today, if the Westbank Indian Band wanted to go and get some money, who would they go to? They wouldn't get it on the signing of a Chief or a Councillor. It would have to be my signature if they wanted to get a line of credit. So, you know that's — but it's not necessary that I was involved in the designation of those shares.

Q Okay. So when the shares were bought by the Band, and I'm not talking about the period of about November/December, 1983, did you know about the purchase of the shares before they were bought?

A No, I did not.

Q So you weren't privy to that decision at all?

A No, sir. . . .

Q . . . .Did you have any discussions with Ron Derrickson about the purchase of those shares?

A No, I wouldn't say that I had any discussion. He just told me that they had purchased these shares, and that's all I can recall.

Q And there was a bank loan taken out to finance the purchase of those shares, was there not?

A Probably there was.

(Transcripts: Volume XLVII, pp. 6816–6819)

It is obvious to me that one of the things that a modern, urban band needs is competent and informed financial advice. It did not appear from the record of evidence that there was any attempt made by the Chief or councillors to obtain any financial analysis of this proposed investment. According to Mr. Schwartz, he had no role to play in the matter. Perhaps it was felt by Chief and Council that he had no role to play. But it would seem to me highly desirable that the executive seek out some advice from a professional in the financial area to help them evaluate the investment. I am sure that Mr. Brian Eli and Mr. Harold Derickson would have been reassured by advice from a person accustomed to dealing with investment. Chief Ronald M. Derrickson had a reasonable degree of experience with investment, but because of his own substantial dealings with the Bank, it would have been preferable for him to have had outside advice on the matter.

Modern Indian bands with significant funds to deal with need access to good financial advice. Given the dimensions of the Northland Bank investment transactions, I found the lack of professional financial analysis disquieting.

Although Mr. Schwartz seemed to be described at times as the Band Administrator, it seemed that in his own view of his responsibilities he was more of an office manager. It seems doubtful if there was anybody occupying the sort of position envisaged by Mr. David Sparks of the Department when he set forth in a by-law the job description of a band administrator. That being so, a prudent course for the Band executive to follow would have been to take proper advice from a qualified third party. I am far from certain that any different or better result would necessarily have been reached, but in matters of this sort, not only must those responsible for decisions act with proper motives, but they must also act in such fashion that impropriety cannot be suggested.

That may have been indeed one of the problems with the Northland Bank investment. If there had been some proper analysis of the whole situation, including questions directed to Chief Derrickson about his relationship to the Bank and the like, I am certain that the matter would not have been handled as it was. Any competent financial adviser would have spotted at once the enormous potential for trouble that existed if the matter was not handled with the greatest care and fullest disclosure. Thus, the Chief and councillors would have avoided blundering into a huge public relations nightmare.

I think the motives that induced the Chief and Council to make the Northland investment were understandable and appropriate. Lack of independent analysis of the transaction coupled with failure to disclose the matter properly is anything but praiseworthy — it was a severe lapse of good management and good judgement. Herein, Mr. Ronald M. Derrickson must bear the major burden of blame, for neither of his councillors could have the detailed knowledge that Mr. Derrickson had of his own business affairs. In addition, neither had any substantial background in business, unlike Chief Derrickson who had a reasonable degree of experience in major ventures.

Ultimately, the investment proved to be wholly disastrous in that the shares are worthless. They represent a loss to the Band of something in the order of $1.25 million. However, that is all hindsight, and as we well know, a great many people and corporations lost considerable sums in the collapse of Northland Bank and Canadian Commercial Bank. Many of those people were quite experienced in capital markets. The investment had risks, as do most investments, but there were also significant benefits that the Chief and councillors saw could accrue to the Band as a result of a good banking connection. Those were legitimate considerations for the Band executive. It would be quite wrong to censure their decision on the basis of hindsight.

In fact, significant loans were obtained from the Northland Bank for purchase of the land at Gallagher's Canyon. As well, loan-financing for erection of the Band building and the acquisition of the water slide known as Wild'N'Wet came via Northland Bank. I deal elsewhere in greater detail with Wild'N'Wet in the chapter entitled "Band Investments" (Chapter 5).

At the time of the Northland Bank collapse, the Band, through its solicitor, had deposits in it over and above its share investment of about $3 million. The Band then also had outstanding about $3 million in loans to it or its development company.

Was it prudent for the Band to have placed virtually all its money in the Northland Bank? That, I suppose, is a question that could elicit different answers from different people, depending on their perspective. I am not prepared to say that it was a wrong decision. Mr. Ronald M. Derrickson was a director of the Bank until August 1985. He and his fellow councillors had decided to support the Bank by way of investments and deposits, and to be consistent with that position they elected to support it by being large depositors. Northland Bank did advance significant loan funds to the Band, so to that extent, the strategy that impelled the Chief and councillors on their original course was being realized.

The Band undoubtedly had heavy exposure at this Bank, in the order of something near $4–$4.5 million (including the share investment), but they also had obtained some substantial loans. As I noted above, it appeared to me that in 1987 serious efforts were being made for the parties to settle the debits and credits that existed relative to the deposits versus the loans. It appears that some resolution of that matter may be achievable and I must leave it to the best judgement of those concerned with the Band government to decide what can be achieved in this area. Doubtless no perfect solution can be found, but one can hope that financial harm occasioned to the Band by the Bank failure can be kept within tolerable limits.

The Northland Bank situation disclosed a lamentable failure by the then Chief and councillors to: (1) involve the Band in the decision to invest; and (2) inform the Band in a timely fashion of details relative to the investment.

Did Mr. Ronald M. Derrickson feel unconsciously that because of his extensive personal dealings with Northland Bank there might be criticism of him for investing substantial Band funds in the Bank? I do not think that when the whole picture emerges such criticism would be thought justifiable. But by acting as he did, or to put it more accurately, by failing to act in a certain way, he did a great disservice to himself and his councillors and caused much needless worry to Band members. Great controversy was fuelled by the investment. Had there been a more orderly and open process followed in connection with it, I am confident that much controversy could have been avoided. I hope a lesson can be learned from this course of events so as to avoid similar pitfalls in future.

Chapter 5

Band Investments

The Commission examined certain Band investments from the point of
view of possible conflict of interest. The Westbank Band has been
actively engaged in a number of businesses and investments over the
past fifteen years. In 1974, the Westbank Indian Band Development
Company was incorporated in order to develop what is now called the
Lakeridge Park residential subdivision on Reserve 10. That company
was the first of a number of subsidiary enterprises that the Band created
or acquired. Over the years, the Band, through its development and
construction companies, has operated in the real estate, insurance,
travel, construction, picture framing, personal care, and recreation
fields. These business ventures have met with varying degrees of
success. Recently, the Band has had to cut back on its investments, as
some were just not successful. Others were successful and remain viable.

Indian band investment is an area where one must be cautious. It
differs from non-Indian private investment in that there are instances
where an investment may not appear to be successful based on a purely
economic analysis, but it may have significant side or spin-off benefits.
Ronald Derrickson gave some illuminating testimony about the special
considerations that affect this area of Indian life:

Q Mr. Derrickson, what was the state of affairs as far as the welfare
system in 1976/77 within the reserve?
A Well, I don't know really. I never liked welfare. I never liked that
word and I never liked what it did to our people.
But you know, we've always had that. That's always been a
major part of our funding and a major part of our problem. I can
remember one occasion, Bill Derrickson was Councillor. He was
handling the welfare system and people who make applications.
He went away for two weeks, and during that two weeks
anybody that came in and gave me a hard story I wrote them a
cheque. When he got back I was in trouble right up to here. From
that point on they kept me away from them, because I believed
everything, you know? It just seemed reasonable to me.
I've hated that system, but it's always been a part of our reserve
system. I think it always will be as long as there's an Indian Act,
because welfare has to do with lack of discipline, you know, or
lack of ability or lack of opportunity, lack of confidence or apathy
or all together. It's something I wish there was a cure for, but, you
know, I think the cure for most of that problem is getting rid of
the Indian Act.
I agreed with Harold Derrickson, maybe not the exact way he
would lay it out, but there'll always be welfare and it will always

go as long as we have the present <u>Indian Act</u> and people like, like I say, Mr. Hobbs running our affairs.

Q Mr. Derrickson, you had a belief, or the Council had a belief, that people that were on welfare should endeavour to the best of their ability to contribute to the Band affairs. Is that correct?

A Well, that's right. It's reasonable, if you have somebody who is on welfare, and if he's working for that welfare, for the benefit of the Band, he's a Band member. He'll benefit eventually. Eventually the Band will get into a position where it doesn't need that sort of thing, where the disciplines are created and put into place so people have more pride in themselves and more opportunity.

It's a question of building opportunity. I know the criticisms. It's all right for you to talk. You, you're well off. You're not on welfare. What about us?

But, I mean, it all has to start somewhere. It won't start where we're fighting with each other all the time and where we're not developing opportunities so we can take advantage.

(Transcripts: Volume LXV, pp. 9738–9740)

There is a moral in what Mr. Derrickson says. In effect, in times past (and present), many Indian people have been out of the economic mainstream. To the extent that they can be more successful in the economic sphere, I believe their lives and the lives of their descendants will be enhanced. Alleged failures in this area are not necessarily useless. Those in charge of economic development in Indian bands often have a difficult environment to work in and progress may be somewhat sporadic. There will be higher rates of apparent failure than would make an eagle-eyed accountant happy, but it will have to be recognized that from some failures will come, eventually, new attitudes and a sense of discipline that is a prerequisite for success in any field.

Westbank Indian Band investments grew significantly following settlement of a cut-off lands claim and the resulting influx of capital. The Westbank Reserves were well situated to take advantage of economic growth in the Kelowna area. The local economy grew in the 1970's but maybe not as quickly as some people had anticipated. Some Band members have criticized the former executive for some of its investment decisions and its business management. In particular, the former council's acquisition and management of the Wild'N'Wet Waterslide, Chancery Hair Design Ltd., and Toussowasket Custom Framers Ltd. were called into question during this Inquiry.

It should be noted that there was also an investment made in an interior design business. The executive elected in 1986 decided to close the operation, an action with which the former executive did not agree. I am not disposed to go into this matter in detail, as I think it a matter where reasonable people may differ in assessing the enterprise. I saw no conflict of interest issue; this case simply illustrates the vicissitudes of economic life. One could criticize the former executive for being unduly expansionary, but it could also be argued that the present executive acted too precipitously in closing the design business. In a rising market it pays to be expansionary and in a falling market the conservative investor will do better. In matters economic, timing is everything and time alone can tell whether an individual has talent or simply was lucky in a choice of investments. The design business failed but it may have had legitimate chance of success, offering apparent employment opportunities for Band members, at its inception. I am not inclined to be critical of this particular venture despite its unhappy demise — it was an effort that failed but that, of course, happens to any number of business ventures.

In December 1984, the Westbank Band purchased a 50 per cent interest in a tourist facility known as Wild'N'Wet Waterslide. The Band had entered into an arrangement with the Fort Nelson Band whereby each band would acquire a 50 per cent interest in the enterprise from the previous (non-Indian) owners. Wild'N'Wet was a limited company located on Reserve 9 where it operated under a locatee lease. It had been in operation since approximately 1980 and appeared to have been a viable enterprise. Both bands contributed equally in making a substantial initial payment. The Fort Nelson Band provided approximately $385,000 in cash, while the Westbank Band provided an equivalent value in land. The balance (approximately $900,000) was to be financed by each band obtaining a loan for their respective half interests. Ultimately the Fort Nelson Band did not take down its share of the financing, forcing the Westbank Band to borrow the full amount from the Northland Bank in order to close the transaction with the previous owners.

Some of the property that the Westbank Band traded to the former proprietors as their portion of the down payment was land originally held by former Chief Ron Derrickson. The Band paid Mr. Derrickson $124,000 for two parcels of land located on Reserve 10. It does not appear that the Band purchase of these properties from the Chief was disclosed to the general Band membership. In fact, when the purchase of Wild'N'Wet was discussed at a Band meeting, the impression conveyed was that the Band had only put up land and no cash in the deal. The money paid to Mr. Derrickson by the Band may well have represented fair market value; the vendors of Wild'N'Wet accepted that value. However, the transaction raises questions concerning a conflict of interest situation. Why was land owned by the Chief included in the deal? Could the Band have used other lands and thereby avoided any cash outlay? These are questions that some Band members might well have asked, if given the opportunity. The significant feature was that because the Band was dealing with the Chief, there should have been full disclosure of the structure of the arrangement to the Band membership. Clearly, there was the potential for a conflict of interest, if not an actual conflict, and to avoid any appearance of a lack of propriety, full disclosure was necessary. The Chief, Council, and Band Administrator were amazingly oblivious to the problem and failed to take steps to ensure that the transaction was properly handled.

As previously noted, Wild'N'Wet has a leasehold interest in lands on Reserve 9. Actually, there are two leases involved because the enterprise occupies the properties of two different locatees. The locatees are receiving rental payments. The fact that this Band business is operating under a locatee lease has resulted in a difficult conflict of interest situation. The Band Council, who in effect control the company, had to negotiate on behalf of the company with the two locatees regarding a fair rent. Purportedly acting pursuant to powers granted under Section 60 of the Indian Act, the then Band Council had assumed responsibility for determining rentals on leased land on behalf of the Minister. Thus the Band Council had to consider, on the one hand, the business interests of Wild'N'Wet and its shareholders (ultimately all Band members) and, on the other hand, they had to consider their obligations to the locatees when they determined the rent. In addition to these disparate interests, then Chief Ronald Derrickson undertook the responsibility for negotiating on behalf of the locatee interests. Mr. Derrickson was clearly wearing too many hats. In his evidence he described the difficulty of his position:

> A ...I could have went two ways. I could have hammered the Lessee — or the landowners, the Locatee. I could have hammered them on the rent and run them through the wringer. But what is my obligation as Chief? My obligation as Chief is to — if the owner of Wild'N'Wet had been Len Crosby, you know, I would have been getting —
>
> I mean, I'm getting criticized for doing what I thought was the only thing I could do; find a middle ground that I thought both would buy, that we could handle both ways. I found that middle ground.
>
> If I had not given Mary Eli and Dave Derrickson fair rent, that I considered fair at that time, I would be here — they would have been asking me — I mean, they were your own Band members Ron Derrickson; why wouldn't you treat them fairly? I couldn't win in that situation.
>
> (Transcripts: Volume LXVII, p. 9967)

I agree that he could not win — neither was the Band likely to. This was a case where Mr. Derrickson would have been more prudent to depute a member of the Council to deal with this matter on behalf of the Band if he undertook to act for any of the locatees. Although I recognize that a band has communal and familial features, where significant transactions are being conducted, businesslike procedures must be followed or controversy will occur later. Chief Derrickson was falling into the very trap I have heard the Department criticized for — paternalism. He believed that he and he alone could deal with the issue and keep everyone happy — a sort of "father knows best" attitude. It is an easy trap to fall into and all Indian band executives should be particularly conscious of this lurking danger, given the close-knit nature of a band.

The new rental agreement called for an increase in the annual rent payable to each locatee from $25,000 to $30,000. In addition, each locatee was to receive 5 per cent of the gross receipts of the company. Mr. William Kinsey, C.A., gave evidence regarding the ability of the business to carry the rental increase. He indicated that based on its previous income, the company would have lost money in all but the best years had it then been operating pursuant to the new rental agreement. In Mr. Kinsey's opinion, the requirement to pay 10 per cent of gross receipts in addition to a base rent would seriously impair the company's ability to break even, let alone show a profit. The present Chief, Mr. Robert Louie, expressed concern that the new rental agreement was not negotiated with the best interests of the company (and the Band) in mind. He stated that the company's profits had been steadily declining virtually since its inception. He attributed this to a variety of factors, including growing competition in the area. He said that under the new lease agreement the company had lost money in 1986 and appeared to be heading for a loss situation in the current season as well. Of course, if a business continually loses money it will go bankrupt. If that happens in this case, Mr. Derrickson will be subject to criticism, but it is criticism he will have brought on himself.

In May 1985, the Band purchased, through its development company, Chancery Hair Design Ltd. and Toussowasket Custom Framers Ltd. These two businesses were previously owned by Noll Derriksan, brother of Ronald Derrickson. The transaction was structured as a purchase of all the shares in the two companies. The purchase price for both businesses was $60,000, which was to be paid in three equal instalments. It appears from the somewhat sparse Band records that the purchase price was to be paid partly in cash and partly by an exchange of properties. Both businesses operated from rented premises in the City of Kelowna. Chief Robert Louie gave evidence concerning the poor financial state in which he found the companies upon his election in August 1986. The hairdressing company was apparently averaging losses of approximately $4,000 per month. Eventually, the new administration decided to discontinue the operation; it is difficult to see what else they could have done, given the continuing losses. Toussowasket Custom Framers is still operating, but in a loss situation. Fortunately, it is not a large cash drain.

Subsequent to the purchase of Chancery Hair Design Ltd., the Band changed the name of the company to Hyde Park Image Creators Ltd. The Band also purchased a building in downtown Kelowna as a site from which to operate the new business. Substantial improvements were made to the building, with the total investment in the land, building, and the company approaching $225,000. Although the Band is no longer operating the hairdressing business, it is being carried on by another party in the same building. The Band still owns the land and building and is in a landlord relationship with the new tenant.

It is unclear how the purchase price was arrived at for the two companies. In their evidence, the current Band auditors said that they had difficulty obtaining financial information related to the two businesses. The Band Administrator, Mr. Schwartz, appeared not to be fully informed about their finances. The most recent financial statements available were dated January 31, 1984. As the Band did not purchase the companies until May 1985, that left a gap in the financial information. According to the January 1984 financial statements, both companies were operating at a loss. There was nothing to indicate that the situation had improved by the time of the Band's purchase. Ronald Derrickson stated in his evidence that the businesses were purchased in order to create employment for Band members and that at least one Band member had been employed in each business from time to time. He also said that he had seen financial records from the companies which had been kept by his brother, Noll Derriksan, subsequent to the 1984 statements. According to the evidence of the auditors, however, there was no financial information available to them in the spring of 1986 when they made their inquiries of the Band administration.

Viewed from one perspective, the purchase of these businesses from Noll Derriksan was an attempt to expand the business activity of the Band and to create employment for Band members. The Band was in a relatively flush financial position at the time of the purchase. From another perspective, it could be viewed as unduly favourable treatment of Noll Derriksan at the expense of the Band. It is understandable how some Band members could hold the latter view. The businesses were not in good financial condition nor had they any great prospects when they were purchased. According to Chief Louie's evidence, they continued to be a financial drain during his administration. There did not appear to be any recent audited financial statements available to the Band Council prior to the purchase of the businesses in May 1985. The companies were purchased from the former Chief's brother and the general Band membership was not informed of the purchase until after the fact.

It is difficult to judge at this point whether these were appropriate purchases. The purchase of the building for Chancery Hair Design Ltd. may work out, but this venture into the personal care business was subject to so little analysis that I think it fair to say it was not a model of how to proceed. Business ventures, of course, do not always turn out as well as planned. In this case, it is not clear what information the purchaser acted on in deciding to acquire these businesses. But the main problem with the transaction was that there was an apparent conflict of interest because the Chief and Council were dealing with the Chief's brother. The appearance of conflict was exacerbated by the lack of current financial information on the companies and their past record of poor performance. Given the nature of the transaction and the clear potential for conflict of interest, it was a lapse in good judgement and good management to make the acquisition in such a casual fashion without any noticeable analysis or apparent business plan.

The big pitfall to watch for in band investment policy is conflict of interest. Opportunity for success must be spread evenly throughout a band. Because of the family nature of many, particularly smaller, bands, care must be taken to avoid the appearance of a favoured few (perhaps close relatives of the elected council) having a virtual monopoly on funding for new business or existing enterprises. Likewise, where a band is considering investment in a project, the members of the band executive must be scrupulously careful in their dealings with band or Department funds. These cautions were not always observed at Westbank and the result was controversy and complaint. This was another instance where proper disclosure and an opportunity for the Band membership to debate the proposed course of action would have minimized the likelihood of later objections.

I have commented elsewhere on certain major investments of the Westbank Indian Band, such as the Northland Bank share purchase and the acquisition of the Gallagher's Canyon land. In addition, the Band had a pot pourri of other investments including travel and insurance businesses. Some of them I thought were undertaken more to fill the new Band building than for any logical economic or Band employment reason. There appeared to be lacking any comprehensive economic plan or vision for the Band. Developing bands must pay particular attention to the planning area or their economic progress will suffer. The lack of overall economic planning at Westbank illustrates a frequent weakness of new and developing organizations. Hopefully, the current and future administrations can take heed from the deficiencies of the past to pursue a more orderly course in the future. Band Council, the Administrator and outside professional advisers must together formulate a reasoned course of investment action. Such a course, accompanied by proper disclosure and sensitivity to conflict situations, should ensure that band investment policy is conducted in an orderly fashion and in a fashion that minimizes the likelihood of controversy.

Chapter 6

Accounting Issues

In the production of this chapter, I wish to acknowledge the very substantial contribution of Mr. William D. Kinsey, C.A., who served as Investigative Accountant to the Commission. Mr. Kinsey, who practised for many years with a national firm of accountants, has undertaken numerous investigative assignments for professional bodies and government. Mr. Kinsey had access to Westbank Indian Band financial records as well as the benefit of discussions with past and present auditors. He spoke to the Band Administrator, Band financial staff, and Departmental officials, and attended on several Commission hearings.

It appears that members of the Westbank Indian Band and other interested people have not received a complete picture over the years concerning the Band's economic performance and the management of Band resources. While there will be differences caused by differing individual circumstances, it seems to me that similar problems are likely to arise in other bands as their asset base grows and they become more actively involved in business ventures. I believe that the process of informing Westbank Band members in a meaningful way can be improved by alterations in financial reporting, including greater disclosure of material transactions.

The Westbank Band is a relatively sophisticated band in terms of economic progress and administrative structure. The Band is located in a favourable area for expansion and Band members have been active in the leasing field. There are existing leases for recreational, industrial, and residential use. The latter is the most substantial, encompassing a number of mobile home park operations. Additionally, Westbank has a Band development company which has undertaken, and continues to undertake, subdivision work. The Band development company in turn controls a contracting company which does work for the Band and also seeks additional sources of work beyond Westbank. The Band has built a large new office building on Tsinstikeptum Reserve 10, and is thus in the commercial office leasing business as well. The early 1980's saw a great deal of economic activity on the Reserves. But Band members were not always kept up to date on financial matters — indeed, at times the Department of Indian Affairs and Northern Development found itself less than perfectly informed concerning Band finances.

The Commission has made some comprehensive suggestions with respect to the financial reporting practice of Indian bands in general in Section II of this Report. With respect to the financial reporting of the Westbank Band, the Commission has the following observations:

1) There is a method of accounting in place which is not simple to follow. I believe greater clarity can be achieved.

2) There has been a failure to adequately inform the Band members about the activities of incorporated companies and unincorporated enterprises controlled by the Band.

3) There has been a failure to recognize or deal with apparent problems or inconsistencies disclosed or hinted at in the financial statements. An example is the "minors' trust fund" matter.

4) There has been in a number of instances a failure to inform Band members about significant transactions involving members of the Band government.

While there are some elements of criticism in what follows, I hope that it will be appreciated that it is intended to be constructive criticism directed to areas that could be improved. This improvement is in the interest of more effective management of Band finances and better appreciation by Band members of the economic state of the Band and Band enterprises.

1) Clarity in Accounting

Compliance with the rules of the Department appears to be no guarantee of easy comprehension of financial matters by Westbank Band members. The accounting guides supplied by the Department have been, perhaps understandably, directed mainly toward matters the Department has a direct responsibility for, namely payments made pursuant to agreements with bands. It follows that Band financial statement standards have been heavily focused on satisfying Departmental requirements. For example, when the Department provided money for a particular purpose, the Band's financial statements often disclosed that contribution, and perhaps a number of related contributions, on separate Statements of Revenue and Expenditure. In recent years, the Westbank Band's financial statements have typically contained 28 such schedules.

The Commission has seen, in edited form, some instances of financial statements for other bands where the number of schedules has far exceeded that number. The proliferation of many separate statements may simplify matters for the Department, but it seems to me that it tends to make the series of statements as a whole more difficult for the individual band member to understand. While the problem of multiplicity of statements seems greater in some other bands, this does not mean that the Westbank manner of financial reporting should not change in favour of greater simplicity.

As a general criticism of the Westbank financial statements, and particularly of those statements available to its members, it could be said that the Statements of Revenue and Expenditure contained an overabundance of detail for the Band operating as a Band. However, information about the incorporated and unincorporated operations of the Band was quite sparse. Neither the Band nor its auditors are necessarily to be criticized for the considerable detail contained in the Band's financial statements because the Department requested it. The Department had a legitimate need for information on funds provided. The ideal would be to supply sufficient detail to allow the Department to fulfil its mandate, but not to include such detail that the average Band member is unable to comprehend the overall picture.

I found one feature of the accounting of the Westbank Indian Band to be quite misleading. This feature showed up when certain sums were described as "revenue" when they were not, in fact, "revenue". As related elsewhere in this Report, Indian bands, like government bodies and non-profit organizations, report financial transactions or account for monies received on a "fund" or "modified fund" basis. Such financial reporting usually consists of a number of individual Statements of Revenue and Expenditure, one for each activity or group of activities plus a combined Statement of Revenue and Expenditures embodying the individual statements. In the Westbank Statements of Revenue and Expenditure, surplus and deficit figures for related activity in the prior year are shown. If an activity has realized a surplus in the prior year, the surplus is carried forward and treated as "revenue". If an activity has suffered a deficit in the prior year, the deficit is treated as an expenditure in the current year.

It appears sensible to work on the assumption that the primary purpose of individual revenue and expenditure statements is to indicate how a band has fared in a particular fund for the year in question. The reader of the financial statements is also concerned with the activity of the fund for the year in question, and the method used by the Westbank Indian Band does not reflect a truly accurate picture of that year because activity in previous years is mixed with the current year's activities.

A serious instance of improperly described revenue has been to classify as "revenue" monies received by the Band on behalf of third parties for immediate payment to those third parties. For example, lease payments received on behalf of locatees are included as Band revenue. The reader of the financial statement would assume that those monies belonged to the Band. Another example of improper description is monies funnelled through the "Distributor's Account". That account is a Band account used for money received and disbursed to pay for tax-free purchases by the Band and its members. There is no intention that any profit be made or any loss be incurred on the transactions. In both of the above instances, the Band functions simply as a trustee of the funds. The receipts are not Band revenue, nor are they intended to be Band revenue. In both instances, monies are merely paid through the Band account. The Band can be seen as simply a temporary holder of these funds for other parties and thus the transactions should be kept separate from any report on general Band financial operations.

When transactions are improperly included in revenue, the result has been double counting, and sometimes multiple counting. In such circumstances, the resultant figures can be quite meaningless. In effect, there are greatly overstated revenues and expenditures. This sort of recording can indicate that there is a great deal of activity occurring in certain areas, when in fact nothing that concerns Band finances is occurring.

A reader of Band statements may mistakenly consider as the year's revenue the reported revenue figures which include opening surplus, internal transfers, and monies received in trust or as an agent. This tends to confuse matters and could be taken to indicate, for instance, that the Band had substantial independent means aside from Department funding. Eliminating the irrelevant figures from the financial statements would minimize the likelihood of any such misapprehensions.

I set out hereafter three examples where there was what I would call "double counting", to illustrate the points made above.

a) The first example is a concrete plant which the the Westbank Band operated for a number of years. The plant furnished concrete products required during the development of, among other things, the Lakeridge subdivision. It provided some Band employment, but as market activity decreased it became so uneconomic that it was deemed necessary to close it.
    The following is a simplified summary of the Statement of Revenue and Expenditure for the concrete plant in 1983.

Statement of Revenue and Expenditure for the Year 1983

Revenue	$
Sales	4,233
Internal transfers from other Band funds	24,564
Total Revenue	28,797
Expenditures	
Deficit at end of prior year	17,137
Actual (true) expenditures (total)	14,625
Total expenditures	31,762
Operating loss	
(excess of expenditures over revenue)	2,965

This simplification shows transfers from other funds as part of revenue, and a deficit from the prior year as part of expenditures. But such figures are not needed, nor are they at all useful in giving the true picture of 1983 activities.

I think the appropriate method of handling this Statement of Revenue and Expenditure would be as follows.

Revenue	$
Sales	4,233
Expenditures (summarized)	14,625
Excess of expenditures over revenue (i.e. operating loss)	10,392

As suggested in Section II, the other data can be shown "below the line" but should not affect the year's operating statement.

It can be seen from this example that the stated revenue for the year 1983 was greatly exaggerated and that the expenditures and operating loss were also distorted. This observation should not be taken to be directed at the Band or its auditors. The format used by the Band appears consistent with the format supplied in the Department's 1980 Accounting Guide (Exhibit 43, Section 5). That guide shows incoming inter-fund transfers as "revenue" and outgoing inter-fund transfers as "expenditures". It also shows the prior year's surpluses and deficits as part of revenue. It is apparent to me that this approach to financial reporting is not particularly illuminating and I think the Department guide should be changed so that clarity is enhanced. I expand on these comments in Section II, Part C.

It should be noted that the former Westbank Indian Band auditor actively pressed for clearer standards in Indian band accounting and financial statements. He said in his testimony that he has been frustrated by the lack of progress to date. Individual bands and their auditors must not be left to establish accounting standards wholly on their own. I am heartened to see that there does seem to be some definite impetus from the Department for improvement in standards of accounting, which hopefully will result in improved clarity and ease of comprehension. We are in a transitional period, and methods that were formerly appropriate are becoming less satisfactory for more economically advanced bands such as the Westbank Indian Band.

b) I would like to deal next with an example of the confusion that can be engendered in individuals by such multiple counting as noted above. I had before me in evidence a report made on November 9, 1982 by the then Director of Economic Development for the British Columbia Region of the Department. It was entitled "Some Indicators of Change — Westbank Indian Band" and related to the decade from

1971–72 to 1980–81. Mr. Fred Walchli, the former Regional Director General, said this report was requested because of the concerns that were being voiced about problems, or alleged problems, at Westbank.

The report contained a reference to, and some analysis of, the 1980–81 Band revenues. I quote from page 16 of Exhibit 113, document 72.

Westbank Band Budget

	1971/72	1980/81	1982/83
Band	5,160	1,999,815	3,788,517
Departmental contribution	13,850	900,763	990,586
Total	19,010	1,900,578	4,779,102

(sic; the author is out $1 million in his addition here)

While the table was said to come from the Westbank Band budget, it appears that the 1980/81 figures were drawn from the 1981 Band financial statements rather than from the budget. Leaving aside the inaccuracy of the source and the addition, the report asserts that the Westbank Band was becoming financially independent of the Department. The report indicated that 69% of the total revenue for the year came from non-Departmental sources.

The "Band" revenue figure of $1,999,815 is erroneous. Proper analysis of the financial statements should have revealed to the writer that the money attributed to revenue earned by the Band was overstated. To arrive at the number $1,999,815, there were included such items as opening surpluses, transfers between funds, monies received by the Band as an agent on behalf of locatees, monies received by the Band as agents for other purposes, and inexplicably, the $900,763 figure, which represented the contributions from the Department of Indian Affairs.

After eliminating the above-mentioned items, a closer look at the financial statements would show that the revenue which could be ascribed to the Band was $386,193 and was about 20 per cent of the Band's total revenue rather than 69 per cent, as stated in the report from the Director of Economic Development. I have no reason to believe that he was endeavouring to mislead anyone, but he appears to have been greatly confused about the true state of financial affairs.

c) Another instance of misunderstanding of the Band revenue figures appeared in Mr. Walchli's testimony. He appears to have let the misleading style of financial reporting creep into his thinking. In the course of giving testimony as to the ability of the Westbank Indian Band to support itself from its own revenues, he said: "the intent here was that as bands developed economically and start to generate their own revenue, that they would start taking on paying some of the cost of services. There is a couple of examples I could give you". (Here he dealt with the finances of another band) and then he continued with regard to Westbank: "In terms of Westbank, it went up from somewhere from around, and I think these figures are correct — the Band was contributing back in '75 about $39,000, and at the end of the ten-year period, they were around $3.2 million or somewhere around that, and paying for a lot of their own programs. . . ."

The figure of $3.2 million does not appear in the financial statements for 1985 as revenue. However, assuming that the figure Mr. Walchli gave in evidence was a ballpark figure, he could only get there by the process of double counting previously referred to or by including non-recurring items, such as the proceeds of cut-off claims.

It appears to me that if the Department's Director of Economic Development and the Regional Director General can be led into this state of confusion by the financial statements, there is little, if any, hope that an individual Band member could obtain a true and accurate picture of what was occurring concerning Band finances. This sort of accounting is not helpful in providing information with respect to the real state of affairs of the Band and Band-related entities, and it can, as we have seen, result in serious misapprehension about the actual state of affairs.

2) Failure to Provide Financial Statements and Information about Band Enterprises and Activities

Although there appeared to be excessive detail in some areas, there was a dearth of information in others. The Westbank Band has displayed considerable initiative in undertaking new business ventures. Those initiatives have not always been successful. That is not necessarily to be criticized because the time period examined by the Commission covered some relatively difficult times for the Okanagan area. As stated elsewhere in this Report, the Band was the owner of the Westbank Indian Band Development Company Ltd. (DevCo). The shares in the company were held in trust for the Band. The directors of the company included the Chief and councillors of the Band, and other Band members were also appointed. The Development Company in turn controlled a number of companies which carried on different enterprises for the Band.

There were a number of instances of lendings and borrowings among subsidiaries, the parent company, and the Band. A retrospective look at those transactions does not always provide a logical explanation for them, but presumably those transfers of monies were made on a needs basis. Band members do not appear to have had ready access to the financial statements of DevCo, or to the financial statements of its subsidiaries. This lack of financial information with regard to the Band's business activities may have had a disquieting effect upon those who were not supporters of the Band government of the day. As the dealings of the subsidiaries sometimes involved members of the Band government or their families, the perception of conflict of interest often occurred. More complete standards of disclosure might have cooled some of the rumours. As well, fuller disclosure would ensure that conflict of interest situations would be addressed at the outset.

The statements of the Band itself cannot adequately reflect the corporate activity of its subsidiaries. Band financial statements in later years bordered on the obscure when it came to the activities of businesses owned and operated by the Band. For the year ending March 31, 1985, the sole information in the Band statements was the entry on the balance sheet of:

Investments (Note 4) $1,227,729

Note 4 is reproduced here in its entirety:

4. Investment	$
Westbank Indian Band Development Company Limited (wholly owned subsidiary)	
Shares at cost	5
Advances	(454,892)
Westbank Indian Band Nonprofit Housing Project	
Advances	11,826
Westbank Indian Band Pine Acres Home (formerly Intermediate Care Facility)	
Advances	24,861
W I B CO Construction Ltd.	
Advances	320,019
Lakeridge Realty Ltd.	
Advances	48,831
Northland Bank	
Shares at cost	1,277,079
	1,227,729

The Westbank Indian Band Development Company Limited is wholly owned by the Westbank Indian Band. The shares are held in trust by the directors for the Westbank Indian Band.

In corporate accounting, investments are generally shown on a cost basis or an equity basis. Essentially the former ascribes to an investment its acquisition cost and the latter takes into account in addition a pro rata share of the subsequent earnings or losses. Note 4 is something different. Investments, properly so-called, confer upon the investor some form of property interest. Except for the $5 ascribed for shares in the Westbank Indian Band Development Company and the $1,277,079 ascribed for the Northland Bank shares at cost, the monies listed in Note 4 are not investments. These other amounts apparently represent accounts receivable which were unsecured in any manner, and for which there were no agreed terms of repayment. In some instances repayment was (and is) problematical.

Describing the $454,892 as an advance to the Westbank Indian Band Development Company Ltd. is an unorthodox way to portray the value of an investment and obscures a complicated story. As pointed out elsewhere in the Report, the Westbank Indian Band entered into a 99-year lease arrangement with DevCo. DevCo undertook development of the residential subdivision on Reserve 10 known as "Lakeridge". There remained a large amount of money owing to the Band from DevCo under the head lease. That debt continued to show on the financial statements of DevCo, but was not correspondingly reflected on the statements of the Band. Sometimes it received monies from DevCo and credited them to the lease payments, but the account receivable from DevCo was not shown as such on the Band's financial statements. The $454,892 advance referred to under Note 4 is thought to reflect monies borrowed by DevCo from the Northland Bank, and in turn passed on to the Band and used for erection of the Band office building. The monies owed to the Band under the lease exceeded the monies advanced by DevCo to the Band, so the bracketed numbers are not a true reflection of the state of accounts between those two entities. It seems that even if the approach used in valuing the investment in DevCo were acceptable, the number would not be right.

The value ascribed to the Band-owned corporations appears to be an exercise in netting out the various advances between those corporations. If that was the case, it was both misleading and unorthodox. A different firm of auditors prepared the Band's financial statements for the year ending March 31, 1986. They showed Band investments in a more orthodox way and added an appropriate note to reflect the fact that the Northland Bank shares appeared to be worthless. But a tangled web of intercorporate loans and advances was obscurely portrayed in a single amount on the liabilities side of the Band Balance Sheet, which showed:

"Advances from related entities" $41,285

The audit working papers reflected the following picture:

Amounts payable by the Band: $ $

DevCo (presumably this debt was
created by the borrowing of monies
by DevCo from the Northland Bank and
the use thereof in the construction of
the office building)   653,938

Amounts payable by the Band (cont.):		$	$
Westbank Indian Band Nonprofit Housing Project		47,110	701,048

Amounts receivable by the Band:	$	
Hyde Park Image Creators Inc.	59,002	
Toussowasket Custom Framers Ltd.	15,751	
Lakeridge Realty Ltd. (net)	68,848	
Lakeridge Insurance Services Ltd.	5,000	
Pine Acres Home (a Society)	70,218	
Sookinchute Utility Corp.	1,035	
WIBCO Construction Ltd.	337,992	
Wild'N'Wet Amusement Park Ltd.	101,917	659,763

Advances from related entities, per Balance Sheet		41,285

Source: Auditors' working papers.

These figures were not carried through to the financial statements. The reader of the financial statements would be limited to learning that the Band owed $41,285 to related entities. The reader would not know that DevCo had been borrowing from the Northland Bank and passing those borrowings to the Band for erection of its office building or that there were significant debts owing by the subsidiary to the Band. No ordinary reader would have any inkling of the amounts of money that came from (or went to) the Band entities. Legitimate questions about the appropriateness of making those advances could not be raised because adequate facts were not disclosed.

3) The Failure to Deal with the Apparent Problems or Inconsistencies in the Financial Statements

Since 1980, the Band has made annual per capita payments to individual Band members. The Band and Band Council Resolutions have stated that the per capita payment to underaged members of the Band shall be "credited to a trust account". Generally, the Band has required that parents or guardians of infant Band members apply on their behalf. The application forms included the wording: "I agree that these monies will be deposited in a trust account in the name of the Westbank Indian Band. . .".

From time to time, concerned Band members, particularly those living away from the Reserve, have made inquiries on behalf of their children. Correspondence from the former Chief and the Band Administrator appeared to suggest that some separate fund was in existence.

In a letter sent to a Band member in April 1985, then Chief Ronald Derrickson wrote: "You keep writing about your childrens' Band Grant. We have told you time and time again, the payment of the Grant is not awarded to minors' parents. It is placed in the trust account until the age of nineteen and given only to the children themselves." That letter was copied to the Minister and several senior officials of the Department. In fact, the monies voted for the minors have not been set aside in any specific trust fund.

After 1984, the discerning reader would have seen that the item on the balance sheet titled "Funds Held in Trust for Band Members" was far less than the item on the liability side of the Balance Sheet entitled "Trust Liability". Those items should have been equal. The balance sheet showed the following discrepancies:

Per Balance Sheets

As at March 31	Funds held in trust for Band members	Trust Liability	Shortfall
	A	B	B-A
	$	$	$
1984	372,096	648,833	276,737
1985	275,169	639,123	363,954
1986	27,880	648,155	620,275

There has been some confusion among the Band members as to what became of the minors' trust monies. The simple answer appears to be that they were never set apart in a trust fund. Just after the collapse of the Northland Bank in late 1985, the Westbank Chief and councillors received a letter quoted hereafter in part:

I read the newsletter of October 2/85 regarding the monies in Northland Bank, Edmonton, Alta. I want to know if my son's grant monies were in that Bank when it collapsed. If not, I would like to know where there [sic] situated. . .

The Band Administrator, Mr. Schwartz, answered that letter on November 4, 1985:

Dear Band member:
   Your letter of no date, received on October 31 1985, was referred to Council. . . .
   The grant monies held on behalf of the minors (19 and under) had nothing to do with the bank so indicated in your letter. All payments

have been made and will continue to be made as a minor reaches the age of 19.

We do not issue statements from any bank showing calculated interest for any individual minor until the minor reaches the age of 19, when we get approval to make a pay out.

Counsel for the former Band executive, who also acted for Mr. Schwartz, made the following submission with regard to the minors' trust fund:

> The evidence of Mr. Schwartz and the former Chief Ron Derrickson was that as these commitments came due, they were met and paid by the Band, although a special account was never set up. This problem became known to both the Administrator, Mr. Schwartz, and to the former Chief and councillors at an early stage and was brought to their attention by the auditors. Once this problem became known, there were steps taken to create and fund this special trust account. These monies were to come from the cut-off settlement. These funds have since been approved by the Band and deposited in the Northland Bank. However, these funds were tied up in the Northland Bank negotiations on loans, and these funds have not been released.

It is difficult to reconcile that submission with the assertion of Mr. Schwartz in his 1985 letter that the "grant monies. . .had nothing to do with the bank" (Northland). After hearing from various witnesses concerning the "minors' trust fund", I had the impression that it might be more appropriately termed the "mystery fund". It had a singularly elusive quality and its locus was never fixed, the reason being that the fund never existed. As I said to counsel during the hearings, I was not convinced that there had to be monies placed in trust as a matter of law, but it seems to me quite misleading to describe the future liability as a "trust fund" when in fact it is simply an unfunded liability.

The gist of the evidence of the Administrator and of the former Chief was that although there was no special trust account set aside, it was intended that the liability to minors would be funded from highway monies on deposit with the Northland Bank. This may be difficult to achieve because of the complex nature of the obligations existing between the failed Bank and the Westbank Band and companies. Mr. Schwartz's testimony was that the trust liability now owing is around $700,000 (Transcripts: Volume LIII, p. 7667). The Commission is aware that negotiations have been carried on between the Receivers of the Northland Bank and officials of the Band to resolve outstanding issues. Funds will be available to satisfy this unfunded liability to the extent that former deposits in the Bank can be recovered. Had the Band members been aware that no monies voted for the benefit of minors were being set aside in a separate fund, it might well have affected their decisions on other matters. The use of the term "minors' trust fund" was unfortunate in that it implied such a thing existed.

At a Band general meeting held on December 12, 1983, Band members voted to authorize payment to locatees of the amounts they had agreed to accept in the highway settlement. The money to pay the locatees was drawn, not from the Ministry of Transportation and Highways of British Columbia, but from the proceeds of the cut-off settlement provided by the federal government. Of $3,211,711 paid to locatees, the then Chief's immediate family received $2,139,959 (67%). At this same meeting, the Band members voted a $3,000 per capita distribution to each Band member. The monies for the infant children were to be put in a "special trust account". That was not done and the liability to the minors remains unfunded. Would Band members have taken the same course if they had realized that no separate trust fund existed? Or would they have insisted that the interests of the minors be protected before full payment of large amounts was made to individual adults? These questions can never be answered because disclosure of who was getting what was not made. This was a failure of the then executive.

The financial statements of the Band are provided annually to the Department. Department officials must have reviewed the Band's balance sheet each year. However, no initiative seems to have been taken to notify Band members of the lack of trust funding, or to require or request the Band to describe the grants differently so that the Band members would not be misled. As of August 1987, when the hearings concluded, the unfunded liability still existed. I know that this is a grave concern to the present Band administration.

The Department has recognized that this area of minor trust funds is a concern throughout the country — it is a matter that can arise from time to time in many bands. Counsel for the Department said:

> It is here suggested that a recommendation be made that the Indian Act be amended so as to require that when a band with Section 69 authority is making a distribution of revenue funds to its members, it be required to place in a trust account that portion of the funds attributable to the underage members of the band so that it will be available to them as they reach their majority.

This submission seems sensible to me and I endorse it. I think it would produce great controversy to have a repetition of the Westbank Band's situation, where there is a large unfunded liability and no designated fund to satisfy it. Expectations were created but no adequate steps were taken to ensure that they could be realized.

4) Failure to Disclose Significant Transactions between Members of the Band Government and the Band Itself

As related in other chapters of this Report, there were a number of transactions which could hardly be said to have been conducted on an arm's length basis. In the governance of Indian bands, it would seem virtually impossible to avoid transactions between the band and individuals (and their direct relations) involved in band government. In orthodox accounting, transactions that involve "related parties" are subject to disclosure. The Westbank matters noted below are instances where such disclosure would be called for.

— the purchase of Chancery Hair Design Ltd. (later renamed Hyde Park Image Creators Inc.);
— the purchase of Toussowasket Custom Framers Ltd.;
— the conveyance of a Vancouver condominium from Noll Derriksan to the Band;
— the payment to Chief Derrickson and to Noll Derriksan of substantial sums of money for "severances" arising from the Highway 97 construction;
— truck and other equipment rentals paid to Chief Derrickson and councillor Brian Eli. Evidence was given that Councillor Eli, during the financial years 1982 to 1986, was paid rentals of about $73,000 for the rental of a 1976 three-ton truck. Those payments were made by the Band-owned construction company. It was not clear whether Councillor Eli paid the driver, but the Band appears to have bought the truck several times over;
— payment by the Band to Waterslide Campground Ltd. of $100,000. Those monies were provided by the Ministry of Highways in payment of the McDougall Creek contract and Ronald Derrickson is a principal of Waterslide Campground Ltd.;
— payment by the Band of funds to Chief Derrickson in exchange for land required as initial payment on the Band purchase of Wild'N'Wet waterslide.

The Role of the Department

The Department exercises great influence over band accounting matters and standards of disclosure in financial statements. This influence is exercised through the various editions of *Accounting Guidelines for Indian Bands* in Canada, through Department staff dealing with band staff, and the provision of courses sponsored by the Department. The Department's approach has been heavily focused on information required or desired by the Department. There is little to indicate that the Department has been "watching out" for band members, ensuring that they have been adequately informed about the government of their band and the conduct of band business ventures.

The Department seems to be gradually assuming a less prominent role in the administration of band finances. The newly developed Alternative Funding Arrangements (AFA) will give bands more flexibility to determine the best use of monies and will allow them to plan for periods of up to five years. Obviously, once an Arrangement is in place, less Departmental input will be required. It seems desirable that a way be found to offer non-AFA bands greater flexibility as well. Given such flexibility, adequate and timely disclosure to band members will be increasingly necessary.

The current restructuring of the Department's role already recognizes the new reality. The Departmental people who previously dealt with bands were called "Band Financial Advisers". Today the Departmental people, who have a less active role than their predecessors, are called "Fund Management Officers". This seems to be a recognition that the Department usually cannot provide all the advice bands require because:

— financial statements of band enterprises, incorporated or not, may not be included with the financial information supplied to the Department. That approach is understandable; if there is no Departmental funding involved, there is no "need to know". But without such information any advice may be faulty;
— advising band management in certain areas, especially band enterprises, is likely far beyond the training and experience of many Departmental people, whose required skills are different;
— Departmental staff time may be inadequate to provide the appropriate assistance;
— there is, or could be, concern about civil liability for what is later determined to be "bad" advice;
— there is no guarantee that a band would take the Department's advice.

In earlier days, the Department had very extensive authority over band finances. Today, much greater responsibility and authority is being exercised by band councils. Band members will have to be more vigilant about band affairs. They can only exercise vigilance if they have the means of finding out the facts. Clearer financial reporting is vital for effective self-government.

Chapter 7

Mobile Home Parks

During the period of almost 11 years referred to in the Commission's Terms of Reference, a burgeoning of mobile home parks took place on Westbank Reserve 9. Wisely, the planning and policy of the Band and of the Department of Indian Affairs precluded the development of mobile home parks on Reserve 10.

Reserve 9 is located immediately northeast of the village of Westbank, and before it was augmented by lands acquired in a cut-off settlement, it was a reserve of some 1540 acres.

Both Reserves 9 and 10 were the subject of a planning study by Interform Planning and Design Ltd. in 1973. The plan proposed the development of a model community on Reserve 10, but had more prosaic aspirations for Reserve 9. It described the uses of Reserve 9 at that time as follows:

> Present uses on the land include housing sites, a small amount of farming, some grape production on leased parcels, a mobile home park, a stock car race track at the north end, and a mobile home park and picnic area in the lakeshore area.

The mobile home park at the north end of the Reserve was operated by Park Mobile Homes Sales Ltd., a company owned by the Yorks. The stock car race track was to become the site of the Mt. Boucherie (Toussowasket) mobile home park of Noll Derriksan. The 1973 study described the site on the lakeshore as follows:

> The lakeshore site is presently in use as a mobile home park and campsite. The quality of the park is sub-standard and should be improved as much as possible. However, it should not be expanded beyond present lease limits. Over the coming years, the site will substantially appreciate in value, and the option for better economic use of the general site should be kept open.

The Interform report did not fully anticipate the tremendous growth of the non-Indian population on Reserve 9. It was in 1976 and the immediately ensuing years that the acceleration of mobile home park development took place. That development brought with it many of the political problems that beset Westbank in the period under review (1975–86). The Commission heard that whereas there were about 250 members of the Westbank Indian Band, some 3000 to 5000 non-Indians also resided on Reserves 9 and 10 during this period.

By 1976, the mobile home park was an idea whose time had come for the Okanagan region. A number of parks were developed on lands owned by Chief Ron Derrickson, his brother Noll (a former Chief), and his father Theodore. The lands on the southern lakeshore flats were lands of the Tomat family which were to be divided into three parks and part of a fourth.

A Mr. Schlief commenced the development of a mobile home park on Reserve 10 on lands occupied by Henry and Millie Jack as locatees. It appears that the then Regional Director General of Indian Affairs, Mr. Fred Walchli, and Chief Derrickson moved quickly, if not somewhat arbitrarily, to stop that development.

Save for the York family, the mobile home park operators had few apparent problems with the Band or with the Department of Indian Affairs during the 1970's. The problems that beset the mobile home park operators in the early 1980's could have been foreseen by anyone who was aware of the Yorks' situation, but that knowledge was not widespread.

As noted elsewhere in this Report, the relationship between the Yorks, on the one hand, and Noll Derriksan and the Westbank Indian Band on the other, had become confrontational and antagonistic by 1977. In 1977, the Department confirmed the allotment of a Band road to Noll Derriksan, which had the potential effect of barring legal access to a substantial portion of the Yorks' (Park Mobile) mobile home park. The strip of land which was an unused Band road was allotted to Noll Derriksan. He, in turn, took legal proceedings against Park Mobile Home Sales Ltd. to remove encroachments from the road and to effect cancellation of the lease alleging purported lease violations. Having permitted the allotment of the roadway to Noll Derriksan, the Department was quick to support Noll Derriksan and the Band government in negotiating a higher rent, using the roadway as a bargaining feature.

Otherwise, however, mobile home park operators developed and operated their businesses in fairly stable circumstances. In late 1976, when Ronald Derrickson became Chief, a major expansion of mobile home parks on Reserve 9 was under way. Mr. Derrickson himself was the locatee of lands that had been leased to (1) Golden Acres Ltd., a company of the Crosby family, (2) Mr. and Mrs. Jack Alexander, who developed a mobile home park by the name of Pineridge Estates, and (3) part of a development by Westgate Developments Ltd., a company of the late Mr. Ted Zelmer. Elsewhere on the Reserve, Noll Derriksan was the locatee for Park Mobile Homes Ltd. and for Toussowasket Enterprises Ltd.

When Ronald Derrickson came to power in 1976, the terms of most of the leases had been agreed upon earlier. It appears that the new

Chief thought the rents being paid by the park operators were too low, but it was several years before the mechanisms in place would permit rents to be raised.

A feature of the mobile park scene at that time was the assertion of jurisdiction over mobile home parks on Indian reserves by the British Columbia Rentalsman. Rent controls had been imposed at Westbank and the Rentalsman's jurisdiction had been affirmed by the British Columbia Court of Appeal in the case of Park Mobile Home Sales Ltd. v. LeGreely, a decision of the B.C. Court of Appeal reported at (1978) 85 D.L.R. (3rd) 618. That decision was reaffirmed by Mr. Justice Locke in March 1982 in a case involving the Mt. Boucherie Park.

The former Chief's view of the fairness of the rents was cogently stated in testimony he gave before the Commission. He said:

> ...one of my concerns has always been that we have many Band members who are in effect millionaires, if you look at their land holdings. Many Band members are millionaires, yet they're on welfare.
> That's a crime. That's a damn crime, that people with that kind of land holdings and that kind of potential should be on welfare. It is a worse crime when some trailer park operator has these and is using these to his advantage and not returning a fair rental.

Chief Derrickson recounted in evidence how the Band had dealt with the so-called Voth lease (the lease by the lakeshore on Reserve 9). Mr. Voth apparently held a head lease and had two sub-lessees, with all three parties operating mobile home parks. Mr. Derrickson gave testimony that rents for the locatees were increased substantially. When asked by his counsel about this matter, he gave the following answer:

> Q Now when you say substantially increased, you're not talking in terms of 10 or 20 per cent or 25 per cent. You're talking about 3 or 4 times or perhaps even higher than what they were paying previously. Is that correct?
> A Maybe even 5 or 6 times.

When the time came to review the rents, the methods used by Mr. Derrickson to increase them were ingenious and bold. Mr. Derrickson relied, to some extent, on the patina of authority conferred upon the Chief and council by the Department of Indian Affairs. In most instances, he purported to act under the "1977 Agreement". He also relied to some extent upon what some operators perceived as discriminatory use of by-laws and he was not above using hyperbole. To some people, he seemed omnipotent. The former Regional Director General, Fred Walchli, gave evidence with respect to powers conferred upon the Chief and council:

> Any activities the Westbank Band undertook by way of land administration were controlled by the Department, and they did not

have authority under this agreement to execute or cancel any agreements. That remained with the Department.

At the Commission hearings, the Department took the position that authority was never given to the Westbank Band under the 1977 Agreement to do anything but administer leases, and while they could discuss rent, they did not have rent fixing authority.

That position was belied by the conduct of the Department, which at times acted to create the impression that the Chief had the power, while at the same time it consciously withheld such power. In any event, Chief Derrickson asserted decision-making powers. The Chief was of the view that the mobile home park operators had signed their leases of their own free will with legal advice.

His major move towards rent increases occurred in late 1981 and early 1982. Notices were sent to all the mobile home park operators in 1981 and ultimately a meeting was held between the Chief and the operators in early October 1981. At that time the usual monthly rents charged were in the vicinity of $90–120 per mobile home pad. To some extent the level of rents depended upon the rules and practices of the British Columbia Rentalsman. The lessors had to limit rental increases to a maximum percentage unless they received approval from the Rentalsman for a larger increase. As previously mentioned, the B.C. Rentalsman had been successful in asserting his jurisdiction when challenged. As long as that jurisdiction was maintained, rental increases would be limited.

Among those present at the meeting convened by the Chief were the Yorks, Ted Zelmer, Leonard Crosby, the Lauriaults, the Lidsters, Val Spring and Councillor Brian Eli. Those assembled were told that the Band had passed its own Rentalsman by-law and that the B.C. Rentalsman had no jurisdiction on Band land. According to Mr. Lauriault, the Chief explained at the meeting:

> that they now had their own powers and that they could set the rents on Indian land. The Chief said that part of the rent increase was to upgrade that area of the Reserve, in other words, sewer and water, etc. . . .

The Chief announced that pad rents for all mobile home parks would be increased to $150 a month. At the same time he said that the leases with the mobile home operators would be modified so that in lieu of the fixed rent, there would be an alternative rental of 20 per cent of the gross receipts, whichever was greater.

The mobile home park operators were supplied with notices to be forwarded to all their tenants to the effect that the rents were to be raised to $150 per month. These notices contained a note at the bottom of the page:

The Westbank Indian Band Council under by-law 1981–03 have established by Resolution that mobile home park owners who are situated on Reserve property are to increase pad fees to a minimum of $150 per month.

Not only was the power of the Band Council to pass such a resolution legally non-existent, there also was no by-law 1981–03. Such a by-law had been passed by the Council on July 28, 1981, but it apparently had been disallowed by the Department. However, it appears that the rejected by-law was distributed as though it was in force. The by-law recited in its preamble that the Band had been granted Section 60(1) powers under the Indian Act, which was not the fact. It called for the appointment of a "Band Rentalsman". It gave the Rentalsman wide powers of investigation, including the powers and privileges, of a Commissioner under the Inquiries Act. This by-law also gave the Band Rentalsman jurisdiction to make orders in a wide variety of circumstances. It empowered him to establish maximum percentage rent increases and to "review, exclude or declare unenforceable any covenant in a lease permit or agreement, which he finds to be unreasonable in the circumstances".

At the meeting, Mr. Crosby requested an authenticated copy of the by-law and received it. This document, which was entered in evidence, was purportedly passed by Council and was signed by the Chief and the then councillors. Mr. Crosby, at the meeting, persisted and asked for some indication of approval by the Department. According to Mr. Crosby, the Chief said "no, they didn't have it right now because the by-law had to be sent back to change one or two words. . .". Mr. Crosby was left with the impression, however, that the by-law had been approved or authenticated in Ottawa.

Some park operators distributed the notices of rental increases which resulted in considerable turmoil. The tenants of the parks did not welcome this initiative of the Chief. It appears the measure was largely effective in establishing a temporary increase in rents in the various parks. The results were not quite what the Chief may have envisioned. The British Columbia Rentalsman continued to assert his jurisdiction and certain rollbacks were made. The B.C. Rentalsman continued to impede efforts to increase rents at the parks.

The tactics used by the Chief in 1981 and 1982 resulted in significant increases in the rent paid by such operators as the Alexanders, the Zelmers, and the Lidsters, all of whom came to terms with the Band about that time. It might be said that in achieving those rent increases, the Chief played hard ball. The Alexander example is illustrative.

The Alexanders

Mr. Alexander and his wife Barbara are the operators of Pineridge Estates. The Alexanders negotiated with Ronald Derrickson in 1976 to lease some 21 acres of land on which Mr. Derrickson was locatee. The lease was dated June 21, 1976, and the rental for the first five-year period was set at $9,654.30 per annum. The lease contained a further provision that the rent would be revised every five years. Specifically, the lease stated that "the Minister or his authorized representative may determine and fix the yearly rent for the second or any subsequent five-year period". The rent was to be "the amount which is, on the 90 days before the five-year period begins, in the opinion of the Minister a fair market rent for the land leased, on the terms and conditions contained in this lease, and enjoying all the services and amenities then existing, but ignoring the value of any permanent improvements made on the land by the tenant". The lease document provided for an appeal to the Federal Court within 60 days after a rental determination.

The lease contained a provision which allowed the lessee to take water from McDougall Creek. There was inadequate water supply for this area, which poses an ongoing problem for the Alexanders. I comment on possible action to alleviate such problems in Appendix C of this Report.

The Alexanders operated the park without serious problems for some time. In 1980, they received a letter from the Chief, with a *Vancouver Sun* article entitled "B.C. Rentalsman Scalped by Indian Act" enclosed. An arrow was opposite a paragraph which read:

> A section of the century old Federal Indian Act allows Indian Bands to ignore provincial, residential tenancy laws and treat non-Indian tenants on their land any way they please.

In February 1981, the Alexanders received the following letter:

February 12, 1981

"DOUBLE REGISTERED"

Jack Ellis Alexander and
Barbara Alexander
RR #1 Boucherie Rd.
Westbank, B.C.
V0H 2A0

Dear Sir:

Re: Rent Review
    Lease No. 49610
    Portion of Lot 45, Indian Reserve No. 9

This is to advise that the subject leasehold property rental is to be reviewed on May 1, 1981.

The new rental has been set on behalf of the Minister at Forty two thousand nine hundred eight ($42,908.00) Dollars per annum for the next five year term.

If you should disagree with the amount set please refer to Page 4(i) wherein you may refer this matter to the Federal Court of Canada under Section 17 of the Federal Court Act. This may not be referred to the Federal Court unless the new amount requested by the Minister is paid first.

Should you agree with the amount set, please make an appointment with this office and a modification agreement to the lease will be drafted.

Yours very truly.

WESTBANK INDIAN COUNCIL

"Ronald M. Derrickson"

Chief Ronald M. Derrickson.

178

The letter was sent double registered and was copied to Mr. S. McCullough, a member of the Lands, Reserves and Trusts Directorate at Indian Affairs. The letter did not say who had set the rent on behalf of the Minister. It would seem it was Ronald Derrickson. Nothing in Mr. Alexander's 1976 lease required that the new rental be embodied in a modification agreement. Modification agreements became the mechanism for achieving a percentage rental as an alternative to a fixed rental.

Mr. Alexander took the letter of February 12, 1981 to the Kelowna law firm of Salloum, Doak. Mr. Welder, who was then an articled student, handled this matter. The Alexanders next received this letter:

March 27, 1981

"DOUBLE REGISTERED"

Jack Ellis & Barbara Alexander
RR # 1, Boucherie Rd.
Westbank, B.C.
V0H 2A0

Dear Sir:

Reference is made to our letter to you dated Feb. 12, 1981, suggesting the new rental figure for the next five year period of your lease and also to our recent telephone conversation wherein you promised to speak to me within three (3) days of our conversation.

As three weeks have now passed and we have not heard from you, we are withdrawing our offer of rental to you but not our notice of rental increase.

I am therefore instructing the Band Appraiser, Robert Dephyffer to do an appraisal of the entire property as per the conditions of the lease. This appraisal is to be done solely for the purpose of establishing a rent in the Federal Court of Canada. We are now at the stage of negotiating rents in amounts up to $2,500.00 per acre per annum or 25% of the gross receipts whichever is the greater.

Because of the extreme cost of a Federal Court appraisal the Westbank Indian Council cannot consider our previous offer. I would advise you to get legal advice and supply the name of your legal Counsel to the Westbank Indian Band so we can have the Dept. of Justice make contact with them as to the court date and to advise you of the conditions you must meet before you take this matter to the Federal Court if this is indeed your choice.

Yours very truly,

WESTBANK INDIAN COUNCIL

"Barbara DeSchutter"
"for" Chief Ronald M. Derrickson

RMD/bdes

Mr. Welder made a counter-offer which was ultimately rejected. Before it was rejected, the Alexanders received a barrage of correspondence calling for approvals from the Dominion Fire Marshall and the Department of Health and Welfare, asking for soil tests, insurance policies, surveys, and plans. Correspondence was copied to the FBDB, the Band solicitor, and officials in the Department, and was to continue until the rent issue was settled. It seemed unusual that these issues were raised five years after the mobile home park was in place, and terminated when the rent issue was settled. During the course of this correspondence the Alexanders complied with each request, only to be met with requests for further information. Another letter was sent to Mr. Alexander asking that he evict certain tenants whose children had allegedly damaged fourplex buildings near the Alexanders' mobile home park. Those fourplexes were owned by the Chief.

An interesting aspect of the settlement of the Alexanders' rent was the role played by the Regional Director General of Indian Affairs.

In a letter dated May 22, 1981, Mr. Welder (by then having been called to the bar) wrote:

> You refer in your letter of May 21 to your letter of February 12, 1981. In that letter you stated that you would be setting the rent on behalf of the Ministry at $42,908. Under the terms of the lease the Minister or his authorized representative may determine and fix the yearly rent for the second or any subsequent five year period, either before or after the five year period has begun. In this regard we would request that you provide us with written authorization from the Minister that appoints you his representative to fix the yearly rent on this lease.

Evidence of the authority was soon forthcoming. The Regional Director General wrote a letter as follows:

"VIA LOOMIS"

May 26th, 1981

Westbank Indian Band Council,
Box 850,
Westbank, B.C.
V0H 2A0

Attention: Chief R. Derrickson

Dear Chief Derrickson:

Questions continue to be raised by several leasehold occupiers of your reserve lands as to the authority provided to your Band through the Band Council to manage and control alienated lands.

Your Band has been declared as having reached an advanced stage of development and has subsequently been granted certain authorities and responsibilities by both the Minister and the Regional Director General. These authorities include the responsibility of managing and controlling revenue monies, including the collection of rentals due to the Band and Band Members; the responsibility for managing, negotiating and enforcing lease and permit agreements entered into by the Crown for the direct benefit of the Band and Band Members; and the responsibility for managing and administering all surrendered reserve lands through the Band Council on behalf of the Department.

It is intended that this letter be used in those instances where the authority and responsibilities of the Westbank Indian Band Council might be questioned.

Yours truly,

"F. J. Walchli"

F. J. Walchli,
Regional Director General,
British Columbia Region

By letter dated May 28, 1981 Chief Derrickson sent a copy of Mr. Walchli's letter to the Alexanders' solicitors, and the Band solicitor Mr. Graham Allen wrote to the Alexanders' solicitors on June 2 in part as follows:

> The Westbank Indian Council has referred to my attention its file concerning the May 1, 1981 rental review for Lease No. 49610, held by your clients Mr. and Mrs. J. Alexander.
>
> My understanding of the situation is that, by rent notice dated February 12, 1981 received by Mr. and Mrs. Alexander on February 18th, Chief R.M. Derrickson gave notice that the yearly rent for the five year period commencing from May 1, 1981 had been determined and fixed at $42,908.00 pursuant to the provisions of subsections 1(e) and 1(f) of the Lease. Chief Derrickson's authority to give such notice is clearly acknowledged in the attached letter of May 26, 1981 from Mr. F. J. Walchli, Regional Director General of the B.C. Region, Department of Indian Affairs.

Mr. Allen went on to take the position that the time within which an appeal should have been taken was 60 days after February 18 and that the payment of $42,908 was a prerequisite to the taking of the appeal. He concluded:

> It is my opinion that Mr. and Mrs. Alexander have failed to pay rent as required by the terms and conditions of lease No. 49610. I have accordingly advised my client, the Westbank Indian Council, that, if it so wished, it is now in a position to seek immediate cancellation of this Lease.

When carefully perused, Mr. Walchli's letter does not clearly acknowledge the Band's authority to set the rent under the Alexander lease. It is easy to see, however, that the letter could create such an impression. I cannot help thinking that it was intended to give an impression that the Chief had quite wide- ranging authority.

It is a fact that the Band had been declared "as having reached an advanced state of development". That declaration was made in accordance with Section 83(1) of the Indian Act, which provides that where such a declaration is made by the Governor in Council, a band may make and pass by-laws on certain subjects. The Band had been granted certain authorities and responsibilities in the "1977 Agreement" executed by the Regional Director General on behalf of the Government of Canada. The Band also had been granted, under Section 53(1) of the Indian Act, powers which authorized it to manage and administer surrendered lands. The Band also had authority to manage and control their revenue monies under Section 69 of the Indian Act.

The question of fixing rents was not addressed in the 1977 Agreement and I do not believe it was intended to transfer this function. The power to fix rents under the Alexander lease and other Westbank leases does not appear to have been expressly delegated by the Minister or the Department to the Band executive or Band. The authority to determine the rent for ensuing five-year periods under the Westbank leases arose from the contract documents and, in the terms of most leases, it was given to "the Minister or his authorized representative". That phrase could mean several things. It could mean the Minister or someone designated by him specifically for that purpose; or it could mean an appropriate official within the Department. If it means the former, the Minister never authorized anyone to exercise the power. If it means the second, it is not clear that the power could be delegated to someone outside the Department. I think the general intention of the agreements was to have this function reside in a Departmental official. I incline to the view that it would be possible under such phraseology to give to an outsider the power to fix rents. I would think that the Department would want to carefully consider any such appointment or delegation. In any event, not even a purported delegation was made. What did happen was that the Department stood idly by watching Chief Derrickson purport to exercise rent-fixing authority. The Alexanders' solicitors did commence action in Federal Court, but did not carry it to a conclusion. Ultimately, the Alexanders succumbed to the negotiation techniques of Chief Derrickson. Mr. Alexander gave evidence of a meeting between himself and Chief Derrickson:

Q Will you tell us what you remember of that meeting?
A Well, I was at the Band office, and we were talking about taking it to Federal Court, and Ron Derrickson said I can break you because. . . .
Q Pardon me?
A Ron Derrickson said I can break you because it doesn't cost me anything in court and it's costing you $1,000 a day. He just came right out and said he could break me.

Mr. Alexander said in evidence: "I didn't have any money to carry on, and I knew what it was going to cost me per day in court, and I couldn't afford to take the chance." He agreed to pay the $42,908 per annum, or 20 per cent of his gross receipts, whichever was greater. As it happens, he has only had to pay the $42,908 per year. In the ensuing five years, Mr. Alexander managed to pay the rent (with some difficulty). He encountered some problems with the supply of water and he has suffered some ill health. Not the least of his problems in obtaining water was the shift of McDougall Creek, referred to in Appendix C of this Report. The shift appears to have deprived him of water he was expecting to receive under his lease.

In 1985, the Band was granted certain management powers regarding Band lands under Section 60 of the Indian Act. There was no specific reference in the powers conferred to fix rents under leases of Band lands. On April 1, 1986, Mr. Alexander received a letter which included the following paragraph:

> This letter will serve as your official notice under the terms and conditions of your lease, that your rent will be reviewed for the next five-year term. Without formal appraisal, but in line with negotiated settlements with other leases in the area, the new rental for the period May 1, 1986 to April 30, 1991 has been set on behalf of the Minister at $69,712.50 or 25% of the gross annual receipts, whichever is the greater.

That letter was brought to the attention of David Crombie, the then Minister of Indian Affairs, who in a letter to the Chief asked him to revoke the letter of April 1. Since that time, the question of Mr. Alexander's rent appears to have been on hold. Given the background, it is not difficult to foresee future problems.

Leonard Crosby

The antagonism between former Chief Derrickson and some operators of mobile home parks was most notably displayed in the case of Mr. Derrickson and Mr. Leonard Crosby.

As noted in the Introduction to this Report, Mr. Crosby entered into his first lease on Westbank Reserve 9 in 1969. He was then serving in the R.C.M.P. and stationed in Kelowna. At the time Mr. Crosby obtained his first lease on Reserve 9, the Band had surrendered both Reserves to the federal government for leasing. Strictly speaking, there were no locatees. However, it appears that individual Indians were recognized as having possessory rights over specific parcels of land. Departmental correspondence at the time refers to equitable rights, which I take to be a recognition that certain Indians were entitled to the use of, or revenue from, certain properties. Mr. Crosby negotiated with Ronald Derrickson for a lease on a 3.5-acre parcel for which Mr. Derrickson had only recently acquired "equitable rights" from his father, Theodore Derrickson. The first lease on the property was dated August 25, 1969, and was for 50 years. About a year later, Mr. Crosby assigned that lease to a company called Golden Acres Ltd.

Initially, Mr. Crosby pursued his original intention, which was to build a retirement village. But that purpose had altered by the mid-1970's, when the original concept did not appear economically feasible. He maintained the concept of a retirement village, but opted for the then popular idea of developing a mobile home park. He decided to develop such a park, limiting it to double-wide mobile homes and an adult clientele. It today appears to be a well-planned and well-run operation.

Mr. Crosby negotiated a new lease with Ron Derrickson for an expanded area of 7.5 acres and installed 35 mobile home pads. The site work was done in 1976, at which time the market appears to have been improving. This continued until 1977 and then the market dropped off dramatically. In about 1979, the market became better again and, in fact, 1980–81 was very good indeed for park operators. The years thereafter have been considerably more wintry on the economic front.

In good times, the mobile home park business was a good one. Mobile home dealers would pay "patch fees", i.e., cash payments to a developer to encourage him to have more lots available. Whether they were occupied by a tenant or not, dealers would pay rents on the pads from the day those pads were created. In 1980 and 1981, developers were being paid premiums of $1000–4000 per pad by mobile home producers and distributors.

When the market again "took off", Mr. Crosby negotiated a lease for an additional 15.5 acres adjacent to his existing park (the "B" lease). He negotiated with Ron Derrickson, who acted on behalf of his father, Theodore Derrickson, the locatee of the land involved. The Crown, on behalf of the locatee, entered into a lease which was dated June 15, 1980 and which ran for a period of 45 years and 7 months from February 1, 1976. It contained a feature which, with variations, was incorporated into a number of Westbank leases thereafter. In that lease, Mr. Crosby agreed to pay an "annual base ground rent" or 20 per cent of the gross receipts, whichever was greater. The lease went into effect without any hitches and Mr. Crosby embarked on a major expansion of his park. He borrowed a substantial amount of money for development from the Royal Bank of Canada.

While he was negotiating the lease for the new land with Chief Derrickson, discussions apparently occurred about incorporating an alternative rental based on a percentage of gross receipts into his earlier lease (the "A" lease). It seems, however, that Mr. Crosby would not agree to apply a percentage rental to the permanent buildings he had built on the land covered by the "A" lease.

Mr. Crosby received a letter which purported to set the rental for the ensuing five-year period.

June 17, 1981

DOUBLE REGISTERED

Golden Acres Ltd.
RR # 1, Boucherie Rd.
Westbank, B.C.
V0H 2A0

Attention: L. Crosby

Dear Sir:

Re: Lease No. 47959

This is to advise the subject lease is now due for review and the new rent for the second five year period has been set on behalf of the Minister at Sixteen Thousand Eight Hundred Ninety Eight ($16,898.00) Dollars per annum or 20% of the gross receipts earned in that year, whichever is the greater.

Accordingly, we enclose a set of modification agreements which we will require that you execute and return to this office within seven (7) days of receipt.

If you have any questions herein, please do not hesitate to contact the writer.

Yours very truly,

WESTBANK INDIAN COUNCIL

"Ronald M. Derrickson"

Chief Ronald M. Derrickson

RMD/bdes
encl.

Accompanying the letter was a short agreement entitled "Modification Agreement". After reciting the description of the lease and the power of the Minister to set the annual rent payable during the second five-year period, the operative part of the agreement read:

> For the term commencing September 1, 1981 and terminating August 31, 1986, the rental of Sixteen Thousand Eight Hundred and Ninety Eight Dollars ($16,898.00) per annum or 20 per cent of gross receipts earned in that year, whichever is greater.

It should be noted that while the lease in question authorized the Minister to set a new rent at five-year intervals using a criterion for valuation set out in the lease, nothing in the lease contemplated the imposition of a percentage rent.

In July, a letter was delivered to Mr. Crosby:

July 16, 1981

BY HAND
Golden Acres Ltd.
R.R. #1
Westbank, B.C.

Dear Sirs:

Re: Lease No. 47959
    Lot 24–2-1 to 24–2-7 I.R. 9

This letter is to advise you that the above lease is due and payable on September 1, 1981 in the amount of $16,898.00.

Please have your <u>certified</u> cheque made payable to the Westbank Indian Council.

Thank you

Yours very truly,

WESTBANK INDIAN COUNCIL

"Ronald M. Derrickson"

RMD/hd
C.C. Ronald M. Derrickson

RECEIPT ACKNOWLEDGED
"Leonard Crosby"
"24 July 81"

Sometime in late summer, Mr. Crosby was requested to go to the Band office. When he arrived, Mr. Sheldon McCullough of the Department of Indian Affairs was there. The Chief presented Mr. Crosby with a new lease for signature, which incorporated provisions setting the base rent of $16,898 or 20 per cent of the gross annual receipts, whichever was the greater. He spoke with the Chief and then separately with Mr. McCullough. Mr. McCullough tried to prevail upon Mr. Crosby to sign the lease. However, Mr. Crosby did not, and left the meeting. Mr. Crosby's objection to the percentage rent appears to have been more a question of the basis upon which it would be calculated, rather than on the principle of a percentage rent itself. It appears that he might have agreed to pay a percentage of the gross in his "A" lease if the permanent buildings had been excluded from the computation of rent.

In early October 1981, the Chief convened the meeting of the mobile home park operators noted earlier. While at that meeting, Mr. Crosby raised a question about the authenticity of the Band's "Rentalsman by-law". The break between Mr. Crosby and Chief Derrickson was yet to occur. The break came later that month.

On approximately October 22, the Chief and Mr. Crosby met to discuss a number of issues that required resolution. While the meeting started on a cordial enough basis, it did not continue that way.

Mr. Crosby made notes of the meeting. He testified that the Chief said in the course of the meeting:

> I find it necessary to threaten, bully, lie, and cheat, and do many other things to get my own way. . .I manage all right. Nothing is done around here without my okay. I run the whole show, including the Council, Vancouver or the Minister, and you know that too.

They discussed the 20 per cent of gross receipts proposed for the rental under the "A" lease. It was apparent that Chief Derrickson felt that the buildings were to be included in such an agreement. Mr. Crosby asserted that he had never agreed to their inclusion. As reported by Mr. Crosby, the conversation continued as follows:

> Ron: Yes you did, I'll prove it. Barb, bring me the new lease on Golden Acres.
> Barbara: Here are the leases, but they were never signed.
> Ron: Well, God damn here, throw these in the garbage. You know what this means, don't you? You are going to be God damn sorry if you don't sign that lease, you're the one that's going to have to take the consequences and live with that. If you don't sign, we have nothing to discuss.

Not only was that the end of the discussion, the two men have not talked to each other since. They have communicated in writing, and Mr. Crosby has communicated continuously with the Department of Indian Affairs, the Minister of Indian Affairs, and with a number of Members of Parliament. The former Chief has communicated through the same avenues, and through the media. As I observed the two individuals during the hearings, it seemed to me that here were two people born to ruffle each other's feelings. Mr. Crosby is a man who likes order and careful procedure. Mr. Derrickson is a "let's get it done" type, much less interested in procedure. Mr. Crosby once wrote to Mr. Derrickson suggesting some third party might intervene, such as Mr. Theodore Derrickson or Mr. Noll Derriksan. I think it close to impossible for these two strong-willed individuals to sort things out directly between themselves. They were born to clash.

In December 1981, the Chief took an unusual step and wrote Mr. Crosby's banker, the Royal Bank, which held security by way of mortgages and a debenture on Mr. Crosby's property. The letter read as follows:

December 4, 1981

Royal Bank of Canada
#30 Orchard Park Shopping Centre
Highway 97.
North Kelowna, British Columbia

Dear Sirs:

Re: Golden Acres Ltd.
    Lease No. 47959
    Lots 24-2–1, 24-2–2, 25-2–3, 24-2–4, 24-2–5,
    24-2–6 and 24-2–7, Tsinstikeptum I.R. No. 9

As you are the mortgagor of the subject lease, we are hereby advising you the lease between the Crown and Golden Acres is no longer in good standing because Golden Acres Ltd. have not signed the renewal of the lease.

Yours very truly,

WESTBANK INDIAN COUNCIL

"Ronald M. Derrickson"

It was copied to Golden Acres Ltd. and to Mr. McCullough of Indian Affairs.

A reading of the Golden Acres lease in question would have disclosed that there was no obligation upon Golden Acres Ltd. to sign any "renewal" of the lease, but the Royal Bank took the statement seriously and replied in part: "In view of the seriousness of your letter, we have frozen our client's credit lines until this matter is resolved and hopefully an agreement can be reached shortly."

This exchange of correspondence took place while Mr. Crosby was developing his new mobile home park, and was substantially reliant on bank credit. Mr. Crosby travelled to Vancouver and met with Mr. McCullough and then with Mr. Peter Clark, who at that time held the position of Acting Director, Lands, Reserves and Trusts, B.C. Region. Mr. Clark wrote to the Westbank Indian Council on December 17, 1981:

> On checking our files and the Land Registry in Ottawa it is apparent that the above-noted lease is in good standing and is fully paid. No steps have been taken or any actions requested that would lead us to believe that grounds were available to consider termination.
> It may be that your observations were based on wrong information. We are not aware of any subsequent agreement that would lead to a revised lease agreement.

That letter was copied to the Royal Bank and to Golden Acres Ltd.

At that time, the source of the Chief's authority was the 1977 Agreement. In effect, the Chief and Council were acting as agents for the Crown. The Chief's letter to the Bank alleging default apparently caused some difficulty to Mr. Crosby and his company. The comments contained in the letter of December 17, 1981 was the only rebuke the Department administered, and the Bank would advance Mr. Crosby no further monies until late in February. Mr. Crosby wrote a lengthy letter dated February 17, 1982 to the Minister of Indian Affairs, a copy of which is set out at the end of this chapter. I will comment upon this letter further when I deal with the Westside Mobile Home Park Owners' Association.

Mr. Crosby paid his rental instalment on the "A" lease on the September 1, 1982. Chief Derrickson accepted the cheque, but wrote:

> perusal of this lease agreement does not reflect this amount, therefore we are accepting this rent on account pending resolution of your five-year review of rent by respective solicitors.

It would appear that Mr. Crosby was acting on the Chief's letters of June and July 1981 and that the Chief considered the determination of the rent still an open question.

Another year passed. On August 31, 1983, Chief Derrickson wrote to Golden Acres Ltd., enclosing an appraisal done by a Mr. Harck and saying:

> In view of the fact that we have been unable to come to an agreement on the rent for the five-year period commencing September 1, 1981, we completed this certified appraisal, and now formally advise you that the rent for the five-year period commencing September 1, 1981 has been determined on behalf of Her Majesty the Queen at $28,500 per annum.

The same day, Mr. Clark, as Director of Lands, Reserves and Trusts, sent a telex to Golden Acres Ltd. saying inter alia:

> On behalf of the Minister, the rental is hereby established at $28,500 per annum. Please provide a cheque for the outstanding amount of dollars. . .

Mr. Clark confirmed the telex by a letter of September 1, reasserting the establishment of the rental at $28,500 per annum and asking for the arrears for the past several years.

The rentals on the "A" lease were the subject of a trial in Federal Court in the fall of 1987. As of the date of writing, no decision has been handed down. I understand that in addition to what rental should be fixed for the five years following September 1, 1981, the rentals for the five-year period following September 1, 1986 were also in issue. Regardless of the eventual result of court proceedings, it must be said that it is almost impossible to run a business where the owner's profit, if any, lies in the spread between the rentals he receives and the rentals he pays when the amounts are determined some six or seven years after the effective date of the rental increase.

Under the "B" lease, questions arose as to the method and timing of payments of the anticipated 20 per cent of gross revenues. Perhaps because of those problems, Mr. Crosby chose to send instalments to the Department rather than to the Band Council. Letters were sent to the Department in an attempt to reach an agreement as to the time and manner in which those monies were to be paid. Mr. Crosby received unhelpful replies. Then, without any forewarning, the Department sent a letter signed by Mr. John Evans dated December 22, 1983 cancelling the "B" lease for failure to pay the rent and demanding possession of the lands and premises. The letter was meant to be a formal termination of the lease and copies were sent to the Royal Bank and other interested parties. It seems the Chief was upset because the rentals were being forwarded to the Department and not to the Band. It also seems the Department would do his bidding without reflection.

The lease was probably cancelled because Mr. Crosby chose to make his payments to the Department. That may have been petulance on his part, but it should be remembered that the Department itself was not clear about the limits of the authority it had conferred. That renders it difficult to criticize people for their actions in dealing with the Department and the Band. The cancellation of the lease, albeit without legal justification, caused a flurry of solicitors' letters. Ultimately Mr. Crosby's solicitors received a letter from the Department of Justice which confirmed that the notice of cancellation had been withdrawn. With the series of investigations into Westbank affairs that were then in train, the high degree of publicity of Westbank matters, and the interest taken by parliamentarians, it is surprising that the Department would make such an error. Such action could only deepen Mr. Crosby's suspicions concerning the Department.

As I said, the rental for the Crosby lease was the subject of court proceedings in the fall of 1987. There have been remarkably few court references, but it is hoped that if they are necessary in the future, they will be tried more expeditiously.

The Commission heard evidence on the progress to effect rent revisions under the mobile home park leases. Commission Counsel intentionally did not delve into the merits of the individual revisions. There is litigation pending and some negotiations are always taking place. It was felt that examination of the merits of the individual rent increases would have extended the hearings of the Commission unreasonably into the future on issues that must be resolved either by agreement of the parties or by third party (court) intervention.

However, in its submission, the Department of Indian Affairs ventured into the subject of rental increases and was highly critical of the mobile home park operators. The Department took the position that the park operators, while complaining of extortionate rent increases, were themselves "ripping off" their own tenants. The Department's written submission said in part:

> One observation must be made about the trailer park operators who, through Mr. Len Crosby, complained to Members of Parliament about the lease rental increases imposed by Chief Derrickson. From the statements they gave to Mr. Crosby which he passed on to the Members of Parliament, and from Mr. Crosby's own statements, the obvious inference was that Chief Derrickson was demanding extortionate rental increases. A desperate picture of trailer park operators being put out of business by these increases was painted by Mr. Crosby and his fellow operators. What they did not tell the Members of Parliament was that they were using these rent increases to justify to the Rentalsman applications for additional rent increases to the residents of their trailer parks. They also kept silent the fact they were pocketing the increased rentals from their residents, while at the same time refusing to pay the increases on their own leases.

In the course of the cross-examination of one of the mobile home park operators, Mr. Val Spring, counsel for the Department took the position that Mr. Spring was withholding information or had withheld information about applications that he had made to the Rentalsman for rent increases. Counsel for the former Band executive, in cross-examining the same witness, took the position that there was some obligation on Mr. Spring to set apart rental monies he had collected from his tenants and accused him of "ripping off" his tenants. Similar suggestions were given some currency in the press at the time of the controversy and were not justified.

The suggestions made in the Department's submission and the tenor of the cross-examinations showed a limited understanding of the rental control system that was in effect at the material time. They overlooked the primary problem, which was the failure of the Department to set rents, as it was obliged to do under certain leases.

Until 1984, a system of rent control was in force in British Columbia. The system governed both the amount of rental increases that could be made and timing of those increases. Landlords, without approval, were entitled to a general, flat percentage increase once a year, and a provision existed for exceeding the prescribed percentage with the approval of the Rentalsman in unusual circumstances. Those circumstances included any unusual increase in the landlord's costs.

Two of the persons who applied for such increases were Mr. Don Lauriault, the operator of the Billabong Mobile Home Park, and Mr. Val Spring, the operator of the Jubilee Mobile Home Park through his company, Acres Holdings Limited.

Donald Lauriault

Mr. Lauriault purchased the company that operates the Billabong Mobile Home in 1980 after he had retired from the RCAF. The Billabong Park occupies close to thirteen acres. It has seventy-seven pads, an office, and a sixty-five-site campground. The property is charged with a first mortgage in favour of RoyNat and a second mortgage in favour of the vendor of the park. The purchase price was $400,000, with Mr. Lauriault having made a $65,000 cash down payment.

Mr. Lauriault attended the meeting between mobile home park operators and the Chief in early October 1981, where operators were told that pad rents were to be increased to $150 per month. This posed a dilemma for them indeed, because they felt constrained by the rules of the British Columbia Rentalsman even though Chief Derrickson was asserting his jurisdiction to have a Band Rentalsman increase rents.

Mr. Lauriault issued Notices of Rental Increase in February 1982, but his rental increases were disallowed or rolled back by the B.C.

Rentalsman. As noted earlier, the decision of Mr. Justice Locke in March 1982 confirmed the B.C. Rentalsman's jurisdiction.

In 1984, the lease under which Mr. Lauriault operated Billabong Mobile Home Park was due for a rent revision effective September 1, 1984. In August, Mr. Lauriault spoke with Chief Derrickson who proposed a new lease at $3,250 per month per acre (which would have amounted to $41,600 per annum) or 25 per cent of the gross, whichever was the greater. It appears that Mr. Lauriault's anniversary date for rental increases under the B.C. Rentalsman's jurisdiction was July 1 of each year and September 1, 1984 was the date on which the new rental for the park itself was to be fixed. In anticipation of the eventuality he might have to pay $41,600 per annum, Mr. Lauriault sought and obtained a rental increase. The Rentalsman's Order approving the increase contemplated a rollback in the event Mr. Lauriault succeeded in paying less money for rent.

One thing changed and another never happened. The B.C. Rentalsman's jurisdiction over rents throughout the province was withdrawn and the Minister or the Department never fixed the rent to be paid in accordance with the terms of Mr. Lauriault's lease. Some time later, and well beyond the 180 day limit in the lease within which rental increases were to be imposed, Chief Derrickson wrote to Mr. Lauriault's solicitors, purportedly fixing the new rental at $41,781 per annum or 25 per cent of the gross annual receipts, whichever was the greater as at September 1, 1984.

This apparent determination of the rent by Chief Derrickson may be subject to several defects which are yet to be resolved, namely:

1. Chief Derrickson's authority to determine rents is doubtful, as there does not appear to have been a legal delegation of the power to set rent.
2. The time within which the rent should have been determined had expired by the time Chief Derrickson asserted what the rent would be.
3. The lease does not appear to contemplate the imposition of a percentage of gross receipts as a rental.

What at first blush may appear to be a windfall to Mr. Lauriault is not perceived as such by him. He continues to be in a state of grave uncertainty as to what figure his rent will ultimately be set at. In the meantime, Mr. Lauriault's financing has expired and he has been called upon by RoyNat, the lender under the first charge against the property, as well as by the vendor who holds the second mortgage. He cannot secure refinancing while the question of his rental remains unresolved and it would be advantageous to have that matter settled. This does not appear to be one of those problems which time improves.

Val Spring

As noted above, Mr. Spring was subject to accusations of "rip off" and the suggestion that he should be holding monies received from rent increases in a trust account. The accusation of a "rip off" is unfair, as the main problem lies with the Minister and the Department. As to the suggestion that monies should be isolated in anticipation of a rent increase, there is no legal obligation to do so, even though commercial prudence might recommend it.

Mr. Spring is the proprietor of the Jubilee Mobile Home Estates through Acres Holdings Limited. The park is on lands registered in the name of the estate of Band member Ellen Tomat, and her heirs are entitled to the revenue from the park. Mr. Spring bought the operation for $385,000 and gave back a $300,000 mortgage. The property was not fully developed; there was room for a substantial number of additional mobile home pads. The unoccupied part of the leased lot contains 7.29 acres.

When Mr. Spring bought the park, the annual rental charged to the operator was $17,720 per annum subject to revision every five years. The lease was due for revision on September 1, 1984.

Expecting to be able to put mobile home pads on the unoccupied land, Mr. Spring went to OPEC Engineering Limited in 1981 to request them to draw up a plan for a park extension. OPEC Engineering was a Kelowna firm which was often engaged by the Band and sometimes acted for people dealing with the Band. OPEC informed Mr. Spring that the Westbank Indian Band wanted $1,500 per pad for "future fire protection". At that point, Mr. Spring had hoped to put in forty more pads and this change would have cost him about $60,000. The OPEC letter said:

> As was discussed with you previously, the Westbank Indian Band required that all new developments on the Reserve provide a minimum fire protection as outlined in their Development By-law.

It is not unreasonable to impose such a cost upon a developer, but in the welter of by-laws passed by the Band, there does not appear to be a by-law that would authorize such a charge. The parties assumed there was a by-law that authorized the imposition of a $1,500 per pad charge. The only by-law that comes close was By-law 1979–12, the Band's subdivision by-law. It provided that a subdivider "shall provide water distribution. . .to serve all parcels created by a subdivision".

However, Mr. Spring was not developing a subdivision as that term is usually understood, and it appears that By-law 1979–12 did not apply. The Commission was not informed of any other by-law that could apply. In any event, Mr. Spring's proposed additions to his park did not proceed.

Like Mr. Lauriault, Mr. Spring attempted to raise the rents for his mobile home pads to $150 per month after the October 1981 meeting with Chief Derrickson. However, the B.C. Rentalsman's office rolled back the rents and Mr. Spring said he was left with "an accountant's nightmare". Some tenants had refused to pay the increase and those who had paid were entitled to have the increases returned.

Mr. Spring had additional reasons than the demands for fire protection not to proceed with his development in 1981. Shortly thereafter, there was a downturn in the economy and difficulties were encountered in securing financing for developments on Indian lands.

In 1983, Mr. Spring proposed to Chief Derrickson that he develop his vacant land into a par three golf course. The Chief suggested that he enter into two new leases, one for the existing mobile home park, and the other for the proposed golf course. Both leases were to be $3,000 per acre or 25 per cent of the gross, but Chief Derrickson was prepared to allow an abatement for the first two years on the par three golf course. He and Mr. Spring did not come to terms, however, so that development did not take place.

The first time Mr. Spring applied to the Rentalsman for a rental increase, it was in anticipation of paying higher rents under a revised lease and charging the higher pad rents Chief Derrickson called for at the meeting in October 1981. When the time came for the rent revision due on September 1, 1984, Mr. Spring gave a Notice of Rental Increase in anticipation of the Minister fixing the rent in accordance with the lease. Under Mr. Spring's lease, the rent is to be reviewed by the Minister or his authorized representative within 180 days of the rent renewal date. Prior to September 1, 1984, there was a relatively continuous exchange of correspondence — much of which pertained to who should negotiate the rent on behalf of the landlord.

Mr. Crosby, on behalf of Mr. Spring and as President of the Mobile Home Park Owners' Association, wrote a letter dated July 20, 1984 to the Department in Ottawa. That letter is reproduced at the end of this chapter. In the letter, he puts the position of the park operators as follows:

> In our opinion the problems we are facing have arisen simply because the Department has not in the past lived up to their undertaking to 'set the rent'.

Mr. Crosby went on to argue that the rent proposed by the Band would amount to something well in excess of Mr. Spring's previous year's total net income and concluded:

> These matters are related only to give you some indication as to the gravity and extreme urgency of the situation and that the Department

address the problem on a 'most urgent' basis. Please wire your response.

Mr. Crosby's letter was answered by a letter dated August 14, 1984 and signed by Mr. F. Singleton for Mr. J. Leask, the Director General of Reserves and Trusts, which said, in part:

It is also the practice of the Department to encourage the Band Council and/or the locatee to negotiate with the lessee in order to arrive at a mutually agreeable rent. I therefore urge the lessee to continue to negotiate with Chief Derrickson and the Westbank Band. In the event that no agreement is reached, then this Department has the responsibility to review the rent determined to be acceptable to the Band, in order to see that it is generally in accordance with the terms of the lease.

It would seem that the Department confused its good intentions with its legal obligations. Those legal obligations called for it to set the rent within 180 days of September 1, 1984, and the Department failed to do so.

On June 6, 1985, an Order-in-Council was passed conferring certain land management authorities upon the Band pursuant to Section 60 of the Indian Act. On September 5, 1985, Chief Derrickson wrote to the solicitors for Mr. Spring and Acres Holdings Limited, purporting to set the rent on behalf of the Minister at $57,274 per annum or 25 per cent of the gross annual receipts — whichever was the greater as at September 1, 1984. That declaration on behalf of the Minister suffered from the same infirmities that I have pointed out with regard to the Billabong-Lauriault lease.

In his testimony before the Commission, Mr. Spring did not appear to take the position that the time had expired for a rental increase. The five-year period to which such a rent increase would apply is now more than half over and the matter is still to be resolved. A fair measure of uncertainty shrouds this matter. I could not perceive that Mr. Spring was attempting to "rip off" anyone. He was castigated as a poor operator by Mr. Derrickson. His park did not appear to be as conspicuously well run as the Crosby operation. But whether he is a good or bad operator is aside altogether from allegations that he was acting dishonestly. I believe he was doing his best to attempt to survive as an independent operator in the midst of a welter of confusing and confused directives from a number of sources, including the Department, the B.C. Rentalsman, and the Chief. As I said, to this day it is impossible for him to know precisely what his rent bill ultimately will amount to.

In 1985, a study was made of the Westbank Band's problems by Mr. Singleton of the Department, assisted by Mr. Preston and Mr. Reecke, both lawyers practising in British Columbia. From that study came a suggestion that the Band might purchase all mobile home parks on

Reserve 9. That suggestion did not proceed to implementation. I have said elsewhere in this Report that such a course of action might resolve some local grievances, but it would raise grave policy questions for government.

The Westside Mobile Home Park Owners' Association

Until 1981, the operators of the mobile home parks were not a cohesive group and to some extent, they regarded themselves as competitors. Certain events in late 1981 and 1982 on the Westbank Reserves created quite a flurry of media coverage, coupled with representations to civil servants, Members of Parliament, and Cabinet Ministers. The park operators who followed Chief Derrickson's program of increasing the pad rental to $150 per month were to encounter B.C. Rentalsman-ordered rollbacks of those increases. Towards the end of February 1982, the park operators met and decided to form an association. A solicitor was hired and the Association was incorporated on July 19, 1982. The original members appear to have been Leonard Crosby, Donald Lauriault, Ted Zelmer, Jack Alexander, Bruce York, James Lidster, and Val Spring. James Lidster later resigned, as did Bruce York when he was charged in connection with an assault on Chief Derrickson.

As noted elsewhere, the early months of 1982 were turbulent times at Westbank. The local press often reported on tenants' complaints and related matters concerning the Band and park operators. A decision in the case of <u>Mathews</u> and <u>Toussowasket Enterprises Ltd.</u> was rendered in early March 1982. The Judge found substantially in the B.C. Rentalsman's (tenants') favour. The question of the surrender of the Toussowasket lease and the resultant defeat of the claim of Donaldson Engineering Ltd. (described in the Toussowasket chapter) was agitating the Department. Members of Parliament were raising Westbank issues with the Minister of Indian Affairs. In May 1982, the Parliamentary Standing Committee on Indian Affairs held several hearings which touched upon British Columbia and the Westbank Band in particular.

Against this background, Mr. Peter Clark, the Regional Director of Lands, Revenues and Trusts, was sent from Vancouver to meet with certain persons concerned with Westbank issues. On May 17, 1982, he met with Mr. Crosby and Mr. and Mrs. York, representing the Mobile Home Park Owners' Association. Mr. Crosby had written a letter to the Minister dated May 14, 1982 which had not yet been dispatched. (A copy of that letter is reproduced at the end of this chapter.) Mr. Crosby gave evidence that he reviewed the letter and its contents with Mr. Clark. The letter contained a number of allegations on which I heard evidence and some on which I did not. I do not consider the letter as any evidence in itself of the truth of the allegations made therein. However, it gives some idea of the matters that concerned the park operators at the time. In that letter, Mr. Crosby dealt with the complaints of Jack

Alexander, Val Spring, and another operator with regard to impost fees for "future fire protection". Mr. Crosby reviewed several problems concerning the Yorks, which included delay in securing approvals and interference with installation of public utilities. He also adverted to complaints of people who had begun to install mobile home parks but had failed to complete them. As a conclusion to this lengthy letter, he wrote:

> There is already some evidence to support the view that the overall circumstances may, if properly investigated, disclose a conspiracy to defraud. Park owners feel unable to make a direct criminal complaint at this time without the knowledge that an investigation might provide. It will not assist us if criminal action is taken and in fact such action could result in the often-used excuse for the lack of any official action in the interim, this is something we cannot abide with. We require action to resolve past injustice and hopefully prevent the current and future continuation of civil wrong.

Mr. Clark gave evidence about the meeting, saying:

> I was surprised that there were so few of the mobile home park owners that were in attendance at that meeting. . .and that the concerns that were expressed then were all concerns that had been previously expressed or provided through other letters to the Department or other channels, and that there was really nothing that was new.

When questioned by counsel for the Department, Mr. Clark answered:

> Q Using your best judgement, can you please advise the Commissioner as to your impression of the claims of the Yorks and Mr. Crosby at that.
> A I wasn't, as I said, I wasn't impressed by them at all, and felt that the great majority of the claims were. . .or concerns were the type that were of a niggling nature that you quite often get between landlord and tenant, but nothing of any sort or great substance at all.

In the spring and summer of 1982, representations by the park operators and tenants were forwarded to the Minister, officials of the Department, the press, and whoever would listen. It is fair to say that the Regional Director of Lands, Revenues and Trusts was then, and remained, impervious to the complaints of the park operators. The situation at Westbank continued to be an unhappy one and controversy continued. Although I think it unfortunate if Mr. Clark left the operators with the impression that their complaints were "niggling", I have some sympathy for the position he found himself in. The problem that the Department often faces is the fact that it is a department of government. Therefore people assume it is a representative of all citizens. In the case of the Department of Indian Affairs, its first and foremost duty is to Indian people. Mr. Crosby was in error if he viewed it as having the same obligations to him and his group as it had to Indian people. In Appendix B of my Report I make some comments about a possible approach to dispute resolution relative to Indian affairs. This approach may lighten the conflict burden that Departmental officials in the position of Mr. Clark often face.

The Park Owners' Association, with Mr. Crosby acting as spokesman, engaged in continuous correspondence on various matters of concern. It queried the validity and application of by-laws on the Reserve as well as the licence fees and charges set by the Band, and it brought to the attention of the appropriate authorities such matters as encroachments by the Department of Highways on the leased land of the park operators. Most of all, however, it queried the process of rent review and determination.

In the letter referred to above, Mr. Leask expressed the view that rents should be the subject of negotiation and agreement with the assistance of the Department, but that was not the way things happened. In practice, negotiations began with the issuance of a Rent Notice which was put forward as the Minister's determination. Any negotiations took place thereafter. With the rent having already been set, the park operators felt they were negotiating from a very difficult position.

In 1985, Mr. Singleton of the Department in Ottawa, came to Kelowna several times and met with the park opertors. Mr. Crosby also met with Messrs. Preston and Reecke, who were assisting Mr. Singleton in the aforementioned study. This study culminated in the recommendation that the mobile home parks be purchased by the Band. Appraisals were done to lay the groundwork, but no further actions appear to have occurred towards implementation of this recommendation.

I cannot leave the question of the Park Owners' Association and the park operators without criticism of one aspect of their activity. I have appended to this chapter several letters from Mr. Crosby to the Minister of Indian Affairs. It will be seen that some of the correspondence is strongly worded. Mr. Crosby's letter of February 17, 1982, which was the first of many letters, contained the following passage on the first page:

I have personal knowledge of the following allegations:

(1) Attempted extortion.
(2) He [Chief Ron Derrickson] is attempting to use the minister's appointment as an Agent of the Crown for personal gain.
(3) By printing known lies while ostensibly performing duties as an Agent of the Crown he has committed a civil wrong for which the Crown could be held liable.

(4) He is causing the Crown to be in violation of a lease which was entered into.

(5) By unethical conduct of breach of trust he is causing his own people and the Crown to be held in disrepute.

The full letter is set out at the end of this chapter.

Counsel for the former Band executive cross-examined Mr. Crosby on this letter in an attempt to ascertain what was referred to in those five allegations. Apparently the attempted extortion referred to discriminatory application of permit fees called for under the by-law. Mr. Crosby referred to the different amounts charged to Mr. Zelmer, to himself, and to the Yorks — all of whom were engaged in comparable developments. Under the heading of attempted extortion, Mr. Crosby also pointed to the allegedly false representations made by Chief Derrickson when he said that powers under Section 60(1) of the Indian Act had been conferred upon the Band. As to the use of the Minister's appointment as agent of the Crown for personal gain, Mr. Crosby pointed to Chief Derrickson's setting of rent for leases of land of which the Chief himself was the locatee. The "printing of known lies" referred to claims made by the Chief that the Band had Section 60 authority when it did not. The "causing of the Crown to be in violation of a lease" was the purported breach of the lessor's covenant for quiet enjoyment when the Department allowed the allocation to Noll Derriksan of the Band road, causing potential access difficulty to some of the York property. The "unethical conduct" and "breach of trust" referred to the representation made by the Chief that the Band Rentalsman by-law was in effect when, in fact, it had not been approved by the Department. In the body of the letter, Mr. Crosby expressed the opinion that the letter written by Chief Derrickson to the Manager of the Royal Bank of Canada stating that his (Crosby's) lease was in default could be a "civil or criminal wrong".

These allegations, which raised the spectre of crime, were reckless when cast in this manner. Such allegations should not be made lightly, particularly by a former senior NCO of the R.C.M.P. While questions could be raised about the ethics of the conduct referred to, the instances do not seem to merit the allegations of criminal conduct. A little knowledge can be a dangerous thing. Mr. Crosby had some knowledge of the Criminal Code. I felt he was taking phraseology from the Code and endeavouring to elevate the activities he accused Chief Derrickson of into breaches of the Code. The Chief may have been overly aggressive at times (as I said, he and Mr. Crosby seemed destined to clash with each other), but it was unfair of Mr. Crosby to suggest that the Chief was carrying on in a criminal fashion.

Another letter on which Mr. Crosby was cross-examined extensively was one he wrote to the Minister on May 6, 1986. Included in that letter was this strongly worded passage:

> We are concerned that inquiries to examine abuse of power to identify responsibility for actions or inactions of personnel within your Department (DIAND) will of necessity, identify circumstances of suspected criminal opportunity to cover evidence or establish alibis. I feel that criminal investigation is warranted and that it should occur before or at least at the same time as any other inquiry.

These words again imply that the Band administration or the Department was wallowing in a quagmire of crime. The facts were otherwise.

The letter of May 6, 1986 and its appendix are reproduced at the end of this chapter. The allegations of criminality in that letter and appendix can be summarized. The "false representations of fact" referred to Chief Derrickson's letter to the Royal Bank alleging that Mr. Crosby's lease was in default; "false documents" referred to the circulation of the non-existent Band Rentalsman by-law and the zoning by-law relating to mobile home parks; and the "attempt to defeat the course of justice" referred to the surrender of the Toussowasket lease. Mr. Crosby referred to the seeking of an impost fee from Acres Holdings Ltd. for future fire protection as a possible conspiracy to attempt to obtain funds by fraud. No evidence was tendered before me of any fraud involving the collection of rentals.

The demanding or receiving of a benefit under Section 383 of the Criminal Code refers to the offence sometimes termed "secret commissions" or "commercial bribery". I heard from Mr. Andrew Archondous, who could not give first hand evidence on that subject, and Mr. Ward Kiehlbauch's evidence would not sustain such a charge against any member of the Band administration or government. The proposed invocation of the mischief and criminal breach of contract sections referred to in Mr. Crosby's appendix represents imaginative application of the criminal law. No criminal lawyer of any experience would have any difficulty in exploding the notion that the facts supported any such charges.

Criminal interpretations placed upon events did not assist in shedding light on anything, but they escalated the temperature. It is clear that the events cited in Mr. Crosby's correspondence could only marginally be considered crimes, and in the event that criminal proceedings were ever instituted, a conviction for any of the above allegations would be highly improbable. To say this is not to overlook that there were ethical questions raised by those events. It will be appreciated that there were things that were wrong at Westbank, and some people feared that even worse things were happening. Mr. Crosby explained his allegations in cross-examination as follows:

> What we were trying to get throughout this whole matter is for someone from the Department, not necessarily to take what I say to

be true or false, but to come out and at least look into the matter and find out what in heaven's name has happened.

The difficulty that arose, however, was that some persons may have read the material supplied without the caveats to which they should have been subject.

Counsel for the former Band executive was highly critical of Mr. Crosby's correspondence. I think the criticism was warranted. The letters contained a substratum of fact but superimposed thereon was a compendium of accusations that suggested Chief Derrickson was conducting a concerted campaign of lawlessness. While the former Chief may well finish dead last in a diplomacy stakes race, it was unfair to him to suggest that he was continually in breach of some of the more arcane sections of the Criminal Code. As a former law enforcement officer, Mr. Crosby should have been more careful in his use of language to Members of Parliament and others. Not only was this unfair to Chief Derrickson, it was unfair to those parliamentarians who were apprised of the allegations. They have a duty to heed the concerns of constituents and where there was such a pall of verbal smoke they would be led, naturally, to fear that there was a large fire indeed. I was not persuaded that Chief Derrickson had infringed the Criminal Code as alleged. The use of such inflammatory language by Mr. Crosby was not supported by the facts.

The Crosby-Derrickson confrontation seemed to arise out of the very different perspectives of the two men. Mr. Crosby appeared greatly attached to procedure. His method of expression tended to circumlocution and the ornate. Mr. Derrickson was inclined to be a verbal bully in his correspondence. He was not one to stand on ceremony. Putting Mr. Crosby and Mr. Derrickson together was like combining flame and gas. There were many other factors listed elsewhere in this Report that led to troubles at Westbank, but clearly the severe clash of personalities between these two men was at the heart of much controversy. It is unlikely they will ever be able to co-exist peacefully. Their view of how things should be done diverge so far that it is nearly impossible for them to communicate. Both appear to have a grudging respect for the other. Mr. Derrickson views Mr. Crosby's operation as a credit to the Reserve. Mr. Crosby doubtless views the former Chief as a person who has sought to advance the fortunes of the Westbank Band. But it seems likely that their differences will have to be sorted out by third parties — for instance, the rent review matter has been the subject of a hearing in Federal Court. The history of their relationship leads me to believe that any direct dealing between them will tend to generate friction and controversy. Both are too rigid in their thinking to accommodate the other and I do not foresee that they will be able to adjust their differences on their own.

20 July 84

Dept. of Indian & Northern Affairs
Ottawa, Ont.
Att; Mr. J. Leask

Dear Sir;   Acres Holding Ltd. Lease # 69732
                             I.R. # 9, Westbank, B.C.

1. This is in respect to the matter of a Rent Review of the above noted lease which is due 1 Sept 1984.

2. The lessee has received correspondence from the band which has been replied to. Copies of the correspondence to date are attached.

3. The lessee has forwarded correspondence to your Dept in Ottawa on this matter some time ago but has not received a reply. I have discussed it with Mr. Doug MacKay at your Vancouver Office but he would not commit himself to make any direct response as to what your Department is going to do or refrain from doing and told me that he would refer the matter to yourself. Mr. MacKay did tell me that the Departments position now is that the Band does not have authority under Section 60 of the Act in respect to unsurrendered lands. I understood this to mean that the Band does not have the authority to set the rents. Is that correct? You will appreciate that this would be a very great change as to what has been allowed to be practiced on this reserve for the past number of years.

4. You will appreciate from the correspondence that the band does not agree to that interpertation and proposes to set the rent unilaterally, as they have been allowed to do in the past. In view of the Ministers contractual obligation to "set the rent" would you please clarify as to who is to perform this duty.

5. We fully expect and encourage the band to make a written submission to the Department concerning the rent and the reasons in support thereof. All the park owners are asking for is that the rent be set by the Department and not the Band because the latter gives rise to a direct "conflict of interest". We expect that the person assigned this task is a qualified licensed appraiser who is instructed to make an "arms length" determination of "fair rent" without being influenced by the desires of either party and that he follows the policy guidelines of the department in respect to rent renewals.

6. In our opinion the problems we are having have arisen simply because the department has not in the past lived up to their undertaking to "set the rent". It will now require an on site examination of the facts. The park owners are prepared to open their books and make full

disclosure of all of the circumstances, which effect value, in order to assist your department.

7. The Band by previous correspondence and recently by direct statement to Mr. Perry have said that the new rent will be 3200. per acre per year. If applied to Acres Holdings Ltd then that will increase their lease rental fee from 17 to 77 thousand dollars. Even if you take the position that the owner should not receive any benefits whatever in respect to his investment, we can prove that such rent would amount to something in excess of 20 thousand dollars of his previous years total Net Income.

Not only that — but the terms of the lease would require that such sum be paid in full prior to being able to refer the matter to the Federal Court. What financial institution would loan funds which would enable him to appeal to the courts?

These matters are related only to give you some indication as to the gravity and extreme urgency of the situation and that the Department address the problem on a "Most Urgent" basis.

Please wire your response.

L.R. Crosby — President
Mobile Park Owners Assoc.
S-17, C-1, Westbank, B.C. V0H 2A0
Phone; 768–4222

14/5/82

The Minister
Indian and Northern Affairs
Les Terrasses de la Chaudiere
Ottawa, Ontario
K1A 0H4

Attention: Roy T. Jacobs — Special Assistance — Portfolio.

Re: Golden Acres Ltd. — L.R. Crosby
I.R. #9, Westbank, B.C.

1. Further to my letter of 17 Feb 82 and to your replies of 1 Mar and 19 April. Also please refer to the letter of Mr. J.D. Leask dated 30 Mar which was sent to Mr. Fred King MP with a copy to yourself.

2. Sir: The principal facts of my complaint are that an agent of the Minister is committing a civil or criminal wrong in respect to administering I.R. #9. This was brought to the attention of your department in Vancouver in Dec 81 and to the Minister himself in Feb 82. The urgency of the matter has been repeatedly stressed and is acknowledged by yourself. Nothing substantive has been done. This is an ongoing matter with damages being incurred daily and after months of waiting I believe it is fair comment to observe that some persons apparently are not interested if taxpayers funds are needlessly spent to defend or compensate. It is highly probable that some affected persons will seek civil redress against the Crown. This could have been easily avoided in the first place with a little common sense and prompt attention to the departments responsibilities. Some letters have been sent but no one to date has addressed himself to the principals of the complaint. Mr. King MP has attempted to assist but meetings are cancelled or attendance is not forthcoming. Mr. Clarke DIAND Vancouver has been here in the interim and also cancelled out an arranged meeting.

3. I and Mr. King have repeatedly pressed for an investigation to no avail. As a citizen I cannot do it. "Investigation" to me means to obtain all of the information from all sources and in particular to question the complainants simply because not everything can be imparted by way of correspondence. In your letter of 19 April you state "our field officers are investigation the matter again with the band council". It is very nieve for anyone to think they are going to get the facts from them. "Again" denotes to me that it has been alleged that the matter has been investigated — this simply is not so in my opinion as no-one has come to see me or any other persons who have complained. A "review" of these matters from an office desk is simply not sufficient and will accomplish nothing.

4. Prior to recent weeks Mobile Park Owners acted individually and did not necessarily have knowledge of what was happening to others. We now have an association registered Provincially. An exchange of information, since my last writing, discloses many irregularities and circumstances which appear to be unlawful. To relate them in detail is too demanding and I will only outline the principal facts. Each of the parties concerned have told me they are prepared to substantiate these matters to any official person or body who may attend.

5. Paradise Mobile Park — Clint Miller — Previous Owner. Now in bankruptcy not available for interview. The Chief demanded and received $18000. from him for "future fire protection" as a condition to granting him permission to utilize the remaining land he had under lease for an extension of a mobile park. Such Band action is not authorized by any existing By-Law or regulation. OPEC Engineering assisted the Chief in this action by claiming that this was necessary due to provisions of a Band By-Law. A fraudulent misrepresentation of fact. This can be confirmed partially be copies of correspondence and by interviewing Darcy O'Keefe an agent for the receiver.

6. Jubilee Mobile Park — Val Spring — owner. Has an unused portion of land under lease. When he enquiried from the Chief about getting their approval to expand his park he was tolda he would have to pay $60,000. to the band "for future fire protection" in order to get such permission. He did not do so. The chief attempted to get him to agree to a new lease partly by indicating by-law 1981–03 was operative.

7. Pine-Ridge Estates — Jack Alexander — Owner. This park was built some 5 years ago. When the rental review came about in spring of 1981 the owner voiced objections to the huge increase and indicated an appeal to the court. Up until that time no requests had been made of him — however as soon as he commenced the appeal he began receiving letters from the Building Inspector, Health Dept and OPEC Engineering requiring such things as prior engineering plans, as-built plans, re-survey etc etc. As soon as he abandoned his appeal all enquiries ceased. Circumstances where alledged administrative requirement and threats are used as a means to force agreement to terms of a new lease. Also in part by pretending that By-Law 1981–03 was in effect he obtained a new lease with this party. This man also received a letter from the Royal Bank asking him to pay his 1982 rent direct to the Band who enclosed a document signed by the Chief whereby he assigned these rents to the Bank prior to the time that they were due and payable to the Crown under the lease.

8. Westgate Mobile Park — Ted Zellmar — Owner. The Chief induced him to enter into a new lease partly on the strength of the fact that By-Law 1981–03 was operative. The Band received $590. as a development fee from him. He was not required to pay for "future fire

protection", to provide large water storage, to keep a green park area, or to make his paved roads wider than 20 feet.

9. Billabong Mobile Park — Don Lauriault — Owner. The Chief attempted to get him to agree to a new lease partly on the strength of the fact that by-law 1981–03 was in force.

10. Westview Village Park — Park Mobile Home Sales Ltd., Bruce York — Owner.

Mr. King MP has given particulars of this complaint to your department. It is a lengthy and involved matter but some of the points are as follows; By delaying approvals for development plans he attempted to cause the owner to be in default of the terms of his sub-lease which had a time limit. It would then have reverted to the Chiefs brother. Failing in that regard he attempted to buy it for $1,400,000. far below fair value and threatens to cause his lease rent on the next review (1982) to be set so high that it couldnt be afforded if he refused to sell. When this failed he ignores the fact that the band has accepted a $500.00 "development permit" fee and says a mistake was made and the total fees in respect to the 80 some lot extension to his park is now $31,000. The owner disputes these fees so the Chief caused a Band Council Resolution to be sent to B.C. Hydro and B.C. Telephone denying them the right to enter band property to serve this development. Up to the present time he has been successful in this ploy. The owner offered to put the disputed fees in trust to await the outcome of a hearing in respect to these fees which are demanded pursuant to By-Law 1979–15. This is refused. The Band will not alledge a By-Law violation in court simply I suggest because they are aware that the By-Law is worthless. The by-law was never approved by the Minister and by default therefor falls under Section 81 of the act which does not authorize such a By-Law. He has effectively prevented this man from carrying on his normal business since Nov 1981 and it continues to this day. All of this conveniently at a time when the Band itself is attempting to obtain customers for their own park next door. Recently also the Band offers customers a $2000. rebate on anyone locating a mobile home in their park or Westbrook Estates park located on each side of Mr. Yorks park. Such rebate of course does not apply to any other parks. This is only a small part of his complaint. Call it attempted extortion or whatever you like but it is clearly, in my opinion, unlawful.

11. Westbrook Mobile Park — Tomasina Invest. Co — Owner Gary Hsu is one of a number of the directors. Before Chief Ron Derrickson would submit this lease application he personally demanded and received a benefit of $11,000 as a condition thereof. This was done by way of the fact that HSU owned a house which he had a buyers offer on for $151,000. The Chief wanted this house for his enstranged wife and family. HSU sold it to him for $140,000. on the strength of the fact that

this was required of him in order to obtain the lease for this park area. Andrew Archondoas was a partner of HSU at that time and is a witness. The lease was obtained by HSU and Archondoas was active in the matter until the Chief demanded a $50,000. deposit prior to the lease having been signed. Archondoas would not agree to this and became cautious and backed out of his part in the deal and quit his interest and funds expended in favour of HSU. The terms of the lease had all been agreed to and HSU was deeply involved financially — he formed a company which is the present owner — when the lease was finally presented to him it contained a condition that the company had to pay the band 20% of gross sales profits — a matter which he had previously understood was not required. He received an ultimatum to sign it or else. Because of his deep involvement he was coerced into signing or loosing everything. A person may say this was a misunderstanding or a mistake but I now know of at least four occasions when this same "mistake" had been made. It is part of the scam and the "similar Acts" are evidence of intent as opposed to mistake. Another "benefit" received by the Chief dealing with this park is that the directors provided him and his lady friend with an expense paid trip to Hawian Islands. It is because of this benefit and the 20% of sales that this park was included in the $2000. so called rebate scheme.

12. Edmundo Barone and Tosh Naka in 1981 were interested in building a mobile park. The chief showed them a site owned by Harry Derrickson. Terms and conditions were discussed and agreed. They proceeded with planning and engineering and when this was completed they were assured that all was in order and a deposit of $10,000. was insisted on. Then they were offered a further five acres adjoining to make a larger park. The same terms and conditions were agreed to. There was an old house on the property and it was agreed between the parties that it had no value over and above the agreed lease costs. When the lease was presented to Barone for signature it was not as agreed in fact it required that he pay an additional $20,000. for the old house. Barone would not sign the lease. The ultimatum was sign it or loose your deposit. He did not sign it and none of the funds have been returned. Exaggerated and untruthful matters were alluded to by the Chief in selling this proposal.

13. Golden Acres Ltd — L.R. Crosby — Owner. My complaint has been previously outlined to you. Further to the matter of "consent" in selling my holdings. I asked Mr. Clark, DIAND about this matter and he replied that it Quote "cannot be denied without good reason so long as it is consistent with the covenants of the head lease" unquote. I take this as "policy". This policy is being refused here by the chief and he is using it as another tool to obtain personal financial benefit. Who is right. One the matter of park area to be retained in a mobile park. On 17 June 1980 I received a copy of the By-Law # 1979/80–11 from the bank with covering correspondence signed by the Chief. Among other things it requires Mobile Home Parks to retain 7.5% of the total area to

be retained as an open area. In my planning I followed this rule. Now I find out that such a By-Law was never passed nor was it ever approved by the Minister and to my knowledge simply does not exist. I also find that the adjoining park expanded during the same period was not required to keep any open area whatever. A similar situation exists in respect to the water fire storage I was required to build and the width of the roads etc. These discrepancies are directly attributable to the Chief and council and resulted in about 50,000. unnecessary construction costs plus depriving me of an additional monthly income of about 1000. per month for the remaining 40 years of the lease.

14. The Band By-Laws are being used as the means or justification for collecting large sums of moiney from developers and mobile park residents as evidenced in previous paragraphs. Where is the authority for fees for "future fire protection", park areas etc etc. If they do exist why are they not applied the same to everyone? The band demands building permits for all additions to mobile homes and quotes by-Law 1979–15 as the authority. Again as per para 10 — there is no such authority. DIAND have advised that quote "Although the Minister may dissallow a By-Law, he seldom does, leaving it to the court to decide whether or not a by-law is intra-vires of the Act" Unquote. Please re-examine that policy in the light of the facts outlined herein. What would really assist would be for your legal department to examine all By-Laws originating from this band and provide an opinion to the Band and the park Owners Association as to what if any are applicable to Mobile Home Parks and our tenants.

15. Mr. Clarks letter of 16 Feb 82 stated quote "By certain authori- ties the Westbank Band was advised that it should undertake the administration of leases and other land agreements so long as the general terms and policy of the Government under the Indian Act was adhered to. In the Absence of an Official Departmental Officer the Band has undertaken to assume Departmental Responsibilities in return for funding and training." Unquote. Enquiries from the band as to their authority resulted in the following; Quote "the Westbank Indian Band is delegated to act on behalf of the Minister in certain instances so the band is an agent of the Minister". Unquote. It would assist us if we were advised precisely what authority has been assigned to them.

16. Mr. King MP informed me that the Minister enquired as why his department should be concerned or involved in the matter of my complaint. I could only reply that the contents of this letter will vividly display facts which I trust are not the general terms and policy of his department. Nor, I trust, is he likely to condone unlawful behaviour on the part of someone acting as his agent.

17. There is already some evidence to support the view that the overall circumstance may, if properly investigated, disclose a conspiracy

to defraud. Park Owners feel unable to make such a direct criminal complaint at this time without the knowledge that an investigation may provide. It will not assist us if Criminal action is taken and in fact such action could result in the often used excuse for the lack of any official action in the interim, this is something we cannot abide with. We require action to resolve past injustice and hopefully prevent the current and future continuation of civil wrong.

18. Could you please assist my by providing the names and mailing addresses of all members of the House Standing Committee on Indian Affairs. Thank you.

L.   R.   Crosby

17 Feb 82

The Minister of Indian Affairs
Ottawa, Ontario.

Dear Sir: Re: Golden Acres Ltd.
                             I.R. #9, Westbank, B.C.

After much thought I reluctantly wish to bring to your attention an intolerable situation which has arisen as a result of the administration on this reserve. The reputation of your department and the Crown has been and is presently being severely damaged principaly because of the actions of one person Chief Ronald Derrickson hereafter called the "chief". He may purport to be trying to help his people but the methods used are doing much more harm to the reputation of Indian people in general and this reserve in particular. Much more could be written that would be hearsay on my part so I will refrain from those items other than to say that I believe an investigation would find many of them to be true and I can refer you to a number of sources.

I have personal knowledge of the following allegations;
(1)   Attempted extortion
(2)   He is attempting to use the ministers appointment as an Agent of the Crown for personal gain.
(3)   By printing known lies while ostensibly performing duties as an Agent of the Crown he has committed a civil wrong for which the Crown could be held liable.
(4)   He is causing the Crown to be in violation of a lease which was entered into.
(5)   By unethical conduct or breach of trust he is causing his own people and the Crown to be held in disrepute.

(2) In 1969–70 I leased 3.5 acres from the Crown — the chief was locatee. I started to build permanent buildings thereon — some were completed. For a number of reasons I sought and obtained permission to convert to a mobile home park. In 1976 I wanted to expand — his father owned the adjoining land but instead of leasing it from him the chief bought it from him and leased it to me. This was a further 4 acres making a total of 7.5 acres. I developed this and as long as the lease was being administered by your department (DIAND) there were no problems, there was a good working relationship, without conflict of any description. In 1979 his father Ted Derrickson started to develop adjoining land but for some reason did not pursue it and asked me if I wanted to lease an additional 6.27 hectares. There were many negotiations but it is suffice to say I leased the land and during 1981 I embarked on a park extension costing some $300,000.

3. During these negotiations the possibility of changing the existing lease #47959 from a straight land rental basis to one of shared rental

income. I indicated I would give this consideration provided it did not entail giving away the rental income from two duplexes I had built or effecting my brothers home. Lease #47959 came up for rental review 1 Sept 86 — In July I received a letter from the band setting the rent for that lease at $16898.per year. I considered it to be fair and in line with other mobile parks so I paid it without comment or discussion. Prior to 1 Sept I was asked to come to the band office — I did — and met with the chief and Mr. McCullough. At that time the new proposed lease was first presented to me and I was expected to sign it right away. I was surprised to find that even a cursory examination revealed that it required me to give away a 20% interest in all buildings including my brothers home and also to share any income the buildings produced. I said I could not sign it — they were very busy with a number of leases — so Mr. McCullough and I had a seperate discussion about the matter out in the entrance foyer. He can confirm that I did not agree to the new lease.

4. I next had contact with the Chief on 22 Oct 81 when I went to his office to get clarification on some other matters — during the conversation I observed that he had become very arrogant. He said "I make all the decisions originating from the band, Vancouver or the Department of Indian Affairs," also "I run the whole show around here" and he has "found it necessary to threaten, bully, lie and cheat and to anything else necessary to get my own way". I was alarmed and disappointed in these statements and immediately resolved to make notes of this conversation and to thereafter require confirmation in writing in respect to anything he told me.

5. Also on 22 Oct 81 he said something about the effect of the new lease — I told him again that I could not and had not signed the new lease he proposed. He at first argued that I had signed the new lease — I told him I had not. He became angry and called his secretary to check the file — when she confirmed that it had not been signed he said — "you are going to be dam sorry if you dont sign that lease", also "you are going to have to take the consequences and live with it" and to his secretary "here Barb throw these dam things in the wastepaper basket". I say those are threats made in an attempt to acquire personal gain — this is borne out by his subsequent letters of the 4th and 17th Dec 81 which were sent out without notice to or any further contact with me whatsoever after the 22 Oct 81 conversation.

6. During the summer the chief was aware that I was relying somewhat on the sub-leasing the two duplexes I had built in order to have sufficient development capital. Also that people by the name of Windsor had given the company funds which would be used towards the costs of a sub-lease. Under the head lease I must have "Consent" to sublease so in dealing with the Windsors it was made clear that unless and until the "consent" was satisfied and the sub-lease actually

registered as such then the funds were to be a direct demand loan to the company. I have on three occasions in the past sub-leased other parcels of land within the head lease with the consent of your department and I anticipated no undue problems. I asked my counsel to draft the sub-lease but he exprienced difficulty and delay in getting the chiefs approval. Finally the Windsor's became upset at the delays and other unfavorable publicity arising from the administration of the band and they asked for the return of their loan — it was paid. The chief is not aware of this latter fact.

7. Therefor the situation prior to 4 Dec 81 is that the chief is aware I had encountered expenses and circumstances which would make me financially vulnerable. He was aware I had not signed the new lease and that I had paid the rent on lease #47959 because as locatee he had received it himself. Despite these facts he wrote a letter to the Royal Bank in Kelowna at the Branch I deal with and therein made the known false statement —

"Lease #47959" "between the Crown and Golden Acres is no longer in good standing because Golden Acres Ltd., have not signed the renewal of the lease".

The letter indicated thereon that a copy was sent to Vancouver DIAND Att. Mr. McCullough. The Band being notified by an agent of the Crown took this matter very seriously. They are aware of my lease and in fact have a copy of it. The bank replied to the letter as follows; "It has been our opinion that the captioned client hald a long term lease and no renewals were necessary. Please provide us with a copy of the renewal lease at your earliest opportunity, pointing out, if any, the changes it will make to the lease now in effect." also "In view of the seriousness of your letter, we have frozen our clients credit lines until this matter is resolved". The chief did not reply in writing to the bank but he did phone and I am told he had some excuse but in fact he did not send a copy of the "renewal of lease". I suggest this was because there simply is no such form required and he didnt want to show the bank that the form he referred to was in fact a new lease.

To make certain there was no mistake about what he wanted signed — I went to see him — he was present but would not see me nor could I make an appointment. I phoned his secretary Barb — I wasnt allowed to speak to the Chief so I told her I wanted to be certain in my own mind that there was no mistake about what he wanted signed — I asked if it was a renewal of lease or some other form or whether or not it was the new lease that I had already refused to sign. She said just a minute — she spoke to someone near at hand and told me "no — it is the new lease he is talking about." I wrote a letter to the band stating that their letter of 4 Dec — "is neither technically or legally correct. In my opinion the letter and the circumstances leading up to it may be a civil or criminal wrong A CIVIL OR CRIMINAL WRONG and one that may bring into serious question the business ethics of the band chief and council.

On the 17 Dec 81 I made a special trip to Vancouver DIAND. I spoke to Mr. McCullough — there was no copy of the letter on file so I gave him one. He didnt want to talk to me on the matter saying he was assigned to some other department. In answer to my problem it was indicated to me that I could seek civil redress. I was referred to Mr. Clark — I told him about my problems and received gaurded sympathy but no indication of action. I finally requested that in view of the urgency it would assist if he wrote a letter to my bank indicating the status of the lease. I called back later to pick it up since copies were for me and the bank — it was addressed to the band.

8. On 22 Dec 81 I received a letter from the band dated 17 Dec 81 and again a copy sent to my bank and DIAND Vancouver Att. S. McCullough. It was full of false statements some being:
"any debenture requires the Westbank Indian Band to give notice to the bank if problems arise concerning the lease"
"you agreed to a new lease"
"Your questionable sale to the Windsor's"
**"Under the lease you have 60 days to refer the matter to the Federal Court if you disagree with the rent. You have failed to give this notice"
"you have built and sold illegal duplexes and have accepted money from the Windsors when you cannot convey title and the lease prevents you from subleasing without ministerial consent."
"we can in effect cancel your lease for the above illegal infractions and we therefor suggest you execute the lease as previous agreed".

** while the statement itself is true it conveys to my bank that there was some disagreement over the rent which is false. It artfully neglects to say it was in fact paid.

9. I did not answer to the band on their letter of 17 Dec as it appeared obvious that such action would only result in a further tirade of lies. I wrote to DIAND Vancouver outlining the allegations and reasons why they were false — this was on the 18 Jan 82 I indicated in that letter some of the problems we face on this reserve — when I didnt get an answer by the 10 Feb I phoned and Mr. Clark disclaimed any knowledge of the letter but promised to look into it. On 17th Feb I phoned again and was told a reply had been prepared that day. Mr. Clark is coming to Kelowna on the 24 Feb and I have made arrangements to pick him up at the Airport. I will give him a copy of this letter and make myself available to answer any questions he may have. I'm sorry — I should have added to para 7 that the letter from Mr. Clark to the Band et al states in part "It is apparent that the above-noted lease is in good standing".

10. The lease states that before I can deal with it I must first have "consent first sought and obtained". Because of my predicament I asked the band in a letter of 4 Jan 82 for consent to sell. In his reply of 14 Jan the chief says;

"if the lease is in good standing consent is standard procedure. The property may be listed and an agreement for sale signed before obtaining a consent ".

I'm not going to be held to ransom over the matter of consent. I asked for consent and it has not been granted. Also it would be highly unfair if not illegal for the locatee to insist in changing the conditions of lease before agreeing to consent to a new lease for a new owner. I predict this will happen. The chief also says in the letter;

"We are still waiting for you to come to the band office to sign the agreement to put your lease in good standing. The rental review is not complete and therefor I will have no opiton but to refer the entire lease to the Federal Court of Canada and the band solicitor if this is not cleared up completely within seven days of receipt of this letter. Many steps have been taken by your company which are not consistent with the lease clauses and we feel this new lease will solve all of these problems".

That sure isnt saying much for the ethics or integrity of an agent of the Minister but it does further clarify his intent and purpose. All of this is written long after he has been told by DIAND in Vancouver that the lease is in good standing. The reference to "rental review" is in respect to lease #47959 with the implied threat that it can THAT IT CAN be re-opened again and a higher rent demanded. I am not concerned about the other threat simply because I have abided by the lease. But it appears likely that he intends to further harass me at every opportunity in an attempt to find something wrong with the development.

11. In response to his letter I asked my solicitor to arrange for a meeting in the hope that perhaps he could better explain my inability to conform to his wishes — I am told he refused to meet with us saying he didnt need any advise on how to run his business and words to the effect that while we might win this round he would get even when the next rent review comes up. Throughout this matter I have been unable to satisfy myself that the remainder of the band council are aware and condone what has been done. All of the letters are signed by the chiefallegedly on behalf of the Council. I did ask him in a previous letter whether he was writing as locatee or on behalf of council but he did not answer. In view of this I have again on 17 Feb 82 sent a letter requesting a meeting with council. My previous similar request of 11 Dec 81 has not been granted.

12. So that is the situation in chronological order as of this date. My bank is still withholding my credit even though there is a debenture in place for security and I cannot at this moment meet my committments. Perhaps a complete retraction of the false statements, an apology and some assurance to my bank that adequate supervision will return to this reserve might assist the present situation, however, I am satisfied their decision arises from the general reliability of the band administration and from more than this single occurrence. To suggest, as before, that I take civil action is really an abrogation of the departments undertaking to me.

13. The chief has misled or lied to me in the past but I have known him long enough to evaluate what he says. New developers, if what they relate is true, have been subjected to what may amount to fraudulent misrepresentation of facts to entice them to invest. Other investors, like myself relied more on the conditions of lease and the fact that I was leasing it from the Crown and not the band or chief. I was totally unaware until Dec 81 that DIAND had in fact began to divest themselves of their undertakings in the leases by passing the administration of the leases over to the local band council. This may not mean much to your department and you may have a legal right to appoint whoever you wish to act as an agent of the Crown but to me and other investors this was a very serious step to take without first advising the other party to our agreements. Could we not, at the very least, have been advised of your intentions? I for one would never have leased the lands If I had prior knowledge of that fact. On this reserve alone there must be 40 millions of dollars invested largely on the basis of our reliance on the integrity of your department. The band are not required to consider our interests as they are not elected by or required in any manner to hear our submissions. In a development they put up their land but experience has taught them they will never loose their land — in fact I and other taxpayers will pay to ensure that fact. They may sign the leases to indicate agreement but they give no covenant nor is their any penalty to require them to live up to the lease. When they administer it they have nothing to loose and some will always be inclined to do anything legal or otherwise to enhance their income and power. They are well aware and rely on the fact that it usually will cost an individual lessee more to appeal to the court than what is at stake realizing as they do that in doing so they will incur the rath of the locatee and council.

In all sincerity I must submit that it is morally wrong for your department to act as a leasing agent for the Indians if you dont intend to administer the leases. This is directly misleading investors. Where a band administration demonstrates an abuse of authority or a lack of integrity to administer the leases then their appointment to act as an agent of the crown should be immediately suspended pending an investigation. To do otherwise is to invite public criticism of your department and the Crown.

14. The Queen gave a covenant to the company that "it will peaceably hold the land without unlawful interruption by the Crown ". I will concede that the "unlawful interruption" is yet to be established before the courts but perhaps what is of equal importance is whether or not the Minister, now being aware of the facts, intends to wait until the irrevocable damage is done. I cannot overstate the urgent need to immediately resolve this matter. What is at stake, in my situation alone, is the nearly one million dollar replacement value of my development and the revenue therefrom which I might normally expect over the remaining 40 years of the lease.

15. The chief openly states that he makes all band decisions and I believe this to be the truth. There are very few voting band members — I have been told fifty some — I believe council members are simply overwhelmed by the chiefs methods and are totally incapable to oppose him. Also between relatives, friends and those band members who have benefitted financially during his tenure he has little to fear about any re-election. He is totally blind to the damage he is causing. Even his father has expressed concern to me about what he is doing.

16. In addition to the above matters — What is he doing?

Practically daily there is a press release, T.V. interview, court appearance, newspaper interview etc in a running fued between anyone or anything which he doesnt agree with. Particularily involving the mobile home and park industry which ironically supplies the majority of the bands income. Media comments atributed to him or the band council include;

"the mobile tenants are going to live by our rules"
"we are going to form our own local government and have complete control over everything"
"all non-band members on the reserve are here illegally and must get a license to remain"
"We are going to control all the rents on the reserve" "have our own rentalsman"

and on and on almost daily until it has reached the point where potential residents in a mobile park have as a first question? Is this on Westbank Indian Land? and they do not locate because of that fact. How much fiscal damage has been done — it is impossible to estimate. Many residents are pensioners who become very upset because of the uncertainty etc. Some claim this has caused a heart attack and other illnesses. Names can be provided. This is not surprising when the band lawyer stated in public —

"four thousand Westside residents could be forced to leave their homes because their occupancy of 17 mobile home parks on the Westbank Indian Band Reserve is illegal" according to the press.

Mobile parks on the reserve are decorated with "For Sale" signs wherever they signs are not prohibited by previously agreed to park rules. One park reports 32 signs out of a total of 72 units. Many parks themselves are for sale but no buyers simply because no financial institution will loan risk capital on this reserve.

17. Adding to the above problems is the following;

None band members resident are being subjected to an array of By-Laws etc purported to be for one purpose or another but in fact they are being used almost exclusively to produce band revenue and nothing else; Examples

In expanding my park a lease was agreed upon but no advice given in respect to a development permit until you are too far along to back out then a fee of $2600. demanded.

Building Permits: likewise no prior notice then a fee of $25.00 average each for "inspection fees". Last year 25 of my new tenants obtained the permits but to my knowledge not a single inspection was carried out by the band.

By-Law 1981–02 — Land is leased for a purpose and a fee — occupancy allowed and encouraged then after tenants are located they propose this by-law to require $10. per person per year for a license for something previously agreed to. Thus creating a tidy, after the fact, annual land income of some $40,000. The chief also told me that it would apply to mobile parks but not to other non-band residents elsewhere on the reserve.

Registering Debenture: A by-law requiring a registration fee five times greater than a similar fee required Provincially and this for a service provided by your own Government department. Resulting in my case to being billed for $1000. for the band to act as a totally unnecessary forwarding agent.

18. Despite the length of this letter I trust you will appreciate that I have not included all of the facts or circumstances but I trust there is sufficient for you to make a decision. Also please appreciate my position that as long as the chief remains in his present position it will, during or after any investigation, be an impossible situation for me to be subject to his administration because despite the request hereby made for confidentiallity any enquiries will in time indicate the source. I request that Vancouver DIAND re-assume the administration of my lease as originally undertaken.

19. I feel that I have been very badly dealt with during this matter including the departments total inaction to date — some two months after first notified. I would like to think there is a means open for a reasonable person to seek redress without having to rely on public opinion or expose. My immediate problem is a $35000. paving bill received 21 Dec 81 (after credit freeze). It is two months overdue and the firm are pressing. Since the delay is not of my doing is there any manner you could assist me to meet this committment and ensure solvency until this matter is resolved?

Yours Truly,

L.R. Crosby — President
Golden Acres Ltd.,
R.R. # 1, S-17 C-1
Westbank, B.C.

Before finishing this letter and having reference to para.9. Mr. CLARK'S secretary phoned to tell me that he was too busy to meet with me on the 24 Feb. I indicated the urgent nature of this matter to no avail.

The Hon. David Crombie
Minister of Indian Affairs
Parliament Buildings
Ottawa, Ontario. K1A OH4.   6 May 86

Sir;   Re: I.R. #9, Westbank, B.C.

1. We are concerned that enquiries to examine abuse of power or to identify responsibility for actions or inactions of personnel within your department (DIA) will, of necessity, identify circumstances of suspected criminal offences. Those suspected are thereby provided an opportunity to cover evidence or establish alibis. I feel a criminal investigation is warranted and that it should occur before or at least at the same time as any other enquiry.

2. Other reports previously supplied to DIA include an opinion by Dept. of Justice — " (T.Marsh) is of the opinion that the B.C. Region could be seen as conspiring with it's tenant — — " While neither may be a person, the principals involved can be parties to the offence or an accessory after the fact.

Other suspicious circumstances were identified. Despite these facts, no investigation, worthy of the name, was ever done. This led to, and continues to cause, accusations of "cover-up" and the DIA "peek-a-boo" look at events does not deal with the situation. It appears to be that whenever enquiries are made the person assigned is not from given the necessary authority to do the job, is prevented from completing the job or if the results are unfavorable, then nothing is done and the matter is approached by some other manner when the issue isn't abandoned.

I will attempt to briefly correlate some of the suspected criminal offences arising from circumstances reported to or known by our association members.

Using the brief provided to your office on 1 Oct 84, as a reference the attached summary is provided.

3. Surely DIA must be responsible for the protection of public funds both in direct expenditure and/or liabilities incurred. These simply are not met if DIA fail to cause an investigation in circumstances where there is reasonable grounds to suspect that an offence, civil or criminal, was committed by an employee, agent or appointee. All matters reported arise directly from the Band being allowed or authorized to assume certain administration duties and they, to my knowledge, still possess this authority. This authority should be cancelled forthwith and then the investigation and/or enquiry, done. There is a fine line between suspicion and belief which can only be dealt with after a genuine investigation. An independent investigation is necessary in order to provide credence to any subsequent decision — Without it — indeci-

sion, distrust and accusations prevail. I believe the issue must be faced squarely in order to best serve the interests of the band, the department and others.

4. Much of the evidence avilable now may lack the clarity that was available initially. The unreasonable delays already experienced severely hamper the quality of justice.

Since the suspicions are primarily directed toward persons connected, directly or indirectly with your department I consider it appropriate to refer the matter directly to you. Please advise me if, in your opinion, these matters should, more properly, be directed to the Provincial Attorney General's Department.

Yours Truly

(L. R. Crosby) President
Westbank Mobile Park Owners Association.

SUMMARY — REFERENCE 1 OCT 84 —
BRIEF TO MINISTER

(1) Person(s) comprising the Band Council or the principals of related firms are hereafter referred to as "Band" — made a false misrepresentation of fact (Exh A-4 & A-5) as to the status of the Golden Acres Lease for the apparent purpose of acquiring a new lease which could provide greater personal benefits. This causes suspicions that the offence of attempted fraud may have been committed. There may also be a defamatory libel or an attempt to extort by that means.

(2) The Band appears to have published and distributed an apparent false document (Exh A-22) and caused or attempted to cause other persons to act upon it. This is suspect to be Forgery or Uttering. (Golden Acres et al)

(3) The Band apparently published a false document (by-Law 1979–80–11) (Exh A-20) and cause or attempted to cause persons to act on it. (Park Mobile)

(4) The Band may have conspired with DIA or other persons in an attempt to defeat the course of justice in circumventing a BC Supreme Court ruling — "Rentalsman issue" and/or a creditor, Dondaldson Engineering Ltd. (Hobbs)

(5) The Band appears to have attempted to obtain money from Thomasina Investments Ltd., by falsely pretending that a debenture registration fee was payable pursuant to by-law when it appears that such a by-law is non-existent. (Hsu et al).

(6) The Band apparently attempted to obtain $60,000 (later reduced to $40,000) from Acres Holdings Ltd by reason of a development by-law — an examination of all purported By-Laws fails to disclose such a particular requirement. This demand originates in part from Okanagan Planning & Engineering Co. Ltd (OPEC) or at least from a principal or employee of that firm — which incidentally the Band insisted that developers use for planning etc. Later there is reason to believe an employee of OPEC also worked with the Band. This and other circumstances gives rise to the suspicion that the latter persons may be part of a conspiracy to attempt to obtain such funds by fraud. (Acres Holdings — also Exh A-19)

(7) A welfare fraud suspicion is reported to Mr. Leask, DIA on 17 Sept 84 — by way of a letter — a copy of which is attached. There is suspicion of Conspiracy between the Band welfare person and/or Mr. Monti who reportedly collects rents etc., on behalf of the Band Chief. The Band Chief owns or has an interest in the firm which possess the building concerned. The matter is not investigated.

(8) The Band is suspected of demanding or receiving a benefit relating to the affairs or business of his principal, namely; the Crown. (S.383) DIA officials were made aware of these suspicions and are privy to the offence. (Thomasina — HSU, ARCHONDOAS, KIEHL-BAUCH).

(9) The Band is suspected of numerous incidents of what may be Mischief — in respect to the lawful use, enjoyment or operation of property. There is also the suggestion or suspicion that DIA person(s) by ommitting to do an act that was their duty to do — may be deemed to have caused the occurrence of the event. (S.386) — Example; DIA allow or cause a Band road (governed by Sec. 34 of Indian Act) to be transferred by the Band Chief, from Band Road Lands, to Band Chief as locatee. This allowed the locatee to claim a right of possession of property which disected and landlocked a portion of an existing mobile home park which had previously been sub-leased by the locatee's company to Park Mobile Home Sales Ltd. DIA then actively assist the Band in demanding fees for the right to use such road. The time element and other factors suggest these occurrences may have been part of a pre-conceived plan which was successfully used in the sense that large sums of money were directly or indirectly obtained by this means. (Park Mobile — YORK).

(10) The Band appears to bear responsibility for what may be a Criminal Breach of Contract (S.380) when they as an employee or agent of the Minister of the Crown deprived to a great extent some inhabitants of a mobile park of their supply of electical power or water. (Park Mobile — York, Alexander).

These are only a part of what can be suspected from the information contained in the reference brief. There are reasonable grounds for these suspicions which are in part documented. No one knows, at this point in time, if an investigation will provide sufficient evidence on which to base any charges, however, I believe that justice and fairness to both the Band and others concerned requires a complete investigation.

Other members of Parliament who have personally interviewed some of the complainants in this matter are: John Frazer, Lorne McCuish and Fred King. Other members who have some personal knowledge of portions of the circumstances are Frank Oberle and Dr. Lorne Greenaway.

Chapter 8

Departmental Responses to Westbank Matters

This Commission was asked to ascertain whether there were any improprieties on the part of members of the Department of Indian Affairs. Counsel were of the view that the word improprieties referred to major transgressions such as criminal acts, acts of deliberate cover-up or perhaps acts which would justify the dismissal of a civil servant. In those senses, I cannot say that improprieties occurred.

Another question posed in the terms of reference was whether the Department's responsibilities and functions were carried out in accordance with law, established policy or generally accepted standards of competence and fairness.

The failures of the Department, if they could be summarized, were not those of malevolence, but rather failures to fully perceive responsibilities. On occasion the Department or its members suffered impaired vision in the good cause of devolution. Sometimes problems arose from the Department's failure to make timely adjustments when the implementation of devolution took unforeseen turns. I felt that at times the Department allowed its judgement to be influenced by a strong and aggressive chief who came to power after the wave of unrest that swept through British Columbia in 1975.

In 1975, an event occurred that was central to the problems at Westbank. That year the Vernon office of the Kootenay-Okanagan District was occupied by Indian bands and organizations and shortly thereafter the office was closed down permanently. The events at Westbank in the years following 1975 took place against a background of change in Indian politics, in governmental policy, and in the organization of the Department of Indian Affairs.

Governmental Policy — The Change from Paternalism

In 1963, the federal government introduced a welfare program for Native Indians at rates comparable to the provinces. This was perhaps the beginning of greater assistance to Indian people. The federal government also made commitments to provide other social programs and economic development and assistance. Funds were provided for education, and some steps were taken towards remedying the poor conditions that prevailed on many reserves.

In 1969, the federal government issued a White Paper entitled "Statement of the Government of Canada on Indian Policy, 1969". The ideal championed in that White Paper was the removal of the legislative and constitutional basis of discrimination. The Paper proposed the abolition of the Indian Act and that Indians should own their own lands. One feature of the Paper that provoked controversy was a proposal that services provided for Indians should be provided through the same channels as services provided to all other Canadians. For example, welfare and education would be channelled through provincial governments. The Paper promised funds for economic development and it promised special help for those who were most disadvantaged.

The Indian community was quick to condemn the White Paper. It was construed by many to point towards integration and assimilation. The strong reaction led to a shift in government direction that sought to achieve, as one witness described it, "the preservation of a separate Indian identity within Canadian society".

At the same time, Indian people were becoming increasingly aware of their ability to manage their own affairs and to govern themselves. Indian people sought self-government and governmental policy moved to accommodate those desires to some extent.

Witnesses at the Commission hearings referred to a Treasury Board Minute of 1974 which authorized the Department to transfer the administration of many programs from the Department itself to Indian organizations. Perhaps that Treasury Board Minute was a watershed, for prior to that time the Department of Indian Affairs was primarily responsible for the delivery of services to Indian bands. After that time, more and more program delivery was carried out by Indian bands and organizations.

The organization of the Department of Indian Affairs went through a number of changes in the 1960's and 1970's. Prior to those years, the Department operated on the concept of the Indian agency. In British Columbia (and elsewhere), the province was divided into districts; the District Manager had complete responsibility and virtually controlled what went on among Indian bands and their members. Authority was centralized in Ottawa. In the 1960's and 1970's, there was a significant reallocation of authority which gave greater authority to the regions.

In the mid-1970's, the B.C. Region was organized into the following significant sections: Reserves and Trusts, Economic Development, Local Government, Education and Engineering. The names of the sections were to change from time to time, often according to Departmental policy changes and shifts in headquarters (Ottawa) organization. The Regional Director General was responsible for matters beyond the daily functions of the Regional office, while the Director of Operations looked after the internal management of the Regional office.

With the Vernon district office closed, the district functions were transferred to Vancouver. There is now a "Central District" office in Vancouver which administers the day-to-day affairs of Okanagan bands where the administration has not devolved upon the bands themselves. Many Indians appear satisfied that the District office be so far away. Perhaps they perceive they have greater control over their own destiny under this arrangement.

The shift in governmental policy towards transferring programs to Indian control has been accompanied by a significant decrease in the number of employees of the Department. Mr. Fred Walchli, former Regional Director General, said:

> During that period, we moved to complete, to the extent possible, the transfer of all programs. When I left the Department [1983], there were...only about 13% of the budget which could be transferred...all 194 bands were now operating programs...At that time, there were 23 tribal councils...

He summarized the period of change as follows:

> ...over the last eighteen years, we had moved from a position where we were in confrontation with the Indian people on virtually everything, to a point where we were in harmony, at least with their goals. To illustrate what I mean; initially, back in the '60's and '70's we were moving along, integrating Indian children into provincial schools. The Indian objective was control of Indian education. So, we were on a collision course.
> Prior to 1973, the Government of Canada refused to recognize land claims. In 1973 the government brought in a policy to support the resolution of land claims. Prior — in the early '60's, or rather late '60's and early '70's, Indian self-government was no more than a dream by some Indian people. The Department had virtual control over the lives of the Indian people.
> By the end of the era, what happened was that the Indian direction and the Department's direction were in harmony to the extent that they at least agreed on the objectives. We agree on the objectives of Indian self-government. We agree on the objectives of improved socio-economic conditions for reserves. We agree on the settlement of land claims. We agree on the need for an economic basis for reserves. There are still a lot of disagreement as to how these are to be accomplished, but those are issues which are currently being negotiated, either in the Constitutional forum or in the — through other policy discussions.

The Westbank Indian Band

In many respects, the Westbank Band was on the cutting edge of the new developments. As noted elsewhere in the Report, it moved forward more quickly than many bands. It is a band which, according to the evidence, contains some 250 band members. There are two occupied reserves, Reserves 9 and 10, with some 3000–5000 people who are non-Native living on the Reserves. Some reside in a number of mobile home parks on Reserve 9 and others live in an attractive subdivision on Reserve 10. To some extent, Westbank issues have developed because of the Band's semi-urban location and because of initiatives taken by the Band government. Many of the problems found at Westbank may well be indicators of issues that will arise in other places. Mr. Walchli adverted to this when he said:

> The problems in Westbank have been highlighted primarily because they have moved faster and further than most other band councils.

As narrated in the Introduction to this Report, the Westbank Band has only existed as a separate band of Indians since 1962, when it separated from the Okanagan Band. Two persons participating in the initiative for separation were the parents of Ronald Derrickson and Noll Derriksan. The two sons have been chiefs for significant periods since the Band's inception. The family appears to be capable and intelligent. By 1970, a large amount of valuable land on the two Reserves had been acquired by one or other members of the family. Resentments were kindled because of this.

The Thornton Report

Allegations of undue acquisitions of land by Noll Derriksan, Ronald Derrickson and other family members were being made as early as 1970. Those allegations became the subject of an investigation and report by Mr. Herb Thornton of the Department of Justice.

Mr. Thornton looked at the acquisition of a number of parcels of land by members of the Derrickson family to determine whether any impropriety had occurred. He looked at a number of transactions where land had been obtained by the Derricksons through allotment. With respect to those allotments he said:

> It will be seen that several of the above 20 parcels of land were allocated to the Derricksons by the Westbank Council, and that the Derricksons have always been members of the Council. In spite of this, I am unable to find any impropriety in the allocations, because the regulations under the Indian Act regulating procedure at Band Council meetings do not prevent a council member from acting, even when he has a direct interest in the subject-matter.

Section 19 of the Regulations (B.C. 1953–1313) reads:

> 19. Every member present when a question is put shall vote thereon unless the council shall excuse them, or unless he is personally interested in the question, in which case he shall not be obligated to vote.

The regulation in question has yet to be changed. It is doubtful that anyone today would view that regulation as a satisfactory guideline concerning conflict of interest. While policy circulars impose higher obligations upon the band, the regulation as such remains. Hopefully, the experience of this Commission and certain of the recommendations I make will tend to sensitize bands and the Department to this problem. As lands become more valuable, the loose practices of the past in this area are no longer to be tolerated.

The Regional Director General and the Westbank Band

Mr. Fred Walchli had been with the Department of Indian Affairs for ten years when he returned to Vancouver in 1976. He had spent the previous several years as Regional Director General in Alberta. Mr. Walchli's advancement in the Department had been rapid and he had dealt with some significant matters in Alberta. Prior to becoming Regional Director General in Alberta, he had been with the Department as a Land Use Officer in British Columbia. In that time, he had become cognizant of many of the problems peculiar to British Columbia.

The period he had spent in Alberta was a period of turbulence which was, to some extent, paralleled in British Columbia. After the closing of the Vernon district office in 1975, the functions of that office were not quickly absorbed by the Vancouver office. It seems there was something of a bureaucratic void and a backlog of work tended to accumulate.

Mr. Walchli returned to Vancouver in 1976. In the fall of 1976, Ronald Derrickson was elected Chief of the Westbank Band. Shortly thereafter Mr. Walchli met with Noll Derriksan, the former Chief, and Ron Derrickson, the newly elected Chief.

Mr. Walchli gave evidence of the meeting between himself and the two brothers:

> Q Maybe you could just carry on with that thought, Mr. Walchli, and tell the Commissioner about some early meetings that you had with Mr. Derrickson shortly after he took over his new responsibilities as Chief?
>
> A Yes. In the fall sometime, I don't recall the date. I think it was in October; it may have been in November, but one day I got a call from Noll Derriksan who I actually knew better than Ron, and he phoned me up and asked if they could meet with me. I said yes. They came to Vancouver equipped with a number of financial statements, and Ron, as Chief, told me that he had reviewed the state of the Westbank Band, had looked at the development company; found they were $1.3 million in the hole; looked at the state of the housing program; had looked at the welfare administration, and that had been the subject of an investigation in 1975.

> After having looked at it, he said to me, "Had I known that the situation was this bad, I would not have run for Chief". He said, "I could better deploy my time elsewhere", pursuing his own business interests. We talked about what had to be done on the Reserves; what had to be done to rescue the development company, to set up the new administration.
>
> I encouraged him to stay on and I committed the Department to do whatever we could to help him straighten up the mess he found in Westbank. (My underlining)
>
> (Transcripts: Volume XXXII, pp. 4417–4418)

The problems Mr. Walchli discovered and continued to have with regard to Toussowasket, Noll Derriksan's mobile home park, are dealt with in Chapter 2.

The Westbank Indian Band Development Company debt of $1.3 million was incurred during the development of Lakeridge Park, sometimes called the "Sookinchute" property development. Lakeridge Park subdivision is a quality housing subdivision on Reserve 10, located on a ridge overlooking Okanagan Lake. Subdivision work had been started and much work had been done prior to 1976. A large amount of money had been borrowed by the Development Company, the Band subsidiary that leased the land from the Band under a long-term lease for the purpose of development. According to contemporary financial statements, the federal government was obliged under a guarantee to the extent of three quarters of the $1.3 million debt.

There were cost over-runs on the subdivision and allegations of faulty work were made against the engineers. These allegations became the subject of litigation. The late 1970's saw several years of economic down turn that caused problems in selling the development. Money had been spent in anticipation of lot sales, but sales were anything but robust.

The decision to continue with the subdivision turned out to be justified. Lakeridge Park became a successful and attractive subdivision. As an economic venture it was not an unqualified success as the Band did not realize all the lease payments owed to it, but it would seem that funds acquired by the Westbank Indian Band Development Company were used in business ventures operated by the Band. Those ventures have provided employment for and developed entrepreneurial skills in some Band members.

The 1977 Agreement

On April 1, 1977, Mr. Walchli, on behalf of the Department of Indian Affairs, entered into an agreement with the Westbank Indian Band which allowed the Westbank Indian Band Council to perform certain functions pertaining to land management, band membership, and estate administration. Under the Agreement, the Band Council undertook to perform specified duties, which duties had formerly been administered through the Department. The Department agreed to provide the funding, training and technical support necessary for the performance of the duties. The Agreement expressly stipulated that the Minister was to retain the responsibilities assigned to him under law regarding the administration of lands, membership and estates.

The 1977 Agreement reflected a general Departmental policy of transferring the administration of government services and programs to local Indian governments (band or tribal councils). The implementation of that policy was somewhat hastened following the closure of many district offices as a consequence of the 1975 controversies. The Vernon office, for instance, served twelve bands, including the Westbank Band, in the Kootenay-Okanagan District. It was closed in the summer of 1975 in the wake of the province-wide demonstrations by Indian bands and organizations protesting inter alia, government funding policies. The District office in Vernon was one of several that was occupied by protesters. It was never re-opened due to widespread opposition in the Kootenay-Okanagan area bands who were seeking greater degrees of autonomy.

The Vernon office had employed a staff to administer land matters but certain bands in the district felt that the level of service was poor. They preferred to administer their own affairs, provided sufficient funds were made available to them. The Department was faced with a choice. It could re-open the office over the protests of the clients it was to serve or it could accede to the request that many functions formerly performed by that office be transferred to Indian administration. The Department chose to follow the latter course. I heard evidence during the course of the Inquiry that the Westbank Band was virtually the only band in the district that favoured the retention of the Vernon office.

The foundation for the transfer of land management responsibilities had been laid before 1977. In the late 1960's, the Department of Indian Affairs had embarked on a policy designed to promote greater Indian participation in the governance of their own affairs. The transfer of the administration of some programs and services from the Department to band councils was seen as an initial step towards accomplishing this goal. In order to transfer the program administration and provide related funding to Indian bands, it was necessary to obtain the approval of Treasury Board. Prior to 1974, Treasury Board approval had been obtained on an ad hoc basis, but in about 1974 the Department put forward an expanded proposal to transfer more programs to band administration. The Department obtained approval from Treasury Board to transfer the requisite funds to band councils. The programs and functions that the Department proposed to transfer comprised a long list of services of the sort commonly provided by local governments. However, due to statutory responsibilities imposed upon the Minister, certain functions had to be retained by the Department.

Having obtained approval in principle to transfer federal funds to bands in order that they might take on additional administrative functions, the Department proceeded to identify which matters were appropriate for transfer and to decide on the format for devolution. In response to the protests of 1975, the then Minister, Hon. Judd Buchanan, prepared a general policy statement which was endorsed by Cabinet. This statement set forth the changing direction of government-Indian relations. Because it is an important and seminal statement for all Indian bands and councils in Canada, I set it out at the end of this chapter. It represented a sea change in the relation between the federal government and Indian people and was as well a portent of the changing relationship between Indian people and non-Indian people in Canada. It was a marker on the road to "self-government". It contains the considerable amount of general expressions of goodwill commonly found in governmental policy documents, but it does in its essential lineaments outline the new order to be followed vis-à-vis Indian people. Stripped of circumlocution, it proposes a move away from a too paternalistic approach (the bad past) to a realization of self-determination status (the good future).

While the Minister's statement has useful features as a statement of broad policy, it obviously is of limited practical use in guiding the people in the field as to what precisely is to be done. The Department could not, nor could it be expected to, change direction immediately. Organizations are people and relationships take time to accommodate any new direction of such a fundamental nature. Today, over ten years later debate continues to reverberate about the pace of change and the role of the Department. It is of interest to note that Mr. Fred Walchli arrived on the B.C. scene as Regional Director General almost at the very moment that the new order was being announced. He was expected to lead the Department and the various groups for which it had responsibility to the promised land — it would not always be clear, however, in just which direction lay that land!

The Minister, in the policy paper, prescribed generally greater participation by Indians in decisions affecting their lives at the national, provincial, and band levels. The proposed policy called for a continuing transfer of programs and resources to band councils and envisaged an enlargement of band powers in conjunction with revisions to the Indian Act. The Department was to be transformed in such a way that it would become an enabling or supportive body rather than a direct provider of services. Although the contemplated revision of the Act has not yet occurred, devolution continued to be a major emphasis of the Department. Departmental officials sought to devise methods by which the responsibilities of band councils could be expanded under the existing legislation. In 1976, a series of policy guidelines or "circulars" were published. These prescribed methods for the devolution of programs and funds to "Indian local governments" (the "D Circulars"). Program Circular D-1 expressed, inter alia, the basic policy that:

Indian Bands have the right to exercise the fullest degree of responsibility for local government that is consistent both with law, and the customs and traditions of the Band, (para. 3.1)

And further that:

Indian Bands can exercise this right and its related obligation without: . . .relieving the Federal Government of its responsibilities to meet commitments under law or various treaties . . . (para. 3.2 (b))

The policy thrust was that Indian bands should be encouraged to manage their own affairs. The granting of increased autonomy was, however, subject to continuing federal responsibility for existing commitments. Further, the Department would retain ultimate responsibility under law for certain programs despite portions of program administration being transferred to local government. Related policy guidelines prescribed which functions could be transferred and how appropriate funding was to be provided and accounted for. Program Circular D-4 stipulated that whenever the Department contributed to the cost of local services administered by a band, a "local service agreement" was to be entered into. The local service agreements were to define specific duties and obligations to be performed, financial controls, and any other necessary terms and conditions related to specific programs. The agreements might be recorded by way of formal agreement or by a Band Council Resolution.

Counsel for the Department said in his submission:

As a result of the (1975) uprising, several District Offices including the Central District Office were closed. This had a serious effect on all of the Bands serviced by the District offices. It meant that the services which were originally performed out of District offices such as estates and land matters were being neglected. Although there had been discussions regarding transferring those services over to the Bands, it was not until early 1977 that anything was accomplished. This left a vacuum for approximately two years.

It is necessary to appreciate this atmosphere within the Indian community and the dramatic changes that were occurring in government policy in order to fully understand the actions of departmental employees throughout this era and the years following. The following factors need to be kept in mind.

1. The structure of the Department was such that its personnel within the Department were much more familiar with providing rather than transferring, services to Indian people.

2. The Indian Act was enacted during an era when paternalism governed the relationship between Indians and non-Indians, and therefore the move to devolution meant that policy guidelines and departmental directives became the "guiding light" for the departmental employees carrying out the Department's role in the devolution process.

3. The changeover in the basic policy regulating Indian peoples was not only dramatic but it happened over a relatively short period of time.

4. The Indian community was becoming a significant political force which continually applied pressure on the politicians and departmental employees to quicken the devolution process.

5. With the changeover in policy, departmental employees were sailing into uncharted waters where trial by error became the norm rather than the exception.

THE 1977 AGREEMENT

A. Background

With particular reference to the British Columbia region of the Department, significant factors from a regional perspective at the time the 1977 Agreement was negotiated and entered into included the following:

1. The region was under pressure from Ottawa to implement the devolution process as quickly as possible;

2. There were important and necessary services which were originally provided to the Westbank Indian Band through the Central District Office which were being negotiated as a result of the closure of the Central District Office;

3. There had been a commitment made to Bands in the Central District that the services originally performed by the District Office would be transferred to those Bands;

4. The atmosphere between the Department of Indian Affairs and the Indian community in British Columbia was tense and there were factions within many Bands including the Westbank Band which were pushing for the dismantling of the Department of Indian Affairs;

5. The region was faced with an aggressive and intelligent Chief of the Westbank Indian Band whose priority was the development of the reserve lands.

The 1977 Agreement was a "local service agreement" which specifically governed the transfer of certain lands, membership and estates functions to the Westbank Band. It was a formal written agreement. Similar local service agreements were concluded with some other bands in the Kootenay-Okanagan District by less formal means through a Band Council Resolution. This Agreement really confirmed and formalized the de facto situation that had evolved consequent upon the closure of the Vernon office. The Regional Director for British Columbia, Mr. Wight, had informed the bands in the Kootenay-Okanagan District shortly after the closure that they would have to take on certain land management functions previously provided by the District Office. The Regional Office lacked sufficient resources to perform all services previously done at the district level. After the bands in the District complained that they were not receiving any funds for this extra responsibility, the local service agreements provided the basis for Departmental funding. In this fashion, the Kootenay-Okanagan bands were among the earliest bands in Canada to participate in the transfer of responsibility relating to land management and administration.

The Westbank 1977 Agreement was largely drafted by Mr. Peter Clark, then employed by the Department as a "special project officer". A short time after, he became Director of Lands, Membership and Estates for the B.C. Region. Included in the specific duties that the Band Council was to perform were various administrative functions associated with land management — record keeping, rental notices, rental collection and the like. Also the Band Council was authorized to "negotiate with lessees and permittees as to revision of rentals, new rentals, and enforcement of terms and conditions in agreements." This language has been the subject of considerable controversy as to just who had the power to finally determine rents payable under leases and to undertake enforcement procedures for alleged breaches of covenants in leases.

The Agreement contained the following clause:

NOTWITHSTANDING any clause in this Agreement, the Minister must maintain his responsibility for the administration of lands, estates and membership within the statutory provisions of the Indian Act and the practices which have been introduced subsequent to the passing of the Indian Act but which have received Treasury Board approval and take whatever action he deems necessary to carry out this responsibility.

This clause may have been intended to specify that the Department was not transferring any Ministerial authorities to the Band Council. In 1977, Mr. Walchli advised Mr. Mackie, the Assistant Deputy Minister, on the issue as follows:

In August of 1975 the District Office for the Kootenay-Okanagan Band was closed. At the time of closure no suitable arrangements were developed to provide for administration of lands, estates and memberships. Consequently much of the work was done by the Band Councils and their administration without being compensated for ... the failure to come to grips with this issue is a major stumbling block to the Department establishing effective working relationships with the Bands. In addition the Land Administration for which the Department has the obligation is not being carried out. I therefore agreed with the District Council that we would compensate the Bands for the work that they have done to date and that we would enter into an agreement with them to provide District-type land administration services starting April 1, 1977...

It should be clearly understood that the proposed arrangement does not constitute a transfer of the Minister's authority to carry out his responsibilities for land administration. It in fact is a service agreement for the Bands to provide the same level of services previously carried out by our District Office. (Exhibit 113, Document 30)

There are specific mechanisms in the Indian Act which allow for the transfer of control and management over reserve lands to a band. Under Section 60, the Governor in Council may grant a band the right to control and manage its reserve lands. This allows a band to exercise certain powers formerly reserved to the Minister. In addition, Section 53 of the Act allows the Minister to appoint a person (often the Chief and/or councillors of the band) to "manage, sell, lease, or otherwise dispose of surrendered lands". These statutory authorities are distinct from a local service agreement, such as the 1977 Agreement. As indicated by Mr. Walchli in the aforementioned letter, the 1977 Agreement did not constitute a transfer of Ministerial authority. The Westbank Band eventually received authority pursuant to Section 53 to manage their surrendered lands (primarily the Lakeridge Park subdivision) in October 1980. They did not receive authority pursuant to Section 60 of the Act until June 1985.

The Westbank Band had applied for Section 53 and 60 authority as early as 1978. While they waited for the granting of these authorities, the Chief and Council undertook certain land administration functions under the authority of the 1977 Agreement. Chief Derrickson sought to interpret the transfer of administrative functions under that agreement as the grant of quite extensive authority over lands at Westbank. In his evidence before the Commission, he said that the Band had more power under the 1977 Agreement than they had under Section 60. If that be so, one might ask, why proceed to ask for Section 60 authority? I think Mr. Derrickson was indulging in wishful thinking if he was serious in his assertion concerning the 1977 Agreement and the breadth of authority granted thereunder.

Mr. Clark, who drafted the 1977 Agreement and who served as the Director of Lands, Membership and Estates (now Lands, Revenues and Trusts) in the B.C. Region from 1977 until 1983, gave evidence before the Commission. He was asked to explain the intention and operation of the Agreement with respect to, inter alia, cancellation of leases. After referring to the notwithstanding clause, noted above, Commission Counsel put the following questions and received the following answers from Mr. Clark:

> Q I take it then, when you drafted this document, it was your intention that the Department maintain all of the statutory responsibilities and not devolve any of those statutory responsibilities upon the Band other than duties of an administrative type; is that a fair statement of the theme of this document?
>
> A Yes, I think the Treasury Board authority clearly stated there were certain things that a Band that could not be devolved at that time, and that included, certainly, the signing of agreements on behalf of the Crown, and that's exactly what I think was envisaged in there; that those were the statutory things that had to remain with the Department.

Q The signing of agreements on behalf of the Crown?

A Yes.

Q Was not given to the Band under this agreement?

A That's right.

Q And were there any other significant functions that were withheld?

A Not that I can recall directly. Well, there was the estate program which was a little different, although there was a considerable amount of reference to it in the Appendix A. That was another part of the program that could not devolve, and so that was something that had to be maintained under those Sections of the Act to the appropriate administrators of estates.

Q All right. For the time being let's just deal with the land function, in any event, because that's what I am concerned with at this point in time.

What about giving notice of termination, or cancellation of leases, how did you view that?

A It was one that was used with a certain amount of, I suppose, discretion, or flexibility between ourselves, as to, if, in fact, rentals had not been paid properly on time, the Band who were collecting those were really the only people is a position to know of that, and we suggested that they take appropriate actions at that time to ensure that the lease was managed properly.

Q All right. What about the power if you give notice terminating a lease, how did you view that?

A That was again an area which was not that clear. We generally followed the approach that maybe the Band council, in those instances, should, if they felt it was appropriate and proper, give notice, but they should inform us at the same time, so that we could, in fact, provide a separate notice.

Q Now, which one did you consider legally effective?

A I don't know whether I consider it, really from the point of view of legally effective, I — difficult to answer that one. I suppose, you know, I found that the practice was accepted by many lessees, or not many, but certain lessees where a Band did cancel, that that was accepted, so I found that that obviously was a process which was acceptable on cancelling. On the other hand there were other lessees that, in these, and other Bands, which didn't like that process, and wrote to my office asking whether, in fact, this was proper, and we would then send out maybe a second notice.

Q Going back to this agreement, is the question of giving notice of cancellation or termination of leases addressed at all in this agreement, in any part of it?

THE COMMISSIONER: You are referring to the —

MR. ROWAN: To the 1977 —

THE COMMISSIONER: — the 1977 Agreement, is that it?

Q Yes, document 23, Exhibit 108?

A It was referred to generally, in I think, one of the subparagraphs on the — which one it was regarding enforcement in terms of leases, which was —

Q You refer perhaps to Appendix A?

A Yes, number three, I think.

Q Number three, which states: "Negotiate with lessees and permittees, as to revision of new rentals, and enforcement of terms and conditions and agreements". Now, whatever is meant by that, it doesn't expressly confer a right to terminate or cancel leases, for non-performance of covenants, you would agree with that?

A Well, the intention was that that was the — that it would provide the Band with that authority to enforce all those terms and conditions and agreements as they were managing.

Q It was your intention?

A That's right.

Q As draftsman of this agreement that the Band have the power to terminate or cancel leases, do I have that right?

A No. To enforce those terms as far as providing that to it, as I said before, if there was difficulties, they would then come back to the Department for a second letter, or reinforcement on that basis, so that, in fact, there would be no problems. We didn't cancel many leases; there weren't very many leases that were, in fact, terminated or surrendered or cancelled in the Department over the time I was there, there were maybe three or four or five, which were all with agreement, so it really was not something that was considered as a major workload of any event.

Q All right. When you used the word "enforcement" in paragraph three, what did you have in mind? What duties did you have in mind as far as the Band was concerned?

A Well, there were many clauses that were put into leases, which were certain obligations and responsibilities of parties, and because there had to be some way of insuring that, in fact, the leases were controlled. I can't remember all of the clauses, but there were clauses like in agricultural leases, not allowing you, you know, weeds to grow, and there were clauses in other leases about insurance requirements to be in place for any buildings to a certain amount of money, and liability insurance, and those were some of the enforcement that had to be done locally.

(Transcripts: Volume XLIX, pp. 7035–7039)

From Mr. Clark's evidence, it is apparent that the respective areas of authority of the Band Council and the Department under the Agreement were not fully defined. The ambiguity of the language in the 1977 Agreement eventually led to confusion over who had the authority to exercise certain decisions concerning the management of leases on Reserve 9. This uncertainty in turn gave rise to controversy, conflict and litigation over the ensuing years.

It is not particularly surprising that the Agreement would have a certain degree of imprecision. These were early days in the devolution process. It should, however, have been evident to the Department by the early 1980's that it was desirable to have the respective spheres of authority more precisely defined. This is but another example of the Department's reluctance to deal more firmly with a strong chief who was inclined to interpret and exercise his authority to the fullest. Perhaps the regional office of the Department was hoping for an earlier grant of Section 60 authority which would have legitimized the situation.

The closure of the District Office and the implementation of the 1977 Agreement created the framework for a new order but it was a new order with very sparse guidelines. One hesitates to be too critical of the local people who were in the eye of the various political storms that have revolved around Indian Affairs in the last decade. It would obviously have been preferable, however, if a more precise definition of authority had been spelled out before matters reached the stage they ultimately did at Westbank.

As noted above, the original direction of government had been to grant increased authority and to concurrently do some revision of the Indian Act. That revision has not proved to be a politically easy task — perhaps not surprisingly, there is a distinct lack of unanimity among Indian people concerning possible changes to the Act. The advent of the Charter and increasing controversy over the limits of self-government have not made the achieving of progress on revisions easier. I comment in Section II of the Report on some areas of the Indian Act that I think might usefully be examined with a view to amendment.

While I do not wish to be unduly critical of those in the Vancouver office of the Department who were faced with the many complications arising from the enhanced speed of devolution, I do think that there were warning signs that all was not well at Westbank. Mr. Crosby's correspondence is not a model of brevity or always a dispassionate recital of the facts, but clearly there was a problem of serious dimensions relating to the administration of the mobile home park leases. The evidence of Mr. Nick Dachyshyn, a proposed partner of the Yorks, concerning his frustrations with finishing additions to a mobile home park illustrates the curious lethargy of the Department in coming to grips with a situation that was far from healthy.

Self-government, to the extent that the term denotes the ordering of their own affairs within the context of Canadian society by Indian people, is a laudable aim. But government must also be responsible. The picture that emerged from the narrative of Mr. Dachyshyn appeared to be one of a rather petulant despotism on the part of the Chief which was in no whit discouraged by the supine posture of the Department. It is not to be wondered at that ill feelings continued to grow at Westbank.

The 1977 Agreement was a step on the path to giving the Westbank Indian Band greater control over its land and destiny. But it did not mean that the Department had no role to play. When a band has Section 53 and 60 authority, it can then act more or less completely as an autonomous body with respect to leasing matters. Where there is a power vacuum, a strong figure will attempt to fill that vacuum. Chief Ronald Derrickson was such a person. While his motives may have been good, his rather abrasive approach caused a great deal of friction with lessees on the Reserve. Perhaps the closure of the Vernon office contributed to difficulties. After 1975 there was not the same degree of

Departmental presence. After 1977 there was even less. Given the difficulties faced in the 1975 turbulence, I have considerable sympathy for the Department's reluctance to be embroiled in leasing controversy at Westbank. But by adopting too much of a laissez-faire attitude, the Department lost touch with what was happening. Getting no adequate response from the Department, people began to go the political route. That route is open to any citizen but when it is utilized in what should be primarily commercial issues, undesirable consequences may follow. I think we have seen the results of that at Westbank. Things can get blown out of all due proportion. Commercial disputes should be settled by commercial means — political involvement all too often involves partisan controversy that can impede any resolution of the original difficulty.

There is this consideration too. Bureaucrats are only human and if their decisions are always being questioned at the political level, morale is sapped. There is much to be said for a policy of trying to solve problems at the local rather than the national level. I comment on a possible approach to this continuing problem in Appendix B of this Report.

The Devolution of Statutory Authority

By 1978, augmentation of the Westbank Band's authority over land administration was being considered. Two sections of the Indian Act are germane. Section 53(1) touches upon the administration of surrendered lands and Section 60 upon lands on reserves occupied by the band. Section 53(1) reads:

> 53.(1) The Minister or a person appointed by him for the purpose may manage, sell, lease or otherwise dispose of surrendered land in accordance with this Act and the terms of the surrender.

Section 60 reads:

> 60.(1) The Governor in Council may at the request of a band grant to the band the right to exercise such control and management over lands on the reserve occupied by that band as the Governor in Council considers desirable.

The 1977 Agreement did not, by its written terms, confer upon the Westbank Band any powers of final decision-making in land matters. As early as 1978, the question of the authority to "determine" rentals was being considered by Mr. Peter Clark, who wrote to the Chief in a letter dated March 13, 1978:

> I think, that based upon your record whilst in office since November 1976, that it would be most sensible for the Westbank Indian Band to manage and administer their reserve lands. This would immediately resolve the problems that occur regarding the authority to negotiate, renegotiate, review and determine rentals with lessees of the Crown.

His letter outlined the procedure to be followed to acquire Section 53 authority and contemplated further, the granting of Section 60 authority.

In September of 1978, the Band passed a resolution seeking authority under both Section 53 and Section 60.

It seems the Department was more inclined to grant authority under Section 53(1) than under Section 60. In 1979, Mr. Clark passed the resolutions on to Ottawa, specifically recommending that the Minister confer authority under Section 53(1) limited to Reserve 10 lands. The "surrendered land" on Reserve 9 included land on which Park Mobile Home Sales Ltd., the Yorks' company, operated a mobile home park, and doubtless Mr. Clark was keenly aware of the problems that continued to emanate from the Derrickson-York controversy. In any event, when power was devolved under Section 53(1) it was given in respect of both Reserves 9 and 10. It was contained in a Minister's letter, signed by the Honourable John Munro, dated October 6, 1980. A copy of the letter is reproduced at the end of this chapter.

A legal question was raised as to whether or not a changing group of persons such as "the Chief and Councillors, from time to time. . ." can be a "person". That may some day be litigated. It seems to me the potential problem could be cured by some legislative housekeeping to provide for devolution of the power to band councils as a council.

In 1981, controversy involving the mobile home park operators and tenants began to be visible. As related in the chapter on the mobile home parks, a number of leases were due for rent revision in 1981. Some of these revisions were achieved, but some revisions are still not resolved today.

Chief Derrickson took a very expansive view of the powers that were conferred upon him and his council. One of the exacerbating features of the devolution of powers to the Westbank Band to administer and manage its lands was the Department's failure to communicate in a complete and timely manner to the persons with whom they had contracted (lessees), the delegation of powers. The only formal notice the Westbank lessees received from the Department was a notice given in 1977 to pay their rents to the Band. On several occasions when requests were received about the Band's authority, the replies tended to be lacking in clarity. Examples include Mr. Walchli's letter to Mr. Jack Alexander's solicitors referred to in the mobile home park chapter, and Mr. Clark's letter on the Sun Country lease referred to later in this chapter. I think that in large measure the lack of clarity reflected a lack of direction at all levels of the Department. Everyone knew they were embarked on a new course, but the voyage was interspersed with frequent fog banks.

244

After Chief Derrickson had written to Mr. Crosby's bank wrongly stating that Mr. Crosby's lease was in default, Mr. Crosby made inquiries of the Department about the Chief's authority.

By letter dated February 16, 1982, Mr. Clark advised him:

> Since the closure of the Indian District office in Vernon, those Bands previously serviced by Federal officers have generally been allowed to undertake their own administration. By certain authorities the Westbank Band was advised that it should undertake the administration of leases and other land agreements so long as the general terms and policy of the Government under the Indian Act were adhered to.

On the subject of by-laws questioned by Mr. Crosby, Mr. Clark responded:

> Although there may be legal uncertainties, it would seem practical to either abide by the Band by-laws that have Ministerial Consent and are thus Federal law or to legally contest the by-laws.

Perhaps the Department could not give more explicit answers because it had not clearly thought out all the implications of its devolution policy, but it might be noted that the policy and its implementation had by then been in effect for some years.

The Department did not move hastily with respect to Section 60 powers. Mr. J. Leask, Director General of Reserves and Trusts in Ottawa, wrote to Mr. Walchli on April 30, 1980, setting out a comprehensive list of all the powers that they were considering transferring. A copy of the letter follows this chapter.

It is important to note, in view of the chaotic events about to take place in Westbank, that no mention was made of the power to set revised rents. It appears to have been assumed that function was covered by one of the statutory powers to be conferred. What was overlooked was that the power to revise rents in the leases was established under the contracts. The power may have originated in the legislation empowering the Minister to act, but the actual obligation or duty, of necessity, flowed from the wording of the particular lease or contract itself.

In 1985, the Governor in Council conferred Section 60 powers upon the Westbank Band. The Order-in-Council is set out fully at the end of this chapter. All parties seem to have viewed the Section 60 grant as one of almost unlimited amplitude.

The Band had first requested Section 60 powers by the vote of September 1978. Perhaps because of the multitude of problems, allegations, accusations, and counter-accusations that had occurred, the granting of Section 60 authority was delayed. There seems to have been little doubt about the administrative ability of the government and the Westbank Band Council to handle land management, but there might have been doubts as to whether the powers would be used in a wise and restrained fashion.

Most of the leases with which the Commission was concerned contained a provision that the rent would be revised at five-year intervals. The basis on which the new rent was to be determined was spelled out (sometimes far from perfectly) in the leases themselves.

The person who was to exercise the rent revision was the "Minister" or in some cases "the Minister or his authorized representative". In the leases where the "Minister" had the power, the document was silent as to his power to delegate. The word could be interpreted to include the appropriate officer within the Department, whoever that might be, but using this definition the power was unlikely to be construed to extend to persons outside the Department. In leases where the power to revise rents was conferred on the "Minister or his representative", or the "Minister or his agent", delegation could have been effected by a simple letter of authority. The Commission saw no evidence of this having been done.

Subject to the caveat to be mentioned shortly, the powers that may be conferred under Section 60 are wide and likely would allow a delegation of power to exercise the powers and rights created under contract. However, if it was intended to convey those powers and rights to the Chief and Council, that was not done in the Order-in-Council. It was worded to limit the powers of control and management to statutory powers. Those created by contract, if they could be delegated, were not expressly delegated by any Order-in-Council.

One of the mobile home park operators raised questions concerning the extent of the authority granted under Section 60. He pointed to the wording of this section which applied to "lands in the reserve occupied by that band" and argued that the Band no longer could be said to "occupy" the mobile home park lands. This is a plausible argument, and it may prove well founded. I would not want to come to any firm conclusion on this question without full argument, but I note it to show that there can be difficult questions raised in respect of the grant of Section 60 authorities. Each Section 60 authority must fully take into consideration the particular circumstances of the Band. Some legislative housekeeping may be thought desirable to enhance the ability of the Department to grant sufficient authority to bands to minimize the opportunity for arguments such as the one noted above.

The Sun Country Lease

Few persons would quarrel with the policy of the Department and the government to confer upon Indian bands such powers as are required for them to govern themselves. But there is a danger that existing obligations can be overlooked at the time of such transfers. I cite as an example the considerable degree of confusion that arose from a lease that was granted of certain reserve lands on Okanagan Lake just south of the Kelowna Bridge. On this site a marina was and is operated. The locatee is Ronald Derrickson. In 1972, the Crown gave a lease to a parcel designated FF-1, together with an accredited area of land designated GJ-1, to a Robert Henry Hebenton, who in turn assigned his lease to a company called Heb's Marina Limited. The Federal Business Development Bank held security over the lease of that property. The lease was later assigned to Sun Country Sports and Marine Ltd. Sun Country Sports and Marine Ltd. did not prosper, and the FBDB appointed Coopers & Lybrand Ltd. as receiver. The receiver wanted to realize on the security of the lease.

It appears that during the course of the receivership the locatee, through the Westbank Band Council, gave a notice cancelling the lease even though the rent had been paid until the following year. Coopers & Lybrand Ltd. inquired of the Department of Indian Affairs as to whether or not the Chief and Council had the power to terminate the lease. It appears that oral advice was given that the Band did have such power. On the basis of that advice, the receiver sold the chattels only of the marina to Madsen Marina Ltd., who proposed to take over and operate the marina. More could have been realized from the insolvent company if there were an existing lease to sell. After the sale of chattels was concluded, the receiver had occasion to question the oral advice it had received as to the extent of the Westbank Band's power to terminate the lease.

Mr. Peter Clark wrote to Coopers & Lybrand Ltd. on September 30, 1980, setting out his understanding of the matters to that point. He said in part:

> Our file includes a copy of letter addressed to Sun Country Sports and Marine Ltd. from the Westbank Band Council dated June 2, 1980 cancelling the lease. I understand that you were advised that this was a proper and effective notice by a member of the Department of Indian Affairs, although I'm unable to discover a letter confirming this.
>
> It is my understanding from considerable experience in handling Crown leases that only Indian Bands that have received authority by Section 53 or Section 60 of the Indian Act have such powers of cancellation. Although the Westbank Indian Band have granted approval to their council for such authority, the necessary Ministerial letters and supporting Order-in-Council have yet to be granted.

The receiver and its solicitors interpreted that letter as a statement by the Department that the Chief and Council had no such power. Their interpretation of the facts was succinctly stated in a letter of December 17, 1980 from their solicitors to the Department to the attention of Mr. Clark, saying in part:

As you are aware, Mr. Derrickson as Locatee of the Indian Reserve Lands purported to terminate the leasehold interest of Sun Country in the said lands. We wrote to you in July of 1980, requesting you to advise us as to whether or not Mr. Derrickson had the authority to terminate the lease. You failed to respond by letter to those inquiries, however, you did advise Messrs. Powroznik and Todd of Coopers & Lybrand Limited, the Receiver-Manager of Sun Country that Derrickson had such authority. On that basis, the assets of Sun Country were disposed of and a new lease was entered into between Mr. Madsen, the purchaser of the assets of Sun Country and Chief Derrickson on behalf of the Westbank Indian Reserve. Subsequently and in particular on or about September 26, 1980, you advised that Mr. Derrickson had no authority to terminate the leasehold interest of Sun Country. You further advised, that in your view the lease between Sun Country and the Department of Indian Affairs with regard to the Indian Reserve Lands was still current and subsisting. We asked you to confirm that advice in writing. Inasmuch as you failed to confirm that advice in writing within a week's time, the writer forwarded to your offices a letter on October 3, 1980, confirming his understanding of what had been discussed at the meeting held in the offices of Coopers & Lybrand on September 26, 1980. Though no reply was received to the writer's letter of October 3, 1980, Mr. Powroznik of Coopers & Lybrand Limited received a letter from your offices dated September 30, 1980, which neither confirmed nor disaffirmed whether Mr. Derrickson had authority to terminate the leasehold interest of Sun Country. In the letter, you did indicate, however, that though the Westbank Indian Band had granted authority to their Counsel to manage Indian Lands such authority had not been supported by the necessary Ministerial letters and supporting Orders-in-Council. The suggestion in that letter is that Mr. Derrickson had no authority to terminate the leasehold interest of Sun Country.

The fat was now in the fire. The Commission heard that Chief Derrickson was highly displeased with the Department for furnishing ammunition to the receiver. Mr. Clark had to endeavour to quiet this controversy.

Mr. Clark wrote a letter to the receiver on December 23, 1980 in which he said in part:

...I am now at last able to clarify the position with respect to the authority of the Westbank Indian Band. As stated in the third paragraph of my letter of September 30th, 1980, it was my understanding that no Bands other than those given authority under Section 53 or 60 of the Indian Act were in any position to manage leases or other contracts on behalf of the Crown. However, I have had brought to my attention information that in the case of several Bands in the previous Okanagan District (an Administrative District of the Indian Affairs Branch) clearly establishes that the Westbank Band were provided with authority in various areas of Band management in 1976. Included in this authority were provisions to undertake other matters related to land management. In view of some difficulties encountered by the Westbank Council, a clearer authority is being provided to them by Order-in-Council.

I am, therefore, satisfied that the Westbank Band acted properly in this case and I apologize for my lack of clarity over the past two months. . . .

The letter is a remarkable piece of bureaucratic obfuscation. It is even more remarkable when it is borne in mind that Mr. Clark was in charge of the transfer of land management to the Band, and that he was the author of the 1977 Agreement between the Westbank Band and the Department of Indian Affairs. This matter is illustrative of the somewhat elusive nature of the parameters of the 1977 Agreement. It also illustrates the fact that uncertainty can cause harm to band long-term business, for the receiver must have felt a measure of frustration from its experience here.

In time, the receiver's solicitors came to the view that the termination of the Sun Country lease was without legal authority. Litigation ensued, with Mr. John McAfee of Kelowna acting as counsel for both the federal government and the Band. Chief Ronald Derrickson was the locatee of the land in question.

On March 23, 1983, the Westbank Indian Band Council approved a settlement of the claim by Coopers & Lybrand Ltd. pursuant to which the sum of $27,500 was to be paid to the receiver. On the same day, the Regional Director General, Mr. Walchli, sent a memo to Mr. Clark. It reads as follows:

I am told that the lease for Sun Country marina has now been settled out of court. The settlement arrived at is $27,500, and the legal costs associated with this are $17,000. As you know this action could have been continued in the Federal Court with the Department of Indian Affairs being joined, given the weak position we apparently were in over the lack of clear direction to the Chief of the Band regarding his authority to cancel such a lease. The Band lawyer felt it was better to settle out of court and we have agreed with this decision. It will now be necessary to compensate the Band in some manner for both the legal fees and the out of court settlement. I wish to discuss this with you as soon as possible.

It appears the Band was reimbursed for that settlement and for their legal fees by a contribution agreement dated July 13, 1983. One of the signatories was Fred J. Walchli, for the Minister. The contribution agreement provided the Band with a total sum of $48,000 and described the monies paid thereunder as "to manage band lands, $44,000" and "to administer the estates of deceased band members and to maintain the Indian Register for the Band, $4,000". The money was paid in part to settle the controversy that had erupted, but it must be remembered that the problems arose in large measure because of the uncertainty of the Department as to the extent of Band powers under the 1977 Agreement.

Funding of Legal Costs and Litigation

The Sun Country matter was the background for several questions as to the propriety of funding litigation for locatees. The documents provided to the Commission tended to show the federal government paid damages arising from the uncertainty of the Department and because of the Chief's unwarranted exercise of authority. Mr. Clark explained the government's payment of those damages by saying that the Department felt responsible because it had not adequately supervised a lease in which a building was erected beyond the surveyed boundaries of the lots (presumably a boathouse). That explanation did not appear in the documentation seen by the Commission. I think there was a problem with a building being located on property not held by the locatee, but the real reason for payment seems to have been to get out of the lease cancellation difficulty.

It appears from the evidence I heard that the Department of Justice will act whenever the Crown is involved in litigation, or alternatively, it will appoint an outside solicitor to act as an agent of the federal government in some cases. In the Sun Country matter, solicitors fees were paid to the Band as a contribution toward land management. Undoubtedly there will be legitimate costs from time to time for solicitors, real estate agents, real estate appraisers, accountants, and perhaps other professionals. It may be that those professional fees can be categorized as land management but it seems to me that the Department would be well advised to spell out the real purpose for which monies were paid and not hide behind a general category of land management. To categorize a damage settlement as was done in this case is to fail to give a complete picture of events.

When professional services are rendered, it is important that they be accurately described. There can be a potential problem with, for instance, full Departmental funding of locatee legal costs. On a number of occasions it has been suggested that the threat of litigation in which the locatee is supplied with a lawyer at no cost and a lessee has to pay his own full legal costs is unfair. Not only can it be unfair, it is unbusinesslike, for the usual pressures towards settlement do not exist. One party has nothing to lose by way of costs, while the other does. I think bands (and individuals) need access to professional advisers and I do not want to foreclose the ability of the Department to assist those who need it. But there is something troubling about the Department fully funding a well-off locatee who could afford to bear some of the burden. As I have said, settlements of lawsuits can be enhanced by the economic pressure of costs on both parties and I would be sorry to see the Department preventing a timely resolution of disputes. This is one of those rare areas where there should be a "means" test in the interests of equity and the efficient working of the litigation process.

Westbank Indian Band By-Laws

An example of the failure to follow through on an otherwise commendable initiative was the Department's handling of the by-law issue. To understand the issue, one should consider what was hapening in land use control in British Columbia in the year 1979 (the year the by-laws were drawn). In the years that preceded the drawing of those Westbank by-laws, British Columbia municipalities were struggling with the mechanics of recovering from developers the costs of development. Municipalities charged fees or costs which became known as "impost fees" and the fairness of those fees were called into question. Municipalities would zone land in a manner that forced developers to come to the municipality to approve any proposed use. The price of municipal approval was the imposition of significant costs upon the developer.

In 1977, a series of amendments to the British Columbia Municipal Act under Section 702AA, 702B, 702C, and Section 711 were passed to bring into effect a regime that sought to provide clarity, legitimacy and fairness for such charges. Development charges could only be levied for specific purposes. Under Section 702C(4), it was provided that such charges could be made:

> for the sole purpose of providing funds to assist the Municipality in paying the capital cost of providing, altering, or expanding sewage, water, drainage and highway facilities and public open space, or any of them in order to serve, directly or indirectly, the development in respect of which the charges are imposed.

The charges to be made were subject to the approval of a provincial official called the Inspector of Municipalities and an elaborate regime was worked out to ensure that the costs were fairly imposed and apportioned.

The Land Control By-laws drafted by the Department of Indian Affairs for the Westbank Band were based on by-laws passed by some British Columbia municipalities. To render them intelligible, one has to be cognizant of the legislation which empowered British Columbia municipalities to pass those by-laws. Only then might they have meaning.

Against that background, it is difficult to accede to the Department's position that it would approve by-laws and wait for a court challenge. It may well be that those responsible for approval did not have a full grip on the by-laws. Chief Derrickson said in his testimony he did not fully understand the by-laws and he may not have been alone.

In 1973, a firm called Interform Planning and Design Ltd. was commissioned to study the development potential of Reserves 9 and 10. At that time the provincial government was in the midst of implementing a policy to preserve agricultural land. Of course, the measures instituted could not apply to Indian lands. One of the results of this provincial initiative was to enhance the value of Indian lands immediately adjacent to urban areas. As we have seen, the Westbank lands fell into this category, being across Okanagan Lake from Kelowna.

The Interform report was conservative in its projections for Reserve 9. It recommended a quite comprehensive scheme of urban development for Reserve 10, foreseeing a "new town". It suggested a plan for a developed town with all the functions required to serve 10,000 people. The plan called for a town centre containing shopping facilities, recreational facilities and business and personal services. There was to be an 18-hole golf course, substantial residential development, and a full infrastructure of new roads, power, water, and sewage.

The then undeveloped state of Reserve 10 presented advantages. The report said:

> One of the key advantages in this unique opportunity of community building is the inherent freedom to develop a design without the restrictions of the usual codes, regulations, and entrenched standards that can prevent innovation or simple improvement in design and economy.
>
> Normally, communities are not designed, but assembled by a process of designating land use zones, density limits, minimum lot sizes, set-backs, servicing standards, and other matters. Regulating in such a way usually precludes strong positive conceptual ideas of community design.

Only the Lakeridge subdivision was constructed; otherwise the 1973 plan has not been realized to date. A short while later it had become apparent that there was a weaker market for residential development than had been expected. Demand had apparently shifted to property for recreational development. In the late 1970's, another report was commissioned to examine the development of Reserve 10. In the new report, a change in the residential mix took into account the proposed highway development and included a site for a hotel and convention centre. This plan has not progressed to date.

A concomitant of plan development is a by-law regime. Attention was focused on this problem in 1977 when Mr. Schlief tried to develop a mobile home park on Reserve 10 lands allocated to Henry and Millie Jack. The Band Chief and the Regional Director General joined forces to prevent further development of the park, but the incident highlighted the need for effective controls.

Mr. David Sparks had become Director of Local Government in the B.C. Region in January 1977, with the responsibility "to assist Indian Bands to put together administrations that could handle programs that the federal government was transferring to the Indians to administer...". It fell to him to develop a by-law regime to facilitate development on the Westbank Reserves. Mr. Sparks had a great deal of academic and practical experience to equip him for the task. Perhaps his most worthwhile experience in this regard was that acquired while working as an administrator for the Municipality of Surrey. He had worked for that municipality at a time when it was undergoing rapid growth as a suburb of Vancouver.

In early 1979, and several times throughout that year, he met with Chief Derrickson, and in the fall of 1979 certain by-laws were presented to the Band Council. In creating a set of by-laws for the projected modern, urban community, he was seriously hampered by legislation that was less than adequate to authorize their enactment. Band by-laws are enacted under the authority of Section 81 and, in the case of some bands, Section 83 of the Indian Act. Westbank is one of the bands that has power under Section 83. Mr. Sparks could have also been inhibited by Departmental doubts about the applicability of band by-laws to surrendered lands. That problem is touched upon elsewhere herein. In any event, a comprehensive group of by-laws was provided to the Band Council in the fall of 1979. The by-laws Mr. Sparks produced were enacted with the significant exception of the zoning by-law.

Despite the lack of any apparent authority in the Indian Act, Mr. Sparks can be credited with some creative draftsmanship. As he explained in his evidence:

> There was no specific legislative base for an official community plan within the Indian Act, but there is a provision that councils can enact by-laws to preserve law and order. So we created a by-law which regulated council and its employees to only do those things which comply — they conformed with the plan without council taking action to amend the by-law.

The Community Plan By-Law

The Community Plan by-law to secure compliance with the "official plan" made it an offence for the Band government and Band agents and employees to act contrary to the official plan. The Commission was not made aware of any test of the by-law. Perhaps the by-law had a salutary effect. However, the way things really worked, any project that was to take place during the regime of Chief Derrickson required his approval or sanction. The need for the by-law was superseded so the opportunity for contesting it has yet to arise.

Band Council Procedure By-Law, 1979–10

The Band Council Procedure by-law contained provisions with respect to conflicts of interest. Under the heading "Disclosure of Conflict of Interest" the following provisions were enacted:

11.1 A member of Council shall disclose any conflict of interest prior to voting on any matter in which he, a member of his immediate family or relative living with the member will benefit by financial gain.

11.2 As soon as a member of Council is aware of having a conflict of interest in any matter brought before Council, he will immediately make full disclosure by signifying his interest, and, if the Council by resolution so directs, leave the meeting until after the matter has been decided.

With respect to those provisions, Mr. Sparks gave evidence:

This is a problem that you have when you have a small council. It's very difficult to, just in the normal course of business, for there not to be almost a continuing conflict of interest.

So, what we did, we provided in the by-law that where the conflict, as it's defined there, exists, that the councillor who is in conflict must make it known, it must be recorded in the minutes and, if he was requested by the balance of the council, he is to leave the council proceedings.

I have commented elsewhere in my Report on the failure of individuals at Westbank to be sensitive to conflict of interest problems. The Department is to be commended for the efforts of Mr. Sparks to put a proper law in place, but no law will work unless there is the will to enforce compliance with its provisions. I elsewhere adopt certain suggestions by counsel for the Department to deal with this pervasive problem.

Band Administration By-Law, 1979–04, and Administration and Management By-Law, 1979–09

Mr. Sparks explained the by-laws relating to procedure and administration as an endeavour to distinguish between the executive branch and the administrative branch of band government. In speaking of the by-laws defining the position of Band Administrator, he explained:

Well, what this does is separate the doing role of local government from the planning and decision role. The planning and decision role is the responsibility of the elected council. They're the people that can plan, make the decisions, and put those decisions in some form of resolution or by-laws or legislation. The administrative role, carrying those decisions out, is for somebody else, and this particular by-law foresaw that all of the decisions of council would be carried out by the administrator, or somebody hired by him, or appointed by him, or who is technically competent to do the job.

Those objectives were sometimes sacrificed under the administration of a strong Chief. The author of the administrative and procedural by-laws wished to have a definite and structured form of government to ensure stability and continuity. This process, of course, takes time. I did not gain the impression that it had progressed to any great degree at Westbank in the era under review. Although a Departmental official had created a by-law, I do not feel the Department did much follow-up in this area at Westbank.

Land Control By-Laws

In this category there was included:

— 1979–11 zoning by-law,
— 1979–12 subdivision by-law,
— 1979–05 permit application fee,
— 1979–05 development permits.

In preparing this package of by-laws, Mr. Sparks undoubtedly called upon his experience in Surrey. Surrey underwent tremendous growth during the period he worked there. The municipality had little land of its own, and at the time of the municipality's expansion it expected difficulty in controlling development. Much land had been agricultural. A rigid zoning and development by-law regime was enacted, with the municipal government of the time working on the basis of what they called "down zoning". Land was zoned at a lower level than its designation under the official community plan. This forced developers to approach the municipal council to seek re-zoning in order to develop. The necessity to seek approval gave the municipal administration the ability to deal with developers. The result was (with some legal set-backs) that the municipality was placed in a position where it could control the type of development and ensure that developments were paid for by developers rather than by the municipality itself. Of course, this can cause friction between government and developers, but that is something that has to be worked out in the normal process. What must be avoided in this area is the appearance of arbitrariness or a lack of even-handed treatment of different persons similarly situated.

It was Mr. Spark's intention for Westbank that the bulk of the lands that were not in present use would be zoned as comprehensive development zones in accordance with the official plan. Under the by-law regime, developers would pay for the infrastructure costs for roads, sidewalks, and the installation of utilities.

The package of by-laws relating to land control were interdependent, incorporating the others by reference. It is not clear just what happened to the zoning by-law. Mr. Sparks gave evidence that it "never went forward". One person said it was passed by the Band Council but it never reached Ottawa. Chief Derrickson seemed to be of the opinion that it had been sent to Ottawa and disapproved. As far as Commission Counsel could determine, the by-law was never in force. The failure to have the zoning by-law in force threw into doubt the legal efficacy of some other by-laws, particularly the development permit by-law. Whoever in the Department looked at the by-laws for approval should have noted that the latter by-law was conditioned on the existence of the zoning and subdivision by-law. Perhaps the by-laws were not carefully perused when they were forwarded to Ottawa for approval or rejection. The policy of letting by-laws stand until they are challenged in court should not mean that care is not required at the enactment stage. Court challenges are an expensive corrective.

The Development Permit By-Law

When a developer sought a zoning change or wished to effect a subdivision of land the legislative scheme seemed to call upon him to secure a development permit. I say "seemed" because the wording of the by-law is imperfect as to imposing the obligation of payment. I do not propose to go into a lengthy textual analysis of the by-laws, but I commend this matter to the Band government for closer study.

It has been alleged the Band applied the development permit by-law in a discriminatory manner. For comparable developments taking place in the same time frame, it was said that Ted Zelmer was charged $590, Len Crosby $2,600, and the Yorks $14,000. I think a considerable source of this complaint was the fact that the by-law regime was just coming into force — thus it might apply to one development just shortly after another one to which it would not apply. Difficulties often arise in such a transitional period. The Yorks were not conspicuously co-operative with the Band government and doubtless received no "breaks". Regardless of the merits of that controversy, it seems to me that difficulties could have been avoided by a more open and orderly procedure for initiating and putting by-laws in force. It think a great deal of confusion arose at Westbank because of the absence of Mr. Sparks at crucial times due to a transfer. I do not say this in a critical spirit, because personnel cannot always be static, but I urge the Department to try to ensure better continuity in such major undertakings in future to prevent the sort of confusion attendant upon this process at Westbank.

The faults of this group of by-laws are several. The package, never fully enacted, was not clear whether the fees charged in some of the by-laws are meant to be cumulative or whether payment of one sufficed for the fee claimed under another. Further, without a definition of such words as "subdivision" and "development", no one knows what they apply to. That lack of understanding has reduced these by-laws to erratic revenue-raising devices.

Because people doing business with the Band have only felt secure in doing their business with the blessing of the Chief, the land control by-laws have not been as important as they might have been. On the other hand, if the by-laws were understood and fairly applied, it would inject stability into Band affairs that would benefit the Band immensely.

Community Control for Health and Public Welfare

This third group of by-laws Mr. Sparks prepared included:

— 1979–03 waterworks regulation,
— 1979–06 soil removal,
— 1979–08 construction regulations,
— 1980–02 business licenses,
— 1979–01 housing standards.

Only the waterworks regulation by-law came into question during the hearings. The manner in which it was passed could be considered by some as an awkward attempt at expropriation. Section 1 of the by-law provided:

> All water under, within, upon, or which may be conveyed on or to the Reserve shall be the property of and under the control of the Band, except as provided herein, and shown on Schedule F attached hereto.

Schedule F referred to a number of individually owned water systems. These systems listed belonged to members of the Band. Systems owned by lessees were not mentioned. Mr. Sparks gave evidence that it was intended that existing water systems would be exempted and left in the hands of their owners. When the by-law was forwarded to the Band, it was expected they would list all the existing water systems in Schedule F. The net result was a literal declaration of Band ownership of those water systems which was likely legally ineffective.

The thinking behind the waterworks by-law was that the Band would buy water from nearby water districts and supply it to residents and occupants of the Reserves. That prospect still exists and the supply of water will undoubtedly be a long-term concern. I address this question of water supply in Appendix C to the Report.

The Rentalsman By-Law

Perhaps the most remarkable of the by-laws passed was by-law 1981–03 which purported to give the Band Council power to set the rents. The Band Rentalsman had almost unlimited powers in matters affecting landlords and tenants, including the powers of "reviewing and excluding or declaring unenforceable any covenant in a lease, permit or agreement. . .which he finds to be unreasonable under the circumstances".

The Rentalsman by-law permitted the "discontinuance of a service or facility reasonably related to the use and enjoyment of residential premises occupied under a lease, permit, or agreement. . ." It included "terminating occupation of residential premises occupied under a lease, permit, or agreement. . .".

The powers of inquiry and decision were wide. This by-law (or the purported by-law) was used in an attempt to increase pad rentals charged to mobile home park tenants at levels far higher than had hitherto been in effect.

Although the Rentalsman by-law had apparently been disapproved, it was distributed as though it was valid. Rental notices increasing rentals to $150 per pad per month were distributed to the tenants of some of the mobile home parks. An outpouring of media coverage and litigation followed. The Band government had created an issue that spawned immense controversy. The Department once again was drawn into a battle not of its own making. The by-law in question was clearly excessive and was properly disallowed — I was never able to ascertain where it originated.

The Application of the By-Laws

A number of complaints made about the by-laws were related to their alleged discriminatory application. In fact, the by-laws, as by-laws, were not as important as people think. What was important was their invocation by the Band from time to time to justify financial charges. The $1,500 per pad sought as a prerequisite for Mr. Spring's development on the Jubilee Mobile Home Park does not seem to have been founded on any existing by-law. The increase of rents to $150 per pad was not founded on any existing by-law. I understand the development charges levied against Park Mobile Home Sales Ltd. are in question before the courts.

As I have said, it was to be regretted that after Mr. Sparks had drafted the by-laws, he was transferred from British Columbia and was not available to supervise their implementation. That implementation was not orderly and for that the Department must bear some responsibility.

To the Band government, the by-laws seem to have had value as follows. In practice, virtually every decision to build or develop was subject to the Chief's approval. The land development by-laws were used primarily as a revenue-raising device, and to some extent, the confusion surrounding the by-laws allowed the Chief to impose his will on any development taking place on the Reserves.

The passage of a sophisticated set of by-laws with an inadequate legislative base can only inhibit development of Indian lands, for no one knows what the rules are. No one knows whether the rules are valid, and the Department's policy of allowing by-laws to be passed and leaving them in place until judicially challenged is a policy that can spawn problems. There is so much doubt surrounding the rules for development that uncertainty about by-laws may well inhibit development. This is an area of the Indian Act that again is rudimentary. I am confident this area can and will be improved by current ongoing initiatives.

The Regulatory Vacuum: The Problem of Surrendered Lands

In his testimony, Mr. Sparks adverted to a problem that has concerned Indian Affairs personnel for some years. It is a matter that seems to call for legislative remedy but has not been addressed in that manner. The question is whether or not bands have the power to apply their by-laws to surrendered or conditionally surrendered lands. There is a large body of opinion in the Department that thinks bands do not have that power and the problem is referred to as "a regulatory vacuum".

Many parcels of land on the Westbank Reserves are leased under locatee leases under Section 58(3) of the Indian Act. Aside from use of this section, Indian lands are usually conditionally surrendered before they can be leased to non-Indians. Bands may not have power to pass by-laws governing those lands. Probably no one else does either. The problem was seriously considered from 1975 to 1977. At that time, there was ongoing correspondence between several Ministers of Indian Affairs and Mr. Andrew Charles, then the Coordinator of the Alliance of British Columbia Bands.

The Associate Deputy Minister of the Department of Justice wrote to Mr. Charles in 1975 advising that band councils lacked proper regulatory power under Section 81 or Section 83 of the Indian Act over lands surrendered for leasing. He was of the view that Section 73(3) of the Indian Act, which allows the Governor in Council to make orders and regulations to carry out the purposes and provisions of the Indian Act, might not suffice to allow the Governor in Council to pass regulations and make orders with regard to surrendered lands.

The Minister of the day, the Honourable Judd Buchanan, wrote to Andrew Charles as follows:

> As Mr. P. Ollivier explained in his letter of September 24th, the opinion of officers of the Department of Justice is that the Governor-in-Council does not have authority to regulate the use of surrendered lands, and that specific legislative authority is therefore required. I am very concerned, as you are, about this regulatory vacuum. Officers of that Department are responsible for advising Federal Departments on all matters of law and, in this case, they have informed me of a legal problem which prevents my Department from pursuing a course of action consistent with our policy of promoting

local government. In view of this, I intend to ask the National Indian Brotherhood to support my request to Parliament for permissive legislation, which will allow Bands to assume as much responsibility as possible, consistent with good administrative practices, for the management and control of reserve lands, and lands surrendered for leasing. I say 'permissive' legislation because I believe these changes would be welcomed by many other Bands, and the amendment would also allow them to assume this responsibility.

In the meantime, I would suggest that part of the problem could be overcome by including in all future leases a covenant by the lessee that the Band by-laws are to be deemed applicable to him, and that he will comply with them as a condition of the lease.

In his testimony, Mr. Sparks expressed the view that incorporating a covenant to abide by such by-laws, regardless of their validity, would not provide a solution to the problem. It was his view that such a covenant would only give the landlord the right to terminate the lease, an unappealing prospect. It does not appear the recommendation was incorporated into any Westbank leases for the Commission did not see any such lease.

In 1977, the then Minister Warren Allmand took up the same question and wrote Mr. Charles the following letter:

This is to follow up on my special assistant's letter to you of November 3rd, 1976 regarding the legal status of surrendered land which you raised in your letter of October 19th, 1976.

Although my predecessor, Mr. Buchanan, felt at one time the simplest way of overcoming the so-called "regulatory vacuum" was to amend the Indian Act, there have been a number of developments since as well as a great deal of research done on the topic. As a consequence, I have asked my officials and those of the Justice Department to finalize work on an Order-in-Council which, if approved pursuant to Section 73(3) of the Indian Act, would enable me or my designee (i.e. the Indian Band through its Council) to regulate activities on surrendered Indian Lands. These regulations will be broad and will cover such aspects as sanitation, health, pollution, building codes enforcement, etc. While I am aware there is a possibility the regulations may not stand the full test of a Court of Law if they are challenged, I am nevertheless more inclined to adopting that route rather than opting for the more complex and lengthy process of amending the present legislation.

In addition, I want you to know that, as far as is legally possible, I will base departmental policies and practices on the premise that Indian lands that have been conditionally surrendered did not cease to be reserve lands. For example, if a Band Council made a by-law pursuant to Section 81 and 83 purporting to regulate or affect surrendered lands, I would not disallow the by-law for that reason alone. The fact remains, however, that the Band would be taking its own chances with respect to enforceability.

I hope that the above interim measures will serve the purposes intended pending appropriate amendments to the Indian Act.

Mr. Allmand seemed to express the view that conditionally surrendered lands could be subject to by-laws. He also seemed to be of the view that the government could and would pass regulations under Section 73(3) of the Indian Act. Regulations under Section 73(3) were apparently not passed.

It would be sensible to eliminate the doubts in this cloudy area. It is difficult to commend the view that "the band would be taking its own chances with respect to enforceability". Neither the bands nor their lessees should be placed in such a position. It is bad business for either party, and to leave such basic questions in doubt inhibits the development of Indian lands for those bands that seek it. I am hopeful that present initiatives relating to surrendered lands will dispel some of the difficulties of band governments in this area. Doubts about law-making capacity would tend to impede greater self direction.

For many initiatives the Department is to be commended. The submissions of the Department's counsel that times were rapidly changing and there were bound to be errors can be readily appreciated. If the Department is to be faulted, it is for failing to make appropriate adjustments when errors arose.

Complaints to Parliamentarians

As I have said in the Introduction to this Report, the basic evidentiary approach taken by the Commission was to avoid hearsay evidence. Issues arose on a number of occasions concerning matters of evidence. One such occasion concerned the possible testimony of parliamentarians past and present.

Commission Counsel investigated the question and discovered that no Members of Parliament had any first hand evidence concerning relevant matters at Westbank. Concern was expressed by counsel for the former Band executive and counsel for the Department to the effect that it would be most undesirable to have persons coming forward after the Inquiry with any new allegations of wrongdoing. I agree.

Counsel to the former Regional Director General put the matter in these terms:

> I put to Commission Counsel, and I believe that he passed that on to them; if not, I would like it to go on the record that the invitation go out to them, to bring forward any evidence which they may have, which will in any way touch upon the terms of reference of this Commission of Inquiry, and that they be advised that their failure to do so will be taken as an admission on their part, that there is no such evidence in existence, not only in a form about which they could speak personally, but in regard to which there are others known to them who may be able to testify.

Research by Commission Counsel showed that no Members of Parliament had any admissible evidence to tender nor were they aware of others who could testify. Certain statements had been made in the House of Commons that to me were unduly alarmist in nature, given the nature of the evidence I heard. I think that in large measure, the rather lurid tone of these statements originated from the activities of the Action Committee. The letters of Mr. Crosby may also have furnished some basis for the belief that matters at Westbank were in a sorry state. The allegations included extortion, murder and others that proved not sustainable. With regard to many of the allegations, after hearing evidence in the Inquiry, I concluded that there was much rumour, but a lack of proven facts.

Counsel to the Department made what I feel is a sensible suggestion. He submitted that the Commission should put on record that it should be accepted as a fact that Members of Parliament were not in possession of any facts concerning any wrongdoing that were not placed before the Commission. In other words, I have heard everything relevant there is to hear and if someone should attempt hereafter to come forward with "new" material they should not be listened to. I adopt those comments of counsel to the Department. I am satisfied that every relevant lead has been investigated and that the "whole story" has been looked into. I am satisfied that there is nothing further that could usefully be examined. The allegations have all been considered. There is nothing more to be said.

Minister
Indian and Northern Affairs

Ministre
Affaires indiennes et du Nord

Headquarters Directors General
Regional Directors General

Ottawa, Ontario K1A 0H3
July 26, 1976

About a year ago the Department was asked by the Government to review the current relationship between the Government and the status Indians in the light of the Government's current responsibilities for them. The attached paper which is a product of that review has been approved by Cabinet. It proposes specific action to strengthen the relationship and improve the situation of the Indian people. It provides a broad framework in which to develop the Government-Indian relationship in future by shaping policies and programs jointly, and to rationalize and stimulate policies and activities that have been emerging in recent years.

This approach is based on the concept of Indian identity within Canadian society rather than a separation from Canadian society or assimilation into it. The concept envisages that there would continue to be recognition for Indian status, treaty rights and special privileges resulting from land claims settlement and that there would also be programs and services based on need because of the disadvantaged situation of many Indian communities and individuals.

The diversities of need, aspiration and attitude among Indians in all parts of Canada rule out a single strategy that would be universal and uniform in its application. Policy/program initiatives or responses to be applied in any given location or set of circumstances must derive from consultations with the Indian group directly affected and would involve agreement on objectives and shared responsibility for implementation at appropriate levels.

The emphasis of the approach is on processes of joint participation in policy/program developments with organized Indian leadership at all levels. In conveying to you this paper, I intend that you should be guided at all times by this approach, the various implications of which are summarized in the paper. The approach would also serve as a broad policy framework for all Federal departments and agencies having programs that affect status Indians, with heavy emphasis on systematic consultation among departments concerned both in Ottawa and in the field.

"Judd Buchanan"

encl.

Judd Buchanan

MAIN ELEMENTS OF GOVERNMENT-INDIAN RELATIONSHIP

Indian Identity
within
Canadian Society

Group Continuity	— Full citizenship — Indian Act status — Treaty rights — Special privileges — Reserved lands — Local government	
Political change	— Revised Indian Act — NIB and affiliates funded — NIB-Cabinet process — Tripartite mechanisms in provinces — Enlarged band powers — Access to media — Representation in advisory bodies	P O L I C Y
Personal Fulfilment	— Safeguards for Indian languages and other cultural values — Indian group activities under multicultural program. — Special assistance for education/ training — Local self-determination — Transitional services to facilitate mobility — Hunting/fishing safeguards	
Social Equity	— Social services on and off reserves. — Federally assisted education — Preference in employment — Joint housing approach with deep subsidy — Assured access to provincial programs and services off-reserves	
Environmental Concerns	— Environmental protection for Indian lands — Involvement in environmental protection and planning — Employment in national parks, tourism, game control.	P R O G R A M
Economic Strength	— Reserve lands and other band assets — Proceeds from claims settlement (package) — Economic development assistance — Special counselling/training — Contract preferences — Tax privileges for reserve lands	

APPROACH TO GOVERNMENT-INDIAN RELATIONSHIP

Introduction

The principal means of concerting policies, programs and resources is to achieve an agreed policy approach. As the established authority and responsibility centre for status Indians, the Federal Government must assume part of the initiative in seeking to define the aims and shape of policies applied to Indian questions. Given the undertaking and need to consult with the Indian people concerned, this process of definition can best be accomplished through joint working arrangements with representatives of the Indian people, operating at various levels of contact. Through these arrangements the objectives, goals, priorities and methods for policy and programs alike can be worked out jointly and systematically, with emphasis on the acknowledged need for sensitivity and flexibility.

The underlying assumption of this approach is that some degree of Indian status will continue, certainly as long as it is perceived as needed both by the Government and by people recognized as "Indian" under Canadian law. The Government's relationship with the group recognized as status Indians is based on the concept of Indian identity within Canadian society rather than on separation from Canadian society or on assimilation into it.

Policy Framework

Indian identity within Canadian society is dynamic and flexible in its expression and evolution. It partakes of the Indian concept of citizen plus but both these concepts need to be given shape and dimension in policy terms. To begin with, neither concept implies a standard formula, set of criteria, or rules of universal and uniform application to all Indian groups in the country. The co-existence of Indian communities — within Indian society and in their relation to the larger Canadian society — that are markedly different in economic potential and social conditon, is an inescapable fact at present and an inevitable likelihood in the foreseeable future. The main elements of Government-Indian relationship are illustrated on the following page.

The first three elements relate mainly to policy content and emphasis, taking particular account of Indian status. The second three embrace programs that apply generally to disadvantaged Canadians, including status Indians.

The listing of main elements (which is indicative and not exhaustive) suggests areas of choice for various Indian communities and implies a range of gradations to accommodate the diversities of situation in which Indian people find themselves. It envisages that there would continue to be recognition for Indian status, treaty rights and special privileges resulting from land claims settlements. There would also be programs and services based on need because of the disadvantaged situation of many Indian communities and individuals. Within Indian communities, based on the concept of band/reserve, the widest opportunity would exist for local self-determination and control of Indian affairs. It follows from all that has been said about flexibility and sensitivity, that every Indian band in Canada would not make the same choices — some bands might prefer to remain remote, others to join in the regional milieu where they are located.

Strategy

— The diversities of need, aspiration and attitude among Indians in all parts of Canada rule out a single strategy that would be universal and uniform in its application.

— The strategy, must be sensitive and flexible enough to facilitate a policy/program initiative or response that meets circumstances found in a broad spectrum of Indian communities, categorized by economic and human potential.

— The strategy to be applied in any given location or set of circumstances must derive from consultations with the Indian group directly affected and would involve ageement on objectives, goal-setting and shared responsibility for implementation, at appropriate levels of relationship.

Processes

In the past two years, a system of joint working arrangements at various levels, involving the Government and representatives of status Indians, has been emerging. The institutions that are taking shape at each level need to be defined as to role and mandate, along the following lines:

i) At the national level, the Joint NIB-Cabinet Committee has been established. As agreed, the Joint Committee should concern itself with major policy issues that emerge in the course of the Government-Indian relationship. These issues, which can be proposed by either side, constitute the agenda of the Joint Committee and become the subject of detailed consideration by Joint Working Groups established for that purpose. To expedite and facilitate the whole process, the Joint Committee has established (a) a Joint Sub-Committee of three Ministers and three Indian leaders, and (b) a Canadian Indian Rights Commission. In addition, there are joint working groups on specific subjects (e.g. housing, economic development) whose work so far has not required the consideration of the Joint Committee. The objective of the Joint Committee process is to enable the Government and Indian leaders to work cooperatively toward the betterment of the Indian people through joint deliberation at the policy level. (The relationships in the process are shown in Diagram I, next page).

ii) At the provincial level, tripartite arrangements do exist but in this area further thought, experimentation and action are needed to arrive at suitable arrangements to accommodate particular needs and situations in the various provinces. Involving representation from the Federal Government, the provincial government(s) concerned and the provincial association, their provincial role is to give joint advice and assistance for policy/program implementation for bands in the various provinces. A key function would be to see that Federal/Provincial Programs, available to Indian people, dovetailed to ensure optimum effectiveness and avoid duplication and waste. The emphasis is more likely to be on broad guidance than on program delivery and an essential requirement would be the continuing consent of the Indian bands concerned to these arrangements and to the advice emanating from them. A joint study of program management in Saskatchewan now underway with the Federation of Saskatchewan Indians, is one example of explorations in this direction.

iii) At the band level, the process of transferring programs and resources would continue to grow at a pace determined by the capability and desire of bands concerned to assume control of their own affairs, including program delivery. The enlargement of band powers to facilitate this process would continue to be a top priority in the consideration of revisions to the Indian Act, with sufficient permissiveness to allow application of specific sections of the Act to bands wishing and able to take advantage of them. DIAND advice and support to all bands would be consistent with their development potential, their requirement for assistance and their choice as regards relationship with DIAND (e.g. as hired or seconded band officials; as consultants; as regional or district administrators). Diagram II, illustrates the transfer of responsibility to bands.

Other processes for consultation and negotiation are currently in place and they too significantly affect the relationship between the Government and the Indian people. The participation of the Treasury Board is considered whenever the consultations and negotiations referred to below occur on items that imply a disbursement of funds. For purposes of this paper they can be grouped in three main categories:

i) Consultations and Negotiations Concerning Comprehensive Claims

These are the discussions, and more specifically the actual negotiations, that are taking place in areas where traditional

Indian interest in lands—deriving from historic occupancy and use—has been lost or interfered with without adequate compensation; and has not been the subject of any Treaty nor superseded by law. The approach to settlement is based on established Government policy that agreements should be negotiated with the Indian groups concerned and incorporated in Federal legislation. The areas concerned included lands in northern Quebec, the Yukon and Northwest Territories and British Columbia. In all these areas the provincial/territorial government is directly concerned with and involved in the negotiations because the settlements envisaged call for a package of proposals including various categories of Indian lands, cash compensation, resource revenue-sharing, and Indian participation in both economic development and local government.

ii)   Processes for Settling Specific Claims

Widespread discussions have been held about another broad category of Indian claims, known as specific claims, which relate to such matters as residual land entitlement under Treaties, the interpretation and administration of the Indian Act, other alleged injustices in past dealings with Indian groups. The claims relate to the Government's commitment to discharge lawful obligations and some of them may require action in the courts (many are considered to be non-justiciable). A priority concern of the Joint NIB-Cabinet Committee is to ascertain whether principles and processes can be devised for settling specific claims through various other approaches such as arbitration, conciliation, negotiation; and a supportive Canadian Indian Rights Commission is being established. Since third-party interests are frequently involved and since these claims affect bands in most parts of the country, the claims and processes of settlement bear heavily on the relationship between Indians as a group and Canadian society.

iii)   DIAND Consultations

There are a whole range of major items (housing, Indian education, economic development, Indian community affairs, off-reserve services) that are the subject of on-going consultation/negotiation at various levels of the relationship with status Indians. Such consultations in the past have tended to lack cohesion and rationale. It is mainly to achieve order and system in the evolution and administration of these major programs of DIAND that this Memorandum gives primary attention to the organization of the Indian/Government relationship at various levels and to refining the DIAND mandate to accord with needs and activities at those levels.

The DIAND mandate would continue to be re-shaped to serve the requirements of policy and strategy outlined in the preceding paragraphs. DIAND would serve as a source of ideas, initiatives and improvements in policies and programs, proposed from the Government side at appropriate levels. It would consult with departments and agencies concerned about the co-ordination of federal programs affecting Indians and those involving Federal-Provincial cooperation. It would provide information and other assistance to Indian groups advancing claims. It would discharge managerial responsibility on the Government side for the financial and administrative support required by policies, strategies and programs affecting the Government-Indian relationship.

Interdepartmental machinery at senior level is needed to coordinate the Federal effort to improve the relationship with the Indian people, along the lines indicated. The NIB-Cabinet process involves continuing participation of six to twelve Ministers whose responsibilities embrace programs of actual or potential benefit to the status Indians. Some of the Departments (but not all) are currently involved in the joint working groups already established under the NIB-Cabinet Committee (notably Justice, Treasury Board, Secretary of State and DIAND); and in other consultations about particular projects such as housing (CMHC), economic development (DREE) and native employment (M&I, PSC). Additional joint working groups will be needed as the process extends to new areas of concern. The key to interdepartmental consultation and coordination of the policies and activities of departments and agencies with programs concerning Indians, may be to establish an interdepartmental committee, but for the moment interdepartmental working arrangements should be linked firmly to the NIB-Cabinet process. The nucleus would be drawn from those departments whose Ministers are in regular attendance at meetings of the NIB-Cabinet Committee. Corresponding coordinative bodies will be needed at regional level as Government-Indian mechanisms evolve there.

Sources of Funding

For carrying out Indian policies and programs, the following funding sources should be fully explored to see whether and how greater effectiveness can be achieved in the pursuit of jointly agreed objectives:

i)   Direct support for special programs and services, e.g. DIAND, NHW.

ii) Resources available to Indians from programs of general application, both Federal and provincial.

iii) Proceeds from claims settlement.

iv) Indian land and other band assets.

v) Core-funding of Indian associations and organizations including bands.

Greater benefits should result from systematic joint planning and cost-sharing arrangements of various kinds. As long as the Indian groups concerned were directly involved in the planning and broad management, through the various joint working arrangements, there is every reason to assume that greater program effectiveness would result. At the same time the relationship between the Government and the Indians would improve through this practice of cooperation.

Assessment of the Approach

The essence of this approach is joint participation at all levels of contact between Government and Indian representatives. It gives solid substance to the Government-Indian relationship in five significant ways:

i) It affords a distinct and relevant role to Indian leaders within their own sphere of influence and competence; and at the same time enables Government managers to see more clearly and more fully appreciate their respective responsibilities, role and mandate in the course of dialogue and joint enterprise with Indian counterparts. The more representative the Indian leadership the more effective their contribution will be.

ii) It affords real opportunities for exercising freedom of choice by the Indian leaders and groups directly affected by such choice. Choices exist on major questions at the national level in the consultative process under the NIB-Cabinet Committee process, even more apparently at band level in the face of clearly differing situations found there. All such choices would emerge from joint consideration of alternatives.

iii) It promotes sensitivity and flexibility of response to needs and aspirations at the various levels; where objectives, goals, priorities and courses of action can be set by the leaders and in the areas directly affected. Their knowledge and experience of local situations, problems and people can be effectively blended with the know-how, advice and resources (including services) available from whatever government source.

iv) It encourages and strengthens a sense of responsibility and accountability on both sides of the relationship; and opportunity to refine that sense into solid and effective management practices.

v) It helps to give reality to the promise of participation, to build the self-confidence and self-reliance of Indian leaders at all levels, and generally to yield psychological benefits to the Indian people that could be as important to them as the substantive achievements flowing from the process.

Finally, it permits consensus to develop at all levels and at a pace consistent with perceived need. Through communication, and the evolution of policy at the higher levels, such consensus as may be reached at band level can be strengthened and broadened—accepting always that universality and uniformity in Indian affairs are probably no more desirable than they are attainable. At the same time, as the consensus evolves among Indians, it can spread among and within the ranks of Government representatives dealing with the Indians directly affected by it, at the various levels and from level to level.

Foreseeable disadvantages of the approach proposed are:

— It could lead to lengthy and diffused discussions resulting from a whole range of causes but principally perhaps because people on both sides were unfamiliar with the process, distrustful of it and certain participants, and generally skeptical.

— It could founder on rivalries that exist among Indian leaders and groups—and are not unknown in interdepartmental circles.

— It could degenerate into perfunctory meetings staged mainly for short-term political gains on both sides.

— It could, if a tight rein were not held firmly, lead to increasing demands for more money to mount bigger and better meetings.

— It could lead to expectations and demands from other native groups, notably Métis and non-status Indians, for corresponding treatment. In the case of the Inuit, their relationship and treatment in future is likely to be found in arrangements reached in the agreement on land claims settlements.

Financial Implications

The main trusts of this approach do not call for any major new expenditures for programs affecting status Indians although it is recognized that additional costs may result from more vigorous consultation processes. The basic aim of the policy and strategy proposed is to get greater effectiveness from programs now in place through agreed commitment to program objectives, through more efficient application of resources, and through joint planning of programs for implementing agreed policies. This paper is prepared in full awareness of the galloping inflation in costs for Indian programs and of the continuing need for restraint in government spending.

Federal Government expenditures for Indian-oriented policy and programs are likely to be heavy for some time to come. Some indication of the magnitude is suggested by principal items; the Indian affairs budget; the major costs for claims settlements foreseen; Indian housing prospects including the needed catch-up during the next five years; the core-funding of the National Indian Brotherhood and affiliated associations; claims research funding and related claims activity. Other Federal departments and agencies also commit substantial resources to programs for natives, although the proportion devoted to status Indians cannot always be identified precisely.

Federal-Provincial and Territorial Relations

The provinces are increasingly affected by Indian relationships with the Federal Government, and this has produced some strain between Federal and provincial authorities at senior levels. The main issues stem from land claims, including residual land entitlement under treaties.

The provincial tendency to portray status Indians as the sole responsibility of the Federal Government—for example in not fulfilling Canada Assistance Plan agreements—adds to the friction between the two levels of government. Some provincial policies and programs that directly affect the rights of status Indians and their lands have been pursued without consultation, or with only token consultation involving Indian representatives. There is, however, increasing recognition by provinces and acceptance by Indians, that provincial governments have a legitimate interest and share in dealing with Indian problems.

Public disturbance resulting from Indian unrest, office occupation and other obstructions have been a further source of irritation in Federal-Provincial relations, e.g. Kenora. Some provincial governments have been slow to recognize that their stake in achieving peaceful relationships with Indian groups ranks with that of the Federal Government.

The same kind of situation prevails in both the Yukon and Northwest Territories with effects that are more acute. Ethnic tensions are running high in both Territories, mainly because of land claims and associated assertions about native rights. The problems of relationship are made more complex and potentially more serious than those in the South because native people form a much higher proportion of the population than in any other part of Canada—in the Northwest Territories the Indian, Inuit and Métis people outnumber the white population at the present time. Conscious of this unique situation, the native associations in both Territories are seeking special arrangements and institutions for local government that will serve to entrench their position. The Inuit land claim calls for the creation of a new territory North of the treeline, with important federal-territorial implications that need only be flagged here.

Conclusions

In many ways this paper is a summary statement of conclusions about the Government-Indian relationship: about what it is at the present time; about where it appears to be heading; and about how it can be developed in future. Some of these conclusions are quite solidly based in experiences of the past five years, others are tentative, even debatable. A conscious effort has been made to present them in a way that emphasizes their significance in relation to each other and in terms of their possible impact on the relationship in future.

It is no accident that the emphasis in the approach is on processes. To begin with, it is abundantly clear that in the practical workings of this difficult relationship, involving two societies deeply divided by cultural differences and a long history of conflict, process can be very important, perhaps paramount. If the paternalism of the past is to give way to real partnership, requiring full commitment and cooperation from all its participants, the Indians must be satisfied above all that they are participating with some sense of equality.

The road to their self-reliance lies somewhere along those processes of joint participation, now being practised, proposed and explored in depth. It is a learning process for all concerned and one that may have lessons for wider application in contemporary government.

It follows that most of the substantive policy (and ultimately program) developments lie beneath the surface of the large and uneven profile of the Government-Indian relationship. They can and must be uncovered through joint exploration and experiment at the various levels of contact and communication.

These processes of participation are modular not hierarchical, decentralized rather than uniform, top-down and bottoms-up at the same time and in different ways. This paper seeks to show how they all relate, without trying to draw them too tightly together, with what could only be premature and probably counter-productive prejudgments.

This paper begins as a response to a government request for a composite report on the relationship. It is intended as well to assist individual Departments in assessing the Government's and their own responsibility, role and contribution for improving the situation of Indian citizens within Canadian society. It is the foundation for future policy and program adjustments, affecting that situation and the Government-Indian relationship. It is neither a blueprint nor a prophecy for success. But it is an honest effort to get greater effectiveness out of tight resources, through processes of working with, rather than against, organized Indian leadership, wherever it is located.

DIAGRAM I

JOINT NIB-CABINET COMMITTEE STRUCTURE

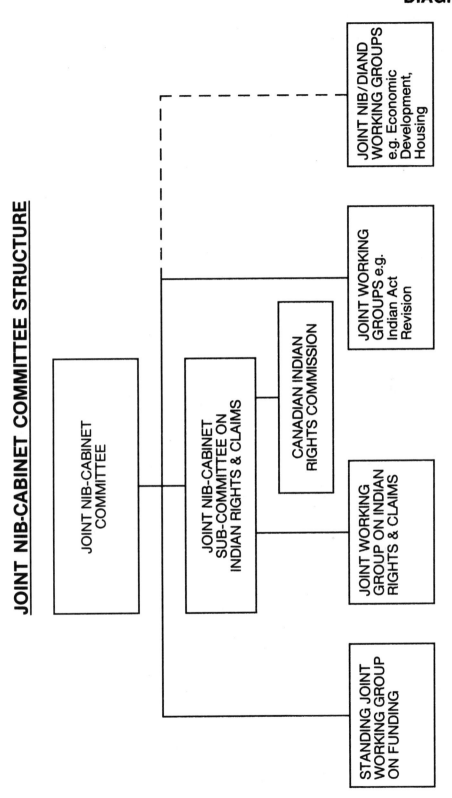

JOINT NIB/DIAND WORKING GROUPS e.g. Economic Development, Housing

JOINT WORKING GROUPS e.g. Indian Act Revision

JOINT NIB-CABINET COMMITTEE

JOINT NIB-CABINET SUB-COMMITTEE ON INDIAN RIGHTS & CLAIMS

CANADIAN INDIAN RIGHTS COMMISSION

JOINT WORKING GROUP ON INDIAN RIGHTS & CLAIMS

STANDING JOINT WORKING GROUP ON FUNDING

DIAGRAM II

Indian and Eskimo Affairs Program
SUMMARY OF BAND MANAGED FUNDS
1971-72 through 1976-77

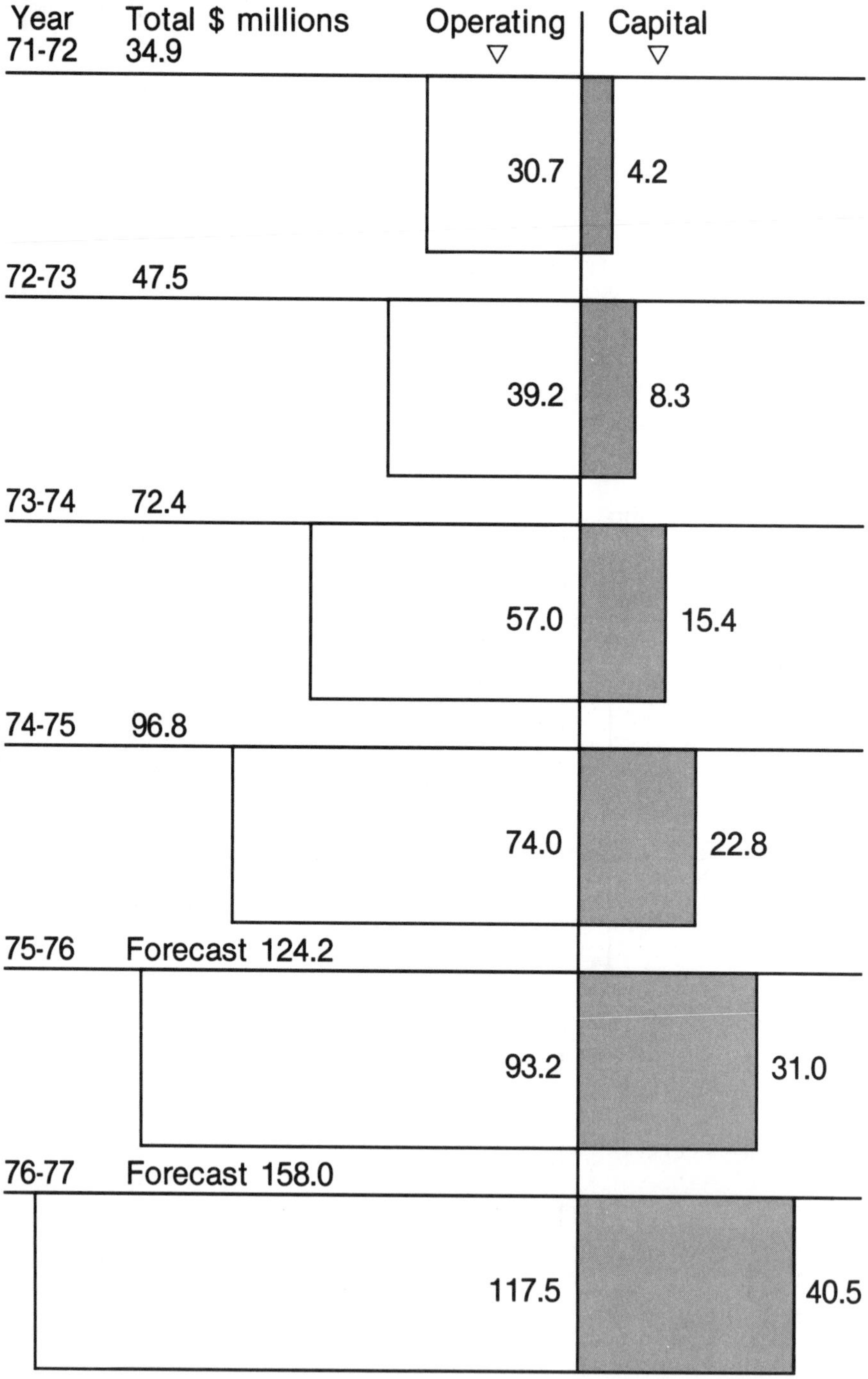

Year	Total $ millions	Operating ▽	Capital ▽
71-72	34.9	30.7	4.2
72-73	47.5	39.2	8.3
73-74	72.4	57.0	15.4
74-75	96.8	74.0	22.8
75-76	Forecast 124.2	93.2	31.0
76-77	Forecast 158.0	117.5	40.5

 Minister
Indian and Northern Affairs Canada

Ministre
Affaires indiennes et du Nord Canada

Oct 6 1980

Westbank Indian Band
Box 850,
Westbank, B.C.
V0H 2A0

Dear Sirs:

Appointment in Respect of Surrendered Lands

Under the authority conferred on me by Section 53 of the Indian Act, I hereby appoint The Chief and the Councillors of the Westbank Indian Band, from time to time, jointly with respect to the signing of leases, rights of way, easements and licences of occupation, to manage, in accordance with the Indian Act and the terms of the surrender, the lands that have been set aside for the Westbank Indian Band which have been or may hereafter be surrendered. It is understood that:

(1) The Westbank Band Council shall have the necessary record system and all encumbrances will be submitted to the Indian Land Registry office in Ottawa for registration;

(2) The documents to be signed will first be acknowledged by the Band Council to be in the best interests of the Band;

(3) The Westbank Band Members shall be responsible for the actions taken by the person given this authority as stipulated in Band Council Resolution No. 1/278 dated September 5, 1978;

(4) The maximum term or period of any lease, right of way, easement or licence of occupation will not exceed the surrender term;

(5) Forms exemplifying the contract are to be the standard lease/permit forms pre-approved by the Minister or his authorized representative;

(6) The authority granted will extend only to those parcels or tracts of land that are specifically described by a plan of survey.

The Chief and Councillors of the Westbank Band will have the authority to carry out the powers granted on each occasion the authority is exercised and will be authorized on behalf of, and in the name of the Minister of Indian Affairs and Northern Development to execute such leases, rights of way, easements, licences of occupation and other instruments and documents as may be required in the carrying out of such authority.

Yours sincerely,

"John C. Munro"

John C. Munro

▌◆▌ Indian and Northern   Affaires indiennes
      Affairs Canada   et du Nord Canada

TO BE SENT BY DEX   Ottawa, Ontario K1A 0H4
AS SOON AS POSSIBLE

April 30, 1980

Mr. F.J. Walchli,
Regional Director General,
Indian and Inuit Affairs,
B.C. Regional Office,
P.O. Box 10061,
700 West Georgia Street,
VANCOUVER, B.C.   Our File: 901/36–15
V7Y 1C1

Management of Reserves and Surrendered Lands
under Sections 60 and 53(1), Westbank Band.

    We have received a telex (copy attached) from Chief Ronald M.
Derrickson, Westbank Band, inquiring about the Band's request for
authority to manage their lands under Section 60 and 53(1). I have
asked Chief Derrickson to discuss the matter with you.

    The Departmental Management Committee approved a policy
proposal whereby the following specific powers under Section 60 of the
Indian Act with respect to the management of reserve lands may be
delegated to Indian Bands:

Section 18(2)

— to exercise the Minister's authority to authorize the use of reserve
    lands for schools, health projects, burial grounds, parks and
    playgrounds.

Any authority granted would be subject to the proviso that where an
Indian, immediately prior to such taking, was entitled to possession of
the lands in question, the Minister will retain authority to fix the
compensation payable to him in the event the Band and the individual
disagreed on the amount payable for such taking.

Section 19

— to allow an Indian Band to authorize surveys and subdivisions of
    reserve lands.

Sections 20, 24 and 49

— to exercise the Minister's authority to approve land transactions between Band members and between a member and his Band.

Any authority granted would be subject to the proviso that when an allotment is made to a sitting member of the Band Council or his family, the allotment is to be approved by a majority vote of the electors of the Band. This is to avoid any possible allegations of conflict of interest. Further, if approval is to be withheld under Sections 24 and 49 the Minister must be notified.

Section 25(1)

— to exercise the Ministerial authority to extend the time limit (up to 1 year) wherein an Indian who ceases to be entitled to reside on a reserve may dispose of his/her interest.

Sections 28(2), 58(1), 58(3), 58(4)

— to authorize Bands to execute on behalf of the Crown instruments disposing of interests in reserve lands by way of leases, licences and permits, to non-Band members.

This grant of authority to be subject to the following minimum conditions:

a) the authority granted would be for specific managerial activity — i.e. agricultural, recreational, residential, commercial, etc.

b) the maximum term or period would not exceed 21 years.

c) forms exemplifying the contract, to be those approved by the Minister and Justice. In cases where standard lease/permit forms will not adequately describe the proposed transaction, the Band land manager, with the assistance of Regional officers will draft a suitable document which Region will submit to Justice for approval.

d) the authority to be granted be limited to specific parcels or tracts of land. (There will be no blanket authority for all lands set apart for the Band).

In addition, the Departmental Management Committee approved the proposal that when requested, the Minister is prepared to extend the authority outlined above to a Band to enter into leases and/or permits with non-Indians for surrendered lands under Section 53(1) of the Act. This authority will be transferred on the proviso that the Band can provide some kind of surety by way of bond or other assurance.

Any powers granted to a Band pursuant to Section 60 or 53(1) must be specifically requested, and approved by a majority of the electors of the Band. The majority of the electors of the Band would also have to approve the delegation of its authority to the Band Council. In addition, a Band seeking such authority will have to have demonstrated that it has the necessary technical, financial and managerial capacity to assume some or all of these authorities.

Undoubtedly some Bands may seek funding from the Department to assume delegated authority particularly for those areas of Indian land administration that are non-revenue generating. If this is the case and inasmuch as there are no funds at Headquarters for this purpose, the Region should ensure that they have the necessary monies available in their budgets to deal with the request.

Upon certification that the above conditions have been met, and upon your recommendations with respect to the request, I am prepared to initiate the appropriate Headquarters action.

> "J.D. Leask"
> J.D. Leask
> Director General,
> Reserves and Trusts.

ATT.

CC: J.D. Nicholson,
    Assistant Deputy Minister —
    (Indian and Inuit Affairs)

CANADA

PRIVY COUNCIL • CONSEIL PRIVÉ

P.C. 1985-1836
6 June, 1985

WHEREAS the Westbank Band of Indians by a Band vote held on October 11, 1984 requested that the Band be granted the right described in Schedule "A" hereto to exercise the control and management over the lands in the Indian Reserves occupied by that Band.

THEREFORE, HER EXCELLENCY THE GOVERNOR GENERAL IN COUNCIL, on the recommendation of the Minister of Indian Affairs and Northern Development, pursuant to subsection 60(1) of the Indian Act, is pleased hereby to grant to the Westbank Band of Indians the right to exercise such control and management over the Indian Reserves occupied by that Band as is set out in Schedule "A" hereto.

CERTIFIED TO BE A TRUE COPY - COPIE CERTIFIÉE CONFORME

CLERK OF THE PRIVY COUNCIL - LE GREFFIER DU CONSEIL PRIVÉ

280

P.C. 1985-1836

This is Schedule "A" to Order in Council P.C. 1984

WHEREAS Section 60 of the Indian Act provides that:

1) the Governor in Council may at the request of a band grant to the band the right to exercise such control and management over lands in the reserve occupied by that band as the Governor in Council considers desirable;

2) the Governor in Council may at any time withdraw from a band a right conferred upon the band under subsection (1);

THAT the Westbank Indian Band requested the Governor in Council grant to it the right to exercise such control and management over lands in Tsinstikeptum Indian Reserve No. 8, Tsinstikeptum Indian Reserve No. 9 and Tsinstikeptum Indian Reserve No. 10, which rights are more particularly set out in Appendix A to this schedule.

THAT the Westbank Indian Band requested that the duly elected Chief and Council of the Band be authorized to exercise these rights on behalf of the Band and be authorized to approve such leases, permits, assignments, consents and other instruments and documents as may be required in carrying out the authorities delegated to the Band;

THAT the approval by the duly elected Chief and Council of the Westbank Indian Band of any such documents or instruments shall constitute an acknowledgement that the document or instrument is in the best interests of the Band;

THAT such signing officer(s) as may be designated from time to time by the Westbank Band Council are authorized to execute such instruments and documents as may be required in the exercise of such authority, subject, in each case, to the prior approval of an absolute majority of the Chief and Councillors of the Westbank Indian Band;

THAT all payments provided for in the said documents shall be paid in the name of the Westbank Indian Band. Should any payments be thirty days in arrears, or should the Band Council consider that a permit or lease is in default by reason of a breach of covenant, the Band Council shall refer the matter, and all pertinent information in the Band's possession, to the Regional Director, Reserves and Trusts.

THAT the Band Council shall keep accounting records for leases or permits entered into, rentals received, receivable and overdue; shall operate a lease billing system; shall be responsible for collecting rentals under routine collection procedures; and shall submit quarterly a detailed aged listing of rentals receivable and collection action taken to the Regional Director, Reserves and Trusts.

.../2

THAT the Band Council shall forward duplicate originals of all documents granting interests in their reserve lands to the Indian Land Registry in Ottawa for registration;

THAT no member of the Band Council shall have a vote in the exercise by the Band Council of any authority provided for under this delegation in which he or she has a personal interest, either direct or indirect;

THAT the Band Council shall establish and maintain a land management records system;

THAT the Band Council shall make available to the Band members and a designated officer of the Minister all records, financial statements and audits and other information as may be necessary to enable the Minister to monitor the exercise of the authorities delegated to the Band.

P.C. 1985-1836

This is Appendix "A" to Schedule "A" to Order in Council P.C. 1984

The Band may exercise the power given to the Minister:

1. a) by subsection 18(2) of the Indian Act to authorize the use of
       lands in the reserve for the purpose of Indian schools,
       Indian burial grounds, Indian health projects, or any other
       purpose that is for the general welfare of the Band. This
       authority is subject to the proviso that where an Indian,
       immediately prior to such taking, was entitled to the
       possession of such lands, compensation for such use shall be
       paid to the Indian by the Band, or failing agreement, in such
       amount as the Minister directs;

    b) by Section 19(a) of the Indian Act to authorize surveys for
       lands in the reserve and the preparation of plans and reports
       with respect thereto;

    c) by Section 19(b) of the Indian Act to divide the reserve into
       lots or other subdivision;

    d) by Section 19(c) of the Indian Act to determine the location
       and direct the construction of roads in the reserve;

    e) by subsections 20(1) and 20(2) of the Indian Act to approve
       the allotment of land in a reserve to Band members and to
       approve the issuance of Certificates of Possession.

    f) by subsection 20(4) of the Indian Act to withhold approval
       for the allotment of land and authorise temporary occupation
       under prescribed terms and conditions. This authority is
       subject to the proviso that when approval is so withheld, the
       Band must notify the individual Indian and the Minister, in
       writing within 30 days, of the grounds for withholding
       approval, and of the individual's right of appeal to the
       Minister. Disputes will be settled by the Minister.

    g) by subsections 20(5) and 20(6) of the Indian Act to extend
       the term of Certificates of Occupation for a period not
       exceeding two years and at the expiry of this time to approve
       or reject the allotment. Refusal under subsection 20(6)(b)
       is subject to the same proviso with respect to written
       notification of the grounds for refusal and the right of
       appeal to the Minister as applies to refusals under
       subsection 20(4);

    h) by Section 24 of the Indian Act to approve transfers of land
       between Band members or between a member and his Band;

- 2 -

i) by subsection 25(1) of the Indian Act to extend the time
   limit wherein an Indian who ceases to be entitled to reside
   on a reserve may dispose of his or her interest;

j) by subsection 28(2) of the Indian Act to authorize by permit
   in writing any person to occupy or use the reserve or to
   reside or otherwise exercise rights on the reserve;

k) by subsection 58(1)(b) of the Indian Act where land in the
   reserve is uncultivated or unused and is in the lawful
   possession of any individual, to grant a lease of such land
   for agricultural or grazing purposes or for any purpose that
   is for the benefit of the person in possession;

l) by subsection 58(1)(c) of the Indian Act where land in the
   reserve is uncultivated or unused and is not in the lawful
   possession of any individual, to grant for the benefit of the
   Band a lease of such land for agricultural or grazing
   purposes;

m) by subsection 58(3) of the Indian Act to lease for the
   benefit of any Indian, upon his application for that purpose,
   the land of which he is lawfully in possession without the
   land being surrendered;

n) by subsection 58(4) of the Indian Act to dispose of the
   property mentioned therein which is on the reserve and issue
   the permits mentioned therein subject to the Minister's power
   to determine the division of the proceeds where the Band and
   the individual Indian in actual possession cannot agree.

2. It is understood and agreed that the exercise of the powers
   referred to in paragraph 1(a) through 1(n) is subject to the
   following conditions;

   i)   unless changed by policy of the Department of Indian
          Affairs, the maximum term of any lease or permit will not
          exceed 21 years, including renewals, without consultation
          with Reserves and Trusts, Ottawa;

   (ii)   all leases or permits for terms of more than 5 years will
          contain a periodic five year fee or rent review clause,
          unless rent is pre-paid for the entire term;

   (iii) no action to recover overdue lease monies or permit fees
          will be taken without the approval of the Department of
          Indian Affairs on the advice of the Department of
          Justice;

   (iv)   the exercise of the authority will be in accordance with
          applicable Departmental policies and procedures in force
          from time to time.

Chapter 9

The Highway 97 Project: Compensation

From 1978 to 1983, the Westbank Indian Band Council was involved in negotiations with the Provincial Ministry of Transportation and Highways concerning the acquisition of Reserve lands for highway construction purposes. The Ministry wanted to widen and upgrade Highway 97, which passes through Tsinstikeptum Reserves 9 and 10. In addition to the widening of Highway 97, other public roads which passed through the Reserve were to be upgraded or rerouted at the same time as the main highway project was being done. A major issue in negotiations was the amount of compensation to be paid to the Band or to individual locatees in exchange for land taken or affected. Various other matters such as the location of intersections and access roads, cattle guards, fencing, and the accretion of new lands to the Reserves were also agreed on between the Band and the Ministry negotiators.

There were two settlements, one for each Reserve. The negotiations concerning Reserve 10 were completed by the spring of 1983. The negotiations concerning highway construction through Reserve 9 were completed by July 1983, using the earlier negotiations as a model. The acquisition of reserve lands by the Province for highway purposes is not complete until the lands are transferred by federal Order-in-Council. This final step in the procedure, which should be relatively straightforward, has proven to be slower than expected. Although negotiations were concluded on Reserve 10 in 1983, the Order-in-Council transferring the lands was not passed until 1985. The Order-in-Council for Reserve 9 has still not been passed.

I propose to deal chiefly with matters related to Reserve 9 as there did not seem to be any particular matters of significance to the Commission that emerged from the Reserve 10 negotiations. The resolution of certain land issues arising out of the highway project on Reserve 9 appeared necessary to investigate and comment upon because conflict of interest issues were present.

Mr. Donald MacSween, who conducted negotiations on behalf of the Ministry of Highways, gave evidence before the Commission. Speaking of the negotiations concerning Reserve 9, Mr. MacSween described how the Ministry had negotiated a comprehensive agreement with the Band Council to cover all aspects of compensation and construction specifications. The Ministry agreed that the Band Council would obtain releases from affected locatees and lessees on the Reserve in exchange for a global sum of money. The total amount involved in the Reserve 9 settlement was approximately $3.5 million. After obtaining the required releases, the Band Council would then be in a position to transfer title to the Province for all of the land required for highway purposes.

Mr. MacSween noted that this procedure simplified matters very much for the Ministry of Highways. Usually they would have to negotiate with at least three parties when acquiring land on an Indian reserve — the band council, individual locatees, and any lessees affected. The settlement procedure innovated at Westbank was a new departure in negotiations between the Ministry of Highways and Indian bands in British Columbia. While it may have simplified matters from the provincial perspective, the procedure placed considerable responsibility on the Westbank Band Council. Under the arrangement, it was agreed that the Ministry would not enter into negotiations with individual locatees. Instead, the Band Council would conduct these negotiations. This put the Band Council in the position of negotiating with individual members and concurrently representing all Band members. Because of the closeknit nature of a smaller-sized band, the Council did not wish to drive hard bargains with individuals. However, all compensation negotiated had to be satisfied out of the global sum available. Any money not required to be paid to individuals could be expected to accrue to the membership generally. Council had a delicate task to perform — it could not be too tight-fisted with individuals but at the same time, it had a duty to conserve funds to be applied for the general purposes of the Band.

The $3.5 million settlement on Reserve 9 included a number of items, the largest of which was compensation to be paid to individual locatees. Locatees received compensation for both lands taken for highway purposes and for lands lost or affected by what is termed "severance". Most of the land on that Reserve had been previously allotted to individual locatees. Consequently, individuals received most of the compensation. Since there remained only a small portion of unallotted lands on Reserve 9 affected by the highway construction, the Band received little compensation. Some money was required to satisfy damage claims of lessees and to pay for construction work to be performed by the Band or others.

In arriving at a final figure, provincial negotiators ascribed values to properties on the Reserve. These values ranged from $20,000 per acre to $90,000 per acre. The disparity in values depended on a variety of factors, including proposed use, distance from the main highway, and total amount of land being acquired. Mr. MacSween said that in dealing with reserve lands, he did not have any zoning by-laws or regulations to rely upon in determining land values based on the highest and best use. Nevertheless, values were eventually arrived at based on the best information available. Negotiators got some guidance from the overall development plan applicable to the Reserve and also considered specific plans for individual parcels of land. For example, a figure of

$90,000 per acre was attributed to Lot 15–5 on Reserve 9. This was land held by Ronald Derrickson. A high value was attributed to this land because of Mr. Derrickson's intention to construct a shopping centre on it. Ultimately, the shopping centre plan had to be deferred, but at the time of the negotiations it was a contemplated project. I was told it was deferred because of the construction of a large new shopping centre in the nearby village of Westbank.

The amounts allocated in the global settlement to cover construction costs were calculated with the assistance of Ministry engineers. Provincial negotiators estimated the cost of work required to satisfy claims of lessees where businesses were likely to be affected by the highway construction. Ronald Derrickson said in his evidence that the Band Council did not feel constrained by the Ministry of Highway's valuations or calculations. These were useful guides when the Band Council conducted negotiations with locatees and lessees, but it was the responsibility of the Band Council to divide the global amount as it saw fit. This allowed the Band Council a certain amount of flexibility. If they felt that the Ministry evaluation was low or high on an individual property, they could make such adjustments as they felt proper. The only limitation was that the global figure would have to suffice to satisfy all claims. It is, of course, understandable that in discussing a compensation figure for an individual locatee, Band Council negotiators and the locatee would often differ — the final figure in each case would reflect the agreement reached between Band negotiators and locatee.

The settlement monies were to be held in trust by the then Band solicitor pending passage of the federal Order-in-Council transferring the lands to the Province of British Columbia. It was agreed that certain specified amounts could be released in construction draws following the completion of individual projects. It was contemplated that the monies payable to locatees and lessees would remain in trust until the federal Order-in-Council was passed. These monies were deposited into an account at the Northland Bank.

As previously noted, the Order-in-Council transferring the highway lands on Reserve 9 has yet to be passed. The Band used Band funds from another source to pay the highway compensation claims of Reserve 9 locatees in December 1983. The Westbank Band had recently received a substantial money settlement from its "cut-off" lands claim and voted to utilize the "cut-off" monies to compensate locatees of land taken for highway purposes. Highway settlement funds held in trust at Northland Bank were to be credited to the Band when the Order-in-Council was passed. By December 1983, the Band Council had completed negotiations with locatees on Reserve 9 and had obtained or was obtaining the necessary releases. The locatees were able to be paid more quickly than would have been the case if they had been forced to wait for the passage of the Order-in-Council. The accelerated payment process was clearly a utilization of general Band funds to pay the locatees and this was, of course, a benefit to affected locatees. Those who had substantial land holdings in the highway corridor were the major beneficiaries of these accelerated payments.

At the Band meeting, before a vote on the issue was held, some Band members expressed concern that a large sum of the Band's revenue monies would be tied up pending issuance of the required Order-in-Council. It was noted at the meeting that some $2.5 million of Band funds would be required to pay out various locatees. However, it does not appear that the total figure was broken down to disclose roughly how much compensation would be paid to individual locatees. Because they were voting on such a substantial commitment of general Band funds, I believe that the members should have had true, full, and plain disclosure of who was getting what. Under the terms of the negotiated settlement, the Band Council had in hand a global sum to obtain the necessary releases and to complete specified construction works. As Ron Derrickson said in his evidence, if Council could negotiate efficiently, there would be money left over for the benefit of the Band. Band records indicate that the total money paid out to locatees exceeded the amount the Ministry of Highways would have been prepared to pay under this head. The Band Council, of course, was not bound by the Ministry's figures when negotiating with any individual locatee but was only limited by the total settlement figure. Additional sums paid to locatees of course diminished the amount of money that would be available for use by the Band. Because of this and the very large sum of cut-off money being utilized, it appears to me that Band members required full information on payment details in order to make a fully informed choice on the issue of using the cut-off funds to pay locatees for land (or severances) on Reserve 9. Full disclosure should also have included Ministry of Highways valuations.

Ron Derrickson was the recipient of a substantial amount of the compensation funds. His brother, Noll Derriksan, also received significant compensation as the result of highway construction. Since both individuals have large land holdings on Reserve 9, it was to be expected that their lands would be affected by the highway project. Included in the compensation they received were monies payable for losses apparently incurred due to the severance of properties. I comment hereafter on two of the severances for which compensation was paid by the Band, which severances were examined in some detail during this Inquiry.

Ron Derrickson received $112,500 for 1.25 acres of land that was part of Lot 15–5. Noll Derriksan received approximately $60,000 for three acres of land which had been separated from two large parcels of land which he owned. The construction of East Boundary Road caused the severance of Noll Derriksan's properties. Generally the road did not encroach upon the Reserve. However, in order to avoid a rock outcrop at the base of Mt. Boucherie, it was necessary to encroach upon Noll Derriksan's property. In both cases the amount of land involved was rather large to be described as a severance. These respective severances remained in the possession of the locatees (Ron Derrickson and Noll Derriksan), but they were compensated for the loss. Neither severance had been recognized as compensable by provincial highway negotiators. It should be noted that there was disagreement between the provincial negotiators and the Band Council over just what would be described as a "severance" for purposes of compensation.

Mr. MacSween described how the Ministry of Highways dealt with severances. In cases where a roadway crossed an individual's property in such a way that it severed a small portion of that property from the larger portion, the land owner would be compensated for the severed portion. The Province would purchase the severed portion because the roadwork would have rendered it useless to the original owner. However, because they were dealing with Indian lands, the Ministry decided to pay compensation for any severance, but did not take title to the land.

Compensation for damage caused by severance is recognized under the general law regarding injurious affection. The policy described by Mr. MacSween, of purchasing unusable severed portions, may be viewed as one way of dealing with a loss caused by severance rendering land unusable. Generally, the term "severance" relates to a small separated portion of one property that becomes detached following an expropriation. Where a property is severed by a roadway, the owner may claim compensation for loss or injury caused to his remaining lands. In order to establish a claim for injurious affection, the owner must demonstrate that the property has been rendered less useful as a result of the expropriation. A claim for injurious affection may be set off against any enhanced value resulting from the expropriation. For example, the construction of a roadway may have the affect of severing part of the property, but the value of some or all of the remaining property may be increased because of improved access to a public road.

Under the terms of the negotiated settlement, the provincial government offered a lump sum of money to the Band Council, which would in turn purchase the lands required for highways from the locatees. The Band, as owner of all lands required for highway purposes, would then be in a position to agree to the transfer of those lands to the provincial government. Due to this arrangement, the Band became the owner of any severed portions of lots and could deal with them as it saw fit. The policy adopted by the Band Council was to transfer the small severed portions to the adjacent land holder. The Band Council and the Ministry differed on the size of parcels which could be termed compensable severances. The Ministry of Highways would only recognize very small parcels as severances. Generally, if a severed portion was so small as to be rendered unusable, compensation would be paid for the loss. The Band Council was prepared to recognize larger portions as compensable severances.

The negotiators for the Province did recognize some severances that required compensation, but the Band Council felt that there were additional cases which should qualify. The final sum agreed upon included compensation for all losses, including severances. Only the small severances were considered by provincial authorities in arriving at their final figure. Since the Ministry of Highways did not recognize certain of the severances when they calculated the total settlement sum, it would appear that had Ron Derrickson or Noll Derriksan dealt directly with the Ministry of Highways as individual locatees, they would not have received compensation for some "severances". However, because it fell to the Band Council to deal with the individual locatee claims, both Ron Derrickson and his brother Noll Derriksan were able to receive additional compensation.

The compensation claimed by Ron Derrickson and Noll Derriksan may fall under a broad category of injurious affection. Even if matters are viewed from this perspective, the claims appear difficult to fit into the traditional doctrine. In both instances examined, it is difficult to identify any resultant injury that would justify the compensation received.

Band Policy Regarding Severances

Ron Derrickson and Brian Eli testified regarding the Band's policy with respect to compensation payable for severances. Mr. Eli stated that the Band Council and the Ministry of Highways often disagreed as to what would be classed as a compensable severance. If the severed portion was large enough to be of economic use, provincial negotiators would not recognize that severance as being a compensable loss. The Band Council felt it was undesirable to have one locatee in possession of a small portion of land which, as a result of road construction, was logically contiguous to a larger property in the possession of a different locatee. Mr. Eli explained that that situation could result in some problems for the locatee of the larger parcel. He said, for example, that the locatee of the smaller portion could seriously affect the value and use of the larger portion by not maintaining the small lot or by allowing debris to accumulate. Also, because the smaller portion would always be adjacent to the roadway, a situation might arise where access to the roadway from the larger parcel could be hindered. It was feared that the development plans of a locatee might be unreasonably interfered with by the holder of the smaller parcel. In order to prevent such problems from arising, it was the Band Council's policy to purchase the smaller severed portion from the original locatee, and then to add it to the dominant parcel that was on the same side of the road as the severance. The locatee of the dominant parcel received the benefit of this additional land. The Band Council's policy did not fix a maximum limit on the size of parcels which could be described as severances.

The reasoning behind the Band Council's policy makes sense where there are two locatees involved. However, the logic is much less compelling where both the holder of the severed portion and the holder of the adjoining portion are the same. In that case, locatee X loses a portion of land from his lot on one side of the road, but he adds that same amount of land to his lot on the other side of the road. He has suffered no loss of total area. According to the evidence of Brian Eli and Ron Derrickson, the Band policy was followed regardless of whether there were two locatees involved or only one. As long as there were two separate lots involved, the policy was "blind" as to the ownership of the lots. Mr. Eli defended this application of the policy, arguing that it had to be implemented in this way or else the Band Council could be criticized for being inconsistent. While that position can be urged, it seems to me that it rather ignores the original reason the Band adopted the policy, namely to prevent a different locatee from hampering the use of the larger parcel. The policy of the Band tended to generate windfall profits for those who had substantial numbers of parcels affected by highway construction.

During the negotiations between the Band Council and the Ministry of Highways, the ownership of the various parcels affected by the roadworks was not revealed. Mr. MacSween testified that he was unaware of which locatee owned which lot. At that stage of the negotiations, it made sense that the Band would not reveal who was in possession of each parcel. However, once negotiations occurred at the local level as the Band Council negotiated compensation with various locatees, they would be aware of who was in possession of which lots. This information would have been significant in determining what should be Council's policy regarding individual severances, depending on whether or not the same locatee held the properties on both sides of the completed roadway.

Ron Derrickson's Severance

The severance for which Ron Derrickson received $112,500 is a flat, triangular piece of land which formerly was part of Lot 15–5. The 1.25-acre severance was created by the construction of the new Bering Road, which crossed the lot diagonally. Immediately to the north of the parcel is Lot 15–2, and immediately to the east is Lot 15–1. Ron Derrickson was the locatee of both these adjacent lots. Lot 15–1 was under lease at the time to a company which operated an amusement park known as "Old MacDonald's Farm". Lot 15–2 was under lease to a corporation controlled by Ron Derrickson and was in use as a drive-in theatre. Mr.

Derrickson had the choice of either leaving that severed portion of Lot 15–5 as it was or being compensated by the Band for the 1.25-acre severance based on the figure of $90,000 per acre. That value was arrived at based on the proposed use of the land for a shopping centre. Ron Derrickson was compensated for the land as though he had lost it, when in fact he retained possession of the land. He said, though, that he felt the separated land was less useful to him because it accrued to the Old MacDonald Farm property, which property was already under a long-term lease. He felt he would not get any additional rent for the land under the then existing lease.

During the course of his testimony, Ron Derrickson was asked to explain why the Band Council's severance policy was applied in the case of the 1.25-acre parcel. He said that everyone else who had a severed portion added to their lands "got something for nothing", so why shouldn't he? He was apparently referring to the fact that those persons who held the larger parcels and received the benefit of a smaller severed portion being added to their lands did not have to pay anything for the extra land they gained. However, in those cases the individuals did not also receive compensation for the land they gained. The land that they gained had formerly been in possession of another locatee, and that locatee had received compensation for land that he had truly lost. Mr. Derrickson, on the other hand, never lost possession of the 1.25-acre parcel. He simply had the boundaries of an adjacent lot resurveyed to include the 1.25 acres.

Mr. Derrickson said that the lots that were immediately adjacent to the 1.25-acre parcel were under long-term lease to third parties. By adding the parcel to Lot 15–1, he did not expect any extra income to be generated from the lease to Old MacDonald's Farm. Consequently, he maintained, he had suffered a loss. I think that, in his own mind, he was convinced that he had been adversely affected.

I am not convinced that the reasons he advanced in favour of compensation are persuasive. The total transaction has to be considered, both the positive and negative aspects. The severance of Lot 15–5 resulted from the construction of Bering Road. Mr. MacSween testified that the Ministry of Highways did not intend to build Bering Road, but that the Band had pressed for its construction. As part of the overall settlement, the provincial authorities agreed to pay for the construction of Bering Road. Ron Derrickson testified that the road construction on Lot 15 was specifically designed to service his proposed shopping centre. The construction of Bering Road would enhance the land in question for future development because there would be better access to all lands. The road that created the severance at Lot 15–5 was constructed at the request of Band Council in order to enhance the development potential of that land. That was a benefit to Mr. Derrickson because of the improved access. However, besides receiving this benefit to his land, Mr. Derrickson received an added bonus when he was compensated for the

1.25-acre severance. The Ministry of Highways had agreed to pay compensation for the construction of the road and for land taken for the roadway. However, they did not consider that there was a compensable severance created by the construction. The size of the "severance" exceeded what the Ministry normally termed a severance. Ron Derrickson claimed and was compensated handsomely for the 1.25-acre parcel.

Mr. Derrickson's claim for compensation for severance in these circumstances seemed to me to be overreaching. Any injury caused by having the smaller parcel severed by the roadway appears to me to be set off by the consideration that the remaining property became much more usable. The parcel of severed land seems to me to be large enough to support some separate commercial use. It fronts on a public road and is near the growing village of Westbank.

Mr. Derrickson would have had the option of leaving the property as it was, but he chose to consolidate it with his adjacent Lot 15–1, which was at that time under long-term lease. If he felt he suffered a loss as a result of amalgamating the property with another of his properties under lease, any such loss would appear to be the result of his choice. If Mr. Derrickson suffered some loss of value as the result of the severance that is not matched by the increased value of the shopping centre parcel, compensation should have been calculated considering the pluses and minuses of the global transaction. In the end, Mr. Derrickson was compensated for the parcel at the $90,000 per acre rate as if he had lost the use of the land completely. That seems to me to be an imprecise assessment of any loss since it fails to consider the total transaction. I think that if the matter had been considered in this way, the Band could well have had some of these funds accruing to it, and as chief executive officer of the Band, the Chief should have had a more enlightened perspective in this particular instance. Council members are not to be unduly penalized simply because they are office holders, but their conduct must be scrupulously correct as an example to their constituents.

Noll Derriksan's Severance

Mr. Noll Derriksan received approximately $60,000 for three acres of land which the Band Council classed as a severance. This land was not recognized by the provincial negotiators as being a compensable severance. The severance was the result of the construction of East Boundary Road, which crossed Lots 33 and 34, located on the extreme northeast corner of Reserve 9. Prior to construction of the roadway, the three-acre parcel formed a physically distinct portion of Noll Derriksan's properties. The land in question is a rocky (and apparently unusable) outcrop at the base of Mt. Boucherie. Mr. Brian Eli was a councillor at the time when negotiations with locatees were conducted.

He told the Inquiry that he and Ron Derrickson were "primarily responsible" for negotiations on Reserve 9. He dealt with Noll Derriksan concerning the compensation to be paid for this severance. He was uncertain whether Ronald Derrickson had any input into this matter. In his evidence, Mr. Eli described the land as "a sheer rock pile" and said that he could not recall precisely how the value was arrived at for this land. However, he said the payment of compensation for this parcel was consistent with the Band Council's policy concerning severances. He said:

> A The position we took was that it didn't matter who was locatee, we were going on properties, boundaries, and we followed that same circumstances as we did on #10. We just carried it over to #9 continuously. We never diverted from our initial policy or direction that we took at that time. I couldn't even say it was a policy; it was just the direction that the Council took.
>
> (Transcripts: Volume LXIII, p. 9298)

He noted in re-examination by counsel for the former Band executive that the value attributed to the three acres was at the lower end of the scale of land values for Reserves 9 and 10 in the highway negotiations.

The Council policy or position with respect to compensating locatees for severances does not entirely fit this situation because there is no other locatee land adjacent to the severed portion. Mr. Eli was not sure whether Noll Derriksan would remain in possession of the land or whether it would be transferred to the Band. However, it appeared to me that the land in question is of little use or value, regardless of who possesses it. It is difficult to understand how a roadway passing in front of this "rock pile" could diminish the value of the property. Why then did the Band Council agree to pay $60,000 compensation? The only justification offered by Mr. Eli was that the Band Council policy was being implemented consistently. Mr. Eli was questioned by Commission Counsel regarding the decision to recognize the "rock pile" as a severance and to pay compensation to Noll Derriksan for it. The following passages deal with the matter:

> Q Another one I would like to have you look at is Map #10, and if I have it right, that's the one that you spoke of yesterday as a rock pile?
> A Yes.
> Q Now, looking at that, that's right on the boundary of the Reserve, isn't it?
> A Yes. That's East Boundary.
> Q East Boundary Road?
> A Yes, East Boundary and east of I.R. 9.
> Q Okay. And then you see on the Map #10, you see the road going around the rockpile?
> A Yes.
> Q Now there are two, there are actually two parcels of land there?

A Yes.

Q And one of those is approximately two acres of land, and one is a little under one acre of land, I think, if my information is correct. Do I have that correctly?

A I will have to go on your — I don't have —

Q Okay, if you will take that for the time being?

A Yeah.

Q And one, the note has 2.04 and the other has .97. Now, is that land good for anything?

A If you blast the rock, I guess.

Q Pardon me?

A If you blast the rock and sell it, I guess.

Q But other than that it doesn't have a high commercial value?

A No.

Q Now, I understand that there was approximately $60,000 paid for that particular severance?

A I couldn't recall unless I seen the documentation.

Q Okay.

A To refresh my memory.

Q But if you take my word for it for the time being my note is $60,200 for that parcel of land.

A Yeah. . . .

Q Okay. So what you have got is a pile of rock —

A And nobody wants it.

Q Nobody wants it, and it costs $60,000?

A Yeah. Nobody wants it other than the Band, I should say.

(Transcripts: Volume LXIII, p. 9303–9304, 9308)

It is not apparent to me that anyone would covet this unlovely parcel of land unless it contained a deposit of platinum! It appears to be presently unusable and I have difficulty appreciating what economic use could be made of it in the future. The payment of $60,000 compensation for these pieces of "severed" land seemed to me unjustifiable.

Effects of Severance Payments

As previously noted, neither the "rock pile" nor the 1.25-acre parcel owned by Ron Derrickson were classed as severances by the provincial negotiators. Compensation for these severances was not included in their calculations when arriving at the total sum to be paid for settlement. The Band Council was not bound by the Ministry of Highways detailed calculations. However, they were working with the same global figure when it came time to negotiate with the locatees and lessees. Had the Band Council simply distributed the total sum among the various locatees and lessees according to the Ministry of Highways calculations, there would not have been any funds designated to pay for these two severances. In his evidence on this issue, Ron Derrickson explained how extra money was found to compensate the locatees over and above the amounts calculated by the Ministry of Highways. He stated that there were areas in the overall settlement where the Band

Council had a lot of leeway. For example, if the Band Council could negotiate efficiently with the various lessees and satisfy their claims with less money, then they would have a surplus to use in other areas. Claims of lessees were related to physical damage or disruption caused by the construction works. The Ministry of Highways had recognized this situation and had provided funds in the settlement to cover damages to improvements on leased lands. If the Band could get the lessees to settle for less, or if through the Band construction company they could do whatever work was necessary for less money than the Ministry of Highways had estimated, perhaps there would be some money left over. As Ron Derrickson put it:

> Well, that's what I keep trying to say. Everybody is hung up on the fact that there is some valuations done, and we should have been sticking with them. I would have never agreed to that. I would have never agreed to that, because that would have put us back in the negotiations. The fact is that we had a global figure; one figure that covered everything. Now, if we were efficient in negotiating the improvements, and negotiating the prices with the locatees, and so forth, we would have something left for the Band at the end.
> (Transcripts: Volume LXVI, p. 9911)

Additional funds expended to pay these severance payments to Ron Derrickson and to his brother Noll Derriksan diminished any sum available to the Band for general Band purposes. Given all the circumstances, I do not view the payment of compensation for these properties as equitable to the Band membership as a whole.

A potential source of extra money for severance payments was surplus funds resulting from Band negotiations with particular lessees. For instance, the Ministry of Highways had agreed that the Band would be responsible for dealing with the lessee who operated under the corporate name of Park Mobile Home Sales Ltd. and that an additional sum would be added to the global amount for this purpose. It was further agreed that should a lesser sum be sufficient to satisfy the claims of any particular lessee, then the Band could use resulting surplus funds to compensate locatees for severances which the Band recognized, but which the Ministry of Highways did not.

The mobile home park that was operated by Park Mobile Home Sales Ltd. was sold prior to the commencement of highway construction. The new lessee, Mr. John Ross, gave evidence before the Commission. He indicated that he was still involved in negotiations with the Band Council regarding compensation for alleged damages caused to his enterprise by the highway construction. Mr. Ross said that the Band had performed some work for him. It was a condition of the agreement between the provincial government and the Westbank Band that in exchange for the global sum received from the Ministry, the Band would obtain necessary releases from all locatees and lessees. If Mr.

Ross still has any outstanding claim, there is a possibility that the Band may have to utilize Band funds to resolve it. If extra money to pay for severances came from this portion of the global fund, such allocation could have a negative impact on current Band finances.

Another source of "extra money" could have been monies left over from construction projects that were the responsibility of the Band. For example, the Band received money to cover the cost of fencing and clearing work. The Band negotiated for this work to create employment and therefore put money into the pockets of Band members. If there were any profits from these projects, either the Band or its construction company would benefit. If extra money to pay for the severances came from this source, it came at the expense of the Band or its construction company.

Wherever the funds were allocated from in the global settlement to cover any compensation paid to Ron Derrickson and Noll Derriksan for these severances, they were a potential source of benefit for the Band. The rationale for payment of compensation for these two severances was dubious, since there was little or no apparent loss involved. The payment may have been made as a result of the application of Band policy concerning severances, but it lacked compelling logic. As Chief of the Band, Ron Derrickson should have appreciated that in the case of the 1.25-acre parcel, uncritical application of the Band's severance policy was poor policy. In fact, the blind application of the policy could adversely affect Band finances.

By claiming and accepting the payment of $112,500 for the severance on Lot 15-5, it does not appear that Ron Derrickson, as Chief, paid due regard to the wider interests of the Band. Rather, he viewed the situation solely from the perspective of Ron Derrickson the locatee, and realized a financial windfall. I believe that he failed here to be properly sensible of his position in the course that he followed. Similarly, Noll Derriksan, who was a former Chief of the Band, might be expected to appreciate that he was receiving a windfall at the expense of the Band. I doubt that the former Chief would have any valid complaint about a "lack of consistency" had Council declined to designate the "rock pile" as a compensable severance. Some nominal payment might have been justifiable, but $60,000 for that patch of rock seemed to me not supportable.

I do not wish to be unduly critical of Ronald Derrickson in this matter, as he worked hard in negotiations with the Ministry of Highways. There, his aggressive stance was desirable for the Band. It was, of course, also beneficial to him as a substantial locatee on Reserve 9. Perhaps he unconsciously felt that he should have his negotiating efforts recognized. Whatever his reasoning, I think he demonstrated a lack of sensibility to his position in the Band.

The chief executive of any organization must always be conscious of his particular position of influence. His conduct must set the tone for those subordinate to him. He must be careful to take no undue advantage of his position. Ronald Derrickson must have been aware that his position in the Band was a special one calling for restraint of a high order. It placed Councillor Eli in a difficult position to be negotiating with his Chief. The Chief had to be careful to refrain from overreaching. Subtle pressures can be present when a subordinate is negotiating with a superior officer.

All of us fail at times to live up to our ideals, but we ought to keep these ideals before us and always try to do better. In the case of those in elective office, such individuals must realize that they set the tone for the organization. Their conduct can be a force for good or ill and it should be seen to be principled and above reproach.

Former Chief Ron Derrickson was not and is not a poor man. In economic matters that concerned the Band, it behooved him to exercise a high measure of self-restraint and probity. Any perceived failure by him to so act could tend to lower the esteem in which Band government ought to be held.

The necessity for the observance of high standards of conduct by those in band government is especially important in the present day. The Government of Canada has been for some time moving towards giving greater self-determination to Native people. This is a desirable course. If independence is to flourish, there must exist confidence that those in power in the new order will conduct affairs in a highly principled manner. If it is perceived that elective office is an opportunity for personal enrichment, untold harm can be done to progress towards self-government. Government must be seen to be exercised in the interest of the electorate, not the self-interest of the elected.

I was somewhat taken aback by some evidence given by a person who was in the group politically opposed to former Chief Derrickson. This person said that she felt the Indian Act Section 60 powers (regarding land management) could be entrusted to the present administration, but that she doubted the wisdom of granting such power to the previous executive. On the face of it, I thought such an assertion lacked logic and smacked of unreasoning partisanship. But, on further reflection, I concluded that there may be a lesson to be drawn from the expression of such a sentiment. It betrays a lack of confidence in government that I found disquieting. But, if the electors perceived a lack of evenhandedness in the conduct of administration, such feelings could be understood. There should be no room for people to entertain such sentiments. There will be political divisions in all organizations. What is intolerable is that there be concerns about the probity of an administration. To me, the worrisome thing about the payments for these severances was that they could raise questions about the conduct and motives of the administration. That is something no government can afford.

Indian leadership at the present time is going through a period of increasing scrutiny. Is the new order going to be a fit replacement for earlier direction by the Department? Can the electors feel that their interest will be well served? Or will there be a tyranny of the majority or of those in power at a given period? These are legitimate questions and to the extent that doubts about Indian government exist, there will be some corresponding slowdown in progress towards effective self-government. I would be sorry to see obstacles on what I think is a good and hopeful course. Any actions that could foster doubts about the probity of local Indian government are liable to hinder progress towards self-government.

Restraint and a high sense of responsibility are vital ingredients of Indian band leaders in the present era. Indian leaders today are very much a city set upon a hill and their actions must be free of any taint of dubious conduct. There must be no lack of confidence in their fitness to govern.

Former Chief Derrickson placed before me some very eloquent words of a former president of the United States, Theodore Roosevelt. The gist of those remarks was that it was better to labour mightily to achieve great things than to languish by undue timidity. I agree with the former Chief that those are worthy sentiments, but I might also commend to him a study of the career of an even earlier president, General George Washington. While President Washington was a rather aggressive speculator in lands west of the Allegheny Mountains in his earlier years, he was as President very sensible of his need to be an example of proper conduct to his countrymen. That sense of a leader's responsibility is an example that band executives and, indeed, all elected representatives can usefully bear in mind.

I would not characterize the Chief's actions on this severance issue as one of gross abuse of office. But I must say that I found his performance in this area rather disappointing. I think he could have and should have done better. He was unfair to Mr. Eli, he was unfair to the Band, and ultimately he was, in the largest sense, unfair to himself. It is matters like this that can lead to the sort of unedifying comments that emanated from the so-called "Action Committee". I believe that, on reflection, Mr. Derrickson will perceive that his conduct here fell short of that standard one would wish to see adhered to by band executives. His failure may have been in large measure unconscious, but it should be a salutary example to those who come after, so that criticism and controversy are not engendered concerning those people who have the opportunity to advance or hinder the cause of Indian self-government by their conduct in elective office.

Chapter 10

Highway Contracts

As a result of the proposed improvement of Highway 97 through the Okanagan Valley, the Westbank Indian Band was involved in the early 1980's in a series of negotiations with the B.C. Ministry of Transportation and Highways concerning highway construction on Tsinstikeptum Reserves 9 and 10. These negotiations culminated in agreements being signed by the Band, the Department of Indian Affairs, and the Ministry of Highways dealing with various aspects of compensation as well as special construction arrangements.

Mr. Ronald Derrickson was Chief of the Band at this time. He testified that in the highways negotiations, he sought to obtain as much construction work as he could for the Band and Band members. The Band did succeed in obtaining contracts for some portions of the highway-related construction on both Reserves. As one example, the Band was paid to perform preparatory clearing and slashing work for road construction on Reserve 10. During the highway improvement project, WIBCO Construction (WIBCO), a Band-owned construction company, came into being to undertake highway and general construction work. Mr. Derrickson said it began to operate in late 1982. With respect to Reserve 9 highway works, the Band or WIBCO undertook a number of projects including clearing, fencing, secondary road construction, and certain drainage works. In addition to this work, the Band or WIBCO were on the lookout for further contracts in order that profits could be made and Band members given employment. Chief Derrickson said he was always in favour of getting Band members working to instil in individuals a more active economic spirit. It was also desirable for the Band construction company to develop a good track record, giving it the ability to perform a wider range of contracts in the future.

Ronald Derrickson has, over the years, been involved in a number of business enterprises including construction. He was interested in land development and had been involved with the Lakeridge Park subdivision. To a greater extent than most people in the Band, he was aware of how contracts could be awarded and was dealing with contracts generally on the highway improvement project.

Evidence presented at the Inquiry revealed that Mr. Derrickson received significant benefits from two highway-related contracts, one being a contract for sign removal and relocation, primarily on Reserve 10, and the other being a contract for the re-channelling of McDougall Creek on Reserve 9. Each of these projects had a gross value of approximately $100,000. At all times while the negotiations were under way and at the time these contracts were obtained and performed, Mr. Derrickson occupied the office of Chief of the Westbank Indian Band. Mr. Derrickson's personal involvement in these contracts needed to be examined in the context of a possible abuse of office.

It would appear that Mr. Derrickson was engaging in an enterprise similar to the Band, namely obtaining and completing highway-related contracts. He played a leading role in the general negotiations with the Ministry of Highways concerning the terms and conditions of the transfer to the Province of Reserve lands for highway purposes. In the context of securities law, for instance, he could be classed as an "insider" who knew the deal and the people involved in the negotiations. It was a situation in which he would have to take special care to avoid any potential conflict of interest that could engender allegations that he was abusing his position.

The Sign Contract

Highway construction operations on Reserve 10 began in 1981. Through discussion with the Ministry of Highways, the Westbank Band obtained a contract for much of the initial clearing of work sites. The head construction contract had been awarded by tender to Cantex Engineering and Construction Ltd. (Cantex), a construction company based in nearby Penticton. Following normal practice, Cantex engaged various sub-contractors to perform various segments of this major highway improvement project. One task to be completed under the umbrella of the head contract was the relocation of a number of billboard signs along the route of the new highway through Reserve 10. Because the main highway was being widened and sound berms were to be constructed in some places, the existing billboards had to be relocated. In some cases signs had to be elevated so that they could be seen above the raised sound berms on the side of the new highway. The sub-contract for this particular project was obtained by Mr. Mervin Fiessel of Kelowna, a long-time friend and business associate of then Chief Derrickson. Chief Derrickson said he assisted Mr. Fiessel by providing the necessary financial backing for him to qualify for the contract. Because of a marital split and businesses reverses, Mr. Fiessel was in a poor financial situation around this time. He also owed a substantial sum of money to Mr. Derrickson. I was told that these debts arose when Mr. Fiessel was unable to contribute his share in ventures in which he had been a partner of Mr. Derrickson. He said he owed Mr. Derrickson "a tremendous amount". Counsel for the former Band executive cross-examined Mr. Fiessel as follows:

> Q Mr. Fiessel, over the last number of years, probably 10 years or more, you have been involved in a number of business transactions with Ron Derrickson?

A Yes.

Q And you are still involved in a number of business transactions with Ron Derrickson?

A Yes, yes.

Q And during that period of time, you have been involved in not just one or two business projects, but probably multiple business projects, is that correct?

A Yes.

Q Louder?

A Yes.

Q Now, during the 1981/82 period of time when this particular contract was being handled, you chose to handle this particular contract by depositing the funds into an account, which is referred to as Salmon River Ranches?

A Exactly.

Q And that was an account that was controlled, in effect, the signing officer was Ron Derrickson?

A Right.

Q Now, could you tell me without going into a lot of detail as to why you chose that particular route at that point in time?

A The reason I chose that is the Royal Bank of Canada, we had a number of properties together and the interest payments were due and coming out of Ron's Salmon River account. At that point I was going through a divorce and everything that I was working on is basically gone into his account and my wife was trying to attach everything of mine.

Q So you were using that particular business account for business transactions because of this particular domestic situation that you were in?

A Domestic and also Ron was carrying the properties we had together.

Q Now, when you say carrying, was there monies owed by you, personally, to Ron Derrickson as a result of business transactions that you were involved with?

A Yes, a tremendous amount.

Q And what you were trying to do was you were endeavouring to repay Ron Derrickson those monies that you owed him?

A Right.

Q And, in effect, you received credit for those monies?

A Right.

Q With Ron Derrickson?

A Right.

(Transcripts: Volume LXXIV, pp. 11095–11097)

Mr. Fiessel gave evidence concerning how he obtained and managed the sign relocation contract. He stated that he had an oral agreement with Cantex to perform the necessary work on a cost-plus basis. The scope of the contract is perhaps most succinctly set out in the evidence of Mr. Victor Davies of Cantex during his cross-examination by counsel for the former Band executive:

Q Mr. Davies, when you state that this was a cost-plus contract, it appears to me that what was happening here was that you hired

Mr. Fiessel Construction to act as a supervisor for the relocation of these particular signs, and when you made that agreement with Mr. Fiessel, you must have either discussed or agreed with him certain rates that would be charged for his services and for the services of other people that he'd require, is that correct?

A   I personally didn't, but I believe our supervisory people on staff would have agreed with him what his hourly rate would be as a supervisor, plus what his hourly rate would be for the labour that he supplied.

Q   Yes, and the equipment that he supplied?

A   Yes, generally, if there was any supplied by him, yes.

Q   And you assume that because you look at the invoices and that's the way it was billed and that's the way it was paid by your company and certainly you wouldn't have asked him to bill it that way and you wouldn't have paid it in that manner if that wasn't the nature of the agreement between yourself and Mr. Fiessel?

A   Yes.

Q   So when you go back and review those documents, it indicates to you that someone in your company made an agreement with Mr. Fiessel to supervise and to pay those rates that were set out in the various invoices?

A   To supervise and employ the people to do the work; to do it all as a collective unit.

Q   Now, Mr. Davies, then your company, in turn, was paid, according to what you have been able to determine from your research, by the Department of Highways for this particular work?

A   That's correct. We would have submitted those daily time cards or chits, if you will, that were turned in, we would have submitted those to the Ministry for their approval.

(Transcripts: Volume LXXIV, pp. 11076–11077)

Mr. Fiessel invoiced Cantex periodically for labour and material used on the job. Cantex then issued a cheque to Mr. Fiessel. These cheques were deposited into the bank account of Salmon River Ranches, an account at the Royal Bank in Kelowna held by Ronald Derrickson. The total value of highway project cheques which were put into this bank account totalled about $100,000. Expenses incurred in the performance of the contract were paid from this account. In other words, this account was apparently used as the contract account. The estimated profit from the job was approximately $40,000 according to Mr. Fiessel's testimony. Mr. Fiessel said in cross-examination by counsel for the former executive that he was not paid anything by Salmon River Ranches for his services, but that the monies he received and deposited to Salmon River Ranches were utilized to repay the monies he owed Mr. Derrickson. Although Mr. Fiessel appeared to be the contractor, the financial matters relating to the contract were handled through this account of then Chief Derrickson.

Mr. Derrickson was questioned about the sign relocation contract and why the sign contract monies were deposited to his Salmon River Ranches account:

Q Now, at some point in time, we have seen from the evidence —
probably in the fall of 1981 — there were certain funds deposited
in an account of Salmon River Ranches by Mr. Fiessel.

Were you aware of that at that time? That that account was
being used by Mr. Fiessel?

A Yes. He didn't deposit them in the account. When he got the
contract from Cantex — and as far as I can remember, you know,
and that's all I can tell you is what I remember — Merv made an
agreement, or had a contract with a guy by the name of Peter
Doyle, who was the superintendent for Cantex at that time.

Peter Doyle gave — he discussed this contract with Peter Doyle
and got it, and then Merv was — he wasn't financially able to
carry the contract himself, from my recollection, and so he came
to me; if I would fund the contract.

Now, you know, at that time, you know, I was delighted to fund
the contract because I wanted to grab the profit from it because
he owed me a lot of money.

(Transcripts: Volume LXXV, pp. 11170–11171)

Cantex was unaware of Ronald Derrickson's involvement in this
matter, as were the members of the Westbank Indian Band. To the
world at large, it appeared that Mr. Fiessel was the only person
involved, given that he managed the contract and received cheques
payable to himself. He arranged for labourers to work on the project
and organized the necessary equipment and materials. The only
indication of Mr. Derrickson's involvement was the fact that cheques
received by Mr. Fiessel on account of the contract were deposited into
the Salmon River Ranches account. The ultimate beneficiary of the
proceeds of the contract was, of course, Mr. Derrickson through this
bank account. Mr. Derrickson was an undisclosed beneficiary. Only
after evidence was led before the Commission were the full facts of this
sign contract made public.

Ronald Derrickson said that during the highway negotiations he had
sought to obtain for the Band a contract for relocation of the billboards,
but that he was unable to do so. In response to questions asked by his
counsel, Mr. Derrickson described this contract:

A The only involvement I had with that sign removal contract, when
we were negotiating with the Department of Highways, we had
requested that the Band get that contract, and when the contract
was let, they omitted us from it; and we were furious about it, but
there was nothing we could do.

Q I would like to back up and just go into that in a little more detail,
Mr. Derrickson. When you say "we", you as Chief, and the
councillors were negotiating with the Department of Highways,
and you wanted that part of the work — that is, taking down the
signs and putting up the signs again — included in the work that
was to be done by the Westbank Indian Band?

A Not only that — yes, but not only that, we requested that the
highway project be broken up into a smaller contract, so we could

qualify under our bonding to handle some of them smaller contracts on the reserve, but we never got any of it.

The only thing we got was a clearing and grubbing contract.

(Transcripts: Volume LXXV, p. 11169)

Mr. Derrickson said that when the main contract had been awarded by the Ministry of Highways to the Cantex company, he did not enter into discussions with Cantex for sub-contracting the work. He said that if anyone from Council had approached Cantex in order to obtain work for Band members, it would likely have been Brian Eli. There is a brief reference to contacting Cantex with regard to relocation of highway signs in the Band Council minutes dated November 9, 1981. Under Item 5 in the minutes, there is the following notation:

In regard to relocating the highway signs, agreement to be negotiated with Cantex using Band members for labour.

There was no evidence that any action was ever taken to obtain the sub-contract for the Band from Cantex. I found this to be somewhat surprising in view of Mr. Derrickson's professed concern about getting employment for Band members to the maximum extent possible. As we have seen, Mr. Fiessel obtained this sub-contract for sign relocation work. According to the invoices which Mr. Fiessel submitted to Cantex, he commenced work on the project on November 11, 1981. Mr. Fiessel was asked by Commission Counsel about the sub-contract from Cantex:

Q How did you meet or come to get hold of that contractor?

A How did I get a hold of Cantex?

Q Yes, what was the origin of the contract?

A Well, I was around while the negotiations on the highways were going and I knew they were — the sign contracts were coming up and I think Brian Eli said, why don't you go over there and maybe get a job with Cantex, you know, raising the signs or moving the signs. I went over to Cantex yard, which was on Boucherie Road; they had a trailer set up there and I met a fellow, the supervisor, and asked them if there was anything in the construction end of it.

Q Yes?

A And that's how the deal was actually consummated. He drove me through the site and looked at the signs and asked me to give him sort of a ball park figure to move the signs back, I think it was 20, 30, 40 feet, in that neighbourhood.

Q Who was the person you dealt with?

A Pete Doyle.

Q And was he at that time associated with Cantex?

A Yes.

Q Was there any requisite or stipulations with regard to using Band labour in the original negotiations with Cantex?

A Basically, I don't believe there was, I can't remember at all.

Q This was all done orally, was it?

A Yes, it was.

Q Nothing was, as far as the original contract was concerned, nothing was committed to writing at all?
A Nothing at all.

(Transcripts: Volume LXXIV, p. 11081)

Mr. Fiessel said he had some Band members working on the project from time to time. Their wages were paid by the Band. The Band does not appear to have been reimbursed by either Mr. Fiessel or Salmon River Ranches (Mr. Derrickson) for these wages. Mr. Fiessel said in his evidence:

Q And you deposited those cheques, or you caused those cheques to be deposited to a bank account known as the Salmon River Ranches band account?
A That's true.
Q Now, the expenses, or certain expenses, were paid out of the Salmon River band account?
A All of the expenses, I believe.
Q Now, I want to deal with specifically wages that were paid to Band members who worked on the job.
A Okay.
Q Now, how was that handled administratively?
A Administratively, it was — Brian came to me and asked me if I could use some local Native people to work on the signs. And I said, well, I had a pretty full staff that was with me on a daily basis, and I said anytime I could use a Native person, I would definitely use them. During the course of the whole sign contract, once we got into the higher removals, I couldn't get hardly anybody to work on them, because we were using scaffolding up to 40, 50 feet high.
   Robert was basically the bravest guy to go up there. I know there was a couple that we used, and my agreement was with Norm Schwartz that any of the Band members that I used that he would keep track of it and bill Salmon River Ranches for me, whenever we used a member and then he would bill and I just handed the bills right to Barb De Schutter...

(Transcripts: Volume LXXIV, p. 11084)

At least three Band members were employed from time to time on the contract at rates ranging from $5.00 an hour to $6.50 per hour and the total amount of wages paid by the Band for this project was said to be in the neighbourhood of $1,000. Mr. Fiessel invoiced Cantex for his labourers at the rate of $15 per hour. This was a supervisory type of contract where Mr. Fiessel obtained the labourers and supervised the sign removal and relocation. Then he charged a fee for his time and a surcharge for the labour he employed. I think it could be best characterized as a cost-plus contract and as I understand it, that is how Mr. Fiessel viewed it. Clearly, from the profits realized, it would have been a desirable contract for the Band to obtain.

Ron Derrickson said that he had no direct involvement with obtaining employment for Band members on the sign project since employment matters would normally be dealt with by Councillor Eli. I can appreciate that there would be a division of labour in any organization, but the Westbank Indian Band in those days was not such a large organization that Mr. Eli and Mr. Derrickson would have been operating entirely separate and apart. Mr. Fiessel stated that Brian Eli came to him after he had secured the contract with a request that he consider using Band members as labourers on the project. This was in accord with general Band policy at that time — namely to seek out maximum employment opportunities for Band members on highway jobs. Mr. Fiessel agreed to contact Mr. Eli whenever he was in need of extra help on the project. Mr. Fiessel stated that he had worked out an arrangement with Mr. Norm Schwartz, the Band Administrator, that the Band would keep track of the hours worked by its members, and then bill Mr. Fiessel for that amount, plus an additional 5 per cent. Mrs. Linda Grover, the Band bookkeeper, was called as a witness. She said that she had searched the Band financial records and could find no evidence that the amounts paid by the Band for wages on the sign project had ever been billed or repaid. She said this sort of matter would be "under the direction of Chief and Council or Norm [Schwartz] to tell us to bill them and who to bill for..." (Transcripts: Volume LXXIV, p. 11145). Mrs. Grover stated that she could not recall whether she knew in 1981 that Merv Fiessel held the sign contract personally or whether he was working for the Band. She said that Merv Fiessel had often done work for the Band. She was not aware that the monies paid to Mr. Fiessel under the Cantex contract flowed through to the Salmon River Ranches account.

Mr. Bruce Swite, a Westbank Band member, was employed on the sign relocation project for several weeks. In his testimony he stated that he got the job by phoning the Band office and talking to Brian Eli. Mr. Eli instructed him to report to the job site to work under the supervision of Mr. Fiessel. Mr. Swite stated that he was paid by the Westbank Indian Band for the time that he worked on the project.

It was not unusual at that time for Mr. Fiessel to undertake projects for the Westbank Indian Band. He stated in his evidence that at the same time that he worked on the sign relocation project, he was engaged by the Band to construct a fire hall, and he had also done some construction work in the Band housing subdivision. However, with regard to the sign relocation contract, it is clear that Mr. Fiessel was not working for the Band, but rather in a personal capacity. Because of the arrangement that he had negotiated with Mr. Derrickson, it could be said that Mr. Fiessel was working for Mr. Derrickson. Mr. Derrickson took no direct part in any negotiations between Mr. Fiessel and Cantex about the contract. But in fact, because he financed the contract and monies from Cantex flowed to him, the contract was in reality his. Mr. Fiessel was his nominee or alter ego.

As noted above, it appears from the Band Council minutes that the Council considered approaching Cantex to obtain the sign relocation work. The minutes indicate the subject was raised and thus the Chief and Council would be aware of the possibility of obtaining work for Band members on this project. Councillor Eli, according to Mr. Fiessel, advised him that he might successfully bid on the sub-contract. Since the Band had used Mr. Fiessel as a supervisor for construction projects before, it appears that the Band Council would have had the opportunity to ask Mr. Fiessel to work on behalf of the Band in regard to the Cantex contract.

Mr. Fiessel said that he was not in a financial position to undertake the contract alone, so he turned to Ronald Derrickson to seek his assistance in providing financial backing. Mr. Fiessel and Mr. Derrickson had been long-time business associates. Mr. Derrickson testified that he was pleased to back him because Mr. Fiessel owed him a considerable sum of money and this would enable him to be repaid (presumably by having control of the contract proceeds). Because Mr. Derrickson's participation in the contract was kept from public view, it could be inferred that his role as beneficiary under the contract was intentionally hidden. The route of payment was Cantex to Fiessel. No monies flowed from Salmon River Ranches to pay for Band labour. The bank transactions were known only to Mr. Fiessel and Mr. Derrickson. This transaction clearly seemed to be a case where the former Chief was in a position where his interest and the Band's were at cross-purposes, and for this reason I found it necessary to investigate the transaction. It seemed to be a breach of the fiduciary obligation owed by the Chief to the Band. An executive of government is not allowed to profit from an enterprise where he is in competition with his government. Nor can he use his position to obtain financial benefits which are not disclosed.

It was submitted by Commission Counsel that the situation with respect to the sign removal contract was generally analogous to the Ontario case of The Queen v. Arnoldi (1893) 23 O.R. 201. In that case an officer of the federal public service was charged with the offence of "misbehaviour in office". This is comparable to the offence of breach of trust of office now found in Section 111 of the Criminal Code of Canada.

> 111. Every official who, in connection with the duties of his office, commits fraud or a breach of trust is guilty of an indictable offence and is liable to imprisonment for five years, whether or not the fraud or breach of trust would be an offence if it were committed in relation to a private person.

The accused, Arnoldi, was Chief Mechanical Engineer of the Department of Public Works. His duties included the hiring of contractors and equipment and the auditing of accounts. One of the vessels that was used in certain dredging operations was actually owned by him. It had been registered in another name apparently in order to conceal the true situation with regard to its ownership. Mr. Arnoldi received funds from the contract. It was acknowledged that there was no suggestion of excess profit or overcharging. The invoices would not disclose his involvement in the contract since it was let under another name. Arnoldi was convicted at trial of misbehaviour in office, with the presiding judge reserving certain questions for the decision of the Divisional Court.

It was argued in the Divisional Court by counsel for Arnoldi that there was no proof of any duty resting on the accused which his conduct contravened, and because everyone in the Department of Public Works knew what was being done, his intention was fair and honest. It was suggested by one member of the court during argument that Arnoldi could not retain any profits from the transaction for the same reason that a trustee is not allowed to retain profits as against his beneficiary.

It was argued for the Crown that the question was not one of financial damages, but rather misbehaviour in office to the detriment of the public. It was said that if there was an injury which would be a breach of trust or an injury of a private nature, such matters would not be criminal, but, if it concerned the public and was an evil example to the public, it would be criminal. Reasons for Judgement in the Divisional Court were given by the two judges who sat on the case, Chancellor Boyd and Mr. Justice Meredith.

Chancellor Boyd said this (pp. 208–9 of the report) in the law reports:

> The main facts on which the reserved question of law arises, may be briefly abstracted: An office in the public service of Canada, charged with the expenditure and audit of public moneys, certifies to the justness and accuracy of a series of accounts as for services rendered by contractors with the government, and thereby received for himself payment for these services. The defendant having charge of public dredging in Quebec and Ontario, used his own steam yacht for the purpose of towing the dredges from place to place, and of furnishing them with supplies during the working season, and also used a storehouse of his own in Ottawa for the purpose of housing plant and machinery connected with the dredges during the winter. The steam yacht, a tug, was registered in the name of first one and then another of the defendant's friends, and accounts were made out in their names for the use of the steam yacht (not including fuel and wages, which were paid in a manner not complained of or objectionable). Accounts for the storage were sent out in the name of a third friend of the defendant. These names were used in order that "newspaper notoriety" might be avoided, and not with a view of making any dishonest gains out of the department. The services were rendered, and no undue gains were made by the defendant.
>
> Upon this statement of facts, it is urged that no criminal offence exists, because it is essential that pecuniary damage should result to

the public by reason of the irregular conduct of the officer. But in my opinion the gravity of this administrative transgression is not to be measured by mere ascertained pecuniary results. The defendant was tempted to do what he did by the prospect of gain, — he profited by his own dereliction of duty, and to accomplish his purpose it was necessary to conceal the actual transaction. This was misbehaviour in office, which is an indictable offence at common law.

The duty of the defendant was to audit the special accounts, of which he had personal cognizance as a government official, and to verify their propriety and correctness. He was placed between the contractors and the public represented by the government, in order that the claims of the one might be checked out and the rights of the other protected. This work of public audit (not less, if not more, than that of private audit), must be a real service in which no concealed pecuniary self-interest should bias the judgement of the officer, and in which the substantial truth of every transaction should be made to appear. Publicity is the preservative of free institutions; any scheme which is devised to keep from the public information to which the public is entitled, in so far as it succeeds, is prejudicial to the well-being of the community. <u>Let the defendant's example be followed so that each trusted officer might work for himself and for private ends, then the whole public service would be honeycombed with corruption</u>. . . . (My underlining)

The Chancellor further said (at p. 212):

Where there is a breach of trust, fraud, or imposition in a matter concerning the public, though as between individuals it would only be actionable, yet as between the King and the subject, it is indictable. That such should be the rule. . . is essential to the existence of the country.

I take the other case cited from the State trials, <u>Rex</u> v. <u>Valentine Jones</u>, (1807) 31 St. Tr. 257, to be in principle a decision on all fours with the case in hand. The gist of the complaint was, that the defendant being the Commissary General of stores, colluded with one Higgins for the supply of public stores so that he, the defendant, might share the profits with Higgins. There was no charge of exorbitant profit. The only provision made was for sharing a fair mercantile profit. The fact that the scheme was so worked as to result in abnormal profits was treated as only an aggravation of the offence. (See pages 283, 289, 299, 313, 334.)

Therefore I conclude that the element of profit more than ordinary is immaterial, except as a circumstance to be regarded in mitigation of the defendant's conduct, to which due weight will be given when judgement is pronounced against him.

The gravity of the matter is not so much in its merely profitable aspect as in the misuse of power entrusted to the defendant for the public benefit, for the furtherance of personal ends. Public example requires the infliction of punishment when public confidence has thus been abused, and my judgement is, that conviction should be sustained.

Mr. Justice Meredith, in a short concurring judgement, said that this was not a case where proof of undue gain was necessary, nor was proof of knowledge of the facts by the defendant's superior officer any defence to the charge. He said that Arnoldi had been rightly convicted of misbehaviour in office.

Counsel for the former Band executive submitted that the Arnoldi case was distinguishable because that case involved "an element of deceit, it involves an element of somebody doing something wrong". Counsel for the former executive went on to say that "Ron Derrickson had a clear responsibility. . .that his personal interests did not conflict with the Band's". The Arnoldi case is a leading case in the area of the required standard of conduct of government officials in Canada. It is open to serious doubt that the Arnoldi case would be applicable to a chief or a member of the band council of an Indian band in Canada because such an elected officer is not expressly included within the definition of "official" in the applicable part of the Criminal Code, and the case authorities do not suggest that a member of a band executive would be found to be an "official".

The Arnoldi case is, however, highly relevant in defining the standards that should be adhered to by someone who is in the position of a fiduciary. The offence of which Arnoldi was found guilty predated the Criminal Code. The present Code offence is described as a breach of trust of office. Counsel for the Department said in his submission to the Commission:

> It is suggested that the Commission consider recommending that Section 112 of the Criminal Code of Canada be amended so as to include band chiefs, councillors and officials in the definition section. This would then provide a criminal sanction against councillors, chiefs and officials of bands abusing their positions as described in Section 112 of the Criminal Code.

I think this submission has merit. I rather think that perhaps counsel meant to refer to Section 111, but obviously both Sections 112 and 111 are directed to wrongful behaviour by public officials or by those having dealings with public officials. As counsel for the Department said, we need a less cumbersome process than a Royal Commission to address problems of conflict of interest or abuse of office. There must be available a simple mechanism to address such problems, which may be expected to arise more frequently with the increasing economic activity of Indian bands. It appears to me desirable that Parliament take steps to change the relevant definition section of the Criminal Code so that "official" includes a chief or a member of a band council.

In the Arnoldi case, the accused had concealed his involvement in the dredging transaction in order to gain a financial benefit to which he would not otherwise have been entitled. He was responsible for auditing all accounts for work done, and was thus in point of fact auditing his own account. The Court viewed the audit function of the accused as further aggravating his deceit regarding the true ownership of the tugboat. The facts of the <u>Arnoldi</u> case are, in a number of ways, similar to that of Salmon River Ranches' involvement with the sign relocation contract. In both instances, a person who occupied a public position received a financial benefit while occupying his office. In both instances, a measure of concealment was used.

Counsel for the former Band executive submitted that the reasoning in the <u>Arnoldi</u> case was inapplicable to the Salmon River Ranches matter because there was complete disclosure. However, it will be remembered that the Court in <u>Arnoldi</u> held that disclosure to superiors was not an answer to the charge. In any event, there was precious little disclosure here because the whole transaction was done out of sight of the Band membership and ostensibly in the name of Mr. Fiessel. It was submitted that since the Band had earlier sought to get the contract and failed, any duty Mr. Derrickson owed to the Band with respect to that contract was at an end. Counsel summarized his argument as follows:

> Now, had Mr. Derrickson been in a situation where he was competing with the Band and had entered into this business relationship with Mr. Fiessel, then I agree that there would probably be a conflict of interest, but that's not what the evidence disclosed.
> It disclosed that it was history as far as the Band was concerned and Mr. Fiessel got the contract.

I was not wholly convinced the Band could not have obtained the contract. If there was a financing problem as indicated by Mr. Fiessel, could not that difficulty have been overcome? But in any event, I do not understand the gravamen of the offence in <u>Arnoldi</u> to have involved his competing with the government, but rather the use of his position to enhance his personal fortune. He tried to conceal his role in events by disguising the ownership of the vessel.

It may have been politically undesirable to make public the fact that Ronald Derrickson was receiving benefits under this contract. It was noted in <u>Arnoldi</u> that one reason why different names were used was to avoid "newspaper notoriety" I should think that it would be a feature in many secret contracts that different names would be used and usually there would be some element of concealment. One such feature was present here, namely an element of concealment of the real transaction. I can understand that Mr. Fiessel's marital problems might have led him to be secretive, but I saw no logical reason for Chief Derrickson's failure to make the fullest disclosure of the true position.

Clearly there was an element of conflict of interest in this case. I found it curious that there was a failure to ensure that Band members' wages were properly debited back to Mr. Derrickson. One would reasonably expect that in such a delicate situation, both Chief Derrickson and the Band Administrator, Mr. Schwartz, would have taken some pains to see that there were no mix-ups that could lead to a suggestion that the Chief was profiting from Band labour without proper reimbursement to the Band.

This whole transaction was handled in a highly suspicious fashion. Mr. Fiessel said he wanted to keep the matter hidden from public view, apparently in order to avoid problems with his estranged spouse. He thus had a motive for depositing the contract cheques into an account other than his own. But the very opposite would have been true for Chief Derrickson. It is obvious that if an outsider had known of these payments flowing surreptitiously into the Chief's bank account, searching questions would have been asked about what was transpiring. Here was a profitable contract that was a possible source of good income to the Band. Mr. Fiessel, a friend and business partner of the Chief, obtains it and financing is furnished by the Chief. It appears to be a clear breach of the fiduciary duty owed by an elected official. From the perspective of Chief Derrickson, it seems to me that it was essential for him to have been very "up front" about this transaction. It should, as a minimum, have been fully documented in Band Council minutes and made clear to Mr. Schwartz and others that, in fact, this particular contract was being funded by Chief Derrickson. I find it hard to believe that if Mr. Schwartz had a true view of matters he would not have been vigilant in ensuring that proper chargebacks were made to Salmon River Ranches. There should have been scrupulous regard paid to keeping track of the time of Band members and charging it back to the Chief. Because the matter was done so secretively, not even the accounting staff at the Band offices realized that there should be a chargeback to Chief Derrickson. To me, it was relatively unimportant that the Band may have realized some financial loss on this labour payment mix-up — the sum was small and such errors in themselves are insignificant. Far more troubling was the inference that the oversight was the result of deliberate concealment in order to keep from Band view the true nature of the transaction.

I can only conclude that Chief Derrickson was sensitive to the fact that he might be criticized for appropriating the benefit of a contract that was said to have returned many thousand dollars' profit to Mr. Fiessel and thus ultimately to Mr. Derrickson himself.

If the Band was unable to obtain this contract, that circumstance could not be altered. It must be remembered that in 1981 the Band had not yet received the substantial funds that it had after 1983. The work was probably of a slightly more substantial nature than clearing and grubbing and may have required some financial strength to stand behind the contract and ensure performance. In this respect, the former Chief may have been in a more advantageous position financially than the Band at that time. I could not be sure, therefore, that it was clearly a case where the Chief had taken this opportunity away from the Band and was in competition with the Band. But the way in which the transaction was handled could only lead to the belief that something wrongful was occurring. There was an element of deceit in the proceedings in the use of Mr. Fiessel's name to mask the reality of the transaction. Valuable benefits were obtained. The real deal was not disclosed.

There may be nothing to be criticized where a person occupying a fiduciary position takes the benefit of a contract if the beneficiary, person, or corporation to whom he or she owes a duty is unable to undertake the venture themselves. In company law, the wrongful appropriation of profits of a venture is sometimes referred to as the "corporate opportunity doctrine". Encompassed in this phrase is the idea that it is not permissible for a person in a fiduciary position to use that position to the detriment of the party to whom duties are owed. The law of equity has always frowned on any element of competition between trustee and beneficiary and there is a heavy onus on a person in a fiduciary position to justify benefits received where there is any benefit obtained. Where a person occupies a position in government, specific rules prohibit such conduct as the acceptance of benefits. I think that on the facts of this case there could have been made a prima facie case of breach of trust in office if former Chief Derrickson had been within that class of officials who fall within the parameters of Section 111 of the Criminal Code. Chief Derrickson was owed money by Mr. Fiessel. He had strong motives to wish to obtain the benefit of that contract for Mr. Fiessel and thus have Mr. Fiessel repay some of his outstanding debt. It may have been permissible for him to obtain the benefit of this contract, but only, in my view, if the fullest disclosure had been made at least to the Council. The better practice would have been to obtain informed Band consent by a Band vote, but in situations of urgency, this may not always be possible. As it was, the matter was done in a secretive, wholly unacceptable way. I found this case to be a very troubling instance where Chief Derrickson was acting in total disregard of his obligations as Chief of the Band. It was an instance where there was a conflict of interest that the Chief failed to resolve, or indeed even address. Secrecy is often a badge of fraud. This matter was kept secret. The failure to disclose the true state of affairs prompts but one conclusion: the former Chief feared disclosure of his true role in events and was conscious of wrongdoing.

Because Mr. Fiessel had inadequate funds to obtain this contract, he had to approach Chief Derrickson. In effect, he was the alter ego of Chief Derrickson in performing this contract. I have said elsewhere that I do not think it fair to prevent people in band office from obtaining legitimate business advantages. What must be avoided is acting in secret. At the very least, Chief Derrickson should have called in Mr. Schwartz, Mr. Eli, and the other councillor of the day and described in plain terms exactly what was occurring. It should have been recorded in full detail in the minutes that such disclosure or discussion had occurred and that, the Band being unable or unwilling to take on this contract, it was therefore acceptable for the Chief to become involved through Mr. Fiessel. The way in which this situation was handled indicates a desire to keep the facts from public scrutiny. It was not easy for investigative staff of the Commission to unearth the matter, and no satisfactory explanation was ever tendered as to why there was such confusion in the Band office over reimbursement of monies paid to Band members who worked for Mr. Fiessel on the sign contract. As I have said, given the delicate circumstances, I would have expected Mr. Derrickson to have actively overseen the matter to ensure that no criticism could be directed towards him regarding use of Band funds or labour.

I view this case as an abuse of office. Problems could have been avoided by adopting the precautions I have set forth above. If a government official had behaved in this way, he probably would have found himself facing a charge of breach of trust in office. If there was no wrongful intent on the part of Mr. Derrickson, his behaviour was certainly bizarre for an elected official. While Chief Derrickson may not have been a detail man, it was my impression that he was usually quite astute in keeping track of Band business. He was alert, for instance, in lease negotiations and was an articulate correspondent. The concealment of his involvement gives the matter a sinister appearance and this illustrates the need for greater disclosure, which I address in Section II, Part C of the Report. The grave lapses in proper procedure should be a salutary warning to those in elective office about how not to behave. Band members appear to have had no access to the facts. There was a failure to document the matter in Band records. No Band Council Resolution dealt with it. This conduct is best categorized as an abuse of office and no chief should ever act this way.

The McDougall Creek Re-Channelling

Mr. Derrickson was also involved in a highways-related contract on Reserve 9. As part of the negotiations with the Ministry of Highways concerning highway construction, the Band obtained the contract for the diversion of McDougall Creek near Lower Boucherie Road on Reserve 9.

The contract price for the diversion was $100,000. This item was included in an agreement between the Band and the Ministry of Highways in the following terms:

> The Ministry will place $100,000.00 in the trust account of the Band's solicitor, in addition to the Compensation Price, for the purpose of allowing the Band to make drainage improvements on Lot 45 and, possibly, Lot 44, with the channel to be kept within Lot 45.

... It is agreed that the channel shall not encroach upon the highway right-of-way except at Stn. 45 + 50 where the watercourse will cross the proposed new highway in a culvert to be supplied and installed by the Ministry, at its own cost, at the time of highway construction. The Band may draw from the $100,000.00 as construction proceeds, on 30 day draws in accordance with standard construction practice.

Mr. MacSween, the negotiator for the Ministry, explained what the works generally involved. A new segment of a secondary road (Lower Boucherie Road) crossed McDougall Creek. It was proposed that the creek should flow under the roadway through one large culvert. However, in order to ensure that the creek flowed through the culvert, it was necessary to divert the channel of the creek bed towards that culvert. It was agreed that the Band would be responsible for the work. As I understood it, the Highways Ministry would be dealing with the culvert work.

Although this contract was to be with the Band, it appeared from Band financial records that in fact two payments of $50,000 each had been made by the Band to a company called Waterslide Campground Ltd. This was a company in which Mr. Fiessel and Mr. Derrickson were interested. Because of the apparent conflict, Commission Counsel had this matter investigated. When questioned by Commission Counsel, former Chief Derrickson seemed unable to be precise about the amount of money owed to his company by WIBCO — this debt was said to have been the basis for the transfer of the contract from the Band (or WIBCO, the Band construction company) to Waterslide Campground Ltd. Once again, there seemed to be a lack of documentation of any such agreement.

A What happened, it was negotiated as a part of the overall negotiations.
Q Yes.
A And at that time, I don't know where to start and finish on this one.
Q I could give you some paper, but that's —
A No, no. Before the negotiations I guess were completed, the Band, our company had a contract with Matsqui.
Q That is the construction company?
A WIBCO, WIBCO the general contracting company.
Q Yes.
A And they had a pipe contract to put in 36-inch main lines right down to the river, or to the inlet, or to somewhere.
Q Yes.
A It was about a mile and a half of main line, and they needed a piece of equipment for that. It was a bonded contract that we won as low bidders and —
THE COMMISSIONER: Who were you contracting for? Who was WIBCO contracting with?
THE WITNESS: The City of Matsqui, or the Municipality of Matsqui, or whatever they call it.

THE COMMISSIONER: Yes.

THE WITNESS: And they were the low bidders and they got the job, but they had to — you know, WIBCO was not a company that had much equipment. We generally leased everything we had.

And when we won the contract, you know, we knew it was a tight contract financially, we were going to have to really perform to do it, so Peter Doyle, who was our superintendent for WIBCO, and Dave Derrickson, went to Edmonton to an auction sale and picked up a 1066.

Q What sort of equipment is that?

A It's an excavator.

Q Yes?

A It is probably one of the — the second or third largest excavator made. The reason they bought it was because they wouldn't have to — with the size of that excavator, they would be able to eliminate two cranes to put in the big concrete pipes, and they are very, very heavy. They are almost as heavy as a boxcar to put in.

So the excavator could dig the land, dig the ditches and the ditches were something like 30 feet deep or 28 feet deep, and so — we bought the excavator.

Q That is the construction company?

A No.

Q Oh, yourself?

A Actually —

Q And this was bought in Waterslide Campgrounds, was it not?

A I don't know where it was bought. We bought it in Edmonton and shipped it to Matsqui, and it worked there. They lost money on the Matsqui job, something like — oh, I can't remember offhand — but I know it was over $100,000 they lost on that job, and I had something like, and again I forget the exact figures, maybe a couple of hundred thousand dollars coming to me in rentals for that equipment, 150.

So the Band made me a deal, if I would knock off fees off of that, off of that hoe, I would get the McDougall Creek contract, and so I did. And I can't remember — I phoned Barb De Schutter and asked her, because somebody had told me you were going to ask this question.

Q Yes.

A I asked her and she said I knocked off $50,000 of that Matsqui contract.

Q You knocked off $50,000 off your bill to Matsqui?

A Yes, to WIBCO.

Q Yes, WIBCO to you for that equipment?

A Yes, yes.

Q So you knocked off $50,000 off that bill.

A And the other problem is, before I would buy the machine, they had to pay, number one the hauling, and it's always the way from the point of where you rent it from, and return. In that case it was from Edmonton, they had to pay for it to Matsqui, and then from Matsqui back to Kelowna — or Edmonton, but I didn't want to — well, I wasn't sure whether I wanted to take it back to Edmonton. I might take it back and sell it.

But anyways, we brought it back. They were paid the hauling back to Kelowna, and then it would do the McDougall Creek job, and that's basically what the story was.

Q Okay. Your real bill to WIBCO, that is the bill for leasing the machine to WIBCO, and for whatever expenses you had for hauling back and forth —

A Yes. They had to do any repairs on the machine too while they had it.

Q All right. Now, what do you say your real bill to WIBCO was?

A Offhand I don't know. I think it was close to $200,000, but I am not sure.

Q $200,000 was —

A Let me finish what I was saying before, though.

Q Okay.

A I checked with Barb DeSchutter and she said I had taken $50,000 off of them. Well, I talked to either Harold or Brian, I can't remember, and they thought it was 25 off of that bill. Whatever it was, the 25 or 50 that I deducted off the bill, was if I got the McDougall Creek, that's what was offered to me to do it.

Q Okay. So you yourself got the McDougall Creek contract?

A Yes.

Q And you did, yourself, the McDougall Creek contract?

A Did the job, yes.

Q And you did it —

A I hired a friend of mine to oversee it, actually there were about five or six people, or seven people working on it, including about five Band members.

Q Okay. Who did the overseeing of the contract?

A A Lyle Shunter.

Q And you would have paid Mr. Shunter out of your own pocket?

A Oh, sure.

(Transcripts: Volume LXXI, pp. 10759–10763)

From the limited documentation that did exist, it appeared that in April and May 1983, heavy equipment was rented from Waterslide Campground Ltd. to WIBCO for a total amount of $48,000. This was apparently for the use of this equipment on the Matsqui project. Mr. Derrickson, in his testimony quoted above, seemed to hold the view that the total bill from Waterslide Campground Ltd. to WIBCO was in the order of $200,000 — whether it was $200,000 or $48,000, the significant figure would appear to be the outstanding debt of $23,097.50. In August 1983, an agreement was entered into, the text of which I set out hereafter:

This agreement made this 11th day of August, 1983

BETWEEN: Ronald Michael Derrickson, Mervin Fiessel
Waterslide Campground Ltd., and Merv Fiessel
Construction

OF THE FIRST PART

and   W I B CO. Construction Ltd. and the Westbank
                   Indian Band

OF THE SECOND PART

WHEREAS:

1. The parties of the first part supplied equipment in the form of a 1066 Hoe, a John Deere 555 Loader, etc. in accordance with an agreement with the parties of the second part, as per schedule "A" attached hereto marked Equipment Rental: From Waterslide Campground to WIBCO Construction Ltd. for period April 23, 1983 to May 28, 1983.

2. The parties of the second part acknowledge they are unable to pay the parties of the first part the full amount owing because of cost overruns.

3. The parties of the first part hereby agrees to accept as payment in full the sum of Twenty-five Thousand ($25,000.00) dollars of the total amount due from the Matsqui contract and further agrees to cancel the balance of $23,097.50 from the invoice.

4. In consideration of the above, the parties of the second part, their heirs, executors, administrators and assigns release and forever discharge the parties of the first part from any and all expenditures and work done for either parties, all actions, causes of actions, claims and demands, whether known or unknown, suspected or unsuspected, whatsoever and wheresoever which hereafter can, shall or may have and which have arisen out of or resulted in any way from or developed from or related in any way whatsoever to the herein parties up to and including this date.

SIGNED, SEALED AND
DELIVERED

"Barb DeSchutter"   "Ronald M. Derrickson"
In the presence of

On behalf of the Westbank Indian Band and W I B CO. Construction Ltd.

"Brian Eli"

"H.J. Derickson"

It appears that to satisfy the then outstanding $48,000 debt, the parties agreed that WIBCO would pay $25,000 and that the remaining debt of $23,097.50 would be cancelled. According to Mr. Derrickson, it was further agreed that WIBCO and the Band would allow the diversion contract for McDougall Creek to be obtained by Waterslide Campground Ltd. Presumably this was to compensate Waterslide Campground (Derrickson and Fiessel) for any loss sustained by reason of not receiving the full sum due on the equipment rental debt. One is left to wonder why such agreement was never documented. It would have been a simple matter to recite it in the text of the agreement set out above. The evidence does not disclose the total amount of profit realized on this contract, but it was clear that Ronald Derrickson wished to obtain the contract and viewed it as a source of profit. No breakdown of the costing on this contract was furnished, so it was not possible to determine the precise amount that accrued to Waterslide Campground Ltd. on a net basis. If it generated profit on any similar scale as the sign contract, it was a highly desirable contract to obtain.

While the financial details of this contract are more sparse than in the case of the sign removal contract, there are obvious problems with this particular transaction. The contract was clearly available to the Band and/or to its construction company, WIBCO. That was the original agreement with the Ministry. There was no suggestion that the Band could not obtain this contract, as was said to be the case with the sign contract. The benefit of the contract was appropriated by Waterslide Campground Ltd., the ultimate beneficiaries being Mr. Derrickson and Mr. Fiessel. Again, if Mr. Fiessel was heavily indebted to Mr. Derrickson, as he testified, then the ultimate beneficiary of the funds would be Mr. Derrickson. At all material times, Mr. Derrickson was Chief of the Westbank Indian Band and a major negotiator for the Band with the Ministry of Highways. This was a situation that called for complete disclosure, proper documentation, and an indication from the Band (or at a minimum, Band Council) that it was acceptable for this benefit to accrue to Waterslide Campground Ltd.

I am at a loss to understand why there was no documentation of any agreement by the Band and WIBCO to assign the benefit of this contract to Waterslide Campground Ltd. The only related document is the agreement of August 11, 1983, which simply recites that $23,097.50 is being forgiven and that the parties release each other mutually from all actions, etc. There is nothing in this particular document that reflects in any way the alleged agreement to permit the contract to be obtained by Waterslide Campground Ltd.

Unlike the situation in the sign relocation contract, there does not appear to have been any potential problem with the Band or its construction company obtaining the benefit of this contract. Here again there was a total failure of disclosure to the Band and there was absolutely nothing documented, either in any Band Council minutes or any written agreement setting forth an understanding between the Band Council and Waterslide Campground Ltd. that this contract should be assigned. Given the clear conflict of interest, these omissions were obvious lapses of proper procedure or, indeed, of any procedure.

It is surprising, to say the least, that the Band Administrator would not have recognized this problem. As I have said in connection with the sign contract, it would seem to me desirable that the Band should have had a chance to comment on the situation to ameliorate the problem of conflict of interest. At a bare minimum, there should have been full documentation of the authorization by members of the Band executive, excluding Chief Derrickson, to assign this contract to Waterslide Campground Ltd. As it stands, there seems to have been a bare-faced appropriation of a contract and its proceeds from the Band and WIBCO by Waterslide Campground Ltd. Here is an absolute failure by the Band Council, the Chief, and the Band Administrator to pay the least regard to an obvious conflict of interest situation and to take steps to ensure that the matter was handled appropriately.

Another disquieting feature of this transaction is the fact that Waterslide Campground Ltd. did not furnish any accounting, then or later, for the financial experience on this contract. For instance, it may be that the true profit was $80,000, or it may be that it was $10,000. There is nothing in the record, either by way of documentary evidence or any evidence adduced that would satisfy any of these questions. And Band members have a right to get the answers to such questions. It seems to me quite wrong for the Chief of the Band to be receiving a contract of this sort when there is no disclosure as to the actual profitability. If the facts are not known, then no judgement can be made by Band members or by other Council members as to the propriety or otherwise of the arrangement.

The situation was not improved by the wording of the Band Council Resolution of October 24, 1983 concerning the matter. It says: "be it resolved that subject to the approval of the Province of British Columbia, we hereby approve the release of the funds held in trust by Mr. Allen of a construction draw in the amount of $50,000 made payable to the Westbank Indian Band". That Resolution was signed by the two Band councillors and Chief Derrickson. Likewise, the Band Council Resolution of November 25, 1983 concerning the final $50,000 draw is signed by Chief Derrickson and the two councillors and simply recites that the work has been done to the satisfaction of the Ministry of Highways and the Westbank Indian Band. It appears that the Band Administrator, Mr. Schwartz, was involved in at least one of the construction draws because his name appears on one of the authorizing vouchers. Also, there is, upon inspection of the documentation (Exhibit 205), an element of non-disclosure approaching deceit. As I said, the original arrangement with the Ministry called for the Band to do the work. The wording of the Band Council Resolutions makes no disclosure of the change — indeed, the Band Council Resolution of

October 24, 1983 gives the impression that the Band was doing the work.

The failure of all concerned to be alive to this conflict of interest is breath-taking. It is quite inconceivable to me that any official of a government, be it municipal, provincial, or federal, could escape prosecution for breach of trust of his office in the circumstances that are disclosed here by the records, or perhaps more properly, by the lack of records. Where there is such a plain and obvious conflict of interest, it would require the most scrupulous documentation and open procedure to make it clear to all that there was no sinister conduct. Counsel for the former Band executive said in his submission before the Commission relative to the McDougall Creek situation:

> The Band company wasn't in a position to pay that money; an agreement was made, and my understanding, Mr. Commissioner, and you may wish to review this in the evidence because I can't put my finger on it at the moment, but my understanding was also that the Band was not in a position to perform that contract at that point in time; that Mr. Derrickson gave evidence that for whatever reason, the Band equipment was not available to perform that contract at that point in time, and therefore it arose that he would use his equipment to complete that particular contract, and there would be a set-off in reference to the monies that were owed for the rental of the particular equipment.
> Again, I would respectfully suggest that there was complete disclosure on that matter, and it was known to all parties involved as to what the deal was and the nature of the transaction.

I am doubtful that the facts support this submission. It seemed to me that the Band or WIBCO was in a position to undertake this contract. No written agreement was ever produced setting out an understanding between either the Band or WIBCO and Waterslide Campground Ltd. Given the obvious conflict of interest that existed here, I found that omission surprising.

With regard to the submission that there was complete disclosure on this matter, it can only be said that the matter was handled less surreptitiously than the sign relocation contract. Cheques flowed to Waterslide Campground Ltd. through the Band office after the Ministry of Highways had paid the funds to the Band. But there was an almost total failure of disclosure in this matter, or at least of any meaningful disclosure. No one in the Band, save perhaps a Council member familiar with the highway agreement, would have understood what was really happening.

I think that this situation falls into the category of abuse of office regardless of whether or not there was some financial basis for the Waterslide Campground Ltd. to be awarded this contract (because of the less than full rental payments on the earlier contract). Mr.

Derrickson failed to disclose this matter properly to the Band, and there was further failure to document any agreement in even the most rudimentary way. As I have said before, if potential or actual benefit is to be appropriated by a Chief or a sitting member of council, there must be clear disclosure and full documentation of any agreement made to permit this benefit. Band members have a right to know what their executive is doing. They may or may not agree with the transaction, but they should certainly have the transaction brought to their attention. Only in this way can conflict be dealt with and obviated. The conduct in the McDougall Creek case is the sort of procedure that casts a band government in a bad light and is ultimately harmful to progress towards self-government.

The point of the matter is that if these situations are properly documented and the other council members, as a minimum, concur that certain actions should be taken, then it will be plain that the issue has at least been considered. Regarding the McDougall Creek contract, there is absolutely no indication that the matter was examined in any informed or orderly way, and one is left with the inference that the contract was simply "scooped" by the company in which Mr. Fiessel and Mr. Derrickson were interested. This is an obvious case of competition between an agency of the incumbent Chief with the Band and WIBCO, and was, of course, quite impermissible because of the fiduciary relationship of the executive to the Band. It could only be rendered permissible by informed consent, preferably of the Band, but at a bare minimum by those members of the executive who had no financial interest in the contract.

Matters relating to both the sign relocation contract and the McDougall Creek diversion were handled extremely poorly by the Band executive, and in particular by former Chief Derrickson. Despite the clear and obvious conflict of interest that existed, no steps were taken to deal with the conflicts. There were no steps taken to deal with conflict of interest situations; indeed, I am not sure that anyone in control at Westbank even recognized or understood what a conflict of interest situation was. I cannot believe that Chief Derrickson, with his extensive business background and experience, was not aware of the need to be more forthright in dealing with such situations. I am also disappointed that the Band Administrator failed to advise elected officials concerning their responsibilities. The lapses here were obvious and severe. It is hard for me to appreciate how a former member of the Department, which Mr. Schwartz was, could fail to recognize the difficulty and advise on a proper course of disclosure and documentation. He may not have been fully aware of the sign contract problems, but he apparently was involved in some of the paperwork on the McDougall Creek payments.

Both the sign contract and the McDougall Creek contract were cases in which abuse of office occurred. They are models of how an elected member of a band executive ought not to act. The Department should take steps to make plain to band councils throughout the country the nature of conflict of interest, asking council members and chiefs to be vigilant in this area to avoid a repetition of the conduct in these two instances at Westbank. I hope education suffices — if not, it may be necessary to resort to the stronger measure of prosecution suggested by counsel for the Department.

Chapter 11

Possible Abuse of Department Funding

Pursuant to the Department's policy of devolving the administration of programs to band councils, the Westbank Indian Band administers a Social Assistance program for eligible recipients living on the Reserves. The Band Council employs a Social Assistance Coordinator to oversee the management of this program. The Department furnishes a manual setting out the rules and procedures for the guidance of the Band and also provides funding to cover the costs involved.

Evidence brought before this Inquiry revealed that funds from the Social Assistance Program had been used to pay for television receivers known as "satellite dishes". These receivers were purchased for various Band members resident at the Band housing subdivision on Reserve 9. Mr. Brian Eli, a former Councillor of the Band, gave evidence concerning the purchase of these satellite dishes for various Band members and how it was planned to recoup costs from Social Assistance funds.

Mr. Eli stated that he had developed a plan to purchase a number of satellite dishes to enable residents in the Band subdivision to improve television reception at homes in the area. He explained that television reception was a problem in this subdivision because of the interference caused by the proximity of Mt. Boucherie. Cable television services were either unavailable or very expensive. Due to a volume purchase, Mr. Eli had managed to get what he considered to be a very good price on satellite dishes. The proposal was that the Band would purchase the dishes and enter into contracts with the recipients (Band members) to pay the money back over a period of time. Mr. Eli planned to structure the debt as a second mortgage on Band housing and to require residents to pay an additional amount of "rent" each month until the cost of the dish was reimbursed to the Band. However, when the plan was presented to the Council, Chief Derrickson expressed reservations about the purchase. Mr. Derrickson was concerned that the Band would not be repaid. He perceived a potential difficulty in the case of some residents of the Band subdivision who were not regularly employed. In those cases where purchasers were receiving Social Assistance, Mr. Eli proposed that the second mortgage would be included in the shelter cost component of their monthly allowance.

The Commission heard evidence from Mrs. Rose Derrickson, Councillor and current Social Assistance Coordinator for the Band. She had assumed the duties of Coordinator in the fall of 1986 and had sought the advice of Departmental staff on various matters pertaining to the Social Assistance program at Westbank as she became familiar with her responsibilities. She realized that Social Assistance funds had been used to purchase satellite dishes for certain Band members from April 1984 through June 1986.

Mr. Gordon Van der Sar, a Social Assistance Adviser from the Vancouver District Office, visited Westbank in November 1986. It had come to his attention that certain members of the Westbank Indian Band who were receiving Social Assistance had purchased satellite dishes apparently using public funds. He asked Rose Derrickson about the matter and she said that while she could confirm that payments of some sort had occurred, she was unaware of the full details of the purchases because they had taken place before she assumed her duties. She was under the impression that the use of Social Assistance funds for that purpose had been approved by the Department. Mr. Van der Sar did not think that this was a permitted use of funds and wished to have the matter further investigated. He instructed her to make a complete analysis of Social Assistance files and Band financial records to determine how Social Assistance funds had been utilized.

Mrs. Derrickson related in her evidence how the purchase plan had operated. The terms of each individual contract required that monthly payments of $200 be made for a total of fifteen months, commencing in April 1984. In those cases where a purchaser was receiving Social Assistance, this $200 monthly payment was recorded as a "shelter cost" in the Band's Social Assistance files. In some cases, the $200 payment was described as "second mortgage". In each case, the $200 item shown as a shelter cost was followed by the letters "PD". This was a notation to pay the $200 directly to the Westbank Indian Band. The $200 monthly payment was charged against the Social Assistance funds that were available to the Band, and credited to the Westbank Indian Band's account as a payment on the individual's satellite dish contract with the Band.

Eleven persons who obtained satellite dishes were receiving Social Assistance during the entire fifteen-month period of the contract. There were other instances where purchasers of satellite dishes had received Social Assistance funds from time to time during the contract. While they were receiving Social Assistance, the $200 monthly payment was paid directly to the Band from the Social Assistance funds.

Each month the Band sent to the Department an accounting of monies spent on the Social Assistance program. The Department then reimbursed the Band for the full amount it had expended. There was no specific reference to the expenditure of Social Assistance funds for satellite dishes on these monthly accounting statements, and indeed the monthly reports are not detailed enough to show that kind of information. The individual Social Assistance files may have revealed a payment as a second mortgage, but there was no reference in the individual files to a purchase of a satellite dish on behalf of a recipient of Social Assistance.

Mr. Van der Sar stated that he had done a review of the Westbank Band Social Assistance files in the late spring of 1986, following a request from Chief Derrickson for a general review. He took a random sampling of 10 per cent of the case load and subsequently reported on the management of the Social Assistance program at Westbank. Mr. Van der Sar did not discover that Social Assistance funds were being used to purchase satellite dishes during the course of his review, nor were the purchases brought to his attention. After his review, he indicated to the Band administration that he felt generally comfortable about the operation of this program.

Mr. Van der Sar did indicate that, as a result of his review, he was concerned that the Social Assistance records did not contain sufficient back-up information to justify the shelter costs shown for each recipient. Of the files he had reviewed, some had shown this $200 payment under "shelter cost". He testified that he did not know what the notation "$200 PD" meant. As noted, some of the forms showed the $200 figure as a second mortgage as well as the direct payment notation. Mr. Van der Sar said that the "$200 PD" notation would not have caused him any particular concern or alarm, as there are cases in which payments are made directly to a third party. He testified that he was unaware of this use of Social Assistance funds prior to visiting the Westbank Band again in November 1986 to review programs. He said that the use of Social Assistance funds to purchase items such as satellite dishes would not be an authorized expenditure under this program. He was unpleasantly surprised to discover what the "200 P.D." notations signified.

Former Councillor Eli testified that he had sought and obtained Departmental approval to use Social Assistance funds for the purchase of the equipment. He said that he had received this approval from the late Mr. Simon Muldoe, former District Manager for the Department of Indian Affairs Central District. He said in cross-examination by counsel for the Department:

Q Who was at that visit?
A Myself, Norm Schwartz and Simon Muldoe.
Q Just the three of you?
A Yes, in his office.
(Transcripts: Volume LXII, p. 9115)

Mr. Norman Schwartz, Band Administrator, also gave evidence about the satellite dish purchases. He stated that he and Mr. Eli had met with Mr. Muldoe and Ms. Donna Moroz before proceeding with purchase of the satellite dishes. He said in answer to a question by counsel for the former Band executive:

A ...If I remember correctly, Brian Eli and myself did speak to Simon Muldoe. In fact, we didn't go down there specifically for that purpose, but we did talk to him about it and mentioned it to him. We also spoke to Donna Moroz on it. They indicated very clearly in regard to any of the ones that were on SA that —

Q If I could just stop you there for a moment. "SA", social assistance?

A Social assistance.

Q Yes, all right.

A We have to go back further than that, though. When the original concept of the satellite dishes came up there was no intent for any of the social assistance people to have the satellite dishes. What happened was a letter was sent out to the Band subdivision, and the letter was sent out by — I think it was under Brian's signature —- by Heidi Simkins, who was an employee, indicating that anybody in the Band subdivision that required a satellite dish, to let them know, because they were under the impression that they could get some satellite dishes quite a bit cheaper.

(Transcripts: Volume LIII, p. 7337)

Mr. Muldoe died in the fall of 1985, but Ms. Moroz was available to testify before the Inquiry. She had been employed with the Department of Indian Affairs Central District as the Superintendent of Social Services, although she is no longer with the Department. She said that she did not take part in any meeting with Mr. Schwartz or Mr. Eli where the purchase of satellite dishes was discussed. She said when questioned by counsel for the Department:

Q And, you have described earlier, Mr. Muldoe's position. Do you have any meetings of any kind with Mr. Muldoe present and Mr. Eli and Mr. Schwartz?

A No, I did not.

Q Did you, yourself, discuss with Mr. Eli and Mr. Schwartz, a proposal, or one or the other of them, a proposal of the nature that I have just described?

A No, I did not.

Q Had such a proposal been put to you, would you have approved it?

A Absolutely not.

Q And why not?

A Well, it certainly would not be within the regulations of the Department to accept payment for satellite dishes out of welfare funds. This is definitely not the purpose to which welfare funds are to be put.

(Transcripts: Volume LXIX, p. 10407)

Ms. Moroz acknowledged under cross-examination by counsel for the former executive that while she could not recall taking part in a meeting with Mr. Muldoe, Mr. Schwartz, and Mr. Eli concerning the purchase of satellite dishes, she had on occasion seen Mr. Muldoe about the office around this time. I think she was acknowledging that it might have been possible for Mr. Muldoe to meet with Messrs. Schwartz and Eli on some occasion when she was not present.

It seems quite improbable to me that the use of Social Assistance funds to purchase these satellite dishes would have been knowingly approved by an official of the Department of Indian Affairs. Mr. Schwartz and Mr. Eli may have believed that Mr. Muldoe had given approval in principle to the plan, but it was my very clear impression from the evidence of Mr. Van der Sar and Ms. Moroz that this was not a course that would generally find favour with the Department. I think Chief Derrickson was aware of the dubious nature of this proceeding and carefully refrained from endorsing it. Given the nature of the planned purchase, it seems elementary to me that it would be the practice of officials involved to carefully document this matter in order to be able to fend off possible criticism of such an expenditure. The absence of such documentation speaks louder in this case than any of the evidence I heard. I have serious doubts that Mr. Muldoe ever approved of this expenditure and I think former Chief Derrickson was showing good sense in steering well clear of this potential minefield.

The scheme to purchase satellite dishes for residents of the Band subdivision was for their benefit in that it was intended to improve the quality of life of Band members who otherwise would not enjoy the range of television programming that was available to other persons resident in the general area. When Mr. Eli and Mr. Schwartz proposed the plan, they felt that those less fortunate persons who relied on Social Assistance for their only source of income should also be able to enjoy the benefits of good television reception.

I have considerable sympathy for the sentiments that underlay this foray into creative accounting. Individuals receiving assistance should not be made to feel like second-class people, nor should their children be deprived of advantages. The problem with this matter was that it was reflected but dimly on the books — it appeared surreptitious. Also, here was a relatively well-off band getting an apparent advantage from the Department of Indian Affairs. Was it really fair? Surely there were other alternatives available to the Band Council. This may have been a case where the Band itself should have provided funding. For example, the Band might have voted the funds from its own revenue account rather than making the purchases out of public funds. Here would have been a worthy cause for the application of some of the cut-off funds.

One cannot fault the recipients of the satellite dishes for participation in the plan. The persons responsible for administering the Social Assistance program instigated the purchase and worked out the repayment plan. The average recipient of Social Assistance would naturally presume that everything was "above board". I certainly do not recommend that the Department should take any action concerning the individual recipients.

This scheme was a half-baked one and ultimately not in the best interests of Indian bands in Canada. The purchase of the satellite dishes became a matter of controversy at Westbank. The Westbank Indian Action and Advisory Council specifically mentioned the use of Social Assistance funds for the purchase of the satellite dishes as a grievance against the former Chief and Council. Public censure is to be expected when public funds are put to such a use. It is essential that those persons responsible for managing public funds have a clear understanding of what is and what is not appropriate expenditure. This is especially so when they are charged with managing a program like Social Assistance, where flexibility in rules demands responsibility in judgement.

But let it be said that the Department should manifest a degree of flexibility in its allocation of Social Assistance resources. Putting some money into improving the quality of life is as necessary as meeting bare necessities. I trust that legitimate requests can be approved by Departmental officials, but in so doing there must be a rough equality of treatment for all entitled. Also, the matter must be handled in a completely frank and honest manner and properly documented. The way in which the matter was handled here was not a model for the future.

Mr. Eli and Mr. Schwartz failed to document this program in any satisfactory fashion. A moment's reflection by either must have made it clear to them that this sort of matter had great potential for trouble. Mr. Schwartz especially is to be faulted for this lapse. He was the Band Administrator and was there to advise and inform the elected officials. He was a former member of the Department. With his experience, I find it absolutely inexplicable that he failed to document the purchase of these satellite dishes in a proper and detailed fashion. Such failures can put a band in a bad light and lead to unnecessary controversy, as was the case in this instance.

Chapter 12

Controversy at Westbank: The Action Committee

Mr. Ronald M. Derrickson served as Chief of the Westbank Band from 1976 until 1986, a period of some ten years. Not surprisingly, certain dissatisfactions and grievances developed over that period of time. In political life, it is not possible to keep all of the people happy all of the time. Mr. Derrickson was a controversial figure, and some of the projects and policies which he implemented or attempted to implement caused a certain amount of resentment on the part of some Band members. Near the end of Mr. Derrickson's last term as Chief in 1986, a number of Band members who were dissatisfied with the administration of Band affairs formed a group that styled itself the Westbank Indian Action and Advisory Council (hereinafter sometimes called the "Action Committee"). Assisted by a person who is not a band member, one Nicholas P. Kayban, the group prepared a petition to the Minister of Indian Affairs calling for the removal of the then Chief and Council. The group also sought to involve Members of Parliament in the affairs of the Westbank Indian Band.

The Westbank Indian Action and Advisory Council may be best described as a loosely knit group of political opponents of Ron Derrickson. In petitions and press releases, the group listed a number of general and specific grievances and made allegations of wrongdoing on the part of the Band executive. The activities of the Action Committee appeared to peak during the spring of 1986 and abated following the election of the new Chief and Council in the summer of 1986.

The operations of the Action Committee were not unlike those of previous dissident groups at Westbank. The Commission heard evidence from Band members Mary Eli and Millie Jack, who described the activities of former dissident groups from 1972 to 1976. Some were pushing for more development and were dissatisfied with the lack of progress by the then Chief and Council. Petitions were organized and news releases were given to the media, very much like the mode of action undertaken by the Action Committee. I got the impression that political feeling at Westbank could be quite intense and sometimes could lead to actions that one might term "overenthusiastic".

Present Chief Robert Louie gave evidence of his past experience on the Band Council and on the Board of Directors of the Band's development company in the mid-1970's. Apparently a group of Band members, unhappy with the way that Band land development was progressing, had spread reports that the Band was in a bankrupt situation, thus threatening the viability of the development company. The Council of that day considered legal action against those who had made such statements, but decided against it.

I understand legal proceedings were commenced arising from the statements made by the Westbank Indian Action and Advisory Council. Comments were made to the press and others about Band management and personnel, comments which have resulted in the lawsuit filed by former Chief Derrickson and councillors for damages for defamation.

The 1986 dissident group appears to have been motivated by a number of specific concerns which arose from a variety of circumstances. Some Band members had long-standing grievances about the distribution of Reserve land, or the proposed use of Reserve land. Others were concerned about a lack of disclosure of Band business affairs to the general membership, or a general lack of communication between the executive and membership. The lack of full information in turn spawned rumour and innuendo, but perhaps the main catalyst of serious discontent was the Band's greatly increased wealth resulting from a cut-off claims settlement and funds received for land acquired for highway use. As might be expected on reserves where substantial portions of land are held by individual locatees, not all members of the Westbank Band were as fortunate as some of their neighbours, depending on the location of their land. Some may have felt "left out" in terms of the compensation received. And, of course, there was the collapse of the Northland Bank, an institution in which the Band had a significant financial investment. Band finances were more robust and those in political opposition to Ron Derrickson were increasingly concerned or professed to be concerned about the stewardship of Band funds. The Band had a considerable amount of its money either invested in or on deposit with Northland Bank. The Bank failure in September 1985 created serious concern and unrest on the part of many Band members. There were additional specific complaints which were articulated through the various petitions and press releases, but the particular outburst of protest in the spring of 1986 can only be fully understood when seen in context against a background of political frustration, lack of confidence in the Band executive, and apparent financial catastrophe.

The role of Nicholas Kayban in organizing and encouraging the dissident Band members was quite significant. Mr. Kayban testified that he first made contact with some dissatisfied Westbank Band members in October 1985, and agreed to help them have their grievances addressed through the assistance of his alleged political connections. During the winter and spring of 1986, Mr. Kayban met with groups of Band members on several occasions. He eventually asked them to sign a petition authorizing him to act on their behalf. Once he received this request in writing, Mr. Kayban became actively involved with the group as a self-styled consultant. He forwarded the group's request to have him act on their behalf, together with his acceptance, to Mr. Fred King, M.P. (whose riding included Westbank), in order that he could put their concerns before the Minister of Indian Affairs. Both Mr. Kayban and the Band members were hoping for some financial assistance, although it is not clear from precisely what source. The Action Committee sought funding to help them advance their cause and have their grievances heard. Mr. Kayban was hoping that funds would be available to pay for his services. It was he who suggested that the group list their concerns in a petition to be forwarded to the Minister.

After the petition had been circulated and numerous Band members had signed it, Mr. Kayban delivered it to Ottawa. Mr. Kayban discussed the petition and promoted the group's cause with several Members of Parliament, including Mr. King, Dr. Lorne Greenaway, and Mr. David Kilgour. Dr. Greenaway was a member of the Standing Committee on Indian Affairs and Mr. Kilgour was then the parliamentary secretary to the Minister of Indian Affairs and Northern Development.

Perhaps in a misguided effort to augment the political pressure, Mr. Kayban and some members of the dissident group drafted a document containing several specific allegations of wrongdoing, which Mr. Kayban delivered to a Kelowna radio station. Shortly afterwards, Mr. Kayban, accompanied by several members of the group, travelled to Edmonton to meet with Mr. Kilgour. They sought his assistance in addressing their grievances. By this time the Action and Advisory Council had achieved a certain visibility. They had also accumulated some debts in the process as legal and other bills mounted. When it became clear to Mr. Kayban that the group could not expect any special funding, he became disenchanted with the cause. By then a lawsuit had been filed against some members of the group and Mr. Kayban.

He began to distance himself from the group in June 1986 when it became apparent that he might not be paid for his services. The petition, which was signed by a large number of Band members and forwarded with the "press release" to the Minister in the spring of 1986, was entered as an exhibit during the course of this Inquiry. While the written documents provide some insight into the nature of the complaints of the dissident group, the Commission also heard evidence from several Band members who had signed the petition. The petition requested the removal from office of Chief Derrickson and his councillors. A number of complaints were enumerated as follows:

— failure to hold regular Band meetings;
— misappropriation of Band property and assets;
— illegal enforcement of Band by-laws, such as the Rentalsman by-law;

— fraudulent representation of the Westbank Indian Band;
— failure to consult with and advise Band members of Band dealings and business affairs such as the removal of band assets from the province without knowledge or consent of Band members — Northland Bank.

These broadly worded grievances apparently held different meanings for different people. Ms. Barbara Coble testified that she was not satisfied with the number of Band meetings that were held during the year. She felt that there was a continuing failure to consult the membership on the part of the Chief and councillors. She believed that the purchase of shares by the Band in the Northland Bank amounted to a "misappropriation" of Band assets. As well, she stated that the Chief was guilty of fraudulent representation of the Band because of statements he made concerning the Band and the wealth of its members to the media, which statements she believed painted a picture that was far from accurate. She said only a few Band members were wealthy and that an overly optimistic picture had been painted of the Band as a group of wealthy people.

Ms. Coble was concerned about the purchase of several businesses by the Band. She felt there was lack of disclosure to the Band membership regarding details of those purchases and that there was considerable division among Band members. She said she had been opposed to the granting of Section 60 authority to the Band in 1985 when Mr. Derrickson was Chief, as she did not feel comfortable that the then Chief and Council should have the extensive land management powers conferred under Section 60 of the Indian Act. She was sufficiently concerned to circulate a petition among Band members to counteract the Band vote which had been taken, which had been in favour of the Band receiving Section 60 authority. She maintained that many Band members did not attend Band meetings because they did not like to vote (as the voting was usually done) by a show of hands. She testified that many Band members felt intimidated at Band meetings and consequently stayed away. Ms. Coble suggested that voting at Band meetings should be done by secret ballot. I must say that this suggestion is one that I think has merit — it seems to me that it would enhance the democratic process and I recommend it for consideration and possible adoption by this Band and others in Canada.

Mrs. Rose Derrickson (a past and present Band councillor) also gave evidence as to why she signed the petition. She felt that Band meetings were held too infrequently and was concerned with how welfare monies were being managed, in particular the use of social assistance funds to purchase satellite dishes for some Band members and to pay for paving driveways. In addition, she expressed concern about how the previous Band Council had obtained funds from the provincial government to build a community centre, though it was not in fact built. I looked into this matter, and while I think the then Band executive congratulated itself about getting the facilities funded to a greater degree than was appropriate in view of the modest results, I was satisfied that funds obtained were spent for the welfare of the Band. Mrs. Derrickson listed both these concerns as falling within the category of "misappropriation of assets" and "fraudulent representation" of the Band. She was also greatly concerned about the collapse of the Northland Bank as it affected Band fortunes. She was aware that the Band had funds on deposit there, and she feared that a significant loss of funds could occur to the great detriment of the Band. Her concerns here were not misplaced and to this day that matter is not wholly resolved. I deal with Northland Bank issues in some detail in Chapter 4.

Present Chief Robert Louie's main concern was that the Band Council had used Band money to purchase shares in the Northland Bank without prior consultation with the Band membership at large. His concerns about the need for fuller explanation and investigation of the transaction were heightened because he was aware that Mr. Ron Derrickson had been a director of the Northland Bank. Mr. Louie was also doubtful about the existence of an alleged fund which was said to have been placed "in trust" for minors. The fund was to have originated from various per capita distributions made over the years. His concerns about the existence or safety of that fund were compounded by the demise of the Northland Bank. He did not feel that Band members had been given a clear picture of Band investments.

Mr. Louie had been a long-time political opponent of Mr. Ronald Derrickson, having run in opposition to Mr. Derrickson in two previous Band elections. He recalled an incident which led to a political falling out between the two men, which is illustrative of the kind of division caused by some of Mr. Derrickson's development initiatives on the Reserves. In 1976, Mr. Derrickson apparently was pressuring Robert Louie to prevail on his grandmother to join in the overall development plan for Reserve 10. That would have involved agreeing to turn the Louie farm into a golf course, a plan to which Mrs. Louie was decidedly not partial. After she had expressed her wishes to her grandson, Mr. Louie was not disposed to put further pressure on her. This stance was said to be not pleasing to Mr. Derrickson. Because of the pressures he felt himself under, Mr. Louie said he elected to resign his post on the Board of Directors of the Band Development Company. This was the company chiefly concerned with development of the Lakeridge Park subdivision.

On numerous occasions during the course of this Inquiry, it was suggested that there is a basic division among the Westbank Band members between those who favoured development and those who did not. While there are obviously differences of opinion among Band members over the issue of development of Reserve lands, it did not appear to be simply a dispute between those in favour of development and those opposed. Rather, there was and is a division of opinion as to how development is to take place, including what type of development and when and where it is to occur. There is no agreement in place to equitably distribute the proceeds from developments on locatee lands. Without such an agreement, a situation could arise where the land-owner who has a golf course, for example, could receive far less than one who has a resort hotel, even though one development complements the other and the comprehensive plan may be viewed as one for the common good and prosperity of all Band members. Perhaps it is natural that there would be opposition by some locatees to develop their lands for the "common good" when an appropriate revenue-sharing scheme is not yet fully worked out. Indian reserves are not the only places where development proposals divide communities. Such differences of opinion are common to many communities.

Mr. Larry Derrickson, a cousin of the former Chief, gave evidence during the Inquiry. He testified that he believed that in the past the former Chief had interfered with certain dealings involving family land. Mr. Derrickson's evidence and that of his brother, Mr. Dave Derrickson, illustrated how politics can become entangled with family relationships. Larry and Dave Derrickson held and hold a joint interest in a small but valuable piece of property on Reserve 9. According to their evidence, Dave Derrickson had at one time agreed to transfer his share in that property to Larry Derrickson. Transfer papers were duly drawn up and signed by both brothers. Larry believed that the deal was complete except for final processing by the Department of Indian Affairs. However, without telling Larry, Dave Derrickson apparently changed his mind about the deal and sought the intervention of then Chief Ron Derrickson to stop the transfer from being approved. Ms. Barbara Shmigelsky, secretary to Chief Derrickson at the material time, said that she had no recollection of Chief Derrickson interfering in the matter but that for some unknown reason, the transfer was never processed at the Department of Indian Affairs. Because of the unavailability of Mr. Sheldon McCullough as a witness (due to illness), the Commission is unable to say just why this transfer was not completed. Larry Derrickson suspected that some pressure had been applied to "gum up the works" on the transfer but the Commission could not find evidence to support wrongful interference by the Band executive.

The transfer was never completed and the landholding situation between the two brothers has remained the same to the present. Larry Derrickson testified that he and his brother had a falling out some years ago and that Dave had a very close friendship with Ron Derrickson. The land transfer controversy and other political differences, including Larry's involvement with the Westbank Indian Action and Advisory Council, not only pushed Larry politically farther apart from his cousin Ron Derrickson, but also, regrettably, resulted in a widening rift in the relationship between the two brothers.

When Larry Derrickson was asked what he understood when he signed the petition, he too referred to the purchase of shares in the Northland Bank without the knowledge of the Band membership as amounting to a misappropriation of Band assets. He also objected to the Band Council's purchase of lands at Gallagher's Canyon without seeking more specific approval of the transaction from Band members.

Analysis of Complaints

Many of the complaints in the Action Committee petition appeared to reflect concerns that Band members were not being sufficiently consulted or informed regarding major expenditures of Band funds. These concerns were raised to a high pitch by the collapse of the Northland Bank, and the resulting fear for the security of the Band's funds. Combined with these concerns was a feeling of distrust or lack of confidence in the executive, a situation not all that unusual among those in political opposition. By way of contrast, Mary Eli and Millie Jack testified that they had no concern over the major land purchase or the purchase of shares in the Northland Bank because they supported and trusted Ronald Derrickson. They felt that he was a very capable Chief, was always accessible, and that they could always get any information they wanted. Ronald Derrickson is a decisive and dynamic personality and is perhaps the sort of individual who invokes both strong loyalties and strong animosities. Feelings appear to have been running at a high, almost fever, pitch at Westbank in early 1986. The body politic was in a state of ferment.

The perceived lack of sufficient information on issues of concern common to all Band members was a recurrent theme in the complaints of the Action Committee. Perhaps it is for that reason that the failure to hold regular Band meetings headed the list of grievances on the petition. Although the lack of confidence of those in political opposition may never be cured by greater information, there can also be created a level of distrust when there is a lack of knowledge and understanding of basic facts. Perfection is never attainable, but these feelings can be ameliorated by the dissemination of more information on Band business to all Band members through a regular reporting process. I do not believe that it is necessary to call endless Band meetings, but some are appropriate. The Band should only be called together for matters of major significance. It seems to me, however, that a system of annual reporting (as recommended in Section II of this Report), perhaps coupled with the use of a periodical newsletter in more economically active bands, could be a force for good government and more stability on reserves. If the "in" group treats everything like a state secret, there is necessarily going to be suspicion and dissatisfaction. When a lack of information is combined with a lack of confidence, there can be rampant speculation and wild rumours. As the rumour mill grinds on, petty disputes are blown out of all proportion. When that happens, foolish action like the petition and press release can be the end result. Controversy is the lifeblood of politics, it is sometimes said, but when it reaches the pitch it did at Westbank, it can be ultimately harmful to Band interests.

In reviewing the written words on the petition and the so-called press release and comparing these to the evidence that was led, it seems to me that there is lack of unanimity as to the meanings of words such as "misappropriation" and "fraudulent representation". These words very often connote quite wrongful conduct. Perhaps they were chosen for their shock value, as they appear unduly harsh to describe the activities in question. However, it appeared to me that some Band members did not fully comprehend the meaning or use of some of those words. For example, Barbara Coble appeared wholly sincere in her assertion that when Chief Derrickson made unduly favourable statements of fact concerning life at Westbank, he was guilty of "fraudulent representation of the Westbank Band". That point of view may be sustainable, but I believe most people would view it as a somewhat extravagant use of language. The former Chief is certainly not a man inclined to understatement, but I would not characterize painting too rosy a picture as "fraudulent" — perhaps Ms. Coble would have been more accurate in characterizing such comments as a "misstatement" or "wrongful description".

The petition was drawn up at the suggestion of and with the assistance of Mr. Nicholas Kayban. Perhaps the choice of words may in part be explained by his rather aggressive political approach. Mr. Kayban said he was directly involved with the release of certain statements to the news media. Although he testified that he was assured that all of the allegations that were put forward could be supported by evidence, he apparently failed to make any serious inquiry to test the accuracy of the allegations. Given the nature of the allegations, I found his failure in this regard surprising. His decision to make public the allegations without obtaining proper evidence of their veracity is in no way commendable. Mr. Kayban apologized to the Commission for his actions. His apologies could more appropriately be directed to the former Chief and Council and to those Band members whom he purported to serve but only misserved. He proved not to be a force for rational debate and discussion at Westbank.

Band members who signed the petition said that it was intended to be given to the Minister in confidence. It called for the removal of the Chief and Council, but primarily it was a request for an investigation into Band affairs. It may be viewed as a political protest by a group of dissatisfied Band members to the Minister of Indian Affairs. Because of the historical relationship between Native people and the Crown, represented by the Minister, the direct petition seems to be an often-used method for airing grievances. Whether it is a desirable or useful method is highly questionable. While the choice of words was intemperate, given the generality of the phrasing of complaints, it is unlikely that officials of the Department of Indian Affairs would take those words at face value or necessarily view matters in a particularly sinister light. Phrased as the petition was, it could only be acted upon after further investigation. That is what the petitioners apparently had in mind.

The sudden influx of revenue into the Band coffers, and then the equally sudden prospect of losing it all with the collapse of the Northland Bank, may be in part an explanation for the alarmist tone of these public pronouncements. Frustration is rarely the parent of clear thought — add to it an apprehension of economic catastrophe and one has a recipe for trouble. The political climate at Westbank in early 1986 was one of hostility, almost of hatred in certain cases. No doubt some had personal grudges against the former Chief and Council. Mr. Kayban stepped in, apparently to help, but I believe his main object was to help himself — in the end he proved simply to be a mischief-maker. Under his direction, the Westbank Indian Action and Advisory Council became quite vociferous. Their language became saturated with hyperbole lightly interspersed with fact. Perhaps those directly involved in the matter will, on sober reflection, realize that scurrilous abuse is always to be avoided in discussing public issues. A decent regard for the facts is preferable to accusations founded on slender grounds. While debate must be free, it should also be conducted on a higher plane than the "petition" and the "press release". The Action Committee would have done better to stay out of action if that was to be their modus operandi.

The fact that so many Band members would sign a petition, primarily aimed at having an independent person or body investigate the affairs of their Band, was evidence of the existence of a serious malady in the body politic at Westbank. However, as I have said, political debate on reserves can become quite intense because political power can mean so much in economic terms. It must be remembered too, that Mr. Derrickson was a strong personality who could arouse animosities. I doubt that matters would have gotten so far out of hand as they did if Mr. Kayban had not been involved. Events at Westbank moved quickly, and perhaps too quickly for some, in the decade 1976–86. One witness used the term "pilot project" — was Westbank a pilot project? It was in the vanguard of change certainly. Certain lessees and members of the Band apparently lost faith in the Vancouver office of the Department. There came to exist a perception that nothing could be done through that office as there did not seem to be an adequate system in place to address grievances at that level. Protests then were made to headquarters in Ottawa. This perception clearly was an underlying factor in the formation of the Action Committee. My view is that the sort of problems we saw at Westbank could be developing in many bands across Canada as they become more economically advanced. In the next section of this Report, I make some suggestions that may help to defuse these situations before they reach the sorry state that affairs came to at Westbank.

SECTION II

The Question of Change:

Indian Law and Policy in Canada

Preface

Certain provisions of the Indian Act, and policies of the Department of Indian Affairs and Northern Development as they concerned the Westbank Indian Band, have been discussed in Section I of this Report. Part IV of the Terms of Reference of this Commission deals with broader issues and reads as follows:

> to recommend any changes to the Indian Act relating to the management of lands, Indian monies and by-laws, or to the policies or the procedures of DIAND in relation to the said matters, or any remedies to specific problems that may seem appropriate having regard to the Government's established policy of supporting and strengthening Indian self-government on Indian lands.

During the first phase of the hearings, I was advised of some difficulties encountered by band members, band executives, and the Department relating to the administration of the Act and Departmental policies. Specific hearings were convened under Part IV to consider whether any recommendations for changes could or should be made pursuant to the Commission's Terms of Reference. Major Indian groups in British Columbia were invited to participate and were requested to make such submissions as they deemed appropriate. Before proceeding to the question of possible recommendations, I think we must consider the present Act and current conditions.

The Act exhibits a basic structure that has often been described as paternalistic. The complex series of statutory changes made over many decades relating to Indian affairs is narrated in the historical abstract included in this Report (Appendix A). I acknowledge with thanks the great assistance of Professor Hamar Foster in the preparation of the historical abstract. As is said in that Appendix, the history of the Indian Act is in many respects a history of the tension between wardship and independence, or the tension between protection of Native peoples and their assimilation into European culture. That kind of tension is still evident today in the desire of Native people to preserve their land base and traditional culture while continuing efforts to achieve self-government and economic self-sufficiency. These tensions can never be entirely resolved, as human affairs are always subject to a certain amount of tension or conflict. Times change. The problems of one era are not the problems of another. Human nature does not change, but the economic and social landscape changes and so the precise nature of perceived problems are often quite different in one era than in an earlier period.

The situation of some bands has changed beyond recognition since 1951 when the last major reforms of the Indian Act were enacted.

Other bands have not changed much at all. The Department today is adopting a much different posture than it did 35 years ago. These factors do not mean that everything must be changed, but the present situation must be considered in order to assess the adequacy of the existing legislative regime. It may be that certain changes can be recommended that will enhance the lives of Native people and that may also help to ensure the maintenance of a good relationship between Native and non-Native people in Canada.

The <u>Indian Act</u> has changed little since 1951 — indeed, substantial portions of the Act are rooted in the nineteenth century. There is, of course, nothing inherently wrong with this. Change for the sake of change is pointless and the general concerns for the well-being of Native people that underlie the <u>Indian Act</u> are not greatly different today from what they were in earlier times. I am inclined to be cautious in considering what should be done under Part IV of my Terms of Reference. Change that is too sudden is hard to digest and seems to me likely to be unpalatable to a broad spectrum of people. But if, after hearing submissions and reflecting on issues, I do have a clear impression that a certain area can be improved or specific problems alleviated, to fail to speak out would not be consistent with my duty.

Efforts for Change Since 1960

From 1960 to the present, the history of attempts at legislative change or reform is a narrative of sincere efforts all too often falling short of the sought-after improvement.

Chief Joe Mathias' personal experience in these efforts strikingly demonstrates this fact. He related his involvement in a Ministerial Committee on Indian Affairs in 1969, the preparation of the famous (or infamous) White Paper on Indian affairs in that year and the 1975 Committee which met with the members of Cabinet then responsible for Indian affairs on the subject of statutory reform. He was engaged from 1977 to 1980 as a policy analyst dealing with the Indian Act. In this capacity, he naturally had extensive consultations with the Department. He outlined to us the considerable efforts made by the Indian people to communicate their concerns to the Parliamentary Committee which produced the *Penner Report* of 1983. All of these studies and proposals were aimed at identifying areas of concern or making recommendations for change. Aside from some amendments flowing from the requirements of the Charter of Rights and Freedoms, there has not been much concluded legislative activity since 1951. However, there has been a fair degree of policy change by the Department in response to the changed climate or direction of Indian affairs in the past several years.

It is safe to say that, since approximately the mid-1960's, certain problem areas of Indian affairs and Indian legislation have become more visible. The White Paper of 1969 entitled "Choosing the Path" addressed a number of the topics touched on in this Report. It created a reaction which led the federal government to embark on a more active policy of devolution to Indian bands and associations in the 1970's. That policy continues to the present.

The *Penner Report* dealt with a wide spectrum of issues and made some far-reaching recommendations for change. The Report touches on the current suggestions for change advocated by Indian people. While it may have had certain effects on policy implementation by the Department, it does not appear that any substantial legislative or constitutional changes have yet resulted from the Report.

Proposed Bill C-52, which received first reading in June 1984, was seen by the Department to be at least a partial solution to some of the more obvious areas of concern to Native people and Native leaders. The Department was, and is, aware that slow progress on change had been caused largely by demands that there be consensus on the part of all of the affected groups before any substantial amendment of the existing Indian Act could be undertaken. That Bill would have, amongst other things, enabled bands to opt out of the Indian Act's limitations by adopting self-government in accordance with the terms of the proposed legislation. The Bill was not enacted because the government of the day was not returned to office in the general election of September 1984.

Recent efforts for change have not borne much fruit. For present purposes, I think it is important to examine why change has proved difficult to effect. The history of the past decade as disclosed in the Westbank phase of the hearings disclosed major alterations in the content and application of Department policies with virtually no significant statutory alteration. This situation could lead to an uncomfortable hiatus. A Departmental official, speaking of the legislative base for by-laws, said that there is a very slender legislative base for many by-laws he considered desirable. This is true also for policies based on other portions of the Act.

During the hearings, it was often said that the long standing relationship between Native people and the federal government is unique and special. It has features that are not just legal and historical but also traditional. Long standing relationships are unlikely to be fundamentally altered without pain and some sense of dislocation. Mankind is an animal that, in common with all nature, is disposed against rapid change. This is true in the political sphere as well. The *Penner Report* endorses many suggestions for change from national Indian organizations. Some of the recommendations are likely to raise divisive political issues. It may be that the government will implement certain of those recommendations, but I would think that in areas where fundamental change was contemplated, it would wish to ensure there was a strong sentiment in the Canadian community that supported the change. I cannot say when or to what extent any such alterations will occur. For the purposes of this Report, I cannot assume that such alterations are imminent.

Any new structure must allow various cultural and historical differences to be accommodated in the legal framework. This will require statutory alteration which is responsive to the real differences in culture and aspirations of the bands and individuals from Newfoundland to British Columbia and the Territories. Total unanimity is probably a chimera, as anyone who has worked on a large committee will doubtless appreciate. Some general sense that a change is progressive or desirable seems likely to be the extent of support for any alteration.

Parliament should ensure that the statutory structure in place at a given time accommodates as much as possible the needs of all Canadians, both Indians and non-Indians, from the point of view of certainty, clarity, and fairness in the administration of Indian affairs.

This task must take account of the limits of the possible or the probable, and cannot be indefinitely deferred in hopes of the arrival of a new Jerusalem. Certain areas can probably be chosen where improvements can be effected without being insensible of the past or stultifying the possibilities for the future growth of self-government.

Recent and Ongoing Legislative and Policy Initiatives

At the outset of my appointment as Commissioner, the Department made many of their people available for interviews and briefings on contemporary concerns within the Department. Two formal briefing sessions were held with members of the Department, one before and one after the hearings convened. Hearings were held specifically to entertain submissions from Indian groups relative to possible changes in the Indian Act and Departmental policy. These hearings followed the conclusion of the hearings on Westbank issues.

The Departmental briefings were very helpful, and crystallized what issues concerning change are common to the majority of bands across the country, and which were unique to Westbank. I think it is widely acknowledged that many difficulties experienced at Westbank are harbingers of future difficulties, and arose largely from the fact that Westbank has been a band at the forefront of development in economic and social terms since the mid-1970's. Mr. David Sparks, of the Department, said in his evidence that Westbank was one of the first bands to be interested in implementing a comprehensive by-law regime. Many aspects of the Westbank situation which were unique in 1977 are more common now, and may be commonplace by 1997. In this sense we have an opportunity to learn from history without having to live through it first.

The briefings included a wide range of policy and statutory considerations such as:

(1) the "Kamloops Amendments";
(2) land, revenues, and trusts;
(3) Indian land issues, including registry and land management matters;
(4) policies and administrative procedures relating to Indian monies;
(5) downsizing and devolution; and
(6) self-government by means of specific legislation.

1. The Kamloops Amendments

I was told that the Kamloops Amendments had their genesis in the desire of the Kamloops Band and their Chief, Clarence "Manny" Jules, that the Band's by-law powers include taxation powers. This would enable the Kamloops Band to raise revenue to provide services on industrial lands within its reserve. The Kamloops Reserve, which is adjacent to the City of Kamloops, has had a substantial industrial park on its land for many years. Industrial parks are normally located on conditionally surrendered lands. Under present legislation, the precise status of these lands vis-à-vis the remaining lands of the reserve is uncertain. There are substantial doubts as to whether or not band by-laws will apply to surrendered lands, since the latter may not have the character of "land in the reserve" for such purposes. It was a matter of concern to the Kamloops Band that provincial jurisdiction should extend over non-Indians who operated businesses on surrendered land. The apparent purpose of provincial taxation was to raise funds for local governments for the provision of services, but services were not in fact being provided from such funds to the lands in the park. I was told that, possibly as a consequence, a majority of such taxes are in default across the province and that only .33 per cent of provincial tax revenues is attributable to this source. The Kamloops Amendments received the support of the vast majority of bands in Canada and are presently before the House of Commons.

These amendments are designed to alleviate doubts concerning the power of a band council to exercise jurisdiction over conditionally surrendered lands, which will become known as "designated lands". By obtaining this jurisdiction, it is contemplated that a band council will be able to levy a form of tax to raise revenue. I think this is likely to substantially alter the relationship between band councils and lessees and residents of surrendered lands. In effect, it will enhance the jurisdiction of the band council over surrendered land. I think it means that bands and provincial governments will have to work out methods to handle taxation between them in this area; both will have jurisdiction, but the job may be better done by those on the scene, namely the band councils. The objects in view — better services and more equitable taxation — are worthy ones, but taxes are always a thorny issue and I foresee a certain amount of skirmishing before solutions are found to the problems arising from such amendments. I support the thrust of the amendments, but I do not expect the road to realization to be always smooth.

2. Lands, Revenues, and Trusts

The Minister has initiated a comprehensive review of matters dealing with statutory provisions and Departmental policy concerning lands, revenues, and trusts. Requests for proposals from contractors were issued on June 1, 1987, and the initial contracts have since been awarded.

This comprehensive review will deal with administration, policy, and statutory concerns. The matters under consideration include the land

registry, land management and entitlement, environmental considerations, trust monies, estates, Indian government, and litigation. The
project has been divided into two phases. The first phase will summarize
and analyze previous studies relating to operational and management
issues of the lands, revenues, and trusts sector, and will identify
priorities for remedial action. This phase is intended to include an
analysis of whether previous studies have been sufficiently comprehensive to identify clearly the problems to be addressed, and whether
proposed solutions are feasible given the current legislative base and the
resources available.

The second phase will include the development of an implementation
plan for approval by the Deputy Minister. Upon completion of the
second phase, a searching review of the terms of the implementation
plan will be undertaken by the Comptroller General, an advisory
committee, and members of the Department. The Report of this
Commission doubtless will form part of the input to the advisory
committee and the contractors carrying out the comprehensive review.
The planned review seems designed to focus mainly on issues of business
management and the reconciliation of competing priorities. I think the
approach taken is sensible in that the review is wide-ranging and seeks
to involve a wide spectrum of the Indian community. The danger is that
issues will be studied to death. I hope, from this Report and the
comprehensive review, that some useful changes to legislation and
policy can be achieved within a reasonable time frame.

The management difficulties of administering many existing policies
are acute and appear to be growing more rather than less difficult.
Management solutions, however, ought not to be confused with
fundamental policy decisions, which must, of necessity, be made by
those with political responsibility to the Indian groups and the country
as a whole. There is a tendency in the present circumstances for any
large organization to generate one study after another when the political
will and initiative is not present to propose and implement solutions to
recognized problems. Evidence of this tendency is the fact that there are
currently some thirty policy reviews under way in the Department. For
the reasons stated below, I think major problems can be delineated and
solutions to problems in the area of lands, revenues, and trusts can be
well under way before the end of this decade. I therefore encourage
swift completion of this comprehensive review and implementation of
recommendations, which will include timely decisions by the Minister
and the government on the political aspects of matters.

3. Indian Land Issues

(a) Indian Lands Act

An Indian Lands Act has been proposed in draft form. While it is
widely felt that this is a useful change, difficulty has been encountered

in finding the political impetus and the necessary time to devote to its passage through Parliament. The present Act is not a very comprehensive one for the present era. It can be made to work for less developed bands, but it tends to be a bit "horse-and-buggy" for more developed bands. A comprehensive Lands Act would seem to make good sense. Land is, as I have said elsewhere, the foundation of Indian economic development.

The extent of a statutory vacuum relating to land issues is made apparent by the proposed contents of the draft Indian Lands Act which include:

(a) how, and by whom, title to Indian lands should be held;
(b) the nature and extent of band powers over the control, management and administration of their lands;
(c) the nature and extent of the Crown's responsibilities with respect to reserve lands;
(d) the legal capacity of bands and band executives;
(e) the acquisition by band members of rights in reserve lands, and the better definition of those rights;
(f) transfer or other disposal of individual rights in reserve lands;
(g) alienation of band lands to non-Indians;
(h) the taking without consent of reserve lands by third parties;
(i) the system for registering interest in Indian lands; and
(j) the control and management of monies (capital and revenue) generated from the granting of rights or interests in reserve lands.

Many of these subjects are dealt with rather lightly in the present Act. I think a separate Act would make for greater clarity and better definition of the respective interests of the band, the Department, and individuals in reserve and surrendered or "designated" lands.

If these subjects can be addressed in a separate Indian Lands Act, then many of the provisions relating to land in the existing Act could be repealed. Land issues are important to Indian bands and individuals, and a separate Act should also make it easier for borrowers and lenders and their solicitors to deal with conveyancing and security issues if the subject-matter is contained in one statute rather than scattered about a general statute, as is the case in the present Act. I therefore would be inclined to press on with this initiative. I think it would create a better environment for land development by those bands that are well situated for development activity and I do not see it as harmful to the status quo for less favourably situated bands.

(b) Reserve Land Registry

The various briefings I had regarding the present system of land holdings under the Indian Act indicated that there is much need for improvement in the existing Land Registry system. The Act provides for the establishment of a Land Registry system in fairly rudimentary terms:

> 21. There shall be kept in the Department a register' to be known as the Reserve Land Register, in which shall be entered particulars relating to Certificates of Possession, and Certificates of Occupation, and other transactions respecting lands in a reserve.

> 55. (1) There shall be kept in the Department a register, to be known as the Surrendered Lands Register, in which shall be entered particulars in connection with any lease or other disposition of surrendered lands by the Minister or any assignment thereof.

> (2) A conditional assignment shall not be registered.

> (3) Registration of an assignment may be refused until proof of its execution has been furnished.

> (4) An assignment registered under this section is valid against an unregistered assignment or an assignment subsequently registered.

In 1983, the Land Registry was automated and I have the impression that reasonable progress is being made on this front. As there is a wide range in the needs of less developed and more developed bands, the Department has had to be sensitive to these differing needs. For largely historical reasons, the use of the provincial registry systems appears to be unacceptable to a majority of Indian groups. It must also be recognized that there are some fundamental differences between tenure under the Torrens system and that created under the Indian Act. There has been some past use of the provincial system in British Columbia

The Department is cognizant of the fact that a number of bands are involved in what is termed "buckshee leasing". A buckshee lease is an irregular (and unregisterable) lease of reserve lands. Chief Sophie Pierre from the Kootenay Tribal Council said that to her knowledge one rural band wants little to do with the Indian Land Registry system and finds it can operate satisfactorily with irregular leases. This may be a feasible solution in a rural area, but obviously it will not work for developments requiring financing. A primary reason for the use of buckshee leases would appear to be the perceived bureaucratic hurdles imposed by the Department under the present system.

Leasing applications and the transfer and assignment of leases are generally subject to approval by the Minister. Longer-term leases require Department of Justice advice. As a result of recent court experience, the Department is being cautious and is closely analyzing longer-term leases. Business opportunities may be lost because of the time constraints imposed by the bureaucratic structure. What was not clear to me, however, was whether this was a good or a bad thing. In the experience of many bands, businessmen who are not prepared to wait for the required analyses and approvals are often businessmen with whom it would be best not to deal. On the other hand, in the business world, opportunities often must be seized upon without delay and development opportunities may be lost if no adjustment in the time required to review and evaluate proposals is made. My impression is that the present registry system is quite overextended and should be upgraded to make it less arcane and more responsive.

The present Act is not adequate with respect to the registration of interests in lands. Obviously, if an Indian Lands Act were to be passed, it should include more comprehensive provisions in this area. But even without legislative amendment, I think the registration system can be improved administratively and technically. At one time I was inclined to think some form of integration into the provincial systems would be best, given that local lawyers and business people would be familiar with the local system. But I doubt that this solution is achievable and I believe that historical and political realities militate in favour of upgrading the Registry.

4. Indian Monies

The Department is presently faced with internal and external pressure for a liberalization of the treatment of Indian capital monies. There was some pressure to pay out capital monies to bands when long-term rates paid on trust funds by the government were low. This has been the case particularly with some Alberta bands which possess large sums of capital money generated from oil and gas revenues. Capital monies were transferred to the Samson Trust Company, but a few years later the Department decided that the Minister could not delegate his trust functions to a trust company and that such payments were outside the scope of the Act.

The dramatic increase in the Department's role as trustee is evident from the following graphs:

TRUST FUNDS

TREND OF INDIAN BAND FUNDS ON DEPOSIT
1975 TO MARCH 31, 1987

$ Millions

900
800
700
600
500
400
300
200
100
0

75 76 77 78 79 80 81 82 83 84 85 86 87

— Dept. of Indian Affairs

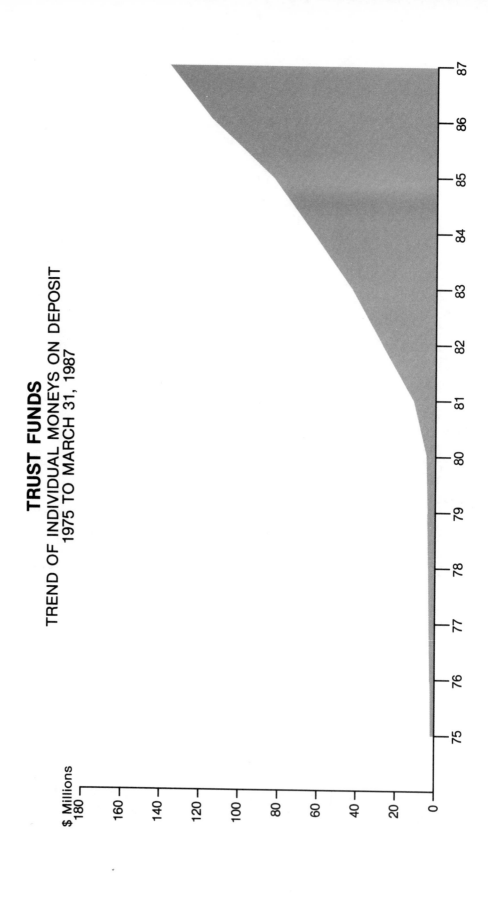

TRUST FUNDS

TREND OF INDIVIDUAL MONEYS ON DEPOSIT
1975 TO MARCH 31, 1987

$ Millions

TRUST FUNDS
TREND OF MONEYS HELD IN SUSPENSE
1975 TO MARCH 31, 1987

$ Millions

25 — 20 — 15 — 10 — 5 — 0

75 76 77 78 79 80 81 82 83 84 85 86 87

— Dept. of Indian Affairs

The *Penner Report* of 1983 recommended that the Minister not be liable for capital monies transferred to bands. The *Neilson Report* of 1985 recommended that the Department improve its management and conduct of its monies-handling functions.

I was told that the vast majority of bands want greater flexibility in disbursement of their capital money and in the application of those monies to various projects. Pressure of this nature is substantial from B.C. and Alberta Indian bands and is expected to increase if assets increase as a result of litigation over land claims and related law suits.

The Department has continued to be cautious concerning the investment of capital monies. Because of the importance of these funds to the band members who depend upon them, the caution is understandable. I was told that the Department of Justice has rendered an opinion that the term "expenditure" under Section 64 of the Indian Act does not permit the Minister to invest capital monies outside of the Consolidated Revenue Fund. I have discussed some of the considerations arising from the Guerin case elsewhere in this Report. The past cannot be changed, but it is clear that the Department is more alive to its possible legal liability than formerly. This awareness is positive to the extent that the Department is more diligent in safeguarding the interests of Indian people, but there is a danger that undue apprehension will result in a paralysis in decision-making. Guerin, like all judgements, must be looked at in the context of the particular facts found in the case. The fact that liability was found there does not mean that timely decision-making by the Department is at an end or that every expenditure or lease proposal should be analyzed to death. At times during the course of the Inquiry, I got the distinct impression that the Department was over-reacting to Guerin.

The extent of per capita distributions of capital money to Indians has increased dramatically. In 1985/86, one hundred and nine million dollars ($109,000,000) in capital funds were transferred to Indians, primarily in Alberta. In 1986/87, it is contemplated that there will have been seventy million dollars ($70,000,000) in per capita distributions of capital to Indians.

Presently, distributions of minors' capital money are limited to a stipulated amount per capita per year. The concern in relation to such distributions is whether payments to minors should be based on need or whether the band should be entitled to ask for them as of right. Advice received from legal counsel to the Department has been to the effect that requests for distribution should be related to the needs of the infant rather than to the fact that there are monies available for possible distribution.

There could be social difficulties arising out of the pressure on minors to obtain per capita distributions through early marriage or other means of bypassing the protections against capital distributions to minors. Minors are minors, whether they are Indian or non-Indian, and the experience of the law is that the showering of too much money on the young is pernicious to their welfare. This is an area that has to be closely monitored by the Department and the bands concerned to ensure that the interests of minors are properly safeguarded.

The possible taxability of capital monies is also a concern because the payment of capital monies may expose the bands to paying taxes on interest earned off reserve lands. For this reason, the headquarters of an Indian trust company incorporated in Alberta was transferred to a reserve. Capital, like land, is a patrimony. Its proper use and conservation is a joint concern of the Department and bands, and I speak elsewhere of some issues that ought to be addressed in this area.

5. *Downsizing and Devolution*

Downsizing and devolution of services are two major changes that have occurred in the Department of Indian Affairs in recent years. Downsizing refers to the reduction in Department staff levels, while devolution refers to the transfer of responsibility for delivery of services to the bands themselves. These two processes are related in that they have been occurring simultaneously. The Department has sought and obtained substantial additional funding from the Treasury Board for the cost of transferring the administration of services to the bands. Arrangements whereby bands receive funds for both the actual cost of services and the cost of administration have been one result of reform, and it appears to be present policy to maximize alternative funding arrangements to the fullest extent compatible with the willingness and ability of bands to receive funds under such arrangements.

A brief history of the transfer of programs and services has been summarized as follows:

Prior to 1956	The Department delivers services directly to individual Indians.
1956	Limited funding provided to Indian band councils for the establishment of school committees.
1956–64	More transfers of funds from the Department to bands for the management and delivery of programs (e.g. education).
1964	The Department received Cabinet approval for a policy respecting the funding of Indian community development plans.
1964–79	Over 30 separate authorities received for program transfers.

1968	Grants to Bands Policy formulated.
1979	Treasury Board approves the first set of Terms and Conditions for contributions to Indian bands and organizations.
1986	Seventy-five per cent of Indian and Inuit Affairs Program budget administered by bands (59%) or provinces (16%). The Department, therefore, administers 25 per cent of services.

The transfer of specialized advisory services to bands or tribal councils has increased rapidly in recent years without any significant alteration of program policies. The preconditions for transfer have been worked out on a policy basis with the Department, whose role has decreased as devolution has proceeded. Since the concept of devolution involves the transfer of programs to non-government employees, and since devolution is an option for both parties, a growing Departmental concern has been the need to adequately assess whether the groups applying for devolved powers are prepared to undertake the necessary responsibility, and also to review whether material problems occur in respect of the powers which have been transferred. The devolution process is desirable and should be encouraged, but a measure of restraint and understanding on the part of both the Department and bands is called for — the Department's task is not rendered any easier by the fact that there is a considerable degree of diversity between the development levels and aspirations of different bands in different regions of Canada.

The issue of whether services should be transferred to individual bands rather than to tribal councils or similar groups of bands is a current topic of debate between bands and the Department. For some specialist roles, many bands do not have a sufficient level of activity to support a full-time person and, of course, specialized personnel who are available and can work satisfactorily with the band governments can be hard to find. There have been less than ten land management transfers across the country. Somewhat less than ten per cent of the bands in Canada are presently in possession of Section 53 (management of surrendered lands) and Section 60 (management of band lands) authority under the Act.

The factors which the Department has taken into account in considering transfers include the desire of a band for such powers, changes within the political structure in a band, technical competence, liquidity of a band's resources, and the perceived risk level to the Department. The Westbank experience illustrated some of the issues that can arise when transfers occur. I encourage the Department to move as quickly as it can in this area — there may be teething troubles but increased responsibility is, in my view, a positive step for Indian people.

There has been no downsizing of the Department with respect to the lands, revenues, and trusts functions and apparently none is planned. This seems sensible to me, as it would be false economy to try to run a shoestring operation in an area of such vital concern to all bands. These functions will alter with time, but given the likelihood of greatly increased development of Indian lands, I think that the need for Departmental advisory resources will grow despite some decrease in direct administrative functions.

I have been advised that the first comprehensive alternative funding arrangement was recently concluded with a West Coast band. It has been negotiated to cover a three-year period with block funds provided for all the federally funded functions of the band. As with any initiative, there have been difficulties with the implementation of alternative funding arrangements. I think that this sort of arrangement is the likely order of the future and it will be necessary to endure a certain amount of trial and error until the most acceptable solutions are found.

The Department is in the first year of a five-year comprehensive services transfer plan, during which a total of two hundred and eighty million dollars ($280,000,000) will be spent on devolution, including incremental costs, front end costs, and salary conversions.

After having prepared and submitted proposals for the transfer of services to bands and tribal councils, the Department appreciated the need for a comprehensive framework for such service transfers. Indeed, the Treasury Board at one point refused approval of further transfers until a comprehensive plan was put in place. The plan is ambitious. The Corporate Management Plan of April 1987 defines transferable programs as follows:

> Transferable programs and services are those so indicated under current legislation, program authorities and policies. This includes nearly all programs and services within the Indian and Inuit affairs program but excludes the Minister's residual responsibilities under the Indian Act and other legislation, as well as remaining administrative and management functions, including the administration of financial transfers to Indian bands.

The transfer program specifically did not address policy issues, Indian child care agencies, management development programs, the Indian economic development fund, and other similar programs already in place.

The downsizing and devolution processes are intended to be financially neutral in the sense that the funds anticipated to be expended by the Department are in fact transferred to the band or tribal councils for the purpose of administering the same services.

Since devolution involves a sacrifice of some efficiencies of scale and involves a considerable degree of transference and education, the expected costs of transfer exceed the costs of present administration. It has been recognized that devolution of a program may require additional funding and standards for increases have been set. This process is not a means by which Native peoples will either be encouraged or permitted to obtain additional funding indirectly when such funds are unavailable through direct grant or other programs. The success of the downsizing efforts can be overemphasized by not having regard to the high degree of downsizing directly attributable to the transfer of educational services. Outside those services, downsizing has been reasonably modest.

6. Self-Government

Part IV of the Commission's Terms of Reference instructs me to have regard for the "established policy of supporting and strengthening Indian self-government on Indian lands". Before proceeding, I wish to comment on the meaning of that term.

Self-government as a concept was dealt with in submissions before me by numerous members of the Department, both past and present. While the general concept of self-government as the transfer of legislative and executive authority to Indian bands and tribal councils is clear, the expression or understanding of the concept varies widely.

Almost all members of Indian groups who appeared before me spoke of the right to self-government and some spoke of the right of self-determination. Chief Mathias said to me that:

> True Indian self-government must, and can, only be founded upon a legal and political relationship that recognizes Indian nations as nations. True self-government cannot be granted to Indian peoples under the Indian Act. Nor can it be based on a relationship whereby the ultimate authority over issues that are critical to the survival of Indian nations rests with non-Indians.
> Indian self-government can only have legitimacy if it is founded upon the constitutional recognition of Indian governments and Indian jurisdictions as a third order of government. . . .
> Moreover, Indian self-government can only be legitimate if the form and jurisdictions of the respective governments are determined through negotiations that culminate in treaties. Treaties represent the true government to government relationship that has historically existed, and is necessary for legitimate Indian self-government.

The concept of self-determination is, of course, a concept in public international law. Article 1(2) of the U.N. Charter proclaimed that one purpose of the United Nations was to "develop friendly relations among nations based on respect for the principle of equal rights and self-determination of peoples . . .". This right is expressed in Article 55 of the U.N. Charter and has been confirmed by that body on a number of occasions.

The definition of the right of self-determination is as broad and embracing as the definitions of self-government:

> All peoples have the right to self-determination; by virtue of that right they freely determine their political status and freely pursue their economic, social, and cultural development. (Declaration 1514 (XV) December 14, 1960)

Self-government is an emotive phrase like "liberty, equality, fraternity". It can mean different things to different people. Clearly, it denotes freedom and responsibility. The concept of self-government has been much to the fore in recent constitutional discussions. The delicate political question is always how to afford maximum freedom without undue Balkanization.

I have from time to time used the term self-direction rather than self-government. Some of the Native claims clearly fall outside the scope of any modern state's ability or willingness to permit autonomous governments within its structure. I think, however, that the Indian people's desire for self-direction for the purpose of ensuring their uniqueness as peoples can be well accommodated within the Canadian Constitution and Canadian culture. In the absence of constitutional amendments removing Section 91(24) from the <u>Constitution Act, 1867</u>, Parliament will remain sovereign in respect of the governance of Indian affairs in this country. However, Parliament may delegate substantial aspects of that sovereignty to the Indian peoples themselves so that they can direct their own affairs. I think it should be acknowledged, however, that this is because the Indian peoples are part of Canada rather than because of their separateness. Ultimately, under the Constitution, Parliament is responsibile for ensuring that the powers vested in Indian people will accrue to their benefit. That responsibility cannot be abdicated and, accordingly, self-government or self-direction is a process which must be administered by the Department in consultation with the Indian people, taking into consideration the capabilities of the bands or groups seeking additional powers. The process is an evolving one and I think it is desirable that Indian people have the necessary freedom and authority to achieve the best use of their lives. The move to self-direction and away from any degree of dependency is always to be encouraged. The Department has recently established an Assistant Deputy Minister of Self-Government as both a practical and symbolic elevation of the importance of the policy within the Department.

I think it is vital that there be a statutory structure for conferring self-government on Indian bands and tribal councils. The issues of devolution of services and self-government are, of course, integrally related. As already noted, devolution should help promote conditions which will assist bands in acquiring the personnel, expertise, and experience to ensure a successful transition to self-government. With respect to self-government, however, the terms of the Indian Act are not consistent with the surrender or delegation of ultimate authority by the Minister to Indian governments. I was told that approximately 40 proposals for self-government have been received and are currently under consideration. The Department estimates that 125 to 130 bands are presently interested in obtaining some degree of self-government.

The two bands which have succeeded in obtaining self-government are those covered by the Sechelt Act, S.C. 1984–85–86, c. 93 and the Cree-Naskapi (of Quebec) Act, S.C. 1984, c. 18. Some comment is appropriate regarding each of these Acts.

The Sechelt Act covers virtually any service concerning Indian land and peoples. This Act created a fully mature Indian government operating generally like a municipal government relative to the legislative jurisdiction of the federal and provincial governments. The Act required enabling legislation from both the federal and provincial governments to fully realize its purposes.

In relation to financing, the Sechelt peoples have received block transfers of funds fixed upon the cost of services in a base year and escalated by factors related to population and the Consumer Price Index. The Sechelt community is entitled under the arrangement to allocate the funds as they see fit, and pursuant to these arrangements the Council has been required to define its accountability to the Sechelt people. The Sechelt Constitution has in practical terms required the Council to obtain the advice and consent of the members for proposed expenditures at an annual or special band meeting called for that purpose. As I have said elsewhere, this new financial responsibility puts increased pressure on a band executive to manage band finances effectively.

The Cree-Naskapi Act essentially takes the Cree-Naskapi peoples out of the Indian Act, but is reasonably limited in its provisions. Health services have been transferred to the Province of Quebec and education services are being funded and supported by a separate Board of Education.

The Department cannot be precise, but it estimates that approximately 15 to 20 bands will be in a position to assume self-government within the next five years. Co-ordination with provincial legislatures is, in some cases, anathema to the bands and, in others, difficult to obtain given the present provisions of the Act. Of course, federal-provincial relations are not always unruffled and it is to be expected that there will be a fair measure of friction in provincial-Indian relations for years to come. This is simply a fact of the political process.

Different bands have indicated different desires in relation to the fundamental incidents of land title. I was informed that the Inuvialuat will be adopting a fee simple concept of property and that the fee simple is proposed to be vested within the government itself rather than through any third party. As a consequence, however, other forms of protection for the long-term interests of the members with respect to the land have been substituted. I deal in some detail with land issues later.

PART B

Scope of Possible Changes

Scope of Recommendations

Many of the witnesses referred to the quite broad scope of Part IV of the Terms of Reference. Chief Mathias stated that any Royal Commission looking into Indian affairs considering recommendations as broad as those contemplated by Part IV ought to hold hearings across Canada and consult with all bands and all national Indian groups. Certain members of the Department expressed concern that the evidence before this Commission did not justify sweeping recommendations for change.

I recognize that many of the issues investigated relate to the local and individual circumstances of the Westbank Indian Band. One must always be careful in moving from the particular to the general. Matters discussed in submissions relating to Part IV of this Commission were not proved in any formal sense. I found the Westbank background material valuable in giving some concrete context to certain issues considered at the Part IV stage. Several factors have caused me to make recommendations regarding general matters concerning the Act and Departmental policy.

During the course of the hearings and submissions, it became clear that many of the difficulties discussed before the Commission related to fundamental problems arising from the Act or its administration. During the Part IV hearings, it became possible to better distinguish problems unique to Westbank. There is little debate about the appropriateness of the Indian Act to present circumstances: people seemed to agree that serious difficulties have been and are presently being experienced. There was a lack of consensus as to whether this was because of the general thrust of the Act or specific defects in the legislation exacerbated by the passage of time since changes to the legislation have occurred. Current debate concerns the processes and solutions which might be adopted to overcome the widely acknowledged problems.

There has not been a Royal Commission to study Indian affairs in the recent past. As its major task, this Commission examined issues raised about the Westbank Band, its governance, and issues relating to lessees on the Westbank Reserves. While I am keenly aware that many problems encountered at Westbank may be of a purely local nature, the history there can be helpful in pointing to areas where weaknesses exist in statutory provisions or Departmental policy. The Westbank Band was, and is, quite active in the economic sphere and some of its controversies over the past decade could be faced by other bands in varying degrees as they become more active in business. It would be regrettable if the information gleaned from this Inquiry was not used to try to decrease the likelihood of future difficulty in other instances. I heed the caution of Chief Mathias. In an ideal world, one would have time for the widest study and consultation. Then one could recommend on a very wide spectrum and in greater detail. But time and resources are finite. I have heard enough that I feel confident in addressing certain aspects of the Act and Departmental policy. It must be remembered that I did not range the country far and wide, but I did have a quite concentrated course of learning about one band and the Department — the Inquiry perforce illuminated many areas of interest to bands and individuals beyond the confines of Westbank. I do not intend to refrain from any activity under my mandate in Part IV, but I bear in mind that my mandate is not unbounded.

I noted earlier that several policy groups are presently considering changes to the Indian Act and Departmental policies, and that a wide-ranging review of lands, reserves, and trusts is presently proceeding under the direction of the Office of the Comptroller General. My recommendations are intended to enhance and complement such endeavours. I have tried to address problems which in my opinion are so systemic and clear that they cannot fail to be a concern to many bands in Canada and to persons concerned with the administration of Indian affairs.

Summary of Submissions

Submissions concerning the issues raised by Part IV were invited from all significant Indian organizations in British Columbia and their views were received formally as well as informally. As well, the views of many individuals, both Indian and non-Indian, were made known to me during the course of the Inquiry.

(a) Department of Indian Affairs and Northern
Development

Members of the Department urged that this Commission recommend improvements in discrete areas such as:

  (i) definition and enforcement of spousal rights upon marriage breakdown;
 (ii) per capita distributions to minors;
(iii) Indian land registry;
 (iv) the definition and expansion of band taxation powers;
  (v) the creation of a clear policy and statutory structure for devolution.

The Commission was also asked to consider carefully whether the Department should remove itself from Indian affairs at the operational level at the same pace as has been the trend in recent years. It was suggested that so long as the Department is responsible for the review of substantive policy questions such as money issues, it requires regular local contact with the bands involved. While the closure of local offices has solved political controversy in many areas, it has not been always a happy experience for those dependent on the local services. Some local offices have been de facto reopened by the assignment of staff without declaring them to be, in fact, local offices. The last ten years have been transitional, certainly in British Columbia, and I think that if there is found to be a need for greater local presence, no one should be afraid to call a spade a spade. Modern communications have made it easy to operate from central locations, but a knowledge of actual conditions "in the field" is often valuable in being sensitive to potential sources of controversy.

The role of settlement monies in the economic futures of bands was addressed by many, and concern was expressed that such monies not be a one-generation payment, but rather the foundation for a band's economic future. People were anxious to ensure that capital be preserved by provisions in any settlement to insulate the monies from too easy alienation. This is a thorny problem. I think bands must be given a fair measure of freedom to run their own operations, but if a band is clearly not advanced, then the Department must play a more aggressive role in seeing that a prudent financial course is charted.

Many people urged upon the Commission the process of statutory reform which had its premature end in Bill C-52. In their view, it is important to pass similar enabling legislation to allow bands to exercise self-government free of the restrictions and antiquated structure of the existing Indian Act.

The Commission carried out quite a detailed review of the procedures applicable to Indian band by-laws. It was suggested that, with respect to taxation by-laws, there should be a procedure to allow some by-laws to be set aside by the Minister or some other independent authority so as to avoid the difficulties of taxation without representation. I gather that certain present proposed legislation is addressing the matter in part through an advisory board to review tax issues. Perhaps a form of review by the Minister or a board would be workable, but I would also want there to be an opportunity to appeal to the courts.

Counsel for the Department provided a written submission outlining recommendations which were felt to be justified by the evidence and submissions heard during the Inquiry. While the Department was careful to point out that there should be some limitation on the scope of recommendations made by the Commission, it was submitted that recommendations could be made along the following lines:

(i) There ought to be more extensive and flexible provisions for the devolution of powers. The Department submitted that a provision that the Minister delegate his functions to the band by agreement is the most desirable solution to this difficulty.

(ii) The by-law powers of bands ought to be expanded as suggested in the Kamloops amendments.

(iii) Band governments should have jurisdiction over conditionally surrendered lands within the boundaries of reserves as suggested in the Kamloops amendments.

(iv) The Indian Land Registry should be upgraded and the powers and duties of that office should be specified in greater detail.

(v) The Department should clarify policies as to the length and conditions of leases for the economic development of reserve lands.

(vi) There should be sufficient funding allocated to cope with the needs of Indian bands for training and support services while they are assuming devolved powers.

(vii) The Criminal Code should be amended so that band chiefs and councillors could be subject to a criminal sanction in the same way that non-Indian governmental officials are subject to such sanctions for misbehaviour in office.

(viii) Bands should be required to hold funds attributable to minors in trust so that funds would be safeguarded for the benefit of the minors when they attain their majority.

All of these submissions have merit and I address many of them later. The forthright way in which the Department acknowledges the extent of its difficulties indicates a likelihood of constructive change. Troubles cannot be overcome until they are recognized as such. Whatever the past history of the Department, it is clear that there is a desire to take steps to enhance the position of Indian people. The Department recognizes that it cannot be oblivious to the interests of non-Indians, but it is clearly of the view that its prime responsibility must be for Native aspirations.

(b) Assembly of First Nations

The Assembly of First Nations appeared before me through Chief Joe Mathias of the Squamish Indian Band. The Assembly of First Nations expressed its reservations about this Commission being vested with the broad powers enumerated under Part IV, and pointed out that the problems of the Westbank Indian Band were fundamentally local in nature. In its submission, the objectives of this Commission were limited to a purely local inquiry.

Chief Mathias' submission suggested that Part IV was too broad and vague to allow for meaningful Indian input and that a wider-ranging Inquiry would have to be established before fundamental reforms could be made. In this submission, the implication in Part IV that the Department has any role in supporting and strengthening Indian self-government is not well founded. Chief Mathias submitted that the Indian Act is hundred-year-old legislation rooted in both a colonial and a racist mentality.

As I have already stated, Chief Mathias submitted that Indian self-government must be founded on a legal and political relationship that recognizes nations as nations. In his words:

> True self-government cannot be granted to Indian peoples under the Indian Act. Nor can it be based on a relationship whereby the ultimate authority over issues that are critical to the survival of Indian nations rests with non-Indians.

The objectionable features of the Indian Act highlighted by Chief Mathias relate to its limited jurisdiction, provision for ministerial vetoes, and the power of Parliament to amend the Act.

He expressed the view that Indian self-government can only obtain legitimacy if it is founded upon a treaty which arises out of a constitutional recognition of Indian governments and jurisdictions as a third order of government in Canada.

Chief Mathias also stated that the problems of past mismanagement affect every Indian band in Canada, and that the existing specific claims process is inadequate and underfunded in its ability to deal with these disputes. This, according to his submission, is the cause of increasing litigation against the Department.

(c) Kamloops Indian Band

Chief Clarence "Manny" Jules of the Kamloops Indian Band appeared before me in his personal capacity. He outlined the procedure by which he was able to obtain the consent and support of the vast majority of Indian bands in Canada to the amendments known as the Kamloops Amendments.

Chief Jules gave some background information about the Kamloops Band. He noted that, as with many bands, the Kamloops Band had lost some of its reserve lands between 1900 and 1930. As early as 1932, the Band commenced leasing Reserve lands to non-Indians. Until the 1950's, many people in the Band occupied a communal village. At present, as a result of allotments made primarily in the 1950's, most of the arable land within the Kamloops Reserve is subject to Certificates of Possession held by approximately 40 people. The Band has an unemployment rate of approximately 60 per cent, but the Band government is moving aggressively to promote employment.

Within the Kamloops Band there is a considerable measure of accountability between the Band Council and the members, including the provision of audited statements to Band members concerning the Band's financial affairs. The Band Council is often asked questions arising from these financial statements. In addition, the Band has a financial manager.

The leasing which has taken place on the Kamloops Reserve has been for the purpose of farming, logging, and industrial park leases. There were approximately nine surrenders of band lands up to 1980. The largest surrender occurred in 1960 for the purpose of developing the Mount Paul Industrial Park. As a result of the absence of funding, and the absence of the jurisdiction to levy taxes for the purpose of providing municipal services, it took over 20 years to install street lighting, municipal roads and other services in the industrial park.

According to Chief Jules' submission, Indian reserves tend to be isolated and exist in a type of purgatory in relation to municipal government. He stated that one problem is that band councils lack clear jurisdiction over surrendered lands. He felt strongly that it is necessary to have jurisdiction over both surrendered and non-surrendered band lands.

Chief Jules expressed the view that under the Act the Minister should retain a fiduciary responsibility relating to financial transactions involving surrendered lands. He agreed, however, that if power was devolved to the band, it could then be argued that the band would have to accept greater responsibility.

According to Chief Jules, the long-term impact of economic decisions is fundamentally a band decision. With respect to conflict of interest issues, he said the situation in his Band is that there are four councillors and one Chief. It is a council procedure that no Chief or councillor can participate in decisions involving their immediate family. Chief Jules stated that he and most members of the council are related in one way or another to most, if not all, of the Band members. He himself is related directly or by marriage to all but one or two families in the Band. I have spoken elsewhere of conflict of interest issues. This is one of the thorniest issues that faces Indian bands. Eternal vigilance seems to be demanded to ensure that controversy is avoided in this area and the familial nature of bands always makes this a difficult problem in band government, according to Chief Jules.

The Kamloops Band charges a five per cent administration fee for the administration of locatee leases. In Chief Jules' view, the taxation of Indian peoples by band councils may eventually become politically palatable as bands develop and achieve a stronger economic base. In his experience, while the band council presently has that power under

Section 83 of the Act, it has not been an acceptable political position to date to use taxation powers.

Chief Jules felt that the council's power to impose taxation on non-Indians using lands for commercial purposes will have to be administered responsibly to avoid Indian bands pricing themselves out of the market. While he accepted that there was an inherent tension in taxation without full electoral representation, he felt that, ultimately, market forces would restrain Indian governments when they were inclined to be too aggressive.

The Kamloops Band seeks to maintain contact with non-Indian lessees through a leaseholders' association which meets annually, as well as through continuing close relationships with individual leaseholders. There will often be tensions between landlord and tenant and in Chief Jules' opinion, it is vital that communications between the parties be preserved.

In his experience, the main obstacle to statutory or political reforms is the absence of a coherent political will on the part of the federal government and Indian people. He feels it is necessary to develop a consensus for change at the band level on a topic-by-topic basis. This would suggest that the Commission recommend that a timetable of reforms based upon priorities and prospects of success be prepared and urged upon government. According to Chief Jules, that timetable should include the following:

1. taxation powers;
2. land management powers;
3. land registry system;
4. zoning;
5. control of land at the band level; and
6. control of education at the band level.

In his opinion, the bands and band councils suffer from the absence of any legislative mandate to do much of what the federal government handles on their behalf. He felt it might be useful to have enabling legislation to allow bands to opt into systems in which there is a legislative framework for those functions they assume from the federal government.

Another concern Chief Jules expressed is that additional funds are required in order to carry out devolution or self-government schemes. For self-government by the Kamloops Band in terms of land management, the Kamloops Band had prepared and presented a budget of $80,000 per annum for land management purposes under Section 53 and Section 60. The Department approved only $30,000 for these purposes.

(d) Westbank Indian Band

In his Part IV submission to me, Chief Louie of the Westbank Indian Band stated that the recommendations made should be related to the fact that this Commission was basically a B.C. Commission.

He noted that there is a great disparity between bands' needs, aspirations, and endowments, both with respect to people and natural resources. He expressed support for the Kamloops Amendments and the opinion that Westbank needs its own separate statutory structure of self-government. He said that Westbank's concept of self-government is not altogether the same as the Sechelt model. He noted as an aside that the process of developing a tailor-made statute can be complicated and expensive. I comment on this problem later and suggest a possible solution.

Chief Louie said that self-sufficiency is a part of self-government and presupposes the ability to raise revenue from whatever sources. He felt it was important to learn lessons from the Alaska experience. He said land claims could be a powerful tool for self-sufficiency of Indian bands.

Chief Louie dealt with what he perceived to be certain day-to-day problems of administration under the Indian Act with respect to the time and resources available. He said some of these difficulties are as follows:

   (i) the Act must embrace bands that require great attention and involvement by the Department as well as bands which require virtually no intervention;
   (ii) the by-law taxation powers promoted by the Kamloops Band should be adopted;
   (iii) bands should be given clear jurisdiction with respect to surrendered lands;
   (iv) the system for the expenditure of capital monies should be better defined;
   (v) the land registry system can and should be improved;
   (vi) There should be protection for bands which pass zoning by-laws analogous to the protection afforded by Section 972 of the B.C. Municipal Act, R.S.B.C. 1979, c. 290.

Chief Louie stated that approximately 80 per cent of his time is spent on land management matters, and that in the 1985/86 fiscal year approximately 100 transactions occurred on surrendered lands. Chief Louie also asked that I recommend the restoration of land management powers to the Westbank Band and the provision of adequate funding for the administration of those powers.

(e) Kootenay Indian Area Council

Chief Sophie Pierre of the St. Mary's Band, accompanied by Chief Paul Sam of the Shuswap Band, appeared before me on behalf of the Kootenay Indian Area Council. She strongly urged that I endorse the recommendations of the Special Committee on Indian self-government, otherwise known as the *Penner Report*.

Chief Pierre urged that I recommend that Parliament occupy the field of legislation in relation to Indians and then vacate that area of jurisdiction to recognized Indian governments. The legislation recommended by the *Penner Report*, it will be remembered, included the following:

(i) the enactment of an Indian First Nations Recognition Act, committing the federal government to recognize Indian governments accountable to Indian peoples;

(ii) legislation authorizing the federal government to enter into agreements with recognized Indian First Nation Governments as to the jurisdiction that each Indian government wished to occupy;

(iii) legislation under the authority of Section 91(24) of the Constitution Act, 1867, designed to occupy all areas of competence necessary to permit Indian First Nations to govern themselves effectively, and to ensure that provincial laws would not apply on Indian lands except with the agreement of the Indian First Nations' governments.

Chief Pierre submitted that it is important that the Penner recommendations regarding the scope of powers allowed to First Nations be adopted. Those recommendations included provision that full legislative and policy-making powers be vested in the Indian Nations and that full control over the territory and resources within reserve boundaries be provided to First Nations' governments. The *Penner Report* recommended that the exact scope of jurisdiction should be decided by negotiation with representatives of the First Nations and that the First Nations governments should at least have the authority to legislate in such areas as social and cultural development, including education and family relations, land and resource use, revenue-raising, economic and commercial development, and justice and law enforcement.

Chief Pierre also emphasized the Penner recommendations relating to providing a better economic base for First Nations by providing such additional lands and monies as are necessary to ensure their self-sufficiency. In her submission, accountability of the First Nations must be primarily to their own constituents, and accountability to the federal government should be limited to the use of public funds.

With respect to the particular circumstances of the St. Mary's Band, Chief Pierre had several interesting observations. Principal among these was the degree to which this Band operates its affairs without regard to the provisions of the Indian Act. In particular, leases of Band lands tend to be buckshee leases on a sharecropper basis. Chief Pierre stated that this is linked to the inefficiencies in the administration of the agricultural leases by the Department, and unhappy experiences which the Band members had in the 1950's and 1960's.

Chief Sam, also of the Kootenay Indian Area Council, submitted to me that a troubling problem for the Shuswap Band is the need for lands and monies to accommodate the increase in population due to the expansion of membership under Bill C-31. He expressed frustration at the delay in receiving monies which were promised to bands that opened their membership to new members under Bill C-31.

Chief Sam stated that many of the water licences in favour of the Band had fallen into default as a result of the administration by Departmental officials in the 1950's and the 1960's. As a consequence, his Band had numerous difficulties in relation to water supply. He adverted to this as an example of what was felt to be neglect of Indian interests in that area.

The Necessity of Reform

A complex legal structure such as that existing under the Indian Act should not be changed unless it is demonstrably inadequate. Witnesses before the Commission agreed that any reform of the Indian Act is likely to attract a considerable degree of political debate and possibly controversy. Nevertheless, nearly all groups affected by the Indian Act are opposed to certain of its provisions in one way or another. The degree to which the Act has become archaic is one reason why reform has become more rather than less difficult.

Since the basic philosophy of the Act is considered outdated, minor reforms seem inconsequential; yet major reforms excite such great concern that they are perceived to be politically unattractive. The patriation of the Canadian Constitution, culminating in the Constitution Act, 1982, provided for constitutional recognition of aboriginal rights. The precise delineation of these rights remains to be worked out. The position of most of the national groups representing status Indians in Canada now appears to be that any future reforms should take place on a constitutional level rather than by Parliament acting pursuant to its legislative authority under the Constitution Act, 1867. Yet the evidence of the difficulties at Westbank has led me to conclude that some reform of the Act or of the legislative structure of Indian affairs would assist the federal government to better fulfil its mandate of government in this area. Such changes are not likely to be a satisfactory global solution to the question of the position of Indian people in Canada, but I think some useful progress can be made in specific areas.

The Indian Act and Departmental Practice: The Widening Gyre

In several important respects, the provisions of the Indian Act and Departmental practice have diverged to such an extent that some Indian Affairs policies lack sufficient statutory foundation. This is not surprising, given the relative antiquity of the Act and the dramatic changes that have occurred since 1975 in the direction of Indian affairs. This comment does not apply to all of the many policies and programs administered by the Department throughout Canada. However, the areas of deficiency are important ones — lands and monies — and in these areas there is a very real danger that the federal government is operating outside a proper statutory basis. Mr. Fred Walchli, former Regional Director General in B.C., commented on the difficulties that he faced in trying to implement the devolution policies of the Department as a first step towards self-government:

> Well, we do not have, and did not have at the time, a legislative base for Indian self-government. All the authorities — that were available to us were derived from the Indian Act or from government policy or from certain decisions made by the Treasury Board.
>
> In a sense it would have been desirable to have a proper legislative base. We did not have it. So, the approach the Department was following was to use the authorities of the Indian Act to the extent that that was possible, to use policies that were approved by Cabinet and eventually Parliament, and to use the Treasury Board to give certain authorities to bands to manage money.
>
> So, the approach we were following basically said we will transfer the management of programs to Indian control. We will provide administrative overhead support to pay for their staff. We will permit the passing of by-laws in order to provide some kind of legislative base at the band level. We pursued those kind of avenues.
>
> So, basically we explored every possibility to develop what could be called Indian self-government, to give them the authority and the power where possible to manage their own affairs, to manage the funds, to make their own decisions.
>
> My mandate was to push that for all it was worth. We were to use whatever authorities we had to transfer responsibility and power to the Indian band councils. That's what we did.
>
> (Transcripts: Volume XXXVI, pp. 5024–5025)

It was often expressed to me in the hearings that a "liberal" or "creative" interpretation of the Act had been adopted. It was usually in a positive direction. The comments serve, however, to show that the garment of the Act is being stretched, and worn by the Department in ways not contemplated by its draftsmen.

Many of the witnesses testified to the archaic character of the Indian Act. Chief Clarence "Manny" Jules of the Kamloops Band referred to the fact that dealings in lands are characterized as "surrenders" by the Act. That term is not appropriate and the word has unfortunate connotations. The government appears committed to change it. I endorse that commitment.

The fundamental property concept in the Act is that assets are held by the Crown for the benefit of individual band members or of bands as a whole. Slightly in excess of one billion dollars is presently held in trust by the Department in favour of Indian bands. Savings accounts for minors, accounts for adopted Indians or Indian children, and estate accounts are other examples of the active trust responsibility of the Minister.

The Minister's dominion over property relating to Indians is far-reaching. Lands in a reserve are held by Her Majesty. The Minister is responsible for the management, sale, or other disposition of surrendered lands (Section 53). Virtually all land transactions require the Minister's involvement. Wills executed by an individual Indian are subject to the Minister's approval (Section 45(3)) and distribution of property on an intestacy is provided for in the Act. The Minister is authorized to operate farms on reserves (Section 71). There is scarcely any aspect of the economic life of an Indian band or its members in which the Minister (Department) is not assigned an active (and hence potentially intrusive) role.

The principal significance of this framework is that while there is an elaborate structure in the Act relating to the areas of Indian government to be carried on by the Crown, very little is spelled out as to the band government's responsibility. Yet today the trend is away from government by the Department to government by bands or band associations such as tribal councils. It is rather as if colonial laws were all that a newly independent republic possessed. The emphasis would be wrong. That seems to be the case with legislation pertaining to Indian affairs.

The government's established policy of supporting and strengthening Indian self-government on Indian lands is thus in conflict with the underlying philosophy of the Indian Act, which remains paternalistic and intrusive in the lives of Indians. But I am not an advocate of undue change. It may be that fundamental alterations ultimately can be achieved by the constitutional modes proposed by certain Native leaders. I simply observe that it has not yet been achieved and because of the fundamental nature of certain of the proposed changes, speedy resolution may not be the order of the day. There are problems existing today. It would be good to address them today. Amendments to existing legislation may not make a perfect world, but they can help make a better world for those affected by the current legislation.

Departmental policy and practice has travelled a considerable distance on the road towards Indian self-government, with significant devolution of federal powers and programs to Indian bands and tribal councils. The significant downsizing of the Department and hence its abilities to administer programs has been matched by an expansion of resources to bands and tribal councils to perform similar functions. From a situation where virtually all programs and services were administered by the Department as late as the mid-1960's, some 75 per cent of the Indian Affairs budget is now administered by bands or provinces. This entire process has, however, proceeded without significant statutory alteration.

The treatment of Indian capital monies illustrates the difficulties that the Indian Act presents for current Departmental policies. The provisions of the Act relating to money are not detailed and comprehensive. The fundamental distinction for administrative purposes is the distinction between Indian and non-Indian monies. In relation to non-Indian monies paid out of the Consolidated Revenue Fund, the Department has moved towards block funding of federal programs and has encouraged the devolution of Departmental programs to band councils or tribal councils.

The Act defines Indian monies as "all monies collected, received or held by Her Majesty for the use and benefit of Indians or bands". The Indian Act does not define or provide much assistance in defining non-Indian monies, and the definition of Indian monies is not of great assistance as the phrase "collected, received or held" is extremely broad. Given that all contracts relating to land are executed by the Crown, monies paid under most leases are, in all likelihood, Indian monies.

The distinction between revenue and capital is one which has a broadly understood meaning in the accounting profession. It is not necessarily the same as that contained in Section 62 of the Indian Act. The Department has adopted a somewhat flexible definition in the distinction between capital and revenue, often with an eye to the Indian Act's limitations in respect of the band's powers over capital monies. For instance, it appeared that in determining what portion of the Westbank cut-off monies was to be treated as capital, a restrictive definition of capital was adopted. The statutory distinction between revenue and capital, combined with the band's powers under Section 69 to control its revenue monies, creates an inevitable tension between the band and the Department regarding the characterization of monies as revenue rather than capital. Because it is often desirable to denote funds as "revenue", there can be a measure of artificiality imposed on transactions. Inadequate legislative provisions, like hard cases, can make for bad law and doubtful precedent.

Section 64 of the Act contains the provisions permitting the expenditure of capital monies. Section 64(1) states that:

With the consent of the council of a band, the Minister may authorize and direct the expenditure of capital monies of the band. . .
[for a variety of construction and purchase objectives]
(k) for any other purpose that, in the opinion of the Minister, is for the benefit of the band.

Departmental policy now is to allow bands as great a role as possible in determining the direction and expenditure of capital monies. This policy seems desirable and ought to be encouraged.

A difficulty which arises out of Section 64 concerns the Department's practice of paying capital monies to the band under Section 64(1)(k) for purposes defined and supervised by the band. The Department's policy of granting band councils greater responsibility in this area conflicts with the statutory provision that the Minister "authorize and direct the expenditure of capital monies". The general provision under Section 64(1)(k) is tied and limited to purposes that ". . .in the opinion of the Minister. . ." are for the benefit of the band. The listing contained under Section 64(1)(b)-(j) suggests that such expenditures must be related to specific projects and objectives both authorized and directed by the Minister and the Department. Nothing in Section 64 expressly allows the band to undertake responsibility for the collection, investment, and reinvestment of capital monies. The thrust of this section is out of step with what is in fact happening.

The difficulty with the conflict between the terms of the Act and Departmental policy is that capital monies are for the benefit of all members of the band. The statutory provisions under the Indian Act, however archaic, appear to be directed to protecting the interests of band members in capital monies. By receding from the statutory role of authorizing and directing the expenditure of capital monies, the Minister and the Department may find themselves subject to attack from dissenting band members who become unhappy with the results of the application of sums of capital money. Such complaints have been voiced and may become the subject of litigation against the Department.

For present purposes, I point out only that the treatment of monies under the Act creates a statutory obstacle to the structure which the Department considers advisable for the treatment and funding of Indian government. Departmental policy has departed so far from the scheme of management provided for under the Act that I think it fair to say that the Department is operating more on the basis of policy than pursuant to the legislation. Ron Derrickson commented to me during the hearings that at times it appeared that the administration of Indian Affairs was "all policy and no law". Certainly in this area that comment would be applicable. I do not criticize the Department for fostering the policy of giving greater authority to bands, but because Departmental practice has moved beyond the apparent statutory boundaries, there is a danger that legislative reform will become less of a necessity as those structures of the Act which are inconsistent with current policy are ignored rather than changed. Any serious divergence between Departmental practice and statutory authorization has several unacceptable consequences for the conduct of Indian affairs; some of these are:

(a) growth of a perception on the part of Indian groups that what cannot be obtained directly under the Indian Act can often be obtained indirectly by seeking an alteration in Departmental practice;
(b) continuing difficulties occasioned to officials of the Department responsible for the administration of Indian Affairs — what are the limits of authority?;
(c) an inadequate public debate within Canada as a whole relating to the proper treatment of Indians under the federal jurisdiction relating to Indians and their property.

At the same time, the legal responsibility of the Department relating to the administration of Indian lands and monies has become recognized as having significant private law consequences. In Guerin v. The Queen [1984] 2 S.C.R. 335, 55 N.R. 161, mentioned above, the Supreme Court of Canada held that the Minister, in relation to a conditional surrender of lands, had a fiduciary duty to band members to ensure that a reasonable rate of return was obtained for the rental of certain lands. I have been advised that a number of claims are being advanced against the Department based on alleged breach of such fiduciary duty. As many as 300 actions are said to have been commenced against the Department since the decision was handed down in Guerin, and as many as 2,000 potential claims involving breach of fiduciary duty, aboriginal land claims, and treaty claims have been identified. It has been estimated by the Department that the liabilities of the Crown may be in excess of a billion dollars with respect to these actions. With increasing awareness of legal remedies, suits against the Department become more likely for any perceived wrongdoing. A lack of congruence between policy and statutory provisions can lead to later problems. If the Act is out of step with desirable practice, the Act should be brought into line so that initiative is not stultified.

Some of those who appeared before me referred to the fundamental nature of the fiduciary duty of the Minister in relation to administration of the Indian Act. Few witnesses were prepared to accept any abatement of this fiduciary duty towards Indian lands or monies. The existence of such a duty in the past is a fact. Whether there will be any changes in the future consequent upon the changing relationship between the Department and individual bands remains to be worked out.

The Department, for understandable reasons, has adopted the position that the informed consent of a band or band council regarding proposed economic activities approved by the Minister is an answer to any subsequent allegation of breach of fiduciary duty. Whether or not this is so in all cases, the process of devolution is seen as being an honourable means by which future litigation between the bands and the Minister may be avoided. The Department and bands are endeavouring to arrive at a consensus on this topic. I am sure some agreements will be reached. In other cases, litigation may be the answer. It must be acknowledged that no one suggested to me that the right already existing be abridged or curtailed in any way. The concern is for the future.

I think the Department's concern about the ambit of the Guerin judgement has a reasonable basis. The fundamental change of perspective wrought by that decision is the acknowledgement that in its dealing with Indian lands, the Department is acting as a private trustee, fiduciary, or agent of the band. In this sense, the Minister is no longer just politically responsible. As Mr. Justice Dickson said in Guerin at page 170 (55 N.R.):

[34] In my view, the nature of Indian title and the framework of the statutory scheme established for disposing of Indian land places upon the Crown an equitable obligation, enforceable for the benefit of the Indians. This obligation does not amount to a trust in the private law sense. It is rather a fiduciary duty. If, however, the Crown breaches this fiduciary duty, it will be liable to the Indians in the same way and to the same extent as if such a trust were in effect.
[35] The fiduciary relationship between the Crown and the Indians has its roots in the concept of aboriginal, native or Indian title. The fact that Indian bands have a certain interest in lands does not, however, in itself give rise to a fiduciary relationship between the Indians and the Crown. The conclusion that the Crown is a fiduciary depends upon the further proposition that the Indian interest in the land is inalienable except upon surrender to the Crown.
[36] An Indian band is prohibited from directly transferring its interest to a third party. Any sale or lease of land can only be carried out after a surrender has taken place, with the Crown then acting on the band's behalf. The Crown first took this responsibility upon itself in the Royal Proclamation of 1763. It is still recognized in the surrender provisions of the Indian Act. The surrender requirement, and the responsibility it entails, are the source of a distinct fiduciary obligation owed by the Crown to the Indians.

Several sections of the Act confer powers on the Minister to deal with, approve, or reject proposals concerning lands and monies. While the law undoubtedly will evolve, I think Guerin has dramatically altered the economic consequences of misadministration under the Act. Obviously not all cases will succeed. In a recent decision, Apsassin et al. v. The Queen, Unreported, November 4, 1987, the Federal Court denied the very substantial relief claimed against the Crown. In that case, Addy J. held that on the facts there had been a valid consent to the surrender for sale of reserve land which much later was discovered to overlie large amounts of oil and gas.

The evidence in the Apsassin case demonstrates the difficulties occasioned to all parties in dealing with such claims. The surrender took place in 1948 and many potential witnesses had died prior to trial. The living witnesses were nearly all elderly. Since many surrenders occurred prior to 1950, it is to be expected that these difficulties will be common. The learned trial judge followed the Guerin judgement and held that there had been a breach of duty, but he found against the plaintiffs on major issues of liability and limitations. He said at page 28 of the Reasons for Judgement:

> I must hasten to state however, that, wherever advice is sought or whenever it is proferred, regardless of whether or not it is sought or where action is taken, there exists a duty on the Crown to take reasonable care in offering the advice to or in taking any action on behalf of the Indians. Whether or not reasonable care and prudence has been exercised will of course depend on all of the circumstances of the case at that time and, among those circumstances, one must of course include as most important any lack of awareness, knowledge, comprehension, sophistication, ingenuity or resourcefulness on the part of the Indians of which the Crown might reasonably be expected to be aware. Since this situation exists in the case at bar, the duty on the Crown is an onerous one, a breach of which will bring into play the appropriate legal and equitable remedies.
>
> Where there does exist a true fiduciary relationship such as in the case at bar, following the 1945 surrender, the same high degree of prudence and care must be exercised in dealing with the subject matter to which the fiduciary duty relates, as in the case of a true trust (refer Guerin et al. v. The Queen, supra at page 376). The test to be applied is an objective one: good faith and a clear conscience will not suffice. It is also similar to a trust in another respect: where a trustee is in any way interested in the subject matter of the trust, there rests upon him a special onus of establishing that all of the rights and interests both present and future of the beneficiary are protected and are given full and absolute priority and that the subject matter is dealt with for the latter's benefit and to the exclusion of the trustee's interest to the extent that there might be a conflict. A similar onus rests on the Crown in the case at bar regarding the equitable obligation which it owed the plaintiffs.

Concerning the consequences of self-government for bands, the Apsassin decision highlights the obvious: if a band gives its informed consent to any dealing in its land or monies, or conducts the transaction itself, then the Department, subject to statutory impediments, is not likely to be fixed with liability if decisions later turn out to be unfortunate or erroneous.

Whatever the full extent of the doctrine reflected in Guerin, it seems likely that the existence of these substantial liabilities will, in the near future, make some changes in the Act a government priority. The amount of potential liability already apprehended by the Department cannot be reconciled with granting self-government without a future abatement in the legal liability that has existed to date.

Counsel for the Department suggested that Guerin should be looked at in context. By that I think he meant it had to be viewed in light of the particular (and somewhat unusual) facts that were found to exist in that case. The courts can and will work out the ramifications of that decision based on the various fact patterns that come before them in future cases. It would be unfortunate if considerations arising from that case paralyzed progressive action on behalf of the Department.

In order to minimize the likelihood that the Department will feel unduly constrained by fears of being sued, I think it is important that the Act be brought into accord with desirable practice. Cases such as Guerin and Apsassin have simply highlighted the need for the Department to proceed prudently and in conformity with the law. To the extent that practice diverges from the wording of the statute, the Department is placed at risk. Because of the dramatic alteration in perceptions occasioned by the recent decisions, statutory reform has become imperative. Failure to do so may be a serious impediment to continued momentum toward self-government.

Indian Ambitions and Statutory Obstacles

Notwithstanding the Department's gradual development of self-government as a fundamental policy in its administration of the Indian Act, Indian bands, tribal councils, and national groups have experienced a degree of frustration in obtaining what they regard as the necessary attributes of self-government. A large obstacle to greater self-government is the present statutory structure of the Indian Act. Many Departmental policies and practices have been changed in terms of the fundamental limitations arising from the Indian Act. But there have been occasions when the Department has not been prepared to accommodate Indian groups because of statutory limitations. In this sense, therefore, the Indian Act represents a substantial statutory obstacle to the fulfilment of the Department's policy of and the Indian groups' desire for self-government.

Many Indian groups have taken the position that the Indian Act itself is, as a whole, archaic and unworkable, and that the only appropriate reform is a constitutional amendment. Any such reform would, of course, result in the repeal of the current Indian Act and/or the replacement of it by constitutional arrangements arrived at by Indian people and governments. It is apparent that Indian ambitions cannot be achieved without a significant change to the Indian Act.

Furthermore, Indian ambitions for self-government are also hampered by an inadequate structure for Indian government under the Act. In other words, it is not only the Act's assignment of responsibilities that is troublesome; the Act's inadequate definition of band government and its duties and responsibilities means that changes should provide a coherent legal structure to underpin Indian government as well as to address the transfer of responsibilities.

The Structure of Reform

As I have already indicated, there is a substantial division of opinion among those concerned with Indian affairs policy as to the method by which changes can best be effected. This issue is obviously fundamental to the question of change and my views are as follows.

A. Constitutional Agreement

In 1982, in the process which resulted in the Canada Act (1982) and the patriation of the Canadian Constitution, Indian groups succeeded in having express constitutional recognition of the existence of aboriginal and treaty rights. Section 35 of the Constitution Act, (1982) states as follows:

(1) The existing aboriginal and treaty rights of the aboriginal peoples of Canada are hereby recognized and affirmed.
(2) In this Act, "aboriginal peoples of Canada" includes the Indian, Inuit and Metis peoples of Canada.
(3) For greater certainty, in subsection (1) "treaty rights" includes rights that now exist by way of land claims agreements or may be so acquired.
(4) Notwithstanding any other provision of this Act, the aboriginal and treaty rights referred to in subsection (1) are guaranteed equally to male and female persons.

As literature on the subject shows, the legal interpretation and effect of Section 35 continues to be the subject of considerable political and legal controversy. The constitutional conferences convened pursuant to Section 37.1 of the Constitution Act, (1982) (now lapsed) resulted in no concluded constitutional arrangements being made between the Indian peoples and the federal and provincial levels of government. I heard the result of those conferences referred to as a "stand-off" and a "stalemate". The governments, federal and provincial, have no further express constitutional requirements to consider constitutional amendments in this area. Several national Indian groups have concluded that reform of the Indian Act pursuant to the federal responsibility for Indian affairs under Section 91(24) of the <u>Constitution Act</u>, (1867) is not a politically desirable objective and that the only acceptable reform would be new constitutional arrangements with the federal and provincial governments. This is not only because of a general desire for self-government, but also because of the trend towards demanding recognition of the right to be considered sovereign peoples. Because of the necessity for constitutional amendments passed pursuant to Section 39 of the <u>Constitution Act</u>, (1982), the constitutionalization of a structure for the regulation and government of Indian affairs has become substantially complicated by the involvement of the provincial governments. At the same time, the emerging concept of Indian self-government makes it evident that as a matter of policy, many Indian groups do not want to participate in or initiate reforms by Parliament under Section 91(24) of the <u>Constitution Act</u>, (1867).

It is not possible at the present time to assert with any degree of confidence what will be the outcome of future constitutional conferences. But the possibility of future constitutional agreement should not necessarily preclude progress on specific statutory reform. There has been a quite dramatic change in Departmental policies and funding practices in the past ten years. The federal government has a present constitutional responsibility in relation to the government of Indian affairs. That responsibility cannot be ignored simply because alternate arrangements may, at some point in the future, be arrived at by all those responsible for constitutional amendments. As it is widely acknowledged that the <u>Indian Act</u> is not in accord with the realities of the present situation, I recommend that legislative reforms be initiated and pursued by the federal government acting under its existing constitutional authority. As I noted above, I have a great concern that if this is not done, the current fear of exposure to liability will cause a slowdown in desirable Departmental initiative. This would not be in the interest of those chiefly concerned, the Native Indians of Canada.

B. Legislative Changes

A significant issue relating to the structure of any changes is whether they should proceed on a case-by-case basis or whether the federal government should seek to effect a wholesale revision of the <u>Indian Act</u>. The alternatives available to the federal government and the desirability of different courses of action can be briefly summarized.

(i) Legislative Patches to the Indian Act

Amendments are in the process of being made relating to band council powers and responsibilities with respect to by-laws and taxation. A national consensus emerged within a brief period supporting those amendments. There was sufficient support to give the measures some legislative priority. Compared to changes which will affect the basic structure of the Indian Act, such reforms are feasible and should be pursued. Many of the reforms discussed in earlier parts of this Report and outlined below can be effected in omnibus legislation that will bring the Act into closer accord with modern practices. The result will be a proper legislative underpinning for current practice and policy. Such changes should be regarded as the minimum necessary to avoid the sorts of problems that have occurred and are likely to occur in future if no action is taken.

(ii) Alternative Statutory Schemes

One of the most innovative changes in Indian affairs suggested in the past fifteen years has been the concept of enabling legislation which would permit bands that are dissatisfied with the structure of the Indian Act to accept options relating to either (a) self-created mechanisms of self-government involving provincial and federal enabling legislation, such as the Sechelt Indian Band Self-Government Act, S.C. 1984-85-86, c. 27 and Sechelt Indian Government District Enabling Act, S.B.C. 1987, c. 16, or (b) enabling legislation which would be an alternative to the Indian Act, such as Bill C-52. There is merit in both approaches. With respect to individual statutes providing for self-government for individual bands, little comment is required. As noted earlier, it is estimated by the Department that 15–20 bands could pursue this route in the next five years. This process can be made available to bands to create a structure of self-government expressly tailored to their unique circumstances. No encouragement is necessary, for it is clear that a number of bands will pursue this process in the near future. The main drawback that I see is the large number of separate statutes — what about amendment? Will a future government balk at the idea of as many separate statutes as may be required? And, as Chief Louie of Westbank noted, the exercise of putting a separate statute in place is time-consuming and costly.

The idea of alternative statutory schemes for Indian government reached its high point in Bill C-52, which was designed to provide an alternative scheme to that presented by the Indian Act. Such an alternative could be opted into by bands wishing to avoid the constraints of the Indian Act. The Bill was drafted and placed on the parliamentary order paper without substantial consultation with major Indian groups. Since bands would not be compelled to opt into the new structure, the Minister apparently considered it appropriate to pursue this avenue without the more time-consuming process of consultation occurring beforehand. Each band was to be granted a broad area of self-definition in relation to its constitution under the proposed Act. The Bill failed passage because the government of the day was defeated in a general election.

Certain obvious defects of the <u>Indian Act</u> can be addressed by selective legislative amendment. On the other hand, an alternative statutory scheme, such as Bill C-52, aimed at creating a more up-to-date structure for Indian government would be an option available to bands who wanted to pursue it. Some people want change. Some do not. Modest alterations to the present Act (probably coupled with the enactment of a separate Indian Lands Act), plus an innovative optional statute such as Bill C-52, should satisfy both constituencies to the extent possible short of full self-government obtained by treaty or constitutional agreement. I am not optimistic that the latter is likely to happen in the immediate future. It may never happen. The present climate calls for some changes and I think the less dramatic ones can be achieved.

PART C

Recommendations for Interim Changes

I have decided to make specific recommendations for change in three principle areas. First, I make several recommendations intended to rationalize and clarify the structure of statute law and policy governing Indian lands. Second, I make a number of recommendations concerning sections of the Indian Act and practice relating to monies. Third, I make several recommendations relating to the powers and responsibilities of Indian governments and the Department's role in the process.

In relation to land, I have endeavoured to make recommendations which reconcile the patchwork of provisions in this area, with a view to creating an atmosphere of certainty, fairness, and opportunity. In relation to Indian monies, I have urged that the protective provisions of the Indian Act be adhered to and that fundamental change receive legislative support by means of self-government to be undertaken at a band's option. Finally, in relation to Indian governments, I recommend that their powers be enhanced, and that this enhancement take place in a framework of openness and accountability to band members.

Some of the difficulties which have been identified give rise to reasonably short-term solutions. In the event that some of the all-embracing proposals for reform are immediately acted upon, these short-term remedies would no longer be necessary. Some bands may wish to opt out of the present system. To accommodate this, I recommend that the present Act be amended and that new optional legislation be put in place. New comprehensive legislation should substitute, for the existing structure, an optional structure which would enable bands to assume devolved powers over federal programs and to exercise self-government or self-direction, which has been sought for some time. Appropriate amendments to the present Act would abolish some of the shortcomings and inconsistencies within the present structure. Bands wishing to stay within the existing Act would have a better version to work with.

I think it important to keep these two processes separate. If, as was agreed by virtually all of the parties before me, the Indian Act cannot be amended to eliminate its inherent paternalism, then I think it important that the differences between the present structure and the new structure be clearly demarcated by law and practice. Bands that are comfortable with the present system should continue to have the assurance and support of that system. Bands which want to undertake greater governance of their own affairs should be able to assume greater powers and, of course, greater responsibilities. A number of bands have both the capacity and the desire to assume those powers and responsibilities and I think it is incumbent upon Parliament to provide a suitable structure within which those ambitions can be realized.

Whether self-government is realized by way of constitutional amendment or statute, either specific to individual bands or generally, it is clear that the process will take time for even the most advanced bands who already have a plan of action. There are, meanwhile, some changes which appear to me necessary regarding the present legislation pending the arrival of a form or forms of self-government. The process of devolution, which was begun more than ten years ago and continues today, suffers in several aspects from lack of a legislative base. The process of devolution has been very useful in preparing Indian bands for greater self-direction. I hope and expect that the following suggested changes will bring the statute law more into accord with present policies aimed at strengthening and supporting Indian initiatives for self-government.

Land Matters

A. General Issues of Land Title and Tenure

The present Act has a regrettable lack of clarity concerning land tenures, title, and other interests in land. The legal title to reserve lands is vested in the Crown, but the beneficial interest in such lands resides in the band for whose use and benefit the reserve has been set apart. The band's interest in the reserve lands is held in common for all band members. This communal interest is affected by the provisions of Section 20 of the Act, which allows individual band members to acquire an interest in a portion of the reserve. An individual locatee who holds a Certificate of Possession acquires certain rights of use and occupation which may be transferred to another band member by sale, devise, or descent. These rights can override any interest of the band in the land covered by the Certificate of Possession (Boyer v. A.G. Canada (1986) 65 N.R. 305, at 311). Cultural forces apparently have created the perception on reserves that the holder of a Certificate of Possession is the holder of something approaching a fee simple or absolute title to the lands.

There appear to be several inconsistencies in how the Indian Act delineates the individual interest and the band interest in the same land. For example, the band may, by a vote of its members, surrender its reserve lands absolutely or conditionally, including lands that are held under a Certificate of Possession. At present, conditional surrenders for leasing are made. The holder of the Certificate of Possession (known as the locatee) may be compensated for improvements on the land, but it is uncertain whether he has the right to be compensated for his loss of use of the land. A locatee is prohibited from disposing of his interest to a non-member (Section 28), and may be forced to turn over his interest to the band if he ceases to be entitled to reside on the reserve (Section 25). On the other hand, by Section 58(3) of the Act, a locatee may apply to the Minister to lease the land for his sole benefit, and band council and other band members may have no right in law to approve or disapprove of that lease — Boyer v. A.G. Canada above. When the Minister, acting for a locatee, enters into long-term leases, such as a 99-year lease for residential development, a substantial issue arises as to whether this is an effective avoidance of the surrender process. Lands under such leases are clearly alienated for a lengthy period and if substantial portions are so leased, the reserve may lose its character. I adverted to this sort of issue earlier in this Report when discussing a proposed lengthening of the head lease at Mt. Boucherie Mobile Home Park.

The Boyer case in the Federal Court of Canada addressed a locatee lease issue. A band member sought approval of a 21-year locatee lease of land intended to be used for a full-service marina. The band administration opposed the lease and refused consent. The Minister effected the lease. The band administration sued. The band's position was that such a lease improperly avoided the surrender process, but Marceau, J. of the Federal Court of Appeal rejected that submission. His Lordship did say, however, that a longer term might involve a violation of the intent of the statute:

> When a lease is entered into pursuant to s.58(3), the circumstances are different altogether: no alienation is contemplated, the right to be transferred temporarily is the right to use which belongs to the individual Indian in possession and no interest of the Band can be affected (I repeat that of course I am talking about interest in a technical and legal sense; it is obvious that morally speaking the Band may always be concerned by the behaviour and attitude of its members). In my view, when he acts under s.58(3), the duty of the Minister is, so to speak, only toward the law: he cannot go beyond the power granted to him, which he would do if, under the guise of a lease, he was to proceed to what would be, for all practical purposes, an alienation of the land (certainly not the case here, the lease being for a term of 21 years with no special renewal clause); and he cannot let extraneous consideration enter into the exercise of this discretion, which would be the case if he was to take into account anything other than the benefit of the Indian in lawful possession of the land and at whose request he is acting. The duty of the Minister is simply not towards the Band. (supra, at 311–12)

The Court held that the 21-year lease did not infringe the surrender requirements and sustained the lease. The result could have been different if the lease had been long-term and amounted to a form of absolute alienation of the land.

In some respects the interest of a locatee is similar to the interests of a holder of a fee simple interest. The surrender provisions of the Act and the legal authority of the band to surrender locatee land notwithstanding the wishes of a locatee creates a measure of uncertainty about the precise interest of the holder of a Certificate of Possession. With the growth of commercial and residential leasing on reserves, such collisions of interests will become more common and it would be desirable to address them now so that the position is clarified.

Another difficulty with respect to the present land regime is that of administering the Act. So long as there are inconsistencies and uncertainties, there will be administrative difficulties. Absence of clear band jurisdiction over surrendered land has created great uncertainty as to regulation of business enterprises on surrendered lands. Coupled with the absence of a taxation power, the normal municipal efforts to create an environment conducive to the development of industrial or business activities is lacking on most reserves. Some of these difficulties will be ameliorated by the Kamloops Amendments. These proposed amendments do not, however, address all of the uncertainties concerning land tenure that inhere in the present statute.

Another difficulty of administration concerns the Minister's involvement in almost all dealings with land. The Minister is often required to exercise discretion where there is a conflict or potential conflict between the collective and individual uses of the land. The Department historically has been responsive to cultural shifts. Recently this has favoured the collective interests of the band as expressed by band councils. It places the Department in a most invidious position if it tries to reconcile the locatee's interest and a band's interest in lands. If there is a degree of uncertainty, it tends to furnish ammunition to both sides to indict the Department. The clearer the demarcation, the less room for controversy.

Perhaps the most fundamental difficulty in relation to the development of band lands is attracting private financing. Bands such as the Westbank Band should have the opportunity to grant security over their lands so that good development is encouraged. Indian people appear unanimous in their desire to preserve in the band, ultimate title in band lands. However, as noted by several witnesses, some Indian people want greater freedom to mortgage their property. Such financing, of course, carries with it the consequences of default. Indian or non-Indian businesses located on band lands will, like businesses elsewhere, fail on occasion. Lending institutions will not advance monies without some assurance that they can deal freely with the security interest being granted to them. Accordingly, steps must be taken in the case of long-term leases to afford lending institutions a clear method by which they can execute upon the remaining term of any lease and thus realize on the property that was posted as security for a loan. The present Act is less than perfect in its delineation of the respective interests in lands and it fails to provide for realization.

I recommend that more detailed legislative provisions be enacted to clarify the different interests in Indian lands, in order to enhance the ability to obtain financing for projects on Indian lands.

The proposed Kamloops Amendments (which I deal with later in more detail) would extend the definition of "reserve" to expressly include conditionally surrendered (designated) lands and at the same time stipulate that the prohibition against mortgaging Indian real property on a reserve would be relaxed. This would not affect the underlying band interest, and would permit a leasehold interest to be mortgaged and subject to a form of execution. At Westbank, many of the developments on the reserve lands were by way of locatee lease. If a lender takes security on a locatee lease, he must be able to realize on his security should the borrower default on the secured loan.

The Toussowasket mobile home park development at Westbank illustrates potential problems that can arise regarding security on locatee leases. The locatee decided to develop his land through a company which he controlled (Toussowasket Enterprises Ltd.). His company took a locatee lease on the property and offered that leasehold interest as security to lenders. Evidence adduced before the Inquiry indicated that there were problems with one lender's security because the development lacked proper access. The mobile home park went into receivership. The Band Council refused to approve any assignment of the leasehold interest by the holder of the security. At the time, it was Department policy to request approval from the band council before permitting any assignment of a leasehold interest in reserve lands. The current Department policy on assignments of leasehold interest apparently has changed. This policy is set out in the *Land Management and Procedures Manual*:

> 6.6.1(d) <u>Band Council Consent</u>. It is a matter of program policy to obtain the written concurrence of the Band Council, and the Locatee where applicable, to the proposed disposition. Some Bands and some Locatees have required that assignees, sub-lessees, mortgagors etc., pay considerable sums to individual Indians as a condition precedent to their recommendation for approval of a proposed transaction between two non-Indian holders of an interest under a lease. There is no provision under the <u>Indian Act</u> to support such a practice. Obtaining the written concurrence from Band Councils and Locatees is a policy of courtesy to the beneficial users of Indian Reserve land, and the Minister or his representative has no authority to capriciously refuse approval of such dispositions of leasehold interest without firm and substantial reasons, none of which comprise a failure to pay for concurrence from Bands or individual Locatees. Where there are substantiated reasons for disapproving a proposed disposition or encumbrance of leasehold interest, such reasons and recommendations must be submitted to the Minister or his delegated representative for consideration. Where a Band Council or Locatee does not, for any reason, provide concurrence or substantiated reasons for non-

recurrence within a reasonable period of time, having regard for the circumstances, a letter over the signature of the Regional Director General should be forwarded to the Band Council outlining that the Minister may not, unless specifically authorized by the terms of the head lease, arbitrarily refuse his approval and registration of the documents evidencing the disposition of the leasehold interest.

As long as the above procedure is followed, it would appear that a secured creditor who is attempting to realize on his security by assigning the leasehold interest to a third party will be successful. However, the events at Westbank demonstrate that substantial pressure may be placed on the Department to deny a secured lender full freedom to realize on his security.

I have considered whether anything needs to be done where bands have authority to manage their lands. I think that in cases where new enterprises are being established on such lands, all must clearly understand who they are dealing with and who will be able to provide such safeguards as are deemed necessary. Where the Department is contemplating the grant of authorities to a band on whose reserve(s) there are a number of tenants, it would seem a sensible precondition to require the band to covenant with the existing operators to not unreasonably refuse consent to dispositions. That seems to be a method to prevent future controversy.

I recommend that the current Departmental policy regarding band council approval of dispositions relating to locatee lands be continued, and that the Department discourage councils from creating administrative delays in the approval of such dispositions, especially concerning realization of security interests.

B. Locatee Leases

The pattern of land holding across the country varies from region to region. While allotments are used by approximately 80 per cent of the bands in B.C. and 80 per cent of the bands in the Maritimes, fewer than 20 per cent of the prairie bands have used them as a means of dividing land. Many of these differences stem from cultural traditions, but they also arise out of the economic circumstances of the band. Allocation of land to locatees was very much the norm at Westbank.

By leasing his land pursuant to Section 58(3) of the Indian Act, a locatee may receive substantial personal benefits. In many cases, locatee lands are leased for many years. Depending on the kind of development, a long-term lease may be required in order for developers to secure adequate financing. The present policy of the Department is to allow locatee leases up to 21 years in length, subject to approval by the band council. Leases over 21 years require a band vote for approval. This appears analogous to the requirement for band approval to surrenders.

The Department also encourages bands to establish a revenue-sharing policy whereby some percentage of the rent received by a locatee accrues to the benefit of the band.

In the Boyer decision discussed above, the Court considered the conflict between the band's communal interest in all of its lands and the individual interest of a locatee. The band argued that the locatee lease provisions were inconsistent with the surrender provisions of the Act and, because a locatee lease was a disposition of band lands, the band wanted to have final say about whether a locatee lease would be granted. The Court held that since the specific provision in the Act governing locatee leases (Section 58(3)) excluded any role of the band or band council in granting the lease, the band council was not entitled to any veto power. In the case of a locatee lease, the individual interest prevailed over the general interest of the band in all its lands. The only caveat the Court placed on this reasoning was to the effect that if the term of a lease was so long as to amount to an alienation of the land, then surrender considerations could arise.

At Westbank, the Band membership held a vote on the issue of locatee leases and revenue-sharing. A large majority of the eligible voters voted in support of the following resolution:

1. That the terms and conditions of individual Locatee leases on our Reserves need only be approved by the Band Council and not by a majority of Electors.
2. That the Locatees leasing their land under Section 58.(3) of the Indian Act should be entitled to receive all the rentals from such leases and should not have to pay any percentage to the Band.
3. That neither the Band nor the Department should interfere with a person's personal and fundamental right to provide for his/her children in the manner he/she considers appropriate.

The Department has apparently abided by the wishes of the Westbank Band as expressed in that Band vote held on February 21, 1980. The first item of the Band resolution appears to overrule the present national policy of the Department to require a band vote on any locatee lease that exceeds a term of 21 years. I think that a major consideration underlying this Departmental policy is a fear of potential liability based on an allegation of breach of fiduciary duty.

I believe that the policy of the Department should be to require a band vote to approve locatee leases only for leases over 45 years. A policy requiring locatee leases exceeding 45 years to receive the support of a majority of band members would allow members to become fully informed about long-term development proposals and to consider the possible consequences of any such proposed development. Because a long-term lease will affect the use of band lands for many years, it is appropriate that the membership at large be given some input into the

396

decision to lease. When band lands are leased for long terms, a conditional surrender is required and the surrender provisions of the Indian Act require a band vote on the terms of any conditional surrender. A locatee lease for 99 years is as much an alienation of band lands as is a conditional surrender for 99 years. While the band interest in locatee lands is residual in nature, there is a vital interest of band members to be addressed if the nature/character of the reserve is to be altered. The democratic process demands that band members should have some say in such matters.

I understand why the Department is nervous about leasing matters. Nonetheless, I think locatees need a measure of freedom. At some point, their absolute rights collide with wider band interests. In Boyer, 21 years was not regarded as an alienation. My sense is that 45 years is roughly the transition point. I believe that amendment of Section 58 may be necessary to achieve the object suggested and to put the matter beyond controversy. Bands opting out (as adverted to earlier in the Report) of the Indian Act will have to consider whether they wish to adopt a more or less stringent approach to this question. This is the sort of issue that will be of concern to more developed or advanced bands. It only arises where Certificates of Possession are in existence. David Sparks said:

> Westbank, and through the Okanagan Valley, there are a large number of location certificates. There are a large number of location certificates on certain reserves in the south end of Vancouver Island. There are virtually no location certificates in either Manitoba, Saskatchewan, or Alberta, or Northern Ontario. There are a large number of location certificates on reserves in southern Ontario, and also a fair number in the Maritimes.
> It's a pattern, and I don't know why it goes that way.

Is it any accident that many areas where there is a preference for Certificates of Possession are areas of more valuable land? If the above suggestions are adopted, I think a workable compromise between band interests and individual interests can be effected.

One further matter deserves mention. A pre-paid long-term locatee lease is not economically different from a sale, but its use may permit individuals to avoid the surrender process and the economic consequences of surrender. In order to fund band management of reserve lands, I think that band governments have the right and obligation to seek a portion of lease revenue to compensate for the band's loss of its residual interest in leased lands. This can assist self-government to be realized in its fiscal as well as its administrative respects.

I recommend that the Department encourage bands to consider the implications of long-term locatee leases on band revenues.

C. Land Leasing

The negotiation and setting of rents on leased reserve land was a source of controversy and conflict at Westbank. The majority of land leases there stipulate that rent be reviewed at five-year intervals. Under the terms of the lease contracts, the Minister or his authorized representative was designated as the authority to determine the rent. If a party was not satisfied with the rent as determined by the Minister, he could appeal to the Federal Court. However, typically, before a lessee could appeal to the Federal Court, and pending its decision, he was required to pay such rent as had been determined by the Minister or his authorized representative. In order to ensure that the rent review process works well, it is important that the parties have a rent fixing procedure that is both efficient and fair.

In the recent past at Westbank there has been some confusion concerning just who has the power to fix or determine rents — the Band Council or the Minister as represented by an official of the regional office. This confusion may have been contributed to by the Department's policy of devolving additional administrative functions to Indian bands. Pursuant to the terms of the 1977 Agreement, the Department of Indian Affairs agreed that the Westbank Band Council would, inter alia:

> Negotiate with lessees and permittees as to revision of rentals, new rentals and enforcement of terms and conditions in agreements.

Then Chief Ronald Derrickson not only negotiated with lessees but also undertook to determine rental rates on a number of occasions. In one case, Mr. Derrickson purported to determine the rent for one lessee at figure X. Two years later, the Department purported to determine the rent on the same lease in a higher amount. The matter remains unresolved even though these events occurred in the early 1980's.

It seems to me that it would be beneficial for all parties if in ordinary cases a single authority for determining the rent could be clearly spelled out and adhered to. Because of the nature of reserve land, all leases are made in the name of the Crown. The Minister or his appointed agent is given authority to fix or determine the rent. This appears to be a contractual matter agreed to by the contracting parties. Because the Crown holds reserve land for the benefit of a band, the Minister has a duty to act in the best interests of the band or band members with regard to any land transactions (Guerin v. The Queen (1984) 2 S.C.R. 55 N.R.161). As noted above, the Minister also appears in the usual case to have a contractual right or duty to determine rent according to the terms of the lease. These duties need not be in conflict. By setting the rent according to the terms of the lease, the Minister or his authorized representative is acting according to law. Clearly, it is in the best interests of the locatee or the band to have the rent determined according to law. Therefore, by setting the rent pursuant to the terms of the lease, the Minister or his authorized representative will never on that account be acting contrary to the Indian interest. However, the person setting the rent must have a scrupulous regard for the economic welfare of the locatee or the band, as the case may be.

How is the Minister or his authorized representative to arrive at an appropriate rent? There must be sufficient expertise available to enable them to properly determine the rental figure for the succeeding period. The Lands, Revenues and Trusts (L.R.&T.) branch of the Department is responsible for managing Indian lands. Because of the crucial importance of the reserve land base to the social and economic well-being of Indian people, it is essential that the L.R.&T. branch have access to professional advice from persons with special expertise and training.

I recommend that the Department of Indian Affairs employ contract counsel to deal with matters such as lease negotiations and litigation arising therefrom.

Such a resource group of experienced professionals should be empowered to act on behalf of locatees in the negotiation process and in other matters involving the use and management of land. Normally, such services should be available to bands and locatees through band councils. The lawyers in the first instance would liaise with the council on the matter. This would allow participation by both the locatee and band council in the negotiation and rent-fixing process. Access to appraisal and legal expertise is necessary if the interests of Indian people are to be properly protected. In cases where the parties could not agree on a rent before the contractual deadline, it would still be the duty of the Minister or his authorized representative to set the rent. They would determine the amount having regard to the best advice and information available. If the Department has the ability to draw upon the expertise of a skilled group of professionals specializing in leasing matters, the Minister will be better informed when determining rents. This is not to say that L.R.&T. are not served by good and dedicated people today — I simply say that the growing complexities of Indian economic affairs demand more sophisticated resources.

By their nature, most land transactions require legal expertise. At the present time the Department of Indian Affairs, like all federal government departments, depends generally upon the Department of Justice for legal advice. For a variety of reasons, the Department of Justice is not always best suited to deal with lease negotiations and litigation. I note certain material that was placed before the Commission (A Review of Land Management and Development Policies, Nov. 21, 1983 in Exhibit 198). This material was produced by a special steering committee chaired by Mr. Gilbert Joe of the Sechelt Band. The report of the committee contained, among other things, the following comments:

The Role of the Federal Justice Department in Band Affairs Should be Restricted to the Absolute Minimum Necessary "for Saving Harmless the Crown".

From the information available to this Committee, it would appear that the Regional Office of the Department of Justice was first brought onto the scene in the early part of 1972. By Pink Circular No. 979 dated March 29, 1972, Larry E. Wight, Regional Director of Indian Affairs, British Columbia Region, announced to his program managers "that all future legal services from this Region will be obtained in Vancouver". Mr. Wight spoke of "this new working relationship" and mentioned that "this pilot program for the British Columbia Region" would be watched very closely in Ottawa ". . . as a model on which to base the direction of legal services in other Regions". Finally, he urged the ". . . proper use of our new Legal Advisors for the British Columbia Region". Attached to this Policy Circular was a copy of Mr. Wight's letter to the Justice Department confirming that legal assistance would be required in a number of specified areas including land transactions, negotiations for "major projects", resource agreements and assistance in the drafting of Band by-laws.

In answer to an enquiry from the Union of B.C. Indian Chiefs, N.D. Mullins, Q.C., Director of the Justice Department's Vancouver Regional Office, wrote in February 1973 explaining his view of his Department's duties and responsibilities "in relation to Indian reserve land and Indian matters in British Columbia". Perhaps the most illuminating paragraph from Mr. Mullins' letter is the following:

> To expedite our processing of Indian land matters, I find it easiest to look on Indian reserves as land which belongs to the Crown, that all alienation of the title to Reserve lands by lease or otherwise must be done in the name of the Crown, and all actions to enforce rights in relation to the Reserves should be brought in the name of the Crown. The legal service functions of the Department of Justice are not and ought not to be political in nature and thus we try to avoid becoming involved in such problems as claims of aboriginal title, or that Reserve lands are held by the Crown in trust for the Indians.

In responding to the specific questions submitted by the Union, he summarized his comments as follows:

> 1. In the final analysis we must take our instructions from the Department of Indian Affairs and Northern Development.
> 2. Title to Indian reserves is vested in Her Majesty and it is Her interests which we must preserve and protect. However, Her primary interests in such lands is that they be used for the benefit of Indians and consequently that is also the interest of the Department of Justice.
> 3. We can best perform our legal functions if we have direct dealing with the Indians and Departmental officials during the whole program of economic development of Reserve lands.

Mr. Wight circulated a copy of this letter with his Pink Circular No. 1012, commenting that "... the services being provided by the Department of Justice are fairly clearly defined in their letter and we should regard this as their role in handling land matters until further clarification is received.." However, he cautioned against involving the Justice lawyers in all negotiations as he did not consider their Regional Office to be "adequately staffed to fill this role for some 400 or 500 land transactions yearly" although he did believe it to be "a good idea for major developments." John Ciaccia, Assistant Deputy Minister of Indian Affairs, was not necessarily even convinced of this. In a discerning directive of "cautionary remarks" to Mr. Wight, he agreed that cases should be referred to Mr. Mullins for his review but that Regional Indian Affairs should retain the prerogative of referring to D.I.A. headquarters any opinions that were not appropriate to their Department's relationship with Indian people. In Mr. Ciaccia's words: "Our responsibility is to service the needs of the Indian people, whereas Justice is responsible for saving harmless the Crown. Therefore, conflicts of interest are possible..."

... The Justice Department must be relegated to its only proper role, that of acting solely as legal advisor protecting the interests of Her Majesty. Until we can achieve self-government, our principal objective, the intrusion of the Justice Department lawyers into our affairs should be kept to the absolute minimum necessary for them to protect the Crown...

In addition to the foregoing conflict considerations, the Department of Justice is often not called upon until lease disputes have reached the litigation stage; undue time may be consumed while the assigned lawyer familiarizes himself with the salient aspects of the case. Clearly, the Indian interest is not always identical to the concerns of the Crown, as the comments quoted above illustrate. Thus, involvement of the Department of Justice as advocate for a band or locatee may not be appropriate. The Indian client may not always feel that the Department of Justice is working only in his interest. Such a perception makes the task of counsel nearly impossible. Where there is the possibility of divided allegiance, the better course is to take steps to resolve the conflict. There is always going to be a possible conflict in having Justice act as the lawyer in these matters — the suggestion I am making appears to me to be a practical method of avoiding the conflict and ensuring fair and competent handling of land issues.

Under the proposed system, both the locatee (band), and the lessee (or counsel for the lessee) would have the benefit of dealing with professionals devoted solely to the resolution of issues arising from leases on reserve lands. The lessee would know who he was dealing with throughout the negotiation process. The locatee (band) would receive expert advice; and the availability of such expertise at an early stage of negotiations should promote a timely and fair resolution of issues. Of course, if a locatee (band) wished to turn to outside advisers, he (it) should be able, at his (its) own expense, to do so.

If rental issues cannot be resolved and the matter proceeds to litigation, a court will be the ultimate arbiter. It can award costs to the successful party. In a case where a locatee or a band has unreasonably insisted that the rent be set at an unrealistic figure and has pursued the matter unsuccessfully in court, the Crown should have the ability to seek recovery of any costs awarded against Her Majesty. These cases probably would be quite rare because in many instances the Crown might feel that there had been a legitimate issue to be tried and would not seek recovery of costs. But in order to deal with instances of unreason or intransigence, the remedy should be available.

As I said above, land is a crucial underpinning to the well-being of Indian people. Money and resources expended in the better utilization of this precious resource will be handsomely repaid. I make these suggestions with a view to increasing the efficiency of utilization of the Indian land resource.

D. Management and Control of Reserve Lands

The Indian Act provides for the transfer of some of the Minister's powers over the management and control of reserve land and surrendered reserve lands to a band. The Department is of the view that by Section 53 of the Act, a band may assume management and control over its conditionally surrendered lands. Section 53 reads as follows:

> 53. (1) The Minister or a person appointed by him for the purpose may manage, sell, lease or otherwise dispose of surrendered lands in accordance with this Act and the terms of the surrender.
> (2) Where the original purchaser of surrendered lands is dead and the heir, assignee or devisee of the original purchaser applies for a grant of the lands, the Minister may, upon receipt of proof in such manner as he directs and requires in support of any claim for the grant and upon being satisfied that the claim has been equitably and justly established, allow the claim and authorize a grant to issue accordingly.
> (3) No person who is appointed to manage, sell, lease or otherwise dispose of surrendered lands or who is an officer or servant of Her Majesty employed in the Department may, except with the approval of the Governor in Council, acquire directly or indirectly an interest in surrendered lands.

Although Section 53 does not specifically provide that the Minister may delegate his powers of management of surrendered lands to a band or band council, in practice this is often done. The section contemplates that the Minister may appoint a person for the purpose of managing, etc., surrendered lands. At Westbank, the Minister appointed the Band Council to manage its surrendered lands. There is, however, some uncertainty as to whether the section in fact permits the Minister to appoint a body such as a band council.

I recommend that Section 53 of the Indian Act be amended to specifically authorize the Minister to appoint a band council to manage surrendered lands of the band.

Under Section 53(3) any person who is appointed to manage surrendered lands is prohibited from having any interest in those surrendered lands. The prohibition does not make sense when a band council has been appointed to manage the surrendered lands. That subsection therefore should be consequentially amended to except a band council from the general prohibition. Members of council would of course continue to be subject to the general law concerning conflict of interest.

Pursuant to Section 60 of the Act, a band may be granted the power to manage and control its own lands. That section reads as follows:

> 60. (1) The Governor in Council may at the request of a band grant to the band the right to exercise such control and management over lands in the reserve occupied by that band as the Governor in Council considers desirable.
>
> (2) The Governor in Council may at any time withdraw from a band a right conferred upon the band under subsection(1).

It should be noted that the right to manage and control reserve lands can be granted to the band as opposed to a band council. Section 2(3) of the Act states that when a power is conferred upon a band, it must be exercised pursuant to the consent of a majority of the band's electors, and when a power is conferred upon a band council, it must be exercised pursuant to a majority vote of the council quorum. The current practice of the Department is to require the band to vote on the request to obtain Section 60 land management powers. If the band wants to delegate its powers to the band council, it expresses that wish in the vote. This was done at Westbank when the Band received Section 60 powers. The Act does not expressly permit a delegation of powers from the band to the band council. In addition to the problem created by the legal principle that a delegate cannot subdelegate his powers, the statute seems to indicate quite clearly that a power conferred upon a band by any provision of the Act can be exercised only by a majority of the band's electors. It seems to me reasonable that certain powers of management and control over band lands can be more conveniently handled by the band council. However, because reserve lands are set apart for the benefit of all band members in common, and because the land base is so crucial to the economic well-being of band members, it is important that the membership at large should have a voice in major decisions affecting reserve lands. Therefore, I do not recommend that the wording of Section 60 simply be changed to allow the Governor in Council to bestow the power of management and control on a band council directly. If those powers are to be transferred from the Minister, they ought to be transferred to the band as a whole.

I recommend that Section 60 be amended to specifically allow an Indian band to further delegate some or all of its powers of management and control of reserve lands to the band council. The terms of any subdelegation should specify the limits of authority bestowed upon the band council and stipulate in what circumstances a band vote should be held on decisions relating to the management or control of reserve lands.

E. Allotments

An issue that can cause controversy among band members is the question of land allotments. As I have noted elsewhere, land forms the great underlying economic base for Indian people. Accordingly, any dealing in that precious commodity very much affects their well-being. Later in this Report I suggest that band councils should prepare an annual report to keep band members properly advised of band business generally.

I recommend that all land allotments be specifically noted in the annual report prepared by any band.

Special care must be taken where there is an allotment of land being made by a band to a member of the band executive or to a member of the immediate family of an executive member. In those instances, it would seem desirable to provide notice to band members of the proposed course of action so that the matter may be raised before the band council in somewhat the same method that certain zoning matters are raised before municipal councils. I doubt that I could analogize band government to a municipal government generally, but it does seem to me that the sort of procedure used in municipal zoning matters (dealing with land) would be a useful model in the case of allotments to band executive members or their immediate families.

It seems undesirable to require that there be a formal band vote held for such allotments because that could be overkill in matters not of sufficient general interest to call for the consideration of the whole band. But, it may well be the case that certain individuals in the band would be interested in or object to the proposed allotment. In order to ensure that there be no foundation for an allegation of favouritism or undue influence, such allotments should be raised in public before the band council for the benefit of interested parties. There ought to be sufficient notice given to all band members of any proposed allotment, together with sufficient details of the proposal, to enable members to reach an informed decision on the issue.

I recommend that fair public hearing procedures relating to allotments to band executive members and their immediate family be provided for either by statute or by regulation.

A simple remedy for failure to follow such a procedure would be to make provision for a court to declare an allotment void if the appropriate procedure had not been followed. Obviously this would have to be subject to some limitation period. The court should be endowed with the power or discretion to excuse good faith exceptions or procedural errors of a minor nature. There must be a balancing of the interests of fairness and the operative necessities of band government.

I recommend that a right of appeal be provided regarding an allotment of lands to a member of the executive or an immediate family member of such executive, and that a court be entitled to declare an allotment void for failure to follow the prescribed procedures, with the discretion to dismiss appeals where any error that occurred was made in good faith or was of a minor nature.

F. Land Registry

A general refrain by many witnesses was that the present system of registration under the Indian Act needs improvement. The Act itself provides for the establishment of a Land Registry system in simple terms:

> 21. There shall be kept in the Department a register, to be known as the Reserve Land Register, in which shall be entered particulars relating to Certificates of Possession and Certificates of Occupation and other transactions respecting land in a reserve.
> 55. (1) There shall be kept in the Department a register, to be known as the Surrendered Lands Register, in which shall be entered particulars in connection with any lease or other disposition of surrendered lands by the Minister or any assignment thereof.
> (2) A conditional assignment shall not be registered.
> (3) Registration of an assignment may be refused until proof of its execution has been furnished.
> (4) An assignment registered under this section is valid against an unregistered assignment of an assignment subsequently registered.

For reasons which are largely historical, the use of the provincial registry systems appears to be considered unacceptable by most of the Indian groups involved. There has been some use of the provincial system in British Columbia.

The Department recognizes that a number of bands issue "buckshee" leases. A "buckshee" lease is an unregistered lease of reserve lands. The primary reason for the use of "buckshee" leases would appear to be the perceived bureaucratic requirements of the Department under the present system. Lease applications and the transfer and assignment of leases are subject to approval by the Minister. Long-term leases under current policy require Department of Justice advice. If it is perceived that the registration system is too expensive or unwieldy, there will be a tendency to try to operate outside the system. This is not the best practice because of the inherent illegality of these "buckshee" leases. The Registry system must be made more accessible and efficient so that it can be utilized by bands at varying stages of development.

I suggest below that a separate statute dealing with Indian land is needed. The Department seems to be of the view that legislative change is necessary with respect to land. The present Act is quite skeletal in its provision for land registration. It appears to me that a major interim measure required is additional funding to upgrade the present system in Ottawa. I think the system must be enhanced because I have no basis for believing that integration into the provincial systems is likely soon.

I recommend that additional funding be provided to improve the operation of the Indian Land Registry and that the necessary regulations for its more effective operation be enacted.

G. An Indian Lands Act

I have noted difficulties with the present Indian Act and policy relating to the system of land interests, locatee leases, the management of lands, allotments, the granting and administration of leases, and the Indian Land Registry. Indian land matters are dealt with quite sparsely in the present Act and as I mentioned in Part A of Section II, an Indian Lands Act has been proposed. I believe that such an Act should be passed. I hasten to say that this is consistent with the process of self-government. Such a statute would address a multitude of existing issues and would afford a coherent legal structure for all bands across Canada. I think the present statutory provisions are too rudimentary for the age in which we live. As I said earlier, such an approach should be of assistance to the better utilization of Indian lands.

I recommend the enactment of a comprehensive Indian Lands Act.

Indian Monies

A. Revenue Monies

The Indian Act defines Indian monies as: "all monies collected, received or held by Her Majesty for the use and benefit of Indians or bands". The Act further distinguishes capital and revenue Indian monies in Section 62:

> All Indian moneys derived from the sale of surrendered lands or the sale of capital assets of a band shall be deemed to be capital moneys of the band and all Indian moneys other than capital moneys shall be deemed to be revenue moneys of the band.

By Section 69 of the Act, the Governor in Council may by order permit a band to control, manage, and expend its own revenue monies. There is no equivalent provision to grant a band control over its own capital monies. Naturally, Indian bands prefer to have control of their monies. I noted earlier that the lack of any provision to allow bands to control their own capital monies had led to pressure on the Department to categorize monies as revenue rather than as capital.

Any power to manage and control revenue monies that may be given, pursuant to Section 69, is given to a band and not to the band council. In this respect, Section 69 is similar to Section 60, referred to above. I was told that most bands have been granted the power to control their own revenue money under Section 69. In practice, however, the day-to-day management of revenue monies is undertaken by the band council as opposed to the band as a whole. It makes sense that the power to manage and expend certain sums of the band's revenue monies should be delegated to the band council, which is charged with the day-to-day administration of band affairs. As counsel for the Department of Indian Affairs submitted to me, it does not make sense that a band vote should be required every time that it is necessary to purchase a new box of pencils for use at the band office. Still, I think it important that the band members should have adequate input on the expenditure of resources which belong to the band as a whole. For example, I was told that some bands hold a vote on a proposed annual budget and authorize the band council to undertake the expenditures indicated in that budget. This seems to be a reasonable way of providing the band members with general input while allowing the band executive to make day-to-day decisions regarding the expenditure of specific funds. I think that with respect to major investments of band funds, the band membership should be consulted prior to the investment and their support should be obtained. Failure to do so in certain cases at Westbank fuelled much controversy. Such failure in any band is a potential source of trouble.

My recommendation regarding Section 69 is similar to my recommendation regarding Section 60 in that I believe that the power should continue to be granted in the first instance to the band as opposed to the band council. However, Section 69 should be amended specifically to allow for the band members to subdelegate certain of those powers to the band council. It would be up to individual bands to decide what terms of limitation, if any, to impose, but possible terms of the subdelegation could limit the band council's power of expenditure to certain dollar amounts or require band approval in potential conflict of interest situations.

I recommend that Section 69 of the <u>Indian Act</u> be amended to allow a delegation of power by the band to the band council, subject to such terms and conditions as are deemed fit by the band.

B. *Capital Monies*

As noted in the submissions before me, the Department is faced with pressures for change and a liberalization of the treatment of Indian capital monies. These pressures are evidenced by the demands for transfers of capital monies, and by the requests for per capita capital distributions under Section 64(1)(a) of the Indian Act.

As I noted earlier, there was pressure to pay out capital monies to bands during a time when long-term rates paid by government on trust funds were low. This sort of controversy continues to simmer to the present day, and there is considerable debate concerning the role of the band and the role of the Minister in dealing with capital funds. The Act here, too, is quite paternalistic and rudimentary in its treatment of this subject. It is out of step with economically advanced bands. A significant number of bands want more flexibility regarding the use of capital money on band projects; those wishes should be satisfied as much as possible. There is considerable tension about this issue between wealthy bands and the Department and early resolution of this tension is desirable.

Section 64 of the Indian Act contains provisions permitting the expenditure of capital monies:

> 64. (1) With the consent of the council of a band, the Minister may authorize and direct the expenditure of capital moneys of the band.
>
> (*a*) to distribute per capita to the members of the band an amount not exceeding fifty per cent of the capital moneys of the band derived from the sale of surrendered lands;
>
> (*b*) to construct and maintain roads, bridges, ditches and water courses on the reserves or on surrendered lands;
>
> (*c*) to construct and maintain outer boundary fences on reserves;
>
> (*d*) to purchase land for use by the band as a reserve or as an addition to a reserve;
>
> (*e*) to purchase for the band the interest of a member of the band in lands on a reserve;
>
> (*f*) to purchase livestock and farm implements, farm equipment, or machinery for the band;
>
> (*g*) to construct and maintain on or in connection with a reserve such permanent improvements or works as in the opinion of the Minister will be of permanent value to the band or will constitute a capital investment;
>
> (*h*) to make to members of the band, for the purpose of promoting the welfare of the band, loans not exceeding one-half of the total value of
>
>> (i) the chattels owned by the borrower, and
>> (ii) the land with respect to which he holds or is eligible to receive a Certificate of Possession,
>
> and may charge interest and take security therefor;
>
> (*i*) to meet expenses necessarily incidental to the management of lands on a reserve, surrendered lands and any band property;

(*j*) to construct houses for members of the band, to make loans to members of the band for building purposes with or without security and to provide for the guarantee of loans made to members of the band for building purposes; and

(*k*) for any other purpose that in the opinion of the Minister is for the benefit of the band.

Department policy now is to allow bands a greater role in determining the direction and expenditure of their capital monies.

One difficulty with Section 64 is the Department's practice of paying over capital monies to the band under Section 64(1)(k) for purposes which are defined and supervised by the band. The Department's policy of granting band council greater responsibility in this area conflicts with the statutory directive that the Minister "authorize and direct the expenditure of capital monies". As I have said before, by surrendering its statutory role of authorizing and directing the expenditure of capital monies, the Minister and the Department may leave themselves open to legal attack.

From the Westbank experience, I think it can be said that the Department has on occasion taken an expansive view as to what constitutes revenue monies as opposed to capital monies. I know that the motivation was sincere, but there is a danger that the Department can be too easily persuaded to follow a course that may properly require full band consideration. I think it important that the Department recognize its responsibility to band members so as to ensure that revenue monies are truly only those monies which are not related to or arise out of capital assets.

Several concrete examples of this conflict between capital and revenue emerged at the hearings. With respect to a matter in Ontario, it was said that a settlement of an aboriginal rights claim was characterized as being 90 per cent revenue monies. That allocation relative to the settlement of an aboriginal or fiduciary claim may well be the result of a desire to avoid the strictures of the present Act concerning capital monies.

With respect to Westbank, the Band wished the compensation monies for the highway project on Reserve 10 to be classified and paid as revenue monies to the Band. The written agreement between the Department, the Ministry of Highways, and the Band contemplated that those monies could be treated as revenue monies. The Department was reluctant to have the monies so treated, but the episode displays the pressures and pitfalls in this area. I see no reason why Indian bands should not be given greater control over the management and expenditure of their capital monies.

I recommend that the <u>Indian Act</u> be amended to allow bands to more effectively control and manage their capital monies.

Any new provision could be similar to that found in Section 69; however, I believe that safeguards should again be included to protect the interests of all band members. It would not be wise to allow a band council which may represent a small portion of the band's current political and social thinking to have untrammelled governance of the assets that could be the major basis of the band's economic future. Therefore, in order to afford some measure of protection to the capital assets of the band, I think that any amendment should stipulate that bands could only expend capital monies on capital projects. Such a stipulation would be consistent with the philosophy underlying the present Section 64.

Evidence adduced at the Inquiry revealed that many bands do not treat capital and revenue monies separately once they have received authorization for the expenditure of capital monies pursuant to Section 64. If bands are to be given the right to control and manage the expenditure of their own capital monies, they must account for these monies separately from their revenue monies. A suggestion that might be considered is whether it would be advisable for there to be an officer similar to a provincial Inspector of Municipalities. Such an officer would have a similar responsibility to ensure that bands' capital monies were separately accounted for and expended only for the purpose of capital projects.

Section 64(1)(a) allows for a per capita distribution to members of the band of an amount not exceeding 50 per cent of the capital monies derived from the sale of surrendered lands. This per capita payment is in no way related to capital projects of the band. The subsection is an anomaly among the several other subsections, all of which are related to capital projects. As I have noted in Appendix A to this Report dealing with statutory history, the original purpose of the per capita distribution was to encourage bands to alienate (sell) their reserve lands. Originally, the permitted yearly per capita distribution was only 10 per cent. It was raised to 50 per cent in an effort to encourage Indian bands to surrender their lands for sale. Today it is unusual in the extreme to have reserve lands surrendered for sale. Both the Department and Indian people are firmly opposed to such sales. The rationale for the practice of paying per capita monies has thus been wholly repudiated and is in fact contrary to present policy. The per capita payments practice therefore needs to be re-examined.

The reason having vanished, why should per capita distribution remain one of the permissible expenditures of capital monies? The underlying philosophy of the per capita payment — to encourage Indian bands to sell their reserve lands — is repugnant to the interests and the aspirations of Indian people today. The legal maxim that when the reason ceases, the law should cease seems to be applicable here. If a band chooses to make a per capita distribution of its monies to individual band members, such a payment could be made out of the revenue monies of the band.

I recommend that the provision permitting a per capita distribution from a band's capital monies be repealed.

I would like also to see the money (and the responsibility therefor) transferred to bands. Occasionally bands might decide to authorize per capita payments, but it should be recognized that this would be unusual. A good analogy would be the provisions in a will enabling trustees to encroach on capital for the extraordinary expenses of a beneficiary. The danger with per capita payments as a matter of course is that the practice can destroy the corpus of the fund too quickly. What is left for future generations?

C. Band Financial Accounting and Disclosure

It is not unusual for Indian bands to have a great many transactions with individual members of the band. Because of the familial nature of a band, it is also not unusual for there to be a wide spectrum of interrelationships between band members, either by blood or marriage. Because of this fact, it is obvious that many transactions could be described as not being at arm's length. This situation is simply a fact of life in a great many bands. Counsel for the former Band executive at Westbank brought out in cross-examination the fact that in a number of bands, one or two large families may be very substantial property owners and may also have a dominating influence on the political direction of the band.

When bands were not engaged in any significant way in economic enterprise, those close relationships did not pose the sort of problems that can arise today in a modern band which is more active economically. As land becomes more valuable — Westbank is a good example — serious questions can arise as to dealings in that land. Allegations may be made that the band is preferring one person or one group of persons over another. It may be thought that the Chief and council show favouritism to a certain group within the band. This favouritism could take the form of the allocation of housing, the allocation of development funds, or access to opportunities for band- or Department-funded employment. Undoubtedly there is a legitimate area of patronage that may be utilized by government at whatever level. But there is also a duty to be fair, as well as the duty of any government to ensure that those governed can have access to a sufficient range of information to dispel suggestions that there is corruption in band administration. The democratic process demands no less.

It was suggested during the Inquiry that in order to obviate conflicts of interest in band government some new set of guidelines or rules would have to be designed and put in place. I doubt that any new or particular code needs to be formulated or promulgated. Simplicity is a great virtue in these matters. It is a bit like the message in the Gospels

— it is not that the standards are unknown — the difficulty is in having proper standards observed.

Due regard must be had to the nature of a band and band government. Bands vary quite widely in size and economic activity. We should not be looking for something that would unduly hamper the efficient operation of band government, nor would one wish to discourage capable people from running for positions as band Chief or band councillors. Many instances can afford an opportunity for possible conflict of interest. Certain of these matters will be more theoretical than real, and it is necessary that we limit ourselves to those that are truly matters of some substance. It appears to me that the first order of business in considering this question is the area of band reporting. To me, this encompasses two areas — financial statements and an annual report to band members. I heard evidence from a number of accountants who gave evidence before the Commission. Mr. William Kinsey, C.A., an experienced investigative accountant, served as an adviser to the Commission. An extensive amount of material was filed during the Inquiry relating to accounting practices and financial statements of Indian bands.

Mr. Patrick Lett, an individual with wide experience in band auditing, gave evidence before the Commission. He has long thought that band accounting standards could be improved across Canada. This is a new and developing area and obviously no wholly perfect guidelines can ever be devised. Also, since government is moving towards what is known as alternative or block funding arrangements, there has to be some flexibility of approach by those in the accounting profession to ensure that the whole process is kept understandable and that unnecessary detail is avoided. One criticism that Mr. Kinsey has found valid is that financial statements of bands often tend to be too diffuse. By that, I mean that there is multiplicity of schedules. This can cause much difficulty to the average band member who wishes to have a meaningful appreciation of just what is the state of band finances. I set out hereafter a detailed commentary on some of the defects that are noted to exist relative to current accounting practices, coupled with suggestions for practical improvements to ensure that greater clarity may be achieved in the future.

Concerning the question of fuller disclosure to band members of the operations of their governing body, it appears to me that there should be disclosure of a number of items that are of concern generally to members of the band. In format, I would urge that a type of annual report be published for band members. Such a report should be sent or delivered to every band member of adult age. This is a vital necessity of democratic government in Indian communities, and questions of economics should not be allowed to impede a proper flow of information. I cannot think that the cost of any such report would be very steep, but I believe that it would be a legitimate item for the Department to fund in each and every case so that there would be no fiscal excuse for the failure to have this sort of information disseminated to the constituents of each band. There are certain sensitive items that might well be deemed not necessary to be disclosed. For instance, when dealing with social welfare issues, this Commission endeavoured to exercise a measure of discretion. This is not the sort of payment I would be concerned about or that any band member need be much concerned about in dollar terms, and it is the sort of area where reporting of sums received would add nothing to the information dissemination process but would simply be material to titillate the curious.

The general rule should be that there is full disclosure of all transactions between the band, the Department, and individuals in the band where economic considerations of any substance are involved. With regard to a band executive, I should think that there ought to be a disclosure of honorariums or salaries received, expenses reimbursed, and allied items such as car leases, subsidized housing, and like benefits. While I do not wish to impose unduly onerous burdens on anyone inclined to run for public office in the Indian community, there is now a wide range of disclosure requirements in non-Indian legislative bodies, and as Indian communities have increasing self-direction and self-government, those sort of requirements become more needed for the proper operation of such governments.

Another area in which disclosure is desirable is that concerning real estate acquisitions and disposals when the band is dealing with band members or when a member of the band executive is dealing in land. I would not think that transactions wherein the band is acting on behalf of a locatee on a lease matter would be of materiality requiring disclosure. A disclosure rule would, of course, apply when dealings occurred between the band and people who were members of the executive or who were immediate relatives of members of the executive. Obviously, because of the wide familial relationships in many bands, it would not be sensible to have these matters pursued to undue lengths (second cousins and the like), but clearly where dealings occur with close relatives of a council member or Chief, such dealings can be of material interest and ought to be disclosed to band membership.

The principle underlying this concept is that a measure of publicity is the life-blood of democracy. The experience of mankind is that if individuals know that their acts are going to come under public scrutiny, they will be less likely to act contrary to the broad public interest. The best form of control is obviously self-control and it is a truism that self-control can be fostered and encouraged by the certainty that one's actions will not go unnoticed or unremarked. It will cause those charged with the conduct of public affairs to act truly in the public interest. At the same time, it is obviously undesirable that peoples' private lives be dissected in excruciating detail and that the task of governing be thereby rendered so unattractive that capable people are discouraged from seeking elective office.

I perceive no insuperable difficulties if this approach is taken to the question of appropriate disclosure of business matters relating to bands and individuals. Any enforcement mechanism should be kept simple. It would be a very simple matter to have inserted in the Act the requirement that once a year the band executive publish a report setting out these matters. Failure by band council to do so could be made subject to a modest penalty along the line of summary convictions matters — I doubt that most fair-minded band councils would have any objection to this sort of disclosure in any event and I would think that the need for enforcement by prosecution would be quite rare.

I have addressed the above remarks chiefly to the question of any possible conflict of interest. It seems to me that before I leave the subject of reporting generally to band membership, I should refer briefly to some matters that I touch on elsewhere in the Report. These concern significant financial transactions of the band. It appears to me that if a significant sum of band capital is being expended or invested, that is a matter that calls for input and direction from the band. One would expect that when such issues arose there would be convened a meeting of the band membership. Such a meeting would precede the actual implementation of the investment or undertaking under consideration. It seems to me that it would be appropriate that in any annual report addressed to the band membership there should be set forth in some detail how the project was implemented and the results to date of the action taken or investment made.

No analogy is ever perfect, but in casting about for some effective method of ensuring that band members were kept up-to-date with regard to occurrences affecting their lives, I considered how it was done in other organizations. A number of self-governing professions send out an annual report to their membership. This seems to me to be a useful way to keep members up-to-date on events occurring in their organization. As Indian bands and tribal groupings become more self-governing entities, I think that there will be an increasing necessity for the executive to keep membership informed in a timely way as to what is happening vis-à-vis their government. Steps will also have to be taken, as I have noted, to ensure that proper standards of disclosure are in place.

It is apparent to me that Indian bands and Indian governments will become more active and prominent in this country. It may be too soon to say that they are "self-governments", whatever that somewhat emotive term may mean, but it is clear that, increasingly, band councils and tribal councils will be more significant forces in the lives of Indian people generally.

The Department of Indian Affairs and Northern Development is becoming a less active presence in their lives. In earlier days when the Department was more or less the whole show, there were certain checks and balances that rested upon that Department as an arm of government. It was subject to ministerial responsibility, for one thing. Also it was subject to certain examination or auditing by parliamentary committees or by entities such as the Auditor General. As the Department ceases to be the main governing authority for Indian people, it appears to me that a new system of checks and balances will have to be devised to ensure that the new mode of government is fair and is seen to be fair. I think a government that is truly responsible has gone a great distance towards being an appropriate and fair government. At the end of the day, individual bands must decide on what is acceptable behaviour for their government. But electors can only make rational choices in this area if there is enough material available to make an informed choice.

It will, of course, be up to the individual voter of the various reserves to satisfy himself or herself as to who is an appropriate candidate for government. If the voters, having the raw material, namely information to work with, cannot make the appropriate choice, then that is a problem that they will have to grapple with like any other democratic group. It appears to me that if this mode of operation is followed, namely disclosure in an ample manner of band business and of matters that could be said to be possible conflict of interest situations, then there will be little opportunity for the fuelling of controversy and conflict on reserves.

I recommend that statutory provision be made for an annual report to be furnished by band councils to band members. I further recommend that the Department follow up any such legislation to ensure that band members are kept apprised of the activities of their government.

I saw a considerable amount of controversy at Westbank. There was a surfeit of rumour. This may largely have been caused by the rapid escalation in economic fortune of that band and its expansion in terms of economic and political power. Perhaps this experience at Westbank was rather exceptional and many other bands will not see such dramatic change. However, we cannot ignore the fact that Indian economic life is going to become more active and more significant, and we must now endeavour to fashion certain tools to aid in coping with the stresses and strains that are bound to arise in future. Obviously it would be highly undesirable to have a Commission frequently appointed to inquire into matters concerning individual Indian bands. Royal Commissions ought not to be invoked if other methods can be utilized. If structures can be put in place that can ensure an orderly democratic process, then opportunities for conflict and controversy could be reduced to a minimum. It appears to me that if the sort of structure and reporting system that I have recommended in general terms is put in place, then there will be a mechanism whereby the searchlight of publicity will have a salutary effect on local Indian government at the grassroots level.

D. Band Accounting Matters

In this section I have not made specific recommendations because I think this is an area where recommendations must be developed by people with specific accounting expertise. I set out the following discussion for study and hopefully for implementation of the suggestions it contains.

Some problems concerning the financial statements of the Westbank Indian Band are ones that may arise for other bands as they enter into more extensive and varied business ventures. To understand the problems of financial reporting for Indian bands, the Commission sought, and was given, access to "mock-ups" of financial statements of other Indian bands. Mock-ups were copies of financial statements from which the particulars of the band and the dollar amounts were removed. By this device, the method of accounting was made apparent and the privacy of the respective bands was preserved. The Commission accountant, Mr. William D. Kinsey, C.A., had access to certain financial records of the Westbank Indian Band, and the Department of Indian Affairs provided to the Commission accounting materials and information. Mr. Kinsey has been of considerable assistance to me in addressing the questions of possible improvements in the accounting and disclosure areas.

Accounting guidelines on a national basis have been supplied to Indian bands. I understand that some regional supplements or modifications have been authorized from time to time. The first guide seen by the Commission was the Department's *Guide to Year-End Band Audits, 1979-80* (Exhibit 43, Section 1). The main guide now available is *Accounting Guide for Indian Bands in Canada* which was reissued in January 1987 (hereinafter sometimes referred to as "the 1987 *Accounting Guide*"). This was the first update done since November 1980. At about the time the Commission was looking into the question of financial reporting, the Department issued an *Audit Guide for Alternative Funding Arrangements* (hereinafter sometimes referred to as the "*AFA Guide*"). This latter guide was based on work that had been done for the Department by the Ottawa office of Coopers and Lybrand, and is intended to apply to bands opting for funding under the New Alternative Funding Arrangements Program.

Accounting for Government Funding

When the Government of Canada supplies monies to organizations or individuals, it does so by way of grants or contributions. A grant could be loosely defined as an unconditional payment without an audit requirement. There is a greater formality associated with contributions. Contributions are payments made subject to conditions. Contributions are generally the subject-matter of a written agreement and payments made thereunder are subject to audit. The funding for Indian bands heretofore has been made primarily under contribution agreements. The monies supplied thereunder have to be used for the purposes for which those monies were designated and recipients are required to substantiate that use.

Following upon the Penner Report and some studies made by the federal government, the Department has now established new methods of financing and reporting for some bands, i.e., the alternative funding arrangements mentioned above. Under those arrangements, a sum of money is given to a band to cover a wide range of expenditures. The band determines how the money will be spent and is not required to refund any portion of it. Similarly, any overspending remains the band's responsibility: the Department will not add to the amount agreed. Alternative Funding Arrangements are expected to be agreed upon for periods as long as five years after the initial phase-in period. It is thought that the new program will result in greater financial flexibility for Indian bands entering into those arrangements. It has become necessary to establish a new system of accountability for the money supplied. It appears to me that this new approach to funding is consistent with the encouragement of greater self-direction of bands. Reporting requirements are being simplified but, of course, a heavier responsibility will rest upon band executives to be effective financial managers.

This change marks a significant departure from the previous system of funding Indian bands. One band has made an Alternative Funding Arrangement, and others are expected to do so shortly. The *AFA Guide* lays down new and more easily understood accounting and disclosure standards. It is thought that the report required under the Alternative Funding Arrangements, a "Financial and Statistical Return", will supply the Department of Indian Affairs and Northern Development with the data it requires, i.e., information to show public funds were spent for appropriate purposes and to give some assurance of band solvency. It is hoped also that the new standards will supply band members with adequate information to allow them to be informed judges of the band management and its performance. As the role of the Department as overseer of band finances abates, the task of seeing that funds are properly utilized and distributed devolves more and more to band executives and band electors.

A number of the approaches taken in the *AFA Guide* would alleviate some of the obscurity the Commission found in statements it examined. I feel that some of the approaches to accounting found in the *AFA*

Guide could usefully be adopted even by those bands that do not choose to opt into Alternative Funding Arrangements.

From the study made by the Commission accountant, it does not appear that all bands are consistently following the accounting guidelines established by the Department. As a result, some worthwhile standards of disclosure are treated as optional or ignored; for example, while the Department guidelines call for the disclosure of salaries, honoraria, and travel expenses, the Commission found that those matters were not always disclosed. I think they need to be disclosed on the basis that the electors should know these facts.

I believe that many of the suggestions in the *AFA Guide* are capable of application to band accounting and reporting generally. Under the Alternative Funding Arrangements, compliance with the accounting and disclosure standards is mandatory. Mandatory compliance has not been required under the existing system. I have been advised that all new contribution agreements will also contain a requirement that there be compliance with the accounting guide. It would appear that uniform standards can be established for bands funded under both the old and the new arrangements, and it seems quite feasible for a new guide to be prepared incorporating the suggestions of the *AFA Guide*, the 1987 *Accounting Guide*, and the recommendations of this Commission.

Fund Accounting

Governments at all levels keep their books on what is known as the "fund accounting" basis and Indian bands follow the same practice. Fund accounting presumes that money received for a particular purpose (or a group of similar, related purposes) is kept separate in its own "pot" until paid out for its intended purpose. Properly handled, this makes it easy for the funding agency to determine if funds were spent in the manner originally stipulated.

As practised, fund accounting for Indian bands has the following characteristics, some of which are disadvantageous.

(a) Monies intended for a number of distinct purposes are often deposited in the same bank account, as though many little pots were emptied into a larger one. This makes it possible (and more likely) that some money intended for a particular purpose will be spent for another purpose. The discipline of separate "pots" has been eroded, and may be lost. Money may be spent for something "temporarily" with the good, but unrealized, intention of paying back that money from another source.

(b) Fund accounting considers all incoming monies as revenue and all outgoing monies as expenditures (not expenses). A result is that expenditures having a long useful life (e.g., buildings and major machinery) are simply written off when acquired, not over the years in which they are expected to be useful. There is no recognition of their lasting value. Since revenue for a period of time and the expenses relating to that same period are not "matched", you cannot know whether the organization is "profitable" in the normal commercial sense. This does not matter for non-profit activities (e.g. governments). It does matter, and hence is unsuitable, for commercial operations where profitability should be measured.

The Use of Fund Accounting for Indian Bands

The concepts of fund accounting have been adopted in the Departmental guides and the system prescribed has evolved to meet the Department's need for knowledge. Compliance with the rules of the Department appears to be no guarantee of easy comprehension by band members. The accounting guides have, perhaps understandably, been directed towards matters for which the Department has direct responsibility, i.e., ensuring that bands apply the monies supplied by the Department for the purposes designated.

In the financial statements perused by the Commission accountant, it was found that there was a proliferation of separate Statements of Revenue and Expenditure as part of those financial statements. The Westbank Band's statements generally comprised some 28 to 30 statements. The financial reports of other bands often contained more, and one band had as many as 126 supplementary statements. I am not sure whether I should characterize that as an embarrassment of riches or a plethora of minutiae! It would seem that most of the information in the multitude of statements was set out for purposes of the Department. The problem so many separate statements causes is that the supply of such detail in the financial statements to band members may constitute serious information overload.

A significant issue concerning the presentation of financial statements was raised by the Westbank Band's former auditor. That was the question of whether or not it would be desirable to integrate the reporting of the various commercial ventures with the reporting of the Band by way of consolidated statements. The Westbank Band has been as commercially active as perhaps any Canadian band (save for those bands that draw substantial revenue from oil and gas). In the world of commerce, one often sees the financial statements of groups of corporations prepared on a consolidated basis. In consolidated statements the operations of all entities are considered as one, i.e., the revenues are amalgamated and the expenditures are amalgamated, and internal transactions between the corporations are eliminated. In the words of a Canadian Institute of Chartered Accountants glossary, consolidated statements "ignore the separate legal identities of the companies and show the financial position and operating results of the group as one economic unit".

The consolidated statements did assist in showing the Band's overall financial situation; however, they did not enlighten the reader on the confusing array of intercorporate, interentity, and interfund transfers. Perhaps the consolidation of the Band and the corporate accounts cannot lead to meaningful results because of the different accounting bases utilized, i.e., the fund accounting used by government and non-profit organizations on the one hand, and the traditional commercial accounting bases used for profit-oriented operations on the other.

To some extent, the method of accounting must be a question of professional judgement. Whatever method is used, the performance of the subsidiaries should be shown to band members. To the extent possible, the standards contained in the *Canadian Institute of Chartered Accountants Handbook* should be adopted.

Reference has already been made in the Report to misconceptions created by financial statements in instances where monies were shifted from one fund to another. We have seen elsewhere how the use of this practice at Westbank beguiled the Regional Director General and the Regional Director of Economic Development. Reallocation of monies or resources between activities (sometimes called "transfers between funds") should not be described as revenue of one fund or activity and the expenditure of another. This can lead to double counting and is a potentially confusing feature of many financial statements seen by the Commission. In some statements, the accumulated surplus of a fund at the end of a year was shown as part of the fund's revenue for the next year. This can be misleading about the actual revenue of a fund for a particular year.

The new *AFA Guide* reflects a form of disclosure which avoids the likelihood of misapprehension. Page 23 of that guide is reproduced at the end of this section. It is a reproduction of a sample statement of revenues and expenditures. Transfers between funds are not treated as revenues or expenditures of the fund. Operating results are shown exclusive of those transfers. The transfer between funds is reported after arriving at the excess of revenue over expenditures or vice versa. Put another way — those transfers should be shown "below the line" as illustrated in the *AFA Guide*.

Notes to Financial Statements

The notes to band financial statements and statements of its unincorporated and incorporated activities should clearly disclose the accounting principles and policies applied in preparing the statements. This is particularly necessary because Indian band accounting policies and

420

principles are somewhat different from those in normal commercial practice. Further, the provision of adequate notes can be of great assistance to the non-professional reader.

The following examples, with appropriate amendments, are models for some of the notes for band financial statements.

Note 1: Significant Accounting Principles

    (i) These financial statements are prepared in accordance with generally accepted accounting principles as set out in the *CICA Handbook* except as modified by the *Accounting Guide* issued by the Department of Indian Affairs and Northern Development, issued [date/or revised to date]. These principles are:

        (a) "Fund accounting" concepts apply, and the statements are prepared on an accrual basis.

        (b) Capital assets (fixed assets) are shown as expenditures. Capital assets acquired after [date] are valued at cost and included in the Capital Asset Fund. (See Note (v) below.)

        (c) Depreciation of fixed assets is charged directly against equity in capital assets and is not included in expenditures for the year.

    (ii) Investments, including band-owned or controlled corporations, are shown at cost, except where written down to a lesser amount due to a decline in value, other than a temporary decline. (See also note (iv) below.)

    (iii) Income from investments is recognized when received or when receivable by the band.

    (iv) These statements include band activities other than those conducted through corporations. The activities included are:

        (a) [provide details]
        (b) [provide details]
        (c) [provide details]

        Activities not included, and the reason for their exclusion are:

        (d) [provide details]
        (e) [provide details]

    (v) The capital asset fund consists of capital assets (fixed assets) acquired after [date], together with capital assets previously acquired and specifically identified. Depreciation is charged directly against equity and is therefore not included in expenditures in the year.

    (vi) "Funds on deposit with Indian Affairs" represents capital and revenue monies held on behalf of the band. The "statement of changes in funds on deposit with the Department" shows the amounts received by the band and for which the band is accountable.

Note 2: Significant Accounting Policies

  (i) Investments have been recorded at the lower of cost or market.
 (ii) Depreciation has been charged at the following rates. [provide details]
(iii) Funding received under Departmental agreements is considered revenue when related expenditures are made. Such amounts received but not expended are considered as deferred revenue or amounts repayable to the Department depending on band management's best judgement. Where a loss has been incurred in Department funded activities, the loss is considered to be for the band unless in the best judgement of the band management, the amounts are recoverable from the Department. Such amounts are listed in Note [X] to these financial statements.

There are many other matters that may be an appropriate subject for notes. Those matters are well known to members of the accounting profession and include such things as overdue loans and advances (bad debts), related party transactions, band guarantees, litigation, subsequent events, contingent liabilities, and corrections to prior period earnings. These matters need not be discussed further here because, at a minimum, the same principles of disclosure should apply to Indian bands as are commonly applied to non-Indian commercial enterprises.

For corporations which are owned by or are affiliated with Indian bands, similar considerations would apply. Corporation notes should reflect the following principles:

  (a) Normal, i.e., *CICA Handbook* accounting standards, will apply.
  (b) The equity method of accounting for investments in subsidiary and affiliated corporations will apply. (This is in contrast to the cost basis which is suggested for band statements.)
  (c) Decline in investment values, other than temporary declines, will result in appropriate write-downs of those investments.
  (d) Where consolidated statements are utilized, the basis for consolidation will be disclosed, the names of the consolidated corporations will be provided, and the names of those not consolidated will be given, together with the reasons for not consolidating them.

Supplementary Disclosure

Financial statements in and of themselves will not provide all the information which the reader should have. The Department already asks for some supplementary disclosure. Under the 1987 *Accounting Guide*, the following supplementary information is required:

  (a) Schedule of Fixed Assets costing over $500 showing individual assets and the following when available: year of acquisition, cost, year of disposition, and proceeds.

(b) Schedule of Debts (other than housing loans) owing to the Band Operations Funds, showing the individual debtor for each of the following classes:

(1) Council members
(2) Officers and other employees of the band
(3) Band members.

(c) Schedule of Housing Loans showing names of individuals and amounts of housing loans owing to the Band Operations Fund.

(d) Schedule of New Homes or Major Renovations showing names of individuals who received new homes or major renovations to existing homes during the fiscal year and showing total dollar amount per person.

(e) Schedule of Salaries, Honoraria, and Travel paid to officers and employees of the band.

(f) Schedule of Accounts Receivable, Aged.

(g) Schedule of Accounts Payable Outstanding, Aged.

(h) Schedule of Contingent Liabilities.

(i) Schedule of band leases showing names of individual lessees and amounts of annual rent. This schedule should also indicate the amount in arrears (aged when applicable) as of the date of the balance sheet.

Aside from what the Department requests, it seems to me that individual band members should be given this information. It also seems to me that the following additional matters should be the subject of disclosure to band members:

(a) Payments and benefits made or given to or for council members, band staff, or their immediate families.

(b) Details of any business acquired by the band or its subsidiaries directly or indirectly during the year. This should be accompanied by a brief description of the consideration paid and sufficient details to adequately inform the band members of the nature of the transaction.

(c) Details of allotments of land made during the year together with a statement of the proposed use by the locatee.

(d) Other real estate transactions to which the band is a party.

Some bands are reluctant to supply the Department with information which is felt to be none of the Department's business. It would seem that the Department has two areas of concern that require it to obtain financial data. One is to see that public funds are appropriately spent. The other is to be aware of any impending insolvency of a band. The AFA guidelines should achieve the Department's ends. However, quite apart from the Department, the band members have a need for knowledge, and each band member should have available to him or her adequate information about the band's business activities. There may be times when commercial prudence requires confidentiality, resulting in a delay in the release of information, but in due course band members have a right to know what their government is doing. If adequate information is given to them, responsible self-government is more readily attainable and the Department's role, perceived by many to be paternalistic, can be reduced.

Auditors

Under the current practice of the Department, the auditor's client is the band and not the Department. The audit engagement letter should be prepared by and originate with the auditor rather than the band. This is consistent with normal audit practice. It ensures that the audit engagement is placed on a proper basis from the outset. It is reasonable that the auditor should be authorized to make disclosure to the Department or to other funding agencies of information that concerns the Department or such agencies. Appropriate wording should be included in the engagement letter.

It would seem to me desirable that auditors have the right to attend band meetings at which financial statements on which they have reported are scheduled to be discussed. It goes without saying that the auditor must be independent of the band, council, management, and staff, and of any commercial activities owned or operated by the band.

Where feasible, there should be the equivalent of an audit committee. The inclusion of members outside the band council could provide a somewhat different and valuable perspective on band affairs. There may be individuals in the band who do not feel that they can take on the duties of being a full-time councillor or Chief, but who have valuable skills that could be applied in dealing with financial matters. This is a potential resource, the use of which should be considered by bands. With the growth of self-government, increased use of band personnel is going to be necessary in order to look after functions formerly provided by the Department. The financial management function is vital and all available resources should be utilized.

General Observations and Recommendations

The Commission has the following observations and recommendations to make regarding accounting, auditing, and disclosure:

(a) Band members should be entitled to clear, easily understood financial statements covering all band activities, including band-owned or controlled businesses, whether incorporated or not. There is no reason why band members should not have access to the type of information that is available to public company shareholders or that the public can find out about government-funded entities.

(b) Financial statements alone are not sufficient to provide appropriate disclosure. Supplementary information is required. Much of this information should be provided in an annual report to band members. Specific recommendations on such reporting are made elsewhere in this Report.

(c) Financial statements and schedules prepared for the Department are unlikely to be in the form most suitable for disclosure and presentation to band members. The Department's need for knowledge is not always the same as the band members' need. However, the documents supplied to the Department should be available to band members on request.

(d) Financial information for all band entities should be included in annual financial statements and annual reports. Such information should be provided to band members well in advance of any band meeting where the information is to be discussed. Where feasible, the necessary materials should be mailed to individual band members or families. However, if the material is too bulky, it could be made available at the band office.

(e) Consistent accounting principles and auditing standards should apply regardless of the size of the band or its method of obtaining Departmental funding.

(f) The Department should provide the accounting, auditing, and other disclosure standards in a practical, as well as a theoretical, sense. Band administrators and auditors ought not to have to guess or devise their own methods. Without consistent standards, inconsistencies and misinterpretations are almost bound to occur. The Department should provide a repository of knowledge that helps bands and their auditors to solve their accounting and disclosure problems. Those problems are common to many bands and such a service can be provided without destroying the privacy and anonymity that is desired by bands.

We are in a transitional period. The Department's role is receding but the necessary concomitant is an increased level of awareness and participation by band members. I think the foregoing suggestions will assist that process. I believe a policy of better disclosure can go a long way towards reducing the possibility of unease and unhappiness arising from misinformation or a plain lack of information. As I have said elsewhere, fact is a powerful antidote to rumour.

SAMPLE INDIAN BAND
STATEMENT OF REVENUES AND EXPENDITURES
AS AT MARCH 31, 19X6

	Operating and Maintenance Fund		Restricted Funds (note 7)		Total	
	19X6 $	19X5 $	19X6 $	19X5 $	19X6 $	19X5 $
REVENUE						
Federal government grants and contributions	2,265,000	1,560,000	–	100,000	2,265,000	1,660,000
Provincial government grants and contributions	40,000	–	80,000	–	120,000	–
Other	25,000	10,000	–	–	25,000	10,000
	2,330,000	1,570,000	80,000	100,000	2,410,000	1,670,000
Deferred revenue	–	–	(50,000)	–	–	–
	2,330,000	1,570,000	30,000	100,000	2,360,000	1,670,000
EXPENDITURE						
Operating and maintenance (schedule)						
Social Development	800,000	700,000	–	–	800,000	700,000
Education	250,000	230,000	–	–	250,000	230,000
Economic development	150,000	170,000	–	–	150,000	170,000
Band management	300,000	250,000	–	–	300,000	250,000
Maintenance of capital facilities	40,000	80,000	40,000	–	80,000	80,000
Interest expense	5,000	5,000	–	–	5,000	5,000
Debt repayment — principal	35,000	–	–	–	35,000	–
Capital outlays	770,000	40,000	–	100,000	770,000	140,000
	2,350,000	1,475,000	40,000	100,000	2,390,000	1,575,000
EXCESS (DEFICIENCY) OF REVENUE OVER EXPENDITURE	(20,000)	95,000	(10,000)	–	(30,000)	95,000
TRANSFERS BETWEEN FUNDS	(10,000)	–	10,000	–	–	–
EXCESS (DEFICIENCY) OF REVENUE AND TRANSFERS OVER EXPENDITURES	(30,000)	95,000	–	–	(30,000)	95,000
ACCUMULATED SURPLUS (DEFICIT) — BEGINNING OF YEAR	90,000	(5,000)	–	–	90,000	(5,000)
ACCUMULATED SURPLUS — END OF YEAR	60,000	90,000	–	–	60,000	90,000

SOURCE: *Audit Guide, Alternative Funding Arrangements*, Indian and Northern Affairs Canada, 1986, p. 23.

E. Abuse of Office

In his submission to me, counsel for the Department of Indian Affairs asked that I recommend that the provisions of the Criminal Code dealing with abuse of office by public officials be amended to include band chiefs and councillors. Section 111 of the Criminal Code deals with the offence of breach of trust of office. It reads as follows:

> 111. Every official who, in connection with the duties of his office, commits fraud or a breach of trust is guilty of an indictable offence and is liable to imprisonment for five years, whether or not the fraud or breach of trust would be an offence if it were committed in relation to a private person.

Band members should be afforded the same protection against breach of trust by public officials as is afforded other electors by the Criminal Code. As I have previously noted in my recommendations regarding disclosure, adequate publicity should provide a powerful check on any potential abuse of official power. However, should an abuse of power occur, there should be in place the necessary sanctions. This would provide a mechanism for investigation of allegations of wrongdoing and an avenue for dealing with misbehavior in office.

I recommend that the Criminal Code be amended to include band chiefs and councillors as persons within the category of "official".

Indian Government

A. Band Constitutions

The provisions in the present Act dealing with the structure of Indian government are sparse. There is provision for elections and for band votes in relation to surrendered lands, but not for a band constitution. The provision by which bands may operate in accordance with "custom" appears to have introduced a substantial degree of uncertainty. The customs which bands incorporate may be of recent vintage and have little or no cultural significance. The Sechelt Act and proposed Bill C-52 permitted bands to develop their own constitutions subject to certain required subject-matters and the approval of the Governor in Council. Each provided for recognition of a band as a legal entity with full legal powers.

Once it is accepted that significant areas of authority have been or are going to be devolved to band councils under either the existing Indian Act or under a self-government statute, it becomes important that the relationship between the council and band members become better defined. Some band constitutional format seems to me a sensible method for this definition.

It was apparent from the submissions placed before me that there was substantial variety in the contents of by-laws promulgated by various bands. I had the opportunity to review the procedures and practice followed by the Kamloops Band as a means of evaluating the adequacy of those in force at Westbank. In my view, devolution must be accompanied by express and articulated terms of accountability placed upon band councils. The movement today is away from Department control towards self-direction by bands — a corollary of this is the need for better communication between a band executive and band electors. In this way, band government can be truly responsible.

Some aspects of devolved powers should be vested in the band as a whole rather than in the band council. Examples would be important decisions relating to the expenditure of substantial capital funds, the budgeting of revenue monies, and the management of lands. I note, however, that not all bands will want or need a constitutional framework. The levels of economic and political sophistication of different bands differ quite widely. To give maximum flexibility, I believe some provision should be made in the present Act for a form of constitution for bands wishing to remain under the terms of the present statute. Bands opting for new legislative arrangements will always need a constitutional framework. There is a continuum here that covers a considerable diversity of needs and aspirations — I want to encourage the highest degree of flexibility possible in order to let the individual band do what best suits its electors. If this approach is adopted, I think that progress towards self-government can be made at a pace that is comfortable to all participants. As a general rule, in order to allow for some Department input and advice in this transitional period, any band constitutions passed should be approved by the Governor in Council.

I recommend that legislation be put in place to allow bands to enact comprehensive constitutions which provide for band government and demarcation of authority between band councils and band members.

Voting Rights

One other issue that will have to be considered is whether the franchise should be restricted to members residing on the reserve, having regard to the effects of Bill C-31. Is it fair that members of the band should be disenfranchised simply because there is no space on reserves to accommodate them? This may be particularly a problem where the Chief and council in a highly charged political atmosphere are in a position to exclude individual members from occupation of the reserve.

The eligibility of voters in band elections is presently governed by Section 77 of the Act:

> 77. (1) A member of a band who has attained the age of eighteen years and is ordinarily resident on the reserve is qualified to vote for a person nominated to be chief of the band and, where the reserve for voting purposes consists of one section, to vote for persons nominated as councillors.

(2) A member of a band who is of the full age of eighteen years and is ordinarily resident in a section that has been established for voting purposes is qualified to vote for a person nominated to be councillor to represent that section.

I was told that some bands tend to the view that residency on the reserve ought not to be a requirement of the franchise. I was also told that in the past some bands had rejected the election provisions of the Indian Act and reverted to a "customary" election system in order that they could allow non-resident band members to vote in band elections. When a band operates according to "custom", the band members do not have the safeguards that are generally incorporated into a statutory scheme governing elections. If the residency requirements of Section 77 are forcing some bands to operate outside the election provisions of the Indian Act, perhaps it would be preferable to amend the Act to allow bands a choice with respect to the residency requirement. This problem is coming very much to the fore as a result of the increase in band membership consequent upon Bill C-31. Again, bands should be given maximum flexibility, but I think it is desirable that election procedure be governed by some definite rules. The Act provides a structure. The danger with "custom" is that there may be a government of men and not a government of laws. I believe the present Act must be amended to make it possible to waive the residency requirements.

I recommend that bands be given the express power to waive residency as a condition of the right to vote under the Indian Act.

B. Taxation

As noted earlier in this Report, there is currently a proposal to amend the Indian Act in order to endow bands with the power to impose taxes on residents of conditionally surrendered lands. Band councils presently have the authority under Section 83 of the Act to tax interests in land located on a reserve. Because of the possible distinction between reserve lands and surrendered lands, it is perceived that the power under Section 83 may well not extend to surrendered lands. Therefore, the Kamloops Amendments include a provision to expand the definition of reserve to include conditionally surrendered lands. I do not intend to go into detail regarding the proposed Kamloops Amendments. I approve of the initiative taken there and think that the amendments sought should be supported.

There is a need for care and caution with respect to the impact of the change on non-Indians holding interests on band lands. Existing commitments must be fairly honoured, always bearing in mind that change is inevitable. Lessees on reserves are not different from people subject to municipal laws — these too change. However, there must be an orderly process for such people to have input before and not after decisions are effected. This was one of the irritants at Westbank — unilateral action can result in people feeling that they are being abused.

The Department has recognized that conferring taxation powers on band councils can give rise to an apprehension on the part of non-Indian lessees that they may face taxation without the usual safeguards. It is as basic as the complaint that underlay the American Revolution — "no taxation without representation". This issue must be slowly (and fairly) resolved if controversy is to be avoided.

It may be that the taxation regime will be seen as a source of revenue to bands, and that band government will be perceived as not responsible, in the popular democratic sense, to industrial users of band lands. Chief Jules noted, however, that each band will be subject to the ultimate test of the marketplace, and that if a band taxation regime is inequitable, then that band will not be able to attract desirable tenants to band sites.

The proposed amendments include a taxation advisory board to provide for fairness in the taxation scheme. It was my impression from testimony I heard, however, that the questions which the advisory board will be asked to decide may not relate to the level of taxation, but rather to the fairness of the assessment values in the area. Any such board could have a further role in relation to the approval of by-laws by the Minister or Governor in Council under the Act. The composition and procedures of any such board is not yet fully worked out.

It is difficult to see how the Department will be able to review the level of taxation in any tax law proposed by a band without becoming embroiled once again in the central tensions relating to the Indian aspiration for self-government. On the other hand, to a businessman looking to long-term return on substantial capital investments, if taxation policy forced him to leave the investment and assets he had put into his venture, he would obviously view the system as seriously flawed. Uncertainty regarding land tenure and the reach of band legislation has led to some businesses locating developments on band lands which are not capital-intensive and which can be removed at short notice. It is generally to the advantage of bands to have a system which is perceived as being orderly and fair. Where there is certainty and a perception of equitable dealing, better-quality development proposals can be attracted. A level playing field attracts a better class of developer.

I do not see how some taxation problems can be avoided. While death and taxes are certain, history has not shown either to have a high degree of popularity. It will be a challenge to band councils to provide some assurance to the market-place that taxation levels will be set fairly and responsibly, and that businessmen will not be exploited after a significant commitment of capital and resources on Indian lands. In practical terms, any business establishing long-term capital investment on Indian lands will seek contractual undertakings from the band councils relating to taxation by the band. Rents paid to locatees or to a band can be much affected by the level of taxation imposed by the band. Thus, individual locatees will have a vital interest in taxation issues and this is doubtless a healthy balancing device in the system. In the long run, the market-place must govern, but in the transitional period, there must be Departmental input through a board or agency to ensure that matters are dealt with efficiently and even-handedly. Implementation of legislative initiatives provided for in the Kamloops Amendments will be a testing process for self-government.

If certain difficulties experienced at Westbank are to be avoided, any system put in place must be clearly understood by those subject to it. In present circumstances, this means that measures must be taken to ensure that businessmen are made aware of such risks and uncertainties as may be attendant upon capital investments on Indian reserve lands. No doubt, band governments will be anxious to provide a climate which will adequately respond to the legitimate concerns of businessmen to create a fair and predictable atmosphere for the conduct of business enterprises. The Department should foster this approach, as it represents opportunity for economic progress.

I recommend that the Kamloops Amendments be supported and that the Department furnish technical and advisory assistance to bands to enable the spirit of the Amendments to be realized.

C. By-Laws

Counsel for the Westbank Band noted that there is no specific provision in the Indian Act which protects bands that undertake to enact zoning by-laws. In his submission, he suggests that there ought to be an equivalent provision in the Indian Act to Section 972 of the British Columbia Municipal Act (R.S.B.C. 1979, c. 290). That section provides:

> 972 (1) Compensation is not payable to any person for any reduction in the value of that person's interest in land, or for any loss or damages that result from the adoption of an official community plan, a rural land use bylaw under this Division or the issue of a permit under Division (5).
> (2) Subsection (1) does not apply where the rural land use by-law or by-law under this Division restricts the use of land to a public use.

Counsel submitted that before any band council could safely exercise its by-law powers with respect to zoning, it would be necessary to have statutory protection against claims for injurious affection. If development on reserve land is to proceed in an orderly fashion, some kind of official plan or zoning legislation is usually needed. It seems only fair that band governments should have protection against legal action analogous to that provided by Section 972 of the British Columbia

Municipal Act. However, I also believe that it is essential that all parties who may be affected by zoning decisions of the band council be given an opportunity to air their views before decisions are made. Counsel for the Westbank Band observed that there is no provision in the Indian Act or in regulations that establishes a procedure for the enactment of by-laws. I believe that certain safeguards, such as notice requirements, should be established either in the statute, or by regulation. As noted earlier with respect to decisions of council regarding land allotments, an appropriate remedy for failure to follow the established procedures would be to make provision for a court to quash an improperly enacted by-law.

I recommend that mechanisms be adopted to provide that the by-law powers and legal immunities of a band be similar to those governing municipalities relative to land zoning and land management.

D. The Department's Role after Devolution

Experience suggests that the Department's role after devolution will become more residual in its character. The tension between the Department's role as supervisor and its role as an advocate for Native rights is becoming more apparent with the downsizing of the Department and the increased devolution of programs and services to Indian governments.

I think it important that there be efforts to separate the support and supervisory functions within the Department. In some cases, difficulty has arisen because a number of functions have been exercised by one person. In a broad sense the government is often placed in a conflict position because while it is responsible for improving the position of aboriginal people, at the same time it must also have regard to the interests of all Canadian people. That problem is not unique, however, in any federal system where there are different needs and aspirations of various regions. Those problems can be, and will be, worked out in the normal political process. At the Departmental operating level, however, it can impose considerable hardship on individual officials to operate simultaneously as advocate and watchdog. There is obviously no perfect solution to this dilemma, but with the increasing complexity of Indian affairs, a conscious effort must be made to separate the roles to the maximum extent possible. I am sure that the current internal review referred to earlier will address this issue. I simply flag this as an area that needs to be recognized in the interim. Policies should be developed to minimize these conflicts.

I recommend that the Department implement policies which separate the supervisory functions and the advocacy functions within the Department. To the greatest extent practicable, supervisory functions of the Department should be exercised by individuals other than those responsible for support or advocacy functions.

PART D

Recommendations for Long-Term Changes

In Part C, I dealt with the question of specific changes to existing statutory provisions and policies. I now consider what might be recommended in terms of a new statutory structure to facilitate Indian self-government. In this context, I deal with the need for a statutory basis for self-government and the general form and contents of any such statute.

Statutory Basis for Self-Government

A great many Indian groups are not satisfied with the continuation of the Department's role in Indian government. As was mentioned by many who appeared before me, there is a tremendous spectrum of opinion among the bands in Canada relating to what degree of self-government they seek. It is usually the case that the wealthier bands have been at the forefront in this respect and have strained the capacity of the present system to provide for their aspirations. The process of self-government is heavily constrained at law by the terms of the Indian Act. The Sechelt and the Cree-Naskapi groups were able to have statutes fashioned to deal with their own unique circumstances.

From the experience of the recent past, it seems clear that Indian bands will continue to assume an increasing amount of self-direction. They will have to deal with the everlasting issues of lands and monies. They may also face increases in activity because of the accession of new members, the settlement of court claims, and a general increase in the level of economic activity. These matters will have an impact in greater or lesser degree on different bands, depending on location and numbers, but the trend or tendency towards greater self-government is inexorable.

For many bands, however, the Department's financial trust or fiduciary responsibility recognized in Guerin v. The Queen is a principal concern in relation to the process of devolution or self-government. A large number of claims have been advanced along the lines of the Guerin decision and also a number in relation to aboriginal title. It may be that substantial sums of money will be awarded to some Indian bands in Canada. Any such funds would form part of a band's capital base in the future. Land settlements may affect future development on Indian lands. A larger land base is said to be necessary to provide adequate support for the growing numbers of Indians resulting from an increase in lifespan and the potentially dramatic results of Bill C-31 (An Act to Amend the Indian Act, S.C. 1985, c.27) which gave Indian status to a large number of people formerly not of that status. Chief Sam of the Shuswap Band told me that he did not have the land base to accommodate the large number of people who he anticipated were going to become members of the Band. Many bands have these worrisome problems.

A Report to Parliament published in June 1987 provides objective support for this concern. For example, applicants for status in B.C. number 16,582, as compared with an existing population of 62,393; that is a potential increase of 26 per cent. The figures for Canada are similar in that 90,051 applications have been received compared with an existing population of 355,321, for a potential increase of 25 per cent. Since an unknown number of applications are yet to be received, and since only a small fraction have been processed, the impact of these numbers has yet to be fully felt. Funds allocated to accommodate the financial consequences of Bill C-31 will constitute assets to be utilized in the structure of Indian government.

The importance to Indians and to their economic future of claims against the federal government have caused many groups to be cautious concerning any process of reform which would result in a diminution of the federal government's fiduciary responsibility under the Indian Act. That appears to me to be a legitimate concern. Any legislative changes will have to pass the test of not altering the status quo ante. It would clearly be unfair to try to rewrite the past. It would be unwise not to try to utilize the lessons of the past to do better in the future.

I believe that many of the problems which occurred over time at Westbank either have been or will be encountered by a great many bands in Canada in the future. The rapidity with which problems arise is usually directly linked to the pace of economic change. There are significant differences in the economic prospects of bands in Canada. But that is not surprising. There are significant differences in the economic prospects of many citizens of Canada. A band whose land adjoins a major urban centre is like someone who had the good luck to have his great-grandfather settle on a farm near a large city. Land of modest value later becomes a pearl of great price. As the country grows, a number of bands will be more a part of the economic mainstream. To facilitate economic activity it would be helpful to overhaul some of the more obvious deficiencies of the Indian Act. The Westbank Band is in the forefront of developing bands, but the numbers of bands more active in economic life in Canada is going to show a marked increase before many years pass. Unless the structure of this ancient Act is improved upon, I think that certain difficulties, perhaps in part exemplified at Westbank, will persist in the future. I doubt that any perfect Act can be devised but to do nothing is a counsel of despair. Improvements can and should be made.

Accordingly, I came to the conclusion that I should make some recommendations with respect to possible changes to the institutions and structures relating to self-government. I think governments, Indian and non-Indian, should proceed with all deliberate speed to enhance the position of Indian people in society. It is good for Native people to have pride in their history and background. But they are part of the fabric of Canadian life and we cannot have Indians and non-Indians occupying two solitudes in this vast, rich land.

The underlying concern of the Indian Act remains valid for many Indian people, namely that their precious land heritage not be eroded. But the Act can be improved to make a transition to a more self-directed mode of life a realizable and orderly process. We should encourage changes of direction but I have a distaste for change merely for the sake of change.

Private Acts or Enabling Legislation?

The only successful changes relating to self-government so far have been the Sechelt Act and the Cree-Naskapi Act. The Department of Indian Affairs has continued to negotiate with respect to specific bands in relation to the passage of specific legislation. This is obviously the only course open to it unless steps are taken to pass a general enabling statute to provide a structure within which self-government could be devolved to other bands. The creation of individual statutes for individual bands is one process which affords a means by which self-government is possible. The disadvantages are that the process involved in creating a unique statute is complex and difficult and amendment of the statute could be a problem in the future. From the Department's perspective, the creation of almost 600 private Acts is a daunting prospect. It was clear to me from the submissions made that the cost and burden on Indian bands relating to the achievement of a specific statute can also be a substantial obstacle to achieving self-government. While I do not say that individual Acts should not be passed, I think it desirable that there be a general enabling statute which would permit creation of self-governing Indian groups within a general statutory structure such as that contemplated in proposed Bill C-52. Large or relatively well-off bands may want to look to an individual statute, but there should be an easier and less costly method for smaller and less well-off bands to obtain the benefits of greater self-direction.

In view of my support for enabling legislation, I think it is important to look at proposed Bill C-52 in some detail. This enabling legislation passed first reading but lapsed due to a general election. The draft Act commenced by giving legal recognition to bands which held a referendum seeking recognition as an Indian nation in accordance with the regulations passed pursuant to the Act. The Minister was empowered to enter into an agreement to defray the costs incurred in seeking recognition as well as the costs of activities undertaken in preparation for the exercise of powers by Indian nations and their governments after recognition.

Section 6 of the Bill required an Indian nation to meet certain conditions before recognition. These included:

(a) the existence of a written constitution providing for Indian government with executive and legislative functions consistent with the Charter;

(b) the constitution was to state the membership code, the accountability of the government, clear democratic processes, the publication of laws, the protection of individual and collective rights, the provision of an independent system for reviewing executive decisions, a system of financial accountability, and a mechanism for dealing with abuse of power.

The recognition of the band as legally constituted was to occur by an order issued by the panel constituted by the Act for the purpose of supervising this process.

By Section 9 the constitution of the Indian nation would have been given legal effect. Section 9 also provided for amendments to the Indian band constitution and Section 12 required the Indian band to conduct itself in accordance with its constitution.

Section 13 of the Bill conferred legal capacity on an Indian nation, although its lands could not be pledged, mortgaged, or hypothecated for security. The lands would have continued to be held by the Crown for the use and benefit of the new Indian nations. The legal aspects of title in the Indian Act would, by and large, have continued in force.

The objects of the Indian nation as stated in Section 15 of the Bill included the plenary power to govern the lands and peoples within the territory described by the constitution.

The legislative power of the Indian nation prescribed by Section 16 included power to legislate with respect to education, taxation, charges for public services, voting procedures, membership, imposition of fines, and penalties for breach of laws passed by an Indian nation, and matters coming within the classes of subjects set out in the Bill or agreed to by the Minister. The executive powers of an Indian nation would have included such areas as management and administration of lands, institution of offices, undertaking of public works, social services, economic development and the operation of educational facilities.

The Minister was empowered to enter into any agreement conferring greater power on an Indian nation with the approval of the Governor in Council. The Minister's power to confer those powers was broad and plenary and extended to all matters falling within Section 91(24), being the federal government's power to legislate relative to Indians and Indian lands.

An interrelationship between the Indian Act and the Self-Government Bill was provided by Section 24 of the Bill whereby the Minister could declare all or any provisions of the Indian Act inapplicable.

The Bill provided for the appointment of an Administrator of bankrupt Indian nations, and also contained override provisions permitting the Minister or Governor in Council to disallow laws inconsistent with the Charter or other democratic principles.

Section 39 of the Bill preserved pre-existing rights and interests without defining anew the rights and position of lease holders and locatees. Federal laws of general application would have applied to Indian nations, but provincial laws of general application would not. This would have reversed the situation under Section 88 of the present Act, whereby provincial laws of general application apply to Indians. In my opinion, this provision, which apparently adopted the Penner Committee report recommendation, is inadvisable. To totally exclude provincial legislation, even if constitutional, appears to me a step of doubtful wisdom. For instance, would common law principles be excluded? What would be the commercial effect on reserves? I fear that a legal vacuum could be created. Even if that policy contains some desirable objectives, I think it would harm the Indian people of Canada to be so treated.

I recommend that in any self-government legislation, provincial laws not be generally excluded.

Finally, the panel created pursuant to the Bill was to be a court of record and its constitution and membership was prescribed by the provisions of the Bill.

The Bill has not been renewed. An alternative statutory scheme in which bands can elect to participate seems to me to be preferable to drastic reform of the Indian Act. Some bands in Canada today are partially satisfied with the Indian Act and in spite of its difficulties may prefer this to sweeping change. In relation to the central issues of self-government and self-regulation, it is clear that many bands are not prepared, nor do they desire, to take on all of the devolved powers which have been demanded of the Department by certain bands which have moved rapidly. There is a broad diversity of views on these issues in the Indian community and those views are not always similar even in groups of similar economic advancement.

I recommend that to enhance the progress of self-government there be enacted enabling legislation in addition to individual statutes in order to facilitate bands wishing to adopt self-government.

Funding for Self-Government and Devolution

It is clear that a band's progress towards self-government depends in large measure on the provision of adequate financing for this process. It seems to me that there should be funding allocated for this purpose in the Indian Affairs budget. It is vital to the success of self-government or self-direction initiatives that a band or group of bands possess a sufficient measure of expertise and be properly prepared to accept broader responsibilities. Failure to ensure that a band is properly prepared could result in costly failures.

I recommend that funding be allocated to finance the development of sufficient expertise within Indian bands and associations to enable them to more effectively assume powers of self-government.

Elements of Self-Government

1. Band or Tribal Council Government

One of the difficulties inherent in Indian self-government is that individual bands often lack the personnel resources required for local government administration. This is not only a difficulty in the lack of training of individual Indians, but also stems from the small numbers of people involved. The past ten years have seen a gradual development of tribal councils and organizations of Indian bands in similar geographic and economic situations which facilitates the assumption of self-direction by the groups involved.

I recommend that bands be encouraged to pursue self-government within a tribal council or broader administrative structure.

This recommendation necessarily involves a demarcation between the role of bands and the larger administrative structures relating to the rights and interests in band monies and lands. I think it necessary to preserve the distinct assets of bands unless each band, by majority vote, consents to pooling these assets. As a consequence, there will be a necessary division of authority relating to the use of monies and development of lands within the larger administrative structure.

2. Powers and Responsibilities of Band Members

There has been a growing tendency to devolve responsibility to band or tribal councils for the programs and services which are transferred from the Department. I think that in general this process is to be encouraged. However, there are at least two factors which lead me to recommend that the band as a whole exercise a measure of control over important band decisions. It is clear from the evidence at Westbank, and the submissions to me, that many bands are small in number and that band councils can be susceptible to domination by a strong personality. Equally, it is clear that in politics where there are familial elements involved, the feelings between groups within the band may be very intense and, as a consequence, the band council may have difficulty responding to the interests of all band members. I think it is important that for major decisions concerning the investment of band monies and the use and development of lands, band members be entitled to vote on such issues. This process provides a broader spectrum of opinion and enables electors to have some say in their government. Such an approach, coupled with more effective disclosure, should ensure more efficient working of the democratic process.

I recommend that any enabling statute passed contain provisions to be included in a band constitution requiring that the band as a whole have the power to approve budgets, large capital expenditures and major land decisions.

The present culture which has evolved in relation to band votes should be respected. As noted in the evidence of Ms. Barbara Coble, band members may exercise franchise rights and deprive a Chief and council of a majority vote by absenting themselves from a band general meeting. Accordingly, large pluralities could simply be a reflection that those who opposed the measure being debated had refused to attend. Present statutory requirements calling for a vote of a majority of electors ought not to be disturbed. Different considerations may apply where bands are setting up new constitutions. I simply say that I would not favour changing the present Act concerning this issue.

3. Land

I have already stated that I consider it important that the band as a whole retain authority with respect to major decisions involving land. I have also discussed extensively the inadequacies of the present land regime in Part C of this Report. I consider it important that these land issues be resolved in an <u>Indian Lands Act</u> irrespective of the fortunes of self-government.

In the context of self-government, I think it would be an unhappy consequence if each band could fashion its own land regime. The potential for resulting confusion and uncertainty is great. I think, therefore, that an <u>Indian Lands Act</u> should be of general application to all bands, including those that exercise powers of self-government.

Provision should be made in any <u>Indian Lands Act</u> for the transfer of the Crown interest to bands that are able to assume full title. Pending such transfers, ultimate title should continue to reside in the Crown.

I recommend that bands be afforded the option of assuming fee simple title concurrent with the devolution to them of the powers of self-government.

4. *Money*

The concept underlying the division between capital and revenue monies is that the band's interest as a whole in capital monies is to be safeguarded by the Department's role in reviewing proposed expenditures of capital monies. At present, the band has no statute-authorized role or function relating to the investment of capital monies. I think self-government must confer on the band the power to make all economic decisions, including investments.

It may be that bands will want to delegate to their executive the responsibility for some or all decisions. The nature and extent of such delegation is properly left to the electors. It seems to me that bands would be ill-advised to delegate all economic powers to council. Why? My reasoning is as follows. If the council possesses all of the authority over fiscal matters (such having been delegated by the band), this is a tremendous repository of power in bands with any amount of capital. The extent of the power (real or perceived) means that control of the political levers of power becomes too eagerly sought after. The elected party has little check on its actions. It is in danger of succumbing to the disease identified by Lord Acton in the dictum that "absolute power corrupts absolutely". There is no via media. The "ins" are in absolute control and the "outs" inhabit a region of outer darkness. It is far better to have a measure of band input and control over major decisions. This both provides a wider measure of advice and counsel and is a safety valve to avoid explosions such as I saw at Westbank in the activities of the "Action Committee".

I think it desirable that band approval be obtained for major capital ventures of the band. The delineation of a major versus a minor expenditure will depend on the individual circumstances of the bands. I also think that the Department has a legitimate role in ensuring that there is no wasting or rapid disappearance of capital assets in bands that do not control their own assets. These assets represent not only the band's prospects of independence from the Department, but also the Department's prospects of freedom from wholly subsidizing Indian programs and Indian-based development.

I recommend that approval of major financial transactions be reserved to the band as a whole in bands assuming full self-direction or self-government.

5. Conflicts of Interest

As already noted, there can often arise potential conflicts of interest in a government in which many of the constituents are related. The central remedy in conflict of interest situations is to provide for publication and approval of the course of action suggested by those persons having responsibility for government. In the context of band government, it should not be very difficult to obtain the approval of band members if the proposed course of action is desirable and legitimate. I think it important, therefore, that actions to be taken by members of the council or chiefs in which such executives may have a conflict of interest should be subject to ratification by the membership as a whole. It is not sufficient that the chief or council member who is interested absent himself or herself from the meetings of council at which the matter is considered.

I recommend that in relation to the conferring of benefits or assets upon a member of the band executive or a member of his or her immediate family, decisions should be subject to ratification by the band membership.

6. Democratic Responsibilities

I think that the responsibilities of members of council as fiduciaries in relation to band members ought to be part of any enabling statute. Further, I think it important that band government be responsible to the band membership and that disclosure requirements for major decisions be imposed by the statute itself. This would ensure that band members are adequately informed about important decisions relating to their interests.

I recommend that any self-government statute require that the band constitution prescribe the duties of the band executive and provide for the disclosure of material transactions.

As we have seen at Westbank, band financial statements can be prepared in such a manner as to be unintelligible to the average person. Individual transactions of great importance can be hidden among numbers and verbiage so as to make it difficult for even a professional person to be apprised of what is actually occurring. I think it clear that independent auditors must have a role, as in so many other areas of society, in the handling of funds by local governments on behalf of band members and the Department.

The transfer of discretion in the expenditure of public funds from the Department to large numbers of local governments inevitably will give rise to problems. This is not sufficient cause to reverse the process, but means there is a need for clear statutory duties on the part of band executives and adequate disclosure requirements.

The specific recommendations I make respecting financial disclosure are included in Part C of Section II.

7. *Continuing Role of Government*

As a regime of self-government emerges, I think it will become important that the Department separate its functions and roles with respect to those bands which prefer to stay under the present system from those bands which adopt a mode of self-government. I doubt that the present Act can serve as a half-way house between self-government and the old structure. There are powers in the present Act which may be of assistance in preparing bands for self-government, but the thrust of the Indian Act is contrary to self-government. It is better to fashion new tools for the new order. I think that the comprehensive demands of the process of self-government should not be understated by permitting a limited attempt at self-government under the existing provisions liberally interpreted. That leads to the problem of too much policy and too little law previously discussed.

With respect to the role of the Department in dealing with bands that have assumed a large measure of self-direction, I think that it can continue to have a useful role in such areas as the negotiation of settlements, the monitoring of expenditures of public funds, the maintenance and completion of a federal Indian land register, and the administration of trust accounts not transferred to local government. In the event that bands which choose self-government prefer to retain a system of land title and tenure in which the government remains a trustee, the Department will obviously have some continuing role in surrenders and leasing of lands. As the bands take more ample responsibility for land decisions, the fiduciary duty of the Department will be abated or extinguished.

The prospects of settlement of certain aboriginal and other claims against the federal and provincial governments represent an opportunity for improvement of the difficult economic and social circumstances facing many Indian people in Canada. There is always the danger, however, that benefits realized can too easily fade and the opportunities presented by cash and land settlements could result in little significant improvement in the personal and societal circumstances of Indians in Canada. The history by Thomas Berger, *A Village Journey*, narrating the experience under the Alaska Settlements Act, gives food for thought. Care must be taken to create a proper structure to ensure that capital is not lost and that assets are preserved for the future of the band. As well, those responsible should endeavour to ensure that the monies and lands are used to achieve the collective desires of the Indian peoples themselves rather than any artificial objectives set for them. In a very practical sense, the risks attendant upon receiving significant amounts of money and land, the latter of which may be subject to alienation in one form or another, requires that a system be in place to ensure that lasting benefits can be preserved for this and future generations to the greatest extent possible.

From the perspective of public policy and the Department, I think that it cannot take a too passive role in the administration of settlements of money and land in the future. Until the Department negotiates new structures whereby Indian self-government is fully realized, the Department should remain legally responsible under the present statutory scheme for failures which arise out of negligence or want of due care.

Departmental personnel are divided on the issue of how daring the Department ought to be in relation to surrendering its statutory and traditional roles to band councils and tribal councils. The Department and Indian groups are both presently suffering from a conflict between inconsistent objectives. The Indian groups, for the most part, wish to assume responsibility for their own affairs. At the same time, since the Departmental fiduciary responsibility is presently part of the hope for future economic gains, the Indian groups obviously would like to retain the right to recover compensation from the Department. It is not politically popular to acknowledge that a band's informed decision to follow a certain course of action carries with it a release of the Department's responsibility relating to that decision. Many Indian witnesses before me walked carefully around this issue. I could not blame them. They inhabit an intensely political environment. The Department, if it acts responsibly and in good faith, will fulfil its duty to itself and to bands. Modern bands with professional advisers are very different from older bands in which many people could not write their name. The Department should continue to exercise great care where less advanced bands are involved, but it should not be unduly alarmed about potential suits from those bands that are willing and able to make their own decisions. Courts usually operate in the real world. Absolute jurisdiction over decision making is wholly inconsistent with residual responsibility in the Department.

This is, of course, largely a political conflict rather than a purely legal one. One aspect of the problem can clearly be delineated. Any future attempts at structuring Indian self-government should, for obvious reasons, not affect the existing responsibility of the Department under existing structures to provide compensation for past wrongs. Once that is made clear, then I think it inevitable that the process of Indian self-government will result in an abatement, if not elimination, of the Department's financial responsibility for collective decisions which are made by Indian groups and which result in economic failure. A clear consequence of full responsibility is that Indian groups will have to make their own assessments about what degree of risk they are prepared to assume in relation to their own decisions.

I think there is a clear role for government to see that structures are in place which ensure that no local government or individual imperils the future of a band through risks that are not adequately considered and understood by all those who have a stake in the outcome. A refrain I heard often was that Indian people want to control their own affairs and destiny. They should. However, the present Act is not structured particularly well to ensure that result. I have indicated above some steps that can be taken to advance the progress of self-government. These include some amendments to the present Act, even though the Act is widely criticized and the sentiment is often expressed that its amendment may delay self-government.

I think amendments to the Act could delay self-government if amendments were all that occurred. However, if the comprehensive approach I endorse above is taken, I believe that those who wish to preserve the existing order and those who wish to assume greater or full self-direction can both be accommodated. We can make things better for the more conservative elements and we can make things possible for the more venturesome. I have not conducted hearings across the country, but I have had my staff study materials and solicit views beyond the confines of Westbank, and indeed, beyond the confines of British Columbia. It would be impossible to have conducted this Inquiry without arriving at certain beliefs and conclusions. Having arrived at them, I felt it my duty to pass them on to government. I would hope that many of these recommendations can bear fruit to improve Indian affairs in Canada.

APPENDICES

Appendix A

Lands and Monies under the Indian Act:
Selected Provisions in Historical Perspective

Outline

1. The Indian Act: Its Origins and Development

    (a) Pre-Confederation Roots

        The Maritimes
        Upper and Lower Canada
        The Gradual Civilization Act of 1857

    (b) Dominion Legislation, 1867–1876

    (c) The Indian Act, 1876–1951

        The Indian Act of 1876
        The Indian Act of 1880
        The Indian Advancement Act of 1884
        The Franchise Act of 1885
        Selected Legislative Developments, 1884–1946

    (d) The Special Joint Committee and the 1951 Indian Act

    (e) Some Subsequent Developments

        The Hawthorn Report
        The 1969 Policy Statement
        The 1970's and 1980's

2. Indian Lands at Common Law and under the Indian Act

    (a) The Concept of Surrender
        (i) The Original Meaning
        (ii) The Problem created by Confederation and "St. Catharines Milling and Lumber Co." v. "The Queen in Right of Ontario" (1888), 14 App. Cas. 46 (P.C.)
        (iii) Some Statutory Provisions concerning Surrenders: Sections 2(1), 18(1), 37, 38 and 53(1)

            Reserves and Surrenders
            Conditional Surrenders
        (iv) Where the Underlying Title is in the Federal Crown: the British Columbia Example

            The Pre-Confederation Vancouver Island Treaties
            Colonial Land Policy After Douglas, 1864–1871

Dominion-Provincial Wrangling, 1871–1912
The McKenna-McBride Agreement of 1912
The Railway Belt and the Peace River Block
The Scott-Cathcart Agreement of 1929
Order-in-Council 1036

(b) Communal Title and the Creation of Individual Interests in Reserve Land
(i) The Relationship between Enfranchisement and Individual Property Rights
(ii) Some Statutory Provisions respecting the Possession of Land in Reserves: Sections 20–29

(c) The Management and Disposal of Reserve and Surrendered Lands
(i) The Minister's Authority over Surrendered Lands: Section 53(1) of the Current Act
(ii) The Requirement of Surrender and the Public Purpose Exception: Sections 35 and 37 of the Current Act
(iii) The Exception for Individual Occupants: Section 58(3) of the Current Act

3. Management of Indian Monies
(a) Monies and Surrendered Lands
(b) Capital and Revenue
(c) Loans

Select Bibliography

Lands and Monies under the <u>Indian Act</u>:
Selected Provisions in Historical Perspective

1. The Indian Act: Its Origins and Development

The <u>Indian Act</u> is more than 110 years old, and many of its provisions are even older. The procedures governing surrenders, for example, are rooted in the Royal Proclamation of 1763, and its primary, if not always compatible, goals of protection and assimilation may be found in legislation and treaties that pre-date Confederation. For much of its history it was subject to constant and technically complex tinkering, but it has been thoroughly reviewed and revised only once, in 1946–51. The result of that process was a statute that reflected the same goals as its predecessors and retained many common features. Although several sections that Native peoples found offensive were dropped, most of which dated from the period 1884–1918, and although band council powers were more extensive than before, the final say continued to belong to either the Minister or the Governor in Council. This remains true today.

The main difference between the 1951 Act and what it replaced has been described as the reduction of the Minister's powers to supervisory status with a veto (Tobias 1983: 52). It is also true that earlier, largely unsuccessful, attempts to force assimilation upon Native peoples were abandoned and provisions that authorized the Government to take reserve lands without consent were deleted. Moreover, the current Act authorizes the Governor in Council to grant to a band the right to exercise varying degrees of control over its reserve lands (s.60) and revenue monies (s.69) and, if it has reached "an advanced stage of development," to enact money by-laws as well. The history of the <u>Indian Act</u> is in many respects a history of this tension between wardship and independence, with legislators and Indians often in sharp disagreement as to how independence should be achieved.

(a) Pre-Confederation Roots

Until a few years before Confederation, Indian policy was primarily an imperial responsibility, and therefore, even after the establishment of colonial legislatures, there was little legislation dealing with Indians and Indian lands. In the Maritimes, Upper Canada, and Vancouver Island, treaties were made with the Indians, and although no land was ceded by the Maritime treaties, reserves were set aside there and in Quebec, where there were no treaties at all. One reason for this is that on the Atlantic and in Old Quebec Indian-European relations had developed largely in advance of intense settlement pressures, and probably both sides felt there was sufficient land for all. By the time this was no longer true, the Indians had ceased to be a force to be reckoned with.

The Maritimes

In the early period, what few colonial statutes there were tended to be concerned with selling or giving liquor to Indians or with protecting their reserves from trespass. By the mid-nineteenth century, however, some were becoming a little more ambitious. In Nova Scotia, for example, the legislature passed "An Act to Provide for the Instruction and Permanent Settlement of the Indians" (S.N.S. 1841, c.16), pursuant to which a Commissioner for Indian Affairs supervised, managed and generally protected reserves from "encroachment and alienation" and preserved them for the use of the Indians. Two years later New Brunswick passed a similar law "to regulate the management and disposal of the Indian Reserves in this Province" (S.N.B. 1844, c.47), which permitted the public auction of reserve lands. There was no requirement that the Indians consent, and these statutes, in amended form, remained in force until they were replaced by the first Dominion statute on the subject in 1868. The annual reports of the Nova Scotia Commissioner reveal that in this period "Indian rights were not being respected" (Cumming and Mickenberg 1972: 104).

Upper and Lower Canada

It was the Upper Canadian experience that was most influential in determining the shape of Dominion legislation, however. From the American Revolutionary War onwards there was a series of land cession treaties with the Indians (see under 2(a), below), prompted first by military considerations and then by development and settlement pressures. The views of philanthropic and religious groups, the transfer of Indian affairs from military to civilian control in 1830, and the reports of three royal commissions in the 1840's and 1850's also heralded a period of greater legislative activity. Prior to 1850 and aside from the usual liquor and game laws, the only colonial statute of note was one passed in 1839 "for the protection of the Lands of the Crown in this Province, from Trespass and Injury" (S.U.C. 1839, c.15). Passed to supplement imperial Indian policy, it also provided for Indian Commissioners, but "the sympathies of the enforcing body lay more with the white trespasser than with the Indians" and the depredations against Indian land it was designed to halt continued (INA 1975: 30). Beginning in 1850, the legislatures became more interventionist.

That year saw two statutes that form an important part of the "prehistory" of the <u>Indian Act</u>. "An Act for the Better Protection of the Lands and Property of Indians in Lower Canada" (S.P.C. 1850, c.42) established a Commissioner to manage and dispose of Indian lands and defined "Indian" for the first time. And "An Act for the Better Protection of Indians in Upper Canada from imposition, and the property occupied or enjoyed by them from trespass and injury" (S.P.C. 1850, c.74) made the Commissioners and Indian Superintendents Justices of the Peace with authority to impose punishment for violations of the Act. Among other things, it also exempted Indians from judgement and taxation.

The Gradual Civilization Act of 1857

The most significant of the pre-Confederation statutes, however, was passed in 1857 and it reflected the changes that had been taking place during the preceding three decades. The earlier policy of isolating Indians on remote reserves had not been successful, and there was a new emphasis upon assimilating the Indian as well as protecting and "civilizing" him. This was to be accomplished partly by moving to a policy of smaller reserves nearer to white communities and partly by a policy of enfranchisement (which meant losing Indian status, not gaining the right to vote). If the 1850 laws reveal an increasing involvement of local legislators in Indian policy, the "Act to encourage the gradual civilization of the Indians in this Province, and to amend the laws respecting the Indians" (S.P.C. 1857, c.26) was an even more substantial intervention by the colonial legislature in Indian affairs. Designed to do just what its title promised, it provided an inducement for the enfranchisement its sponsors wished to promote: each enfranchised Indian was to receive an allotment of reserve land and a payment "equal to the principal of the enfranchisee's share of the annuities and other income of the tribe to which he belonged" (INA 1975: 33). The Act has been described in this way:

> After stipulating in the preamble that [it] was designed to encourage civilization of the Indian, remove all legal distinctions between Indians and other Canadians, and integrate them fully into Canadian society, the legislation proceeded to...state that [an Indian] could not be accorded [full] rights and privileges until he could read and write either the French or English language, was free of debt, and of good moral character. If he could meet such criteria, the Indian was then eligible to receive an allotment of [up to fifty acres] of reserve land...and then to be given the franchise. Thus, the legislation to remove all legal distinctions between Indians and Europeans actually established them. In fact, it set standards for acceptance that many, if not most, white colonials could not meet...(Tobias 1983: 42–43)

The Act also provided that an Indian who could not read or write but who could speak either French or English, and who met the other criteria could become enfranchised after satisfactory completion of a period of three years' probation.

The legislators were not the only ones who saw this law as significant. Many Indians regarded the enfranchisement provisions as aimed directly at the destruction of communal land tenure and tribal reserves. A campaign of sorts was launched against it, including a plan to complain to the Prince of Wales. In the words of one commentator:

> A general Indian position emerged in the 1860's. Councils across the colony remained pro-development. They wanted education and agricultural and resource development but would not participate in a system designed, as an Oneida petition said, to "separate our people". Civilization, which they might define as the revitalization of their traditional culture within an agricultural context, they would have; assimilation, the total abandonment of their culture, they would not. The policy of civilization, particularly as it was now centred on enfranchisement, was destined to founder upon the rocks of tribal nationalism. (Milloy 1983: 60)

This has been a constant refrain since the Gradual Civilization Act of 1857. By 1876 very few Indians had applied to be enfranchised, and only one application had been accepted. For some reason, the land this applicant was entitled to by law was never granted to him (Commons Debates 1876: 1037–38). And nearly one hundred years later, when the Minister of Citizenship and Immigration moved second reading of the 1951 Indian Bill, he felt obliged — because of "many protests from Indians" about remarks he had made on an earlier occasion — to explain that by "integration" he did not mean "assimilation" (Commons Debates 1951: 1350). In 1969 Indian associations reacted with even greater vehemence to Ottawa's proposal to do away with special status for Indians altogether (see under (e), below).

A year after the passage of the Gradual Civilization Act, a Special Commission appointed to look into these matters approved in principle of "the gradual destruction of the tribal organization", but recommended against introducing municipal government at that time because of certain American experiences with it. Instead, in 1859 the 1850 and 1857 laws were consolidated by an "Act respecting Civilization and Enfranchisement of certain Indians" (S.P.C. 1859, c.9) and in the following year an "Act respecting the Management of the Indian Lands and Property" (S.P.C. 1860, c.151) made the Commissioner of Crown Lands the Chief Superintendent of Indian Affairs and formalized the surrender process. More significant changes had to await Confederation.

(b) Dominion Legislation, 1867–1876

A year after Confederation, the Secretary of State was made Superintendent of Indian Affairs (S.C. 1868, c.42), and in 1869 an

"Act for the gradual enfranchisement of Indians and the better management of Indian affairs" (S.C. 1869, c.6) introduced a form of the sort of municipal government that the Special Commission of 1858 had recommended against. (If nothing else, the titles of these early statutes appear to reflect an admirable if somewhat perplexing optimism in their repeated determination to do "better".) It instituted the so-called "three year elective system", which required chiefs to be elected for three-year terms and authorized their removal by the Governor for "dishonesty, intemperance or immorality". The elective system applied to a band only if the Governor so ordered, and the Act substituted new but similar provisions respecting enfranchisement. It also lodged a power to regulate a number of minor matters in the "Chiefs of any Tribe in Council", subject to confirmation by the Governor in Council. However, the 1868 law concerning the Department of the Secretary of State retained and increased the much more important powers of the Government over Indian lands and property.

The Gradual Enfranchisement Act (1869) would appear to represent acceptance by the new Dominion Government of the Indian Branch's explanation of why enfranchisement had not worked. In the Branch's view, the traditional Indian leadership was opposed to it and had used their authority to dissuade others from seeking to be enfranchised. Consequently, that leadership had to be gradually replaced by a system of municipal government under departmental control (Milloy 1983: 61–62). This model was continued in the first comprehensive Indian Act in 1876 and its rationale was described by Deputy Superintendent William Spragge in 1871 as follows:

> The Acts framed in the years 1868 and 1869. . .were designed to lead the Indian people by degrees to mingle with the white race in the ordinary avocations of life. It was intended to afford facilities for electing, for a limited period, members of bands to manage, as a Council, local matters — that intelligent, educated men, recognized as chiefs, should carry out the wishes of the male members of mature years in each band, who should be fairly represented in the conduct of their internal affairs. . .Thus establishing a responsible, for an irresponsible system, this provision, by law was designed to pave the way to the establishment of simple municipal institutions. (Excerpted in Daugherty and Madill 1980: 2)

In 1873, a further reorganization of responsibilities took place. A Department of the Interior was established and the Minister of the Interior became, by virtue of his office, Superintendent General of Indian Affairs (S.C. 1873, c.4). The Indian Branch became a separate Department in 1880, although still presided over by the Minister of the Interior, and remained so until it was placed under the Minister of Mines and Resources in 1936. After that it became the responsibility of the Minister of Citizenship and Immigration in 1949 before attaining its present status in 1966. In the 1870's, however, the Department of the

Interior was a logical home for Indian Affairs because the Dominion Government had begun to make treaties with the Indians of the Northwest in order to clear the way for settlement and development. In 1874, Parliament therefore extended its Indian legislation to the new provinces of Manitoba and British Columbia and, ultimately, to the Northwest Territories (S.C. 1874, c.21). It was this extension that prompted the first consolidation of these laws two years later.

(c) The Indian Act, 1876–1951

The Indian Act of 1876

When David Laird, Minister of the Interior and Superintendent General of Indian Affairs, introduced the Indian Act in 1876, he told the House of Commons that:

> [t]he principal object of this Bill is to consolidate the several laws relating to the Indians now on the statute books of the Dominion and the old Provinces of Upper and Lower Canada. We find that there are three different statutes on the Dominion law books as well as portions of several acts that were in operation under the laws of old Canada, which are still in operation. It is advisable to have these consolidated in the interests of the Indian population throughout the Dominion, and have it applied to all the Provinces. (Commons Debates 1876: 342)

As this quotation suggests, the new Indian Act (S.C. 1876, c.18) was directed at consolidation, rather than innovation. But in the process it removed the legislative separation hitherto existing between Indians and Indian lands, and refined and reorganized the provisions respecting surrenders, enfranchisement, band membership, local government, and individualized land holding by way of inheritable location tickets (as to which see under (2), below). The enfranchisement sections did not, however, apply to the "less advanced" western Indians.

The opposition to the enfranchisement procedures of 1857 and 1869 may be the reason that the new Act required band consent to such applications. This met with considerable criticism in the Commons, but the Government resisted pressure to dispense with the consent requirement by pointing out that a scheme unacceptable to the Indians would be undesirable and that amendments could easily be made in the future (Commons Debates 1876: 1036–39). The Act also provided for the enfranchisement of whole bands if a majority of the members requested it, but this provision, like the enfranchisement process generally, was little used (see under 2(b)(i), below).

The Indian Act of 1880

There were a few minor amendments in 1879 and in 1880 the Act was consolidated again (S.C. 1880, c.28), mainly to provide for the reorganization of the administration of the Act by creating a separate Indian Department and to introduce new sections directed at the growing problems in the West. The buffalo were gone and many Indians were facing starvation, there was political unrest, and whisky traders, according to the agents in the field, were doing a brisk business. Many of the new amendments were therefore directed at the control of liquor, prostitution and "other vices". Overall, however, there were few major changes. Enfranchisement continued to be restricted to Indians east of Lake Superior, but the election rules were amended so that, in those bands where the Governor in Council had introduced the elective system, customary "life" chiefs were deprived of their authority unless they had also won election. The 1876 Act had permitted such chiefs to retain their authority until death or resignation, notwithstanding the adoption of the electoral regime. The system was beginning to stiffen.

By 1880, only 57 of approximately 90,000 Indians had been enfranchised, and that figure included children. As one Member of Parliament pointed out, at that rate it would take about 36,000 years to enfranchise the rest (Commons Debates 1880: 1992). The primary reason for such slow progress was that, from the Indian point of view, enfranchisement meant the loss of their land and traditions for very little in return. And from the point of view of the Department, most Indians were not ready for it, anyway. This caused some critics to question the policy that had been pursued over the preceding thirty years, but most were hard-pressed to know what to do instead. Some advocated "wiping out the distinction which exists between the races" and:

> giving the red man all the liberties and rights enjoyed by the white man, and entailing upon him all the responsibilities which attach to those rights and privileges. . .[L]egislation in the direction proposed, old-time legislation, simply means that it will entail upon the people, year after year, and for all time to come, the voting annually of hundreds of thousands of dollars to keep the Indians in the low, degraded state in which they are at present. (Commons Debates 1880: 1990)

Sir John A. Macdonald, however, was both Prime Minister and Minister of the Interior, and he had therefore introduced the Bill. He felt that without this sort of protection the Indians might well "disappear".

The Indian Advancement Act of 1884

In this year the Conservative government introduced a statute that Macdonald described as "experimental". It was, he said, designed to enable:

> the Indians to do by an elective council what the chiefs, by the Statute of 1880, have already the power to do. In some of the tribes or bands, those chiefs are elected now, in others the office is hereditary, and in other bands there is a mixture of both systems. This Bill is to provide that in those larger reserves where the Indians are more advanced in education, and feel more self-confident, more willing to undertake power and self-government, they shall elect their councils much the same as the whites do in the neighbouring townships. (Commons Debates 1884: 539)

The Indian Advancement Act (S.C. 1884, c.28) provided for the election of band councillors for a one-year term and gave councils under the Act significant powers to enact and enforce by-laws, including the power to assess and tax lands of enfranchised Indians and lands held by location ticket. This is now Section 83 of the current Act, concerning money by-laws. The Advancement Act also bestowed a power on the band council to subdivide reserve land for allocation purposes. This sparked some controversy because no guidelines had been set out:

> One of the most difficult questions in the advancement of the Indian and in fitting him to assume the duties of citizenship and manhood, is to be found in the subdivision of reserves. . .The intelligent Indian will, by thrift and industry, acquire the possession of 100 to 200 acres, while others will lose their land. Those frugal Indians are the class fitted to assume the duties of manhood, so they reply: we do not want the privileges of citizenship, which simply means the power to tax us and involves a surrender of more that half the possessions that we have. . .[R]ights which might have been acquired, whether legally or not, but rights recognized on the reserve for years and years, should be protected. It would never do to give six men the power to go and arbitrarily change the bounds. . .(Commons Debates 1884: 540)

Macdonald admitted that permitting elected councils to subdivide reserves could lead to problems, but maintained that this had to be risked if the Indians were to learn municipal government. That it was much of a risk may be doubted, however. By-laws had to be approved and confirmed by the Superintendent General and the Act stipulated that the local Indian agent preside at council meetings. When it was argued that the chief councillor rather than a government functionary ought to do so, Deputy Superintendent Vankoughnet dismissed the suggestion as likely to be "attended with mischievous results" (quoted in INA 1975: 85).

The Act was hardly a resounding success. For it to apply, it had to be requested by the band and authorized by Order-in-Council, and it seems that neither the Indians nor Departmental officials were terribly enthusiastic. By 1898 only four bands in British Columbia, one in Ontario, and one in Quebec had been brought within it, and throughout its entire history (i.e., up to 1951) it was applied to only nine bands, whereas 185 were under the three-year system introduced in 1869. Often its application was highly theoretical as well (Daugherty and Madill 1980: 78; Bartlett 1978: 597). The system was incorporated into the Indian Act proper as Part II in 1906, and forms the basis of Sections 74 to 80 of the current Act, which are an amalgamation of the two pre-existing systems. Elections according to custom are also permitted, and today approximately 40% of Indian bands select their council by this method rather than under the Indian Act.

The debate over the Indian Advancement Act was not without its lighter moments. When a member of the Opposition expressed his support for a clause barring habitual drunkards from holding elected office on council, he suggested this should be extended to whites as well. Why, he asked, should we legislators be "more moral with our Indian friends that with ourselves?" Because, Macdonald replied, it "might diminish the members of the Opposition" (Commons Debates 1884: 542).

The Franchise Act of 1885

This statute constitutes an unusual and brief chapter in the history of Canadian Indian law. From 1885 to 1898, adult Indian males in eastern Canada, whether enfranchised pursuant to the Indian Act or not, could vote in Dominion elections if they met the same, relatively minimal, property qualifications as the whites. This change was effected when the Macdonald government, no longer content to have Dominion elections governed by existing provincial laws, passed the first federal Franchise Act in 1885. It has been suggested, perhaps not without reason, that the Government's expectation was that the Indians would vote for them, and the Bill that was first introduced covered all Indian males over twenty-one. However, the outbreak of the Riel Rebellion soon made this politically inexpedient. After the Opposition inquired whether Poundmaker and Big Bear could go straight "from a scalping party to the polls", Macdonald announced his intention to amend the Bill to exclude the Indians of Manitoba, British Columbia, Keewatin, and the Northwest Territories (Smith 1987: 5).

The Liberal position was that men who were wards of the government and without civic responsibilities could be improperly influenced and therefore should not have the vote. Returned to power in 1896, the Liberals eliminated the separate Dominion franchise in 1898, returning the situation to what it had been thirteen years earlier. The federal franchise was re-established in 1920 but it did not extend to Indians who ordinarily resided on a reserve.

When in 1951 the franchise was again held out to Indians, it was with strings attached. Some Indians had feared in the 1880's that voting would mean subjecting themselves to taxation, but Macdonald assured them that that was not the case. In 1951, however, it was: a waiver of the taxation exemption was a condition of the vote (Bartlett 1985: 583). Finally, in 1960 Indians were able to vote in federal elections on the same terms as other Canadians, eleven years after the Province of British Columbia had granted them the provincial vote.

Selected Legislative Developments, 1884–1946

Three trends stand out in the years between the mid-1880's and the mid-1930's. The first, particularly in the early years, involved attempts to repress by law certain aspects of Indian culture that were seen to inhibit advancement: for example, the criminalization of the potlatch and the Tamanawas dance in 1884, and the Sun dance in 1885. The second is a gradual but steady increase in the discretionary powers vested in the Superintendent General, especially over Indian lands and monies, in order "to overcome the apparently increasing reluctance of band councils to do what the Department deemed desirable" (INA 1975: 105). The third trend, which is closely related to the second, may be described as a steady erosion of reserves. This was done by creating inducements to Indians to surrender their lands, by dispensing with band consent in certain circumstances for the sale, lease, or development of land, and even by outright legislative expropriation. Some examples: the amount of money that the Governor in Council could disburse to band members upon surrendering land was increased from 10 per cent to 50 per cent (S.C. 1906, c.20, s.1); the pressure to dispense with band consent to enfranchisement that had been resisted in 1876 won the day in 1884 (S.C. 1884, c.27, s.16); and in 1911 s.49A was added to the Act, permitting the removal of reserves near larger urban centres without surrender (S.C. 1911, c.14, s.2). These and other examples will be considered in more detail under (2) and (3), below.

There were, of course, other changes, as well. Indians were permitted to devise their land by will, first with band consent, and then without it (S.C. 1884, c.27, s.5; S.C. 1894 c.32, s.1). Compulsory enfranchisement was tried, first in 1920 when Deputy Superintendent General Duncan Campbell Scott decided to "get rid of the Indian problem" and again in 1933 with "greater safeguards" (INA 1975: 121, 127, 131). And with remarkable frequency, other adjustments were made. By the mid-1930's, however, the years of constant tinkering with the Act were over.

(d) The Special Joint Committee and the 1951 Indian Act

After World War II, public (as opposed to official or bureaucratic) attention focussed on Indians in a way that had not happened previously, or at least not since the 1880's. This led to the appointment of a Special Joint Committee of the Senate and House of Commons which sat from 1946 to 1948. This Committee inquired into and reported on Indian administration generally, but with particular emphasis upon matters affecting Indian social and economic status and their "advancement", e.g., treaty rights, band membership, taxes, enfranchisement, the vote, encroachment upon reserves, and education. It was the first time that a serious attempt had been made to do this, and the first time that Indians were consulted in an organized way.

The 1946 hearings dealt with evidence from officials of the Indian Department, and were concerned mainly with their problems: inadequate staffing, low budgets, low salaries, low morale, and so on. In its first report that year the Committee recommended that "no decision affecting the welfare of the Indians...be made without the consent of the band", and this was a principle adopted, even if it was incompletely reflected in the legislation that ultimately resulted (Commons Debates 1946: 5485). The Committee also recommended that responsibility for Indian services be turned over to the provinces.

In 1947, it heard from representatives of a number of Indian bands and associations, a few of which had also made submissions the previous year. More emphasis was put upon the Indian Act itself during these hearings, but mainly in terms of broad principles, e.g., treaty rights, enfranchisement, and the powers of the Superintendent General. Most of the recommendations made by the Committee were concerned with Departmental administration, but it also urged the government — without success — to establish a claims commission for inquiring into treaty and other rights.

In 1948, the Committee spent much more of its time considering how the Act ought to be amended, but most of their deliberations on this topic were in camera and are not recorded in the minutes. In May and June 1948 two reports were submitted, one recommending that Indians be given the vote in Dominion elections, the other that, "with a few exceptions, all sections of the Act be either repealed or amended". This report then went on to make a number of further recommendations, both within and beyond the terms of reference set down in 1946, but these did not involve specific amendments. The Government then drafted a new Act, Bill 267, which it introduced, after enduring considerable criticism for the length of time it was taking, two weeks before Parliament was to prorogue in June 1950.

Both the substance of the Bill and the lack of time that the Government had allotted for consideration of it drew the ire of Committee members, the Opposition, and the press — not to mention the Indians themselves. There were demands that the Bill be held over until the next session, and one Committee member told the House that he was "deeply" disappointed:

> To think that, after all our efforts, the sum total of our reward is this
> contemptible thing we have before us today makes me wonder if I do
> not have to struggle to keep my faith in humanity...I have found no
> evidence of anything in the Bill to help the Indians to help themselves
> beyond what we had in the old Act. (Commons Debates 1950: 3946)

Bill 267 was withdrawn, and a Conference was held with Indian
representatives prior to introducing a second bill the following year.
After some discussion, which is summarized in the 1951 Commons
Debates, Appendix B at 1364–67, the Conference unanimously
approved 103 of the 124 sections of the new Bill (No. 79) and a
majority approved a further 15. Of the remaining six, two dealing with
taxation, the vote, and enfranchisement were unanimously opposed and
four, concerning liquor, were opposed by a majority (Commons Debates
1951: 1351).

Bill 79 was referred to a special committee in April 1951 and was
passed into law in May. Those who had criticized Bill 267 were
generally pleased with the new Act. The restrictions on Indian culture
(the potlatch, etc.) had been removed, and many of the extraordinary
powers to interfere with reserves that had "crept into" the old Act over
the years were gone. The Indian Advancement Act (Part II of the 1906
consolidation) became the local government sections of the new Act and
the council powers provided for there were accordingly extended to
councils under the 1951 law (INA 1975: 165). Considerable authority
did, however, remain with the Governor in Council and the Superintendent General. For example, the former could exempt any band,
Indian, or Indian lands from the operation of most of the Act (s.4(2)).
Proposals to have this power amended to be conditional upon band
consent failed (Commons Debates 1951: 1357, 1530, 1535, 3106–09).

(e) Some Subsequent Developments

One historian of Canadian Indian policy has suggested that the 1951
Act did not repudiate the goal of speedy assimilation, only the means
that had been previously adopted to achieve it. And when it became
clear that the new Act was not much more likely to promote this than
its predecessors, alternative means were sought (Tobias 1983: 53).
Whether or not that is an accurate assessment, some of these means
need to be mentioned briefly.

The Hawthorn Report

Although s.141 of the 1927 Indian Act, which had prohibited the
raising of funds and the obtaining of legal advice for the purpose of
prosecuting land claims, was dropped from the Act in 1951, the Special
Committee's recommendation that a claims commission be established
was rejected by the Liberal government. When a second Joint

Committee in 1959–61 made a similar recommendation, the Conservative government adopted the proposal but fell before introducing the required legislation. The new Liberal administration put forward a modified version of the earlier proposal, but this too was side-tracked, this time by the federal election of 1965.

At about the same time, Dr. H.B. Hawthorn, who had done a report on British Columbia's Indians in the 1950's, was asked to do a further study, and in 1966–67 a two-part report entitled "A Detailed Survey of the Contemporary Indians of Canada" was published. It was not directly concerned with amendments to the Act, but was concerned with the "social, educational and economic situation" of the Indians. The report described the Indians as "citizens plus", and emphasized federal responsibility for Indian affairs. While services were being gradually transferred to the provinces, as the 1946 Special Committee had recommended, there was a need for caution because the provinces lacked administrative and professional expertise in the area:

> The perception that Indians are not really complete provincial citizens because of their special...relation to the federal government easily gets transmuted into the argument that if they wish to receive the same government treatment as other provincial citizens, they will have to give up their special privileges under treaty or the Indian Act. Provincial officials and politicians display a much more assimilative and less protective philosophy to Indians than does the federal government. There is, for example, a fairly general provincial antipathy to the reserve system. Indians, we were told on several occasions, cannot have it both ways and retain their special privileges while simultaneously obtaining the full benefits of provincial citizenship. (Pt.1, ch.17)

The 1969 Policy Statement

It was something of a surprise, therefore, when a few years later the Liberal government produced its White Paper on Indian policy. It proposed the dismantling of the Indian Affairs Branch within five years, the repeal of the Indian Act, the rejection of the land claims and treaties as regressive and the provision of services to Indians through regular provincial agencies. It ignored the "spirit and intent" of the Hawthorn Report and brought an outraged reaction from Indian groups. It represents, together with the decision of the Supreme Court of Canada in Calder v. A.G.B.C., [1973] S.C.R. 313, a major turning point in Canadian Indian history.

The B.C. Indians' Brown Paper, the Alberta Red Paper, and the Manitoba "Wahbung" all argued strongly against it (Daugherty and Madill 1980: 80). As the Indian Chiefs of Alberta put it in their Red Paper, they wanted the Act reviewed, not repealed, and wanted their special status confirmed and entrenched. "The only way to maintain our culture is for us to remain as Indians. To preserve our culture it is necessary to preserve our status, rights, lands and traditions. Our treaties are the bases of our rights" (quoted in Bartlett 1978: 589). Of course, not all Indians have treaties, and not all agreed. But the proposed policy was withdrawn.

The 1970's and 1980's

Thereafter the emphasis shifted from the Indian Act to land claims, treaties, and native self-government and self-determination. It was a considerable departure from the policy announced in 1969. The James Bay Agreement, the Calder case, and the new federal policy on Native claims that was a result are all evidence of this, as is the continuing process of placing aboriginal rights into the Constitution. In 1981, the federal government announced a "re-affirmation" of the Comprehensive Native Claims process begun in 1973 in a publication entitled "In All Fairness: A Native Claims Policy", which was examined in detail a few years later by the Task Force to Review Comprehensive Claims Policy. This body issued a report in 1985 entitled "Living Treaties: Lasting Agreements", which declared the earlier policy defective in a number of respects. It proposed major changes designed to avoid the resort to courts that the Task Force saw the failure of existing policy tending towards, one of which was the negotiation of agreements which do not involve the extinguishment of Indian title. The Sechelt self-government legislation and the 1985 amendments to the Indian Act respecting band membership are also part of this current if controversial trend, and the latter represents one of the very few occasions in the last thirty years when the 1951 Act has been altered.

2. Indian Lands at Common Law and under the Indian Act

Under Section 91(24) of the Constitution Act, 1867, the Parliament of Canada has responsibility for "Indians and Lands reserved for the Indians". Prior to the first federal Indian Act in 1876, the fact that this section allocates legislative jurisdiction over "not one but two subject matters" (Lysyk 1967: 514) was clear: Indians and Indian lands tended to be dealt with in separate statutes. This changed in 1876, and although the primary reason was simply to consolidate the scattered Dominion and pre-Confederation statutes at a time when Parliament was extending its juristiction into newly acquired provinces and territories (House of Commons Debates 1876: 342), the change reflected a philosophical consolidation as well. Since at least 1830, when Indian affairs passed from military to civilian control, the critical importance of Indian lands to the new policy of "protecting, civilizing and assimilating" the Indian had been recognized (Tobias 1983: 39), both as a means of insulating him from corrupt influences and of training him in the property values of European culture. Philanthropic and religious groups were particularly influential in this process. But Indian lands were also important because, as the century progressed, increasing pressure was brought to bear upon governments to open up more of this land for settlement and development. The imperial authorities were aware of this, and in keeping with standard imperial practice at the time, retained responsibility for the Indians notwithstanding the introduction of responsible government in the Canadas. By the 1850's, however, they were no longer willing to bear the expense this entailed, and sought to be relieved of it (British Parliamentary Papers 1856: 247). Accordingly, in 1860 responsibility for the Indian Department was transferred to the Canadian government, a move many Indians saw as giving up control to "the land jobbers" (Milloy 1983: 60).

Introducing the Indian Act of 1880, Sir John A. Macdonald made reference to both these tendencies when he responded to the member from South Brant's contention that government policy, instead of improving and assimilating the Indians, was only "more firmly fastening the shackles of tutelage upon them". Suggesting that his critic's view were politically motivated, he said:

> Disguise it as we may, wherever there is an Indian settlement the whites in the vicinity are very naturally anxious. . .to get rid of the red men, believing and perhaps, truly, that the progress of the locality is retarded by them, and that the sooner they are enfranchised, or deprived of their lands, and allowed to shift for themselves, the better. If the Indians were to disappear from the continent, the Indian question would cease to exist. But we must remember that they are the original owners of the soil, of which they have been dispossessed by the covetousness and ambition of our ancestors. . .[T]he Indians have been great sufferers by the discovery of America, and the transfer to it of a large white population. We are bound to protect them. (House of Commons Debates 1880: 1990–91)

The tensions between protecting and "civilizing" the Indian, and especially between protecting his land and developing it, are reflected in the history of some of the statutory provisions respecting (i) surrenders, (ii) individual title to reserve land, and (iii) the granting and leasing of reserve land without surrender. These will be considered in turn.

(a) The Concept of Surrender

(i) The Original Meaning

In North America the imperial powers, all of whom had to contend with aboriginal peoples, behaved in ways that reflect both similarities and differences between their governmental traditions and the situations in which they found themselves. The French, for example, do not appear to have recognized any form of Indian title, and although lands were set aside for the Indians, no land "surrenders" took place (Stanley 1983: 4). Except for the purposes of the military and the fur trade, Indian relations were more a matter for Church than State, and this largely accounts for the provisions respecting "special reserves" under Indian legislation from Confederation to the present day: such reserves are primarily those in southern Quebec granted to Catholic religious orders (Morse 1985: 510).

The British, on the other hand, were relative latecomers to much of what is now Canada, and the importance of the Indians as allies in their wars against both the French and, later, the Americans, strongly influenced their Native policy. The "nucleus" of an Indian department had been established in the late seventeenth century in the American colonies, and this arrangement was put on a firmer footing in 1755 when two superintendents were appointed who reported to the British military commander in North America. During and immediately after the Seven Years' War, the British promised to protect the lands of their Indian allies, and this promise was formalized in Royal Proclamations in 1761 and 1763 (Hinge, Vol I: 1–7).

The Royal Proclamation of 1763 was by far the more important, and has been described as the "Indian Magna Carta". It established the broad outlines of British Indian policy in North America for years to come. Once regarded as the source of the Indian title that is the subject of land surrenders, Canadian courts now regard it instead as expressing the developing policy of the common law: Guerin et al. v. R. and National Indian Brotherhood, [1984] 6 W.W.R 481 (S.C.C.), per Dickson, J., interpreting the court's earlier decision in Calder v. A.G.B.C., [1973] S.C.R.313. The Royal Proclamation is strong evidence of the importance of the Indians, and in particular the Iroquois Confederacy, to Britain in the eighteenth and early nineteenth centuries. Among other things, it designated a protected Indian Territory into which Europeans could not go without licence and the lands of which could not be settled unless ceded in open assembly to an official authorized to represent the British Crown. These protections survived the Quebec Act of 1774, which removed the land north of the Ohio from the Indian Territory. A.-G. for Ontario v. Bear Island Foundation et al. (1984) 49 O.R. 353 at 376, and Sections 37–41 of the present Indian Act continue to reflect both the policies and the procedures first explicitly laid out in 1763.

However, when the American Revolutionary War ended and Britain gave up its claim to much of the land of its Indian allies, it did so without consulting them and soon found itself looking for land within British North America for both the Indians and the Loyalists. The Proclamation had contemplated the Crown buying lands from Indians "inclined to dispose of them", and therefore every effort was made to see that they were so inclined. Between 1781 and 1836, twenty-three land sales were concluded with the Mississaugas, Chippewas, Ottawas, Potawotomis, and other tribes of Upper Canada (Stanley 1983: 8–9). Increasingly vulnerable after the conclusion of the War of 1812 because their hunting grounds were exhausted and because they had ceased to be important as military allies, the Indians were no longer a force to be reckoned with (Surtees 1983: 65). A policy of placating them with concessions therefore gave way to a policy of obtaining their land and inducting them into British society — should any of them survive what many whites saw as their inevitable extinction.

Before Confederation, however, the situation varied from colony to colony. In Lower Canada the process of settlement had been largely completed during the French regime, and in the Atlantic colonies neither the French nor the British appear to have negotiated land cessions, even after 1763. In the West, with the possible exception of the Selkirk Treaty of 1817, there was insufficient settlement even to raise the issue until the colonies of Red River, Vancouver Island, and British Columbia were established. But in Upper Canada the surrender procedures were followed, and the treaties or land agreements entered into there became important precedents for the numbered Dominion treaties that were negotiated after Confederation.

In Canadian law an Indian treaty, at least for the purposes of Section 88 of the Indian Act, "is an agreement *sui generis* which is neither created nor terminated according to the rules of international law" (Simon v. The Queen (1985), 23 C.C.C.(3d) 238 (S.C.C.) at 252). Equally important, it "embraces all such engagements made by persons in authority as may be brought within the term 'the word of the white man'" (Regina v. White and Bob (1965), 50 D.L.R.(2d) 613 (B.C.C.A.) *per* Norris, J.A. at 648–49, aff'd (1966), 52 D.L.R.(2d) 481). Outside the Maritimes, however, most Indian treaties, however they might be styled, involved the cession of land, and the Upper Canadian ones were no exception.

At first these treaties were on the basis of a single, one-time payment. After the War of 1812, however, the Lords of the Treasury resolved that the cost of purchasing land in Upper Canada ought to be borne locally:

> To provide this revenue, Lieutenant-Governor Maitland proposed to sell a portion of the Indian lands at public auction. Purchasers would be required to pay 10 per cent as a downpayment and carry a mortgage for the balance. However, as long as they paid the annual interest, the principal would not be required. The annual income from interest would then be used to make a payment, in perpetuity, to the Indians who sold their land. (Surtees 1983: 69–70)

In this way the authorities moved from relying exclusively on lump sums to annuities or "treaty money", and from 1818 onwards this was part of the negotiating process.

The Robinson Superior and Robinson Huron treaties of 1850 were particularly important. Named after the man who negotiated them, these treaties extinguished Native title to vast tracts of Indian land and set a pattern for future dealings. As provided for in the Royal Proclamation, the treaties were negotiated at a "public meeting or Assembly" at which the lands were ceded to a representative of the Crown. Reserves were set aside and listed in a schedule, and the Indians undertook not to "sell, lease or otherwise dispose of any portion of their reservations without the consent of the Superintendent General of Indian Affairs. . .(or) at any time (to) hinder or prevent persons from exploring or searching for minerals or other valuable productions in any part of the territory. . .ceded to Her Majesty". In addition to the reserves, the Indians received a lump sum payment and were promised annuities and a continuation of their hunting and fishing rights over the ceded territory, "excepting only such portions. . .as may from time to time be sold or leased to individuals or companies. . .and occupied by them with the consent of the Provincial Government".

The term "surrender", therefore, originally meant the sale of lands traditionally occupied or used by the Indians and the extinguishing of their right of occupation, but not necessarily of their right to hunt and fish. The land could be surrendered only to the Crown and, once surrendered, full legal title was in the Crown. The clarity of this result was clouded, however, both by the division of powers consequent upon Confederation and by the need to manage lands reserved in the treaty process "for the use and benefit" of the Indians occupying them.

(ii) The Problem Created by Confederation and St. Catharines Milling and Lumber Co. v. The Queen in Right of Ontario (1888), 14 App. Cas. 46 (P.C.)

Immediately after Confederation, the procedures for surrendering lands "reserved for the use of the Indians" that had been employed in the Robinson treaties were set out in more detail in Sections 8–10 of "An Act providing for the organization of the Department of the Secretary of State of Canada, and for the management of Indian and Ordinance Lands", S.C. 1868, c. 42. The Act provided that, to be valid, a surrender had to be by a majority of the chiefs at a public assembly held in the presence of the Secretary of State or his duly authorized representative, and the surrender had to be certified on oath before a judge. This was, in essence, the process laid down by the Royal Proclamation of 1763, modified to apply to lands already reserved to Indians pursuant to treaty or otherwise. It was continued in subsequent legislation, up to and including, although in amended form, Section 39 of the present Indian Act.

In the West, however, the treaty process was just beginning, and between 1871 and 1877, the Dominion government negotiated seven numbered treaties with the western Indians in which they ceded land in return for reserves, annuities, hunting and fishing rights and sundry lesser considerations. Unlike the Robinson treaties, the reserves were not confirmed at the time of the treaty; instead, the Crown undertook to confirm them later, i.e., to grant them back to the Indians, after they had been surveyed. This change is significant because it meant that these reserves were made up of land surrendered by treaty, the Indian title to which had been extinguished. This caused some confusion in the early 1880's (see under (iii), below), and is of concern to many Indians today (Living Treaties 1985: 37–38).

One of these numbered treaties, Treaty No. 3 with the Ojibwa Indians in 1873, became the foundation of the Dominion government's position in the St. Catharines case. Relying upon the surrender by the Indians, the Dominion government claimed the right to issue Dominion timber licences in the area. When it was subsequently determined that these lands were within the province of Ontario, the question of the validity of these licences was raised. To succeed in court, therefore, the Dominion government became owner in their place. The Privy Council, however, ruled that the fee in the land had been in the Crown all along, and that only the Indians' right of occupancy, "a personal and usufructuary right", had been surrendered and extinguished by the treaty. Because the land was in Ontario and because Section 109 of the BNA Act was read as bestowing the beneficial interest in such Crown lands upon the province, the Dominion had no authority to grant the licences. Once the Indian title, which was an "interest other than that of the province" under Section 109, was extinguished, full beneficial title vested in the Crown in right of the province.

This created something of a constitutional problem for the Dominion government, charged as it was with responsibility for Indians and lands reserved for Indians. If, upon surrender to the Dominion of land located in a province, the entire beneficial interest in the land vested in the Crown in right of that province, how could the Dominion establish reserves following such a surrender or subsequently dispose of reserve land surrendered pursuant to the Indian Act? Once surrendered, the land was the province's, not the Dominion's, to dispose of. The Privy Council in Ontario Mining Company v. Seybold, [1903] A.C. 73 alluded to these difficulties in a case in which some land surrendered under Treaty No. 3 had been designated a reserve and re-surrendered for sale under the Indian Act of 1880. In ruling against the subsequent sale of the land by the Dominion, Lord Davey reminded Ottawa of the distinction, suggesting that the nature of the Canadian Constitution required Ottawa and the provinces to cooperate in such matters:

[The argument of counsel for the appellants] ignores the effect of the surrender of 1873 as declared in [the St. Catharines Milling case]...Let it be assumed that the Government of the province, taking advantage of the surrender of 1873, came at least under an honourable engagement to fulfill the terms on the faith of which the surrender was made, and, therefore, to concur with the Dominion Government in appropriating certain undefined portions of the surrendered lands as Indian reserves. The result, however, is that the choice and location of the lands to be so appropriated could only be effectively made by the joint action of the two governments. (82–83)

The Privy Council in Seybold described their decision in favour of the province as "a corollary" of their earlier decision in St. Catharines Milling, and a similar result was reached some twenty years later in A.-G. of Quebec and Star Chrome Mining v. A.-G. of Canada, [1921] A.C. 401. The problem was that when Indians surrendered lands occupied or used by them at common law or pursuant to the Royal Proclamation, they invariably did so on the condition that a portion of the land be reserved for their continued use and benefit. If anything, Street, J. of the Ontario Divisional Court put the issue in the Seybold case even more succinctly when he noted that it would be unjust of the province to ignore the terms of the surrender even though they had no legal obligation to do so.

The primary effect of these decisions was "to inhibit the establishment of reserves by the federal government and to preclude the surrender of such lands for the benefit of the Indians" (Morse 1985: 487). Clearly both levels of government had to reach some sort of agreement concerning Indian reserves, and this in fact happened, except in Quebec. Agreements were made with Ontario in 1891, 1894, 1905, 1923 and 1924, with the prairie provinces in 1930, with the Atlantic provinces in 1958–59, and with British Columbia in 1912. The latter was a particularly difficult process, however, and matters were not finally settled in B.C. until 1938 (see under (iv), below).

(iii) Some Statutory Provisions Concerning Surrenders: Sections 2(1), 18(1), 37, 38, and 53(1)

Today the most relevant sections are Section 2(1), which defines "reserve" and "surrendered lands"; Section 18(1), which provides that reserves are held for the "use and benefit" of the Indian bands assigned to them; Section 37, which provides that reserve lands may not be sold or leased without being surrendered, unless the Act otherwise provides; Section 38, which designates surrenders as either "absolute or qualified, conditional or unconditional"; and Section 53(1), which vests the management and disposition of surrendered lands in the Minister. Section 35, which permits reserve land under certain circumstances to be expropriated or used for public purposes, and Section 58(3), which permits the Minister to lease the unsurrendered land of an individual Indian upon request, are more appropriately considered under headings (b) and (c), below. Over time, the effect of St. Catharines Milling and the other cases referred to above seems to have been not only to require federal-provincial cooperation in carving reserves out of land, the underlying title to which is vested in the provincial Crown, but also to highlight a latent ambiguity in these provisions and their predecessors.

Reserves and Surrenders

Section 3(6) of the Indian Act of 1876 defined a reserve as "any tract...of land set apart by treaty or otherwise for the use or benefit of...a particular band of Indians, of which the legal title is in the Crown, but which is unsurrendered..." Which Crown is unspecified, but the final phrase was presumably meant to acknowledge that reserve land set apart by treaty was land, the Native title to which had not been included in the surrender effected by the treaty, as was the case with the Robinson treaties of 1850. There was no definition of "surrendered lands" in the 1876 Act, but "Indian lands" were defined in Section 3(8) as "any reserve or portion of a reserve which has been surrendered to the Crown". By Section 29, such lands were to be "managed, leased, and sold as the Governor in Council may direct".

However, in 1882 the Act, which had been consolidated again in 1880 without affecting these definitions, was amended by deleting the phrase "but which is unsurrendered" in Section 3(6) and substituting the words "and which remains a portion of the said reserve" (S.C. 1882, c.30, s.1). None of the changes effected by the 1882 amending statute were debated in the House of Commons, but in the Senate one member queried the deletion, asserting that the amended section now seemed only to say that "an Indian reserve should be an Indian reserve". He received the following response:

> Many Indian reserves were set apart as such after the territory in which they are situated had been surrendered to the Crown by the Indians, such surrender having embraced with the other land covered thereby the reserves subsequently allotted to the Indians. This is the case with all the Indian reserves in the Northwest Territories and with very many in Manitoba and Keewatin. The Superintendent General considers this amendment necessary to carry out the Act. (Senate Debates 1882: 704)

This excerpt would seem to clarify a change that seems otherwise perplexing (see, for example, the decision of the Supreme Court of Canada in The Queen v. Smith (1983), 47 N.R. 132 at 143–44, where the deletion is incorrectly attributed to the Indian Act of 1886). Because the Dominion numbered treaties involved the surrender of all the Indians' lands, leaving reserves to be confirmed later, legislation that confined reserves to unsurrendered lands could, technically, be construed as excluding the western reserves from the definition. The fact that reserves and reserve land surrendered pursuant to the Indian Act may or may not have been previously surrendered to the Crown by treaty was not acknowledged, therefore, in the Indian Act of 1876.

The 1876 and 1882 definitions were combined in the 1906 Indian Act (R.S.C. 1906, c.81, s.2(i)), and the current definitions of "reserve" and "surrendered lands" — the phrase "Indian lands" was dropped in 1951 — clearly reflect a legislative intent to confine the meaning of "surrendered lands" to lands surrendered pursuant to the Act. However, even here, if the legal result of a surrender is to perfect the title of the provincial Crown, the St. Catharines problem can arise, as in fact it did in Smith, above.

In the judgement of the Court in that case, Estey, J. noted the confusing nature not only of the definition of "surrendered lands" in Section 2(1), but also of the surrender requirement in Section 37 and the authority of the Minister to dispose of surrendered land pursuant to Section 53(1). His remarks with respect to the latter deserve quotation:

> Section 53.(1)...appear[s] to have been based upon an assumption that after the surrender of lands set aside for Indians under s.91(24), some interest therein remains in the government of Canada; or alternatively, that a facilitative surrender has been taken so as to enable the Crown to manage the lands for the continued use and benefit by and of the Indians. The St. Catharines case, of course, has long since decided otherwise when the surrender of the usufructary interest in complete. It may be that s.53 and like provisions in the Indian Act are predicated upon the assumption that lands comprised in the Indian Reserves have been conveyed by the province to the Federal Government. Since these lands would then become public lands of the Government of Canada, Parliament could validly make provision for their continued use under s.91(1A). However, insofar as s.53(1) purports to affect land held by the province, it would be *ultra vires*. (146)

But such situations will be rare because the underlying title to reserve land is generally in the federal Crown, either because the land is federal territory (e.g., the Yukon) or by virtue of the sort of federal-provincial agreement referred to under heading (ii), above.

When one considers the reason for the deletion in 1882 of the phrase "but which is unsurrendered" from the definition of "reserve", the historical depth of the ambiguity becomes clear. Because most of the reserve land in western Canada had been surrendered (in the old sense) before being reserved, the Indian Department, with this meaning in mind, was concerned that these lands would be excluded from the statutory definition. Hence they requested the amendment to ensure they were included. However, the substitution of the words "and which remains a portion of the said reserve" indicated that reserve lands subsequently surrendered pursuant to the Act (i.e., in the newer sense) were *not* to be included in the definition of "reserve". These were defined as "Indian lands" or, since 1951, "surrendered lands". "Surrender" has both an older and a newer connotation — and so, as the excerpt from the Senate debates quoted above reveals, does the term "reserve". Originally it meant land which had not yet been ceded to the Crown, e.g., land within the Indian Territory marked off by the Royal Proclamation. But now it usually means a reserve as contemplated by the Indian Act, which may or may not be composed of land ceded by treaty, depending upon whether there was a treaty, or if there was, what its terms were.

Conditional Surrenders

In addition to a new definition of "surrendered lands", the Indian Act of 1951 (S.C. 1951, c.29, s.38(2)) explicitly acknowledged the concept of a "conditional" or "qualified" surrender, perhaps partly as a result of the discussion concerning what constituted a "total and definitive" surrender in St. Ann's Island Shooting & Fishing Club Ltd. v. The Queen, [1950] S.C.R. 211. The idea that a surrender might be subject to conditions was, of course, nothing new. The Indian Act of 1876 provided that surrendered lands were to be managed as the Governor in Council directed, subject to the conditions of surrender (s.29), and this directive is now section 53(1) of the present Act. As Estey, J. said in Smith, however:

> Whatever 'surrender' may mean in the Indian Act, a surrender in law
> has the immediate result of extinguishing the personal right of the
> Indians to which federal jurisdiction attaches under s.91(24). (at 141)

But if a surrender is conditional or qualified, it can be said that the land in question continues to be "reserved for the Indians" and under federal jurisdiction. The surrender is a legal condition precedent to any dealing in the land but is merely "facilitative", i.e., designed to increase the value of the land to the Indians. Such land, although surrendered, remains land "reserved for the Indians" and is, for example, not subject to municipal zoning by-laws or provincial health regulations: Corporation of Surrey et al. v. Peace Arch Enterprises Ltd. and Surfside Recreations Ltd. (1970), 74 W.W.R. 380 (B.C.C.A.), although this decision should not be compared to Reference re Stony Plain Indian Reserve No.135 (1981), 130 D.L.R. (3D) 636 (Alta. C.A.). In Smith an attempt was made to characterize the surrender in that case as a conditional one, but it did not succeed, a result that strongly suggests that when an outright sale is contemplated the courts will be slow to conclude that the surrender of the usufructary interest has not been complete. Where a lease is concerned, however, the situation is different. As MacLean, J.A. put it in the Peace Arch case:

> In my view the "surrender" under the Indian Act is not a surrender
> as a conveyancer would understand it. The Indians are in effect
> forbidden from leasing or conveying the lands within an Indian
> reserve, and this function must be performed by an official of the
> Government if it is to be performed at all. . .Further, it is to be noted

that the surrender is in favour of Her Majesty "in trust". This obviously means in trust for the Indians. The title which Her Majesty gets under this arrangement is an empty one. (385)

To sum up: the term "surrender" would appear to have at least two meanings. The older of the two refers to the process, first formalized in the Proclamation of 1763, whereby Indians ceded their lands to the Crown by conveyance or treaty, reserving portions of them for their continued use and occupation (as in the Robinson Treaties) or surrendering all the land and receiving a grant of reserve land back from the government (as in the numbered Treaties). To protect the Indians from unscrupulous whites, a surrender could be made only to the Crown and only in a prescribed fashion. The object of this sort of surrender is the complete extinguishment of Native title to the land. The second, newer meaning refers to the process under the Indian Act by which land that is already part of an Indian reserve is surrendered to the Crown either for sale or, much more likely, for lease. Here the object may be extinguishment, but much more often the object of a surrender will be simply to so manage the land as to maximize its economic benefit to the band, without extinguishing the Native title.

(iv) Where the Underlying Title is in the Federal Crown: the British Columbia Example

As stated above, the St. Catharines problem does not arise where the fee simple is in the federal Crown, and over the years agreements were entered into with a number of provinces where by they either agreed to cooperate with federal plans to dispose of surrendered lands or actually transferred title to reserve lands to the federal Crown. In British Columbia this process was a difficult one.

Unlike the prairie provinces, Native title to most of British Columbia has never been ceded by treaty, and whether this title was implicitly extinguished by colonial land legislation is a question that has yet to receive a definitive judicial answer. Only the northeast corner, which was included in Treaty No. 8 in 1899, and approximately one-fortieth of Vancouver Island, ceded to James Douglas in his capacity as HBC Chief Factor (to 1858) and Colonial Governor (1851–64), is subject to treaty.

The Pre-Confederation Vancouver Island Treaties

The fourteen Douglas treaties (1850–54) really fall into two groups, i.e. the eleven negotiated at Fort Victoria, which ceded an arc of land from Sooke to the northern end of the Saanich Peninsula, and the remaining three, two of which concern land at Fort Rupert and one at Nanaimo (Duff 1969). Based upon New Zealand precedents and sharing much in common with the Robinson treaties of the same period, the treaties provided for reserves, lump sum payments, and the preservation of fishing and hunting rights in return for the ceded land. However, they were comparatively informal transactions, and there is reason to believe that the Island Indians understood the significance of them even less well than their prairie and Ontario counterparts. Unlike the treaties made east of the Rockies, there was no provision for regular payments: Douglas appears to have regarded annuities and lump sums as mutually exclusive, and the Indians opted for the latter although he urged them to choose the former. Nor, unlike the Robinson treaties, do the Vancouver Island agreements mention any limitations on the Native right to hunt and fish or explicitly refer to any restrictions on leasing or selling land. Douglas' policy, however, was to lease unused portions of the reserves for the benefit of the Indians (Fisher 1977: 114).

On at least four occasions to date, Canadian courts have pronounced upon these treaties. In Regina v. White and Bob, referred to under heading (i), above, the Supreme Court of Canada confirmed the B.C. Court of Appeal's ruling that the treaty with the Saalequun people of Nanaimo is a treaty under the Indian Act. Similar findings were made in respect of the Sooke agreement in Regina v. Cooper (1968), 1 D.L.R.(3d) 113 (B.C.S.C.) and the North Saanich agreement in Regina v. Bartleman (1984), 55 B.C.L.R. 78 (B.C.C.A.). The provincial government tried recently to relitigate this issue in a lawsuit between the Tsawout, whose ancestors were one of the three tribal groups who signed the North Saanich Treaty in 1852, and a corporation that had received permission from the provincial government to develop a marina in Saanichton Bay. The attempt was unsuccessful because the court ruled that the proposed development would interfere with fishing rights guaranteed by the treaty (Saanichton Marina Ltd. v. Claxton et al., B.C.S.C., 8 October, 1987).

When Douglas was obliged to summon the Colony of Vancouver Island's first legislative assembly in 1856, his treaty-making effectively ceased. Already strapped for funds, Douglas appealed in vain in 1861 to the Colonial Office, but they advised him that such matters were now a matter for the local legislature. The legislature refused to vote money for what they continued to see as an imperial responsibility. With the exception of an island in Barkley Sound that was conveyed in 1859, no more treaties were negotiated on Vancouver Island (Madill 1981: 74). None at all were entered into during the colonial period (1858–71) on mainland British Columbia because, by the time the colony was established in 1858, Douglas was out of funds and the colonial governments which administered Vancouver Island and British Columbia after Douglas' retirement took the position that the policy of extinguishing Native title was inapplicable on the Pacific slope. Much later, when the Nishga and Tshimshian peoples asked Premier Smithe in 1887 for a treaty like the ones they had heard the Dominion government had made with the Indians east of the Rockies, Smithe even went so far as to pretend to them that they had been misinformed (Raunet 1984: 94–98).

Colonial Land Policy after Douglas, 1864–1871

The problems created by the St. Catharines, Seybold, and Star Chrome cases, discussed under (ii), above, were some years in the future when British Columbia joined Confederation in 1871. It is perhaps not surprising, therefore, that the Terms of Union have little to say about Indians and their lands and, indeed, very nearly included nothing at all of the subject (Special Joint Committee 1927: 4–5). Had the Dominion government been better informed about the new province's Indian policy, it is likely that the terms would have been more detailed and the parties less disposed to agree. As it is, Article 13 acknowledges that Indians and their lands are to pass under Dominion jurisdiction and that "a policy as liberal as that hitherto pursued" by the colony will be continued. In order to carry out that policy:

> . . .tracts of land of such extent as it has hitherto been the practice of the British Columbia Government to appropriate for that purpose, shall from time to time be conveyed by the Local Government to the Dominion Government for the use and benefit of the Indians on the application of the Dominion Government. . .

The Article goes on to provide that, in the event of disagreement, problems should be referred to the Secretary of State for the Colonies.

The Dominion government soon discovered just how liberal British Columbia's policy had been and just what its practice respecting allocating reserve land was. Whereas Dominion policy was to extinguish Native title and then allot reserves in the neighbourhood of eighty acres per family, since Douglas retired as governor, the practice in B.C. had been not to bother about Native title and to allot only six to ten acres per family (Bankes 1986: 136). While it is true that Douglas had not negotiated any land surrenders during the last ten years of his terms, he had continued to set aside generous reserves, as he explained in a letter to Dr. I.W. Powell, the first Indian Superintendent:

> . . .in laying out Indian Reserves no specific number of acres was insisted on. The principle followed in all cases was to leave the extent and selection of the land entirely optional with the Indians. . .the surveying officers having instructions to meet their wishes in every particular. . . (Reproduced in Cail 1974: Appendix D, Item 4)

He warned Powell against departing from this practice, but this in fact had already happened, as Douglas no doubt suspected. In 1864, Joseph Trutch had become Chief Commissioner of Lands, and he treated the fact that most of the reserves previously set aside came to only ten acres per family as a matter of policy. He seems to have been appalled by the way the surveyors, following Douglas' instructions, had allotted whatever lands the Indians had requested, and in some areas he even had existing reserves reduced in size. His views may be gleaned from a letter he wrote to Sir John A. Macdonald after he had become B.C.'s first lieutenant governor. Describing most of the new province's Indians as "utter savages", he advised Macdonald that the Canadian approach to Native title would never work in B.C. and should not be adopted (Cail 1974: 181, 298–99). In the years to come, Victoria and the Dominion would clash repeatedly over their respective obligations under the Terms of Union, particularly when there was a Liberal government in Ottawa. It would be sixty-seven years before the lands contemplated by Article 13 would finally be transferred.

Dominion-Provincial Wrangling, 1871–1912

In 1873, B.C. agreed to increase the size of reserves to be allotted in the future to a maximum of twenty acres per family, but Ottawa remained of the opinion that, whatever Article 13 might mean, the province's position was unfair to the Indians. Further counter-proposals were exchanged, and in 1875–76, after the Dominion government had to disallow one B.C. statute dealing with Crown lands because it made no provision for Indians, an agreement was finally reached to appoint a three-man commission to allot reserves. Unfortunately, the provincial government was unhappy with the finding of this commission and accepted none of its proposed reserves. One of the commissioners, Gilbert Sproat, carried on on his own for two years but resigned in frustration in 1880. The reason may be gleaned from a letter, the text of which was read by a Member of Parliament to the House of Commons in April of that year, from an unhappy white resident of British Columbia:

> Mr. Sproat, the Dominion Land agent here, has been making great havoc with the settlement of the lands, giving to Indians all the land that was of any good for settlement and that was not previously preempted. His decisions have caused universal dissatisfaction among the whites. (Commons Debates: 1880: 1693)

At about the same time, feelings were also excited by the prospect of an Indian uprising consequent upon the murder of a constable at Kamloops by a gang of "half breeds". The rebellion, however failed to materialize.

A few days before the letter concerning Sproat was read in the Commons, David Mills, who had been Minister of the Interior in the former Liberal government, raised the ire of Amor de Cosmos by saying that the Terms of Union had completely "overlooked" Indian land claims. He went on:

> I think it is the only instance in the whole history of British colonization in North America, where the Government have

undertaken to deal with the land without first securing the extinction of Indian titles. It is my opinion that the terms and conditions of the Union did not, and in law could not take away the right of the Indians in the soil...*That title is protected by the law...*[The commission was appointed because] the amount of land allotted to [the Indians] was so limited, that it was impossible for them to subsist... (Commons Debates 1880: 1634–35, emphasis added)

De Cosmos regarded this as an insult to the people of British Columbia, who had had "no trouble at all" with the Indians prior to Confederation and who had spend only $500 to $1000 per annum on the Indians compared to the $50,000 now spent by the Dominion. Sproat was accused by another Member from B.C. of giving the Indians whatever they wanted, and a motion for the return of all relevant documents and correspondence was passed.

Sproat was replaced by Peter O'Reilly, whose views were more in line with the province's, and as the white population finally began to exceed the Native population in the 1880's whatever earlier need for prudence may have existed soon lessened considerably (Titley 1986: 136–37). At last progress was being made, "although O'Reilly [resurveyed] lands already allotted by Sproat or the joint commissioners on the ground that they had been improvident, at least in the view of the province" (Bankes 1986: 138). By 1897, most reserves had been laid out. But title remained in the province.

The difficulty was not only that the two sides could not agree on the extent and size of reserves; they also did not agree in their respective interpretations of B.C.'s obligation to transfer the land. British Columbia took the position that it retained a reversionary interest in any lands conveyed, and relied upon a clause in the 1875–76 agreement which stated that "any land taken off a reserve shall revert to the province".

Still, the Terms of Union did contemplate a transfer and the province's so-called reversionary interest was really no different from that enjoyed by the other provinces as a result of Section 109 of the British North America Act and the St. Catharines case. From 1894 onward, Ontario and Ottawa entered into a series of agreements concerning the allocation of reserves, culminating in the 1924 agreement referred to under (ii), above, and in the same period negotiations were proceeding, although somewhat less amicably, in British Columbia. The unresolved problem concerning the province's reversionary interest held up the removal of the Songhees Reserve in Victoria and complicated the question of coal leases in Nanaimo, provoking a request to have the matter referred to the Supreme Court of Canada (Bankes 1986: 139). Instead, an agreement was reached in 1912 that was designed finally to resolve all questions respecting Indian affairs in B.C., except the question of Native or aboriginal title, which the province consistently refused to reopen.

The McKenna-McBride Agreement of 1912

The McKenna-McBride Agreement attempted to deal, by means of another larger commission, both with the allotment of reserves (neither the Native nor the white population, for very different reasons, were happy with the existing situation) and with the question of the provincial reversionary interest. Essentially, it provided that the new Royal Commission would adjust the size of reserves upwards or downwards in terms of the Indians' "reasonable" needs and that the province would then transfer these adjusted reserves to the Dominion. Title would revert to the province only if a particular band became extinct.

Because this process did not deal with aboriginal title and because it resulted in approximately 47,000 acres of valuable land being "cut-off" existing reserves in return for about 87,000 acres of much less valuable land, it was unacceptable to the Indians (La Violette 1961: 135). Moreover, the agreement was said to be "a final adjustment" of all outstanding issues and the requirement that the Indians consent to the changes was subsequently overridden by the British Columbia Indian Lands Settlement Act:

> For the purposes of adjusting. . .the reductions or cutoff from reserves in accordance with the recommendations of the Royal Commission, the Governor in Council may order such reductions or cut-offs to be effected without surrenders of the same by the Indians, notwithstanding any provisions of the Indian Act to the contrary. . . (S.C. 1919–20, c.51, s.3)

These measures continue to be a source of grievance and, indeed, are still being sorted out: see, for example, the Indian Cut-Off Lands Disputes Act, S.B.C. 1982, c.50. In 1920 W.E. Ditchburn of Indian Affairs and Major J.W. Clark for B.C. were appointed to review the Commission's report. It was, however, another sort of "Settlement Act" that helped to cause the implementation of the McKenna-McBride Agreement to be postponed for many years.

The Railway Belt and the Peace River Block

To facilitate the building of the railway that was promised to B.C. at Confederation, the Province had agreed to transfer to the Dominion a strip of land up to forty miles wide along the route of the proposed railway (Terms of Union, Article 11). Unfortunately, by the time Ottawa was finally ready to begin construction it had become aware that much of the land within the Railway Belt was not of the quality it had been led to believe and that B.C. had already alienated 800–900,000 acres of it. In any event, after a couple of false starts, B.C. passed a statute (S.B.C. 1884, c.14) that later came to be known as the Settlement Act, providing for the conveyance to the Dominion of the forty-mile strip (10,976,000 acres) and a block of 3,500,000 acres in the Peace River area, although the latter was not selected until 1907. A further 1,900,000 acres on Vancouver Island was also included, for the construction of the extension of the railway from Esquimalt to Nanaimo (Cail 1974: 137–38n).

By the time of the Royal Commission of 1912–16, therefore, title to both the Peace River Block and the Railway Belt was in the Dominion and Treaty No. 8, which included the surrender of Indian title to northeastern B.C., had been negotiated. The Dominion government had also, pursuant to that treaty, set aside four reserves within the Peace River Block. When Ditchburn and Clark reported in 1923, their agreement was confirmed by both governments except as to the lands covered by Treaty No. 8 and the Railway Belt:

> Ottawa contended that when the belt had been conveyed to the Dominion, the province had lost all claim to reserves already granted and to those that might later be granted within its boundaries. In other words, its reversionary interest did not apply. The royal commission, however, had examined such reserves and had recommended cut-offs in a number of instances. Ottawa suggested that this had been done merely for the sake of consistency and that the cut-offs should not be made. Victoria's viewpoint was quite the opposite. It held that when the railway belt had been created under the act of 1884, its reversionary interest in reserves already laid out within the boundaries of the belt had not been cancelled. (Titley 1986: 148)

The Scott-Cathcart Agreement of 1929

There the matter stood until in 1927, when a further Royal Commission reported that the Railway Belt and the Peace River Block ought to be transferred back to the Province (Cail 1974: 151). Because the provincial authorities had no legal right to such a transfer, their Dominion counterparts "were quick to appreciate the opportunity" this demand presented finally to obtain title to B.C.'s Indian reserves (Bankes 1986: 143). Accordingly, the Dominion agreed to return all unalienated land in these regions, subject to settlement of the reserve issue. Insofar as reserves outside the two problem areas were concerned, the parties agreed in 1929 to a form of conveyance surprisingly favourable to B.C. Although the form reflects the McKenna-McBride Agreement that only the lands of extinct bands will revert to the provincial Crown, one clause permits the province to "resume" up to one-twentieth of the reserve land for public purposes, an arrangement which continues to cause problems today: see Moses v. The Queen, [1977] 4 W.W.R. 474, aff'd [1979] 5 W.W.R. 100 (B.C.C.A.).

Oddly — because title to the Railway Belt and the Peace River Block was already in the Dominion and there was therefore no need to convey them — the agreement went on to provide that, nonetheless, reserves in these areas would be governed by the terms of the new form of conveyance. The Scott-Cathcart Agreement was made effective by Order-in-Council in 1930, the same year that the re-transfer of the Railway Belt and the Peace River Block, excluding the reserves, took place. All this was embodied in the schedule to the Constitution Act, 1930, 20–21 Geo.V (U.K.), c.26, and Article 13 of the Dominion/provincial agreement therein contained reads as follows:

> Nothing in this agreement shall extend to the lands included within Indian Reserves in the Railway Belt and the Peace River Block, but the said reserves shall continue to be vested in Canada in trust for the Indians on the terms and conditions set out in [the Order-in-Council referred to above].

All that remained was for the province to reciprocate and convey the Indian reserves outside of the Railway Belt and the Peace River Block to Canada.

Order-in-Council 1036

Surprisingly, this did not happen. The B.C. government continued to raise questions about reserve size and even about the cut-offs in the former Railway Belt, notwithstanding that the Scott-Cathcart Agreement explicitly excluded these reserves from the transfer. Moreover, the Dominion Order-in-Council regarding the 1916 Royal Commission Report (as amended by Ditchburn and Clark) had refused to go along with cut-offs in the Railway Belt and this had been part of the Agreement (Titley 1986: 159). On these issues Ottawa therefore remained adamant, and after a few more years of bartering mineral and timber rights, B.C. finally conveyed title in its Indian reserves to Ottawa in 1938 (Order-in-Council 1036). In 1961, reserve lands in that part of the province subject to Treaty No. 8 were also conveyed to Ottawa (Order-in-Council 2995), and in 1969 Order-in-Council 1555 deleted the provision concerning extinct bands.

A legal distinction presumably remains between Indian reserves within the Railway Belt and other reserves because the former were not conveyed to Ottawa in 1938; the rights enjoyed by the province in these reserves is by virtue of the agreement between the Dominion and the province that the terms of the standard form conveyance should apply to them (Smith 1986: 20). However, as a result of Order-in-Council 1036 the problem presented by St. Catharines Milling and The Queen v. Smith cannot frustrate the surrender of reserve lands in British Columbia. As Dickson, J. put it in the Guerin case (above, heading (i)):

> When the land in question in St. Catharines Milling was subsequently disencumbered of the native title upon its surrender to the federal government by the Indian occupants in 1873, the entire beneficial

interest in the land was held to have passed, because of the personal and usufructary nature of the Indian's right, to the Province of Ontario under s.109 rather than to Canada. The same constitutional issue arose recently in this court in [the Smith case], in which the court held that the Indian right in a reserve, being personal, could not be transferred to a grantee, whether an individual or the Crown. Upon surrender the right disappeared "in the process of release".

No such constitutional problem arises in the present case, since in 1938 the title to all Indian reserves in British Columbia was transferred by the provincial government to the Crown in right of Canada. (498)

What the English legal historian F.W. Maitland referred to as the feudal "mystery of seisin" clearly lives on in the magical constitutional tangle of Canadian Indian law.

(b) Communal Title and the Creation of Individual Interest in Reserve Land

The inclusion of inheritable location tickets in the Indian Act of 1876, based upon similar provisions introduced seven years earlier, constitutes a statutory announcement of a central policy of the Indian Department: the gradual substitution of individual ownership for customary, communal title to land. By concentrating effective authority over band membership, local government, and land management in the Superintendent General, the authorities hoped to guide the Indians towards eventual assimilation into white society. Individualized title was an essential step in this process, and had been so viewed since at least the 1830's. It was only a step, however, and until they became enfranchised and were granted the title in fee simple, locatees' rights were and are limited. Although there are certainly important exceptions, and although there have been times when this philosophy tended to be contradicted by events, the overall scheme of the Indian Act is to maintain reserve lands intact for the use and benefit of the band for whom the lands were set apart: The Queen v. Devereux (1965), 51 D.L.R.(2d) 546 (S.C.C.) and Joe v. Findlay (1981), 122 D.L.R.(3d) 377 (B.C.C.A.). Probably the most significant statutory exception to this principle today is s.58(3), discussed under (c)(iii), below. Its outer limits remain to be determined.

(i) The Relationship between Enfranchisement and Individual Property Rights

Individual, inheritable rights to land, especially when made devisable by will without band consent in 1894, were seen not only as tending to increase the Indians' attachment to European notions of real property but also to prepare them for assimilation into the wider society through enfranchisement. At first the approach was somewhat different. In the

Gradual Civilization Act of 1857 (S.P.C. 1857, c.26), the colonial legislature provided that any Indian who became enfranchised would be allotted a life estate in up to fifty acres of reserve land. By Section 10 of the statute, this estate could be willed to or inherited by his children, and in their hands it became a fee simple. In this scheme, becoming enfranchised was seen as a prerequisite to becoming a proprietor, as the preamble to both the 1857 Act and the subsequent "Act respecting the Civilization and Enfranchisement of certain Indians" (S.P.C. 1859, c.9) makes clear. The legislation was passed in order to:

> encourage the progress of civilization among the Indian Tribes in this Province, and the gradual removal of all legal distinctions between them and Her Majesty's other Canadian Subjects, and to facilitate the acquisition of property and of the rights accompanying it, by such Individual Members of the said Tribes as are found to desire such encouragement and to have deserved it. . .

First the Indian was, if suitable, to be enfranchised; then, gradually, he and his descendants were to enjoy full rights of property. Because one of the effects of this process was the removal of the land of enfranchised Indians from the reserve and hence the depletion of the band's assets and treaty rights, it met with considerable opposition.

This approach was continued by the first Dominion legislation on the subject, the Gradual Enfranchisement Act of 1869 (S.C. 1869, c.6), which provided for the issuance of letters patent for land held by enfranchised Indians (s.13). But there was a change. The statute deemed an Indian to be lawfully in possession of reserve land which had been subdivided by survey into lots only if the Superintendent General had granted him a "location title", thus extending individualized "ownership" — or at least possession — to Indians who were not enfranchised (s.1). Land held by location title was not transferable and continued to be exempt from seizure for debt, but it could descend to the holder's children upon his death. Unlike the land of an enfranchised Indian, however, the children received only a life estate (s.9). In the 1869 legislation, therefore, individualized property rights could be enjoyed to a certain extent prior to as well as after enfranchisement.

This difference is reflected in the 1876 Act, which appears to distinguish between ordinary location tickets and location tickets issued to "probationary" Indians, i.e., those who have applied for enfranchisement and have been provisionally accepted (s.86). In the former case, the band would "locate" the member on a particular lot and, if the Superintendent General approved, he would issue a location ticket. The land covered by the ticket could be transferred only to an Indian of the same band, and then only if both the band council and the Superintendent General consented (ss.7–9). A band member seeking to be enfranchised, on the other hand, needed the band to consent and to assign him a "suitable allotment of land for that purpose". He then had to be found fit by an official designated by the Superintendent General, who would then grant him a location ticket "as a probationary Indian". After three years of good behaviour, the applicant was entitled to have issued to him letters patent granting him the land in fee simple (ss.86–87). Indians completing this process would then:

> no longer be deemed Indians within the meaning of the laws relating to Indians, except in so far as their right to participate in the annuities and interest monies, and rents and councils of the band of Indians to which they belonged is concerned. . .(s.88)

Further, if the band as a whole decided to allow every member who chose to do so to become enfranchised, an Indian who received letters patent by virtue of the process just described could, by undergoing yet another three-year period of probation, become entitled to receive "his or her share of the capital funds at the credit of the band. . .or. . .of the principal of the annuities of the band", and cease to be an Indian "in every respect" (s.93).

These provisions were explained to the House of Commons, not always very precisely, by the Minister on March 2 and 21, 1876, and other Members noted that both the 1857 and the 1869 schemes had failed (Commons Debates 1876: 342–43, 749–50, and 752–53). So did this one, and mainly for the same reason: bands did not want land removed from the reserve and possibly sold to non-Indians. Consent to individual applications was therefore rarely obtained, and in the nineteenth century only one band availed itself of the second-stage procedure under Section 93. In 1880, a Member of the House suggested another reason for this reluctance to the Commons. After noting that Sir John A. Macdonald's 1876 law, as expected, had been no more successful than his 1857 one, he stated:

> It is said the reason why so few Indians are enfranchised is because they are not fit for the position. With regard to the Six Nation Indians, the fact that the more intelligent and industrious among them have not enfranchisement, under the present law, is the most conclusive proof of their ability to look after their own interests. At present many of this class occupy from 200 to 300 acres of land apiece, were they to be enfranchised, as the law now stands, they would get only their share of the reserve, something less than fifty acres. In such circumstances they are not so foolish as to seek for enfranchisement. (Commons Debates 1880: 1992)

The extent to which this was true of other reserves is not clear. In the West, however, it was not an issue because the Act provided that the enfranchisement sections were not to be applied there until such time as the Governor General proclaimed their extension to those provinces and territories (S.C. 1876, c.18, s.94; R.S.C. 1886, c.43, s.82).

These provisions, as amended from time to time, remained a permanent feature of the Act, and in 1951 a waiting period of ten years between enfranchisement and fee simple title was introduced (S.C. 1951, c.29, s.110). The Minister allowed that this was a more restrictive provision than before, but it was to assure bands that the land would not be sold "immediately upon enfranchisement" (Commons Debates 1951: 1353, 3070, 3082–83). In 1985, the enfranchisement part of the Act was repealed (S.C. 1985, c.27, s.19).

(ii) Some Statutory Provisions Respecting the Possession of Land in Reserves: Sections 20–29 of the Current Act

The scheme laid down in 1876 is essentially that described above: band members were located by the band, and, when the approval of the Superintendent General was obtained, a location ticket issued. One copy was kept by the Department, one was for the local agent (to be copied into the band register, if there was one), and one was for the band member. No holder of a location ticket could be dispossessed of land "on which he or she has improvements, without receiving compensation therefore" (s.6). Location title could be transferred only to another band member if both the council and the Superintendent General consented, and upon death one-third of the holder's interest went to his widow and the rest went to his children, who held "a like estate in such land as their father" (s.9). In 1880, the requirement that the band consent to transfers was deleted (S.C. 1880, c.28, s.19), and over the years there were a number of changes respecting the descent of property, notably an amendment in 1884 permitting locatees, with the consent of the band and the Superintendent General, to devise their land by will (S.C. 1884, c.27, s.5). In 1894, the requirement that the band consent was dropped (S.C. 1894, c.32, s.1). In western Canada, Indians who had, prior to the establishment of a reserve, occupied and improved land subsequently included in a reserve, were to be in the same position as Indians holding land under a location title (s.10). There were no changes when the Act was consolidated for the third time in 1886: R.S.C. 1886, c.43, ss.16–19.

In 1890, however, "Certificates of Occupancy" were introduced for the Indians of Manitoba, Keewatin and the "Western Territories" — a somewhat unusual geographical term. In those areas the Indian Commissioner was authorized, prior to locating an Indian in the usual way, to issue a Certificate of Occupancy for up to 160 acres. This certificate conferred lawful possession of the land upon the holder, but could be cancelled by the Commissioner at any time (S.C. 1890, c.29, s.2). Presumably, this was to impose a sort of probation period even upon Indians who were not seeking enfranchisement; certainly it had that effect.

There were no significant changes in the consolidations of 1906 and 1927, and in 1951 these provisions were put in what is essentially their present form. Certificates of Occupation were no longer confined to the areas named above but could be issued whenever the Minister wished to have more time to consider whether an allotment by a band council should be approved, and location tickets were replaced by Certificates of Possession (s.20). A Department Register for these certificates was required (s.21) and the provisions regarding western Indians' improvements were generalized (s.22). One Indian representative at the Ottawa Conference in 1951 objected to the temporary possession provisions as creating "feelings of insecurity", and argued that, once land had been allotted by a band council, it should not be subject to ministerial conditions. (Conference 1951: 1365).

By Section 29, reserve lands remained exempt from seizure for debt. More significantly, the requirement that an Indian dispossessed of land he had improved be compensated, which had been in the Act since 1876 was substantially altered. In the 1927 consolidation it was provided that:

> ...no Indian shall be dispossessed of any land on which he has improvements, without receiving compensation for such improvements, at a valuation approved by the Superintendent General, from the Indian who obtains the land, or from the funds of the band, as is determined by the Superintendent General. (R.S.C. 1927, c.98, s.21)

In 1951 this became:

> An Indian who is lawfully removed from lands in a reserve upon which he has made *permanent* improvements *may, if the Minister so directs,* be paid compensation in respect thereof in an amount to be determined by the Minister, either from the person who goes into possession or from the funds of the band, at the discretion of the Minister. (S.C. 1951, c.29, s.23, emphasis added)

The improvements now had to be permanent and compensation was no longer mandatory. These changes were carried over into the current Act.

By Section 24 the right of an Indian in lawful possession of reserve lands to transfer his right of possession to another band member (with the consent of the Minister) was expanded to permit a transfer to the band itself, and Section 25 made provision for Indians who ceased to be entitled to live on a reserve to transfer their land, or in default thereof, have it revert to the band and receive compensation for payment improvements. In the House one member objected to this, arguing that ownership of property was "sacred" and that he did not see why the Indian should not be compensated for the land as well as the improvements. The Minister did not really answer this question, but intimated that because a locatee could transfer his land only to another band member, his interest in it was not one that was worthy of compensation.

This did not satisfy his questioner, who replied that the locatee should be entitled to some compensation for the land "if it is his own property". A few moments later, during a discussion about Indian wills, the Minister described the question of the nature of a locatee's interest in his land as "a rather interesting point of law" (Commons Debates 1951: 3064–65).

Sections 26 and 27 provided for the correction of fraud or error in Certificates of Possession or Occupation, and then had to be amended to include location tickets, presumably because the failure to include them had rendered the new provisions largely ineffectual (S.C. 1956, c.40, s.9). Finally, Section 28 rendered void any attempt by a band or band member to permit anyone other than a band member to occupy or use reserve land, except where the Minister authorized such use or occupation in writing. When Indian representatives queried this latter provision, expressing their concern that private use of reserve land should have the sanction of the band council, the response stressed the fact that the Section limited such ministerial permits to periods of no more than one year (Conference 1951: 1366). An amendment a few years later allowed the Minister, if the band consented, to prescribe a longer period (S.C. 1956, c.40, s.10). The effect of this provision is to add a third method of validating non-Indian use of reserve lands, the other two being by surrender and by a lease pursuant to Section 58(3) of the current Act (Sanders 1985: 465), considered under (c)(iii), below.

(c) The Management and Disposal of Reserve and Surrendered Lands

When Clifford Sifton became Minister of the Interior and therefore Superintendent General of Indian Affairs in 1896, he discovered that, contrary to what he had assumed, it was rather difficult for the government to appropriate Indian lands (Hall 1983: 120). But this was already changing. The North West Rebellion in 1885 had hardened hearts, and in the 1890's the pressure upon the government and the Indian Department to open up Indian land for settlement and development intensified. For the next forty years this pressure, and the change in the law it helped to produce, was constant, and the Superintendent General was authorized to do more and more without the consent of the band. In 1895, for example, he was authorized to lease, without surrender, the land of any Indian who applied to him for that purpose (see under (c)(iii), below), and in 1918 to lease, again without surrender, any uncultivated reserve land. This was to prevent the Government's campaign to increase productivity in the West from being put "entirely at the mercy of the Indian bands" (Commons Debates 1918: 1047–48, explaining S.C. 1918, c.26, s.4).

This trend peaked just before the First World War when Section 49A was added to the <u>Indian Act</u>, enabling the government to expropriate certain reserves in violation of treaty and surrender requirements:

> In the case of an Indian reserve which adjoins or is situated wholly or partly within an incorporated town or city...of not less than 8,000...the Governor in Council may...refer to...the Exchequer Court of Canada for inquiry and report the question as to whether it is expedient, having regard to the interest of the public and of the Indians...for whose use the reserve is held, that the Indians should be removed...

The section was enacted to avoid having to pass a special statute each time this needed to be done, and was prompted by an Act that went through Parliament at the same time removing the Songhees from their Reserve in Victoria, B.C. This Reserve, which was situated across from the legislative buildings in Victoria harbour, had been the object of civic enmity (because it was seen as an eyesore and a source of social problems) and envy (because it occupied extremely valuable land) since colonial times. In 1859, Governor Douglas had refused a request by the House of Assembly to have the Indians moved, on the ground that it would be unjust to violate the government's solemn treaty obligations (Fisher 1977: 114). Yet in 1911, this is precisely what was done. "While we wish to pay every respect to treaty right", the Minister of the Interior informed the House, "it is absolutely necessary, in a progressive country, that existing circumstances and ... conditions should be taken account of". The Songhees, he said, were occupying extremely valuable land without making use of it; they would therefore be transferred to new land in Esquimalt and paid compensation (Commons Debates 1911: 7987–88). In a related development a few years later, Parliament authorized the Governor in Council to reduce the size of B.C.'s Indian reserves, again without requiring compliance with the surrender provisions of the Indian Act (S.C. 1919–20, c.51). That action is discussed under (a)(iv), above.

In response to criticism that Section 49A went too far, it was amended to require the Exchequer Court's finding to be referred to Parliament for approval before a removal could proceed (S.C. 1911, c.14, s.2). The section remained in the Act until 1951, when the Minister at that time conceded that it was discriminatory and that the Indians felt it made them "second-class citizens" (Commons Debates 1951: 1355).

By the 1930's, the government had other concerns, and in 1936 the Indian Department once again became a Branch, this time of the Department of Mines and Resources, and the Minister of Mines became the Superintendent General of Indian Affairs (Department of Mines and Resources Act, S.C. 1936, c.33).

(i) The Minister's Authority over Surrendered Lands: Section 53(1) of the Current Act

Governmental authority over the management and disposition of surrendered lands predates Confederation, as the Nova Scotia, New Brunswick, and Upper and Lower Canadian statutes referred to under 1(a), above, make clear. The Lower Canadian law, for example, established a Commissioner to manage and dispose of Indian lands, and its legal effect was considered in the Star Chrome case (see (a)(ii), above). Section 29 of the 1876 Indian Act provided as follows:

> All Indian lands, being reserves or portions of reserves surrendered or to be surrendered to the Crown, shall be deemed to be held for the same purposes as before the passing of this Act; and shall be managed, leased and sold as the Governor in Council may direct, subject to the conditions of surrender, and to the provisions of this Act.

It is essentially the same today, except that this authority since 1951 has reposed in the Minister or his designate: s.53(1). The determination of whether a particular purpose for which reserve land is used is truly for the use and benefit of the band remains with the Governor in Council, however: s.18(1). The historical ambiguity of s.53(1) and its predecessors is discussed under (a)(iii), above.

The Minister also has considerable powers with respect to reserve land, e.g., s.18(2), dealing with schools, burial grounds, health, etc.; s.58(1), dealing with improvements to uncultivated or unused lands and agricultural leases, and s.58(4), concerning the disposition of grass, fallen timber, and gravel, most of which are subject to the consent of the band council. At the Ottawa Conference in 1951, questions were raised about these provisions, and some representatives complained about the manner in which Indian agents had been leasing uncultivated or unused lands. Disposing of sand and gravel without consent was also discussed, and the representatives were assured that it would be done only when, due to absences, there was "undue difficulty or delay" in obtaining band council consent. The Conference was also told that leases granted for such reasons would not be renewed without consent (Conference 1951: 1366).

By virtue of Section 60, the Governor in Council may, should a band so request, confer "such control and management over (reserve lands) occupied by that band as the Governor in Council considers desirable". This authority can also be withdrawn.

(ii) The Requirement of Surrender and the Public Purpose Exception: Sections 35 and 37 of the Current Act

The principle set out in Section 37 is arguably the most fundamental in the Act, forbidding as it does the disposition of any reserve land that has not first been surrendered to the Crown by the band "for whose use and benefit in common (it) was set apart". This principle is, however, subject to exceptions made elsewhere in the Act, notably Sections 35, providing for lands taken for public purposes, and 58(3). These will be considered in turn.

The earliest version of the policy reflected in Section 35 deals, not surprisingly, with railways. The history of the common law world in the nineteenth century is festooned with statutory provisions favouring railways, and Section 25 of the first Dominion Act respecting Indian lands is no exception. I stated simply that if any railway, road, or public work passed through or caused injury to any Indian land, compensation would have to be paid. This same provision, more or less, appears in the 1876, 1880, and 1886 Indian Acts, and then in 1887 it was amended to read that "no portion of any reserve" should be encroached upon in this way without the consent of the Governor in Council, but if any railway, etc. did pass through or cause injury, compensation was required (S.C. 1887, c.33, s.5). The wording of this provision was criticized in the House as being contradictory but, amended only slightly, this is substantially what appears in the 1906 consolidation as well.

In 1911, however, the section was changed into what is essentially its present form by authorizing companies and municipalities with statutory expropriation powers to expropriate reserve lands for public purposes (S.C. 1911, c.14, s.1). The consent of the Governor in Council was required for such expropriation, and in 1951 the special reference to railways, etc. was dropped (S.C. 1951, c.29, s.35). Section 35 was the subject of "a considerable amount of discussion" at the Ottawa Conference, but delegates were assured that the policy behind the section was "not the wholesale acquisition of land" but "the use of lands for public utilities and other similar services". This seemed to satisfy those present and the section was approved (Commons Debates 1951: 1366).

(iii) The Exception for Individual Occupants: Section 58(3) of the Current Act

Section 58(3) provides that the Minister "may lease for the benefit of any Indian upon his application for that purpose, the land of which he is lawfully in possession without the land being surrendered". As stated earlier, this is one of only two ways in which non-Indians can lawfully lease reserve land without it being surrendered. Its history in instructive.

The general principle governing reserve land is that it should not be "sold, alienated, leased, or otherwise disposed of" until it has been surrendered to the Crown by the band for whose "use and benefit" it was set apart (s.37). This principle dates back at least to the Royal Proclamation of 1763, and appears in the first Dominion statute concerning the management of Indian lands in 1868. But in the Indian Act it is subject to statutory exceptions which date from the first Act in 1876, and others were to follow.

The origin of the present Section 58(3) is probably to be found in the Act of 1880, which permitted the Superintendent General to lease without surrender the lands of "aged, sick and infirm Indians and widows and children left without a guardian" for their support (S.C. 1880, c.28, s.36). This was expanded in 1884 to include the land of Indians who were professionals or school teachers, or who worked at a trade that interfered with their "cultivating land on the reserve" (S.C. 1884, c.27, s.8), and then these three new categories were condensed into one, i.e., "occupations" that interfered with cultivation, in 1894 (S.C. 1894, c.32, s.3). In 1898, authority to dispose of wild grass and dead or fallen timber without surrender was also added (S.C. 1898, c.34, s.2).

The most important change had come a few years earlier, however. In 1895, the section was repealed, thus deleting the reference to widows, etc. and occupations that interfered with farming, and a much broader provision was put in its place:

> No reserve or portion of a reserve shall be sold, alienated or leased until the same has been released or surrendered to the Crown for the purposes of this Act; provided that the superintendent general may lease, for the benefit of *any* Indian, *upon his application for that purpose*, and land to which he is entitled *without the same being released or surrendered.* (S.C. 1895, c.35, s.1)

The effect of this was to remove the need to obtain band consent (by way of surrender) to leasing land which had been allotted to a band member and which he wished to lease, so long as the Superintendent General was willing. In the Commons, the change was described as designed to make the law "general", and as prompted by:

> a number of cases [in which] Indians have. . .left the reserve, and under the law, as it at present stands, we are not in a position to lease these lands without the consent of the band. . .[T]he neighbours, through spite or pique, have used sufficient influence to prevent that being done. (Commons Debates 1895: 3933)

That, in any event, was the official view. But dispensing with band consent created its own problems. As others saw it eighty-five years later, when more and more locatees wished to enter into long-term commercial leases, the Crown's obligations to the band respecting the allotted land were not to be regarded as "entirely superceeded" by the allotment. Using this provision to grant leases that are virtual alienations would be "contrary to the spirit" of the Act, at least (Program Circular, Indian and Inuit Affairs, 1980, No. H-7–1 at 2.4 and 3.1). The recent case of Re Boyer and The Queen et al. (1986), 26

D.L.R.(4th) 284 (F.C.A.), however, strongly favours individual over communal property rights insofar as the present s.58(3) is concerned.

In 1919, authority to grant leases for surface mining rights was vested in the Superintendent General, whether anyone had requested this or not (S.C. 1919, c.56, s.1). Compensation was to be provided for any damage caused thereby to an occupant, and in 1938, after the Indian Department had become a branch of the Department of Mines and Resources, provision was made for compensating non-Indian lessees and licensees as well. This amendment went on to distinguish between mineral leases which did, and did not, require a prior surrender (S.C. 1938, c.31, s.1).

In 1951, the section was split, and the first part, which contains the general prohibition against disposition without surrender, became Section 37. The latter part, containing the exception for individual occupants, was moved to the section of the Act dealing with land management, and numbered 58(3). The provisions concerning uncultivated land, and many of, but not all, the other provisions which reposed control in the Superintendent General (now the Minister of Citizenship and Immigration), were replaced by ones requiring the consent of the band council (see under heading (i), above). This was the general thrust of the 1951 reform of the Act, and Sections 37 and 58(3) have not changed since that time.

At the Ottawa Conference in 1951, the question of the meaning of the words "except where this Act otherwise provides" in Section 37 was raised. The answer given by the government was that this referred to action taken under Sections 35 (lands taken for public purposes) and 110(2) (grants to enfranchised Indians). No mention was made of Sections 28(2) or 58(3), perhaps because the concern at that time was with sales rather than leases and licences (Conference 1951: 1366).

3. Management of Indian Monies

Although a definition of Indian lands appeared as early as the first Indian Act in 1876, there was no definition of Indian monies until 1951. In that year, Indian monies were defined as "all monies collected, received or held by [Her] Majesty for the use and benefit of Indians or bands", and so it remains today. This difference between lands and monies is some indication of the relative importance of the two, and the extent to which Indian lands and monies have been related in the past. Unlike Indian lands, however, Indian monies have received comparatively little attention from historians, lawyers, and the courts.

The relevant provisions of the current Act are ss. 61–69. Section 61 is to monies what s.18(1) is to lands: it provides that they are to be expended only for the "the benefit of the Indians or bands for whose use and benefit in common the monies are received or held", and the Governor in Council may determine whether a particular expenditure meets this criterion. The fact that such provisions seem to permit no appeal to the courts of the Governor in Council's determination provoked considerable debate in 1956 (Commons Debates 1956: 7118–19, 7140–43), and s.18(1) was relied upon by the Crown in the <u>Guerin</u> case as negativing any fiduciary obligation. This contention was ultimately rejected in that case, and the gap complained of in 1956 has therefore been at least partially filled.

Section 61(2) provides for interest to be paid on Indian monies held in the Consolidated Revenue Fund at a rate to be fixed by the Governor in Council. In 1951, some of the representatives at the Ottawa Conference wanted this amended to ensure that the rate would never fall below five per cent, but they were unsuccessful (Conference 1951: 1365).

Section 62 distinguishes between capital and revenue monies by providing that all monies derived from the sale of surrendered lands and capital assets of a band are deemed to be capital monies of the band and the rest are revenue monies. The distinction is important because the 1951 Act allocates ministerial power based upon this distinction and because s.69, much like s.60 regarding lands, authorizes the Governor in Council to permit a band "to control, manage, and expend in whole or in part its revenue monies". The first permission was granted in 1959 and by 1971 it had been granted to many bands (Daugherty and Madill 1980: 76). As the schedule to the Indian Bands Revenue Monies Regulations reveals, well over half the bands now enjoy this power.

Sections 64 and 65 deal with the Minister's authority over the capital monies of a band, exercised with the consent of the band council, and s.66 deals similarly with its revenue monies, although here the Minister has more authority to act without consent. Section 68 empowers the Minister to apply the annuity or interest money of an Indian to the support of his spouse or family in a number of circumstances. Aspects of these provisions and others are considered in more detail below.

Speaking generally, the provision of the 1951 Act respecting Indian monies reflect the same tension between wardship and independence that characterizes the rest of the Act, and the same tendency towards the latter. However, the continuing supervisory role of the Minister and the Governor in Council, especially the latter's authority to permit a band to enact money by-laws only if it "has reached an advanced stage of development" (s.83), are indications that much remains unchanged. The Minister of Citizenship and Immigration, anticipating criticism of the amount of ministerial discretion in the proposed 1951 Act, commented on this compromise as follows:

> This bill does continue ministerial discretion, but I assure the House
> that this discretion is very much limited as compared with the present

act; and in committee I am sure we will be prepared to defend such discretion as has been retained. *In particular the Minister is obliged to retain authority over the expenditure of band funds,* for the very simple reason that these monies are in the consolidated revenue fund and there must be some authority for their payment. I would not want to mislead the House. *The ministerial authority does extend to supervision of expenditure of band funds, but I want to assure the House that just as soon as a band demonstrates its ability to handle money it will be given an opportunity of doing so.* (Commons Debates 1951: 1353, emphasis added)

(a) Monies from Land Surrenders

The early legislation did not segregate provisions respecting lands and monies. The first Dominion law to address the subject of monies was the 1868 statute, which constituted the Department of the Secretary of State and provided for "the management of Indian and Ordinance Lands" (S.C. 1868, c.42). Section 7 stipulated that all monies for the "support and benefit" of Indians, including those from the sale of land and timber, should be applied in the same manner as before the Act. Section 11 vested control of these funds in the Governor in Council, authorizing him to direct how the monies should be invested, when payments should be made and assistance given, and how much should be set apart for the management of Indian lands and property. The first Indian Act in 1876 was similar, except that it provided that, at the time of surrender, it could be agreed to pay up to 10 per cent of the proceeds of a sale to the members of the band instead of investing or applying them to other purposes. This figure appears to reflect the treaty-making policy developed when it was decided to move from lump sum payments to annuities after the War of 1812 (see under (2)(a)(i), above). The 1876 Act also required that the proceeds of the sale or lease of any Indian lands, timber, hay, stone, minerals, or "other valuables thereon" should be paid to the Receiver General to the credit of the Indian fund.

The Indian Acts of 1880 and 1886 continued these provisions. There were some minor amendments in 1895 and 1898, and in 1906 the amount that could be paid to band members from land sales was increased to 50 per cent. The reason was, according to the Minister of the Interior, that:

[ten per cent] is very little inducement. . .and we find that there is a very considerable difficulty in securing [the Indians'] consent to any surrender. Some weeks ago. . .it was brought to the attention of the House by several members, especially from the Northwest, that there was a great and pressing need. . .to secure the utilization of the large areas of land held by Indians in their reserves without these reserves being of any value to the Indians and being a detriment to the settlers and to the prosperity and progress of the surrounding country. (Commons Debates 1906: 5422)

For a few more years the rate remained at ten per cent for timber and other property, but the pressure was on. Some members wanted the ceilings raised higher or even removed (Commons Debates 1910: 5926–27), and in 1919, the 50 per cent rate was applied to timber and other property as well as land (S.C. 1919, c.56, s.2). In 1951, this became s.64(a) and the phrase "per capita" was inserted. It is now s.64(1)(a).

(b) Capital and Revenue

Although the use of the term "revenue" is more recent, the first reference to capital appears to be in the enfranchisement provisions of the 1857 Gradual Civilization Act, and these references continue in the statutes that followed. The gist of them is that band capital is not to be eroded without band consent, and this seems to be a reflection of the surrender principle concerning land. The principle itself eroded, however. For example, a section introduced in 1894 authorized the Governor in Council, with the consent of the band, to use the capital monies of that band to purchase reserve lands and to finance permanent improvements and the purchase of cattle (S.C. 1894, c.32, s.11). In 1918, it was amended to allow this to be done without band consent if the refusal of such consent was "detrimental to the progress or welfare of the band" (S.C. 1918, c.26, s.4). It seems reasonable to assume, however, that because Indians had virtually no control over their funds and because most of this money was from the sale of land and land-based resources, there was not a pressing need to attempt a distinction between capital and revenue. It was only then the government decided, in the 1951 Act, to move towards transferring more fiscal control to bands that this became important.

There have always been money provision. The current s.68, for example, has its beginnings in the Indian Act of 1886 (R.S.C. 1886, c.43), which was amended a number of times between 1887 and 1898 to provide for the families of Indians who had offended against contemporary laws and morals. Section 72 of the 1886 Act authorized the Superintendent General to stop the "annuity and interest money" of any Indian who had deserted his family and to apply the monies instead to supporting the family. Section 73 conferred a like power to stop payment where an Indian woman with no children had deserted her husband and was living "immorally" with another man. In 1887, these powers were broadened to include depriving an offending Indian of his right to "participate" in the real property of the band, and in 1894, s.72 was expanded to apply to an Indian whose behaviour caused his wife or family to leave, or who was separated from them by reason of imprisonment. In 1898, the Superintendent was further authorized to stop the monies of an Indian parent of an illegitimate child and to apply them instead to the support of that child. This statute also expanded his authority over "immoral" Indian women that had been conferred in 1886, permitting him to order that their interest and annuities be paid towards the support of any children deserted by them.

Although the notion of an Indian being deprived of "participating" in the real property of the band is somewhat vague, there may be a parallel in the old enfranchisement provisions (see under 2(b)(i), above, and ss.15(5) and 16(2) of the current Act). Under the 1875 Indian Act, an Indian who was a successful applicant for enfranchisement received an allotment of land in fee simple and ceased to be an Indian except insofar as he was entitled to "participate in the annuities and interest monies, and rents and councils" of the band. But at this stage the enfranchisee was not entitled to receive his share of the capital funds of the band and the principal of the annuities. As the Minister put it, if enfranchised Indians wished to "get possession of their share of the invested funds of the land", consent of the band had to be obtained for such a distribution (Commons Debates 1876: 342, 750). This rarely happened.

A number of other references to capital, including the provisions respecting loans dealt with below, are in amendments to the original 1894 provision authorizing the Governor in Council to use band capital to purchase reserve lands, etc. In 1918, for example, the same statute that provided for dispensing with band consent in these circumstances permitted the Superintendent General to lease uncultivated reserve land without a surrender and to authorize the expenditure of "so much of the capital funds of the band as may be necessary" to make the land suitable for agricultural or grazing purposes (S.C. 1918, c.26, s.4). Again, the reason was to prevent "reactionary or recalcitrant Indian bands" from "checking progress" (Commons Debates 1918: 1047–48). These provisions, modified to require the consent of the band council are now ss.58(1) and 64(1)(d) of the Act.

Another amendment to the original power to expend capital was made in 1936, when it was extended to permit using such funds to purchase "the possessory rights of a member of the band in respect of any particular parcel of land on the reserve" (S.C. 1936, c.20, s.3). If an Indian devised land to someone not entitled to live on the reserve, the land had to be sold to someone who was so entitled; there was no provision permitting the band itself to resume the land, however, and this was the point of the change.

Two more provisions that relate to Indian monies that deserve mention were enacted in 1895 and 1910. The first vested authority in the Governor in Council to reduce the purchase money due on sales of Indian lands or to reduce or remit the interest on such money. It also authorized the reduction of rents on leased Indian lands if the Governor in Council found them to be excessive (S.C. 1895, c.35, s.8). All reductions or remissions pursuant to this section had to be reported to Parliament. Pressure from purchasers of uninspected Indian land who had belatedly discovered that they had paid too much was behind this measure. The Indian Department had been "dealing" with the problem for some time, but the Justice Department questioned the legality of reducing the payments without statutory authority (Commons Debates

1895: 3937–38). The concern, no doubt, was that this amounted to a violation of the surrender terms, or put differently, an unauthorized reduction of band capital. Perhaps today it would be characterized as a breach of fiduciary duty within the <u>Guerin</u> principle. The section appears in the 1906 and 1927 consolidations but was dropped in 1951.

The second section rendered invalid any contract of agreement concerning Indian monies or securities, or monies appropriated by Parliament for the benefit of Indians, that was made by chief, councillors, or band members unless it was authorized by the Act or approved in writing by the Superintendent General (S.C. 1910, c.28, s.2). Similar in form to s.28 of the current <u>Indian Act</u> regulating the use and occupation of reserve land, its intent was to clarify and reaffirm the principle that band funds could not be "bartered away" without governmental approval (Commons Debates 1910: 5922–26). There is no precise equivalent in the 1951 Act, although s.61 reflects the same general idea.

As stated earlier, the distinction between capital and revenue is more explicit in the 1951 Act because, unlike the earlier versions of the Act, the government's powers are more precisely organized around this distinction. The earlier laws vested the management of Indian monies in the Governor in Council and then added special powers on an *ad hoc* basis when it appeared that it was necessary to expend the capital of the band. These provisions respecting the sale or development of unsurrendered land and, similarly, could sometimes be exercised without band consent. The 1951 Act, on the other hand, generally transferred these powers from the Governor in Council to the Minister, and this trend was continued, after considerable debate, in 1956 (Commons Debates 1956: 7111–14, 7119–20ff). It then defined capital and revenue monies and set out the Minister's authority over each in separate sections, most but not all of which provided for the consent of the band council. The result suggests that the intent was to rationalize the rather haphazard growth of the preceding sixty years or so, and there is therefore often no precise or direct correlation with earlier versions, as there was in previous consolidations.

It is perhaps useful to note that s.66 is the only section concerned with Indian monies that attracted debate in 1951. Section 66(1) conferred upon the Minister a very general authority, subject to band council consent, to authorize the expenditure of revenue monies to "promote the general progress and welfare of the band or any member of the band" (s.66(1)). It was the subject of debate because there was a concern that it would adversely affect Indian entitlement to social security benefits (Commons Debates 1951: 3067). Some of the delegates to the Ottawa Conference were also concerned about s.66(2) which, in one form or another, had been in the Act since 1886. It authorized the Minister, without consent, to expend band funds for such things as the care of the sick and disabled and the burial of deceased indigent band members, and it was felt that public rather than band funds should be used for these purposes (Conference 1951: 1365).

(c) Loans

It is important to distinguish between loans from band funds and loans from the Consolidated Revenue Fund under s.70.

Loans from band funds have the longer history. They were introduced in 1924 because Indians in financial distress to whom agents had issued special permits to buy farm equipment had apparently run up a number of bad debts. The idea was to provide a loan fund out of the capital monies of the band. Such loans were under the authority of the Governor in Council and required band consent. They were "to promote progress", and could not exceed one-half of the appraised value of the interest of the borrower in the reserve land held by him (S.C. 1924, c.47, s.5). This section became s.64(h) of the 1951 Act and another sub-section was added in 1956 to provide for construction loans, with or without security, to build houses for individual band members, and for the guarantee of loans to band members for building purposes (S.C. 1956, c.40, s.15). It is possible that this was a response of sorts to a complaint made at the Ottawa Conference. At that time a delegate inquired why loans from the Consolidated Revenue Fund could not be used for houses, and the response was that the main objective of the program "was to provide for loans to Indians for *revenue producing projects*, and that housing, unless it were for rental purposes, was not revenue producing" (Conference 1951: 1367, emphasis in original). The 1956 amendment did not, of course, provide for loans from the fund, but it did provide loans for housing. Band fund loans are now dealt with in ss.64(h) and (j).

The quite different Consolidated Revenue Fund loans are dealt with in s.70 of the current Act, which was first enacted as s.94B in 1938 (S.C. 1938, c.31, s.2). It met with general but not unanimous approval (Senate Debates 1938: 472). The section created a "revolving loan fund" originally limited to $350,000, but in 1955 this was increased by way of a separate appropriation to $650,000 (Commons Debates 1956: 5173). In 1956, this was increased again to $1,000,000, this time by an amendment to the Indian Act itself (S.C. 1956, c.40, s.18), and is now at $6,050,000. In 1956, the Minister, the Honourable J.W. Pickersgill, explained that loans made pursuant to this section:

> ...are advanced to Indians to assist them in establishing themselves in agriculture, forestry, fishing, in setting up business in handicrafts, for getting equipment and facilities for guiding, trapping and a good many other...pursuits. The purpose of the loans is to make it possible for Indians — who, because of the protection they are given under the Indian Act, are also under a disability about borrowing in the ordinary way — to get money on reasonable terms in order to

supplement their traditional mode of livelihood. (Commons Debates 1956: 5173–74)

He went on to add that the record of repayment was "remarkably good".

The 1956 amendments, not all of which have been mentioned above, were incorporated into the 1970 consolidation and, except for some changes consequent upon the new band membership rules introduced in 1985 (S.C. 1985, c.27, ss.10–13), the provisions respecting Indian monies in force today are the same. There are very few judicial decisions interpreting these sections. Land issues appear to have generated far more litigation. As bands and Indian entrepreneurs become more active in business, more matters concerning Indian monies may come before the courts.

Select Bibliography

Bankes, N.D. "Indian Resource Rights and Constitutional Enactments in Western Canada, 1871–1930" in Louis Knafla, ed. *Law and Justice in a New Land. Essays in Western Canadian Legal History* (Calgary 1986) at 129–164

Bartlett, Richard H. "The Indian Act of Canada" (1978) 27 *Buffalo Law Review* 581–615

——— "Reserve Lands" in Morse, ed. (see below) at 467–578

——— "Taxation" in Morse, ed. (see below) at 579–616

British Parliamentary Papers: *Correspondence and Papers Relating to Canada 1854–58* (Irish University Press 1969), Vol. 21

Brody, Hugh *Maps and Dreams: Indians and the British Columbia Frontier* (Vancouver 1981)

Brown, Desmond H. "Unpredictable and Uncertain: Criminal Law in the Canadian Northwest before 1886" (1979) 17 *Alberta Law Review* 497–512

Burrell, Gordon J. and Sanders, Doublas E. *Handbook of Case Law on the Indian Act* (Dept. of Indian Affairs and Northern Development 1984)

Cail, Robert E. *Land, Man, and the Law: The Disposal of Crown Lands in British Columbia, 1871–1913* (Vancouver 1974)

Canada: House of Commons Debates (Ottawa 1876–1985)

Canada: Senate Debates (Ottawa 1882)

Canada: Special Joint Committees of the Senate and House of Commons to Inquire into the Claims of the Allied Tribes of British Columbia (Ottawa 1927)

Canada: Special Joint Committees of the Senate and House of Commons to Examine and Consider the Indian Act (Ottawa 1946–48)

Canadian Indian Treaties: The Robinson Treaties, the Numbered Treaties 1–11, and the Chippewa and Mississauga Treaties of 1923

Cumming, Peter A. and Mickenberg, Neil H. *Native Rights in Canada*, 2nd ed. (Toronto 1972)

Daugherty, Wayne and Madill, Dennis *Indian Government under Indian Act Legislation 1868–1951* (Treaties and Historical Research Centre, Dept. of Indian and Northern Affairs 1980)

Duff, Wilson "The Fort Victoria Treaties" (1969) *3 B.C. Studies* 3–57

Fisher, Robin *Contact and Conflict: Indian-European Relations in British Columbia, 1774–1890* (Vancouver 1977)

——— "Joseph Trutch and Indian Land Policy" in Ward, W.P. and Mcdonald, R.A.J., eds. *British Columbia: Historical Readings* (Vancouver 1981) at 154–183

Flanagan, Thomas "From Indian Title to Aboriginal Rights" in Knafla, ed. (see above) at 81–100.

Hall, David J. "Clifford Sifton and Canadian Indian Administration 1896–1905" in Getty, Ian A.L. and Lussier, Antoine S., eds. *As Long as the Sun Shines and Water Flows: A Reader in Canadian Natives Studies* (Vancouver 1983) at 120–144

Hawthorn, H.B., ed. *A Survey of the Contemporary Indians of Canada* (Two Parts, Ottawa 1966 and 1967) [The "Hawthorn Report"]

Hinge, Gail *Consolidation of Indian Legislation* (Dept. of Indian and Northern Affairs), Vol. I: United Kingdom and Canada and Vol. III: Provincial Legislation, pre- and Post-Confederation

Historical Development of the Indian Act, The (Policy, Planning and Research Branch, Dept. of Indian and Northern Affairs, 1975) (Referred to in the text as INA)

In All Fairness. Native Claims Policy: Comprehensive Claims (Ministry of Indian Affairs and Northern Development 1981)

La Violette, F.E. *The Struggle for Survival: Indian Culture and the Protestant Ethic in British Columbia* (Toronto 1973)

Leighton, Douglas "A Victorian Civil Servant at Work: Lawrence Vankoughnet and the Canadian Indian Department 1874–1893" in Getty and Lussier, eds. (see above) at 104–119

Living Treaties, Lasting Agreements (Report of the Task Force to Review Comprehensive Claims Policy 1985)

Lysyk, K. "The Unique Constitutional Position of the Canadian Indian" (1967) *Canadian Bar Review* at 513–553

Madill, Dennis *British Columbia Indian Treaties in Historical Perspective* (Research Branch, Corporate Policy, Indian and Northern Affairs 1980)

Milloy, John S. "The Early Indian Acts: Developmental Strategy and Constitutional Change" in Getty and Lussier, eds. (see above) at 56–64

McNab, David T. "Herman Merivale and Colonial Office Indian Policy in the Mid-Nineteenth Century" in Getty and Lussier, eds. (see above) at 85–103

Morse, Bradford W., ed. *Aboriginal Peoples and the Law: Indian, Metis and Inuit Rights in Canada* (Ottawa 1985) and excerpts selected therein

Raunet, Daniel *Without Surrender, Without Consent: A History of the Nisgha Land Claims* (Vancouver 1984)

Sanders, Douglas "The Application of Provincial Laws" in Morse, ed. (see above) at 452–466

— — — "The Queen's Promises" in Knafla, ed. (see above) at 101–127

Scott, D.C. "Indian Affairs 1763–1841" in *Canada and its Provinces*, Vol. 4 (1913)

Shankel, George Edgar *The Development of Indian Policy in British Columbia* (University of Washington, PhD thesis 1945)

Slattery, Brian "Did France Claim Canada upon 'Discovery'?" in J.M. Bumsted, ed. *Interpreting Canada's Past* (Toronto 1986), Vol. I at 2–26

Smith, Donald B. "Aboriginal Rights a Century Ago: The St. Catharines Milling Case of 1885 Hardened Attitudes Toward Native Land Claims", *The Beaver* (February/March 1987) at 4–15

Smith, Donald M. "Indian Reserves in British Columbia: Historical Background" (Unpublished 1986)

Stanley, George F.G. "As Long as the Sun Shines and Water Flows: An Historical Comment" in Getty and Lussier, eds. (see above) at 1–26

Summary of the Proceedings of a Conference with Representative Indians held in Ottawa, February 28-March 3, 1951 (Commons Debates 1951) at 1364–67

Surtees, Robert J. "Indian Land Cessions in Upper Canada, 1815–1830" in Getty and Lussier, eds. (see above) at 65–84

Titley, E. Brian *A Narrow Vision: Duncan Campbell Scott and the Administration of Indian Affairs in Canada* (Vancouver 1986)

Tobias, John L. "Protection, Civilization, Assimilation: An Outline History of Canada's Indian Polciy" in Getty and Lussier, eds. (see above) at 29–55

Venne, Sharon Helen *Indian Acts and Amendments 1868–1975: An Indexed Collection* (University of Saskatchewan Native Law Centre 1981)

Ware, Reuben *The Lands We Lost: A History of Cut-Off Lands and Land Losses from Indian Reserves in British Columbia* (Union of British Columbia Indian Chiefs, Land Claims Research Centre 1974)

Wildsmith, Bruce H. "Pre-Confederation Treaties" in Morse, ed. (see above) at 122–271

Zlotkin, Norman K. "Post-Confederation Treaties" in Morse, ed. (see above) at 272–407

APPENDIX B

Dispute Resolution

Much of the evidence heard during the course of this Inquiry was related to complaints of one sort or another. I heard from lessees who complained about the actions or inaction of the Band Council or the Department of Indian Affairs. Several Band members testified concerning various grievances related to the administration of Band affairs or, in some cases, related to their dealings with Departmental officials. One purpose of calling a public inquiry into a matter is to have a public airing of complaints or allegations, and to afford those persons who may be the object of complaints an opportunity to respond to them. As I listened to numerous witnesses on a variety of subjects, I could not help but wonder how many of the issues, which were essentially of local interest, could have attained such prominence as to be the subject of a public inquiry. I do not say that the concerns raised by any of the witnesses during this Inquiry were trivial or unworthy of being heard. A small sore can become a serious infection if it is left untreated. To a certain extent, that is what happened at Westbank.

While many of the controversies or disputes that arose at Westbank may be attributable to a clash of particular personalities, I believe that the types of disputes are not uncommon in the administration of Indian affairs. As Indian bands assume more powers and responsibility, either by way of the devolution policy or through self-government, it becomes more likely that band government will become the object of increasing complaints. As is the case with governments everywhere, the greater the influence an authority has over the lives of individuals, the greater is the chance that objections or complaints will arise. In order that governments may carry on their operations in an orderly and efficient manner, it is highly desirable that an effective mechanism be available for the resolution of disputes. If disputes which concern local matters can be dealt with in a timely fashion at the local level, it is in everyone's best interest. Local disputes can become highly politicized and blown out of proportion when the combatants attempt to enlist the support of the Minister or a local Member of Parliament. When local battles are fought at such lofty heights, the fallout can be very disruptive indeed.

Perhaps the reason why disputes of a local nature can become overly complex is that a unique relationship exists between the Department of Indian Affairs and an Indian band. On the one hand, the Department attempts to further Indian self-government, but on the other hand it has certain supervisory functions. Under the current legislative structure, the Department is involved as an intermediary whenever Indian lands are leased. In practical terms, however, it is the Indian band or locatee who has the direct interest and consequently the day-to-day involvement with lessees. Because the Department (Crown) is a party to any lease, it is understandable that the Department will be drawn into some disputes that concern the lease itself. It is also understandable that a lessee may look to the Department for assistance or action in situations where problems arise with the local Indian government. The Department is clearly in a difficult position when disputes arise between lessees and local Indian governments.

Similarly, the Department has a difficult role to play in resolving disputes which may arise between band government and band members. Any active involvement by Departmental officials, no matter how well-intentioned, could be criticized by either side in the dispute. If the Department supports the complainant against the band council, its action may be viewed by the band executive as paternalistic interference. If the Department supports the band council, it may be criticized for ignoring the complaints of the band members.

Local band government disputes often have been brought to the attention of senior Departmental officials or Members of Parliament. During the course of the Inquiry, I was told that it is not unusual for band members to petition the Minister in an attempt to call attention to local problems. I was also told that Ron Derrickson was a very persistent advocate while he was Chief of the Westbank Band, and would not hesitate to bring local matters to the attention of the Regional Director General, or even the Minister. Various non-band members who had problems in their dealings with the Westbank Band and the Department turned to their Members of Parliament in an attempt to resolve a situation which they felt had reached an impasse.

It appears to me that matters which are entirely local in nature are all too often turned into political causes. Why, for example, should the Minister have to deal with a dispute over the administration of one band's water by-law? There must be some method by which disputes and problems concerning local band government matters can be resolved without involving senior officials of the Department or Members of Parliament.

Many provinces in Canada have established an office of ombudsman to serve as a mediator for citizens who feel that they have a complaint against a particular governmental authority. The federal government has not established an office of ombudsman. Because the federal government has legislative jurisdiction concerning Indians and lands reserved for Indians, the services of a provincial ombudsman are not available to residents of Indian reserves who have complaints against the local government. This may be another example of what has been termed the "regulatory vacuum" that exists on Indian reserves.

I believe that the concept of the ombudsman might be usefully employed in the resolution of disputes related to the administration of Indian affairs at the local level. An ombudsman has the quality of impartiality which is necessary for any mediator of disputes. The office of ombudsman is generally endowed with investigative powers, including the power to compel the production of documents and examine witnesses under oath. Often an ombudsman can investigate a complaint and successfully resolve the matter in an informal and unobtrusive manner. I suggest that an office similar to that of the provincial ombudsman be established for the purpose of mediating disputes which may arise from the administration of local Indian government and Indian affairs generally. Such an institution might be called the "Office of the Native Ombudsman".

The Supreme Court of Canada has recently offered the following comments on the goal and purpose of an ombudsman:

> The limitations of courts are also well-known. Litigation can be costly and slow. Only the most serious cases of administrative abuse are therefore likely to find their way into the courts. More importantly, there is simply no remedy at law available in a great many cases.

H.W.R. Wade [*Administrative Law*, 5th ed. (1982), pp. 73–74] describes this problem and the special role the Ombudsman has come to fill:

> But there is a large residue of grievances which fit into none of the regular legal moulds, but are none the less real. A humane system of government must provide some way of assuaging them, both for the sake of justice and because accumulating discontent is a serious clog on administrative efficiency in a democratic country.
>
> The vital necessity is the impartial investigation of complaints... What every form of government needs is some regular and smooth-running mechanism for feeding back the reactions of its disgruntled customers, after impartial assessment, and for correcting whatever may have gone wrong. Nothing of this kind existed in our system before 1968, except in very limited spheres. Yet it is a fundamental need in every system. It was because it filled that need that the device of the ombudsman suddenly attained immense popularity, sweeping round the democratic world and taking root in Britain and in many other countries, as well as inspiring a vast literature.

This problem is also addressed by Professor Donald C. Rowat, in an article entitled *An Ombudsman Scheme for Canada* (1962), 28 Can. J. Econ. & Poli. Sc. 543, at p. 543:

> It is quite possible nowadays for a citizen's right to be accidentally crushed by the vast juggernaut of the government's administrative machine. In this age of the welfare state, thousands of administrative decisions are made each year by governments or their agencies, many of them by lowly officials; and if some of

these decisions are arbitrary or unjustified, there is no easy way for the ordinary citizen to gain redress.

The Ombudsman represents society's response to these problems of potential abuse and of supervision. His unique characteristics render him capable of addressing many of the concerns left untouched by the traditional bureaucratic control devices. He is impartial. His services are free, and available to all. Because he often operates informally, his investigations do not impede the normal processes of government. Most importantly, his powers of investigation can bring to light cases of bureaucratic maladministration that would otherwise pass unnoticed. The Ombudsman "can bring the lamp of scrutiny to otherwise dark places, even over the resistance of those who would draw the blinds": *Re Ombudsman Act* (1970), 10 D.L.R.(3d) 47 at p. 61, 72 W.W.R. 176 (Alta. S.C.) at pp. 192–93, *per* Milvain C.J.T.D. On the other hand, he may find the complaint groundless, not a rare occurrence, in which event his impartial and independent report, absolving the public authority, may well serve to enhance the morale and restore the self-confidence of the public employees impugned.

In short, the powers granted to the Ombudsman allow him to address administrative problems that the courts, the legislature, and the executive cannot effectively resolve.

(Re British Columbia Development Corp. et. al. and Friedmann et. al. [1984] 2 S.C.R. 447 at pp. 460–461).

Although local Indian governments are not as large or complex as provincial governments, an ombudsman or similar official may nevertheless have a valuable role to play in resolving complaints against a band administration or the Department of Indian Affairs. Many of the services local Indian governments provide or will provide to their members and residents are similar to those provided by other governments. Consequently, the band administration may be viewed as the equivalent of other bureaucracies from the perspective of a band member or resident of the reserve. Lessees on the reserve must deal with the band executive with respect to many typically administrative matters. That is a natural consequence of their decision to operate their businesses within the jurisdiction of a local Indian government. The experience at Westbank illustrates the desirability of having some practical mechanism for dispute resolution when a person feels that he or she has a legitimate complaint regarding an administrative matter. It seems to me to be far preferable for a local matter to be resolved through the assistance of an independent mediator rather than via the political route.

Some disputes are of a legal nature and in such cases the parties will have recourse to the courts. In Section II, I have recommended changes to the manner in which lease negotiations are conducted. I see no role for an ombudsman in matters concerning lease negotiations such as the setting of rents. Also, it should be noted that, as in the case of the provincial ombudsman, the jurisdiction of the proposed mediator is best limited to administrative matters. For example, the mediator could not entertain a complaint about the substance of a particular by-law passed by a band council. However, he could properly investigate a complaint regarding the manner in which a particular by-law was being implemented.

In order for the proposed mediator to effectively discharge his duties, I believe that it is necessary that he or she have powers and responsibilities similar to those of an ombudsman. The most important features of a mediator are that he is independent and that he is always perceived to be independent and impartial. Another important feature of the ombudsman, which I suggest be incorporated here, is that his role is limited to that of a persuader and mediator rather than an arbitrator. An ombudsman has no power to compel any government authority to remedy what he perceives to be a wrong. Rather, the ombudsman may only report to the government executive branch, or to the legislature, concerning any intransigence on the part of the governmental authorities. A report to the legislature is usually a measure of last resort, where the ombudsman has failed to resolve a problem and feels that there is a continuing problem which ought to be addressed. The report becomes a matter of public record and the mere threat of such publicity may be sufficient to move a party from an unreasonable position. I believe that it is a particular strength of the ombudsman concept that the ombudsman cannot interfere with the administration of government, but rather must serve as a persuader to attempt to assist members of the public in any disputes that they have with governmental agencies. In this way, the ombudsman can remain an impartial mediator rather than usurping the role of legislator or adjudicator. I therefore suggest that the proposed mediator for Native disputes should not have the power to enforce his view of matters upon a local Indian government or the Department of Indian Affairs.

The Native Ombudsman's powers and duties with respect to administrative matters should be established in general terms. In the British Columbia Development Corporation case noted above, the Supreme Court of Canada considered the meaning of the term "matter of administration" as that term is used in the British Columbia Ombudsman Act. The Ombudsman's investigative authority concerning matters of administration was found in that case to include the power to investigate a complaint concerning any governmental authority engaged in the implementation of government policy. The court would have only excluded the activities of the legislature and the courts from the Ombudsman's jurisdiction. The governmental authorities with which the proposed Native Ombudsman should properly deal are local Indian governments (band or tribal councils) and the Department of Indian Affairs.

Another feature which ought to be part of any mediation system is the preservation of the confidentiality of any information received during the course of an investigation. For example, the British Columbia Ombudsman Act requires that the Ombudsman and every person on his staff maintain confidentiality in respect of all matters that come to their knowledge in the performance of their duties, except under defined circumstances. Certain matters may be disclosed if it is necessary to further an investigation, prosecute an offence under the Act, or establish grounds for conclusions and recommendations made in any report. The British Columbia Ombudsman Act also stipulates that investigations be conducted in private, unless there are special circumstances in which public knowledge is essential in order to further the investigation. Such provisions tend to encourage a more informal and unobtrusive dispute resolution process.

The Office of the Native Ombudsman must be endowed with powers to obtain information such as the power to compel production of documents and to summon and examine under oath any person who, in the opinion of the mediator, is able to give information relevant to the investigation of a complaint. In order to support the powers of the office, there should be created an offence in the nature of a summary conviction for anyone who, without lawful excuse, intentionally obstructs or hinders the Native Ombudsman or his staff in the exercise of any of their powers or duties.

Any complaints that are made should be in writing before they are considered. The Office should have quite a broad discretion to refuse to investigate or to cease investigation of a complaint for specific reasons. For example, if in the opinion of the Native Ombudsman the complaint is frivolous, or if in his opinion further investigation will be of no benefit, then there should be available the option to refuse an investigation or to cease investigation of any matter. However, in such a case, the Ombudsman should have the duty to inform the complainant in writing and give reasons why the matter was not pursued. In order to make the investigation procedure a fair and reasonable one, the authority who is the subject of complaint or investigation must be notified of any pending investigation. It is a feature of the British Columbia legislation that the Ombudsman must consult with the authority under investigation if that authority so requests. As well, where there appears to be grounds for making an adverse report, the Ombudsman must give the interested authority an opportunity to make written or oral representations.

Following any investigation, the Native Ombudsman should inform the complainant of the results of the investigation. Where he believes that the actions or omissions of the authority were contrary to law, unreasonable or otherwise wrong, he should be required to report his opinion to the authority and to make any recommendations that he considers appropriate. If the authority fails to take adequate action within a reasonable time following the recommendations of the

Ombudsman, then the Ombudsman should have the power to report the matter to higher authorities.

The Office of the Native Ombudsman should be established under and report to a Ministry such as the Secretary of State in order that it may be truly independent of the Department of Indian Affairs. Such an office can only be successful if it is seen to be an independent body. The person who is in charge of the Office ought to be appointed only following significant input from the Native community. I suggest that there be at least one branch office established in every region according to need. It would defeat the Office's main purpose — to resolve local disputes — if it were to be only located in Ottawa/Hull.

If an office similar to that of the Provincial Ombudsman can be established to assist in the resolution of disputes connected with local Indian government, there could be many benefits. Because the Office would be independent and impartial and its services would be rendered free of charge, aggrieved persons would be encouraged to resolve disputes through mediation rather than through the Minister's office. Where a complaint is found to be groundless, an impartial and independent report may well serve to vindicate the governmental official whose conduct has been impugned. Such positive feedback can enhance the morale and self-confidence of local governments or Departmental staff. Local Indian governments have experienced substantial growth over the last ten years since the Department began to devolve more responsibility and authority, and there may naturally be some problems adjusting to a new role. An official mediator in the form of an ombudsman could serve a very useful role in ensuring that the administration of Indian governments and Indian affairs runs smoothly and free of the disruptive effects of Departmental investigations or public inquiries. I recommend that serious consideration be given at once to setting up such an office.

Infrastructure on Reserves

A continuing problem to residents in the area of the Westbank Indian
Reserves is the assurance of an adequate water supply. This problem is
particularly pressing on Reserve 9. Mr. Ronald Derrickson described
the situation as he had knowledge of it. It was his thesis that rather than
have a multiplicity of wells (and other individual services such as
garbage collection and the like), that there be a central authority to look
after such matters. That, of course, raises issues of by-laws and
taxation. He said this:

A ...one of the problems we have is we have basically on this
Reserve, 15 or 20 or 30 individual little water systems, which all
get minimum maintenance and minimum care. In many areas of
the trailer parks, there was concern from National Health and
Welfare that eventually the saturation of the lands down there
would cause severe problems with the wells, and it even caused
sewage leakage, eventually into the lake.

The other thing was that the trailer park owners, and rightly so,
you know, have to supply a service, where they have to pay out of
their own pocket, the service of garbage, water, sewer; and each
individual supply his own needs and doing it.

The problem is with the Province of British Columbia, they
don't have any ground water legislation in this province. This is
missing. All the other provinces have ground water legislation; in
other words, the control over who can drill where, and what you
can take out.

In other words, there are certain restrictions in the Province of
Alberta's ground water legislation, so you can't have a situation
that's created, and — I can't remember the golf course name up
there.

Q Shannon Lake?

A Shannon Lake Golf Course, and the Shannon Lake Development,
you have two or three thousand gallon a minute wells that are
pumping onto that golf course, and into the homes, and we have
all these wells. Our main supply of water on this Reserve is from
the well, from the ground water. We have watched, over the last
four to five years, as development increases, on the fringes
especially, on the uplands going northwest, we have watched the
ground water levels dropping year after year after year, to where
our trailer parks and our development are in jeopardy; in jeopardy
of having to close down because there is not enough water to
service the residents in those trailer parks.

The idea of the water by-law was to put in place the regulations
so that we could take over that function and handle it, number
one, more economically. For example, if, say, you know, blankety-

blank trailer park that was on this Reserve, if they were there and they were charging $150 a month, for lack of a better figure, and we wanted to take over the garbage and the water system, the maintenance of the water system, and be responsible for it, then our suggestion to them was they would drop their rates for what it cost them to supply that service.

I mean, a reasonable figure would have to be worked out. If it costs, say, Jack Alexander at Pine Ridge Trailer Park $10 a month from his income, to supply the service of water, the sewer and garbage, we would take over that function, you know, in this case we were only talking about water; we were putting together our garbage collection by-laws — this would in turn, create one uniform company, or utility that can handle this function; it would create employment for our Band members. It would also provide us with the vehicle to get low interest loans and grants relying on the income from the tenants.

In other words, instead of the trailer park owners supplying water, we would, and they would, in turn, reduce their rents and they wouldn't have that responsibility. So, if Jack Alexander ran out of water down there, he could phone up the utility and say, look, I am out of water, it's your responsibility, you're collecting the rates. That, in turn, would allow us to build up enough of a fund, have enough income coming from — and you know, there's several trailer parks on this Reserve — create enough income to eventually put in an overall water system, overall sewer system on this Reserve to supply everybody.

It became — well, I guess I don't have to repeat myself — it became increasingly difficult to try and have an idea like that acceptable to the trailer park owners when we were lashing out at each other all the time.

Q Mr. Derrickson, did you feel at the time that that particular by-law was implemented that it was necessary and important, as far as the Reserve was concerned, at that time?

A Well, I think we have, right today, on this Reserve, a serious water situation. I mean, you know, you hear people say, why those Indians have all that good land, why the hell don't they get off their butts and do something about it. We don't have the infrastructure on this Reserve to take advantage of the opportunity that's there regarding that land. We can't get our share. If we could just get our share in relation to the good land that we hold near that highway corridor, this Band would be well off.

<u>Until we can have the infrastructure, what are you going to do?</u> You can't build a hotel with no water and no sewer; you can't build a shopping centre with no water or no sewer. (My underlining)

(Transcripts: Volume LXVI, pp. 9865–9868)

Chief Robert Louie also told the Inquiry that an adequate water system, particularly for Reserve 9, is badly needed. Because of the nature of the climate in the Okanagan, water supply is a difficulty that is constantly faced with regard to any new development. The problems were not lessened during the past summer, which was unusually dry.

The question of providing adequate infrastructure on Indian reserve lands is becoming more topical. It is obviously more important in the case of those reserves that are ripe for increased development because of their proximity to growing urban areas. The Westbank Reserves fall into this category. The Department has been aware of the necessity for adequate services on reserves for quite some time.

For instance, in a memorandum of June 27, 1973 from Mr. Sparks to Mr. Walchli, who was then the Regional Superintendent of Economic Development for the B.C. Region, Mr. Sparks noted that it was going to be increasingly necessary for adequate infrastructure to be provided for any large-scale development of Indian lands to occur. The required infrastructure would differ depending on the location, climate, and the like.

It is clear that it would greatly assist development on Reserve 9 to have an assured and adequate supply of water. Various mobile home parks are already located on this Reserve, and its lands are becoming more desirable due to its proximity to the Highway 97 corridor and Kelowna. It appears to me that this Reserve has now reached the stage where a comprehensive water system is an essential component of the infrastructure needed to attract continuing development. In the short-term, it may need some government backing (perhaps by way of guarantee as I comment on elsewhere in the Report), but over the long-term such a system should at least partly pay for itself, including its maintenance and operation.

The story of Pineridge Mobile Home Park illustrates the sort of problem that can occur with regard to water supply. Pineridge Park comprises approximately 21 acres located near Lake Okanagan on Reserve 9, the locatee of which is Mr. Ronald M. Derrickson. The Pineridge Park has from its inception been operated by Jack and Barbara Alexander. The original water supply utilized by Pineridge came from wells on the property. These wells depended on springs adjacent to McDougall Creek.

Mr. Derrickson had some rental houses (fourplexes) located just below the Pineridge property, closer to Lake Okanagan. The Band subdivision on Reserve 9 is located above the Pineridge Park property.

In 1982, the Band, Mr. Alexander, and Mr. Derrickson agreed that they would cooperate in building a waterline for the joint benefit of the Band subdivision, Mr. Alexander's park, and Mr. Derrickson's rental properties. The line, which in part traversed Pineridge Park, was installed in approximately 1982. Mr. Alexander utilized it in conjunction with his existing wells until 1984. In 1983–84, he ran into problems with his wells, which were serviced by springs in the McDougall Creek area. Because of the change of course of that creek, necessitated by highway construction, the wells Mr. Alexander had been using were rendered virtually useless and he had to have a new well drilled on adjacent property.

He had an unpleasant surprise, however, in 1984. As noted, he had agreed to contribute to the capital cost of the waterline which he needed to supplement his wells. He was paying part of the cost by monthly payments to the Band. He paid until the events he described in his evidence.

> Q And you did make those payments?
> A I made it up until June 20, 1984 when they shut my water off. I haven't paid them since.
> Q All right. Now, tell us about that. What happened on June 20, 1984?
> A Well, we came home from a school — we were at the school, for the kids, and we came home to no water, because they'd shut the water right off and they'd also drained my tanks down to his fourplexes. We had quite a rough time of it for a while, and we couldn't get that turned on again. We never did.
> Q So, ever since June, 1984 that source of water has been turned off?
> A Right.
> Q Have you had any discussions with Ron Derrickson or any other members of the Council about that?
> A Yes, we've talked about it, but they haven't got the water to supply it.
> Q Who told you that?
> A Ron Derrickson.
>
> (Transcripts: Volume XIII, pp. 1754–1755)

Mr. Alexander told the Inquiry that he had paid about $16,000 of the approximately $20,000 that was his share of the cost of the waterline, but that he had ceased paying after 1984 when the water was cut off.

This situation illustrates one matter that would have to be carefully addressed in the construction and operation of any new water system. It would appear that the water to the Alexander property was cut off in 1984 without any consultation or warning. This was not a desirable method of proceeding, to say the least.

Mr. Alexander, in good faith, contributed a portion of the capital costs to this waterline, and then found himself suddenly cut off from using the water supply. That situation apparently had persisted for three years to the time he gave evidence. Obviously, the Band must have regard to the residences in the subdivision as a priority, but it could scarcely be considered good practice to suddenly shut off the water to Mr. Alexander's property without giving him any warning and the time to make alternate arrangements. Mr. Alexander might feel justifiably ill-treated in that he has provided funds for a capital work which has proved latterly to be of no use or benefit to him. He seemed to be a patient and fair-minded man. He was not as critical as he might have been of the rather high-handed action that appears to have occurred with regard to this water system.

It appears to me that the Department should make immediate efforts to organize a decent water system for Reserve 9. This matter is of vital concern, not only to the Band itself, but to residents on that Reserve. In order to make certain that a system is run in a proper and even-handed and businesslike fashion, it is my view that it should be set up under some sort of body equivalent to a public utilities commission. It seems to me that a body comprising representatives of the Department, the Band, and mobile home park lessees would be required to ensure that the system would be run for the benefit of all interested parties.

I think that the Department will have to assist with a good portion of the initial capital costs. This can be viewed as simply an investment in the future that ultimately will be repaid in many tangible and intangible ways. Of course, there are always more needs than resources. But one of the great needs, as I see it, in Indian communities, is the need to establish a proper economic base. It is the old choice between giving a person a fish or teaching him how to fish. I think that the Westbank Reserves are a good example of a situation where creation of a better infrastructure will be a great engine for economic progress. New developments on the Reserve will just have to pay their rateable portions of capital costs. The ultimate aim should be to make any system self-sustaining by imposts and fees charged to users and developers.

One of the great continuing policy problems for the Department is to know where to best direct its resources. The needs in the differing reserves are many and varied across the country. Choices have to be made. The Department may, from time to time, be criticized for putting money into a reserve which is relatively well off and perhaps not pouring more money into reserves that are very disadvantaged and that have no particularly viable economy. There was continuing debate over that sort of issue in the case of Toussowasket Enterprises.

There never will be a universally popular solution to this sort of dilemma, but I do not think the Department should be criticized for endeavouring to enhance the economic status of the more economically progressive reserves. Indian communities need some joint sense of purpose; as certain reserves progress, they become role models for others. Joint political action is occurring more generally and it is to be hoped that joint economic action can be encouraged. Over the long-term, it should be possible for richer bands to supply capital to other developing reserves. The Department and advanced bands can liaise to work in this direction. A great problem with regard to Indian people throughout Canada has been the dearth of viable economic enterprises.

Bands and locatees with good lands should be encouraged to make the best use of them to provide a better base for themselves and those who come after them.

We had the privilege during the Inquiry of hearing from Senator Len Marchand. He described his early years and how he had obtained an education and participated in political life. His story is but one example to Native people everywhere that doors to advancement need not be closed to them. It is difficult to advance with no economic base. The route to greater self-direction lies in good part through the route of economic self-sufficiency.

Certain individuals at Westbank have made good economic progress. There will always be distinctions in the rate of progress based on differing inherited talent, business opportunities, and life experience. There may be perceived inequities, but there are always those prepared to carp at others who are relatively successful. The answer to such criticism often is, "go and do likewise".

I think it is desirable that the Department furnish technical and economic assistance to bands and individuals who have a demonstrated capability, and who have progressed some distance along the road to economic self-sufficiency. I have said elsewhere that the Department must seek to be involved more as a guarantor than simply as a funding agency. It is vitally important that there be successful Indian role models so that the rising generation can discern ways in which they can make the best use of their lives.

There has been a fair measure of controversy and confrontation between the Westbank Band Council and lessees and residents on Reserve 9. Neither the Band nor the lessees benefit from continuing differences and controversy. A more adequate water system would make this land more attractive for leasing, to the ultimate benefit of the Band and of locatees. Such a system would also enhance the value and amenities of the existing mobile home parks located on Reserve 9.

But any new system must be administered in an even-handed and orderly fashion, unlike the behaviour in the Alexander episode. One problem that surfaced from time to time during the course of the evidence before the Inquiry was what I might term an occasionally inconsistent approach by Band Council to questions of local government and the provision of utilities. Obviously, this sort of an approach can have a very chilling effect on any proper long-term development.

To those who would say that providing assistance for the installation of a water system would show favouritism to this Reserve, I simply say that this Reserve has a critical problem coupled with real opportunity for growth, and it is a matter of prudent investment to put money where you can obtain some tangible results.

It seemed clear from the evidence I heard that unless this issue is addressed in the near future, a very serious situation will arise on Reserve 9. The problem ought to be addressed without delay, and as I noted above, the Department need not feel apologetic about putting some resources into a reserve that does have great potential for development and that has shown significant economic progress.

Although there is a proper role for government in providing certain essential services, I am not at all certain that government does well when it goes beyond that and attempts to take on a role that more properly belongs to private entrepreneurship. For example, it has been suggested that government purchase some or all existing mobile home parks at Westbank. But it was not apparent to me that that was a sound suggestion. It will be remembered that the Band itself resiled from the idea of being in the mobile home park business in 1982 because of perceived problems of management. It seems unlikely that government itself planned to manage the enterprises; the apparent plan was to have the Band or individual locatees run the parks. What level of expertise or experience would be brought to such management? Government, of necessity, would have to be cautious in undertaking to buy enterprises on Indian land with a view to transferring such enterprises over to bands or band members. Where would the process begin or end? Would, for instance, tenants of mobile home parks be well served by such intervention? The question of setting precedents would have to be examined. If problems were encountered on a reserve in the future, it might be suggested that government step in as a purchaser of enterprises if such a course were adopted at Westbank.

It seems to me preferable to have government provide funding for better infrastructure on reserves and leave it to the bands and individual locatees or lessees to inaugurate and operate business enterprises. Ultimately some form of market place economy has to apply if satisfactory economic results are to be obtained. Government may provide technical assistance, guarantees, and the like to be of assistance to enterprise. Bands may have to be more active in the regulatory field to ensure proper development. Government (at all levels) can assist by financial underwriting, by providing a consistent regulatory scheme, and by helping to put in place a proper infrastructure in order to foster better economic development on Indian reserves.

The Department has a difficult task in this time of transition. On the one hand, it is withdrawing from certain traditional functions that it has long performed and is turning over greater responsibility to Indian bands or councils. On the other hand, it has a continuing responsibility to Indian people to look after their economic interests where bands are not economically sophisticated. As well, it has a duty not to withdraw too precipitously from a role in the administration of agreements already in place. The transfer of responsibility to bands must be done in a planned fashion. One can recognize the desire of government not to be unduly involved in private sector matters, but as regards the Department of Indian Affairs and Northern Development, there is a long history of very active involvement in the lives of Native people. The Commission heard on more than one occasion the refrain that the Department should get out of the lives of Indians. Counsel to the former Band executive said this in his submission to me:

> It is my submission that the Indian Act, while competent Federal legislation, is mired in a Victorian mind set. Since the Indian Act has been Canadian law for generations, the attitudes found in it are sedimented Canadian beliefs. The attitude that Indians are not equal to white people is especially visible in Government and specifically in the Department of Indian Affairs and agencies like the R.C.M.P. because they have to "deal with Indians" and operate pursuant to the Indian Act.
>
> (Transcripts: Volume LXXIX, p. 11810)

I think the Department genuinely wishes to step back from any overly active involvement in band affairs. But that process must be gradual and orderly. When there was a general rejection of Departmental involvement in 1975, the result was unhappy. The Department should not be vilified as the oppressor of Indian people — it has, and will have for years to come, a role in their lives. It will always be a delicate task for the Department to tread a line between being, on the one hand, intrusive, and on the other hand, indifferent. It is a resource to be used by bands and a source of stability in the present times of change.

Family Relations Rights on Reserves

During the course of this Inquiry, a number of witnesses voiced concerns about defects in the legislation that applies (or does not apply) to Indian people on reserve lands. For example, there were difficulties in applying Band by-laws to surrendered lands. Some witnesses have adverted to a "regulatory vacuum". As well, because of the separation of powers under the Canadian Constitution, many provincial laws have no application to reserve lands. Under the Constitution, "Indians and lands reserved for Indians" is a heading that falls under exclusive federal legislative jurisdiction.

By Section 88 of the Indian Act, provincial laws of general application are made applicable to Indians to the extent that they are not inconsistent with the Indian Act or any rules, orders, regulations, and by-laws made pursuant to the Act. That section reads:

> 88. Subject to the terms of any treaty and any other Act of the Parliament of Canada, all laws of general application from time to time in force in any province are applicable to and in respect of Indians in the province, except to the extent that such laws are inconsistent with this Act or any order, rule, regulation or by-law made thereunder, and except to the extent that such laws make provision for any matter for which provision is made by or under this Act.

The Canadian Constitutional law doctrine of paramountcy provides that where there is conflict between provincial laws and federal laws, federal law will take precedence.

The constitutional status of reserve lands can be viewed as both an advantage and a disadvantage vis-à-vis the application of provincial laws. In some instances, the non-applicability of provincial laws may make Indian lands more attractive to investors or developers. Indian reserves may be viewed as special status islands not subject to provincial or municipal regulation and the accompanying red tape. But this special status can sometimes be a disadvantage. For example, Mr. Ronald M. Derrickson expressed concern that strata title legislation in force in B.C. was not applicable to Indian lands. While legislation obviously can be a burden to some segments of society, its usual purpose is to remedy some perceived or actual problem in society. Due to the constitutional position of reserve lands, Indian people may not be able to receive the benefit of remedial legislation enacted by provinces to enhance the opportunities or rights of different groups.

In many areas, the <u>Indian Act</u> deals with subject matters that are traditionally in the domain of provincial jurisdiction. It is perhaps not surprising that the current <u>Indian Act</u>, substantially unchanged since 1951, has lagged behind the growing complexities of reserve development and government. The Act is likewise out of step with societal changes. One obvious area where Indian legislation is outdated is in a total absence of recognition of a family law regime. The subject matter of family relations law generally falls within the constitutional sphere of the provinces.

Over the last twenty years there has been an increased awareness of the status and rights of women. Beginning in the 1970's, most provincial governments embarked on a process of legislative reform designed to reflect the principle of the equality of the sexes before the law. One major area which was the subject of reform was family relations. In particular, new provincial laws were enacted to ensure a more equal division of family assets upon the dissolution of a marriage. This new legislation typically allowed women to share more equitably in assets generated during the marriage.

Important aspects of provincial family relations law have been held not to apply to Indians living on reserve lands. It was recently decided by the Supreme Court of Canada that the provisions of the <u>Family Relations Act</u> of British Columbia, which allows a court to order division of family property, did not apply to lands on an Indian reserve. That case involved people from Westbank. The decision is cited as <u>Derrickson</u> v. <u>Derrickson</u> (1986) 26 DLR (4th) 175. Mrs. Rose Derrickson, a party to the action, gave evidence before the Inquiry.

Prior to her marriage, Mrs. Derrickson had been a member of the Okanagan Band. She acquired membership in the Westbank Band upon her marriage to Mr. William Derrickson. At the time of their marriage, the couple did not own property on the Westbank Reserves. Mrs. Derrickson bought some land with assistance from her family. This land was registered in her name and the couple built their home on it. During the course of their marriage, they purchased other properties on Reserve 9 which were registered in the name of Mr. William Derrickson. In her evidence before this Commission, Mrs. Derrickson stated that she felt that all of the property which they had purchased was joint family property. When the marriage broke down, the parties were unable to agree on a division of assets and court proceedings ensued. The matter progressed through the Supreme Court of B.C., the B.C. Court of Appeal and, ultimately, the Supreme Court of Canada.

Mrs. Derrickson sought to have the provisions of the British Columbia <u>Family Relations Act</u> apply to the division of the family property upon the dissolution of the marriage. The applicable sections of that Act are as follows:

43. (1) Subject to this Part, each spouse is entitled to an interest in each family asset on or after March 31, 1979 when

(a) a separation agreement;
(b) a declaratory judgement under section 44;
(c) an order for dissolution of marriage or judicial separation; or
(d) an order declaring the marriage null and void

respecting the marriage is first made.

(2) The interest under subsection (1) is an undivided half interest in the family asset as a tenant in common.

(3) An interest under subsection (1) is subject to:

(a) an order under this Part; or
(b) a marriage agreement or a separation agreement.

(4) This section applies to a marriage entered into before or after this section comes into force.

51. Where the provisions for division of property between spouses under section 43 or their marriage agreement, as the case may be, would be unfair having regard to

(a) the duration of the marriage;
(b) the duration of the period during which the spouses have lived separate and apart;
(c) the date when property was acquired or disposed of;
(d) the extent to which property was acquired by one spouse through inheritance or gift;
(e) the needs of each spouse to become or remain economically independent and self sufficient; or
(f) any other circumstances relating to the acquisition, preservation, maintenance, improvement or use of property or the capacity or liabilities of a spouse,

the Supreme Court, on application, may order that the property covered by section 43 or the marriage agreement, as the case may be, be divided into shares fixed by the court. Additionally or alternatively the court may order that other property not covered by section 43 or the marriage agreement, as the case may be, of one spouse be vested in the other spouse.

52. (1) In proceedings under this Part or on application, the Supreme Court may determine any matter respecting the ownership, right of possession or division of property under this Part, including the vesting of property under section 51, and may make orders which are necessary, reasonable or ancillary to give effect to the determination.

(2) In an order under this section, the court may, without limiting the generality of subsection (1), do one or more of the following:

(a) declare the ownership of or right of possession to property;

(b) order that, on a division of property, title to a specified property granted to a spouse be transferred to, or held in trust for, or vested in the spouse either absolutely, for life or for a term of years;

(c) order a spouse to pay compensation to the other spouse where property has been disposed of, or for the purpose of adjusting the division;

(d) order partition or sale of property and payment to be made out of the proceeds of sale to one or both spouses in specific proportions or amounts;

(e) order that property forming all or part of the share of either or both spouses be transferred to, or in trust for, or vested in a child;

(f) order that a spouse give security for the performance of an obligation imposed by order under this section, including a charge on property; or

(g) where property is owned by spouses as joint tenants, sever the joint tenancy.

This legislation is of general application to persons in the Province of British Columbia. The Supreme Court of British Columbia in the Derrickson case held that this provincial law was inconsistent with the Indian Act. In particular, sections of the Family Relations Act which allowed a judge to make an order respecting the division of immovable property (lands and buildings) were found to be in conflict with the provisions of Section 20 of the Indian Act. That section of the Indian Act deals with the matter of lawful possession of reserve lands.

20. (1) No Indian is lawfully in possession of land in a reserve unless, with the approval of the Minister, possession of the land has been allotted to him by the council of the band.

(2) The Minister may issue to an Indian who is lawfully in possession of land in a reserve a certificate, to be called a Certificate of Possession, as evidence of his right to possession of the land described therein.

(3) For the purposes of this Act, any person who, on the 4th day of September, 1951, held a valid and subsisting Location Ticket issued under "The Indian Act, 1880", or any statute relating to the same subject-matter, shall be deemed to be lawfully in possession of the land to which the location ticket relates and to hold a Certificate of Possession with respect thereto.

(4) Where possession of land in a reserve has been allotted to an Indian by the council of the band, the Minister may, in his discretion, withhold his approval and may authorize the Indian to occupy the land temporarily and may prescribe the conditions as to use and settlement that are to be fulfilled by the Indian before the Minister approves of the allotment.

(5) Where the Minister withholds approval pursuant to subsection (4), he shall issue a Certificate of Occupation to the Indian, and the Certificate entitles the Indian, or those claiming possession by devise or descent, to occupy the land in respect of which it is issued for a period of two years from the date thereof.

(6) The Minister may extend the term of a Certificate of Occupation for a further period not exceeding two years, and may, at the expiration of any period during which a Certificate of Occupation is in force

> (a) approve the allotment by the council of the band and issue a Certificate of Possession if in his opinion the conditions as to use and settlement have been fulfilled; or
> (b) refuse approval of the allotment by the council of the band and declare the land in respect of which the Certificate of Occupation was issued to be available for re-allotment by the council of the band. R.S., c. 149, s. 20.

The effect of the section is that no individual Indian can be in lawful possession of reserve lands without the approval of the Minister. Applying the doctrine of paramountcy, the trial judge concluded that he lacked jurisdiction under the B.C. Family Relations Act to direct a division of reserve lands.

Section 52(2)(c) of the Family Relations Act empowers a court to order one spouse to pay compensation to the other where property has been disposed of or for the purpose of adjusting the division of property. Mrs. Derrickson also sought relief under these provisions of the provincial legislation. The trial judge held that he lacked jurisdiction to order a division of property or to make an order for compensation in lieu of any such division. In the result, Mrs. Derrickson was unable to obtain any sharing of the real property registered in the name of Mr. Derrickson. Similarly, her husband was unable to obtain a court order dividing the property registered in Mrs. Derrickson's name. In terms of land assets, the division of property in effect at the time of the marriage breakdown clearly appeared to favour Mr. Derrickson, but the provincial legislation could not be utilized to provide for a more equitable division of the property between the former spouses.

The Derrickson case went on appeal to the British Columbia Court of Appeal. Mrs. Derrickson did not have adequate financial resources to fully fund an appeal. However, the Department of Indian Affairs felt this was a significant matter so funds were provided to have counsel argue the matter. The British Columbia Court of Appeal agreed with the conclusion of the trial judge that the provincial Family Relations Act could not be invoked to obtain an order for the division of property on an Indian reserve. However, the Court of Appeal differed from the trial judge on the issue of whether or not any order for compensation could be made. In order to get a definite pronouncement on these important issues from the highest court in the land, the Department supported a further appeal to the Supreme Court of Canada.

The judgement of the Supreme Court of Canada was delivered by Mr. Justice Chouinard. He identified the issues facing the court in Derrickson v. Derrickson as follows:

1. Are the provisions of the Family Relations Act applicable of their own force to lands reserved for the Indians?

2. Is the Family Relations Act referentially incorporated in the Indian Act by the application of s. 88 of the latter Act?
This issue in turn breaks down into two:

(a) Does s. 88 of the Indian Act apply to lands reserved for the Indians?
(b) In the affirmative, do the provisions of the Family Relations Act fall within one of the exceptions in s. 88?

3. Can an order for compensation be made in accordance with para. 52(2)(c) of the Family Relations Act with respect to lands on a reserve in lieu of an order directing division of property?

After a full analysis of the provincial legislation and the Indian Act, it was held that the Family Relations Act could not apply of its own force to lands reserved for Indians. Mr. Justice Chouinard found, as had the B.C. Supreme Court and the B.C. Court of Appeal, that there was conflict between the two Acts, and that, by reason of the paramountcy doctrine, the conflicting provisions of the Family Relations Act could not apply to lands on an Indian reserve. This conclusion was reached by the application of settled principles of Canadian constitutional law. The Supreme Court was clearly conscious of the practical difficulties occasioned by the application of those principles in this class of case. Mr. Justice Chouinard stated:

> In reaching this conclusion I am not unmindful of the ensuing consequences for the spouses, arising out of the laws in question, according as real property is located on a reserve or not. In this respect I borrow the following sentence, albeit in a different context, from P.W. Hogg, op. cit., at p. 554:
>
>> Whether such laws are wise or unwise is of course a much-controverted question, but it is not relevant to their constitutional validity.

The Supreme Court agreed with the B.C. Court of Appeal that an order could be made pursuant to Section 52(2)(c) of the provincial Family Relations Act to direct the payment of monetary compensation in lieu of an order for division of immovable property. Although some spouses may benefit in the future from that aspect of the decision, it was not of great practical assistance to Rose Derrickson. In order to obtain a compensation order in lieu of division of lands she would have had to return to the Supreme Court of British Columbia. This would entail further expenditure. Furthermore, it would have to be established that her husband had sufficient liquid resources to comply with any order. Mrs. Derrickson had already run into difficulty in this regard during her first appearance before the British Columbia Supreme Court. If the only substantial asset is real property on a reserve, any enforcement of a compensation order may be practically impossible. Mr. Derrickson had been receiving money from a developer regarding one of his properties, but Mrs. Derrickson could not prove this satisfactorily as there was no registered lease. The fact that there was an unofficial lease arrangement was confirmed by another witness at this Inquiry. Mr. Fred Walchli, at one point in his testimony, termed this type of lease a "buckshee lease".

Mr. Ward Kiehlbauch arrived in the Okanagan area in 1977 in search of a suitable location for a proposed tourist attraction. He was impressed with the tourist facilities already situate on Reserve 9. Through Chief Ron Derrickson he was introduced to Mr. William Derrickson and soon entered into an arrangement to lease certain lands from William Derrickson. Mr. Kiehlbauch planned to construct and operate a recreation project which he proposed to call "Space Trek". Although he had some start-up capital, he had not yet obtained all the financing required for such an ambitious project. According to the evidence of Mr. Kiehlbauch, William Derrickson made a proposal that would ease the financial strain on the project in its developing stages. The locatee was prepared to accept the annual rental in unequal instalments at irregular intervals. Mr. Kiehlbauch was thus afforded an opportunity to pay the rent in such instalments as he could afford, when he could afford them. According to Mr. Kiehlbauch, the reason that Mr. Derrickson was prepared to be so lenient was that he did not want his wife to know about the payments. These sorts of strategies are all too familiar to practitioners at the family bar. By this time, the Derrickson marriage had broken down and legal proceedings were under way. Mrs. Derrickson placed a caveat on the properties which her husband owned. Mr. Derrickson requested Mr. Kiehlbauch not to register any lease. Apparently Mr. Derrickson found that if a lease was registered on the property, his spouse would be more likely to share in some of the income from it. If a lease had been properly registered, payments would usually flow through the Band, which would ultimately then pay the proceeds over to the locatee. Rentals paid on a lease would be duly recorded in the Band office. Apparently Mr. Derrickson felt that if payments went through this pipeline, Mrs. Derrickson would be able to seize all or part of the money. To avoid this, Mr. Derrickson wanted to receive the lease payments "under the table" and Mr. Kiehlbauch agreed to Mr. Derrickson's scheme. This course of action ultimately proved unfortunate for both locatee and lessee. The participants in this covert scheme outsmarted themselves.

No lease was ever registered. Mr. Kiehlbauch had financial difficulty because he was unable to obtain proper financing without a duly registered lease. When he attempted to sell his partially completed project, Mr. Derrickson sought some percentage of the sale proceeds before he would execute a lease. Stalemate ensued and the sale eventually fell through. In the process, animosity arose between Mr. Kiehlbauch and Mr. Derrickson. Ultimately, the undertaking ended in financial disaster for all. Mr. Kiehlbauch departed, leaving behind his partially completed "Space Trek". As a result of his efforts to conceal income from the lease arrangement from his spouse, Mr. Derrickson ended up with no viable lease. Mrs. Derrickson received nothing. Her prospects of receiving any meaningful award of compensation in the future remain uncertain. The Derrickson v. Derrickson case and the story of the Kielbauch development illuminate a continuing problem area in the lives of Indian spouses.

In his evidence before this Commission, Mr. Ronald M. Derrickson complained about the lack of protection afforded to Indian women under the present legislative regime. Responding to questions from his counsel, he gave the following evidence of his role in the Derrickson test case, and his views of what could be done to assist women in a position similar to Mrs. Rose Derrickson:

Q Mr. Derrickson, notwithstanding the difficulties you had with Rose Derrickson, in reference to earlier times in the 1980's and the latter part of the 1980's, did you go to bat for her and seek legal assistance for her to take her case to the Supreme Court of Canada in reference to her domestic problems?

A Yes.

Q Have you continued since that time to try and support her?

A But you know, not only that, but I also went to bat for her husband, that he get legal assistance, because my complaint was that you can't legally support one side — I'm the Chief of the Band — I have no — you know, even though I'm male and maybe I have my male egotism, the fact is that I made sure that not only did she get legal assistance, I made sure that Bill Derrickson got legal assistance.

    I lobbied for that and it was done. Not only that I have since — Rose Derrickson lost that in the Supreme Court of Canada. I've approached Len Marchand and other politicians and senior people to try and see if we could find a good case so that women could regain their rights under the Charter of Rights, their rights to get half of the property or a reasonable settlement if a separation or divorce occurred.

    Because Indian women, although they have got rights back to the reserve, if their husband owns land they have no rights to take part of that land. It's a damn shame. (My underlining)

(Transcripts: Volume LXVII, pp. 9993–9994)

Mr. Derrickson here expresses a concern that is doubtless shared by many persons in the Native community. He took steps to protect and advance the property rights of Indian women in the Derrickson case. Hopefully his determination to ensure that Indian women are treated equally will one day meet with success. However, the Supreme Court of Canada has made it clear that under the existing law, it is not possible for a trial court to order a division of family assets consisting of real property, pursuant to existing provincial family relations legislation.

I have considered this question raised before the Commission concerning better protection for spouses and children when a matrimonial arrangement breaks down. There is nothing contained in the Indian Act, as framed presently, to deal with this issue. I do not understand why it is any less desirable for Indian people to have equivalent legislative safeguards to enhance their lives than it is for non-Indian people.

I suppose that it would be technically possible to add sections to the current Indian Act to provide a family relations code for Native people. There may be hesitancy to do this because it is already such an omnibus statute.

It would also be possible to enact a wholly new federal statute dealing with family law matters. The subject could also be included in any new legislation dealing specifically with Indian lands. The essential problem concerns land so this might be a sensible route to pursue.

There are a host of precedents on the subject matter of family relations law from the various provincial jurisdictions. It should be possible to provide that the law governing family relations in force in each province is applicable to Indian band members living on reserve lands in each province. Using this approach, Indian families would be entitled to the same rights and remedies under the law as other families resident in the various provinces enjoy. Referential incorporation of provincial law in areas where provincial and federal jurisdictions overlap has been employed in the past in order to achieve a uniform legislative scheme.

Section 88 of the Indian Act already provides for incorporation of all provincial laws of general application except where they conflict with the Indian Act. The Supreme Court of Canada has declared that there is a conflict between current provincial family law legislation and the Indian Act. This conflict could be overcome if provincial family relations legislation were expressly adopted by federal statute. Some minor consequential amendments would be required to the present Act (for instance, Sections 20 and 24) in order to remove any conflict and to ensure effective court orders. I doubt that any fair-minded Native person would have any hesitation in endorsing such legislation. The need exists, as demonstrated by Derrickson v. Derrickson. The solution is not hard to find. Steps should be taken to remedy this gap in the law as soon as possible.

APPENDIX E

Conduct of the Inquiry

530

CANADA

PRIVY COUNCIL

Certified to be a true copy of a Minute of a Meeting of the Committee of the Privy Council, approved by Her Excellency the Governor General on the 12th day of August, 1986.

WHEREAS certain matters associated with the Westbank Indian Band of Kelowna, British Columbia have been the subject of public controversy;

WHEREAS there have been allegations of impropriety on the part of officials of the Department of Indian Affairs and Northern Development (DIAND) and of Councillors of the Westbank Indian Band (Band) in connection with the affairs of the Band;

AND WHEREAS three reviews of these matters have been conducted and the resulting reports have been submitted to Ministers of Indian Affairs and Northern Development without resolving the concerns relating to these matters.

THEREFORE, the Committee of the Privy Council, on the recommendation of the Prime Minister, advise that a Commission do issue under Part I of the Inquiries Act and under the Great Seal of Canada appointing Mr. John E. Hall of Vancouver, British Columbia to be Commissioner to inquire into and report on the circumstances of, and factors contributing to, the above-mentioned controversy, allegations and concerns and, without limiting the generality of the foregoing, to inquire into and report upon

(1) the manner in which DIAND, in headquarters and in the regional and district offices, has carried out its responsibilities and functions in relation to the Band and to lessees and residents on reserves of the Band from 1975 to the present, particularly in relation to:

- the financial arrangements and transactions including Indian moneys, with the Band,

- the use of Band lands by Band members, lessees and other residents,

- the review by the Department of all by-laws made by the Band,

../2

P.C. 1986-1816

- 2 -

to determine whether these responsibilities and functions were carried out in accordance with law, established policy and generally accepted standards of competence and fairness;

(2)   the exercise of Band government from 1975 to the present, and in particular:

- whether there has been abuse of office by chiefs or councillors of the Band,

- whether there have been conflicts of interest on the part of chiefs or councillors of the Band and whether any conflict should or could have been avoided,

- consider the impacts of these practices, if any, on the members of the Band and on lessees and other residents of the Westbank Indian Band reserves;

(3)   the activities of lessees and residents of Westbank Indian Band reserves in relation to the Band, the Band Council and Band members, and in particular:

- whether these lessees and residents met their obligations to the Crown and to the Band,

- whether the activities of these lessees and residents contributed to tensions and conflicts with the Band; and

(4)   to recommend any changes to the Indian Act relating to the management of lands, Indian moneys and by-laws, or to the policies or the procedures of DIAND in relation to the said matters, or any remedies to specific problems, that may seem appropriate having regard to the Government's established policy of supporting and strengthening Indian self-government on Indian lands.

.../3

P.C. 1986-1816

- 3 -

The Committee further advises that

(a) the Commissioner be authorized

    (i) to adopt such procedures and methods as he may consider expedient for the proper conduct of the inquiry and to sit at such times and at such places within Canada as he may decide;

    (ii) to engage the services of such staff and counsel as he may consider necessary or advisable, at such rates of remuneration and reimbursement as may be approved by the Treasury Board;

    (iii) to engage the services of such experts and other persons as are referred to in section 11 of the Inquiries Act who shall receive such remuneration and reimbursement as may be approved by the Treasury Board;

    (iv) to rent office space and facilities for the Commission's purposes in accordance with Treasury Board policy; and

(b) The Commissioner be directed to submit a report to the Governor in Council embodying his findings, and recommendations on or before June 30, 1987, and to file with the Clerk of the Privy Council his papers and records as soon as reasonably may be after the conclusion of the inquiry.

CERTIFIED TO BE A TRUE COPY - COPIE CERTIFIÉE CONFORME

CLERK OF THE PRIVY COUNCIL - LE GREFFIER DU CONSEIL PRIVÉ

Hearings Schedule

DATE	LOCATION
1986	
November 12–14	Westbank, B.C.
November 17–20	Westbank, B.C.
December 8–12	Vancouver, B.C.
1987	
February 2–6	Westbank, B.C.
February 9–13	Westbank, B.C.
February 16–19	Westbank, B.C.
March 4–6	Vancouver, B.C.
March 9–13	Vancouver, B.C.
March 24–27	Vancouver, B.C.
March 30-April 2	Westbank, B.C.
April 6–10	Westbank, B.C.
May 11–15	Vancouver, B.C.
May 19–22	Westbank, B.C.
May 25–29	Westbank, B.C.
June 1–5	Westbank, B.C.
June 8–10	Westbank, B.C.
June 22, 24, 25, 30	Vancouver, B.C.
July 2	Vancouver, B.C.
August 11–12	Westbank, B.C.
August 18–21	Vancouver, B.C.
August 24, 26–28	Vancouver, B.C.

Total Number of Hearing Days: 84

Total Number of Exhibits: 225

Total Number of Witnesses: 67

Witnesses and Individuals Appearing Before the Inquiry

Westbank Indian Band Members

Barbara Coble
Harold J. Derickson
Richard N. Derickson
David Derrickson
Larry A. Derrickson
Ronald M. Derrickson
Rose Derrickson
Brian D. Eli
Mary A. Eli
Millie Jack
Chief Robert Louie
Roxanne Lindley
Thomas Lindley
George Michele
Bruce Swite
Lucy W.E. Swite

Mobile Home Park Operators

Jack E. Alexander
Leonard R. Crosby
Nicholas Dachyshyn
Donald A. Lauriault
James B. Lidster
T. Darcy O'Keefe
John K. Ross
Val Spring
Henriette York
Ted Zelmer

Business and Professional People

Andrew T. Archondous
Victor N. Davies
Gordon F. Dixon
Mervin G. Fiessel
Nicholas Kayban
Ward A. Kiehlbauch
Beverly P. Kingsbury
H. Grant Maddock
Dudley A. Pritchard
Edward C. Ross
Robert M. Turik
Derril T. Warren

Department of Indian Affairs Officials (Past and Present)

Dr. Owen A.J. Anderson
Peter J.F. Clark
Frederic R. Drummie
Donald K. Goodwin
Ernest E. Hobbs
H. Alexander McDougal
Donna Moroz
Denis Novak
L. Myler Savill
Arthur S. Silverman
David G. Sparks
Gabor Szalay
Gordon C. Van der Sar
Frederick J. Walchli

Auditors, Accounting Experts and Northland Bank Officials

Kevin E. Berry, C.A.
Martin G. Fortier
Danier T. Hopkins
William D. Kinsey, C.A.
Patrick J. Lett, C.A.
Harold B. McBain
Donald A. Pettman, C.A.

Others

Claire B. Eraut — First Citizens' Fund (B.C.)
Linda Grover — Employee, Westbank Indian Band
Sgt. Leonard H. Nyland — R.C.M.P.
Donald I.F. MacSween — B.C. Department of Highways
Senator Leonard S. Marchand
Robert Sam — First Citizens' Fund (B.C.)
Norman Schwartz — Administrator, Westbank Indian Band
Barbara Shmigelsky — Former Employee, Westbank Indian Band
Sgt. Brian H. Vance — R.C.M.P.

Part IV Submissions

Chief Clarence "Manny" Jules
William D. Kinsey, C.A.
Chief Robert Louie
Chief Joe Mathias
Chief Sophie Pierre
Chief Paul Sam

Final Submissions

Cecil O.D. Branson, Q.C.
Leonard R. Crosby
P. John Landry
John A. McAfee
John S. Maguire
John F. Rowan, Q.C.
Duncan W. Shaw, Q.C.

Counsel Appearing at the Inquiry

Commission of Inquiry	John F. Rowan, Q.C. Donald M. Smith D. Geoffrey Cowper
Department of Indian Affairs and Northern Development	Duncan W. Shaw, Q.C. P. John Landry
F.J. Walchli, Former Regional Director General, Dept. of Indian Affairs	Cecil O.D. Branson, Q.C.
Westbank Indian Band	John S. Maguire
Former Executive of the Westbank Indian Band	John A. McAfee
Touche Ross Ltd., Liquidators of the Northland Bank	Frederick H. Herbert, Q.C. Sharon L. Fugman

Inquiry Staff

Commissioner	John E. Hall, Q.C.
Counsel	John F. Rowan, Q.C. Donald M. Smith D. Geoffrey Cowper
Experts	William D. Kinsey, C.A. — Investigative Accountant John R.D. Iwanson — Investigator
Administration	Maureen E. Cowin — Executive Secretary John T. Laurillard — Hearings Officer Lise M.M. Carrière — Secretary
Report Production	Mary Ann Allen, Marguerite Côté, Marie Dionne, Paul Ollivier, Jean Wilson